NIXON

VOLUME TWO

*The Triumph
of a Politician
1962-1972*

STEPHEN E. AMBROSE

SIMON AND SCHUSTER
NEW YORK • LONDON • TORONTO • SYDNEY • TOKYO

SIMON AND SCHUSTER
Simon & Schuster Building
Rockefeller Center
1230 Avenue of the Americas
New York, New York 10020

Designed by Edith Fowler
Photo section researched and edited by Vincent Virga
Manufactured in the United States of America

10 9 8 7 6 5 4 3 2 1

Library of Congress Cataloging in Publication Data

Ambrose, Stephen E.
  Nixon.

  Includes bibliographies and indexes.
  Contents: v. 1. The education of a politician, 1913–1962—
v. 2. The triumph of a politician, 1962–1972.
  1. Nixon, Richard M. (Richard Milhous), 1913–
2. Presidents—United States—Biography. 3. United States—
Politics and government—1945— . I. Title.
E856.A72 1987 973'.924'092 [B] 86-26126
ISBN 0-671-52836-X (v. 1)
ISBN 0-671-52837-8 (v. 2)

TO ALICE MAYHEW

CONTENTS

Foreword 9

1 The Fast Track, 1963 11
2 Coping with Catastrophe, 1964 38
3 Preparing a Republican Revival, 1965 59
4 The Ninth Campaign, 1966 80
5 Preparing for the Presidency, January–July 1967 102
6 Operation Candor, July–December 1967 118
7 The Primaries, January–May 1968 133
8 The Nomination, June–August 1968 157
9 The Ninth Campaign, Part One, August 9–
   October 14, 1968 177
10 The Ninth Campaign, Part Two,
   October 15–November 6, 1968 201
11 Transition and Inauguration,
   November 6, 1968–January 20, 1969 223
12 Getting Started, January–June 1969 246
13 "Don't Get Rattled—Don't Waver—Don't React"
   July 1–October 15, 1969 280
14 The Silent Majority, October 16–December 31, 1969 305
15 The Cambodian Incursion, January–April 1970 322
16 Reaping the Whirlwind, May–August 1970 347
17 The Tenth Campaign, September–December 1970 373
18 Nixon at Midterm: An Assessment, 1969–1970 402
19 Laos and Other Woes, January–April 1971 413
20 Détente with Russia and China, May–August 1971 439

8 | CONTENTS

21 Tilting at Windmills, September–December 1971   467
22 Politics, Hanoi, Peking, and Busing,
       January–March 1972   493
23 Bombing Hanoi, Mining Haiphong, Toasting in
       Moscow, April–June 1972   525
24 Politics and the Break-in, June–July 1972   552
25 The Conventions, July–August 1972   579
26 The Last Campaign, Part One,
       September 1–October 8, 1972   604
27 The Last Campaign, Part Two,
       October 8–November 7, 1972   627
28 Nixon's First Term: An Assessment, 1969–1972   653

    Notes   663
    Bibliography   700
    Acknowledgments   704
    Index   709

FOREWORD

THIS IS the story that begins with Richard Nixon's drive to the Presidency, which he launched at his self-proclaimed "last press conference" on November 7, 1962. It carries through his campaign and victory in 1968, and covers his actions as President in his first term. It ends on November 7, 1972, the day of his re-election.

The story is based, overwhelmingly, on Richard Nixon's own words, written and spoken, public and private. His published memoirs provide the starting point. They are voluminous, detailed, sometimes almost embarrassingly revealing (certainly more so than any other President's memoirs), and usually reliable on statements of fact. His speeches, averaging almost one per day for the ten years covered in this volume, are available in newspapers and in four volumes of the *Public Papers of the President*. Nixon's private writings consist of tens of thousands of memorandums, hand-scribbled notes and comments, drafts of speeches, and the like. Much of this material remains under seal, as Nixon continues to do legal battle with the National Archives (a situation described on page 558), but a great deal is available to scholars. These private papers give a unique insight into Nixon's instinctive reactions and patterns of thought, his prejudices and convictions, as well as his orders and directives.

Then there are the tape-recorded conversations from the Nixon White House. They present all kinds of problems for scholars (see page 424), and are terribly limited, as only conversations about the Watergate cover-up are available out of the thousands of hours that were taped. Still, the tapes that have been made public are a marvelously rich source. It is less what is said, although that is obviously important, and more the nuances, the tone of voice, the

9

pause, the chuckle, the guffaw, the snarl, the intangibles that impress, inform, and elucidate. Imagine being able to listen to Abraham Lincoln talking to John Hay or John Nicolay; no matter how bad the quality of the tapes, they would give us an insight into Lincoln's style and methods unavailable from any other source. So it is with Nixon.

Beyond Nixon's own words, the story is based on what his closest associates said about him and his actions. No other Administration in American history has produced so much in the way of memoirs by the participants as the Nixon Administration. The reason, at least in part, is obvious: in no other Administration did so many members need so much money for such horrendous legal fees. The Nixon biographer has available the memoirs of Haldeman, Ehrlichman, Magruder, Klein, Stans, Colson, Safire, Price, Dean, Dent, and others.

And, of course, there are Henry Kissinger's memoirs, by far the most voluminous of any Secretary of State. If they are also the most self-serving, they are in addition the most revealing.

As a biographer, I am concerned with what Nixon said and did, planned and hoped, attempted and achieved. As to questions of motive, of why he did what he did, I confess that I do not understand this complex man. It is not news that he was devious, manipulative, driven by unseen and unknowable forces, quick as a summer storm to blame and slow as a glacier melt to forgive, passionate in his hatreds, self-centered, untruthful, untrusting, and at times so despicable that one wants to avert one's eyes in shame and embarrassment. Nor is it news that this same man could be considerate, straightforward, sympathetic, and helpful, or that he was blessed with great talent, a superb intellect, an awesome memory, and a remarkable ability to see things whole, especially on a global scale and with regard to the world balance of power. If he was the ultimate cynic, a President without principle in domestic politics, he was also the ultimate realist, a President without peer in foreign affairs.

Why these contradictions? I don't know. I only know they were there. I see my job as one of pointing them out within the context of explaining what Nixon was doing, with what results.

I wish that I could write shorter books, but once I get going on a subject my curiosity drives me. I discover, for instance, that I want to know what Nixon did, and the only way I can find out is to do the research, then think about what I've found, and then—the crucial step—write it up. For me, the act of writing is the act of learning.

The consequence is that I make heavy demands on my readers. I hope their effort is worthwhile.

CHAPTER ONE

THE FAST TRACK
1963

IN NOVEMBER 1962, at his self-proclaimed "last press conference" following his loss in the California gubernatorial contest, Richard Nixon announced that he was walking out of history. "You won't have Nixon to kick around anymore," he told the press. "Just think how much you're going to be missing." The reporters, in response, wrote his political obituary.

In December 1962, Nixon flew to New York. While there he saw his old friend Bill Rogers, former Attorney General in the Eisenhower Administration. "It's hard now to understand how far down he was," Rogers later observed. "He was broke. He had no future in the field he knew best." Nixon himself said that "as a political force . . . I am through."

But five years later, by the spring of 1968, Nixon had held hundreds of press conferences and was the almost certain Republican nominee for the Presidency. In connection with his campaign, he was writing an introduction to a new paperback edition of *Six Crises*. Bill Safire, one of his speech writers, was helping him. Safire suggested some "fairly frank language." Nixon responded with these passages:

"I wish I could analyze the workings of American democracy and the mystery of public opinion that took a man from 'finished' in 1963 to candidate for the Presidency in 1968. I cannot. Not even a statesman who was also a great historian—Winston Churchill—could adequately explain why, after a decade in political eclipse, he was the one called upon to lead his nation in a time of crisis.

"There is no doubt, however, about what was not the reason

11

for my candidacy today: it was not by dint of my own calculation or efforts. No man, not if he combined the wisdom of Lincoln with the connivance of Machiavelli, could have maneuvered or manipated his way back into the arena."[1]

Nixon's claim that he was but the child of fate, that he had done nothing to bring about his impending nomination by the Republicans, was untrue. In fact, from the beginning of 1963 to the spring of 1968, his actions could not have been better calculated to put him in sight of the nomination. Indeed, he might well have written that neither Lincoln nor Machiavelli could have plotted a campaign for him more successful than the one he directed himself.

He had never thought of himself as finished, not even at his lowest moment, the morning after the California defeat. Nixon used his last press conference as the occasion to stake out his position as the leading Republican critic of President John F. Kennedy's foreign policy, and was bold enough to choose as his issue the very one that he felt had just cost him the California election, the Cuban missile crisis. Nixon asked if Kennedy had made a deal that would allow Khrushchev to "bring an Iron Curtain down around Cuba."

The press had been close to unanimous in praising Kennedy's handling of the crisis, but Nixon saw his vulnerability at once, and immediately made Democratic weakness in standing up to the Communist threat his number-one issue. It stayed there right through to his nomination five and a half years later. The reporters present, and the columnists who commented on Nixon's political demise, missed the story.[2]

The reporters made another misjudgment, brought on by their own sense of self-importance, when they took Nixon at his word. The reason the reporters assumed Nixon had meant it when he said he was through was that he had insulted and attacked the press as he said it. No one could do that and survive in American politics, in the opinion of the press. In charging that the press was biased, untruthful, and vindictive, Nixon had burned his bridges behind him. This saddened some members of the press, Nixon admirers, but it delighted many more.

The story the reporters had missed was that Nixon had just made the press an issue. Nixon knew that the national press did not speak for or to millions of Republicans. He understood and enunciated a point of view: that the press was liberal, Democratic, do-gooder, pro big government and big labor, for high taxes, yet craven in the face of the Communist menace, and always out to give the shaft to Republicans. Nixon received thousands of letters after his blast at the reporters, urging him on. Former President Eisenhower spoke for the party when he commented that "Dick did have a point about bias in reporting and the arrogant sort of journalistic sharp-shooting that occurs daily in all too many publications."[3]

In 1965, Nixon pointed out another advantage of the last press conference. It "served a purpose," he said. "The press had a guilt complex about their inaccuracy [this was an assertion, not a fact, and every reporter in California would have denied it]. Since then, they've been generally more accurate, and far more respectful."[4]

In short, immediately after escaping from the bad dream of actually being governor of California, Nixon began at his last press conference the start of his next campaign. He had known no other life since 1946, and wanted no other, short of occupying the ultimate seat of power itself. Campaigning meant bashing the Democrats and their allies, the reporters. Nixon was the best there was at that, and the one who enjoyed it most. He couldn't imagine living without campaigning, and didn't try to.

He did not have a specific race to aim for. Some parts of him shied away from even the thought of running against Kennedy in 1964, but there was a draw in the other direction too. Kennedy might well be vulnerable by then, and a victory over Kennedy would be a sweet vindication, especially if he could use Cuba to do it, as Kennedy had used Cuba against him in 1960. Still, 1968 looked more realistic, assuming a Kennedy victory in 1964.[5]

But uncertainty about when Nixon would run again should not obscure the fact that he was running, and for nothing short of the Presidency. He was realistic enough to know that his fate rested to a large degree on chance, accident, and luck—just as Churchill's did in the thirties—but then that is always more or less true for all politicians at all times. The point was to be ready to seize opportunities.

Nixon stayed ready, in his usual determined, skillful, and thoughtful way (to his critics, in his usual cynical, hypocritical, power-mad way). But however one views his actions, the point is that they were his actions. There was nothing miraculous about his resurrection. He used his assets shrewdly, and succeeded with the qualities that had made him successful in the past—hard work, boldness, risk taking, and attacking the Democrats.

THERE WAS one other fib at that last press conference. "One last thing," Nixon had said. "What are my plans?" He told the reporters he was going home "to get acquainted with my family again."

That was on Wednesday morning. On Friday morning, leaving Pat and the girls behind, he flew to the Bahamas. His companions were John S. Davies, a quiet, unobtrusive man who had been director of communications in the recent campaign, and Bebe Rebozo, a Miami businessman who was friend and confidant to many high-ranking politicians in both parties.

Davies joined Nixon in Los Angeles. "On the flight down," he later recalled, "there were times he obviously was deep in thought, peering out the window." Davies let him brood. "When he wants to talk and chat, that's fine." Rebozo also did not intrude. "I've seen [Nixon] and Bebe sit in a room for three hours," Senator George Smathers of Florida once remarked, "and neither ever say a word. Nixon's a little bit of a mystic. He gets all his information together, then he meditates and contemplates. And Bebe sits there."

Steve Hess, a young intellectual who sent Nixon political gossip from Washington and assisted him in writing speeches and magazine articles, caught the appeal of these men for Nixon nicely: "He can be comfortable with them. They don't want anything from him, and he doesn't have to be on guard with them. Men like Bebe have an old-shoe quality that helps Nixon relax."[6]

The trio spent three weeks on Paradise Island. Davies described their routine: "The three of us would go swimming in the surf, swapping stories, talking about anything. Then he would get deep in thought and would walk down the beach. We'd wait for him, and sooner or later he would come back."[7]

AFTER EVERY crisis of his life, Nixon had gone for long walks on the beach, figuratively if not literally, to reassess his position and think things through.

He was within two months of his fiftieth birthday. He was robust, free of any major physical problems. He quite rightly chided himself about his lack of exercise, which was limited to occasional games of golf and some swimming, but he was neither a heavy drinker nor a smoker, and he looked and felt fine. His mind was constantly at work, calculating the possibilities, plotting, planning. He threw himself totally into politics, for him by far the most absorbing of all games, so much so that once he woke—more often than not after five hours or less of sleep—his mind began to race, and he was up, ready for that day's battle. He frequently ended the day with phone calls to politicians around the nation, extending into the small hours. He had the physical essentials: good looks, commitment, and sufficient health and stamina to carry him through the rigors of campaigning.

He had many additional assets. He had been a major figure in Washington for longer than any other active national politician. He had served four years in the House, two in the Senate, and eight as

Vice-President. Except for Kennedy, Truman, and Eisenhower, he was the best-known politician in the country. He knew more foreign leaders than any man in America except Eisenhower. He was in the solid position of occupying the broad center ground of the Republican Party, with Senator Barry Goldwater of Arizona off to his right and Governor Nelson Rockefeller of New York off to his left. He had run Jack Kennedy dead even in 1960, despite Democratic victories in the congressional and state elections. He was the legitimate spokesman for the Republican Party, despite the last press conference.

He had serious liabilities. He had lost two elections in a row, and with the 1962 California press conference, he had squandered some of the reputation he had earned as a good loser in 1960. And although what he said delighted most Republicans, it made the Democrats hate him even more, which pointed to his more general problem, that he was the most hated and feared man in America. No one could rouse the Democrats for an all-out effort quite the way Nixon could; thus in California in 1962 a number of reporters commented on the fervor and dedication of the anti-Nixon volunteers in the Pat Brown campaign. This was a consequence of Nixon's campaign style, in which he nearly always exaggerated, and not his policies, which were middle-of-the-road.

But campaigning was almost all he had ever done. One of his shortcomings as a presidential candidate was his complete lack of administrative experience. Except for a supply crew in the Pacific for a year or so in World War II, Nixon had never actually run anything. That was why Eisenhower, in 1956, had urged Nixon to take over the Department of Defense. But Nixon reasoned that the political route was far more profitable and interesting than administration, and insisted on remaining Vice-President, with nothing to do but campaign.

One result of all the time he spent on the chicken-and-peas circuit was that there was scarcely a Republican in the country who didn't owe Dick Nixon a favor or two, or whom he didn't know. Herb Klein once said of Nixon, "I have seen him stand in long reception lines by the hour and remember by name, or at least city, more than half of the thousands he would see."[8]

Nixon also had a large number of important people in the business, legal, and political worlds who thought highly of him. Some were former financial backers, some were insiders from the Eisenhower Administration, some were former aides or associates. Nixon inspired loyalty, just as he earned and held the admiration of those who worked with or for him. These Nixon supporters were by no means ready to see him abandon politics.

He needed an income, and a business expense account for his travels, for, as he never tired of pointing out, he had saved no money in his seventeen years in politics. His girls were growing; he needed to make enough to pay for their education, and to provide for his own and Pat's retirement. As a consultant to the Los Angeles law firm of Adams, Duque, and Hazeltine, he made a substantial salary, but there were overwhelming reasons to get out of California. Neither he nor his family were really Californians anymore—since 1946 they had lived there only the past two years—and the voters of the state had just repudiated him decisively. The California Republican Party was badly split on regional and ideological lines and could not provide him with a base in anything like the way New York provided a base for Rockefeller, or Texas for Vice-President Lyndon Johnson. The law firm could not provide him with worldwide business, nor intimate contact with the big men of the nation. His true home was in the national capital, and his true base was the nation itself.

In deciding where to live, and what to do to make a living, Nixon had many options. At least two universities offered him their presidencies. Chrysler Corporation inquired as to his availability to serve as chairman of the board. Baseball owners wanted to know if he was interested in serving as commissioner of baseball. Bryce Harlow, who had served Eisenhower as White House liaison with Congress, called Nixon's secretary, Rose Mary Woods, around this time with some further suggestions. Harlow thought Nixon ought to consider joining one of the foundations—the Fund for the Republic, or Freedom Foundation—as that would "force him to stay abreast of the things that are going on in the world."

For Nixon, however, none of these possibilities had much appeal, primarily because the leadership of a university or a foundation would prevent him from speaking out as a partisan on the issues of the day, while a business career would not satisfy him. As Harlow put it, "It is difficult to see how he is going to find lasting satisfaction in a strictly mercenary life."[9]

Harlow concluded that the best place for Nixon was in a law firm with some big-business clients. Nixon agreed with that—a major firm would give him income plus time to speak, travel, and study. Where? Only in the East, in New York City or Washington, could he put himself on what he liked to call the "fast track." California was provincial and out of touch. "There was no foreign policy angle in California," one aide pointed out. "It had to be the East. He had to have his cake (money) and eat it too (his interest in foreign policy)."[10]

While Nixon was in the Bahamas, one of his strongest backers,

Elmer Bobst, chairman of the board of the Warner-Lambert Pharmaceutical Company, came to visit and talk. Bobst urged Nixon to go to New York. Nixon liked the idea—he thought of New York as a place where people worked harder, were smarter, and became more successful than anywhere else. New York would give him the advantage of allowing him to claim that by moving to Nelson Rockefeller's state he was "ruling myself out as an active political figure." [11] Actually, he would be ruling himself in, as in New York he could avoid state politics but have instant access to the international media when he commented on foreign policy.

New York had another advantage: he could pretend he was moving there for his family's sake, not his own. For Tricia and Julie, then sixteen and fourteen years of age, the idea of New York was exciting, and they both wanted to get out of California. Pat wanted to get out of politics. Dick told her, when she and the girls joined him for the Thanksgiving holiday in the Bahamas, that a move to New York would be a "clean break with politics," because of Rockefeller's tight control of the party there.[12] They agreed that a move to New York was the right thing, and that they would do it as soon as he could find the right job.

IN JANUARY 1963, Nixon flew to New York to scout the possibilities. He talked to Tom Dewey, who encouraged him to do as he had done, become a New York lawyer. After losing two presidential contests, Dewey had made himself a rich and influential man. In 1952 he had used his influence to get Eisenhower to run, and then to get Nixon selected for Vice-President. Nixon was ready enough to get rich, and eager to follow Dewey's suggestions on how to do it, but Dewey's political style was not his at all. Dewey was a behind-the-scenes manipulator, had been since his 1948 defeat; he hardly ever made public speeches or comments, and had refused a position in Eisenhower's Cabinet. Dewey wanted to be influential. Nixon wanted to be powerful. To get power, he had to remain a public figure, speaking out on the issues of the day.

He needed a job that would give him a big salary, free time, and plenty of overseas travel. It was not an easy assignment for his New York friends scouting for him. "A lot of lawyers didn't want a tiger in their midst," one said later, and another added, "There just weren't too many places where he could get two hundred and fifty thousand dollars and all his time." [13] Bobst finally cleared the way with the firm that handled the Warner-Lambert account, Mudge, Stern, Baldwin, and Todd. It was an old, conservative, and respected but a bit behind-the-times Wall Street firm. Another old Nixon backer, Donald Kendall of Pepsi-Cola, helped Nixon along by promising the firm Pepsi's lucrative legal account. So it was settled. The Nixons would move to New York in the summer, when the girls' school year ended and after a European vacation.

NIXON USED the time between making his decision and actually moving to re-establish his position as Republican spokesman on foreign policy. He began in February, with his first public appearance since the last press conference, on a popular television talk show, the Jack Paar program. Nixon prepared for the show, which was usually played for laughs, with the utmost seriousness. He wrote to dozens of political friends, asking their advice on what to say, then telling them what he would say: that recent announcements from the Kennedy Administration about Soviet troop withdrawals from Cuba were "pure cover-up for what remains a formidable build-up on the island." [14]

On the show, which was aired in March, Nixon told Paar and the 20 million viewers that he had decided to remain in public life as a constructive critic of the Kennedy Administration, and called for a blockade of Cuba until the last Soviet soldier left the island. [15]

In March, Nixon sent a form letter to hundreds of his backers, telling them that he had made a decision to "continue to devote as much of my time as possible to participation in public affairs." He also announced that he intended to do a lot of speaking and traveling over the next few months. [16]

IN FEBRUARY, the Internal Revenue Service began an extensive audit of Nixon's tax returns. For Nixon, it was irritating, time-consuming, and expensive. At the same time the Justice Department, under Attorney General Robert Kennedy, was investigating a loan from Howard Hughes to Donald Nixon, with a view to developing criminal charges of conflict of interest. The probe came up empty, but Nixon naturally resented the attempt to get at him through his family, and complained about the "abuse of the Internal Revenue Service and the Justice Department for political purposes" by the Kennedy Administration. [17]

Kennedy's apparent abuse of power was a private problem; Nixon wanted to go after the President on policy questions. In March, he spent a weekend with Eisenhower in his winter home at Palm Desert, California. The men talked about issues, especially Cuba. Ike was furious with Kennedy for pledging that in return for the removal of Russian missiles from Cuba, the United States would never invade the island. Ike insisted that Kennedy had no right to make such a pledge, that if Kennedy had presented it to the Senate in the form of a treaty he never could have achieved ratification. Contrary to the media's judgment, that Kennedy had won a great victory in the missile crisis, Ike thought he had suffered a bad defeat. Nixon heartily agreed, and told Ike he would hit Kennedy hard on this one.[18]

His opportunity came on April 20, when he spoke to the American Society of Newspaper Editors in Washington. He regarded it as a major speech, and prepared accordingly. He flew to Washington a day early; John C. Whitaker, a Washington-based geologist and Nixon volunteer in 1960, joined him in his hotel room to help out. "From eleven o'clock that night until four in the morning he went over the material," Whitaker recalled, "scribbling away with the old fountain pen on the yellow legal pad. While he wrote, I typed. After a few hours' sleep, he got up again at seven and went until noon, working it over and over."[19]

The result was vintage Nixon. He began with a sort of apology for the last press conference—"I felt like returning for sixteen minutes some of the heat I had been taking for sixteen years"—and a little attempt at a joke, quoting Harry Truman's "If you can't stand the heat, get out of the kitchen" and saying that he had gotten out of the kitchen.

Then he put himself right back in. He said he knew the editors expected him, as "a battle-scarred political veteran," to "pour it on."

"If only I were the 'partisan type,' " he continued, "what a field day I could have!"

He proceeded to have it: "In Cuba we have goofed an invasion, paid tribute to Castro for the prisoners, then given the Soviets squatters' rights in our backyard." He provided other examples of the shortcomings of the Kennedy Administration, three paragraphs' worth, then said he could "see no useful purpose to be served in proceeding in this vein," before proceeding even further in that vein.

He used a favorite Nixon technique—to deny that he was saying what he was saying—and got some revenge in the process. In the 1960 campaign, Kennedy had demanded the release of State Department polls in foreign countries that indicated a fall in American prestige. Foul, Nixon had cried. Now, Nixon said, "I am not going to demand the release of the polls about the decline of American prestige [under Kennedy]. We have enough troubles abroad without running America down at home."

In 1960, Kennedy had charged that the American economy was stagnating because of Republican policies. Now, Nixon said, "Nor do I charge today that because of the failure of our economy to grow as fast as was predicted [by Kennedy] that we are in deadly peril of being outproduced by the Soviet Union" as Kennedy had said in 1960.

Referring implicitly again to Kennedy's '60 campaign, Nixon said, "Nor do I charge that this Administration is trying to appease Mr. Khrushchev." Kennedy's policy was better described as containment, Nixon said, and "because it is essentially defensive in character, it is doomed to failure." As a result of Kennedy's policies, "the Atlantic alliance is in disarray, Cuba is western Russia, and the rest of Latin America is in deadly peril."

In place of containment, Nixon called for a strategy of victory, even though "I know that talk of victory over Communism is not fashionable these days." But he could not accept coexistence, because that was "another word for creeping surrender."

Nixon assured the editors that it was not his purpose to second-guess the Bay of Pigs invasion, or the Cuban missile crisis (where "we proceeded to pull defeat out of the jaws of victory"), but he did want to issue a clear call for action: "We must no longer postpone making a command decision to do whatever is necessary to force the removal of the Soviet beachhead."

He ended with an appeal to the editors to avoid partisanship, to use their "eloquence to stir in the hearts of our people their love for America," and to set a great goal: "Nothing less than a free Russia, a free China, a free Eastern Europe and a free Cuba."

In the question period, Nixon was pressed for examples of what action he would take to free Cuba. He said he could not be specific but declared that he was not calling for "an invasion immediately with maximum power." He thought Kennedy could be defeated in 1964, and suggested a ticket of Goldwater and Rockefeller: "If Jack and Lyndon could get together," he quipped, "Barry and Nelson can." He denied that he had any intention of ever seeking political office again, but as one reporter commented, "Several of his listeners were heard to remark that he sounded for all the world like a man still seeking the presidency."[20]

Nixon was pleased with his effort. He told his backers that "it served the purpose of setting forth some constructive alternatives to present Administration policy."[21]

Of course the opposite was true—the alternatives he had offered were jingoistic and irresponsible and inconsistent. How could he square the call to do "whatever is necessary" to force the Soviet troops out of Cuba with his denial during questions that he was advocating an invasion? How could he label a call to "free Russia" a constructive alternative? But there was one good thing about being in opposition; it freed Nixon to slash and denounce without having to assume any responsibility for his words. Nixon was back in business, at the old stand, and enjoying it hugely. Bashing Kennedy was much more fun than defending Eisenhower.

And more profitable too. Nixon's speech got front-page coverage around the country and inspired many editorials. *The New York Times* gave it the ultimate tribute by reprinting the text. Letters to Nixon from frustrated Republicans who were glad someone had finally laid into Kennedy on Cuba came pouring in.[22]

NIXON SPENT most of the late winter and spring of 1963 on the East Coast, making arrangements for his move to New York and meeting with supporters. He reached an agreement with the law firm whereby he would act as consultant until he had lived in New York for six months and could be admitted to the bar, at which time he would become the senior partner and the name would change. He talked to his publisher, Doubleday, about another book. The idea was that, with the assistance of Steve Hess, he would take on Teddy White, who had enjoyed a fabulous success with *The Making of the President, 1960*. Nixon and Hess proposed to use the White technique in 1964. As Hess explained, "The premise was that it would be much more marvelous to have someone who had gone through it himself, and was no longer a politician, explaining to the rest of the world how the process works."[23]

Nixon was intrigued by the idea. He did not propose to physically cover the campaign himself, as White had done, but to rely on Hess and a research staff to do the legwork and bring him the results. He would then put it together. It was an opportunity to comment at length on Kennedy, in the respected intellectual format of a book, with the benefit of hindsight, and it might be highly profitable. It would allow Nixon to remain at the center of presidential politics without having to run against Kennedy in 1964. Nixon was more than interested, and his talks with Hess and Doubleday moved forward smoothly. By late spring, they had set a date for signing a contract, November 22, 1963.[24] Meanwhile, he signed a contract with *The Saturday Evening Post* for an article on foreign policy.

Pat joined him at Easter time, and they went house hunting. After two days of looking, they found a ten-room apartment that took up the fifth floor of a building at 62nd Street and Fifth Avenue, with a view of Central Park and the Plaza Hotel. It was in rundown condition, but Dick said that "Pat can make anything look good," and they took it.[25] The Nixons sold their house in the Truesdale Estates section of Beverly Hills for $183,000; they paid $135,000 for the New York apartment, and put $50,000 into remodeling. The work included creating servants' quarters, as Nixon had added to his household a Cuban refugee couple, Fina and Manolo Sanchez, as live-in servants. Only later did Nixon learn that the building belonged to Mrs. Mary Clark Rockefeller, who had taken possession as part of her divorce settlement, and that her ex-husband, Governor Rockefeller, and his new wife lived on the twelfth floor of the fourteen-story building.[26]

On May 2, Nixon announced his impending move to New York. He explained that he would "engage in matters relating to the Washington and Paris offices of the firm," which sounded to many reporters like politics and foreign policy, but to others his move seemed to provide proof that he had no presidential ambitions. Rockefeller said it was "wonderful news" that he had Nixon for a neighbor and expressed the hope that Nixon would get back into national politics. Walter Cronkite, on CBS News, reported that Nixon was coming to New York "to establish a base for another try at the Presidency," but Nixon told reporters that he was "not here for any political purpose."[27]

Through May, noncandidate Nixon traveled around the country, meeting with Republican leaders. He held local press conferences, where he ridiculed the notion that he was moving to New York for any purpose other than practicing law. Some reports, he said, had him moving in order to support Rockefeller for the nomination, others that he intended to mastermind a movement to draft Governor George Romney of Michigan, and still others that his plan was to stop Goldwater. But he was not going to do any of that, nor engage in active politics, nor endorse a candidate. "I will support whoever is nominated" was his last word.[28]

Before taking up his work at the law firm, Nixon was "determined to keep a long-standing promise to Pat and the girls" and take them on an extended overseas vacation.[29] On June 12, accompanied by their oldest California friends, Jack and Helene Drown and their daughter, Maureen, they set off for what Julie later described as "the longest unbroken period my father had spent with us in many years."[30]

Nixon's idea of a vacation differed from most people's. He worked as hard during the trip as if he were still Vice-President, and reaped his rewards in American press coverage. What he had learned so well during his years in the Eisenhower Administration still held true—Nixon overseas was newsworthy, and he got much more positive coverage when he talked about foreign policy in a foreign land than when he discussed domestic politics in New York.

Nixon prepared carefully. Through former Secretary of State Christian Herter, he got State Department cooperation; arrangements were made for him to meet with European leaders, and a press conference was set up for him at each stop.[31] He held one at Idlewild Airport before boarding the flight to Lisbon, another on his arrival, another on flying to Madrid, and so on. In Frankfurt, he spoke out against right-wing "nuts or kooks, as we call them in California," and said he was sure Goldwater regarded them as a liability, "just as I do." He repeated that theme in Budapest, and stepped up the pressure on Goldwater, saying, "the Senator should not allow such people to have any part in his campaign."[32]

He was more comfortable talking about Kennedy's shortcomings than about Republican problems. Two days before Nixon left the States, Kennedy had made a dramatic appeal for peace in a major address at American University. The President had spoken strongly in favor of a partial nuclear test ban treaty, covering the atmosphere, under water, and in outer space, but not underground. While Nixon was in Europe, the Soviets had responded favorably to Kennedy's offer. In Vienna, Nixon commented that if Soviet Premier Nikita Khrushchev was ready to agree, fine, but he warned that "we must be under no illusions that this indicates any change in his basic objective, which is to impose Communism on the Western world."

Warming to his favorite subject, Nixon continued, "Too many people today are gloating publicly because the Chinese Communists and the Soviet Communists are having an argument.

"What they fail to realize is that this argument is not about how they can beat each other, but how they could beat us."[33]

In Berlin, Nixon suggested that the United States should "use its power to seek German unification and the extension of freedom to the nations of Eastern Europe."[34] When the test ban treaty was signed in Moscow in mid-July, Nixon announced from Paris his support for it. He urged Republican senators to vote for ratification, pointing out that the treaty had been initially proposed by Eisenhower four years earlier.[35]

"Everywhere we went," Nixon later wrote, "we were received as if I were still Vice President."[36] He met with Francisco Franco in Spain, and on a side trip to Cairo to see the pyramids, he talked with Egyptian President Gamal Nasser. He drew big crowds in Budapest. But best of all, he was President Charles de Gaulle's guest for lunch at the Elysée Palace in Paris.

De Gaulle, in the summer of 1963, was at the height of his power. Awesome in his appearance, he projected a great dignity. With Churchill, Roosevelt, Stalin, Montgomery, and Eisenhower dead or retired, de Gaulle was the last of the World War II giants. Nixon admired him almost without stint. Late in his life Nixon wrote a book entitled *Leaders;* in it he put de Gaulle second only to Churchill among the many world leaders he had known.

They talked politics, in the broadest sense. Nixon spoke enthusiastically of a United States of Europe, long a favorite project of Americans, but de Gaulle was uninterested. He perked up when Nixon suggested that the United States should share its atomic secrets with France, and de Gaulle said he might be willing to sign the nuclear test ban treaty (France was then performing its initial series of tests, which it was conducting in the atmosphere) in return for access to American know-how. They talked about China and its role in the future, of NATO, and of other things.[37]

At the conclusion of the lunch, de Gaulle rose to propose a toast. He said that he knew Nixon had suffered some difficult defeats, but predicted that in the future Nixon would play a great role in "a top capacity."[38]

De Gaulle's toast was heady stuff, as were the receptions from the press and world leaders elsewhere, but while he was in Europe, Nixon got a sharp reminder of the difference between being leader of the opposition and being in power. In June, President Kennedy traveled to Europe, where on the twenty-sixth, in Berlin, he reached one of the high points of his Presidency, and got enormous worldwide press coverage when he declared, *"Ich bin ein Berliner."* Nixon was in Berlin a couple of weeks later; where Kennedy had drawn 150,000 for his speech at the Berlin Wall, Nixon, holding a press conference, drew a dozen reporters. For both men, it was a first view of the Berlin Wall, built by Khrushchev two years earlier as the first barrier in history designed to keep people in rather than their enemies out. Both were appalled by what they saw. In his press conference, Nixon warned against any belief that Khrushchev had "mellowed," and urged Kennedy to seek German unification and the extension of freedom to the nations of Eastern Europe.[39]

IN AUGUST, Nixon went to work at the law firm. He went at the job the way he went after political office, aggressively, with an equal emphasis on hard work and personal contacts. When he was in New York (he was on the road, on business, nearly half the time), he got to his office at 20 Broad Street by 7 A.M. and often stayed until 6 P.M. Business in the firm immediately picked up, especially overseas, and Nixon the corporate lawyer was as instant a success as he had been as Nixon the politician. A major reason was that he was who he was and knew who he knew, but equally important was his ability and his penchant for hard, sustained work. In the short period he spent as an active lawyer, Nixon demonstrated that he could have reached the pinnacle in corporate law practice as well as in politics.

New York State was Rockefeller's base, but within New York City there were dozens of prominent Republicans, many of them former members of the Eisenhower Administration, who had no connection with the state Republican Party. They were men of national affairs who when they heard the word "capital" thought of Washington, not Albany.

Nixon knew them all, of course, and many were his supporters. Those who itched to get back to Washington once again to take charge of the nation's affairs saw Nixon as the man who could get them there. These New York City Republicans rallied around Nixon. They got him into the best clubs, introduced him to the best society, sent business his way.

Dr. Henry Kissinger, Harvard professor and on a retainer from Rockefeller as adviser on foreign policy, moved in different circles and saw it differently. Kissinger later wrote that "when Nixon moved to New York in 1962, he was shunned by the people whose respect he might have expected. . . . He was never invited by what he considered the 'best' families. This rankled and compounded his already strong tendency to see himself beset by enemies." The opposite was more nearly true.[40] Nixon turned down far more invitations than he accepted.

The Eisenhower men Nixon saw regularly in New York included Bill Rogers, Thomas Gates (Secretary of Defense), Gabriel Hauge (economic adviser), Herbert Brownell (Attorney General before Rogers), and Maurice Stans (Director of the Budget), among others. Businessmen who were hefty contributors to the Republican Party and who helped Nixon get started in New York included his former aide Charles McWhorter, now a lawyer for AT&T (and described by *The New York Times* as "a walking encyclopedia of political information who is regarded as one of the most astute strategists in the country"),[41] Roger Blough, chairman of U.S. Steel, Mrs. Ogden Reid of the New York *Herald Tribune,* Horace Flanigan of Manufacturers Hanover Trust, Donald Kendall of Pepsi, George Champion of Chase Manhattan, and Elmer Bobst of Warner-Lambert, among others.

Even Nixon's minister was at the top of the New York ladder; Sunday mornings, Nixon went to hear Norman Vincent Peale preach. In the afternoons, he went to the New York Giants football games; he had a friend on the team, Frank Gifford. Saturday nights he would attend a play or a musical, then go to Toots Shor's place afterward to talk sports.

Nixon the New York lawyer impressed visitors as supremely

happy. He told Peter Kihss, who did a feature story on his life in the city for *The New York Times,* that he found New York "the most challenging and stimulating and fastest track in the world in top corporate and international law." Kihss thought Nixon "never looked more fit or more relaxed."

Nixon told Kihss emphatically that "I came to New York to practice law and not to practice politics." The family too was committed to life in New York. The girls were attending Chapin School, a private girls' school that was Mrs. Kennedy's alma mater. Pat regretted the loss of California sunshine, and confessed "we miss the outdoor barbecue." Apartment living had its drawbacks too: "We haven't got room for a big deep freeze." But overall, she was glad to be out of politics, and enjoyed strolling in the anonymity of the city, with the girls, Checkers, and a new poodle. Shortly after moving into the apartment, Pat told Dick over dinner one night, "I hope we never move again." [42]

In denying that he came to New York for political rather than economic reasons, Nixon repeatedly cited as proof the fact that he had no political staff. Rose Mary Woods was his secretary, as she had been for more than a decade, with Loie Gaunt as her assistant. Steve Hess was also working for Nixon, but as a writer, not a political aide. Otherwise there was no staff.

But attractive as Nixon initially found life in New York City to be, and much as he enjoyed a big income and seeing his firm prosper, and despite what he told Pat and the girls, he never considered abandoning politics, the fastest track of all. Not even during quiet evenings at home, of which there were an increasing number. At first, the Nixons had accepted numerous invitations to balls and other social affairs, but after a couple of months they declined all but a few, to stay home. Nixon would read for three hours or more before going to bed, primarily American history and biography. "It's escapist," Nixon said, "but it also enriches your thought processes." It also increased his already deep knowledge of the recent past, and was in fact the best possible study for a presidential aspirant.

His heroes were Teddy Roosevelt and Woodrow Wilson. He liked TR "because of his great dynamic drive and ability to mobilize a young country . . . and his ability to lead." The attraction of Wilson, Nixon explained, was "his sheer intellectual brilliance. . . . Wilson once wrote a speech at Princeton in which he talked of men of thought and men of action. . . . Teddy Roosevelt was a man of action who could think and Woodrow Wilson was a man of thought who could act." [43]

Nixon's office struck reporter Jules Witcover as "a museum of his past political life . . . a kind of sanctuary for a President-in-exile." It included a pen set from Ike, a landscape by Ike, signed photographs of world leaders, keys to assorted cities, the vice-presidential gavel, and so forth.[44] There were other reminders of who Nixon had been and might be: when he attended football or hockey games, or the theater, or ate in a restaurant, he was always mobbed by autograph seekers and well-wishers. These fans spoke for millions of others, as the Gallup polls made clear: consistently he was the first choice of 25 percent or more of Republicans for the 1964 nomination, some months slightly ahead of Goldwater, sometimes slightly behind, but always far in front of Rockefeller and Romney. Nixon expressed gratification each time a new poll came out, but insisted that he was not a candidate; in response to that standard question in such cases—would he accept a draft?—Nixon's reply was that because he was not a candidate, a draft would be unthinkable.

But he made sure his name stayed in circulation. In September, when Ike gave out a list of ten possible Republican candidates, and did not include Nixon on the list, Nixon moved quickly. At a private dinner with a number of Republican politicians Nixon restated his disinclination to run, but added that "I did think it was a little odd that President Eisenhower didn't include me on his list of 10 'good people' who might make Republican candidates. I thought it was strange."

Nixon's comment reached Eisenhower's ear the next day, as Nixon intended. The former President immediately wrote Nixon to say he could scarcely believe Nixon had been quoted correctly, "because you had frankly told me that you were not available."[45] But Eisenhower also told a reporter the next week that if there were a "sudden wave of support" for Nixon, "there would be no question about his capacity to perform the job." (Once again, Eisenhower had not said he supported Nixon for President, only that Nixon was qualified.) It was around this time that Nixon, fed up with Ike's ambiguity, characterized the former President as "that senile old bastard."[46]

In his speeches (about one a week), Nixon was provocative enough to make all the papers. In October, he criticized Kennedy's decision to sell $250 million in wheat to the Soviet Union as "the major foreign policy mistake of this administration, even more serious than . . . the Bay of Pigs. What we're doing is subsidizing Khrushchev at a time he is in deep economic trouble."[47]

Later in the month, Nixon went to Paris on business for Pepsi. He used the occasion to hold a press conference, where he began by proclaiming, "I am not a candidate for office in 1964," then laid into Kennedy. NATO was in disarray because of Kennedy's blunders, he said, and he also hit Kennedy for the Administration's obvious withdrawal of support for President Ngo Dinh Diem in South Vietnam (Diem was under intense pressure from the Buddhists in his own country and from the Democrats in Washington, who saw his apparently repressive policies and evident inefficiency as the real problem in Vietnam): "I would say that in Vietnam today the choice is not between Diem and somebody better, it is between Diem and somebody infinitely worse." [48]

When he got back to the States, Nixon held another news conference, where he declared that "I have never been abroad when American prestige was lower than it is now." [49]

In October, in *The Saturday Evening Post* (reprinted three months later in *Reader's Digest*), Nixon reported on his European trip. He returned to a theme that had been successful for the Republicans back in 1952, the liberation of Eastern Europe. He wanted to "mobilize" and "arouse" public opinion to "prevent the sellout of the right of 97 million enslaved people in Eastern Europe to be free." He called for a "complete change of direction . . . in U.S. foreign policy," setting a goal of "nothing less than to bring freedom to the communist world." He implicitly but strongly criticized Eisenhower for failing to help the Hungarian uprising in 1956. [50]

By early November, one year after he declared he had held his last press conference, Nixon had held nearly fifty press conferences, plus many interviews, and done considerable writing. He kept his name alive, in sharp contrast to Tom Dewey after 1948. But he was not necessarily speaking falsely when he said he was not running in 1964. As he wrote in his memoirs, he thought "Kennedy would be virtually unbeatable . . . [and] another defeat in 1964 might so brand me with a loser image that I could never recover." [51]

But he had not missed a campaign since 1946. Every even-numbered year he had spent more time on the campaign trail than in his office. If Goldwater and Rockefeller deadlocked, he would be the obvious choice to unify the party and carry the flag. Kennedy might make some egregious blunder between now and the election. Nixon kept himself ready. Meanwhile he got on with his law practice, and prepared to sign the contract with Doubleday to do a commentary on the 1964 campaign, a strong indication that he had little expectation of being the nominee himself.

KENNEDY WAS giving him plenty to write about if he became a commentator, or to oppose if he became the candidate. There was, for example, wiretapping. It was widely rumored in Washington that the Justice Department, through the FBI, was placing bugs and taps on reporters, political opponents, and businessmen. The FBI wiretapped the home and office of Hanson Baldwin, the military-affairs analyst of *The New York Times*. In the April 1963 *Atlantic* magazine, Baldwin published an article that criticized the Administration for the use of the FBI to investigate leaks and to intimidate reporters. The agents used methods that "have smacked of totalitarianism," Baldwin wrote. He charged that their goal was to protect the Administration, not national security.[52]

That fall, Victor Lasky published *J.F.K.: The Man and the Myth*, a decidedly unfriendly biography. Nixon read the book and telephoned Lasky. "That's quite a book," Nixon said. "I've just finished it and, frankly, I never knew what bastards those Kennedys were." Lasky told Nixon that the Kennedys were out to get him, Lasky, that "Bobby's boys" in Justice were digging into his files looking for derogatory material. Nixon was not surprised. He mentioned the tax audit he had undergone, then shrugged: "Oh, what the hell, it's all part of the game, I guess."[53]

Part of the game or not, on November 13 Nixon told his old friend Senator Karl Mundt (R., S.D.) that the recent revelations of wiretapping by the Administration in the "Otepka case" were "shocking."

The case involved Otto F. Otepka, a security evaluations officer in the State Department. He had objected to changes the Democrats had made in security procedures, and he had refused to give a security blessing to a high Kennedy appointee, Walt W. Rostow. Otepka had not called Rostow a Communist, but he cited Communist relatives, associates, and friends of Rostow's and called him a security risk. The Kennedy brothers thought this preposterous.

Otepka had also leaked documents supporting his position to Republicans on the Senate Internal Security Subcommittee. In retaliation, the Kennedy Administration had demoted Otepka, harrassed him, bugged and wiretapped him, and put him under personal surveillance.

The State Department employees who did the bugging and spying flatly denied ever doing such things. But when the subcommittee produced solid evidence of their crimes, they switched stories. Now they admitted the truth but claimed that they got no information from the wiretapping because of "static" on the line. For this reason, they said, they were not guilty of perjury for telling the subcommittee they had not done what they had done, because their efforts had been "ineffective." But even that was a lie—they did get usable tapes.[54]

It was an apparently open-and-shut case of criminal action by the State Department, including illegal entry, illegal wiretapping, and perjury. But Justice brought no charges, made no indictments, except against Otepka, whom it charged with leaking information and documents to the Senate subcommittee.

Nixon was outraged. He called Jimmy Byrnes, a former Democratic Secretary of State, to express his feelings and explore the possibilities of doing something. As Nixon explained in a letter to Mundt the next day, "The key question, it would seem to me, is—who ordered these subordinates to wire-tap their superior and then to commit perjury?" Byrnes had agreed that "this question should be pressed vigorously."

The potential was enormous. If the guilty men could be forced to say who ordered them to break the law, and then to cover up, they could only point up, and it might lead to the Attorney General himself, or the Secretary of State, or . . . who knew?

Nixon was excited by the possibilities, and laid down careful instructions for Mundt to follow. Nixon's premise was that "a couple of lowly clerks would never have taken such risks on their own." The way to force them to talk, Nixon was convinced, was to use the threat of perjury. Show them the threat of perjury "and they will hesitate to run the additional risk of refusing to disclose who was behind the whole operation."[55]

In his reply, Mundt admitted that none of the Republicans on the subcommittee had thought of that approach, and promised to see that it was followed. But he did nothing. Nor did any newspapers take up the case. The story died before it was born.

Nixon, frustrated, was helpless. It was like January 1961, when he had urged Senator Everett Dirksen (R., Ill.) to use the confirmation hearings on Robert Kennedy as Attorney General to ask questions about the Kennedy family fortune. Dirksen had said he would do so, but did not. The Republicans simply did not have the ruthlessness of the Democrats when it came to attacking their enemies, or so it seemed to Nixon. Only by staying active himself in the campaign, either as commentator or candidate, could Nixon bring the peccadilloes of the Kennedys to light.

THE OVERTHROW and assassination of President Diem (November 1–2) also outraged Nixon. "I think our complicity in Diem's murder was a national disgrace," he wrote by hand at the bottom of a letter to Eisenhower three days later.[56] On November 7, he expressed himself more fully in a letter to the head of the Joint House-Senate Republican Committee, Robert Humphreys.

"I personally can't understand why the Republicans are so reluctant to say a good word for Diem," Nixon complained. "He was, after all, a foe of communism and a friend of the United States. If it had not been for him, Viet Nam would be Communist today.

"It is true that some of his extreme policies as well as the antics of his brother and sister-in-law were embarrassing to us. But our heavy-handed complicity in his murder can only have the effect of striking terror in the hearts of leaders of other nations who presumably are our friends." [57]

Eisenhower told Nixon that "I cannot believe any American would have approved the cold-blooded killing of a man who had, after all, shown great courage when he undertook the task of defeating Communism." Ike added that he could not accept that Kennedy would have ordered the murder of a fellow Catholic,[58] but Nixon stuck to his belief that there was American complicity in Diem's assassination.

By this time, a year away from the 1964 election, Nixon's name was, inevitably, popping up again and again in the speculation about the Republican nominee. Campaigning in New Hampshire, Rockefeller said that if a deadlock developed, Nixon "sure would be in the wings, I'll bet you that." And Eisenhower, on CBS's "Face the Nation" on November 10, said that if there were a deadlock, Nixon would be "one of the likely persons to be . . . approached because he is after all a very knowledgeable and very courageous type of person."

Asked to comment, Nixon said of Rockefeller's remark, "I am not a candidate," and added, "This is not a devious, conspiratorial plan on my part to be a candidate." Two days later, he insisted, "My best role is to unite the party after the bloodletting. . . . Anyone in the United States would want to be President, but there is a time and place for everything." He was not, he said, "shaking out there in the wings, wringing my hands, waiting to be called by the party. . . . I'm not going to run." [59] But he did not repudiate Eisenhower's sort-of endorsement. Nixon was a man who kept his options open, ready to seize opportunities.

ON NOVEMBER 21, Nixon was in Dallas for a meeting of Pepsi-Cola bottlers. He found the city seething with hate-filled and violent talk. Just a month earlier in Dallas, Adlai Stevenson had been hit by a placard and spat upon in a right-wing demonstration. Kennedy was scheduled to appear in the city the next day along with Vice-President Johnson and Governor John Connally of Texas. Hostility toward Kennedy apparently was widespread and was prompting some wild talk about demonstrations, "getting Kennedy," and so on.*

---

* Nixon was himself a target. Unknown to him, the morning he arrived in Dallas, Lee Harvey Oswald had set out to kill him, only to be stopped by his wife.[60]

Nixon was appalled. No matter how partisan his speeches, no matter how often he seemed to incite people with his campaign rhetoric, all his life Nixon was firmly opposed to heckling, demonstrations, picketing, and attempts to embarrass or shout down a speaker. Back in early June, at a farewell speech in California, Nixon had spoken out strongly against the NAACP for picketing President Kennedy in Los Angeles.[61] In Dallas, on November 21, Nixon called a news conference, where he urged the citizens to give President Kennedy and his wife "a courteous reception." Those who did otherwise, he said, "harm their own cause and help their opponents."[62]

The morning of November 22, Nixon flew back to New York. He hailed a taxicab at the airport and headed for home. On the way, when the cab stopped for a traffic light, a man rushed over from the curb and asked the driver, "Do you have a radio in your cab? I just heard that Kennedy was shot."

There was no radio. As the cab drove on, Nixon thought, "Oh, my God, it must have been one of the nuts."

The doorman at Nixon's apartment building was crying when Nixon arrived.

"Oh, Mr. Nixon, have you heard, sir?" he sobbed. "It's just terrible. They've killed President Kennedy."

Nixon told interviewers at the time, and later wrote in his memoirs, "I never felt the 'there but for the grace of God go I' reaction to Kennedy's death. . . . I did not think that if I had won in 1960 it would have been I rather than he riding through Dealey Plaza in Dallas at that time, on that day."[63]

But Steve Hess, who arrived at Nixon's apartment a couple of minutes after Nixon got there (they were scheduled to sign the contract with Doubleday), had a different impression. "When he opened the door for me," Hess said, "the first person of his circle to see him, I can assure you that his reaction appeared to me to be, 'There but for the grace of God go I.' He was very shaken."

Nixon got out his attaché case and showed Hess the Dallas morning paper, with the story about his urging respect for the President. Hess felt it was Nixon's way of saying, "You see, I didn't have anything to do with creating this."

Nixon went to the phone. He called J. Edgar Hoover, head of the FBI.

"What happened?" Nixon asked. "Was it one of the right-wing nuts?"

"No," Hoover replied, "it was a Communist."[64]

Hess thought Nixon was somewhat relieved by the news. Together they prepared a statement for the television cameras downstairs. Nixon expressed his grief and his sympathy and concluded, "The greatest tribute we can pay to his memory is in our everyday lives to do everything we can to reduce the forces of hatred which drive men to do such terrible deeds."[65]

Rose Woods came over to the Nixon apartment; at Nixon's request, she phoned Tom Dewey and Roger Blough to cancel a golf date. Other calls cleared Nixon's schedule for the following days, and Rose arranged for a meeting the next morning in Nixon's apartment, a gathering of his major New York supporters, to discuss the implications. Nixon's first speculation was that there would be a "bloodbath" in the Democratic Party, as President Johnson struggled with Attorney General Kennedy for control. Nixon thought it might lead to an Adlai Stevenson nomination for 1964.[66]

That night, before going to bed, Nixon wrote a note to Jacqueline Kennedy. "While the hand of fate made Jack and me political opponents," he said, "I always cherished the fact that we were personal friends from the time we came to the Congress together in 1947."[67]

Hess joined the meeting the following morning: "The politicos were already assessing how this event would affect or re-create the possibilities of Nixon running for President." Nixon had changed his mind about the possibility of a Democratic bloodbath and now thought that Johnson "would have it under control," that the country would unite behind him, and that he was a good enough politician to take advantage of his opportunity. As for his own prospects, Nixon knew it was far too early to tell. Obviously Kennedy's assassination was an event of the first importance that would have innumerable repercussions. It would dramatically affect Nixon. But how, in what ways, could not so soon be seen.

He needed to keep his options open, which meant in these circumstances backing out of the Doubleday contract. Working on such a book would tie him down too firmly at a time when he needed to stay available for whatever might develop.[68]

THE NIXONS went to Washington for Kennedy's funeral. It was not a time for him to be making any public statements, other than to express shock and sympathy. But it was a time for Nixon to think about Kennedy.

The way the press had fawned on Kennedy had made Nixon furious and jealous; all that money and the things Kennedy had gotten away with had made Nixon resentful; Kennedy's policies— backing down at the Bay of Pigs, allowing Soviet troops to remain on Cuban soil, wiretapping his opponents, refusing to tear down the Berlin Wall, the complicity in the assassination of Diem, selling wheat to the Soviet Union—had given Nixon opportunities to criticize President Kennedy, and he had done so with gusto.

Nixon could hardly have avoided feelings of envy about Kennedy's good looks and charm and wit and bearing and money and family—every politician in America felt some envy of the man. But for all that, Nixon said he liked Kennedy and considered him a friend, and he really was not that much different from Kennedy in his policies once he came to power. One of the notable features about Nixon's campaigning in 1963 was the issue over which he did *not* go after Kennedy, even though it was the one on which the Kennedy Administration had broken most sharply with the Eisenhower Administration—greatly increased defense spending and a consequent unbalanced budget. Nor did he criticize Kennedy for getting involved in Vietnam, and sending combat units there, but only for limiting the use of force and abandoning Diem.

So for all their differences on policy questions, and despite their well-known differences of style—Nixon's scowl, Kennedy's smile; Nixon's snarl, Kennedy's quips; Nixon's awkwardness, Kennedy's athletic grace—they were much more alike than they were different.

Nixon, as much as Kennedy, was of that "new generation of Americans—born in this century, tempered by war, disciplined by a hard and bitter peace, proud of our ancient heritage." Out of that experience had come some common assumptions, shared not only by Nixon and Kennedy but by millions of their generation. These assumptions included the belief that America was morally superior to all other nations, that there were no limits to what America could achieve, and that there were no limits on the methods that had to be used to wage the Cold War.

American moral superiority was based, above all else, on the heritage of World War II. At the end of the war, America's prestige had never been higher. The U.S. had provided the tools and the men to save Europe and Russia from Hitler and his Nazis. The U.S. had driven the Japanese out of China, Indochina, Burma, Korea, the Philippines. The U.S. had given the Philippines independence, without forcing the Filipinos to wage a war of national liberation to achieve it. America had asked for nothing for itself in return. Ho Chi Minh, leader of the Vietminh in Vietnam at that time, hailed the Americans as the true friends of the oppressed of the earth. So did such dissimilar men as Charles de Gaulle, Churchill, and on one occasion even Stalin himself. In a world full of hatred, death, destruction, deception, and double-dealing, the United States at the end of World War II was almost universally regarded as the disinterested champion of justice, freedom, and democracy. America was especially seen in that light by Americans.

The idea that anything was possible for the United States, given enough commitment, was also a heritage of World War II. The nation that had been practically unarmed in 1939 had, by 1945, a military preponderance in the world that was unprecedented. And an economic preponderance too, as the American homeland was not just untouched but booming, at a time when much of the rest of the world's industrial capacity was in ashes. Events over the next decade and a half reinforced the sense of power—the great postwar economic boom, stopping Communist aggression in Korea, creating NATO.

By 1960, however, there was an increasing sense of frustration, growing from a feeling that President Eisenhower and the old men who served in his Cabinet had put self-imposed, stuck-in-the-mud limits on the country's approach to its problems. It seemed to younger leaders like Nixon and Kennedy that their elders were so concerned with protecting the profits from World War II that they were neglecting opportunities to invest those profits. In 1960, it was time for the junior officers from the war to take command, to get the country moving again.

The notion that anything goes in the struggle against the enemy was also a World War II legacy. No moral sensibilities had been allowed to stand in the way of the Allied cause, for the quite obvious reason that the opponent was the Gestapo. In a life-and-death struggle, one has no choice. As to assassination, would anyone in the world (other than a few Nazis) have objected had the British or Americans managed to kill Hitler in 1943?

In the postwar period, when Stalin quickly came to seem to Americans to be the next Hitler, and when the NKVD was even more active than the Gestapo (and as evil in its methods), it was inevitable that America would develop a way of fighting the new enemy. Harry Truman got it started; it was called the Central Intelligence Agency. In 1954, in an investigation of the CIA for the Eisenhower Administration, the Doolittle Committee had described the assumptions on which the agency had to operate in chilling words: "We are facing an implacable enemy whose avowed objective is world domination by whatever means and at whatever cost. There are no rules in such a game. Hitherto acceptable norms of human conduct do not apply. We must develop effective espionage and counterespionage services and must learn to subvert, sabotage, and destroy our enemies by more clever, more sophisticated, and more effective methods than those used against us."[69]

By law, the CIA was forbidden to operate within the United States, and in theory that line would keep all distasteful espionage activities overseas. But the extension of these practices (wiretapping, etc.) to domestic enemies was probably inevitable—for one reason, because the technology was there, and the resultant temptation strong—and in any case soon under way. Eisenhower used the FBI to spy on the American Communist Party. Kennedy used the FBI to spy on Martin Luther King, Jr. Johnson would soon be using the FBI to spy on his political enemies, both Democratic (the Mississippi Freedom Democratic Party) and Republican. It was a natural and logical progression.

Nixon and Kennedy shared a legacy and a number of basic assumptions. In this, they were the authentic spokesmen for their generation.

NIXON, in an interview a couple of years after Kennedy's death, tried to speak to the meaning of the event. "When a man is old and dies, that's one thing," Nixon said. "But a young man—the death of a man in his youth, so idealistic, so spirited. . . . I think that was one of the reasons Kennedy's death had a traumatic effect on the country greater than the death of Lincoln. It was not just the death of a man. The end of an era that had just begun . . . "[70]

Aside from his exaggeration about Lincoln's death, Nixon may well have been right on the mark in his judgment about the end of an era. It was not, however, an era that had "just begun"; rather it was the era of the forties and fifties coming to an end. The triumphs of the forties, the supreme self-confidence of the fifties, the extraordinary optimism of the early sixties, all summed up in Kennedy's program of putting a man on the moon, stopping aggression in Vietnam, eliminating poverty and prejudice, quickening the arms race, providing free health care for large segments of the public, and lowering taxes, all at once, were beginning to crumble even before his death.

In the six months since Nixon had moved to New York, the strain and tension produced within the nation by the attempt to reach these goals had led to a series of incidents. On June 11, a Buddhist monk had immolated himself in Saigon in protest against Diem. On June 12, in Jackson, Mississippi, a sniper's rifle bullet had killed civil rights leader Medgar Evers. On August 28, Dr. King had made Negro demands for civil rights into the great moral issue of the day with his "I have a dream" speech at the Lincoln Memorial. On September 15, four little girls had been killed in a Sunday-school bombing of a church in Birmingham, Alabama. On November 1–2, Diem had been toppled and assassinated in Vietnam. By mid-November, the United States had sent sixteen thousand troops to Vietnam.

Kennedy's assassination, and the killing of Lee Harvey Oswald by Jack Ruby a few days later, capped this wave of violence and passion. Those events marked, as Nixon said, the end of an era. They opened to him opportunities that he was quick to seize.

CHAPTER TWO

COPING
WITH CATASTROPHE
1964

IN THE WEEKS following Kennedy's death, Nixon concentrated on his law practice. That December, having completed six months' residence in New York, he was admitted to the bar. His law firm changed its name to Nixon, Mudge, Rose, Guthrie, and Alexander. He was enjoying the Christmas season in the city, with carol-singing parties in the apartment for the girls and his friends.

He had a special reason to celebrate. In order to be admitted to the New York bar, he had had to write an essay on "What do you believe the principles underlying the form of government of the United States to be?" His answer, according to the chairman of the committee on character and fitness, was "the finest he had seen in 28 years," so good that he released it to the press, which published it widely.

Nixon described the principles as decentralization and separation of powers and the balancing of freedom with order. "The American ideal," he wrote, "is that private or individual enterprise should be allowed and encouraged to undertake all functions which it is capable to perform." He thought that "above all else, the framers of the Constitution were fearful of the concentration of power in either individuals or government." The protection of individual rights, he wrote, was guaranteed "by the system itself, which is the most effective safeguard against arbitrary power ever devised by man." [1]

Nixon had chosen his words carefully. His essay was tightly constructed, his conclusion concisely stated. He made his argument with power and passion. He made it clear, without having to say so, that this expression of the American ideal represented exactly his own most deeply held convictions.

The publicity about his essay helped his already flourishing legal practice. His political positioning of himself, meanwhile, continued. In early January, Nixon met with fifteen friends at the Waldorf in New York to discuss his future. Bob Finch and Bob Haldeman from California were there, along with Fred Seaton of Nebraska (Ike's Secretary of the Interior), John Whitaker, Steve Hess, and others. The strategy meeting came to an obvious conclusion: Nixon's only hope in 1964 was a deadlock between Goldwater and Rockefeller. Meanwhile he would not himself be an announced candidate (there was no chance of raising the necessary money, nor any chance that Nixon would take time off from his law practice to campaign in New Hampshire), which meant he need not attack either Goldwater or Rockefeller, but could concentrate on Johnson.

Anyway, he never had the alternative of genuinely taking himself out of the race. Not even a Sherman-like statement could have removed his name from the speculation. He was still the favorite of more Republicans than anyone else, and a mid-January poll had him running better against Johnson than any other man. Coupled with the strong position he held among many Eisenhower people and his own following among the professionals and big-business supporters of the Republican Party, such shows of strength sustained Nixon speculation.

He did his part to keep it alive. On January 9, his fifty-first birthday, he told a reporter that he would "make any sacrifice" to see to it that the GOP nominated "its strongest man." Reminded that the latest Gallup poll showed him two points ahead of Goldwater, Nixon said, "I believe that any man who has become a public figure belongs to the public, and as long as they want him to lead, to lead." Then came the inevitable disclaimer: "Leadership doesn't always involve being a candidate," and an explanation of his role, which was to talk about issues and develop a Republican program. But he also had an aide, Stephen Jones, put together a list of men nominated for the Presidency who had previously lost an election. Nixon sent the list to Raymond Moley to use in his *Newsweek* column.[2]

IN FEBRUARY, Nixon hit the Lincoln's Day circuit. He went to North Carolina for a speech, television interview, and Republican reception, then back to New York City for a fund-raiser, then to Philadelphia for a day of speeches, receptions, and a dinner. A week later it was Cincinnati, then Florida, Minneapolis, Kansas City, and finally Peoria, Illinois.

His message was alarmist. The Kennedy-Johnson Administration, Nixon said, had presided over "the worst series of foreign-policy disasters since World War II. We find we no longer contain Communism but are being contained by it." The President, Nixon charged, "has created an image of weakness and indecision," and he promised that the Republicans would "launch an offensive for victory without war for the forces of freedom." [3]

Early in March, Nixon went to Washington to testify at Senate subcommittee hearings on presidential succession and disability. The setting was the Senate Caucus Room, Congress's grand inquisitorial chamber.

"This is the first time I've ever been present in this room on this side of the table," Nixon quipped as he took the witness chair. "I'm glad I'm here voluntarily, and not under subpoena."

Nixon recommended that the vacancy in the Vice-Presidency be filled by having Johnson name a man who would be subject to the approval of the electoral college of 1960. Russell Baker, who covered the story, wrote that "without a paper before him, Mr. Nixon talked extemporaneously for nearly 30 minutes. His sentences were crisp and direct. . . . It was the measured performance of the constitutional lawyer who has mastered his brief."

But the role that really restored color to Nixon's cheeks, Baker observed, "was that of Presidential noncandidate." When Nixon completed his testimony, reporters came charging up with questions about the presidential race. Baker could see "Nixon's eyes lighting up as the reporters led him through the beloved old political clichés."

One such was that he was "neither encouraging nor discouraging" a write-in vote in New Hampshire, where the primary was a week away. It featured Goldwater versus Rockefeller, with last-minute support for a write-in for Henry Cabot Lodge, Jr., Nixon's running mate in 1960, currently U.S. ambassador to South Vietnam. Nixon also announced that he would not take his name off the Oregon primary ballot because to do so would require him to sign an affidavit that he would not accept the nomination. Nixon said that since he had already declared his willingness to take any Republican assignment, he could not consistently sign the affidavit. [4]

In New Hampshire, on March 10, Lodge won with 33,400 write-in votes. Goldwater got 21,700 votes, and Rockefeller, 19,500. Nixon got 15,700 write-ins. Nixon was unhappy—he had carried the state in 1960—but he knew that Lodge supporters had put $100,000 into their campaign for write-in votes, to his zero, and insisted that he was pleased with the outcome.

What he had to be most pleased about was the miserable showing of both Goldwater and Rockefeller. James Reston wrote that the New Hampshire primary election "virtually eliminates both Senator Goldwater and Governor Rockefeller." Reston predicted a deadlocked convention, with the prize eventually going to Lodge, Nixon, or Governor William Scranton of Pennsylvania.[5]

Nixon knew better than to think either Goldwater or Rockefeller was out of the race; he also knew how to take advantage of their possible deadlock. At a news conference in Newark, where he was speaking at a Republican dinner, Nixon declared, "I feel there is no man in this country who can make a case against Mr. Johnson more effectively than I can." He showed what he meant in his speech: "I warn you that this country could be in for four more years of wheeling and dealing and influence-peddling unprecedented in this country." He said Johnson's foreign policy was allowing the free world to fall into the hands of the Communists, and denounced the Administration's "spending and big government policies."[6]

The next day, March 12, Nixon talked on the telephone to Fred Seaton in Nebraska, site of a May 12 primary. They agreed that Lodge was not going to get anywhere. Nixon asked what chance Seaton thought Scranton had.

"Zero," Seaton replied.

They then agreed that Nixon would not enter the primary in Nebraska, but that Seaton would organize a write-in campaign for him.

Nixon asked if Seaton thought he should run in the Oregon primary.

"If you do," Seaton replied, "you will lose your identity as an available nominee who was doing nothing to seek the place, and if the ball doesn't bounce right after you campaign in Oregon you will be practically a dead duck."[7]

So Nixon wisely stuck to his cautious, noncandidate position. It was a good time to stay low, a time of high passion within the GOP and intense politics in the nation, as Lyndon Johnson began to seize his opportunity. In January, Johnson declared "War on Poverty" as he began his Great Society program of reform and redistribution. He put the initial bill at one billion dollars. He gave enthusiastic support to the Civil Rights Act of 1964. That bill prohibited racial discrimination in employment, places of public accommodation, publicly owned facilities, and federally funded programs. The bill was a big and necessary step forward from the Eisenhower Administration's 1957 civil rights bill, and beyond anything Jack Kennedy had ever proposed.

Johnson's Civil Rights Act was a hard one for any member of

the party of Abraham Lincoln to oppose, but Goldwater did anyway; he voted against it. Nixon avoided comment.

Meanwhile "white backlash" was becoming a political phenomenon. Meanwhile, too, civil rights activists were beginning to picket and heckle Johnson for his failure to act sooner and more decisively, and race riots began in Rochester, New York. Overseas, there had been anti-American riots in Panama, and another coup in Saigon. Castro had tightened his links with Khrushchev in a visit to Moscow, and threatened to cut the water supply to the U.S. naval base at Guantanamo.

THE SPRING of 1964 was a volatile time. Politics was in turmoil; people were divided. This was because fundamental questions were at stake. At home, the question was, What is the role and place of Afro-Americans in the United States? It was a question that cut to the soul of America, because it touched every part of American life—economics, jobs, social life, religion, public facilities, medicine, crime—but most of all, it put the heaviest responsibility for change on that part of the society least able to bear it, the public-school system. No other institution in American life was so vulnerable; no other institution aroused such emotion.

So it was inevitable that passions would run high in 1964. America was not going to achieve a revolutionary change in civil and political rights for Negro Americans without cost. The changes and their cost caused fear. Fear produced motivated voters whose political spokesmen took extreme positions—it was "never" versus "now."

Johnson's position was "now." Nixon's position was "later." This put him squarely in the middle, as a supporter of civil rights, but not quite yet.

Overseas, the question in 1964 was, What is the role and place of the United States in Vietnam? It too cut to the very soul of America; it too touched every part of American life; it too aroused the deepest passions. What was the nature of the Communist threat? How should the United States respond to it? What was the U.S. capable of doing so far from home? What burden were we willing to bear? What was at stake? These questions, and the possible answers to them, also created fear, which produced motivated voters whose political spokesmen took extreme positions—it was "all the way" versus "pull out."

Johnson's position was to "stay the course." This put him squarely in the middle, a supporter of an independent South Vietnam, but not a man to widen the war; rather he would win the hearts and minds of the peasants by building roads and schools.

Nixon's position was "all the way." He was the most hawkish of all national politicians that summer, even including Barry Goldwater. All through 1964, Nixon called for a greater effort.

And so on the great domestic issue of 1964, civil rights, Nixon took what middle ground there was, and Johnson stood at the head of the much larger Left, while on the great international issue, Vietnam, Johnson took what middle ground there was, while Nixon stood at the head of the much larger Right.

As THE CANDIDATES went after one another, Nixon got out of the country. It was a business trip, and if most of the business seemed to be Nixon for President, he did manage to get some work done and to promote Pepsi. He prepared with his usual ruthless efficiency, writing friends for advice on whom to see and what to ask, arranging meetings with foreign leaders.[8] But as he left on March 22, he told reporters at Kennedy Airport (the name had just been changed from Idlewild) that he was going to take a "holiday from politics."[9]

When he got off the plane in Beirut, Lebanon, he told a news conference that he would accept the Republican presidential nomination "if the party leaders ask me to run." Still he insisted that he was making this trip as a businessman; to prove the point, he had a Pepsi bottle at his elbow.[10] In Pakistan, in India, in Malaysia, and in Thailand, he met with the leaders, promoted Pepsi, warned about the Communists, and repeated that he was not a candidate but would run if asked.

In Saigon, Nixon criticized Johnson for his hesitancy in Vietnam. Asked if he expected Vietnam to become an issue in the presidential campaign, Nixon replied with one of his classics: "I hope it doesn't; it will only become an issue if the policy has weaknesses worthy of criticism, if it is plagued with inconsistency, improvisation and uncertainty. That has been the case in the past."

Next, Nixon paraphrased Douglas MacArthur's 1951 statement about Korea: "There is no substitute for victory in South Vietnam."[11]

Through the next two days, as American reporters followed him around Saigon, Nixon called for a greater effort. He talked to Ambassador Lodge, who indicated he thought the big problem in South Vietnam was economic, not military. Nixon was dismayed to discover that Lodge had "been converted by the academic theorists around Johnson who thought that the problem of communism in Southeast Asia could be solved by economic development." Nixon was further dismayed to hear American officers complain that they were being restrained from launching air raids into North Vietnam and ground raids into Laos to cut the Ho Chi Minh Trail, restrained, they speculated, because of politics back home.[12]

Nixon got a lovely opportunity to blast the Democrats when he arrived in Hong Kong. Senator J. William Fulbright (D., Ark.) had recently called for a "review" of U.S. policy toward China, to take advantage of the Sino-Soviet split. Nixon scorned such talk. "This kind of naive woolly-headed thinking is what has plagued U.S. policy," he said. "It would be disastrous to the cause of freedom" for the U.S. to recognize Red China or accept its admission into the United Nations.[13]

From Hong Kong, he was off to the Philippines, then Taiwan for a meeting with Chiang Kai-shek, and finally Tokyo, where he met the leaders of the Japanese government and at the inevitable press conference chose his ground for the 1964 campaign, if he happened to be the candidate.

Nixon announced that he favored extension of the war to North Vietnam. The policy of "restricting the South Vietnamese to simply dealing with the Communist guerrillas in South Vietnam" had shown "little success." Military men in the field had told him that merely increasing economic and military assistance would not suffice unless some countermeasures were taken against the North.[14]

Nixon's call for immediate escalation represented an extreme position on the political spectrum in the spring of 1964, seemingly unlike Nixon, but in fact he had always favored escalation in the war against Communism in Asia, whenever and wherever. But he had not gone public with these views, nor had he done so with regard to Communism in Latin America; in the 1960 campaign he had appeared to take an antiescalation position with regard to Castro, when in fact he was urging Eisenhower to invade Cuba.

So 1964 gave Nixon an opportunity to go public with his long and deeply held views. There was an element of sweet revenge in this: in 1960, Jack Kennedy had charged that the Republicans were not doing enough about the Communist menace, to which Nixon had had to reply, "Yes, we are." Now, in 1964, Nixon could go on the attack with the charge that the Democrats were not doing enough about the Communist menace.

Nixon frequently remarked that when he changed his public posture on a position he liked to leapfrog the next place in line. Thus on Vietnam, in 1964, he leapfrogged Lodge and Rockefeller, who advocated more economic aid and no wider war, to take a position to the right of Goldwater.

Nixon stood where General MacArthur had stood thirteen years earlier, albeit in another part of Asia. On his return, in mid-April, Nixon told reporters in New York that the U.S. should deny the enemy a "privileged sanctuary" in North Vietnam; in Washington, he insisted that "we cannot have a Yalu River concept in South Vietnam." [15]

NIXON'S CALL for action directed against North Vietnam struck a responsive chord among Goldwater Republicans, so it had the political advantage of making Nixon the number-two choice of the Goldwater delegates. They did not much like Nixon, most of them, because of his middle-of-the-road domestic positions, but they would never take Rockefeller, and Nixon's extremism on Vietnam made him acceptable if Goldwater faltered. And there were more Goldwater delegates, in hand, than the combined opposition.

On April 20, an Associated Press poll of Republican county chairmen showed that the party professionals felt Nixon was the "most likely nominee" (526 for Nixon to 427 for Goldwater), but when asked to express a personal preference, the vote was 722 for Goldwater, 301 for Nixon. [16]

In short, if the combined opposition could stop Goldwater, Nixon was a cinch as nominee. But if Nixon did anything to stop Goldwater, he would lose Goldwater's delegates, and thus the nomination. That was the hand he had been dealt, and he needed to play it carefully.

Of course, he did. The first requirement was to prove to the professionals that he still had wide and deep support. The day the AP poll appeared, Nixon got on the telephone to Seaton in Nebraska. Nixon said he was "all for going ahead in Nebraska."

Seaton asked about money. Nixon said he would let William Casey, of the Republican National Committee (RNC), deal with the financial end. But two days later, on April 22, Nixon confessed to Seaton that "the money wasn't easy to get." Casey had reported that some potential donors felt the money should be saved for Oregon, where Nixon's name was on the ballot.

In other words, the donors didn't want to give until Nixon agreed to become an active candidate. That was not what Nixon wanted at all. If money were spent in Oregon, he would have to approve it, which meant he would have to be a candidate, which would have put him in opposition not to Johnson but to Goldwater and Rockefeller.

Nixon, the most eager campaigner of all, had to avoid this campaign at all costs. Thus a write-in campaign in Nebraska was ideal: he did not need to approve it, nor campaign, but under Seaton's expert direction it would show the depth and breadth of Nixon's support. And it would allow him to go head-to-head with Goldwater (Rockefeller had conceded the state and his name was not on the primary ballot; only Goldwater's name and a space for write-ins appeared) without having to say one word against Goldwater.

How much did Seaton need? Nixon asked.

Fifty thousand dollars, Seaton answered.

Nixon went to work, but found it difficult. He spent a fruitless all-day session with New York Republicans, followed by a series of phone calls to California, and some more legwork by Bill Casey. Even with all that, Nixon raised only $20,000.[17]

In relaying this news to Seaton, Rose Woods remarked, "RMN will be in touch again—he is quite concerned about security on these telephone calls—better [for Seaton] to place the calls—Seaton said security ok on his end—he didn't know about the NY end."

Bugged telephone or not, Woods rang off with these words: "RMN wants to go ahead."[18]

So a Nixon campaign, featuring direct mail and local newspaper advertisements, began in Nebraska, where he was not on the ballot, while there was no campaign in Oregon, where he was. If he could run strongly in Nebraska (May 12), where he could claim any vote over 25 percent as a major victory, and in Oregon (May 15), and if Rockefeller beat Goldwater in California (June 2), where no write-ins were allowed and only Goldwater and Rockefeller appeared on the ballot, the convention would deadlock.

He was within sight of his second nomination as the Republican candidate for President. On April 27, he moved to improve his relations with the press. He was speaking at the annual stag dinner of the Gridiron Club in Washington, and made an apology of sorts: "My friends in the press—if I have any. If I haven't any, maybe it is more my fault than theirs. I hope a man can lose his temper once in sixteen years and be forgiven for it."

He gave further evidence of a new Nixon when he turned to Harry Truman and said, "If this party is supposed to be dedicated to love, what better evidence is there than for Harry Truman to take a drink from Dick Nixon without asking someone else to taste it first."

Truman took the offered drink, then shook Nixon's hand, as the reporters and politicians present—a sentimental lot, especially when drinking—rose as one man to applaud heartily.[19]

On May 7, Nixon went to Omaha for a "nonpolitical" speech to the National Conference of Christians and Jews. It got him attention in the Nebraska press, and of course he held a press conference. Nixon said that he was ready to take on Lyndon Johnson if the delegates should decide that he was "best qualified to lead the fight." Five days later, Nebraska Republicans voted 49.5 percent for Goldwater, 31.5 for Nixon, the rest going to Lodge and Rockefeller. The primary came out exactly as Nixon wished—he had shown his strength, and exposed Goldwater's weakness, without campaigning, without his own name on the ballot, and without offending the Goldwater supporters.

Three days later, in Oregon, he got more good news, when Republicans gave Rockefeller (the only candidate to campaign in the state) 93,000 votes to 78,000 for Lodge, 49,800 for Goldwater, and 47,600 for Nixon.[20] Again, Goldwater weakness was exposed, while any victory for Rockefeller was good for Nixon, as Rockefeller had no chance of carrying the convention.

Nixon would not, however, endorse Rockefeller in California, because of the certain reaction of the Goldwater delegates. Rockefeller did ask for Nixon's help, but as Nixon told Eisenhower on the telephone on May 19, he was staying strictly neutral. California looked close, but Rockefeller had the lead. Eisenhower assumed that if the New York governor did carry California, the convention would be "wide open." In that case, Eisenhower said, Nixon might well be the candidate again. Nixon said he thought that was possible.[21]

THROUGH THE second half of May, Nixon could see himself as not just a possible, but rather the likely GOP candidate. It was a happy prospect. Nixon relished the thought of going all out after Johnson. He said that he was the best-qualified man to do so, and he was right, not least because Nixon could get to LBJ in a way that Goldwater never could. When Nixon lashed out, he could count on Johnson to lash back.

Alas, it was the campaign that never was. It would have been quite a show. Nixon would have attacked Johnson for doing too much about poverty and racism at home, and for not doing enough for freedom abroad. Johnson would have attacked Nixon for his lack of heart at home, his recklessness abroad.

So much for the issues. On the personal side the Howard Hughes loan to Nixon's brother Donald surely would have appeared, while Nixon would have made extensive use of Bobby Baker and Walter Jenkins, a Johnson protégé and a White House aide, respectively, accused of influence peddling (Baker) and homosexual acts in public places (Jenkins). Johnson, knowing of Nixon's numerous contacts with disgruntled army officers in Vietnam and civil servants in Washington, would have found a good national-security reason to have the FBI bug Nixon's telephones and otherwise spy on him. And so on—everyone can write his own scenario on how a Johnson-Nixon campaign in 1964 might have gone.

As for the specifics of his attack on Johnson, Nixon spelled them out in articles he wrote that spring for the *Reader's Digest*. The first, which appeared in August, was titled "Needed in Vietnam: The Will to Win," and it amounted to his platform plank. As such, it was his Vietnam policy as of 1964, and therefore deserves some detailed treatment.

He began by recalling Diem's assassination, which he called "one of the blackest moments in the history of American diplomacy," and insisted, "We cannot dodge responsibility for what happened." Nixon claimed that "every military man with whom I talked privately admitted that we are losing the war. But every one of those men believes that it is possible for us to win it . . . and win it decisively." He threw in a bit of hyperbole—"Victory [in Vietnam] is essential to the survival of freedom"—before telling the good news: "We have an unparalleled opportunity to roll back the Communist tide, not only in South Vietnam but in Southeast Asia generally, and indeed in the world as a whole."

As against that bright prospect, he named the dominoes that would fall if America failed to do its duty and South Vietnam fell— Laos, Cambodia, Thailand, Malaysia, Indonesia, the Philippines, Australia, Japan.

"There are those who say," Nixon went on, and Nixon watchers immediately knew that the alternative he was about to present was surely wrong, for whenever "those who say" or "some say" preceded a Nixon sentence, it was a sure thing that whatever they said was wrong. One could also be sure that what "they said" was the "easy way, the politically profitable way," and also sure that nevertheless Nixon would scorn it and take the hard way, the right way.

"There are those who say," Nixon went on, "that this picture is much too dark." Such people "deride the importance of South Vietnam." They wanted to "reach an agreement with our adversaries—as Chamberlain reached an agreement with Hitler at Munich in 1938." The neutralization proposals "some people" were supporting were "but another name for appeasement. It is surrender on the installment plan.

"It would be better to get out voluntarily than to be kicked out," Nixon went on. "In one case, it would be an orderly retreat. In the other, it would be a humiliating defeat."

Not that he was advocating retreat; quite the contrary. "If we are ever to stop the Communist advance in Asia the time is now. The place is Vietnam." He put only one limit on what should be done: "I am firmly opposed to the use of nuclear devices of any sort, not only because of the disastrous effect this would have on world opinion, but because it is wholly unnecessary."

America could win. That was Nixon's message. His method was to eliminate the "privileged sanctuaries" in the North. He was sure of "our ability to destroy these sanctuaries and the enemy's supply routes," because the "top strategists in the Pentagon" had assured him it was so. The Vietcong, isolated, could be rounded up. Meanwhile "we should strengthen the Vietnam air force so that it [could] bomb the roads, bridges and supply routes into South Vietnam," and "extend guerrilla warfare over the border and harass the enemy in the north."

He stopped short of calling for an invasion of the North. He did say, "We must make up our mind to win this war . . . and then instruct our top soldiers to develop the plan for doing so."

In his conclusion, Nixon said that Vietnam was not a test of power but of our "will to win—and the courage to use our power —now."[22]

That was the policy Nixon intended to introduce if he became President in January 1965. The advantage of hindsight makes his proposed little pinprick war of hot pursuit across the DMZ appear hopelessly naïve, but it needs to be recalled that in the spring of 1964 what Nixon was saying in public was matched almost exactly by what Walt Rostow was urging on President Johnson in private. And it is close to what Johnson actually did in 1965. But in 1964 Johnson was saying that to bomb the North would be to widen the war and lead to committing American troops to the battle (a question Nixon did not discuss in his article).

In a second article for the *Reader's Digest*, Nixon took up "Cuba, Castro and John F. Kennedy." In it, he repeated the story (already told in detail in *Six Crises*) about Cuba and the Bay of Pigs and the 1960 campaign, when he had criticized Kennedy for calling for an attack on Cuba: "[My] decision was right from the standpoint of the country. It was wrong politically."

He then faulted Kennedy for failing to provide air support for the Bay of Pigs, and said he had advised the President, in 1961, to "find a proper legal cover and go in." But Kennedy had drawn back from confrontation, and Castro had won.

Coming to the Cuban missile crisis, Nixon wrote that the Democrats had "pull[ed] defeat out of the jaws of victory." The Kennedy Administration had failed to insist on on-site inspection while it had committed the United States to a "no-invasion policy." As a result of "this weak-kneed foreign policy . . . shiploads of Soviet arms have continued to pour into Cuba."

"Where are we now?" Nixon asked in a concluding section. Everywhere he looked, "American weakness and indecision . . . has reduced American prestige to an all-time low. . . . We have been humiliated, frustrated, outguessed and outmaneuvered at every turn. . . . The Cold War isn't thawing; it is burning with a deadly heat. Communism isn't sleeping; it is, as always, plotting, scheming, working, fighting." It was Johnson and the Democrats who were sleeping.[23]

Those were the themes at the end of May 1964 that Nixon intended to use against Johnson—indecision in Vietnam, weakness on Cuba, softness on Communism. They were all Goldwater themes, down to the details, but Nixon could get to Johnson with them in a way that Goldwater could not.

IN POLITICS, as in life, the oddest things can upset the most carefully made plans. In the first two days of June, Nixon went from being the probable nominee to no chance at all, not because of anything he did, or anything Goldwater did, or any major event, but because a baby was born.

Nixon had carefully avoided California. Rockefeller looked like a winner, according to the polls, and even though Goldwater still might have enough delegates for a first-ballot nomination without California, Goldwater himself had stated publicly that a loss in the state would rule him out as a candidate.[24]

But on May 31, the Sunday before the election, Rockefeller's second wife, Happy, had a baby. The candidate flew home to be with her, in the process canceling his last-minute blitz in California. Newspaper photos of the mother and child merely served to remind voters of his recent messy divorce, and cost him votes. Meanwhile, the Goldwater people made an all-out effort those last two days. The result was 51.6 percent for Goldwater, which was 1.5 percent more than he needed to assure himself the Republican nomination.

GOLDWATER'S California victory changed everything for Nixon. He could forget about his own candidacy in 1964 and concentrate on what was good for the GOP. That meant, first of all, facing up to what a Goldwater candidacy meant.

In his acts, his writings, and his speeches, Goldwater had taken himself outside the moderate center, leaving the broad middle ground to Johnson. He called for an abandonment of federal welfare programs, at a pace of cutting back by 10 percent per year. He wanted to make Social Security "flexible and voluntary." He wished to sell the Tennessee Valley Authority to private industry. He opposed the graduated income tax as "repugnant to my notions of justice." He voted against the nuclear test ban treaty, against the Civil Rights Act of 1964, against federal aid to education.[25]

These were all the kinds of issue on which people would cast their votes, and in every case Goldwater represented only the right wing of the Republican Party. And while Nixon, in calling for a worldwide offensive against the Communists, could somehow make himself sound like a responsible statesman facing up to American responsibilities, Goldwater in issuing the same call sounded like an irresponsible adventurer. Goldwater threatened, therefore, not only to lose badly to Johnson, but to drag the rest of the GOP down with him.

These obvious facts occurred to a number of people immediately after California. Eisenhower, in Gettysburg, was dismayed at the prospect of Goldwater. He urged Governor Scranton to enter the contest—and then backed away from endorsing Scranton when the governor did agree. Nixon, initially, would not join a stop-Goldwater movement. At a fund-raiser on Long Island, he pointed out that if the candidate were stopped, "Goldwater people by the millions across the country would sit on their hands. . . . The Republican nomination would not be worth anything at all." His own chances, he said, were "so remote that it isn't worth discussing."[26]

That was realistic enough, but Nixon was never a man to abandon all hope. The stop-Goldwater movement was getting a lot of press coverage, from reporters who fed as well as recorded the rumors. One idea kicking around was a Goldwater-Scranton deadlock, from which Nixon would emerge as the compromise candidate. Nixon did nothing to encourage it, except to say at a press conference on June 7 in Detroit that he would "willingly accept" any assignment the party gave him, and that "if the party should decide on me as its candidate, Mr. Johnson would know he'd been in a fight."[27]

The next day, Nixon met with Scranton in Cleveland, where there was a National Governors' Conference going on, and then with Romney. Nixon urged both men to run. Scranton reported that Nixon asked him to run "to provide some kind of contest at the convention; otherwise they'll be bored and turn it off." To reporters, Nixon said "it would be a tragedy" if Goldwater's views were not "challenged and repudiated."

The following day, Goldwater rejoined that as to the repudiation of his views, "I guess he doesn't know my views very well. I got most of them from him." And he added, "Nixon is sounding more like Harold Stassen every day."[28]

Nixon flew on to Baltimore to catch a plane for London for a two-day business trip. When he got to Baltimore, aide John Whitaker told him, "It's on the radio that Romney's *not* going to run." Nixon was stunned—"What do you mean he's not going to run? He told me he was."[29]

Nixon flew to London, from which place he told the press he would not endorse Scranton, but he welcomed the governor's entry into the race. Goldwater supporters began to charge Nixon with a conspiracy to stop their man, and Goldwater himself complained, "It's just like Nixon to set this up and run off to London." [30]

When he returned to the States, Nixon realized that he had nothing to gain from antagonizing the by-now-certain winner. He could also see, clearly and precisely, the role the situation dictated that he play. After Goldwater led the party into disastrous defeat, Nixon would be the only man available to act as party unifier, to lead the rehabilitation of Republicanism.

To arrange properly for the role, Nixon got RNC Chairman William E. Miller of New York State to switch his place on the convention speaking agenda. Nixon wanted to come after the nomination, instead of before it, to avoid the possibility of any spontaneous activity on his behalf. By coming after Goldwater's nomination, he could introduce the nominee in the role of party healer.

What might happen after that? Jim Bassett, an old Nixon hand and former aide, currently reporting for the Los Angeles *Times*, proved remarkably prescient in his prediction. Behind the scenes in San Francisco, Bassett wrote, "an informal group of erstwhile GOP leaders is earnestly working to make Richard Nixon the party's nominee for President. Not this year, however, but in 1968." They were proceeding on the "melancholy assumption" that Goldwater would take a terrible beating from Johnson and "somebody else will have to pick up the pieces." Who better than Nixon? But to do so, Nixon would have to "vigorously espouse the Goldwater cause, just as the Arizonian himself labored mightily for Nixon in 1960."

After the election, Nixon's role would be to "weld together the dissident elements of right and left. This he would accomplish by persuasion, by conferences, by speech-making, by traveling and by writing, without seeking interim public office as he did, regrettably, two years ago in California. Nixon would, moreover, play a prominent role in the 1966 off-year congressional campaign." [31]

Bassett was right on the mark.

AT THE CONVENTION in San Francisco, Nixon announced his new role at a press conference. He had kind words for both remaining candidates, Goldwater and Scranton, and emphasized that no matter who won, "I for one Republican don't intend to sit it out, take a walk." Asked about Goldwater's ability to handle foreign policy, Nixon began on a disastrous note; the European press, Nixon said, had painted Goldwater as "some kind of nut, a jerk, a wild man." Of course the Europeans were wrong, Nixon quickly added as Goldwater aides seethed—Goldwater was "a reasonable man" who could get for the United States "great respect from its enemies, something we don't have at the present time."[32]

On July 15, in the Cow Palace, the right wing of the Republican Party took control of the convention. The Goldwater delegates were in a vengeful mood. They had seen Bob Taft rebuffed in '48 and '52, and been forced to accept the moderate Nixon in '60, but now their turn had come, and they made the most of it.

Senator Hugh Scott of Pennsylvania, a Scranton supporter, offered an antiextremism plank that singled out the Ku Klux Klan and the John Birch Society. Rockefeller rose to speak for the plank. Boos, hisses, catcalls, cries of "We want Barry" filled the hall. Rockefeller could not go on.

When the vote was called, the delegates gave the Scott proposal a thunderous "No." In the balloting for a nominee, they gave Goldwater a thunderous "Yes."

Nixon's moment had arrived, to introduce the candidate to his adoring followers. Nixon used the moment skillfully, as the opening speech of his 1968 candidacy, and realistically, because if the Republican Party remained as divided as it was at that moment, the 1968 party nomination would be worthless.

He cast himself, in his own words, as the preacher of "the ministry of party unity." He said, "Before this convention we were Goldwater Republicans, Rockefeller Republicans, Scranton Republicans, Lodge Republicans, but now that this convention has met and made its decision, we are Republicans, period, working for Barry Goldwater.

"And to those few, if there are some, who say that they are going to sit it out or take a walk, or even go on a boat ride, I have an answer: in the words of Barry Goldwater in 1960, 'Let's grow up, Republicans, let's go to work'—and we shall win in November!"[33]

Nixon introduced Goldwater, and the Cow Palace went wild. Nixon had given the candidate a priceless opportunity to reach out to the moderate and liberal wings of the party, but he had failed to check with Goldwater on what the senator planned to say. Nixon sat there in growing dismay as the nominee spoke. Goldwater began by casually tossing aside about half the GOP: "Anyone who joins us in all sincerity we welcome," he said. "Those who do not care for our cause we do not expect to enter our ranks in any case."

Nixon, and nearly every Republican from north of the Ohio and east of the Mississippi, sat stunned. Nixon described himself as "almost physically sick" when he heard what came next: "Extremism in the defense of liberty is no vice! Moderation in the pursuit of justice is no virtue!"

The Cow Palace erupted in what one observer called "a truly frightening display of fervor." The Goldwater delegates began shaking their fists defiantly at the press gallery, where the reporters looked on "with awe and some disbelief." [34]

Goldwater's acceptance speech left the Old Guard joyful but the Republican Party in disarray. Eastern and Midwestern Republicans, led by Rockefeller and Romney, refused to endorse or campaign for Goldwater. Republican businessmen began to contribute to and organize for Johnson. Republican candidates around the country had polls that showed Goldwater would drag them down to defeat. What had threatened to be a major setback now loomed as a complete catastrophe.

Nixon was always ready to act in a crisis, in this case as a broker. He called Eisenhower right after the convention to urge Ike to talk to Goldwater. Ike refused to do so until he had a "clarification" of the extremism remark. Nixon said that he would get one.

Nixon then wrote Goldwater, who replied that the thought could be paraphrased "by saying that wholehearted devotion to liberty is unassailable and that halfhearted devotion to justice is indefensible." [35] Whatever that meant, it was good enough for Ike, who then met with Nixon and Goldwater at his office in Gettysburg, where they agreed to a party unity meeting the next week in Hershey, Pennsylvania.

At that meeting, Eisenhower gave Goldwater his blessing. Then Nixon took over. He told the leaders there was room for all in the GOP, that in diversity there was strength. Nixon said, "I want all Republicans to win; I am just as strong for a liberal Republican in New York as I am for a conservative Republican in Texas." And he pledged that he would campaign across the country for Goldwater, full time for five weeks. [36]

ALL THIS Republican activity took place against a series of events at the end of July and the beginning of August that shook the foundations of American politics. Moscow, Hanoi, and Paris joined in a call for an international conference in Geneva to deal with the war in Vietnam. On July 27, Johnson responded, "We do not believe in conferences called to ratify terror," and announced that American military advisers to South Vietnam would be increased by 30 percent, from sixteen thousand to twenty-one thousand.

On August 2, North Vietnamese patrol boats reportedly attacked an American destroyer in the Gulf of Tonkin, an act repeated shortly thereafter against another destroyer. Johnson, outraged, said the American warships were on innocent passage in international waters and that the attacks were unprovoked, assertions that could not withstand later investigation but which were almost universally believed at the time. The President ordered retaliatory air strikes against military targets in North Vietnam.

Nixon supported the President. He said the Communists were testing the United States during the election period, which made it "doubly important to overcompensate with firm action." He said that when Johnson showed strength, "then I'm for it." Nixon's praise never came freely; he could not resist adding, "I think we should have been strong all along."[37]

Johnson introduced in Congress the Gulf of Tonkin Resolution, which gave him authority to use "all necessary measures" to "repel any armed attack" against American forces. To "prevent further aggression," the resolution authorized the President to take "all necessary steps" to protect any nation covered by the Southeast Asia Treaty that might request aid in "defense of its freedom." The resolution passed the House by a vote of 416–0. In the Senate the vote was 88–2 in favor (Democrats Wayne Morse of Oregon and Ernest Gruening of Alaska were the lone dissenters).

It was the decisive moment in the 1964 election. With the Gulf of Tonkin Resolution, Johnson had pulled off a political miracle. He had made himself invulnerable to the criticism that he was shilly-shallying on Vietnam and was too soft on Communism. He appeared tough, determined, in command. Thus was Nixon very lucky he was not the nominee, as Johnson had just stolen his issue.

Nixon was lucky on the domestic front too, where events immediately after the GOP convention demonstrated how explosive the race issue was, and how hard it would have been for Nixon to hold to a position in the center. On July 18, a three-day riot broke out in Harlem. On July 27, a race riot erupted in Rochester; Governor Rockefeller had to send in a thousand National Guardsmen to restore order. On August 4, the bodies of three missing civil rights workers were found in Mississippi, the young activists murdered by racist whites.

Johnson already had a solution for the riots. He called it the War on Poverty, and it seemed to a majority of Americans outside Dixie that his plan was more reasonable and promising and generous and likely to work than anything the GOP had to offer. Johnson was hard to oppose on civil rights, at a time when it was still embarrassing to appeal to a white backlash vote. Television coverage of the white resistance in the South had shown the ugly face of segregation to millions who had been able, previously, to look the other way. Eisenhower declared he would repudiate any Republican who openly courted a white backlash vote.

Goldwater did his best to stay clear of the civil rights issue. Instead, he engaged in star-spangled sloganeering that eschewed complicated issues, calling for a return to never very clearly defined traditional values. He committed gaffes (attacking the anti-poverty program in West Virginia and Social Security in Florida) that made him, unhappily, a near-comic figure.

Nixon defined his own role in the campaign and stuck to it through a grueling thirty-three-day, thirty-six-state speaking tour, with more than 150 appearances. He took a leave from Nixon, Mudge, and took with him on the tour a full staff. Nick Ruwe, who had helped with logistics and advance work in the past, was part of it. So was Dale Grubb, a former Secret Service man who had been with Nixon in Venezuela in 1958. Robert Hill, former ambassador to Mexico, and Charlie McWhorter were also along. So was Rose Mary Woods and another secretary. All but Grubb and the secretaries were donating their time. The RNC was picking up their expenses.

There was nothing notable about his speeches, little to remind voters of the old Nixon. His criticisms of Johnson and the Democrats were, for Nixon, mild and inoffensive. He accused Johnson's running mate, Senator Hubert H. Humphrey of Minnesota, of being a "dedicated radical." He said Johnson was "a political chameleon who changes colors to match his setting." And that was about it. It was almost as if he were saving his ammunition against Johnson for 1968.

He concentrated on helping local Republicans. Although he took care to praise Goldwater at every stop, he managed to do so without associating him with the local man. Then he got into the real business. McCandlish Phillips, covering a speech in Waterloo, Iowa, described his technique: "The wind blew scratchily through the microphone as Mr. Nixon began calling the roll of the state and local candidates, a thing he does with a great deal more than the perfunctory professionalism of duty.

"He finds out facts about their backgrounds—for example, the fact that Mr. Evan Hultman [Republican candidate for governor] was president of the student body at the University of Iowa, a fact that Mr. Nixon said was an 'index of leadership.' "[38]

As he had back in 1958, when he was also campaigning for GOP congressmen in what he knew was a lost cause, Nixon kept up a brave front, predicting Republican victories, seeing a "strong Republican surge" in the closing days of the campaign, but in private he found the experience "frustrating" and "heartbreaking."

He also could not have been unaware that it was wonderfully profitable to him personally, as he piled up chits from Republicans around the country.[39] With Goldwater doing so poorly, and Rockefeller and Romney having eliminated themselves forever by sitting out the campaign, Nixon had become the favorite for the 1968 GOP nomination even before the 1964 election was held.

A threat did appear during the last week of the campaign. Actor Ronald Reagan made a nationwide television broadcast for Goldwater, or rather for a conservative philosophy. He denounced big government and high taxes and praised free enterprise, which he wanted unleashed. He was eloquent, reasonable, sincere, and looked terrific. He could not sell Goldwater, but he did sell himself, starting an immediate demand that he begin a political career.

On November 3, Johnson and the Democrats won an unprecedented victory. In the presidential contest, Johnson got 61 percent and 486 electoral votes to Goldwater's 39 percent and 52 electoral votes. The Democrats picked up two seats in the Senate, to give them a 68–32 majority. In the House, the Republicans lost thirty-eight seats, leaving the Democrats with a stupendous 295–140 majority. More than five hundred seats in state legislatures were lost to the Democrats in the debacle.

Losses of that magnitude could not be sustained without some bloody backbiting. It began the next day. Goldwater, in his concession statement, said that the party would have done better had more Republicans "wholeheartedly" supported the ticket. Rockefeller blamed Goldwater in a statement that was highly critical of the Old Guard. Nixon chose to regard the Rockefeller statement as an attempt to read him out of the party, and responded furiously. He called the governor a "party divider" and a "spoilsport," and said he had no leadership role in the GOP outside New York. Rockefeller responded, "This kind of peevish post-election utterance has unfortunately become typical of Mr. Nixon."[40]

A week after the election, Nixon gave an interview to McCandlish Phillips. He declared that the Republican Party must choose centrist leadership that "will make a place for all responsible points of view," from conservative to liberal, while rejecting right-wing extremism.

"The center does not try to read anybody out of the party," he added. "But the farther you go in either direction, the greater the inclination to read others out." He deplored that sort of "political cannibalism" and repeated, "The center must lead."

Just in case Phillips missed the point, Nixon described himself as on "dead center," and declared that he would devote all his "spare time to the political area."

Turning to lessons from the campaign, Nixon said the chief

one was that the Republican Party was "through forever with any illusions" that there might be political profit in white backlash. Sounding very presidential, Nixon said that "in the world in which we live today extremism—peace at any cost or victory at any price —will destroy freedom because it will destroy the world." The photograph accompanying the interview showed him with a broad grin, looking as fit and happy as he should have been, considering how many things were going his way.[41]

Two days later, Nixon flew off to Tokyo on a business trip. At the press conference at Tokyo Airport, he declared that the GOP needed new blood—but not brand-new. "The leadership itself," he said, "must be new in that it must have broad appeal to all elements of the party, but that does not in itself have to mean new people."[42]

In December, Nixon concentrated on his law practice, and enjoyed the holidays. The big event was the International Debutante Ball at the Astor Hotel on December 29. Tricia Nixon led the parade, escorted by Edward F. Cox. It was a grand occasion, and put a nice cap on the year.

It had been a lucky year, not for the GOP but for Nixon. He had started out seeking a nomination, which, had he gotten it, would have led to his almost certain defeat after the Gulf of Tonkin Resolution. And the Republican catastrophe that resulted from the Goldwater nomination now offered him a way back.

CHAPTER THREE

PREPARING
A REPUBLICAN REVIVAL
1965

IN THIRTY YEARS of active political life, spanning four decades, Nixon had many good times and enjoyable moments along with many bad moments and unhappy times. In that long public life, one of the best of times for Nixon came in 1965–1966, when he held no office and was running for none, yet was able to spend almost full time on politics. Reporters who interviewed him in those years used words that had not been used previously to describe Nixon—fit, happy, relaxed—and would seldom be used after 1967.

In '65 and '66, he had reason to look and feel fit, happy, relaxed. Business could not have been better. He was earning more than $250,000 a year. The law firm left him more than enough time for politics, and it provided almost unlimited opportunities and excuses for foreign travel. He was very much a world figure, a man who could fill a room to overflowing at any capital on either side of the Iron Curtain just by announcing a press conference. He carried himself as if he were leader of the opposition, and was so treated by the press at home and abroad.

Nixon later said that one of his weaknesses during this period was the lack of a political base.[1] Actually, it was a strength, or at least Nixon was able to make it one. First of all, not holding office was an obvious advantage for a man seeking the Presidency. He had the time to travel around the country, meeting GOP leaders, raising money, learning, talking, converting people, things he could not have done as a governor or a senator. By not being on the ballot in 1966, he was able to appear all across the country, the

59

only Republican campaigning on a national basis. He put every Republican in the country into his debt, without risking anything himself.

The timing of events was a boon for Nixon. On one hand, there was a vacuum at the center of the Republican Party. Goldwater knew he could not serve as "titular leader" after the election debacle, and quickly eased himself out of national politics (as signified by his refusal to speak outside Arizona on Lincoln's Birthday, 1965). On the other hand, the Democrats were clearly headed for trouble. Their victory in 1964 contained within it the seeds of destruction; it was too big, it took off too many restraints, it could not be sustained. Nixon, at the beginning of 1965, thought that the Democrats would be guilty of "excesses" that would haunt them by 1966, on which point he proved exactly right.

Put another way, Nixon knew that the Republican Party was far from dead, and that his interests and those of the GOP ran together in a wonderfully fortuitous way. That the GOP was going to revive was obvious. The 61–39 percent vote in the presidential election and the 2–1 Democratic majorities in Congress and the state legislatures were not an authentic representation of the political division of the American people. The pendulum had swung too far, too fast. It had to come back, and it would start in 1966.

What Nixon did in '65 and '66 was put himself in a position to claim the credit for a certain Republican victory in the 1966 congressional elections. It was a brilliant conception, efficiently executed. For example, there were dozens of Republican congressional candidates who had lost close contests because of Goldwater. To keep their spirits up, and to remind them of whom they should blame, Nixon wrote a form letter to the defeated candidates: "It was really a miracle for you to run as well as you did in view of the drag at the top of the ticket." He signed off with a call to "work together" toward a major victory in '66.[2]

Nixon stayed with such men. In the next two years, he spoke before more than four hundred GOP groups in forty states, raising money for local candidates.[3] No one else worked like that for the party, and no one else, save only Ike, drew people as Nixon did.

It was not just that he was a former Vice-President, or that he was so controversial; he was a draw because he was the frontrunner for the Republican nomination. Goldwater made this all but official at a RNC meeting in Chicago on January 22, when he introduced Nixon as the man "who worked harder than any one person for the ticket." Turning to Nixon, Goldwater added, "Dick, I will never forget it. I know that you did it in the interests of the Republican Party and not for any selfish reasons. But if there ever comes a time I can turn those into selfish reasons, I am going to do all I can to see that it comes about."[4]

Thus anointed, Nixon spoke four days later in New York with appropriate authority and alarm about Vietnam. He told a business group that "we are losing the war in Vietnam," and said that American security required that "we end the war by winning it." If not, all of Asia would be lost to the Communists. Nixon proposed to take the war to the North by sustained naval and air bombardment. He was aware of the risks, he said, "but we must realize that there is no easy way out. We either get out, surrender on the installment plan through neutralization, or we find a way to win." Nixon again took care to distance himself from the most extreme hawks—he said it would not be necessary to employ either nuclear weapons or American ground troops.[5]

Thus did Nixon, speaking as leader of the opposition, play a role in forcing Johnson's choices in that winter of '64–'65, as crucial decisions were being made. When Nixon said, in 1969, that he had inherited a war not of his making, he was being too modest. From the time of the Gulf of Tonkin Resolution onward, Nixon spurred Johnson to ever greater involvement in Vietnam. Nixon made it clear that the Republican Party would never criticize Johnson for doing more in Vietnam.

Nixon's hard line on Vietnam helped him immeasurably with the right wing of the GOP, those Goldwater supporters who had always distrusted Nixon because, while he was tough enough with the Communists, he was soft on liberals. As Nixon said of the Goldwater people, "They don't like me, but they tolerate me." Historian David Reinhard wrote that in 1965 "most Right Wing Republicans, all too familiar with Nixonian pragmatism, believed that he would always respond to popular political pressures and that these were now mainly conservative and would remain so."[6]

Among the leading Goldwater supporters who followed the senator's lead and gave Nixon an early endorsement for 1968 were such luminaries as Congressman John Ashbrook of Ohio, Senators Strom Thurmond of South Carolina and John Tower of Texas, and intellectual pundit and polemicist William F. Buckley, Jr. In no case were such men happy with Nixon's position on civil rights or the Great Society programs, but in their view at least Nixon was better than Romney and Rockefeller, and—this is what hooked them—they were as one with Nixon on what to do in Vietnam.

William Rusher later wrote in *National Review* that conservatives who supported Nixon in 1968 owed history an accounting for this "uncharacteristic but unavoidable streak of opportunistic calculation."[7] But why conservatives supported Nixon was no mystery, nor was it opportunistic; they flocked to Nixon because they liked what he said on Vietnam—no compromise, war to the finish, total victory.

In February, the Vietcong shelled the U.S. air base near Pleiku. Johnson ordered retaliatory air raids against North Vietnam. Nixon immediately announced his enthusiastic support, and called for more: "Now that this step has been taken, the United States air and sea power should be used to stop further movement of supplies and men to the Viet Cong."[8]

Three days later, Nixon charged that Johnson's retaliation was insufficient, and demanded a "day by day and night by night" bombing campaign. He was speaking to twelve hundred Republicans at a $100-per-plate fund-raiser at the Bellevue Stratford Hotel in Philadelphia, and the Pennsylvanians roared their approval of his call to arms.[9] He kept it up through the winter, to approving audiences everywhere.

The prevailing mood among Republicans was that it was time to go for victory. Their spokesman for that position was Nixon. So much so that he got a front-page headline in *The New York Times* on February 14: "NIXON IS TAKING G.O.P. LEADERSHIP."[10]

The story noted that Nixon was free to turn the role into "anything he wants to make it." He chose to use it to prod Johnson.

AT THE BEGINNING of spring 1965, reporter Robert Donovan interviewed Nixon in New York. Donovan was struck by how much life in the city agreed with Nixon, "who is now decidedly more relaxed and mellow than he appeared in his political campaigns."

Nixon fairly gushed over life in New York, the competition, the "fast track." Nixon told Donovan that "New York is very cold and very ruthless and very exciting and, therefore, an interesting place to live. . . . The main thing, it is a place where you can't slow down."

Nixon said another appeal of New York was that it was a place that offered tremendous variety and a highly enviable lifestyle for those who could afford it. For the Nixons, this included the Broadway theaters, the Metropolitan Opera, elegant eating places, private clubs, exclusive shops, Madison Square Garden, and the paths of Central Park, all of which absorbed some of the leisure hours of Nixon, his wife, and their daughters.[11]

Not that there were many leisure hours for this family. Julie, sixteen years old, went to the Chapin School; Tricia, nineteen years old, was a student at Finch College in the city. Both girls lived with their parents in the apartment. Both were excellent students, Tricia more serious and tight-lipped than the bubbly Julie.

Pat helped them with their homework, typed term papers, saw to their needs.

But once the excitement of life in Manhattan had worn down, Pat was looking for something to do. During the Goldwater campaign, she had gone down to the office at Nixon, Mudge to help Rose Woods with the mail and the typing. She had answered the phone with her maiden name, "Miss Ryan," and had often stayed at her desk until ten or eleven o'clock in the evening. On Saturdays, she had made the girls come down to help with the mail.[12]

After the campaign, there had been Thanksgiving, then Christmas, but by January, boredom was setting in. "After you've been in political life," she told a friend, "at first you try your hand at charity work, but it's not the commitment of politics. You know, I do get restless."[13]

So it was back to 20 Broad Street, where Miss Ryan took a desk placed inconspicuously in a corner and spent the better part of her days working as a secretary. Her husband and younger daughter worried about her. Julie recorded in her diary how she and her father "took a long walk along Madison Avenue" and agreed "that Mother needed something to do." Nixon told Julie, "We all have to contribute and try if we want to be happy. You must learn to accept things as they are and forge ahead."[14]

For Pat, things were not so simple. She did miss the commitment of politics, and the splendor and fame, but she would be happiest if she never ever had to face another reception line. It was the campaigning she could not stand, the need it brought to put her on public display, which violated her inner, most private self. All those hands, all those smiles, all those empty phrases, all those strangers. Julie loved that part of politics. Nixon, like Pat, hated it. So did Tricia. But Nixon made himself do it, while Tricia just refused to participate. Pat, not surprisingly, was the one caught in the middle.

On a vacation at Key Biscayne in 1966, Pat had a long talk with her daughters. She wondered aloud whether she was "a failure to Daddy" because she refused to participate in the campaigns the way she once did. Julie saw Pat's conflict of "wanting to help him but disliking politics," and felt that her father "must have been aware" of Pat's feelings.[15] Pat said she dreaded the thought of another campaign, but she knew there was no other life for her man. She had heard him say more than once that he did not find his legal work fulfilling, and that if he had only his law practice, he would be mentally dead in two years and physically dead in four.[16] So she went down to the office to do her bit to help make him President, hoping all the while it would never happen, hoping that it would.

• •

THROUGH THE SPRING, Nixon kept up his drumbeat criticism of Johnson on Vietnam. At a press conference in Washington on April 1, he endorsed Johnson's retaliatory raids on North Vietnam but called for more of them, regularly applied. He declared, "The United States cannot afford another defeat in Asia. The United States must find a way to stop indirect aggression. The United States must be prepared to meet the issue squarely and to commit whatever forces are necessary. I would personally support whatever measures are made to achieve this objective." [17]

Two weeks later, the United States carried out its heaviest air raids of the war to date, using some 230 planes to drop napalm on Vietcong strongholds. Nixon was not satisfied; he wanted more raids, and he was ready to increase the commitment of American troops. Whatever move Johnson made in the direction of escalation, Nixon was always one step ahead of him, demanding more.

IN APRIL, on a business trip to Finland for client John Shaheen, who was setting up a pulp mill, Nixon finished his business early and on the spur of the moment decided to go to Moscow to see former Premier Nikita Khrushchev, with whom he had held the famous Kitchen Debate in 1959. Khrushchev was out of power and living in obscurity. The great curiosity Nixon must have had about his old nemesis was enhanced by the publicity possibilities of a meeting, perhaps even another debate.

Nixon got Khrushchev's address from a Canadian reporter. At dinner that evening, with two Soviet Intourist guides, Nixon asked directions to the men's room. He slipped out a back door and took a cab to Khrushchev's apartment house. There were two housekeepers; they insisted that Khrushchev was not home. Nixon, disappointed, left a handwritten note. He never received a reply. [18]

Nixon still managed to get into a public debate in Moscow. He had learned in Latin America in 1958 that nothing beats a university for attention, so he and his companions, including American reporters, took themselves off to Moscow University. His technique in Latin America had been to march directly into a classroom and begin answering questions, but the Russians knew his techniques well, and how to foil them. In this case, the deputy rector greeted Nixon at the gate and took him immediately to his office.

The press followed, and the two men put on a show. The deputy rector said he "did not want to talk about" such things as the Ku Klux Klan or the John Birch Society (a nice use of a typical Nixon technique—to say that you don't want to bring up a subject, which you then name—that perhaps showed how closely the Soviets had studied this man). The deputy rector did want to know "what he should tell his students when they asked, as they often did, how it could happen in a freedom-loving country that a President could be killed?"

Nixon shot back, "What happened to Beria? Why was he killed? Trotsky, what happened to him?" (Beria, First Deputy Premier, had been ousted and then executed in 1953; Trotsky had been assassinated in Mexico in 1940.)

The deputy rector replied, "Trotsky was killed on American territory."

Nixon tried again: "If you want to talk about force, then we should talk about Soviet action against the Freedom Fighters in Hungary [in 1956]." [19]

As a debate, it wasn't much. In 1965, as in 1959, Nixon was talking past rather than communicating with his debate opponent. In 1959, he had learned never to try to talk a Communist out of his beliefs; in 1965, the lesson was never to try to debate with a Communist about the recent past.

Even though he did not see Khrushchev, or get to stand before a class at Moscow University, he did get his picture on the front pages back in the States "debating" the deputy rector. The story that accompanied the photo contained ample reminders of the glorious moment when Nixon had been the man who stood up to Khrushchev, at a time when Khrushchev's name was enough to frighten half the world to death.

In 1959, in his speech on Russian national television to the people of the Soviet Union, Nixon had called *Pravda* a liar. Six years later, *Pravda* got its revenge. In a story on Nixon's visit (with no mention of his attempt to see Khrushchev, nor of the '59 debate, as Khrushchev was now a nonperson), *Pravda* said, "Conceited by the fact that his person still means something, the former Vice President and erstwhile candidate took to advertising himself even if it was scandalous, if only they wrote and talked about him.

"On the street, Nixon for some reason accosted a policeman with stupid questions. He tried to start arguments with strangers and invited them to be his guests.

"In a word, as in a real clown's act, he tried to provide sensational material for the foreign newspapermen who followed on his heels." [20]

WHAT HAD BEEN obvious to Jim Bassett and Dick Nixon as early as July 1964 was by the spring of 1965 becoming obvious to others: that the odds were better than even money that in 1968 Richard Nixon would be the nominee of the Republican Party, that the party would be revived, thanks to victories in the '66 election, and that the Democrats could be in complete disarray between Right and Left over Vietnam and civil rights. In short, even at this early point—taking into account the fact that nothing is ever certain in politics until it happens—Nixon could see himself as President. So whenever he spoke, he stayed at a national or international level, never stooping to squabble in local situations.

As a President-in-waiting, he needed a staff—advance men, researchers, speech writers, press aides, secretaries, the works. For that, he needed money. He turned to Maurice Stans, former Director of the Budget under Eisenhower, current New York businessman, a strong Nixon supporter who was eager to promote the cause. Stans put together a group that included Hobart Lewis of *Reader's Digest;* Peter Flanigan, an investment banker who had worked for Nixon in 1960; Bob Finch, an old Nixon hand who was currently running for lieutenant governor of California; Pat Hillings, who had once held Nixon's original 12th District in California for the Republicans; Charlie McWhorter; and a few others. Among the group was Robert Merriam, a former assistant to Stans in the Eisenhower Administration and a strong Nixon supporter in 1960.

Nixon had to do a bit of persuading to get Merriam to join up. When Stans first brought them together for a meeting in Nixon's New York apartment, Merriam was blunt with Nixon. He said Nixon had refused to accept advice in '60, that he had run a one-man show, that he had as a result made some bad mistakes, and that he, Merriam, didn't want to put his time and money into a Nixon campaign unless he had some assurance that the candidate would open himself to advice.

Nixon was emphatic. He said he recognized the truth of what Merriam said and promised that in the future he would be different. Merriam was convinced, and agreed to help.[21] From then on he was active in raising money, and in joining Stans to give Nixon detailed briefings on the federal budget.

Stans, meanwhile, had put together a "non-political" entity he called the Issues Research Council, which gave Nixon a small research and writing staff. William Safire joined the inner circle and prepared a ten-page paper on the problem of Nixon's image and what had to be done to restore it. This paper became the basis for a charter for the Issues Research Council: "The objective is to restate and reemphasize the candidate's experience and qualifications for public office, and to counter the negative implications of his two election defeats."[22]

The obvious best way to accomplish those goals was to associate Nixon with the coming Republican victory in the '66 elections, which is what the group set out to do. Nixon christened the group the Birdwatchers of '66, a play on the names of Lady Bird, Lynda Bird, and Luci Bird Johnson, and a symbolic recognition that the President, not the Democratic Congress, was the real target.[23]

Safire began to work closely with Nixon, primarily as a speech writer. Their relationship revealed a side of Nixon seldom seen. Safire, for all his self-proclaimed conservative political views, was in many respects the type whom Nixon, at least by reputation, was most likely to hate. Safire was a young Jewish intellectual with a quick wit and a way with words, with a sardonic approach to the hoopla of politics and an honest man's disapproval of the corruption of politics. There was not, on the surface, much to pull Nixon and Safire together. Yet they took an immediate liking to each other, which continued to grow over the years. Safire came to have, and retained, great respect for Nixon the politician and affection for Nixon the man.[24]

Much the same thing happened with Pat Buchanan, a young (twenty-seven-year-old) editorial writer for the St. Louis *Globe-Democrat*, who later joined Safire as a speech writer. Buchanan's politics were far to the right of Safire's, indeed they were far to the right of almost everyone's, but that was not what appealed to Nixon. He liked Buchanan's eccentric mind, his passionate involvement, his wide-ranging knowledge of politics, and his speech-writing ability. And having Safire and Buchanan close to him gave Nixon flexibility—when he wanted a right-wing speech for an Old Guard audience, he could call on Buchanan; when he wanted a moderate talk for a liberal Republican group, he could call on Safire.

Steve Hess, who had been helping Nixon with his writing before 1965, explained some of the factors in Nixon's success in his relationship with his writers. The first was Nixon's high regard for the writing process. Nixon had found writing *Six Crises* to be difficult; he told Hess "it was one of the hardest and most satisfying things I've ever done." So he respected writers and their craft. Second, Nixon worked closely with his speech writers, going over drafts word by word, questioning, judging, inserting, drawing a blue pencil through a line—the most intimate kind of work. Third, Nixon was always generous with his praise. After a major speech, he would call Safire, or Buchanan, or Hess, or whoever helped him write it, to say thanks. Even better, he would refer to a specific line written by his aide, and point out how well it had gone over with the audience, and thank the writer again. For a speech writer in politics, this is a most unusual, and wonderfully heady, experience. Fourth, Nixon was personally fond of his writers, and showed it.

Especially welcome was Nixon's method of payment. "I never set a price," Hess recalled, and Nixon always paid him "far more than I would have asked, or thought I deserved." Hess asked him about it once; Nixon replied, "Oh, well, I would just pay it to the government anyway." When *The Saturday Evening Post* paid Nixon $10,000 for his article on Vietnam, he sent Hess a check for $5,000. This at a time, as Hess recalls, when "you and your wife could take a trip to Europe *and* remodel your home for five thousand dollars, and when the same article under my own name would have gotten one thousand dollars." [25]

In 1965, Safire was able to sell the North American Newspaper Alliance on syndicating a series of ten articles by Nixon on the issues of 1966, for $10,000, which was about as good a deal as could be imagined—Nixon was getting paid for spreading his name and his views in support of Republican candidates. [26]

THROUGH THE SPRING and summer of 1965, America moved more firepower into Vietnam. In June, the President announced that he was authorizing commanders in Vietnam to commit U.S. ground forces to combat, while Defense Secretary Robert McNamara revealed that 21,000 additional U.S. troops were on their way to Vietnam. A month later, Johnson sent another 50,000, to raise the U.S. total to 125,000. Meanwhile, violence at home was escalating on two fronts; 350 antiwar protesters were arrested on August 8 in Washington, while later that week the worst race riots yet broke out in Watts, the Negro section of Los Angeles.

In this tense situation, Nixon elevated himself to the role of number-one critic of Johnson's war, just as he had been back in 1951 the number-one critic of Truman's war. No matter how rapidly Johnson stepped up the bombing campaign, it was not enough to satisfy Nixon; no matter how many troops the President sent to Vietnam, it was not enough to satisfy Nixon.

In August, Nixon went to Asia, to promote Pepsi and do other business. He called it a private, nonpolitical tour—and of course called press conferences at every stop. In Taiwan, after meeting with Chiang Kai-shek, Nixon announced that if Red China dared to intervene in Vietnam, Nationalist China would attack the mainland. [27] In Tokyo, he denounced antiwar demonstrators in the States, saying "they create grave miscalculations in North Vietnam and Communist China as to the will and to the unity of the United States." He denounced the President for his willingness to negotiate with the North Vietnamese, calling it "a sign of weakness that has actually prolonged the war." [28]

At the beginning of September, Nixon spent three days in

South Vietnam. After conferring with American and South Vietnamese officials, Nixon held his press conference and repeated his threat to make Vietnam into an issue if Johnson "continued his talk about negotiations that would reward aggression. All that he does is prolong the war. He encourages our enemies, he discourages our friends and he confuses even the neutrals." Nixon said 125,000 troops would be enough, called yet again for an expanded bombing campaign, and predicted the war would go on for two or even three more years.[29]

This was too much for *The New York Times,* which in an editorial called Nixon "off base" in opposing a settlement based on concessions by both sides, accused him of chasing the "illusion of unconditional surrender by North Vietnam," and labeled his remarks "tragically harmful."[30]

The *Times*'s editorial did not slow Nixon down one bit. Sophisticated East Coast intellectuals might dismiss Nixon's calls for "victory in Vietnam" as unobtainable, but he had been down this path before, with Douglas MacArthur in 1951, and Nixon knew that his constituents wanted victory, identified with victory, would accept nothing less than victory.

When he got back from Asia, Nixon went on NBC's "Meet the Press." He said he was more optimistic than he had been after his last visit to Vietnam, eighteen months ago, because he could foresee a military victory in "two or three years of intensive activity." He called for a bombing campaign against military targets in the Hanoi area and a naval blockade of Haiphong harbor. On the ground, he thought eventually as many as 200,000 men might be needed. On the question of what he meant by "victory," Nixon said he would support a settlement of the kind the Eisenhower Administration had reached in Korea in 1953, in which South Vietnam would retain its independence and security. He did not call for "liberation" of North Vietnam.[31]

As for his own plans, Nixon said that he was a practical man who intended to do whatever he could to strengthen the GOP "so that when we get to 1968, whoever is selected—and it very probably is not going to be me . . . will be able to win, because I feel a certain responsibility . . . for losing the election in 1960 . . . and for the weakness of this party, and I am devoting my efforts to building it up, without regard to what happens to me."

Murray Chotiner summed it up nicely: "He felt the party had been good to him and as a national leader he had to help. If it was helping him politically at the same time, why, that was a calculated risk he'd have to take."[32]

• •

NIXON the noncandidate needed a domestic issue, one as passionate as Vietnam but not as dangerous as race relations. He found it in the antiwar protest movement, which in 1965 was growing rapidly, especially on the campuses. Within that movement, he found the ideal target, a radical young professor of history at a state university, and ideal issues, patriotism and freedom of speech. Nixon was the first national politician to speak out forcefully on these matters, the first to see the political pay dirt in them, the first to see how fundamental these issues were to America's voters.

One of the reasons for Nixon's staying power in national politics was that he knew instinctively what issues moved the average Republican voter—because they were the ones that moved him the most. For all of his political career, Nixon was the authentic spokesman of millions of Americans, most of them Republicans, most of them comfortably middle class, many of them middle-aged and older. Nixon moved in step with these people. When they viewed with alarm, so did he.

Nixon did not create the fears, but he did speak to them and in the process took political advantage of them. One of the big fears Nixon and his voters had in 1965 was what was happening on the college campuses.

They were right to be concerned. The colleges were in the midst of a period of extremely rapid change. The first wave of the postwar Baby Boom generation hit the colleges in 1965. The parents, most of them, were World War II veterans and their wives who had borne the children while still struggling through college. Meanwhile the draft for Vietnam was beginning to reach into the colleges, provoking antiwar demonstrations. And all hell broke loose.

No generation was ever worse prepared to accept the attitudes of the succeeding generation than the World War II parents of the Baby Boom generation. To those parents, it was my country right or wrong, unconditional surrender, crew cuts, bobby sox, coats and ties, responsibility, hard work. When they had been in college, unmarried girls had 10 P.M. curfews, and were grounded for a weekend if they broke the rules. All this was still the case on most campuses in 1963. But by 1965, it was being questioned everywhere, and had been overthrown in many trend-setting schools. Girls lived openly with boys, even in the same dorm. Dress codes were shattered. A new music came to campus as rock and roll and the Beatles replaced love ballads and jazz—all this between '63 and '65.

These, and other social changes, were terribly unsettling to parents. The length of the male students' hair, which in the school year '65–'66 first began to lengthen, was becoming a family dinner-table battleground in millions of homes. A concurrent development —the antiwar movement—made the generation gap much greater, bringing together politics and social mores.

To the parents of the students of 1965, it was inconceivable that any American could fail to do his or her full duty in a war. That being so, they were quite unable to deal with their own children, many of whom not only said they would not do their duty but denounced the war and insisted that America was fighting on the wrong side. Their children questioned patriotism, even laughed at it. They encouraged students to dodge the draft, evade it, cheat it; they demonstrated against their government in the midst of a war.

Millions of Americans were absolutely outraged by these developments. The most privileged generation of kids in history was revolting against those who had brought them the privileges. What could possibly explain such ingratitude?

One answer was drugs. It was in 1965, the year the Baby Boomers started college, that marijuana began to be used widely by students. Another answer was that America's colleges had been taken over by young radical intellectuals who aimed to subvert the youth.

To NIXON and his supporters, it was the radical professors who were the worst. In their view, the young Ph.D.s in America who were undertaking the task of giving the Baby Boomers a college education included many Socialists and not a few Communists. These young radicals were especially prominent in history, political science, and allied fields. They came from all over, but especially from the biggest and most prestigious graduate schools, Berkeley or Madison or Ann Arbor. William A. Williams, at the University of Wisconsin, was one of the leaders; *Studies on the Left,* published by graduate students in Madison, was one of the early publications. There were many other strands, from all over the country; the final product was the New Left.

By 1965, just as the World War II parents started turning over their kids to the colleges for an education, the New Left began doing much of the college teaching in the areas of politics and history. There was much potential for misunderstanding here. The New Left taught that America was imperialist, that America had caused the Cold War, that even in World War II American motives had been selfish and centered on improving capitalist exploitation of the masses around the world, that in Vietnam the Vietcong were freedom fighters while the GIs were suppressing the legitimate desire for national independence.

To most older Americans, such interpretations turned reality completely upside down. It was maddening to them to learn that this was what was being taught in the colleges; it seemed to them to explain, at least in part, how the students could be so misled as to engage in antiwar demonstrations.

There was more infuriating news; in 1965, so-called "teach-ins" began to become popular around the country. These were seminars designed to teach interested and involved students about Vietnam, some of which drew hundreds of students and lasted all night. Very few supporters of the war came to such teach-ins, which became in effect rallies for the antiwar movement. And it was mainly young New Left teachers who organized the affairs.

Conservatives and many moderates felt that somehow someone had snuck up in the night and stolen their colleges and universities from them. And that was the ultimate theft, because what was being stolen was the nation's future. It was Nixon who saw the issue first, and struck hardest.

IN APRIL 1965, at a teach-in at Rutgers University, thirty-four-year-old associate professor of history Eugene D. Genovese said, "Those of you who know me, know that I am a Marxist and a socialist.

"I do not fear or regret the impending Vietcong victory in Vietnam. I welcome it." [33]

There was a gubernatorial election going on in New Jersey that year, matching incumbent Democrat Richard J. Hughes against Republican State Senator Wayne Dumont. Through the summer and into the fall, Dumont had tried to make Genovese an issue, without much success. Governor Hughes had refused to fire Genovese, as Dumont had demanded; indeed, the governor had spoken forthrightly for freedom of speech and academic freedom. Outside New Jersey, Genovese was unknown, and even inside the state his name was hardly on everyone's lips.

One reason was that Dumont had been unable to persuade visiting Republican big shots on the campaign circuit to talk about Genovese. Ike came to New Jersey and refused; so did Governors Scranton, Rockefeller, Romney, and John Chafee of Rhode Island. Kenneth Keating, a former senator from New York, would not touch the issue, nor would New Jersey's own Republican Senator Clifford Case.

These GOP leaders remembered all too well how badly they had been embarrassed by academic-freedom questions back in Joe McCarthy's day. Most of them were on the board of one college or another and knew how much the concept of academic freedom meant to the professors. As Establishment figures themselves, they cared what the professors thought, and probably exaggerated the role the professors could play in the molding of public opinion. So all the top men in the GOP had a chance to take up the Genovese case and refused.

Then came Nixon.

He arrived in New Jersey on October 24, about a week before Election Day, and a few days after Senator Robert Kennedy of New York had made an impassioned defense of academic freedom at Rutgers. Kennedy had said that the Genovese case was the biggest issue in the campaign. This provoked Nixon. It also gave him an opportunity. Dumont was trailing badly in the polls, had no chance to win against a popular incumbent, so there was little reward in campaigning for him—unless Nixon could find a way to speak to the nation through Dumont.

He did. In Morristown, Nixon said that Genovese had a "right to be for segregation or integration, for free love or celibacy, for communism or anarchy, or anything else—in peacetime." But, Nixon went on, "the United States is at war. Genovese is employed by a state university, and he used the state college as a forum to, in effect, give aid and comfort to the enemy."

Nixon's statements in New Jersey through the course of that day showed an astonishing disregard for elementary facts; for example, in this opening paragraph in Morristown: the United States was not at war, and Genovese was not using Rutgers as a forum to give aid to the enemy; he was expressing his personal views at a political rally.

But though that disregard for the elementary facts on Nixon's part drove his enemies into fits of helpless rage, what he said next showed how quickly and expertly he could cut to the heart of the matter and in the process speak for millions upon millions of Americans. Nixon pointed out that "if anyone had welcomed a Nazi victory during World War II there would have been no question about what to do."

Later that day, before a cheering American Legion outing in Flemington, Nixon asked, "Does an individual employed by the state have the right to use his position to give aid and comfort to the enemies of the United States in wartime?"

Some five hundred Legionnaires and their families shouted, "NO! NO! NO!"

Nixon said, "The choice is simple. When it comes between American boys defending freedom of speech and Professor Genovese's rights to use that freedom, I'm for American boys every time." That night, at a press conference, he called on the board of governors of Rutgers to dismiss Genovese immediately.[34]

Just that quickly, Genovese became a national issue, with

Nixon at the center of the action. *The New York Times*, in a stern editorial, admonished Nixon to tread more carefully. "Here is the old Nixon in action," the editors lamented, "posing the spurious choice between freedom of speech for Genovese and 'American boys defending freedom of speech' in Vietnam."[35]

Nixon was not surprised that the *Times* and other Establishment voices were against him. On the ride back to New York, after his day in New Jersey, Nixon had been in high spirits. Bill Safire had been with him, and disapproved of the way Nixon had used early-fifties-style anti-Communism.

"Oh, I know you and the rest of the intellectuals won't like it," Nixon had replied. He said his law partners would not like it either. "But somebody had to take 'em on. Imagine a professor teaching that line to kids."[36]

Nixon's patriotic outrage, Safire was convinced, was entirely genuine. But just as clearly, Nixon knew his constituency. Far from backing down after the *Times* scolded him, Nixon escalated the issue. He sent out hundreds of copies of his New Jersey remarks, with a covering letter, to Republicans and newspaper editors around the country. He wrote a long letter to *The New York Times*. In that letter, read by millions, he made an incredible statement that went unchallenged: "The victory for the Vietcong which Professor Genovese 'welcomes' would mean ultimately the destruction of freedom of speech for all men for all time not only in Asia but in the United States as well."

Kennedy had said that Dumont's demand for Genovese's dismissal was the same as former governor Ross Barnett's demand that professors at the University of Mississippi who advocated integration should be fired. Nixon wrote that Kennedy "completely missed the fundamental distinction," which was that no one would question Genovese's right to advocate "integration or any other controversial issue in *peace time*," but now the country was at war. So the question was, "Does the principle of freedom of speech require that the state subsidize those who would destroy the system of government which protects freedom of speech?"[37]

On Election Day, Governor Hughes won a 300,000-vote victory. At first glance that outcome made it appear that Nixon had chosen a loser for an issue. But Johnson had carried the state by 900,000 a year earlier. Nixon himself was convinced not only that he was right but that most Republicans agreed with him. A few days after the election, he wrote Ike, "I think an increasing number of people throughout the country are beginning to resent the arrogant tactics of the so-called intellectuals who are demonstrating against our Viet Nam policy."[38]

Nixon had settled on his approach to the 1966 congressional campaign: the Democrats were not tough enough with the Communists in Vietnam or with the protesters and radical professors at home.

IN THE FALL of 1965, Nixon denounced not only the New Left and the antiwar movement, but also the Far Right, as symbolized by the John Birch Society. In November, speaking to a Salt Lake City audience of one thousand western Republican leaders, Nixon congratulated the delegates on ridding the GOP of its radical Right and called for a formal renunciation of the Birchers. He said the Democrats faced a far more serious problem with their radical Left and pledged himself to campaign for all Republican nominees in 1966.[39]

Nixon could not take a stand against the Birchers without paying a price, as Ezra Taft Benson reminded him. Benson, once Eisenhower's controversial Secretary of Agriculture, a Salt Lake City businessman, and an elder in the Mormon Church, was a prominent member of the Birch Society. He wrote Nixon that "the time is near when you will regret the false statements being made regarding this organization of loyal and devoted Americans." Benson asserted that Robert Welch, head of the Birch Society, was the only American, other than J. Edgar Hoover, to recognize the Communist threat for what it was.

Nixon replied that Welch had called Ike and Dulles "dedicated conscious agents of the Communist conspiracy." For his part, Nixon said, "I think these are outrageous, malicious, false statements. I am frankly quite surprised that you do not agree."[40]

EXTREMISM WAS increasingly dominating American politics, on the Left as well as the Right, in itself a reflection of the tension of the time and of what was at stake. Fundamental decisions were being made during a period of great flux. On November 24, the Army announced that week's death toll was 240, a new high. On November 30, some fifty thousand Americans marched in a peace demonstration in Washington, another record number.

Things were out of joint elsewhere too: on November 28, Moscow accused Peking of being a threat to international Communism; the following day Peking accused the Soviets of undermining the world revolutionary struggle.

Nixon's contribution to this explosive situation was to add fuel to the flames. In an appearance on CBS's "Face the Nation" on November 21, Nixon said that Johnson's conduct of the war in Vietnam would be a major issue in the 1968 election. He accused

Johnson of allowing America to get "bogged down" in a long and costly ground war and said that military commanders should be given authority to bomb all military targets in and around Hanoi. He dismissed out of hand the threat of a Chinese intervention: China was "a fourth-rate military power." Nixon also urged that the harbor of Haiphong be mined. He denied that he was being bellicose.

Then he said something strange. Asked about his reaction to Representative Gerald R. Ford's (R., Mich.) suggestion that the United States declare war on North Vietnam, Nixon said he would be "strongly opposed." He said a declaration of war would cause diplomatic complications and might lead Hanoi to turn to the Soviet Union and Communist China for open intervention.[41]

Thus did Nixon become part of what might be called the Great Political Evasion of the 1960s, the refusal on the part of Democrats and Republicans alike to confront the Vietnam issue head-on, in an up-or-down vote for war. Had the Congress declared a state of war, much would have been different, from academic cases like Professor Genovese to censorship of reporting from the battlefield.

But an attempt to declare war through a vote in Congress would have surely exposed the deep divisions within the country. As many as one out of four congressmen, perhaps more, would have voted no. So the politicians entered into a conspiracy, albeit unorganized and spontaneous. The doves did not want a vote on war, because they knew they would lose. The hawks did not want a vote on war, because they knew that so narrow a victory on so fundamental a question would be as bad as losing.

The nation never had an occasion to put its elected representatives to the test on the question, Are you for or against the war in Vietnam? As this was the most important political question of the sixties, it is no wonder people got impatient with democracy.

It was contradictory for Nixon to call for victory with one breath and refuse to even consider declaring war with the next. For how could the United States win without declaring war, invading North Vietnam, and occupying Hanoi? Nixon pointed to Korea as the model he had in mind, but the analogy simply was not there. Korea was a peninsula across which a military line had been drawn and trenches dug, so that it was relatively easy to defend against infiltration. Vietnam's borders with Cambodia and Laos were hundreds of miles long; it was useless to even talk about stopping infiltration.

But Nixon was far from being alone on the question of forcing a vote for or against war on North Vietnam. No other politician wanted to press the moment to its crisis either, not even Ford, who told the press later that he had not meant to indicate his own support for a declaration of war.[42]

As the Christmas season of 1965 began, the United States continued to make war in Vietnam, without declaring it, and to escalate, without admitting it. On December 15, the Air Force launched the biggest raid yet (twelve tons of bombs) on industrial targets around Hanoi.

Vietnam made some strange bedfellows and created some odd alliances. At the end of 1965, an outfit calling itself Freedom House issued a statement that declared that while those who opposed American policy in Vietnam had a right to speak out, those who supported the war "have an obligation to shout." George Field, the executive director, said that the prominent men who endorsed the statement had no quarrel with the antiwar protesters. "Instead, we are placing the onus on those who remain silent and fail to make clear the American consensus."

Among the 104 national figures who signed the statement were Richard Nixon and Dean Acheson. They had once been the bitterest of enemies; whatever Acheson had wanted when he was Secretary of State, whether in Asia or in Europe, Nixon opposed. Only Vietnam could have drawn them together.[43]

IN DECEMBER 1965, Nixon published an article in *Reader's Digest* on the specifics of the war in Vietnam and on the general problem of how to relate to aggressive Communism in Asia.

Nixon would negotiate only on the basis of three minimum conditions: that North Vietnam stop its aggression; that South Vietnam's freedom and independence be guaranteed; that there be "no substitute for victory." In other words, no negotiations. Nixon was explicit on the point: "To negotiate in Vietnam would be negotiation of the wrong kind, at the wrong time, at the wrong place." To negotiate with the Vietcong or North Vietnamese before driving them out of South Vietnam "would be like negotiating with Hitler before the German armies had been driven from France."

All this led up to Nixon's rock-solid position on negotiations: "We should negotiate only when our military superiority is so convincing that we can achieve our objective at the conference table." To most people, that sounded more like a surrender than a conference table.

Proponents of negotiation—Nixon cited Senator Fulbright, columnist Walter Lippmann, and Martin Luther King, Jr., by name —were, according to Nixon, actually urging "appeasement and retreat." He forgave them, because they did not understand that the policy they advocated "is filled with far more danger of war." In so saying, Nixon was picking up on a theme that Secretary of State Dean Rusk had been playing, that to sit down with Ho Chi Minh and his cohorts in 1965 was the equivalent of sitting down with Hitler at Munich in 1938. This reasoning linked Ho with Hitler, a thought that was ludicrous. Still, Democrats as well as Republicans made the analogy.

Behind the question of negotiation lay the question, What's at stake here? Nixon, Johnson, Rusk, and the hawks generally responded that the stakes were as high as in World War II. To the doves, that was the grossest exaggeration. Each side overstated its case. Lyndon Johnson's overselling techniques are well known— if we don't fight them there, he warned, next thing we'll be fighting them in San Francisco. Senator Fulbright's response to that was "We go ahead treating this little piss-ant country as though we were up against Russia and China put together."

Nixon was as one with President Johnson on the question of what was at stake. "If the United States gives up on Vietnam," Nixon wrote in the *Digest*, "the Pacific Ocean will become a Red Sea." He explained that "the true enemy behind the Viet Cong and North Vietnam is China. . . . If Vietnam is lost, Red China would gain vast new power." Indonesia, Thailand, Cambodia, and Laos would "inevitably fall under communist domination." Red China would be "only 14 miles from the Philippines and less than 100 miles from Australia."

But with a small investment now, in South Vietnam, America could hold the Reds back. Nixon wrote that the tide had turned in Vietnam (another theme he picked up from Dean Rusk), and "a real victory" was now possible. It would "take two years or more of the hardest kind of fighting. It will require stepped-up air and land attacks." [44]

Thus Nixon at the end of 1965 was harking back to the war of his youth, using images and symbols and a basic frame of reference from World War II to describe and think about Vietnam. For Nixon, victory was possible. It was a question of will. His call was for escalation, immediate and decisive.

Nixon said that his way was "the right way," but the "politically unpopular way." Insofar as there were almost no doves among the Republican politicians, and insofar as Nixon was running for the Republican nomination in 1968, the mind boggles at the alternative suggested by Nixon's logic: suppose he had taken "the easy way" and advocated negotiation and withdrawal. He would have immediately fallen from almost a sure thing for the GOP nomination to no chance whatsoever.

So Nixon stayed well out to Johnson's right, which was hard to do, as Johnson, Rusk, and Rostow were moving very quickly themselves, freezing out Fulbright, condemning Martin Luther King, and attacking the doves. Between them, Nixon and Johnson were fanning the flames in Vietnam to white-hot heat.

CHAPTER FOUR

THE NINTH CAMPAIGN
1966

In 1966, for the first time in a decade, Nixon entered a campaign year full of confidence in himself and his party. A combination of bigger federal deficits, race riots, civil rights demonstrations, unfulfilled promises from the Democrats, and most of all the war in Vietnam and the antiwar movement at home had made the Democrats vulnerable. In an ordinary off-year election, the party in power could expect to lose as many as thirty seats in the House, but 1966 was not an ordinary year. Given the depth of Democratic vulnerability and the magnitude of the Democratic win in 1964, the Republicans could expect to do much better.

Nixon successfully positioned himself as the chief national manager of the Republican resurgence. In part, the role came to him by default. Goldwater, discredited after 1964, stayed away from the national scene. Eisenhower and Dewey were in full retirement. Governors Romney and Rockefeller were busy campaigning in Michigan and New York, while the brightest new light for the GOP, actor Ronald Reagan, who had won many an Old Guard heart with his television appearance on the eve of the '64 election, was running for governor of California.

But Nixon did not just fall into his role through luck or fortunate timing; he actively reached out to seize his opportunity. He did not have to spend nearly all his time in 1966 campaigning for GOP candidates, but he did. He carefully considered his options, decided on his course, and stuck to it, to the great benefit of both himself and the GOP.

He did something else right; he carefully chose those districts in which he campaigned, and for the most part picked districts that were traditionally Republican but had been lost to the Democrats in the Goldwater catastrophe. With or without Nixon, most of these districts were going to go back to the GOP in 1966; by campaigning for the Republican candidate in such districts, Nixon could make it appear that he was the one who made victory possible.

He got going in January, when in a series of speeches on the East Coast he predicted big Republican victories come November. How big? As many as forty to forty-five seats, according to Nixon. This was actually a conservative guess, but the press acted as if Nixon had gone far out on a limb—which was exactly what he wanted the press to do.

Nixon set the tone in an end-of-January appearance on ABC's "Issues and Answers." He laid into LBJ for failing to prosecute the war vigorously enough, and into Senator Fulbright and other anti-war Democrats for taking "the appeasement line" on Vietnam. He called the "appeasers," in his familiar heavy-handed style, "well-intentioned but mistaken" Democrats. Asked how the GOP could make an issue out of Vietnam when most Republicans were supporting the President's policies, Nixon replied, "I hope it will not be an issue. It will become one only if President Johnson fails to take a strong line that will preserve the peace by refusing to reward the aggressors." In other words, Nixon would not make an issue out of Vietnam if Johnson managed to win the war before the election.

Nixon outlined his plans for the year in his appearance on "Issues and Answers." He used lines he would repeat a hundred times over before the campaign ended: "I am a political realist. I do not expect to be a candidate again. I am motivated solely by a desire to strengthen the party so that whoever we nominate in 1968 can win."[1]

In May, in Durham, North Carolina, Nixon said that if the United States adopted "the appeasement line of Senator William Fulbright in Vietnam and cuts and runs we will have a temporary peace and then a certain world war." He said specifically that World War III would come in "four or five years" if Vietnam fell, and warned that the Chinese now had nuclear weapons.[2]

With that apocalyptic view, Nixon felt justified in exposing the enemy wherever he appeared. As one example, he went after the Du Bois Clubs, a Marxist group named for the Negro historian W. E. B. Du Bois, who had died an expatriate in Ghana in 1963. Nixon, in early March, cited the Attorney General's designation of the Du Bois Clubs as a Communist-front organization and then decried the similarity in the pronunciation of Du Bois Clubs and the Boys Clubs of America (of which he was national chairman), saying that the confusion was "an almost classic example of Communist deception and duplicity."[3] It was also an almost classic "only Nixon"; who else but Nixon would have seen this particular danger to the Republic?

But if Nixon was capable of playing to the primitive Right, he was no Joe McCarthy. He wanted the respect and admiration of the intellectuals and the Establishment. He wanted their approval because, although no one could be quite so sarcastic in describing intellectuals (he liked to quote Frederick I, "The surest way to destroy a state is to have it governed by professors"), he respected and admired them, and spoke of himself as one of them. "Some people have said I'm sort of an egghead in the Republican Party," he told Jules Witcover in June, in one of innumerable descriptions of himself as an intellectual. "I wish I had more time to read and write," he continued. "If I had my druthers, I'd like to write two or three books a year, go to one of the fine schools—Oxford, for instance—just teach, read and write. I'd like to do that better than what I'm doing now." He did not say what prevented him from doing it; he did explain that "the appeal of teaching or writing is in being able to take time to contemplate."[4]

In the spring of 1966, Nixon set out to impress those with whom he claimed to identify. In April, he argued his first and only case before the Supreme Court, *Time* v. *Hill*. It was a privacy case involving *Life* magazine coverage of the James Hill family's ordeal (the family had been held at gunpoint in their own home).

According to Nixon, the case involved what Justice Louis Brandeis called "the constitutional right to be let alone." Nixon put a major effort into his preparation, assisted by a young member of Nixon, Mudge, former jazz clarinet player and liberal Democrat Leonard Garment. After he made his argument before the Court, Nixon prepared a long tape analyzing his effort for Garment. His homework, his logic, his presentation, and his commitment all impressed his law partners, the larger New York legal community, and the reporters covering the Supreme Court. Although he eventually lost the case, 5–4, Nixon got from it the respect of his fellow lawyers. He proved what he already knew, that if he had devoted full time to his legal practice, he would have been one of the best.[5]

In June, Nixon went to the University of Rochester to deliver the commencement address. He used the occasion to calm the fears of New York Establishment types who had seen disturbing evidence of the "old" Nixon in his 1965 attack on Professor Genovese. At that time, Nixon had appeared to be joining the anti-intellectuals in his assault on freedom of speech and academic freedom, so much so that there had been widespread opposition on the Rochester campus to his appearance.

Nixon went anyway. He spoke on the subject of academic freedom and free speech. He said that these rights included the freedom "to be against war, to be against this war, to be against the way this war is conducted, to be against the inequities of the draft." They did not include "the right to root for the other side" in Vietnam.

"Any teacher," Nixon said, "who uses the forum of a university to proclaim that he welcomes victory for the enemy in a shooting war crosses the line between liberty and license. If we are to defend academic freedom from encroachment, we must also defend it from its own excesses." A line had to be drawn somewhere, Nixon declared, but no single group had the right or power to draw that line by itself. "Only through the interplay of free discussion can a balance be struck, with each of us willing to speak out on our interpretation of the line that not only limits—but defends—academic freedom."

Thus did Nixon become an improbable champion of academic freedom. He was proud of his effort, and sent copies of his speech to friends and supporters around the country.[6] Eisenhower was unhappy with it. He wrote Nixon, "I am a bit skeptical about the assertion that teachers and students possess a special freedom in America." Eisenhower also strenuously objected to Nixon's statement that academic freedom protected the right of a professor to advocate Communism.[7]

Nixon was experienced at working both sides of the street. Having defended academic freedom and intellectual respectability in Rochester, less than a month later Nixon was in California to speak at a fund-raiser for Reagan. Reagan had accepted support from the California John Birch Society. Asked how he could support the Hollywood actor in view of his own condemnation of the Birch Society, Nixon snapped, "I do not seek to lay down a code of conduct for other candidates." He managed to raise $300,000 for Reagan.[8]

A COUPLE of days after his appearance for Reagan in California, Nixon was in Chicago for a meeting of his informal organization, the Birdwatchers of '66. Two dozen men were present, including Maurice Stans, who was in charge of fund-raising, Peter Flanigan, Fred Seaton, and Bob Merriam. Nixon estimated he would need $100,000 for the summer and fall of 1966 to cover his expenses; together with Stans and Flanigan he went over lists of possible contributors. Nixon had hoped that the RNC would provide him with an airplane, but Chairman Ray Bliss refused on the grounds that to do so would show favoritism for Nixon over other potential candidates in 1968. As Nixon was the only Republican campaigning nationally in 1966, he had good reason to resent Bliss's decision.

Nixon wanted to keep the number of contributors small, and Stans was able to comply; he raised $70,000 from a handful of old Nixon supporters, led by DeWitt Wallace of *Reader's Digest* ($8,500) and Elmer Bobst ($5,000). And the airplane problem was solved by William Lear, who loaned Nixon a six-seat Lear Jet, the identical plane used by James Bond in a recent movie, *Goldfinger*.[9]

Although Nixon had promised Bob Merriam that in 1966, unlike 1960, he would open himself to advice, in fact his staff consisted of advance men, moneymen, and speech writers. He did not seek outside advice; he made up his own mind on the issues and established his own positions. He set Pat Buchanan, who was young, energetic, and highly partisan, to work on "political intelligence." Nixon had always been concerned with what his opponents were doing and saying, but that concern was now becoming a near obsession. John Kennedy had caught him flat-footed in October of 1960 when he called for support for the anti-Castro Cuban rebels. He never wanted to be surprised again; to prevent it, he set Buchanan to following the enemy around.[10]

That used to be John Ehrlichman's job. The young Seattle lawyer had worked for Nixon in 1960, first to provide political intelligence on Rockefeller during the primaries, then as an advance man during the campaign. Ehrlichman had also pitched in during the 1962 campaign for governor in California, and had been with Nixon at the 1964 San Francisco convention the night Goldwater was nominated. Late that evening, when only Charlie McWhorter, Bob Finch, Bob Haldeman, and a few others were present, Nixon —according to Ehrlichman—had gotten drunk, begun slurring his words, and had generally embarrassed the group. So, in 1966, when the Birdwatchers invited him to New York to get on the team, Ehrlichman first insisted on talking privately to Nixon.

They met in Nixon's office. Ehrlichman bluntly told Nixon he was worried about the booze. He said he did not want to invest his time in a presidential campaign "that might well be lost because the candidate was not fully in control of himself."

Nixon faced the issue squarely. He said Ehrlichman's point was well taken, that everyone working for him had "a right to expect . . . that he would keep himself in the best of condition in a campaign."[11]

Ehrlichman later wrote that Nixon kept that promise. And Bob Haldeman, who was in the best position to know, stated flatly: "In all my years with [Nixon] as candidate or as President, I never saw him intoxicated."[12]

During the 1966 campaign, Nixon told a reporter that he sometimes had one beer after speaking, but never any alcohol of any kind before. "When I'm campaigning," he explained, "I live like a Spartan . . . I've seen a lot of people who drink. They get up there and talk too long. I speak without notes, and I can't do that without intense concentration before and during the speech."[13]

Whatever Nixon's problems in life, and Lord knows there were many, alcohol was not one of them.

ONE THING Nixon had that all his opponents envied was his energy. He seemed never to tire, and to be in the air more than he was on the ground. In the last week of June alone, he spoke in Chicago, Detroit, Flint and Bay City, Michigan, Roanoke, Virginia, and Washington, D.C. Reporter David Broder wondered which was the more remarkable, "the tension that drives a man at such a pace," or "the durability of his political appeal." Whatever it was, he thought Nixon never looked better. Broder asked Nixon about the pace; Nixon replied, "I think I do better in adversity than when I am living off the fat of the land." An unnamed staff member on the trip commented, "The man is possessed by a demon."[14]

In July, Nixon was off on another around-the-world tour, with stops in London, Dublin, Paris, Tel Aviv, Karachi, Bangkok, Saigon, Manila, Hong Kong, Tokyo, and Seoul.[15] Pat and the girls went along, but the purpose of the tour was politics, not sight-seeing. Nixon conferred with various leaders at every stop, and held his usual press conference at every airport.

In Saigon, Nixon said he had come to gather political and military information on Vietnam, but quickly added that he had no intention of using the information as ammunition against the Democrats. He then proceeded to use it as ammunition against the Democrats, as he denounced the antiwar critics. He claimed they were "prolonging the war, encouraging the enemy and preventing the very negotiations they say they want." To win the war, Nixon said, America "needed unity of purpose," which could be achieved in November by electing Republicans.[16]

The following day, still in Saigon, Nixon said he could see "no possibility of negotiations," and pitched into Johnson for failing to go after the enemy. He called for "a substantial increase" in troops. The current troop level was 287,000; Nixon wanted 500,000. He also advocated heavier and more frequent air attacks on North Vietnam (on June 30, American bombers had struck oil-storage depots near Hanoi for the first time).[17]

The New York Times, in a lead editorial, took Nixon to task for raising precisely the issue he was insisting should no longer be a subject for debate, the American objective in Vietnam. In calling for more guns and bombs, Nixon was in fact questioning Johnson's pursuit of a negotiated settlement and advocating a quick total victory. The editors commented, "A commitment to endless escalation in pursuit of military victory on the Asian mainland would be a commitment to disaster." [18]

BACK HOME in the States, Nixon went into high gear in his role of architect of party recovery. His schedule had him campaigning in thirty-five states for 105 candidates. "I know," he explained to reporters who asked what good his visits did, "that nobody gets anybody else elected. What I can do is get the candidate exposed to a bigger audience, get him on television and raise some money for his campaign." He claimed too that "I can get the different factions to sit down together. I know the liberal fringe and the conservative fringe have no use for me, but they tolerate me, where they don't tolerate others." [19]

He approached the election as he had approached the previous eight campaigns, as if it were Armageddon. "If we don't have a significant win this fall," he said, "you can forget about the Republican party." He told James Reston that the election "will determine the survival of the Republican party and the two-party system in this country." [20]

Whether they believed such hyperbole or not, Republican candidates were happy to have Nixon come into their districts. He brought publicity unobtainable in any other way; he got the party faithful enthused; he generated funds. He never talked about himself, only about how bad the Democrats were and what a great man the local GOP candidate was. When it was picture-taking time, Nixon would gather the candidates around him. "Make these guys look good," he urged the photographers. "Don't worry about me." He did not discriminate between conservative and liberal Republicans; he insisted that the GOP had room enough for both. "The Democrats always got in bed with each other so they could always keep their noses in the trough," he would say. "Why not Republicans?" [21]

He enjoyed it immensely. Not the backslapping or the handshaking, which he endured, but the opportunity to throw out oneliners thought up by Safire or Buchanan. "Any Republican who believes LBJ is a conservative would believe Richard Burton married Elizabeth Taylor for her money" was one. Another was "Johnson's War on Poverty has become the War on Prosperity."

He looked great. In a column on "The New Nixon," James

Reston, who had in 1962 written Nixon's political obituary, wrote that "Nixon is now a little heavier, a little more relaxed, a little wiser, and a lot richer than the tense and painfully suspicious young man who served two terms as Vice President."[22] John Herbers, who covered Nixon in Wisconsin, North Dakota, Wyoming, Oklahoma, and Nebraska, reported that "at every stop, Mr. Nixon appears relaxed, friendly and articulate. His face is tanned from standing in the sun and he looks as if he is enjoying it all."[23]

It was the same old speech, day after day, but Nixon always managed to get himself up for it, radiating enthusiasm and apparent spontaneity. He would stride out onto the platform, deliberately arriving late and never appearing before everyone else was seated. He did not want long introductions—everyone knew who he was anyway—and he did not make long speeches.

He would open with a joke. One favorite was "I'm a dropout from the Electoral College because I flunked debating," which reminded voters of the 1960 campaign (Nixon characterized that race as "the classic campaign of our era. It is part of everyone's life").[24]

Another opener: Nixon said that after gazing at all the domestic issues the Democrats had created for the Republicans, he felt like "a mosquito in a nudist camp—I don't know where to begin."[25]

Still another: Nixon said he had recently been introduced as "the Vice President of the United States." He went on, "Now, I'm not particularly sensitive. I've been called almost everything. But please don't call me Hubert."[26]

He liked to show that he was up-to-date. The verb "stoned" had taken on a new meaning as marijuana use increased. Nixon played on it at the annual Al Smith dinner in New York City. He opened by saying that contrary to some reports, he and Governor Rockefeller were good friends. Before he left for South America in 1958, Nixon recalled, Rockefeller had suggested that he visit Caracas. Nixon asked why.

"It's a real fun town," Rockefeller replied.

"Boy, was he right," Nixon continued. "I got stoned there."[27]

In a variation on that one, Nixon told the Junior Chamber of Commerce, "I got stoned in Caracas. I'll tell you one thing, it's a lot different from getting stoned at a Jaycee convention." It brought down the house.[28]

There were other openers, some of them even worse, but enough. Nixon's audiences were overwhelmingly Republican, and they loved the material. Once he had them warmed up, he would get into the issues. On the domestic side, he said there were three big ones—inflation and high interest rates, crime in the streets, and labor-management relations. He called for lower spending and warned that the Democrats would raise taxes. But when he abandoned generalities for specifics, he sometimes sounded more liberal than the Democrats. He told an elderly audience in Indiana, for example, that he was proposing legislation to provide automatic cost-of-living increases in Social Security benefits and veterans' pensions.[29]

In foreign affairs, Nixon charged that the Democrats were endangering NATO (by July 1, de Gaulle had pulled French armed forces out of NATO), and thereby encouraging Communist adventurism. But his main theme was Vietnam. Here he was in the happy position of being able to criticize the antiwar Democrats for not supporting the President, and to criticize the President for not prosecuting the war vigorously enough. He was scornful of the optimistic predictions coming from the Administration, such as the light Dean Rusk kept seeing at the end of the tunnel, or Secretary of Defense Robert McNamara's insistence that an important corner had been turned. In August, Nixon told the American Legion Convention that "those who predict the Vietnam war will end in a year or two are smoking opium or taking LSD."

Nixon told the Legionnaires that while it was always a temptation for the opposition to attack the Administration, "it would be wrong to do so at a time when American boys are fighting and dying in Vietnam." He then proceeded to attack the Administration, calling for a major increase in ground strength, for a cutoff of aid to any country trading with the enemy, and a much expanded bombing of North Vietnam.[30]

He was insistent on the last point. In Birmingham, Alabama, he declared that "the bombing of North Vietnam is a case of too little and too late. If it had been done months ago, thousands of American boys wouldn't be dead today."[31]

Reporter Tom Wicker, covering Nixon for *The New York Times,* described him as "obviously in high spirits. He is drawing enthusiastic crowds, delighting audiences with pep talks, a fast flow of political jokes and sledge-hammer blows at President Johnson and the 'rubber stamp' 89th Congress."[32]

He retained his unique ability to drive his opponents to distraction with his contradictions. After laying into Johnson on Vietnam, he would call on Democrats to grant the President "a pause in their criticisms."[33]

NIXON's presumed purpose in 1966 was to help GOP candidates, a position reinforced by his refusal to discuss 1968 and his own chances for nomination. But Broder, Wicker, Reston, Witcover, and other reporters speculated that he was creating a political base for 1968, and that it was the South. He campaigned in all eleven of the former Confederate states, and as Broder noted, "The South provides a base of more than adequate dimensions for a serious bid."[34] There were 279 delegates from the states of the old Confederacy, nearly half the total needed to nominate. Almost all had gone for Goldwater in 1964; in a race between Rockefeller, Romney, and Nixon, Nixon was almost sure to hold them all for himself in 1968.

Goldwater had been the southern favorite because he had voted against the Civil Rights Act of 1964. Nixon was much too smart, and his well-known commitment to civil rights far too well established, for him to follow Goldwater's lead. He urged southern Republicans to drop the race issue from their campaigns, and whenever he spoke in the South he iterated his support of the Civil Rights Act of 1964 and the Voting Rights Act of 1965.

In Mississippi, where the local Republicans had adopted a platform endorsing "segregation of the races as absolutely essential to harmonious racial relations," Nixon was firm and straightforward; he told a Jackson audience that "I am opposed to any segregationist plank in a Republican platform. I would fight it in the national Republican platform and speak against it in any state I appear in."[35] He pitched into the Democrats for failing to speak out against the racist appeals of such gubernatorial candidates as Mrs. Lurleen Wallace in Alabama, Lester Maddox in Georgia, Jim Johnson in Arkansas, and George Mahoney in Maryland.[36]

All of which would seemingly have made Nixon anathema in the South, but it did not, partly because southern Republicans could hardly expect a national candidate to endorse segregation after what happened to Goldwater in 1964, partly because Nixon always softened his message by adding that he was for states' rights and opposed to any attempt by Washington to "dictate" to the South, but mainly because southerners told themselves that Nixon didn't really mean what he said. One Atlanta Republican explained how he thought about it after listening to George Romney lecture on civil rights: "This fellow [Romney] really means it. Dick Nixon comes down South and talks hard on civil rights, but you know he *has* to say what he does, for the Northern press."[37]

That cynical remark seemed to the Nixon haters to be an entirely accurate description of the cynicism of Nixon himself, and perhaps it was, but there was another point of view. Not once, in any southern or northern state, did Nixon make a direct appeal to the white backlash, and he privately as well as publicly told GOP candidates that they could never win by trying to outsegregate the Democrats.

Nixon's appeal to the South was not based on racism. Southerners liked him for his general conservatism, for his denunciation of crime in the streets and of riots (which his critics said was a code for racism), for his outspoken patriotism, and most of all for his insistence on victory in Vietnam.

Southerners also liked Nixon for his friends. Pat Buchanan, along with Tom Charles Huston of the Young Americans for Freedom, arranged for a series of meetings between Nixon and the leading conservative organizations in the country, many of them based in the South or the West. Among the groups represented were the Americans for Conservative Action, the Free Society Association, and the American Conservative Union.[38]

In short, in 1966 Nixon had not only helped revive the Republican Party nationally, he was participating in the building of a new Republican Party in the South, and in the process—to use Murray Chotiner's lovely phrase—taking the risk that all this might help him in 1968.

IF NIXON did win the nomination in 1968, his almost certain opponent would be Lyndon Johnson. The prospect delighted Nixon, because Johnson was vulnerable on so many fronts and because Nixon, more than any other Republican, could goad LBJ into overreacting.

At a meeting in the early fall of the coordinating committee of the RNC, held in New York and attended by Dewey and Eisenhower, among others, Nixon set the tone. He said Republicans in 1966 should campaign against LBJ, not against their local Democratic opponents. He suggested themes worked out by his speech writers, punchy stuff devoid of thought or content, but excellent material for campaigning by slogan ("All the way with LBJ means a five-year war in Asia, a spiraling increase in the cost of living, crime growing six times as fast as the population"; "It is time to call a truce in Johnson's War Against Prosperity and to declare war on Johnson's inflation," and so on).[39]

Nixon was adept at stirring up trouble for the Democrats. In late August, after the Gallup poll showed that Senator Bobby Kennedy had more popularity with Democrats than Vice-President Humphrey, Nixon predicted that LBJ would dump Humphrey for Kennedy as his running mate in 1968. As the relationship between the President and the senator was, at best, strained, Nixon's prediction angered Johnson. At a press conference the following day, Johnson said that Humphrey was a "fine and excellent public servant," and that in selecting his running mate he would "not be guided by either the wishes or the desires or the predictions of an ex-Vice President."[40]

Two days after that, on the NBC "Today" show, Nixon said that although Kennedy "has attacked the President, and has gained much support, including that of the hard-core left," he stuck by his prediction. The political realities, he said, would force Johnson to take Kennedy on the ticket.[41] Nixon kept after it; a week later he told an interviewer, "If Lyndon thinks he's in trouble, if Lyndon thinks he needs Bobby on the ticket to win, he'll sugar-coat him, swallow him and regurgitate him later."[42]

In mid-September, on the CBS program "Face the Nation," Nixon was asked to comment on a recent White House leak that said Johnson was thinking about raising the present troop level of 300,000 to 600,000 or even 750,000. Nixon was nothing if not consistent—whatever Johnson wanted, he was against it. In this case, the man who had been demanding major troop-level increases for the past two years now said, "There is a grave danger at the present time that the Administration will go overboard in increasing American forces in Vietnam. We might be able to win the war, but by doing so we would have on our hands a dependency for a generation to come. That's the wrong way to handle it."[43]

For the next few days, Nixon changed his charge from "Johnson isn't doing enough" to "Johnson is doing too much." He told the Overseas Press Club that Johnson secretly planned to increase troop levels in Vietnam in 1967, and declared, "He owes it to the American people to come clean and tell them exactly what his plans are." Asked if he was accusing the President of deliberate deception, Nixon replied, "I wouldn't charge the President with misleading, because he may not have thought this thing through." Nixon described himself as "distressed" by the rumors of as many as 750,000 Americans in Vietnam and said an increase of such proportions would make South Vietnam into a virtual American dependency. "South Vietnam should still carry the brunt of the responsibility," Nixon said. "We must not get into the position of fighting their war for them."[44] This was his first and only mention of concern for the Army of the Republic of Vietnam (ARVN).

By the end of September, the rumors and leaks from Washington were that Johnson was going to settle for a negotiated peace in 1967. Nixon was against that too. When Johnson offered to go to an international conference in Geneva to settle the war, Nixon said the President should "publicly withdraw and repudiate" the offer.[45] When U.S. Ambassador to the United Nations Arthur Goldberg declared, "We are prepared to order a cessation of all bombing of North Vietnam the moment we are assured privately or otherwise that this step will be answered promptly by a corresponding de-escalation from the other side," Nixon demanded that Goldberg withdraw and repudiate his statement. Nixon feared that in return for halting the bombing, all the United States would get would be a "worthless promise."[46]

In a letter to Eisenhower, Nixon said that Goldberg's statement "runs directly contrary to the principle that you and Foster Dulles insisted upon in dealing with the communists—that we should never rely on communist promises—but should always insist on guaranteed deeds." In his reply, Eisenhower concluded, "Frankly, it seems that the Vietnam War is creating more whimperings and whinings from some frustrated partisans than it's inspiring a unification of all Americans in the solution of a national problem."[47]

At the end of September, Johnson announced that he was going to meet President Nguyen Van Thieu of South Vietnam in Manila in late October. Nixon heard the announcement in Wilmington, Delaware. He responded: "He has put politics ahead of policy so many times that leaders of both parties on Capitol Hill are publicly asking whether in going to the Far East he is even playing politics with world peace."[48]

But quips could not deal with the danger that Johnson might come out of Manila with a communiqué that would translate into Democratic votes in November. One way to undercut Johnson was to set an impossibly high goal for him; Nixon did just that when he proposed that Johnson and Thieu "use this historic occasion as an opportunity to issue a Pacific Charter which would set forth a long range program for peace and freedom in Asia." It called to mind Churchill, Roosevelt, and the Atlantic Charter of 1941, and implied that anything less in the current crisis would be unacceptable.

In a letter to Eisenhower describing these moves, Nixon asserted that his proposed Pacific Charter "represents a responsible and constructive position for members of the Loyal Opposition to take with regard to the Johnson trip."[49]

At a Chicago press conference, Nixon was less statesmanlike: "The timing [of the Manila] conference was certainly not designed to hurt the Democrats, but who is to say? There might have been other genuine reasons for holding it now.

"There have been many firsts in the Johnson Administration, but this is the first time a President may have figured the best way to help his party is to leave the country."[50]

The following day, in Newark, Johnson lashed back. Although he was careful not to use Nixon's name, he said that "a New York lawyer, originally from California," was going around the country predicting big Republican victories. The President taunted Nixon as a "consistently poor political prophet," throwing in Nixon's face the predictions he had made in previous campaigns (such as his prediction that Goldwater would win and that the GOP would gain thirty seats in 1964). The President said that the Republicans were the party of privilege and the party of fear. "Their platform this year is made up of one word. And that word is fear."[51]

A week later, in Wilmington, Delaware, Johnson said that a vote for the Republicans "could cause the nation to falter and fall back and fail in Vietnam." Nixon could not have asked for a better opportunity, save only being criticized by Johnson by name, and he quickly took it. The next day he issued a statement: "This is a vicious, unwarranted and partisan assault upon the Republican party that has given President Johnson the support for the war that his own party has denied him." Then a warning: "With his insensitive attack, President Johnson has gravely jeopardized the bipartisan backing he should have when he goes to Manila." When or how or in what form Johnson ever had bipartisan backing for anything, or could ever hope for it, Nixon did not say; he did demand that Johnson "apologize to the Republican party for his irresponsible charge."[52]

In mid-October, Johnson flew off to Manila, without having apologized and without bipartisan support. While Johnson was gone, Nixon—who was enamored with the idea of loyal opposition —proposed that after the elections President Johnson meet with "representatives of both political parties to develop a strategy for victory in Vietnam within the next year." It sounded very much like the British War Cabinets of 1917–1918 and 1940–1945, in which both parties shared power. Nixon said that the reason for his most unusual proposal was his belief that unless the war was ended before the 1968 presidential contest began, Vietnam would become "a devastating political issue" that would defeat Johnson and drive the Republicans to a "peace campaign and candidate." That development, Nixon said, could be prevented if Johnson called in leading Republicans to work with him "to devise a strategy to end the war."[53]

Johnson did not call.

AT THE END of October 1966, Johnson returned home. He brought with him the Manila Communiqué, which offered an American troop withdrawal from South Vietnam six months after North Vietnam withdrew and ceased all support for the Vietcong.

The proposal never had the slightest chance of acceptance by the Communists, because if implemented, it meant a South Vietnamese victory. But Nixon took it seriously, or rather saw it as an opportunity. He gave considerable thought to his response, and took nearly a week before he issued a statement. When he did, he wanted *The New York Times* to carry the full text, for the prestige of it, and had Safire call Harrison Salisbury, assistant managing editor, who agreed to read and consider the piece carefully. The next morning, the text was in the *Times*.[54]

In his statement, Nixon said that a "Communist victory would most certainly be the result of 'mutual withdrawal'. . ." and therefore condemned the Manila Communiqué. He then asked Johnson a series of questions.

Are we really ready to stand aside and let the Vietcong and ARVN slug it out? Will we limit our military response to the fluctuating intensity of Communist aggression? Or will we escalate in order to shorten the war and reduce American casualties? How many more American troops will victory require? Does the Johnson Administration intend to raise taxes to pay for this war?

Unasked, but implicit throughout, was this question: Are the American people willing to pay the cost of victory?

When Johnson read his *Times* that morning, he was furious with the editors for printing the text of Nixon's statement. "Don't they know it's all a lot of politics?" the President thundered to his press secretary, Bill Moyers.[55]

JOHNSON HAD long since been torturing himself with the questions Nixon asked, questions to which neither he nor Nixon had any answers. Had their positions been reversed, LBJ would have asked President Nixon the identical questions. The sparring between the two men, which really was all a lot of politics, exactly as Johnson said, should not obscure the reality, which was that neither man had a plan for victory, but neither one was ready to pull out short of victory. Both hoped that continued American escalation would sooner or later cause Hanoi to say "ouch" and quit. But that was a hope, not a plan, and unfortunately they argued with each other over the pace of escalation, not the assumption behind it.

Politics had come to prevail over policy in the United States in 1966. This was hardly new, of course, but it is worth pausing briefly to compare 1966 to 1942. In each case, a Democratic President had taken the country into a foreign war a year earlier. But in 1966 the GOP concentrated on criticizing Johnson's conduct of the war, while in 1942 the GOP had questioned basic assumptions, such as how FDR had manipulated America into the war, and whether internationalism was a good thing. In 1966 the GOP accepted Johnson's assumptions and went after him on implementation.

But for another contrast, think of 1952, when the GOP Old Guard was nearly frothing at the mouth as it went after Truman for his conduct of the Korean War. The chief critic was the junior senator from California and vice-presidential nominee, Richard

Nixon. At that time, Nixon had charged that Truman had sold out to the Communists when he agreed to truce talks and accepted a stalemated war in Korea. Nixon had been scornful of the idea of limited war and had urged the "unleashing" of the Nationalist Chinese troops on Formosa, reinforcement of U.N. (read U.S.) troops in Korea, a land offensive to the Yalu, a naval blockade of China, and a bombing of China, possibly with atomic bombs.

Nixon, for all his political convolutions over his long career, had been consistent on this one: for seventeen years, ever since the Communist victory in China, he had been the most prominent and persistent advocate of taking the offensive against Communism in Asia, Europe, or wherever it threatened freedom. At every critical moment—Korea, 1950–53; Dien Bien Phu, 1954; Hungary and Suez, 1956; Cuba, 1959; the Bay of Pigs, 1961; the Berlin Wall, 1961; the Cuban missile crisis, 1962; Vietnam, 1964–66—Nixon had scorned accommodation and negotiation to urge escalation.

The principal political question the United States had been forced to face in the two decades since World War II was how to relate to the Soviet Union and an ever-expanding international Communist movement. Nixon's answer, always, was to relate to the Communists as enemies, just as we related to Hitler and the Nazis. No accommodation, no compromise, only total victory.

People asked of Nixon, "Is he sincere?" The question came up so often because of his many switches on issues, because his body language so often gave the impression that he meant the opposite of what he said, because he so often gave the appearance of cynicism, and just because Nixon was Nixon. But with regard to relating to the Communist menace, one would have to say he was sincere, that here at least he was speaking the truth when he said he was scorning the "easy way, the politically profitable way," to do what he really believed in.

Of course, being Nixon, he was not unaware that being the world's number-one anti-Communist was a great help to him with the Old Guard of the GOP. Goldwater had thought that conservatives alone could carry him to victory in 1964; Rockefeller thought the GOP could win without the conservatives; Nixon, the smartest of the three by far, knew that no Republican could win without solid support from independents and conservative Democrats, but also that no Republican could win without the enthusiastic support of the Old Guard. All his political life, Nixon had acted on that knowledge, using liberal domestic politics to appeal to the independents and Democrats, and his extraordinary belligerency on foreign issues to appeal to the right wing.

Sincerity is not necessarily an admirable trait (the Nazis were sincere, after all). What counts more is intelligence and honesty and concern for the best interests of the country. On these points, Nixon had failed. His intelligence about the enemy in Vietnam was woefully incomplete, and he had an altogether false picture of the Vietcong. He had no understanding of what the victory he was demanding would cost, nor of what the American people could be persuaded to pay. It was irresponsible for Nixon to say that more bombing and more troops could achieve victory in Vietnam. And it was not in the best interests of the nation to so grossly exaggerate what was at stake in Vietnam. The fact that he was hardly alone is no more of an excuse for Nixon than is the fact that he was sincere.

NIXON'S STATEMENT on the Manila Communiqué ran in the *Times* on November 4. That morning, Nixon flew from New York to New Hampshire. As he got into the Lear Jet, Buchanan greeted him with the news of a just-concluded presidential press conference.

"He *hit* us," Buchanan declared, excited. "Jesus, did he hit us. You'll never believe how he hit us."

And Buchanan told Nixon about Johnson's reply to a reporter's request that he comment on Nixon's statement. "I would be glad to comment," Johnson had said. "I do not want to get into a debate on a foreign policy meeting in Manila with a chronic campaigner like Mr. Nixon. He—it's his problem to find fault with his country and his government during a period of October every two years."

Johnson had gone on to sketch out Nixon's political career for the press and television audience: "And if you will look back over his record you will find that's true. He never did really recognize and realize what was going on when he had an official position in the Government. You remember what President Eisenhower said, 'that if you'd give him a week or so he'd figure out what he [Nixon] was doing.' "

That one hurt, even though Johnson got the quote wrong.

Johnson had gone on: "Now since then he has made a temporary stand in California and you saw what the people—what action they took out there. Then he crossed the country to New York and then he went back to San Francisco hoping that he'd be in the wings available if Goldwater stumbled, but Goldwater didn't stumble and now he's out talking about a conference that obviously he is not well-prepared on or informed about.

"Mr. Nixon," Johnson had concluded, "doesn't serve his country well by trying to leave that kind of impression in the hope that he can pick up a precinct or two, or a ward or two."

Even though the President's description of Nixon, while obviously unfriendly, was essentially accurate, Nixon saw this direct attack as a heaven-sent gift. Making the situation even better, Nixon could ignore the substance of Johnson's reply ("Why would we want to stay there if there was no aggression? We wouldn't want to stay there as tourists; we wouldn't want to keep 400,000 men there just to march up and down the runways at Camranh Bay") and respond to the personal attack.[56]

When he got off the plane, Nixon called Safire in New York. "I'm going to be absolutely cool," he said excitedly. "High road. President is tired, after all, it was a long trip. Not answer in kind." Then, obviously elated, he met the press to respond to the attack launched on him by the President. Johnson, Nixon said, had "broken the bipartisan line on Vietnam policy." Smiling and relaxed, he said he would not change his position whatever Johnson called him. His position, he said, was to support the Administration's goal of no reward for aggression while pressing for answers to such questions as how many troops would be needed and whether nondefense spending should be cut to pay for the war.[57]

Safire and the others around Nixon thought that Nixon's goading of Johnson for the past months had finally paid off, that Johnson had lost his temper and with it his political sense. But Safire later talked to two Johnson insiders, Bill Moyers and Joseph Califano, who insisted that Johnson was speaking quite deliberately, that his apparent anger at Nixon was not spontaneous but calculated.

"Johnson thought that Nixon was the most vulnerable man in American politics—he said so that morning," Moyers told Safire. Califano said that Johnson found the idea of running against Nixon in 1968 very appealing. He pointed out the obvious: What could possibly drive antiwar Democrats back to Lyndon more quickly or more certainly than a Nixon candidacy?[58]

There was no one LBJ wanted to run against more than Nixon. He wanted Nixon badly enough to give him a boost when he could. And there was no one Nixon wanted to run against more than LBJ.

Thus did these two bull elks start knocking horns in their opening maneuvers. The final clash for supremacy would come in 1968, and the prospect of a Nixon-Johnson presidential campaign was one for political watchers and aficionados to anticipate with relish. When the rutting season came in the fall of 1968, the rivals would each be in his prime, experienced, glossy, strong, confident, calculating, yet each in a full rutting-season frenzy to win. When they locked horns, it promised to be an earthshaking struggle.

These early clashes featured manipulation, a little pressure here, a little more there. In Waterville, New Hampshire, when a reporter asked Nixon about Johnson's charge that Nixon was playing politics with Vietnam "to pick up a precinct or two," Nixon chuckled and said he would not indulge in personalities. Then he termed Johnson's attack "a shocking display of temper" and suggested that both sides discuss the issue "like gentlemen."

He turned away from the microphone, but was heard by a reporter to ask Buchanan, "Was I too hard on him?"[59]

That night, Eisenhower called Nixon from Gettysburg. "Dick," he said, "I could kick myself every time some jackass brings up that goddamn 'give me a week' business. Johnson has gone too far." He told Nixon he was issuing a statement, which he did the next day; in it, Ike said he had "always had the highest personal and official regard" for Nixon, who "was one of the best informed, most capable and most industrious Vice Presidents in the history of the United States. . . . He was constantly informed of the major problems of the United States during my administration."[60]

As so often in the past, Eisenhower's attempt to set things straight on Nixon's contribution to his Administration was something short of an unqualified endorsement: note that the key verb was "informed," with no implication of participation in decision making.

But never mind; everything else was breaking Nixon's way. He was at the center of national attention in the Sunday newspapers two days before the election. He appeared that day on ABC's "Issues and Answers," and then got a half hour of prime time on NBC sponsored by the RNC (the committee had scheduled a film that included scenes of crime, violence, and the war in Vietnam; Chairman Bliss withdrew it when it was criticized, substituting Nixon).

On "Issues and Answers," Nixon asked Johnson the same questions he had used in commenting on the Manila Communiqué: What kind of a war should we wage in Vietnam? How many men is this war going to require? How do we finance the war? and so on. He accused Johnson of "cheap political demagoguery" and said indignantly that the President "tends to have an attitude that unless you go all the way with LBJ you don't go any of the way. He isn't going to get away with that with me."

On NBC, Nixon opened with remarks that reminded some observers of his Checkers speech of 1952: "I was subjected last week to one of the most savage personal assaults ever leveled by the President of the United States against one of his political opponents. . . .

"I shall answer it not for myself but because of a great principle that is at stake. It is the principle of the right to disagree, the right to dissent."

He closed with a beauty: speaking directly to President Johnson, he said, "I respect you for the great energies you devote to your office, and my respect has not changed because of the personal attack you made on me. You see, I think I can understand how a man can be very, very tired and how his temper can then be very short."[61]

ON MONDAY, Nixon campaigned in Indiana, where he repeated the prediction he had been making all fall—Republicans would pick up forty House seats. *The New York Times*, in its election-eve roundup, predicted twenty-eight House seats to the Republicans, five governorships, and no gains in the Senate.[62]

Tuesday morning, after voting, Nixon caught up on correspondence. He wrote a long letter to Nelson Rockefeller, inviting Rockefeller to meet with him for a talk on foreign policy sometime soon. In his conclusion, Nixon expressed a part of himself he seldom showed, the genuine admiration he had for his longtime rival, Nelson Rockefeller: "When the history of your campaign is written, it will be recorded that win, lose or draw you fought a most gallant battle. It took an incredible amount of courage to look at those unfavorable polls early this year and then to make a horse race out of the contest. There are plenty of people who can put on a good campaign when things are going their way. What separates the men from the boys is that rare ability which you have demonstrated in this contest to fight at your best when the odds were greatest."[63]

On election night, the Birdwatchers of '66 took a suite at the Drake Hotel in New York. Nixon was elated as the results came in; even before the polls closed in California, it was clear that the GOP was winning a major victory. One by one, as the evening wore on, Nixon called the big winners around the country to congratulate them—first Governor Rockefeller in New York; then his brother Winthrop Rockefeller, now governor-elect in Arkansas; Spiro Agnew, governor-elect in Maryland; Governor George Romney, by a landslide in Michigan; Chuck Percy, senator-elect in Illinois; Edward Brooke, senator-elect in Massachusetts. "It's a sweep," he kept repeating. "It's a sweep." After talking to Reagan, Nixon told his aides, "He's all right, Ron is—it's a sweep in California too."[64] Nixon's former campaign manager, Robert Finch, was also a winner—he ran 100,000 votes ahead of Reagan and was the lieutenant governor–elect in California. Nixon called Herb Klein at the San Diego *Union;* to Klein, he sounded "as if he felt rebirth at that moment. I never heard him sound happier."

After the calls to the West Coast, Nixon went home, stopping on the way for spaghetti at El Morocco at 3 A.M. From his apartment, he called back to the Drake, where aide John Sears was keeping track of the latest returns. Nixon had him read the better ones over and over. "We've beaten hell out of them," Nixon told Sears, "and we're going to kill them in '68."[65]

THE REPUBLICANS picked up 47 House seats, 3 Senate seats, 8 governorships, and 540 seats in state legislatures. Nixon's predictions had been, in his words, "vindicated with a vengeance."[66]

The political pundits immediately began their speculation on the Republican nominee for 1968. Tom Wicker saw a three-cornered contest, pitting "the evangelistic Romney and the 'chronic campaigner' Richard Nixon, with Reagan holding the trump cards."[67] *The New York Times* reported that Reagan, "without a day in public office, is already the favorite Presidential candidate of Republican conservatives."[68] Rockefeller took himself out of the running, saying one day after the election that he "unequivocally" would not be a candidate.

However the speculation went, the cold truth was that Nixon was now in the commanding position for the 1968 GOP nomination. One of the hard facts that stood out in the 1966 election was that a GOP House candidate for whom Nixon did not campaign stood only a 45 percent chance of winning, while those for whom Nixon appeared had a 70 percent chance of victory.[69] These were figures not even the most Right Republican would ignore.

At his "Issues and Answers" appearance the Sunday before the election, Nixon had responded to a question from Bill Lawrence about when he was going to start running for President by saying, "After this election, I am going to take a holiday from politics for at least six months." That self-imposed moratorium on political comment did not keep him from issuing a statement a week after the election in which he analyzed the results.

The American people, according to Nixon, had voted for escalation in Vietnam. They wanted more support, rather than less, for the principle of no reward for aggression. The vote showed "a growing desire by Americans to increase our military pressure on the Communists so as to end the war in Vietnam soon." The vote also meant "the revitalization of the two-party system."[70]

He could have added that it meant the revitalization of Richard Nixon. He had brought himself back from the humiliation of the 1962 California governor's race. Through hard work, effrontery, loyalty to the GOP, hard work, brains, brazenness, luck, hard work, and more luck, all capped by the Manila Communiqué extravaganza, Nixon had made himself the leader of the loyal opposition, and had helped set in motion political forces that could soon make the GOP into the ruling party, with Nixon as President.

Nixon did not hold a news conference after the 1966 campaign, but he did grant an interview to Witcover, who asked him to comment on the press. If Nixon was a snarling loser, he was a gracious winner. "The press are good guys," Nixon said, straight-faced. "They're oriented against my views. But I like the battle. I like to take them on in a give-and-take. I used to be too serious about it. Now I treat it as a game. I'm probably more relaxed."

Nixon sometimes said the oddest things. In this case, he told Witcover, "I like the press guys, because I'm basically like them."[71]

IT HAD BEEN a wonderful year for Nixon. It had a perfect ending. On December 29, Julie led fifty-six young women from twelve countries at the twelfth annual International Debutante Ball at the Waldorf-Astoria. The presentation ceremony was carried on New York television.

Julie was a freshman at Smith College. Her escort at the ball was Ike's grandson, David Eisenhower, a freshman at Amherst. They had had their first date on election night, '66, when they got together to listen to the returns. Although they had earlier resisted efforts to bring them together, when they met for the first time as young adults, they found they liked each other immediately.

They certainly had a lot in common, these children of very famous families, accustomed all their lives to being on stage. Both were good-looking, intelligent, clean-cut, intense, conservative— none of the sixties rebelliousness for these two. They were the kind of kids every Republican would like to have for children.

Julie brought David home with her to New York for Thanksgiving. David and "Mr. Nixon" hit it off from the start; they had common obsessions, baseball and politics, and could talk about either one for hours. David returned to the Nixons' apartment for Christmas vacation, then escorted Julie to the ball.[72]

They were irresistible. Their picture appeared on front pages across the country, David in his white tie and tails, but with rumpled hair and a hint of embarrassment as he led Julie by the hand; she in a floor-length traditional debutante white gown, her head held high and flashing a broad smile; Dick and Pat in the balcony overhead looking down, all against a background of national flags. The band played "America the Beautiful."[73]

CHAPTER FIVE

PREPARING
FOR THE PRESIDENCY
January–July 1967

ON JANUARY 7 AND 8, 1967, Nixon met with seven men at the Waldorf Towers in New York, in the suite where Herbert Hoover had once lived, to talk about how to win the 1968 nomination. Nixon had an established practice of planning his campaigns far in advance, in as much detail as possible, and he intended to run his next campaign the same way. That meant, above all, that he was in charge.

He made that clear in the meeting at the Waldorf. Those present were Peter Flanigan, the finance man; Bob Finch, just elected lieutenant governor of California; Tom Evans, from Nixon, Mudge; Jerry Milbank, a Wall Street Republican who had been a fundraiser for Goldwater; Fred LaRue, chairman of the Mississippi Republicans; Peter O'Donnell, chairman of the Texas Republicans; and Safire. ("This is Safire," Nixon had said in introducing him, "absolutely trustworthy, worked with us in '60. But watch what you say, he's a writer." Safire, who had a strong Boswell tendency anyway, took this as an invitation to take notes.) The average age of the men was thirty-nine.

Nixon's opening lines were "The purpose of this group is to begin planning now to win the nomination. . . . It is not the purpose of this group to help me on issues." [1]

IT WAS almost as if the issues didn't matter, and in a real sense they did not, except for the biggest issue of all: Who was going to lead? This meant that insofar as Nixon was concerned, whatever Johnson was for, he was against.

This was especially true on Vietnam. In 1967, Johnson implemented the policy changes Nixon had been demanding for the past two years. He went over to the offensive, by land, sea, and air. In February, in the largest assault of the war, American troops swept the Cambodian border in search of what was described as a secret Vietcong headquarters called the Central Office for South Vietnam (COSVN). Communiqués called the twenty-five-thousand-man offensive a success. That same month, U.S. Navy planes started dropping mines in rivers in the southern part of North Vietnam to impede water traffic.

In May, U.S. jets bombed downtown Hanoi for the first time. In late July, General William Westmoreland asked for 100,000 more men, or a total of 565,000; Johnson promised the requested reinforcements. The bombing of Hanoi was intensified. That fall, U.S. planes began hitting the Haiphong shipyards, while Westmoreland began a ground offensive in the Central Highlands near the Cambodian border.

As the United States escalated in Vietnam, the protest at home intensified, and the split in the body politic deepened and widened, almost to the point of becoming unbridgeable. Various marches against the war culminated on October 21, when fifty thousand or more demonstrators marched on the nation's military headquarters, at the Pentagon. That unprecedented and previously unimaginable event was but a single indication of the passions that had been aroused. Less publicized but more poignant was a mid-August event, when a Michigan couple returned the President's letter of sympathy on their son's death in Vietnam.

As the level of violence rose in Vietnam, so did it rise in the United States. As the cities in Vietnam burned, so did the cities in America. In the summer of 1967 there were race riots in Harlem, in Toledo, Ohio, in Grand Rapids, Michigan, in Newark, New Jersey, and elsewhere. The worst were in Detroit, where thirty-eight were killed and thousands were arrested, where LBJ sent in forty-five hundred paratroopers, and where the television cameras showed American tanks on the streets of an American city pointing their cannons toward American citizens.

That same month, the news services changed their style sheets to substitute "black" for "Negro." Stokely Carmichael, former chairman of the Student Nonviolent Coordinating Committee, called for a "black revolution" from his exile in Havana, and Thurgood Marshall became the first black appointed to the U.S. Supreme Court.

Crosscurrents, tension, passion, divisiveness, and confusion were abroad in the land as people struggled to respond to these momentous changes. The times cried out for leadership. What the country got was Johnson and Nixon.

Nixon, as will be seen, responded to these shocks by making them into campaign issues, a natural enough and fair enough thing for the leader of the opposition to do. What he did not do, most of all with regard to Vietnam, was to re-examine his prior conclusions and recommendations in light of the events of 1967. To repeat, Johnson instituted in Vietnam in 1967 the military policy Nixon had advocated. North Vietnam was getting pounded from the air, the Vietcong was being pounded on the ground, the enemy body count was rising—and yet the enemy was able to match the United States step-by-step up the escalation ladder, and the United States was no closer to winning the war than ever, and the apparent best that the country could look forward to was a stalemate. These results might well have prompted Nixon to think through the whole situation again, but there is no evidence that he did so. Judged by his public statements, the failure of the policy he had advocated gave him no pause whatsoever. He went through the year insistently demanding more escalation in South Vietnam, but still holding back from a declaration of war or an invasion of North Vietnam, or of Cambodia or Laos, to take control of the Ho Chi Minh Trail.

WHAT NIXON wanted from the men at the Waldorf was help in working out a campaign that would lead to the nomination. Nixon judged that Romney was his chief rival, followed by Senator Percy of Illinois and Governor Reagan. He gave Rockefeller no chance at all. As for himself, Nixon said that "my biggest problem is 'Nixon can't win.' "

It had been seventeen years since Nixon had won an election on his own. In his long political career, the only people he had ever beaten head-to-head were poor befuddled Jerry Voorhis for the 12th Congressional District seat in 1946 and that hapless innocent Helen Douglas for the Senate in 1950. Most Republicans believed that he had been a drag on the ticket in '52 and '56. He had lost to Kennedy in 1960 and to Pat Brown in 1962. No wonder Republicans across the country were saying,, "I like Nixon best, but he just can't win."

"If we could convince delegates that Dick could win," Finch declared, "then he's in."

Flanigan pointed out the obvious: that for Nixon to show that he could win, he would have to enter the primaries. There were, in 1968, primaries in a dozen states, but some of those were already tied up by favorite-son candidates, most importantly California for the Republicans by Reagan. The majority of delegates would be picked in the nonprimary states by the state committees. Goldwater had had the nomination practically won in 1964 even before the first primary, because of his strength among delegates selected by the state parties. Nixon was strong enough with most Republican organizations around the country that he could have done the same in 1968, but as noted, that risked winning the nomination but losing the election. He needed momentum going into November 1968, and to get it he needed to prove that he could win, which he could do only through the primaries. There were risks—Flanigan characterized it as the "dangerous route"—but Nixon had no choice.

As with all risks, there were opportunities. The primaries in which Nixon could run head-to-head against Romney, Percy, Rockefeller (if Rockefeller re-entered the race), and any other contenders were New Hampshire (March 12), Wisconsin (April 2), Nebraska (May 14), and Oregon (May 28).

Romney looked to be the toughest opponent, because of his big win in Michigan in 1966. This gave Nixon his opportunity. He doubted that Romney could "hit big-league pitching," meaning that when Romney was subjected to the national press corps he would crack. Thus it was to Nixon's advantage to build up Romney; then Nixon's victory, when it came, would be all the more dramatic.

So when the group at the Waldorf, to a man, urged him to take advantage of his 1966 triumph by immediately hitting the road, with speeches, appearances, TV, interviews, and so forth, Nixon said no. "Let Romney take the point," he insisted. Nixon would maintain his moratorium on politics for six months, meanwhile traveling abroad on fact-finding missions.

"But make no mistake," Nixon went on, "while I am lying back I want you to work your tails off getting the job done. We will have to work harder and better than the other candidates to win." He wanted the group to get going on putting together an organization in every state, complete with advance men, fund-raisers, and campaign managers. "Don't give out any franchises," he said, "but get started contacting the power groups in each state."

Before breaking up the meeting, Nixon went down the list of states and guessed his delegate strength in each one. Safire added up the figures: 603 on the first ballot. Needed to nominate: 667.[2]

ONE THING Nixon and his people badly wanted was a promise of an Eisenhower endorsement. To that end Seaton wrote Ike, in mid-January, asking the former President to commit himself. Eisenhower was enthusiastic in the opening of his reply: "I agree with you about the qualification of Dick Nixon for political office. I cannot think of anyone better prepared than he is to undertake the responsibilities of the Presidency." Then came the same maddening disclaimer: "However, following my usual custom I do not intend—at this moment—to indicate any preference among the potential Republican candidates."[3]

Even without Eisenhower's nod, Nixon's staff grew. Former congressman Robert Ellsworth of Kansas was one addition; Raymond Price was another. Ellsworth, known as a liberal Republican when he was in Congress, was a great admirer of Nixon. Price came on the team as a speech writer. A rather shy, soft-spoken man, Price was a thirty-seven-year-old former chief editorial writer for the now-defunct New York *Herald Tribune*. In his attitudes as in his dress, he personified the Eastern Establishment, as befit a *Herald Tribune* editor. Despite this, he got on well with Nixon, for whom he developed a strong admiration and deep sense of loyalty.

By early March, Stans, Flanigan, Seaton, and the others had expanded the Nixon working group to thirty men. They suffered an immediate setback. Seaton and Stans sent a letter to 408 Eisenhower Administration appointees, who proved to be no more willing to commit themselves to Nixon than their old boss; 85 percent either straddled the question or did not reply. Of those who did answer, only fifty-two said they would support Nixon at this early stage. That only 13 percent of Ike's appointees would support him incensed Nixon.[4]

Well, he had never thought it would be easy. In March, with his organization taking shape as he wanted it to, he prepared for a series of fact-finding trips.

NIXON'S TRIPS, as usual, provided opportunities to learn, to see for himself, to be seen, to generate publicity both in the country he was visiting and back home, to be treated like an actual leader of the opposition or a potential President, to confer with foreign leaders in and out of power, and to project himself to the voters as the most knowledgeable man in America on foreign affairs (which may well have been true). His trips, as usual, had their ups and downs.

Before he left, on March 5, he requested a CIA briefing and was, for the first time, turned down. Then the Polish government denied him a visa. The Russians would let him in, but his specific requests for interviews with Kremlin leaders were not simply ignored, as was customary when the Russians did not choose to comply, but were coldly and publicly rejected.

At Kennedy Airport, Nixon broke his moratorium on politics to comment on Senator Robert Kennedy's call for a bombing halt in North Vietnam: "Johnson is right and Kennedy is wrong." Nixon added that Kennedy's proposal would have the effect of "prolonging the war by encouraging the enemy."[5] And off he flew to Europe, accompanied by Bob Ellsworth.

In Western Europe, the NATO allies felt neglected, or so they told Nixon. They feared America was so overinvolved in Vietnam that it had forgotten its real enemy, the Soviet Union. "Make no mistake about it," Konrad Adenauer declared in Bonn, "they [the Soviets] want the world. The whole world." In Rome, an Italian diplomat told him, "I know the Russians. They are great liars, clever cheaters, and magnificent actors. They cannot be trusted. They consider it their duty to cheat and lie."[6] Nixon was quick to agree with these bloodcurdling assessments.

Then he was off for the enemy's heartland. On March 16 he arrived in Moscow, only to be snubbed. There were no Soviet officials to greet him. Foreign reporters were there; Nixon held an impromptu press conference. "Apparently a Government without an opposition is not willing to recognize the opposition party in another country," he said.[7]

The next morning he flew to Soviet Central Asia to visit Tashkent, Samarkand, and Alma-Ata, within 150 miles of the Chinese border. In Alma-Ata, Nixon—"up to his old tricks," as Tass put it —strode into a marketplace and began confronting citizens with questions about their lives.

But the Russians knew Nixon too well. When he started into the crowd, they produced a crippled World War II veteran, medals and all, who pushed himself in front of Nixon and told him, "Get American troops out of Vietnam." As Nixon began to reply, the veteran waved his empty right sleeve and pointed to his burned-out eye socket. He said he had participated in the end-of-the-war linkup of American and Soviet troops on the Elbe River.

Nixon might well have asked when and where he got such horrible wounds, if he was still fighting with his unit in the last days at the Elbe linkup, but instead compared American aid to Russia in World War II to American aid to South Vietnam. Nixon said, "We too want peace, but it takes two to make peace." The veteran replied, "Yes, and the two are North Vietnam and South Vietnam."[8]

Back in Moscow, on his way west, Nixon paid a visit to Sokolniki Park, where he had had his Kitchen Debate with Khrushchev in 1959. He was getting old enough—he was fifty-four years of age —that he could start paying nostalgic visits to scenes of former triumphs. He tried to re-create the mood of 1959 by engaging a construction engineer on the site in a debate, but it had no sparkle.[9]

In Bucharest, Romania, Secretary General Nicolae Ceaușescu,

who had been sharply critical of the Soviets recently, on issues ranging from economic relations to the Chinese-Soviet conflict, evidently decided to use Nixon's visit to demonstrate his independence from the Russians. There was a full-dress welcome at the airport, a ninety-minute private conference with the Foreign Minister, and a dinner at the Foreign Ministry.[10] Nixon responded warmly to these signs of respect, and he never forgot that, when others turned their backs on him, Ceauşescu and the Romanians treated him royally.

On March 25, he flew back to the States, where he told reporters at Kennedy Airport that "we are entering a new era in relations between the East and the West, an era of great promise and great danger." He urged President Johnson to visit Europe soon to reassure America's allies, and said that one of America's problems was educating the "half-worlders." He described these as people who saw problems only in their areas, such as East Coast residents being concerned only with Europe and westerners only with Asia.[11] That was not much to come back with in the way of new insights or programs after three weeks; the truth was, Nixon had reinforced old prejudices and judgments.

Within a week of his return to New York, Nixon was off again, this time for the Far East, with Ray Price along as his traveling companion. The Asian trip proved to be much more productive in generating new thought, perhaps because the situation was more volatile there, perhaps because Price was along to talk ideas. The direction of his thoughts Nixon would not reveal until later in the year; meanwhile, he listened, as first the Japanese leaders and then Chiang Kai-shek told him to beware the Communist enemy.

In his memoirs, Price has written a vivid description of Nixon's *modus operandi* on these trips. On the plane, he would have Price sit in the aisle seat, so that he served as a buffer between Nixon and other passengers. Nixon traveled with his briefcase on his knee, dipping into it for papers, using it as a writing desk when it was closed. He often sat for long periods staring out the window; then he would suddenly start to talk. Price learned to adjust to his moods.

One of Price's jobs was to brief Nixon on the country they were about to visit, but Price quickly learned that "there was little real need" for a briefing as Nixon already knew the countries, the problems, and the leaders he was going to meet. Still, Nixon wanted every scrap of information he could get.

Once on the ground, Price was impressed by the way Nixon dealt with the various leaders. "There was always mutual deference, and great courtesy, but except in the setting of a lunch or a dinner there was very little small talk." Nixon had a deep interest in the progress of Asia generally and of the host country specifically, Price wrote, and "he also would lead the conversation to the larger world picture, to the possible future roles of China, the Soviet Union, and the United States, and to the impact of those roles on Asia generally."

At the formal dinners, Price was again impressed by Nixon the formal diplomatist. He was a superb toastmaster: "He always spoke extemporaneously, without notes, and invariably his toasts were gracious, knowledgeable, and minutely sensitive to the feelings of the host country."

Nixon was sensitive to the feelings of lesser folks too. In Tokyo, Nixon and Price stayed in the embassy residence, a palatial home previously used by General MacArthur. They were there three days. As they were preparing to leave, Nixon asked to meet the household help, the maids, butlers, cooks, and laundress. He thanked them, as a group and as individuals, and shook hands with each. Later he told Price that he always tried to thank the help wherever he stayed, but especially abroad. "They don't vote," Nixon said, "but it means a lot to them." [12]

When Nixon and Price arrived in Saigon, Nixon held a series of news conferences, intermixed with his interviews and visits to various sites. He was adroit, as always. He urged Democratic critics of the war to declare "a moratorium on the kind of criticism that gives aid and comfort to the enemy." He said the antiwar movement was "the major factor in prolonging the conflict," because it created the "monstrous delusion" that it represented more than a small minority. According to Nixon, 20 percent of the American people, at most, were against the war. He said there was "no question" but that the Communist Party in the States was stimulating the peace movement. In making this charge, Nixon was repeating one that Johnson had initiated and was stressing. Both men were getting that line from their mutual friend J. Edgar Hoover. Nixon termed Martin Luther King's recent strong criticism of the war "very unfortunate." He said that young people had been "dazzled by the beguiling rhetoric of the intellectual community." Catching himself, he said that not all intellectuals opposed the war. He then accused Senators Mike Mansfield (D., Mont.) and Robert Kennedy of being "misinformed but well intentioned." Thus he tied together the Communist Party, U.S.A., the peace movement, Dr. King, the professors, and Senators Mansfield and Kennedy, without once making a direct charge that any of the individuals he named were Communists.

All of which was standard Nixon. So was his call for yet more air strikes (on a day when U.S. planes had knocked out a power plant in Haiphong) and for mining the North Vietnamese harbors. Quite uncharacteristic was his statement, "It can be said now that the defeat of the Communist forces in South Vietnam is inevitable. The only question is, how soon?" [13]

But in his memoirs, Nixon wrote that when he had been in Vietnam in 1967 he concluded the opposite, that a "continuation of the administration's policy of fighting a defensive war of attrition would inevitably lead to defeat." [14]

Which did he really believe? The question is of fundamental importance, as he became the man whose thoughts about the war were more important than those of anyone else.

Did he believe, as he said in Saigon in 1967, that the war was being won? Or did he believe, as he wrote in 1977, that to continue the war at 1967 levels would "inevitably lead to defeat"? And if he believed the latter, what were his thoughts on how high the escalation would have to go before America could hope to prevail?

In his memoirs, Nixon wrote that "they [the Communists] had a total commitment to victory. We had, at most, a partial commitment to avoid defeat." Did not that genuine insight make him wonder how high a price America would be willing to pay? Or to wonder why, after all the oversell of the war engaged in by the Johnson Administration, Americans still had only a partial commitment? Or to re-examine his own assumptions in the aftermath of Johnson's having adopted almost exactly the policies he had been recommending, only to learn that they were not working? Or to conclude that the United States would have to physically occupy Laos and Cambodia if it wanted to win?

The answers are elusive, because Nixon kept his thoughts within himself, and showed what they were in his subsequent actions far more clearly than he ever wrote or talked about them.

HOME FROM ASIA, Nixon was off almost immediately to Latin America. This time his companion was Bebe Rebozo. The two men were spending more time together, and had become jointly involved in real-estate ventures. Nixon had begun some years back purchasing stock in Fisher Island, a development in the Miami harbor area that Rebozo and his banking partners were sponsoring. In February, and again in May, 1967, Nixon bought lots in Key Biscayne, near Rebozo's place, where he had been vacationing for fourteen years. [15]

Although Rebozo was always happy to serve Nixon, whether as translator, aide, or friend, he did not really want to take this trip, as its purpose was to prepare Nixon for the 1968 race, and Rebozo thought he should get out of politics. Just a few months earlier,

Rebozo had informed a group of Nixon supporters, "I told him [Nixon], 'Hell, no, I wouldn't get involved.' I felt it strongly. To me it was a personal thing. I didn't want him or the family to get hurt again. I'd seen what had happened in 1960 and especially in 1962. It just wasn't worth it." [16] Rebozo's concern for Pat and Julie and Tricia was genuine, and greater than his concern for Nixon; he was, as his statement indicated, more like an uncle to the girls than he was their father's friend.

Rebozo especially had Pat in mind. The girls were into their romances and college careers, constantly busy, with little time for reflection. Pat kept herself busy too, making plans for the girls, helping them to manage their ever-expanding activities. But occasionally she did think beyond the next party or ball, and when she did, she was disturbed.

Down in Florida at Christmas, 1966, sitting with her daughters on the beach, Pat had told them she could not face another presidential race. She had spoken of the "humiliation." Through the first half of 1967, it was clear to Julie that Pat was "unmistakably troubled as she faced the prospect of another political race." But with her husband either out of the country or off politicking nearly all the time, she could hardly expect anything else.

That summer, Pat flew alone to California to spend three weeks with her closest and oldest friend, Helene Drown. Helene listened as Pat expressed her doubts about her willingness or ability to go through another campaign. She wanted "peace of mind," she said, and "to lead a normal life."

Helene urged her to reconsider. She pointed out that Pat had long since left the chance for a quiet life in Whittier behind her, that she had always been a woman who thrived on challenges. Helene later explained to Julie why she was so insistent that Pat accept the need for another campaign: "I sensed strongly that Pat still had a deep belief in your father's unique talent. She was sure that he alone was capable of solving some of the problems we were facing in the country then." [17]

Pat kept her own counsel, and prepared herself for the inevitable consultation—there had been one before every campaign— in which her man would say that he was ready to give up all hopes and ambitions for her, if that was what she wanted, and she would reply that his destiny was her fate.

NIXON's Latin-American trip took him to Peru, Chile, Argentina, Brazil, and Mexico. He saw the president in each country and managed to meet private citizens on the streets, with reporters present to record the happening.

One such occurred in Rio de Janeiro, when Nixon plunged

into the slums and began hugging grimy children, shaking hands all around, questioning shopkeepers about business. At one point he stopped to talk with a toothless pregnant woman who had three scrawny waifs clinging to her ragged skirts.

"Let me ask you this," Nixon began, with Rebozo translating, "what do you need most to improve your life?"

"Money," the woman replied without hesitation.

Nixon, a bit startled, stumbled on: "What does your husband do for a living?"

The woman looked puzzled, then began to laugh—she had no husband.

"Thank you very much," said Nixon in turning away.

"May things go well with you," she called as he walked away.

Asked by reporters if she knew who he was, she replied, "I think he's connected with the movies." [18]

Returning to the scene of one of his great crises, Nixon flew into the airport at Lima, Peru, where he had been spat upon nine years earlier. This time there were no crowds or incidents. Nixon threw off his coat, undid his tie, drank local beer, ate Peruvian pastry, laid bricks on a school building under construction, and donated $15 to the same school.[19]

On May 15, at a wrap-up press conference before returning home, Nixon explained what he had learned. He thought it time for the United States to change its Latin-American policy. He praised President Juan Carlos Onganía, head of Argentina's military government, calling him "the right man for Argentina at this moment in its destiny." He explained that "United States–style democracy won't work here. I wish it would."[20]

IN JUNE he was off to Africa, with Pat Buchanan as his companion. His conclusions, as in Latin America, were depressing. He wrote Eisenhower, "It's going to be two generations at best before there is anything we here in the United States would recognize as 'freedom' in Africa, and it's doubtful even then. . . . We shouldn't insist on Western-style democracy everywhere in the world; different systems may be better for other nations in different stages of development."[21]

Back in 1957, at a Cabinet meeting, Eisenhower had said, "The United States could not possibly maintain that freedom—independence—liberty—were necessary to us but not to others."[22] On this occasion, however, he wrote "fine" at the bottom of Nixon's letter.

While Nixon was in Africa, Israel attacked Egypt, Jordan, and Syria. This came as a surprise to Nixon, who had said a week earlier, "In the Middle East, those who want war do not have the power to wage it, and those who do have the power do not want it."[23]

That prediction was as bad as the one he made after the war, on June 21, when he told a press conference in Athens that "there can be no lasting settlement without the joint guarantee of the United States and the Soviet Union." From Athens, he flew on to the capital of the victorious Israelis, Tel Aviv, where he said that Israel had a right to keep her conquered territory "until a settlement insuring her security was reached."[24]

James Reston did a savage commentary on Nixon's travels. "What is he trying to prove?" Reston asked, and answered, "He is trying to prove the new theories of American politics: (a) that motion is progress; (b) that the road to the White House runs through all the other capitals of the world; and (c) that distance lends enchantment. He is proving that he not only knows all the Republican county chairmen of the United States, but all the Prime Ministers of the world as well."

But Reston wondered if there was any meaning to it all, and decided there was none: "There is absolutely no evidence that travel has given him any new or deeper visions of America's problems in the world. . . . He gives us straight Cold War dialogue. . . . Few candidates have ever seen so many new things or had so little new to say about them."

Reston admitted that Nixon was making "steady progress toward the Presidential nomination," and professed himself amazed that this should be happening, especially since Nixon had done it "without any organization, without much money, and without making a single speech anybody can remember."[25]

RESTON WAS wrong on all three points, but Nixon was just as glad that the top political reporter in Washington was not aware of the extent of the Nixon campaign staff and the success of the fund-raising efforts. What hurt was the snide tone of the column, the implication that there was nothing to Nixon but thoughtless slogans. Nixon set out to change that perception. He wanted to show that despite the inanity of his questions, whether on the streets of Moscow or in the slums of Rio, despite the simplicity of the views he expressed in press conferences on complex subjects, he really was a man of substance.

He did so by summing up his conclusions for two elite audiences, first in a speech to a small group of some of the biggest and most powerful businessmen in the country, then in an article for the nation's leading journal of opinion on foreign affairs.

In July, Nixon went to the Bohemian Grove, on the Russian River in northern California, to give the Lakeside Speech, always given by Herbert Hoover before his death in 1964. The members came not just from California, but from across the nation, and included some of the biggest Republican contributors.

Nixon later recalled his speech at the Bohemian Grove as the one that "gave me the most pleasure and satisfaction in my political career."[26] He did not say why. One can suppose that the feeling came from the setting: he stood on the shore of the lake, redwoods towering overhead, his audience seated in a natural amphitheater rising before him. It was at this spot that Nixon had first met Eisenhower, in 1950, and here that Eisenhower had given a speech that had impressed and delighted the millionaires present, and helped start Ike on the road to the White House.[27]

Nixon could hardly have been so pleased with the speech because of its content, which was mainly Cold War generalizations; what he liked was the impression it made on his audience. That impression was a favorable one, naturally enough, since what Nixon said was what the members already thought.

Nixon's theme was change: "Never in human history have more changes taken place in the world in one generation." He took the audience on a tour of the world, in a personal *tour de force*, pointing to the dangers and opportunities on every continent. He urged the need for strong alliances and continued aid to developing nations, but with more emphasis on private than government investment. As to the Soviet Union, Nixon was ready for negotiations on trade and other matters, but in such negotiations Americans should always remember "that our goal is different from theirs. We seek peace as an end in itself. They seek victory, with peace being at this time a means toward that end."

In his conclusion, Nixon said that the survival of peace and freedom in the world depended on American leadership. He saw no limits at all on what America could do, if it but tried: "Our economic superiority is enormous; our military superiority can be whatever we choose to make it." The only question was one of will: "That is whether America has the national character and moral stamina to see us through this long and difficult struggle."[28]

That was a dangerous assumption, that the only question was one of will. It badly oversimplified the terribly complex, and made Nixon sound a bit out of date, more like Kennedy (and himself) in the 1960 campaign. It was as if the intervening seven years had not happened, as if all the high hopes and bright promises of 1960 were still valid. "All You Need Is Love" was the Beatles' answer to the problems of 1967; "All You Need Is Will" was Nixon's.

• •

NIXON's second bid for the respect of America's elite came in the form of an article entitled "Asia After Viet Nam," which Nixon wrote with Ray Price's help and which appeared in the October 1967 issue of the prestigious journal *Foreign Affairs*. It assumed a victory for the United States in South Vietnam in the near future, without being specific on how that was going to be achieved, and speculated on the future of the postwar Asian continent. It contained some insights and some commonplace observations, some useful suggestions and some fanciful ones. But what it established, overall, was that Nixon was the first prominent American politician to see clearly the importance of the emergence of modern Asia. By 1967 everyone could see what a powerful economic force Japan had become; Nixon was the one to point out that Taiwan, Hong Kong, South Korea, Thailand, Singapore, and Malaysia were not far behind the Japanese.

"America is a Pacific power," Nixon declared, but he recognized that there were sharp limits to how much power post-Vietnam America could project into Asia. "One of the legacies of Viet Nam," he wrote, "almost certainly will be a deep reluctance on the part of the United States to become involved once again in a similar intervention on a similar basis." Contradicting what he had said at the Bohemian Grove, he wrote that "other nations must recognize that the role of the United States as world policeman is likely to be limited in the future."

This left Asia open to a simply stated threat: "China's ambitions." To counter Chinese adventurism, Nixon proposed a sort of successor to SEATO, a regional alliance composed of South Korea, Japan, Taiwan, Thailand, Malaysia, South Vietnam, the Philippines, Australia, and New Zealand (and perhaps someday, who could tell, "even India"). It should have both economic and military ties. The United States would not be a member, but should stand ready to come to the assistance of any member of the alliance threatened by internal communist uprisings or external aggression.[29]

As one part of his program, Nixon wanted the restrictions imposed on Japan's military force by the Japanese constitution removed, and Japan allowed/forced to assume its own defense. This included nuclear weapons.[30]

Nixon's call for Japanese rearmament was a reminder of just how long this man had been a participant in international politics, and of how consistent he could be on certain questions. In this case, the first American politician to ever suggest Japanese rearmament had been Dick Nixon, way back in 1953, when he said at a press conference in Tokyo that America had made a mistake in 1946 in imposing the military limitation on the Japanese constitution, and had urged Japanese rearmament.[31]

"Any American policy toward Asia must come urgently to grips with the reality of China," Nixon wrote. "This does not mean," he went on, "rushing to grant recognition to Peking," but it did mean "we simply cannot afford to leave China forever outside the family of nations, there to nurture its fantasies, cherish its hates and threaten its neighbors." These became the most quoted words from an article that did Nixon's reputation immense good with various branches of the Establishment.

In "Asia After Viet Nam," Nixon made it clear that he had no intention of dealing with the Chinese as they were. He also asserted that "the world cannot be safe until China changes. Thus our aim . . . should be to induce change." The ultimate goal was to get the Chinese to turn away from foreign adventuring and turn toward the solution of their own domestic problems.

The obstacles were huge, but time was short. Nixon warned that two events were coming in the seventies that together "could create a crisis of the first order." The first was that the Soviets would reach military parity with the United States, and the second that China would develop significant nuclear capability.

How to get the Chinese to change before the crisis came was the trick. Nixon's answer was the regional alliance, backed by American military and economic support; once it was in place, the members would "no longer furnish tempting targets for Chinese aggression."

Nixon was quite specific about when the new American dialogue with China could begin: when "the leaders in Peking are persuaded to turn their energies inward rather than outward."

"Weary with war, disheartened with allies, disillusioned with aid, dismayed at domestic crises," Nixon wrote in his summary, "many Americans are heeding the call of the new isolationists." He warned against the trend, and called for a Pacific community to match the Atlantic community, with America playing its full role in each.[32]

The article showed that despite Reston's cracks, Nixon had been thinking about what he had seen and learned, and that he was capable of readjusting his thoughts, as even the hint of an accommodation someday with Red China was a near-revolutionary change for Nixon, who since 1950 had been a leader of the China Lobby.

He had made good use of his time, in the first half of 1967, as he traveled around the world to prepare himself for the Presidency.

Whatever critics thought or said about Nixon's performance in foreign policy, it was clear that he made his decisions and recommendations and set his policies on the basis of firsthand observation, knowledge of local situations, and a full course of hard study.

CHAPTER SIX

OPERATION CANDOR
July–December 1967

WHEN HE WAS at the Bohemian Grove, Nixon had a talk with Governor Reagan. Nixon told Reagan that he had "tentative" plans to enter the primaries and that his main goal was to unify the Republican Party so as to beat Johnson. Reagan solemnly agreed that the party came before anything else. He confessed to Nixon that he was surprised, flattered, and somewhat concerned by the talk about his own presidential chances. Then Reagan showed that although he had been in politics for one year to Nixon's twenty-one, he could dissemble as well as the oldest pro. Reagan told Nixon he did not want to be a favorite son, but feared he would have to in order to assure party unity in California.[1]

Next Reagan talked to Senator John Tower of Texas and Governor Claude Kirk of Florida, who were also at the Bohemian Grove. They assured him that the southern Republicans who had provided so critical a portion of Goldwater's troops in '64 were eager to get behind Reagan in '68. Although the southerners would prefer Nixon to either Rockefeller or Romney, their support for Nixon was soft and negative; they figured Nixon was the most conservative Republican candidate they could get who had a chance to win. But Reagan could steal the southerners, and with them plus California he would be in the commanding position. Reagan then put out the word to key conservative Republican leaders to withhold announcing support for Nixon. Reagan said he was not yet a candidate himself, but his "let's wait and see" advice convinced many observers that he was considering becoming an active candidate.[2]

A Reagan candidacy was a real threat to Nixon, because of the phenomenal popularity of the California governor around the country. It was commonly said that Reagan had captured the hearts of conservatives with his election-eve pitch for Goldwater on national TV in 1964, but actually he had much more going for him. For some years past, Reagan's acting career had been less than active, as he had spent his time on the circuit for General Electric, speaking to businessmen's groups around the country. His message was less government and lower taxes, and his audiences loved what he said and the way he said it. He had national support, in other words, before he ever won a single vote.

Reagan had something else almost no other politician in the land enjoyed, instant name recognition. If he was not in the first rank as a movie star, his dozens of films and his years as host of "Death Valley Days" on TV made him known across the land. Along with his good looks, casual ah-shucks manner, and earnest belief in old-time values, Reagan had another great asset—he was governor of California. It was an ideal place for him to be, for two reasons. First, the state was certain to be richer and more populated at the end of his term; put another way, it was well-nigh impossible to fail as the leader of a state that was enjoying a seemingly permanent boom (helped in no small part by the war in Vietnam). Second, being governor put him on a platform from which to preach on one of the most emotional issues of the day, unrest on the campus and its causes. It was an issue Nixon had tried to make his own in New Jersey, in 1965, in the Genovese/Rutgers case, but without complete success.

Reagan had better luck, partly because he had a better target. It was nothing less than the premier institution of higher learning in the state, if not the nation, if not the world, the University of California at Berkeley. Always known for its liberalism, not to say radicalism, Berkeley was nevertheless at the center of the California economic boom, just as the Bechtel Building, named after the Bechtel Corporation, one of the largest defense contractors in the nation, stood at the center of the Berkeley campus.

Californians took great pride in their university; the students took great pride in their tradition of rebelliousness. In 1965, a Free Speech movement broke out on campus, which led to protests and violence and demonstrations, and which undoubtedly helped Reagan beat Pat Brown in 1966. During the campaign Reagan had promised to "clean up the mess at Berkeley," where, he said, there had occurred "sexual orgies so vile I cannot describe them to you."[3]

The next year, as governor, Reagan issued a warning to campus dissidents: "Observe the rules or get out." This line hit exactly the right note so far as millions of Republicans around the country were concerned. The powerful and positive response he received from his attacks on the university encouraged Reagan; he soon charged that universities were "subsidizing intellectual curiosity."[4]

What made all this so passionate was the belief by all parties that nothing less than the future of the society was at stake. To the radicals, the modern state could not exist without the university, and as they hated the modern state, they wanted to destroy the university. To the liberals, civilization without the liberal arts and sciences was unimaginable. To the doves, the way to shut down the Vietnam War was to shut down the ROTC. To conservatives, the apparent triumph of the bearded young professors of history and political science who were all too often leading the demonstrations spelled the end of freedom and democracy.

By going after the campus radicals, Reagan was capturing the conservatives. And doing so actively, as he set off in the summer of 1967 on an extensive speaking schedule, concentrating on the Goldwater strongholds in the Mountain States, the Midwest, and the Deep South. He began broadening his subject matter, and started speaking out on Vietnam.

He immediately took the most hawkish position of any major Republican, going even beyond Nixon in his demands for more firepower. In Cincinnati, he charged that Johnson's policy had led to unnecessary loss of lives. Asked if he considered the President as "directly blameful" for such losses, Reagan gave a Nixon-like reply that the master himself could not have topped: "It's hard to answer that question without it seeming to sound like a terrible accusation. But since as President he would get credit for a victory, I think he must take responsibility for the policy of war and what the results of that policy are. I doubt this was a cold-blooded or callous attempt to sacrifice lives."[5]

When he saw lines like that, or heard Reagan lecture to the university people about their responsibilities, Nixon knew who his chief competitor was, whatever he told the press about Rockefeller or Romney.

NIXON WAS NOT without assets, of course, should Reagan decide to challenge him. The most important of these was Reagan's Johnny-come-lately status, or, reversed, Nixon's decades in politics. Nixon had IOUs all over the country; a poll in late May showed that his lead among Republican county chairmen was almost embarrassing; he was 4–1 ahead of Romney, his nearest competitor, and 10–1 ahead of Reagan.[6]

But Nixon also had reason to fear that at the first sign of his faltering, the southern Republicans would start bolting to Reagan. Such are the vagaries of American politics; to hold his base in the South, Nixon had to win primaries in New Hampshire, Wisconsin, Nebraska, and Oregon. To win in those states, Nixon had to shed his image of "Tricky Dick," the nickname Helen Douglas had hung on him back in 1950. So Nixon went gunning for Tricky Dick, and as usual indulged in overkill.

He called it Operation Candor. It was Nixon giving the appearance of being perfectly clear, absolutely frank, entirely open with every reporter with whom he talked. He would explain, in detail, some of his various political devices and his motives for using them. For example, he told Witcover that the occasional favorable comment about the opposition was "a device, of course, to show I'm fair-minded."

"All right," he told James J. Kilpatrick of *National Review.* "They still call me 'Tricky Dick.' It's a brutal thing to fight. . . . Look at my record on civil rights; and then look at Lyndon's. . . . The carefully cultivated impression is that Nixon is devious. I can overcome this impression in one way only: by absolute candor."[7]

Nixon's idea of candor was to talk politics with reporters. In an interview with Warren Weaver, he said, "More than the others, I have to win every primary. Rockefeller, Percy and Reagan are in an enviable position. They can sit back and see what happens. I can't." He explained that he could not go after delegates in non-primary states, as Goldwater had done so successfully, because for him to win by that method would only reinforce the Tricky Dick image and cause his defeat in November. "I'm not going to the convention as a second or third string candidate to sit on a clump of delegates and try my hand at brokering," he went on. "By that time I'll either be in or out."[8]

"I'm not kidding myself," Nixon said in concluding the Weaver interview. "I suppose my chances of going all the way are maybe one in five, but they're as good as any."

As Weaver got up to leave (they were in Nixon's office, encrusted with memorabilia from his past, almost a museum to the Nixon Vice-Presidency), Nixon looked around wistfully and made his only stab at self-analysis: "Once you get used to the fast track," he said, "it's hard to be entirely happy slowing down."[9]

It was on the stump, even more than to reporters, that Nixon worked Operation Candor. Of course, he made sure people knew how candid he was being, by constantly drawing their attention to it. Some of his oft-used phrases preceding a statement included: "to be perfectly candid," "speaking quite frankly," "putting it bluntly," "let me be quite precise," and "let me make it perfectly clear." In fact, in most cases, he was about to be the opposite. For example, whenever he promised to be "quite precise," he would fly off into a generalization; whenever he promised to make things "perfectly clear," he always left them more opaque than ever.

But this man who was, a year before the convention, the almost certain Republican nominee did not attain that position simply through lies and half-truths to the press and the people. He was, by 1967, a master politician. He could wow them at the Bohemian Grove, bring them to their feet with a mighty roar at the American Legion Convention, and impress the intellectuals who read *Foreign Affairs*. In the sports jargon that he so loved to use, Nixon as a public speaker was a triple threat who touched all the bases.

He was a masterful political speaker for two good reasons. First, he just knew so much. Talking to big-business men or to intellectuals, he could go on for hours without a single note, reeling off statistics on production, population growth, educational levels, and gross national products for nearly every nation in the world, or speculate on this or that political personality in those countries, not on the basis of something he had read but on the basis of personal knowledge. As to American politics, no one, not even the President, knew the players and the game more intimately than Nixon.

Second, Nixon had an instinctive feel for the political responses and prejudices of a broad spectrum of the voting public, heavily but not exclusively the white middle class. Better than anyone else, he knew what those voters feared, and was an authentic spokesman for those fears.

There were other dimensions to Nixon's mastery of politics, including his talent for organization, his attention to detail, his ability at political arithmetic, his self-assurance, and his skillful use of the issues.

Most of all, he worked so hard at his profession; for example, on October 18, having finished business in Washington in mid-morning, Nixon made an unannounced visit to Congress. He stationed himself in the office of Representative Leslie C. Arends of Illinois, the Republican whip, across the hall from the House Chamber, where he received, one by one, the Republican representatives for whom he had campaigned in 1966. *The New York Times* reported that he "was jovial and relaxed and fitted in perfectly with Republican Congressmen who were happily conducting an assault on President Johnson's budget." At the end of the day Nixon met with reporters, telling them that Johnson was "more vulnerable now than President Hoover had been in 1932." "Any Republican," he went on, specifically including himself in that number, "will beat Johnson in 1968." [10]

Back in New York a few days later, Nixon followed up on the visit by writing all the congressmen, saying how much he enjoyed it and that he planned to return soon.[11]

Nixon was also infinitely better organized than any of his opponents. He had speech writers, moneymen, advance men, the works. Politics starts with money in America, and Nixon had one of the best getting it for him in Maurice Stans. Stans knew how to go for the big checks, and Nixon knew how to cooperate in getting them, without compromising himself.

Stans would set up a cocktail party or a lunch with fifteen or twenty potential contributors. Nixon would make an appearance, give a little talk, shake hands, chat for a few minutes, then leave. At that point, Stans and Flanigan moved in. Nixon would not allow them to make promises; he told Stans that he did not want contributions taken from anyone who felt he was entitled to something in return, and he did not want to know who had given how much. He was extremely careful about money: when he wanted to pass on to Stans the name of a prospect, he would write a memo and sign it "DC," presumably meaning his aide Dwight Chapin, but actually a pseudonym so that Nixon's involvement could not be traced. In one such memo "DC" ordered, "Don't take any money under any circumstances from H. L. Hunt."[12] No such memo existed with regard to Howard Hughes.

The Nixon for President Committee was growing and taking on new responsibilities. One of the major additions was a big, gruff, coarse New York lawyer, John Mitchell. He was fifty-four years old, just Nixon's age, and thus unusual—nearly everyone else on Nixon's staff was ten or more years younger than the boss. At the beginning of the year, Mitchell's law firm had merged with Nixon, Mudge. Mitchell became a full partner. His specialty was providing legal advice on bond issues to state and local governments, work that had put him in intimate contact with the powerful in many states. He had impressed Nixon with his network of political contacts and local knowledge. Moving the bonds was the heart blood of local politics, there were profits to be shared for all the insiders, and no one was more inside than Mitchell. His was a cynic's view of politics, which reinforced the cynicism in his personality. From the first, he made a powerful impression on Nixon, and through 1967 moved closer to the Nixon inner circle.

Mitchell had helped draft legislation in Wisconsin establishing a state borrowing agency; in the process he had put many of the state's Republicans in his debt. He took charge of the Nixon organization in the state, and by late July had a full-scale office set up in Madison, staffed by forty-two experienced campaigners, with separate setups in each of the seventy-two counties, the ten congressional districts, and in the twenty largest cities and towns. By fall, Mitchell was extending his activities into other states, almost always drawing in the influential and effective members of the local Republican Establishment. It was an impressive and important performance, and Nixon was pleased and grateful.[13]

Nixon was adding some thinkers as well as doers to his staff. Although he remained, as always, in charge of selecting the issues, he wanted help from idea men. Garment, Chapin, and other aides began making contacts, for example with Martin Anderson, a Columbia University professor and author of a highly critical attack on the urban-renewal program, which he called the "Federal Bulldozer." Anderson introduced Nixon and his aides to the works of Daniel Patrick Moynihan of Harvard, and of other liberal sociologists, that attacked the current welfare system. Nixon aides began saying things like "the present welfare apparatus, developed under the New and Fair Deals, is bankrupt," and suggesting as an alternative a negative income tax, first proposed by a University of Chicago economist, Milton Friedman.[14]

Nixon was not only studying the negative income tax as a way to deal with welfare and the problems of the poor, but looking at other innovative approaches. He was considering a program of federal tax incentives and guarantees to enlist the support of private enterprise in the slums. This implied a willingness to put aside the goal of an integrated society to concentrate on improving conditions in the ghettos. (His own cynicism made it unlikely that he would ever take the lead in such matters. During the 1960 campaign, he had told his staff he would have to do a speech on "all that welfare crap." Herb Klein said Arthur Flemming, head of HEW, referred to such things as "meeting human needs." "I don't care," Nixon said irritably. "It *is* crap.")

"It's important to break down the barriers," Nixon told one reporter, "but the fellow who spends all his time talking about open housing is pursuing a will-o'-the-wisp. I know that that's the exciting way to do things. Marching feet. Protests." But Nixon knew his voters, and knew that way was the wrong way.

"Some people are terrified," he pointed out. "Sooner or later the white community is going to retaliate," he warned, "and all the patient work will be undone. And the majority of law-abiding Negroes are going to take the heat." If he thought there was anything he could do to ward off these unhappy developments, he did not say what it was, except that Negroes should stay where they were and improve their positions from within.

"Take education," Nixon went on, referring to recent court

orders mandating busing to achieve racial balance in the schools. "It is a mistake to think that the problem in education is going to be met by busing. I am convinced that the damage there would far outweigh the benefits, and besides, most of the problems would remain." [15]

What the blacks caught in the ghetto needed, Nixon asserted, was not more Great Society, not more handouts, not buses, but jobs. That meant inducing the business community to invest in the ghettos to create employment. "Jobs is the gut issue," Nixon said. "If you don't have jobs, you don't have housing and you don't get off of welfare." [16]

In interviews, in speeches, and in an article in the October *Reader's Digest*, Nixon explained his position on welfare reform and economic development within the ghetto. He drew heavily on the current academic hot subject, investigated so heavily by Moynihan and others, the Negro family. As Nixon summed up the research and conclusions for *Reader's Digest*, there was a crisis in the Negro family because of a welfare program "that provides money for dependent children only as long as the father stays away from home."

Nixon wrote that welfare reform and capital investment in the areas where blacks lived, while desirable, could not solve the problems of racism and riots by themselves. First, Nixon insisted, the black community had to reject lawlessness and the society as a whole had to re-establish law and order. His constituents, generally, were far more receptive to hearing him talk about law and order than listening to him discuss uplifting the ghetto, so it was law and order that he talked about the most.

In so doing, he indulged his penchant for hyperbole. America had become, according to Nixon, "the most lawless and violent [nation] in the history of free peoples." And "far from being a great society, ours is becoming a lawless society." He denounced the "growing tolerance of lawlessness" among civil rights groups, and "the increasing public acceptance of civil disobedience." He got in a shot at the universities, which had helped blur the distinction between "where civil disobedience may begin and where it must end."

"To the professor objecting to de facto segregation," he said, the line "may be crystal-clear, but the boundaries have become fluid to his students and other listeners. Today in the urban slums the limits of responsible action are all but invisible." His solution to urban riots was simple and straightforward: more police and better pay and training for the law officers. [17] There was a nice parallel here. Nixon advocated bringing the Chinese into the family of nations, once the Chinese had learned how to behave; Nixon advocated bringing the blacks into the body politic, once they had learned how to behave.

These themes received warm receptions. In Waukesha, a suburb of Milwaukee, he got his loudest applause when he condemned what he termed the rising tide of lawlessness and violence in the nation.[18] In New York, in the red-white-and-blue-festooned grand ballroom of the Waldorf, a black-tie audience of the National Association of Manufacturers interrupted him five times with hearty applause as he said things like "the war in Asia is a limited one with limited means and limited goals. The war at home is a war for survival of a free society." He asserted that unless a solution was found to the racial problem in the United States, "it will not matter what happens in Vietnam and elsewhere."[19]

OF COURSE, he could not ignore Vietnam, nor had he any intention of doing so. Through the second half of 1967 it remained his number-one issue. His themes were consistent with what he had been saying all along. He told the fifteen hundred members of the Chicago Executives Club at the Conrad Hilton Hotel that Communist success in Vietnam would constitute a "reward for aggression" that would encourage further "wars of liberation" and thus increase the chances of a much wider conflict. He asserted that Vietnam represented a "turning point" in American history, that the United States had "vital strategic interests" there, and that one of the major failures of the Johnson Administration had been its inability to convince people of the "fundamental strategic importance of Vietnam" to America.

He also continued to assert that the war in Vietnam would be decided not by the struggle between the Vietcong, the North Vietnamese, the South Vietnamese, and the U.S. armed forces, but rather by the American voters in November 1968. "The last desperate hope of North Vietnam," he said in Chicago, "is that they can win politically in the United States what our fighting men are denying them militarily in Vietnam." America could "win the war" in a year or so, he went on, if the North Vietnamese leaders could be made to realize that "regardless of what happens in the American elections, there will be no reward for aggression."[20]

Reporter Robert Semple thought that on Vietnam, Nixon was taking an "immense gamble, hoping that enough people share his conviction that America's Pacific interests are at stake there, that the war is therefore justified, and that it should be pressed to a successful conclusion." Semple pointed out that Nixon's was "a position whose political appeal ultimately depends on the mood of the voters, on the course of the war, on decisions over which he has no control in Hanoi and Washington."[21]

Perhaps it was a gamble (although Nixon would demonstrate a year later that he was not entirely incapable of influencing decisions made in Saigon), but Nixon had no choice. His options did not include taking a cut-and-run position on Vietnam, because his constituents, especially but by no means exclusively in the South, would have deserted him in droves. Beyond that factor, he personally was by no means ready to give up. His basic position on how to end the war remained unchanged: send more bombs to Vietnam and more Republicans to Washington.

ROMNEY WAS HAVING much more trouble with the Vietnam issue than was Nixon. Originally a firm supporter of the war effort, the governor was beginning to have his doubts. His ambiguity cost him dearly when reporters began to press for answers. In the kind of situation in which Nixon excelled, Romney was an innocent lamb —just as Nixon had predicted would be the case.

The worst goof came at the beginning of September, when Romney told the press the original reason for his support of the war was that "I just had the greatest brainwashing that anyone can get when you go over to Vietnam, not only by the generals, but also by the diplomatic corps over there, and they do a very thorough job." Since getting back home he had changed his mind, he said, and no longer thought the war necessary or wise: "I think it was tragic that we became involved in the conflict there."[22]

The word "brainwashing" spelled the end of Romney's chances, although Nixon did all he could to keep the Romney candidacy alive through the early primaries, so that he would have someone to run against and beat.

There was more good luck. In October, Drew Pearson broke in his national column a story that most reporters in California already knew, that there had been a homosexual ring operating within the governor's office. The resulting uproar, excitement, charge, and countercharge hurt Reagan's chances just as he was getting started.[23]

With Romney and Reagan slipping, Nixon was closer than ever to the nomination and therefore in a position in which he could concentrate on Johnson rather than wasting time and energy on Republican opposition. That fall, on the National Educational Television network, Nixon laid down a challenge to the President to debate him in 1968. He argued that the Kennedy-Nixon debates of 1960 "served a great cause in creating tremendous interest in the campaign, also in educating people about the great issues."[24]

He may have allowed himself a shiver of delight as he contemplated the prospect of debating Johnson on national television.

ON SEPTEMBER 30, Hannah Nixon died. She had been in a nursing home in Whittier the past two years, incapable of recognizing visitors, so her death was not unexpected. The Nixons flew to California for the services, which were held in the Friends Church in East Whittier where Nixon had gone to Sunday school. The church brought back a flood of memories and emotions, which came pouring out of Nixon as he shook Billy Graham's hand when he was leaving. Nixon looked at Graham, who had been a friend of his mother's, and the tears broke loose. He put his head on Graham's shoulder and sobbed. Only he knew how lucky he had been to have Hannah Nixon for a mother, only he could guess at how much he owed to her.

In its obituary the AP quoted something Hannah had said in 1960, when asked if she would campaign for her son.

"It's been a campaign since the day he was born," she had replied. "All his life I've been his campaigner."

Nixon, on the flight back to New York after the funeral, thought about his mother's last words to him, spoken two years previously after she had been through an operation and was in terrible pain. Just before going in for the operation, she had read a newspaper column that asserted Nixon was through.

Nixon, at a loss for appropriate words, had said, "Mother, don't give up."

And the woman who had never known the meaning of the word quit, the mother who had given birth to, nurtured, and helped train one of the most remarkable personalities of her time, the saint (it was a word used to describe her by others long before her son used it) who had wiped up her oldest boy's tuberculosis spittle (and that of so many others) in a desperate attempt to give Harold Nixon his fair chance, denying herself meanwhile even the smallest luxury or comfort, the wife who had tamed and civilized Frank Nixon, had pulled herself up in bed. She had looked intently into her son's eyes. For her at least, one may suppose that time no longer existed, that it was not 1965 but 1915, or 1925 or '35 or '45 or '55. Whatever the year, whatever the current crisis, her admonishment to her boy was the same.

"Richard," she had said, "don't *you* give up. Don't let anybody tell you you are through."[25]

ON OCTOBER 17, Nixon went to Gettysburg to confer with Eisenhower. They discussed Vietnam. Ike was talking very tough on Vietnam these days, far tougher than he had been when he was in power. He told Nixon that Johnson had been about a year and a half too late at every stage: in committing U.S. troops, in the bombing, and in building support for the war.

Nixon, in hearty agreement, said he thought the United States should "quarantine North Vietnam by mining its harbors," but Eisenhower drew back at that. He said a blockade could not be justified under international law without a declaration of war, and neither he nor Nixon was ready to face up to that test.[26]

In November, Nixon and Eisenhower had a public disagreement over Vietnam. On the twenty-eighth, in a television interview, Ike said that U.S. troops should be allowed to invade the demilitarized zone in Vietnam and to pursue Communist troops into Cambodia and Laos. Nixon, campaigning in Oregon, was asked to comment. He said that while General Eisenhower was "absolutely right" from a "military standpoint," such a move would be both diplomatically and politically unsound "at this time."

"Moving into the D.M.Z. with ground troops could run a substantial risk of widening the ground conflict in Vietnam—a risk that should be carefully weighed.

"From a political standpoint, I would be very reluctant to take action that would be regarded as an invasion of North Vietnam, Cambodia or Laos."[27]

So Nixon drew the line at widening the war, leaving him only with intensified bombing as a prescription for victory. Along with enough votes in support of the war in 1968, that would convince Hanoi that America would never stop. At that point the Communists would come to the bargaining table, where presumably they would agree to give up their goals in return for a halt to the bombing.

The trouble with that plan was that it was exactly the one Johnson had been using, and it was not working. Nixon, with nothing new to offer, criticized Johnson for having nothing new to offer, while Eisenhower, who had refused to send troops to Vietnam when he was President, now wanted to send them to Laos and Cambodia as well.

THE EISENHOWER-NIXON disagreement was within the family, as it were, because that Thanksgiving, at the Gettysburg farm, David Eisenhower announced that he planned to marry Julie Nixon before graduation from college. Everyone was excited by the news, Mamie Eisenhower the most so. But when Julie told her father, he had so little to say—he hardly looked up from the legal pad he was writing on—that she felt let down and went to her mother for consolation. Pat spoke to her husband.

The next morning, Julie found a note slipped under her door:

Dear Julie,

I suppose no father believes any boy is good enough for his daughter. But I believe both David and you are lucky to have found each other. Fina often says, "Miss Julie always brings life into the home." In the many years ahead you will have your ups and downs but I know you will always "bring life into your home" wherever it is.

Love, Daddy[28]

On November 30, the public announcement was made. The depth of the interest in these two youngsters was shown by the front-page treatment it got in nearly every paper across the country, in most cases complete with a photo (*The New York Times* had three photographs, including one on the front page). Republicans could be forgiven for feeling that this was a marriage made in heaven, one sure to produce GOP Presidents for the twenty-first century.

Nixon, interviewed on television, tried his idea of a joke: "They are both remarkable young people. And I'd say that even if they weren't both Republicans."[29]

The only sour note came from Gettysburg, where General Eisenhower expressed his genuine delight at the fine catch his grandson had made, but then told reporters who suggested that family ties ought to now lead him to endorse Nixon that he would make no endorsement before the party's convention in Miami next August.[30]

EISENHOWER'S COYNESS aside, Nixon's prospects were so good as 1967 drew to an end that James Reston took it for granted that the 1968 campaign would pit Nixon against Johnson. The prospect troubled Reston considerably. "Why Johnson and why Nixon?" He felt "the answer to this is not easy to find, especially if you think about it for at least two minutes."

Reston wrote that he did not mean to imply that Johnson and Nixon were not able men. "They just happen to be the two politicians who inspire more distrust among more people in this country than any other two men in American political life." Reston worried that Johnson might well be able to win a victory at the polls, but he could never be able to muster the support needed to govern.

"Ironically, this is also Nixon's problem," Reston went on, "so the prospect before us is that the two men most likely to be nominated happen to lack exactly the personal characteristics most essential to gain consent for the hard and divisive politics that will face the nation between 1969 and '73."[31]

Reston's accuracy as a prophet was impressive; what was missing was a suggestion of who might be capable of uniting the country and mustering the power to govern in the America of 1969.

BY THE END OF 1967, Nixon had spent nearly every waking minute of the past two years in preparing himself for the 1968 presidential campaign. During the holidays, he was suddenly beset with doubts. On December 22, following a Christmas party, he went into his den, took out a yellow legal pad, and wrote, "I have decided personally against becoming a candidate."

He went on to scribble down the reasons for this incredible decision. He wrote that he did not want to be President in order to *be* someone, that he had lost the spirit and zeal essential to success, that he did not relish the combat, and so on, until, finally, "I don't give a damn."

Not one person close to Nixon would have agreed with any of this; friends and associates would have insisted that in every case the opposite was true. But for Nixon, this sort of thing was a necessary part of gearing up for the campaign. For Nixon, every decision had to be a crisis, every decision had to be a part of a larger drama, even where there was none. He pretended, evidently even to himself, that he was in an agony of indecision.[32]

On Christmas Day, it was time to tell the members of the family he had decided not to run, for their sake. Julie recorded in her diary that "Daddy called Tricia and me in separately and told us that he had decided—almost definitely—not to run. He was very depressed. I had never known him to be depressed before—not even after 1962."

The girls would not hear of it. "If you don't run, Daddy, you really have nothing to live for," Tricia told him. Julie said, "You have to do it for the country." But Pat, when her turn came, held back—a little. She could not bring herself to urge him to run, but she told him she would help if he felt he must.[33]

Not content with these reassurances and demonstrations of support, Nixon went down to Key Biscayne, without his family, on December 28, to make what he grandiloquently called in his memoirs "the most important decision of my life." Billy Graham joined him; Nixon asked advice; Graham said run.

Nixon dragged this out for two more weeks. During that period, he got a letter from his son-in-law-to-be. David Eisenhower wrote that he knew what a thankless business politics was. "My Grandad is now regarded as a simple country bumpkin," David asserted as he revealed some of the bitterness felt in the Eisenhower family at the criticisms of Ike. But David said he also knew the satisfaction that came from serving the country. America needed Nixon's "wisdom and insight," and David urged him to run.[34]

On January 15, at a family gathering, the final scene of the drama was played out. Nixon asked Rose Woods to join the others. Julie described the scene in her diary: "I'll never forget dinner. Daddy called Fina and Manolo in, since they are part of the family too, and asked Fina why she thought he must 'do this terrible thing.' She said that in the world there are few men that are born to do something and that D[addy] was one of them. It brought tears to his eyes and to Mother's too."[35]

Drying his eyes, Nixon announced his decision: "I have decided to go. I have decided to run again."

Eyes turned to Pat. That ever-brave trouper said, "I know what you are asking us to do, and what you are asking of yourself. Now that the decision is made, I will go along with it."[36]

Julie concluded her diary entry, "Deep in my heart, I still think Mother is opposed to running but at least she is reconciled now."[37]

For Nixon, that had been the point of the entire charade. He could go into the climax of 1968 with the knowledge that he had a secure home front.

CHAPTER SEVEN

THE PRIMARIES
JANUARY–MAY 1968

ON JANUARY 16, the morning after he received the family's assurance of support, Nixon was in his office, off and running. He sent out personal letters to Republican politicians across the land, asking them for their support.[1] He got good news from Stans, who reported a $100,000 contribution from James Crosby, head of Mary Carter Paint Company. Nixon gave Stans a piece of good news of his own; his law partners had agreed to release John Mitchell to serve full time as Nixon's "personal Chief of Staff."[2]

Then Nixon joined with his writers to work on his basic all-purpose campaign speech. He had had one in every campaign. He wanted one that was hard-hitting and vote-getting, full of catchy slogans, general enough to let him occupy the broad middle ground, specific enough for him to denounce his opponents as extremists of the Left or Right.

While the candidate composed his speech, his staff worked on a mailing of 150,000 letters to New Hampshire households (about 85 percent of the total in the state), announcing Nixon's entry in the primary. The letter went out at the end of January; in it Nixon told the voters that on their choice depended "peace and freedom in the world." He cited his experience ("During fourteen years in Washington, I learned the awesome nature of the great decisions a President faces") and made a virtue of his time in the political wilderness ("During the past eight years I have had a chance to reflect on the lessons of public office, to measure the nation's tasks and its problems from a fresh perspective. . . . I believe I have found some answers").

133

The letters arrived on February 1; that same day, Nixon's aides at campaign headquarters at 521 Fifth Avenue called a press conference to hand out copies of the letter. They stressed the line that read, "For these critical years, America needs new leadership."[3]

The timing of Nixon's call for "new leadership" was perfect, even if fortuitous. The front page of *The New York Times* the following morning, February 2, 1968, reported a nation in turmoil.

Top left was a story about the alarming growth in the rate of inflation, and the Administration's plan to impose a 10 percent surcharge on income taxes. Next was the story on Nixon's announcement of his candidacy. Then a local report on the city's burgeoning budget problems. Beside the budget item, there was a report on Secretary of Defense Robert McNamara's "farewell address" to the Senate's armed services and defense committees.

McNamara's speech would have been the headline, the right-hand column feature on almost any other day, because in it he said that an era had come to an end. The Soviet Union, McNamara reported, had doubled its force of intercontinental ballistic missiles in the past year and thus had achieved virtual equality with the United States. The resulting nuclear stalemate, McNamara said, was a good thing, because "it is precisely this mutual capability to destroy one another, and conversely, our respective inability to prevent such destruction, that provides us both with the strongest possible motive to avoid a strategic nuclear war."

So after seven years of the most intensive peacetime buildup of America's armed forces in history, the Administration confessed that the Russians had caught up. After all the money that it had spent, the United States was more vulnerable than ever. From now on, America would have to relate to the Soviet Union as a nuclear equal.

Big as that story was, it gave way in placement to a story that was even bigger. The Vietcong had launched a countrywide offensive during the traditional cease-fire observed for the Vietnamese religious holiday of Tet. More than a hundred cities were battlegrounds; the American Embassy in Saigon had been penetrated by a Vietcong suicide squad; General Westmoreland's headquarters and the presidential palace in Saigon were under attack; Vietcong troops had captured the Saigon radio station; President Thieu had declared martial law; the enemy had tightened the siege on the U.S. Marine base at Khe Sanh.

President Johnson was quoted as vowing that "the enemy will fail again and again," because "we Americans will never yield." But the feature photograph (two columns to the right of Nixon's portrait) was of Brigadier General Nguyen Ngoc Loan, national police chief of South Vietnam, in the streets of Saigon, executing an apparent civilian with a pistol shot to the head.[4] (This became one of the most famous photographs of the Vietnam War. It later turned out that the "civilian" was a Vietcong death-squad member who had just shot one of General Loan's relatives.)

Nixon for President; Soviet strategic equality; the Vietcong on the march in far greater numbers and strength than anyone had thought possible. These were ominous portents for the future. They undercut some of the most basic assumptions of the first seven years of the decade—that Nixon was through, that America could outrace the Soviets, and that victory in Vietnam was just around the corner.

It surely was time for new leadership, just as Nixon said.

That afternoon, Nixon strode to the microphones set up before assembled reporters in the meeting room of the Holiday Inn in Manchester, New Hampshire, and began: "Gentlemen, this is *not* my last press conference." He laughed, and the reporters tried to laugh, and he plunged on. He hit his main weakness head-on: "Can Nixon win?" he asked. He wanted to be "quite candid" in his answer, which turned out to be yes.

He would win by demonstrating in the primaries that he was a winner. He got in a dig at Rockefeller, who had announced again that he was withdrawing his name from the Oregon primary, but that he was open to a draft. Nixon said, "I will test my ability . . . in the fires of the primaries, and not just in the smoke-filled rooms of Miami Beach."

Governor George Romney was Nixon's only opponent in New Hampshire. A reporter asked Nixon about Romney's challenge to a debate. Nixon replied, "The great debate of 1968 should be between the Republican nominee and Lyndon Johnson. The only winner of a debate between Republicans—as we learned in 1964 —would be Lyndon Johnson."

Prior to the press conference, while going over his basic speech one more time before giving it that evening at the Highway Hotel in Concord, Nixon had to deal with an unexpected problem. Julie arrived, breathless and excited. She told her father that David Eisenhower had driven her over from Smith College.[5] Nixon frowned. He said he was worried that the press might write that by attending the reception that afternoon, David Eisenhower was implying that his grandfather was endorsing Nixon. Nixon knew how sensitive the former President was in these matters, and that Ike had specifically *not* endorsed him. On the other hand, Nixon mused, if the press found out that David had driven Julie to Manchester and then *not* attended the reception, it might imply a lack of support on Ike's part. Nixon fretted and worried and fussed and finally decided that David should stay.

Nixon introduced him to the press, and when interviewed by reporters, David and Julie announced their plans to marry before graduation from college. Earlier plans had been "indefinite" as to the "when," but now the couple revealed that it would be "quite some time" before their graduations.[6]

One reporter observed, "Julie and David together provided most of the sex appeal—she innocent and vivacious, he innocent and unassuming. His tousled head of hair and open expression quickly won the hearts of the Republican faithful—and, from the accompanying press corps, the nickname 'Howdy Doody.' "[7]

In the speech, delivered before two thousand enthusiastic supporters, Nixon stressed the theme of new leadership to give the country the "lift of a driving dream." He said that the nation was suffering from a "crisis of the spirit." The Johnson Administration, Nixon charged, had lost touch with "the soul of the nation."

Nixon then went after the Democrats, using some of their own most cherished phrases as he did so. "It's time to move on to a new freedom," Nixon declared (Woodrow Wilson's slogan in 1912 had been the "New Freedom"). "The old negative freedoms—freedom from hunger, freedom from want, freedom from fear—are no longer enough." So much for FDR. "The new freedom has to mean freedom for the poor as well as the rich, freedom for black as well as for white; and it has to mean not only freedom from but freedom to. It means freedom to grow, freedom to choose, freedom to travel, freedom to create, freedom to work—and freedom to enjoy the fruits of our labors."

He delivered his peroration with fist-pounding emphasis: "When the strongest nation in the world can be tied down for four years in the war in Vietnam with no end in sight; when the nation with the greatest tradition of respect for the rule of law is plagued by random lawlessness; when the nation that has been a symbol of human liberty is torn apart by racial strife; when the President of the United States cannot travel either at home or abroad without fear of a hostile demonstration, then it is time America had new leadership!"[8]

It was a strong, self-confident demonstration of just how good Nixon could be on the stump. It also demonstrated how closely he had studied Jack Kennedy's techniques and appeals in 1960. (Teddy White, covering the event, was struck by this line: "This country must move again, how long will it take the United States to move?")[9] The stress on fundamental values and the sermonlike quality suited Nixon well. His earnestness and sincerity were plain to see. Although he had said scarcely a word about Vietnam, his audience was enthusiastic. Ike wrote him a glowing letter about his "new freedoms." [10] He was started.

Nixon's New Hampshire campaign was stately, dignified, proud, and slow. In a complete reversal of his 1960 techniques, Nixon stayed away from factory gates, avoided shopping centers, made no effort to press the flesh, appeared in no high-school gyms, all of which Romney was doing to a maximum degree. But Nixon was well known in the state already (could there have been a voter in New Hampshire, indeed in the nation, who did not know Dick Nixon?), and he feared overexposure. When he did appear in public, it was only in large auditoriums, with audiences of never less than a thousand, some as large as twenty-five hundred.

He made an effort to appear statesmanlike, dignified, experienced, and in command, and he succeeded. He spoke without notes, casually.

He hardly wavered from his basic speech, with its emphasis on moral decay and the collapse of the American spirit. He stuck to his generalities. This delighted some voters, but dismayed others. With U.S. troops suffering their heaviest casualties to date in the war, as General Westmoreland pressed a counteroffensive after having stopped the Communists' Tet attack, with major battles raging at Khe Sanh and in Hue, Vietnam was what the audiences wanted to hear about. So did George Romney, who continued to press Nixon for a debate, and who three times in the first week of the campaign demanded that Nixon present a "plan for peace." Nixon's reply was that Republicans should not fight among themselves, while on Vietnam the most he would say was that the American presence there "is the cork in the bottle of Chinese expansion in Asia," coupled with a promise that if elected he would bring sufficient resourcefulness to U.S. diplomacy to prevent any future Vietnams. [11]

Relatively infrequent appearances in New Hampshire (he made twenty altogether) gave Nixon time to rest and to campaign elsewhere, which was one of the major benefits of the new strategy he adopted for 1968. An even greater benefit was that his changed techniques allowed him to go over the heads of the reporters and television commentators directly to the people. He found he liked doing that very much. He got his opportunity to do so by seizing on a plan that Bob Haldeman had suggested to him in a memorandum some months earlier.

Haldeman's memorandum consisted of a brutal criticism of the 1960 campaign and a recommendation for new methods in 1968. No matter how hard a candidate worked, according to Haldeman, he could at best talk directly to a million or two voters, as Nixon had done in 1960. "The reach of the individual campaigner doesn't add up to diddly-squat in votes." Nixon's heroic physical effort had sapped his inner strength and vitality, pushed him beyond the realm of good judgment. "We started Nixon off in 1960 sick and under medication and then we ran his tail off."

The right way, Haldeman wrote, was to use television to the maximum while keeping direct voter and reporter contacts to a minimum. One minute on the network evening news would reach more people than three months of barnstorming. Nixon would have to make only one speech a day to provide the necessary footage.

All this was pretty much Basic Marketing I, and to be expected from an advertising executive at J. Walter Thompson in Los Angeles, on loan to the Nixon campaign. What gave the Haldeman approach life and made it viable was the way in which Nixon's staff fleshed it out. The staff members concerned included Safire, Herb Klein, Len Garment, Haldeman, Harry Treleaven (on loan from J. Walter Thompson), and Frank Shakespeare (a CBS executive on sabbatical).

If Haldeman was right and television was the way to go, the immediate problem was how to use Nixon effectively on the medium. Nixon's reputation was that he was experienced and able, but unelectable, because he handled television badly. When people thought of Nixon and television, they recalled the Checkers speech (by this time an embarrassment to the Republicans), the 1960 debates with Kennedy, and the "last press conference." These were devastating images. On the face of it, Nixon should avoid TV as much as possible.

But the staff realized that there had been specific problems with each case, problems that could be corrected. In the Checkers speech, Nixon was on screen for nearly thirty minutes, with no props; it was the awkwardness of his gestures, the menacing clenched fist, as much as what he said, that caused embarrassment. In the 1960 debates, it was his appearance in the first debate that everyone remembered; he used makeup thereafter and was generally judged to have equaled Kennedy in the three following debates. In the "last press conference," the worst of the three images, the problem was that he was appearing before the press, which brought out the worst in him.

But if Nixon was not all that good by himself, or one-on-one, or with reporters, there were times when he was outstanding. Speaking to large audiences, he was smooth, professional, outgoing, and impressive. His punch lines would make the evening news, and have an impact. Nixon was also good in a small-group situation, so long as that group did not consist of reporters. He had spent much of his life in living rooms with a dozen or so awed supporters, explaining to them how government worked, or a current foreign-policy crisis, or his long-term strategy on this or that issue. He had an ability to simplify and generalize that was entirely convincing, at least to a group of citizens who had little idea of the specifics of what he was talking about. Such groups induced apparent spontaneity, as Nixon would react to the most elementary question as if he was hearing it for the first time. He would ponder a bit, congratulate the questioner on his originality, then give the answer he had given hundreds of times before, complete with some figures and a quotation, as the citizen listened in utter awe.

So the staff decided on a format that came to be called the Hillsboro approach, after the small town in New Hampshire where it was inaugurated. Nixon's people recruited a dozen or so citizens and gathered them together as a panel in the Hillsboro Town Hall. Treleaven and Shakespeare had the lights, TV cameras, and sound equipment ready. Nixon sat down facing the group of panelists and took questions.

They were not all friendly. Although it was later charged that the panelists were handpicked Nixon supporters, in fact the staffers knew that Nixon was often at his best in dealing with hostile questions (assuming that the questioner did not know many details and in any case had no chance to follow up), so they made sure there were critical panelists.

One great beauty of the whole format was that the staff could cut it up into five-minute segments for later broadcasting, leaving the embarrassing or awkward moments in the trash can. Another great beauty was that Nixon would not have to face informed reporters, and could thus avoid the hard questions, such as what he proposed to do in Vietnam. With this format, Nixon could run a national campaign that relied exclusively on staged television events and excluded the press corps.

Despite these appealing features, Nixon originally had resisted the Haldeman approach. For one thing, he was not ready to denounce the 1960 campaign—in his own mind he had won, so he must have done something right. But the staff convinced him to give it a try, and he did at Hillsboro, although he appeared "grouchy" when he walked into the Town Hall. But with no newsmen present, and knowing that reporters and voters would see only what Treleaven and Shakespeare decided to show them, Nixon quickly relaxed. He began to enjoy the procedure, even refused to stop after two hours. In the segments that were later shown to the press, he impressed Teddy White as "crisp, direct, real and convincing."[12]

Nixon was hooked. He stayed with the Hillsboro approach

right to the end of the campaign. Just as Haldeman had suggested, in 1968 he turned his 1960 campaign on its head.

That decision led to another big difference in the two campaigns; the cost of producing and presenting the five-minute segments of Nixon talking to the voters was horrendous. Television campaigns were far more expensive than barnstorming. Fortunately for Nixon, Maurice Stans was there to raise the money to keep the cameras grinding away and to purchase the local TV time.

Stans went after the small as well as the big contributions. He had a "RN Associates" gold lapel pin to award to the first thousand contributors to give $1,000 each. He had a Century Club for those who gave $100,000 or more (eventually twenty-six did). And he had a personal bank account of sufficient size that he could tide the campaign over with a personal loan when necessary—as for example on March 31, when he put up $25,000 to cover some current expenses.[13]

Stans gathered in the money. Between Hillsboro and the Miami convention, the Nixon campaign spent $9 million. Stans covered it all and had some to spare.

The press corps, as a result of the Hillsboro approach, hardly ever got to see Nixon in 1968, and almost never had a chance to ask questions. This naturally infuriated the press corps. Joe McGinniss, in his bitterly sarcastic 1969 book, *The Selling of the President 1968*, expressed the sentiments of many reporters: by refusing to face the press, he wrote, Nixon was presenting a false picture of himself, a package designed to create an image of Nixon that was the opposite of the reality. Nixon was selling a product, not discussing the issues.

The assumption that reporters could have revealed the real Nixon was false. They would have been no more successful in forcing Nixon to reveal himself in the primary season of 1968 than the citizen panelists were. He was a past master at avoiding specific questions with generalizations, a slogan and/or a quotation, or in explaining why he could not answer a question—as for example, what he was thinking about Vietnam.

Through his life, Nixon revealed what he wanted to reveal, and hid what he wanted to hide. The staff had hit on the best way to present their man, but he was still the same old Nixon. Newspaper reporters' indignation to the contrary notwithstanding, the Nixon campaign of 1968 was brilliantly conceived and executed. It was geared specifically to Richard Nixon's strengths and weaknesses, it was well thought out, it had nuances too detailed to go into here, and it was successful.

The staff also did well when it came up with the button and

poster slogan, "Nixon's the One." Like the Hillsboro approach, it fit Nixon perfectly, most of all in its ambiguity.

The polls, and the crowds Nixon drew when he made his speech, indicated that Romney was facing a humiliating defeat. Despite a frantic campaign in New Hampshire and despite access to Rockefeller money (at least according to Nixon,) [14] Romney was down to 10 percent in the polls. At the end of February he pulled out.

Rockefeller immediately let it be known that he would accept a draft, and leaked a poll that showed he had more appeal to independents and Democrats than Nixon did. Nixon countered with a poll of his own that showed him running even with Johnson. [15]

Romney's departure had its effect on the Democratic primary too, because antiwar Republicans who had been supporting Romney now began to look more closely at the apparently quixotic campaign of Senator Eugene McCarthy of Minnesota. McCarthy, with no real staff or money, was taking on Lyndon Johnson, on the single issue of ending the war. Meanwhile former governor George Wallace of Alabama made a long-expected announcement: he was entering the presidential race as head of a third-party (the American Independent Party) ticket.

Johnson was getting battered by both the Left and the Right in his own party. He could console himself with the thought that the same thing had happened to Harry Truman back in 1948, when Henry Wallace organized the Progressive Party on the Left while Senator J. Strom Thurmond ran as the candidate of the Dixiecrats on the Right. Truman had rallied the center and won.

For Nixon, Wallace's entry made for complications, the full extent of which could only be dimly foreseen. Certainly Wallace was going to preempt the extreme Right of the political spectrum on such basic issues as race relations and the war in Vietnam, but Nixon was never going to advocate segregation or a nuclear offensive in Vietnam anyway, so Wallace figured to help as well as hurt, by making Nixon appear more a man of the center.

The battle in Vietnam raged on. The marines at Khe Sanh withstood suicidal enemy attacks; regular North Vietnamese Army units were appearing in increasing numbers; Hue was being fought for almost as Stalingrad had been; casualties were mounting; the President dispatched 10,500 more infantry to the battle, before proclaiming a victory in the Tet offensive; Senator Robert Kennedy said the war could not be won.

Nixon had been as surprised by the Tet offensive as Johnson, Westmoreland, and everyone else. Unlike the men in power, he had time to think before responding.

But no more than the men in power did he know what to think about the meaning of the Tet offensive. Perhaps the enemy had been defeated, as Johnson claimed; perhaps the kill ratio was 20–1 in favor of the American troops, as Westmoreland asserted; it was nevertheless obvious that the Americans were not winning, that the massive influx of American weapons and men into Vietnam in 1967 had not turned the tide. And the panic reaction of the press, television, and the public all indicated that John Kennedy had been wrong when he said back in January 1961 that the United States would "pay any price, bear any burden" to insure the survival of freedom, in Vietnam and elsewhere. There were limits, and they had quite possibly been reached, to what Americans would pay, to the burden they would bear.

The great lesson of Tet was that escalation had not worked, and the meaning of the lesson included this fact: the American political system would not allow further escalation. Another obvious fact was simultaneously emerging: the American economic system was in a state of vulnerable disarray. Johnson's policy of expanding the war while extending the Great Society programs while refusing to raise taxes to pay for either was threatening to create runaway inflation along with uncontrollable deficits.

In sum, the policy Nixon had advocated relentlessly for the past four years fell apart almost at the exact time he began his formal campaign for the Presidency. He needed time to think of a new approach.

His staff, however, was pressing him, insisting that he had to speak out on Vietnam. Herbert Brownell, formerly Ike's Attorney General and an unofficial adviser to the Nixon camp, said that Nixon had to say he would end the war, just as Ike had done back in 1952 with regard to Korea.[16] Safire told Nixon that people wanted hope, that he had an obligation to give it to them, and that as ending the war was what he wanted to do anyway, that was what he should promise.

On March 5, at the American Legion Hall in Hampton, New Hampshire, Nixon interrupted his regular speech to finally speak out on Vietnam. "I pledge to you," he said, "new leadership will end the war and win the peace in the Pacific." He did *not* say, as was later reported and widely believed, that he had "a secret plan to end the war." In fact, he said the opposite: that he had no gimmick, "no push-button technique" to end the war. He did insist that he was not suggesting "withdrawal from Vietnam." However, he continued, "I am saying to you that the war can be ended if we mobilize our economic and political and diplomatic leadership."[17]

That afternoon, Nixon flew to Washington, where he appeared

in the evening at a Republican fund-raiser. The clamor from reporters for clarification of his Hampton remarks on ending the war forced him to be a bit more explicit.

Nixon said that Johnson had placed too much emphasis on the military side and too little on the nonmilitary side. He asserted that the United States should "keep the pressure on" militarily but supplement it with more intensive diplomatic, economic, and political programs. Nixon added that the United States should use leverage to get the Soviet Union to use its power on the side of peace; he referred to such leverage as a possible "key to peace." [18]

Over the next few days, Nixon repeated his pledge to "end the war and win the peace." Indeed, he added to it, reminding his audiences that he had been part of an Administration that had come to power in 1953 in the middle of "another war in Asia. We ended that war and kept the nation out of other wars for eight years. And that's the kind of leadership you'll be voting for this year if you support my ticket." [19] As he continued this campaign, Democrats joined reporters in demanding to know some details of how he proposed to achieve his objectives. Nixon refused to provide any. He explained that to give any details of how he would carry out his pledge would fatally weaken his bargaining position if he became President. "I'm not trying to be coy or political," Nixon coyly said.

Although he refused to talk about his plan, Nixon was fairly specific about what he would not do. He said he would not seek an "unconditional surrender" by North Vietnam, "nor do I want Ho's head on a plate." He would work for an "honorable" bargain that would insure self-determination for South Vietnam, that could not be construed as a "defeat for the United States or a reward for aggression," and that would not lead to "further wars of liberation" in Asia. [20]

He said that the Soviet Union was the key to securing a settlement, and that he would explore fully the various means, military and diplomatic, by which Russia could be "enlisted on the side of peace." He thought the next President should approach the Kremlin with the offer of a "carrot" as well as with a "stick," the carrot being "economic détente" in Europe.

That was as far as he would go. Not even Eisenhower, who wrote to ask for details of Nixon's plan, could elicit a further elucidation. Nixon explained to the former President that he could not be specific, because he did not want to "undercut whatever diplomatic negotiations might be underway at present," and because he did not want to restrict his own negotiating flexibility when he moved into the White House. [21]

Hidden in all the verbiage was a clear-cut change in Nixon's thinking about Vietnam. No longer was he calling for victory. No longer was he calling for escalation. Never before had he suggested cutting a deal with the Russians. For the first time he was using the words "honorable peace," not "victorious peace." Never before had he used the word "withdrawal," and even though he denied that he intended to withdraw, that was the logical outgrowth of his thinking.

Nixon's silence was good politics, as the American effort in Vietnam had reached its turning point. After four years of escalation, Johnson had decided to change the course. The President, confronted with a request from Westmoreland for 206,000 more troops, decided that the limit had been reached and passed. At best, Johnson told Westmoreland on the eve of the New Hampshire primary, he could send another thirty-five thousand men, and he was reluctant to do even that much. A major factor in his decision was the growing strength of the antiwar movement within the United States.

Johnson, for the first time, began to reach out to the North Vietnamese to negotiate seriously. Nixon, excluded from the discussions, was wise to avoid comment, to stay as vague as he could on Vietnam.

Nixon did make one pledge. Once the war in Vietnam was over, he declared, the Selective Service System should be abolished and the nation should rely on a volunteer army of professional, well-paid troops skilled in the techniques of modern warfare. That was a nice touch, coming as it did during a week that Johnson announced he was eliminating the draft deferments for graduate students.

On the law-and-order issue, Nixon was specific on all the details. On March 6, in a radio interview in Keene, New Hampshire, he commented on the recent report of the President's National Advisory Commission on Civil Disorders. The report had put the major share of the blame for urban riots on what it called "white racism," and warned that unless the races reconciled their differences, the nation could divide into two permanent and hostile camps.

Nixon was incensed. "One of the major weaknesses of the President's commission," he said, "is that it, in effect, blames everybody for the riots except the perpetrators of the riots." He also criticized the report for leaning "too much on Federal programs" to achieve housing and jobs for black Americans.[22]

The following night, in a nationwide radio broadcast, Nixon said he intended "to meet force with force, if necessary, in the cities." He urged the government to move swiftly to contain the "planners of violence" before summer; he urged "retaliation against the perpetrators of violence," and wanted it to be "swift and sure." He justified this tough talk by asserting that "the violence being threatened for this summer is more in the nature of a war than a riot. A riot, by definition, is a spontaneous outburst; a war is subject to advance planning."[23]

Nixon was pleased with his effort, and even more so with the response. He wrote Eisenhower, delightedly, that "I have found great audience response to this theme [law and order] in all parts of the country, including areas like New Hampshire where there is virtually no race problem and relatively little crime."[24]

In New Hampshire, on March 12, Nixon got 79 percent of the Republican votes. Even better, his 84,000 votes dwarfed Johnson's 22,000 in the Democratic primary. Best of all, Senator McCarthy, who according to the reporters would do well to get 20 percent of the Democratic vote, had 18,000, or 42 percent. That was enough to allow McCarthy to claim an upset victory, and for the press to write it that way.

Nixon was devastatingly accurate when he commented that the total vote meant "the people of the nation don't want four more years of Johnson in the White House."[25]

But there was another, for Nixon less happy, result of McCarthy's "victory." On March 16, evidently encouraged by the proof that Johnson was vulnerable, Senator Robert Kennedy entered the Democratic race. Nixon was in Portland, Oregon, that day; he watched Kennedy make his announcement on a hotel-room TV. John Ehrlichman, who was present, recalled that when the set was turned off, Nixon sat and stared at the blank screen. He finally shook his head and said, "We've just seen some very terrible forces unleashed. Something bad is going to come of this. God knows where this is going to lead."[26]

Pat Buchanan noticed that a feeling of fear spread quickly among the old Nixon hands from the '60 campaign when Robert Kennedy announced. For his part, Buchanan thought RFK would be the easiest Democrat to beat, but then he had never been through a campaign against a Kennedy.[27]

Nixon's big win on the Republican side in New Hampshire put the pressure on Rockefeller to announce that he was entering the primaries. Nixon expected Rockefeller to do so, and did not particularly fear it. Although the governor had been privately mocking him on his end-the-war-and-win-the-peace "plan," Nixon could handle Rockefeller's questions on Vietnam as easily as he handled those of Romney, the Democrats, and the reporters. But, on March 21, to Nixon's surprise, Rockefeller announced, "I have decided today to reiterate unequivocally that I am not a candidate campaigning directly or indirectly for the presidency of the United States." He said he had taken his name off the ballot in Oregon, swearing by affidavit that "I am not, and will not be, a candidate for the presidency."[28]

Three days earlier, Governor Spiro Agnew of Maryland had formed a Draft Rockefeller Committee. On March 21, he had called reporters into his office to watch with him as Rockefeller announced his plans, fully expecting the New York governor to enter the primaries. Agnew was embarrassed, and angered, when Rockefeller said the opposite. A week later, Nixon met in New York with Agnew. Agnew had a reputation as a moderate or even liberal Republican (he had just defeated a Democratic opponent in Maryland who was an out-and-out racist). Nixon liked the big, strong, good-looking, self-confident governor. He said he was "impressed by his intelligence and poise." Agnew did not pledge his support, but then Nixon did not ask for it, and was satisfied that Agnew praised him in his comments to reporters.[29]

Meanwhile, Nixon was adding some flesh to his Vietnam plan. Campaigning in Wisconsin, he called for an increased use of South Vietnamese soldiers to end the war. He said, "The nation's objective should be to help the South Vietnamese fight the war and not fight it for them.

"If they do not assume the majority of the burden in their own defense," Nixon concluded, "they cannot be saved."[30]

That was not specific enough to justify the claim of an "end the war and win the peace" plan. First, it sounded like Johnson, who had once said that American boys ought not be doing what Asian boys ought to be doing for themselves. Second, turning the war over to the Vietnamese was what Johnson was already doing, as he had shown when he turned down his field commander's request for reinforcements. Third, seeking a negotiated end to the war, implied by Nixon's stress on getting the Russians to help bring about a peace, was also what Johnson was already doing.

Nixon had to say more. But he resisted when his staff pointed this out to him. "It would be better for me not to do anything controversial for the time being," Nixon told Safire over the telephone on March 24. "I don't want to get into the crossfire between LBJ and Bobby—let them hit each other, not me." He did admit, "I don't like this 'secret plan' business." Safire convinced him that he would have to make a major policy speech on Vietnam.

On March 28, after a campaign speech in Milwaukee, Nixon flew to New York to confer with Price, Safire, and Richard Whalen and to work on a text for a nationwide broadcast. They thought about a Nixon idea, to call for a unified command for ARVN and U.S. forces in Vietnam, but scrapped it. Instead, the emphasis was on increasing the air and sea pressure while decreasing the level of "search and destroy" missions, and to use diplomatic pressure and promises to the Soviets and the Chinese to help bring the war to an honorable conclusion.[31]

Nixon's major speech on Vietnam was scheduled for the evening of March 31. That day, President Johnson asked for television time to make a speech to the nation. Nixon canceled his own program. He wanted to wait to hear what Johnson had to say.

Johnson, Nixon guessed, had adopted the very plan Nixon was going to propose. This was no accident—the two men had been together on Vietnam right along, except that Nixon had always been just ahead of Johnson.

Each man realized, in the immediate aftermath of Tet, that Defense Secretary Clifford spoke the truth when he said "more men, more bombs, and more killing" had not worked. Westmoreland was claiming that the United States Army had won a great victory, that the Vietcong, by coming out of their holes, had exposed themselves to American firepower, and thus suffered horrendous casualties, as did the NVA. But both Johnson and Nixon realized that it hardly mattered how many Vietcong or NVA were killed; the enemy could make up the losses in a year or so, meanwhile pulling back to sanctuaries that gave them time to rest and recover and recruit. The only way to end the war was to occupy Laos, Cambodia, and North Vietnam, but Johnson and Nixon explicitly ruled that out.

Westmoreland wanted to compare Tet to the Battle of the Bulge, of December 1944. He pointed out that after the Bulge, General Eisenhower had asked for reinforcements in order to follow up his victory over the Wehrmacht. But the analogy would not hold up, because in January 1945 victory was in sight. One more mighty blow would do it. In March 1968, victory could not be seen even in the far distance, no matter how mighty a blow was struck.

Another problem: the South Vietnamese government had gotten worse instead of better. President Thieu's corruption, his penchant for putting incompetent officers in key positions, his reluctance to broaden his government by taking in members of the opposition, his refusal either to fight or to make concessions that might lead to a negotiated peace, were all maddening. But they were less a consequence of Thieu's personal qualities than they were built into the structure of the situation.

The massive inflow of American money meant that corruption was inevitable. So long as the Americans were eager to "search and destroy," thereby throwing the Vietcong on the defensive and providing relatively complete security for the cities, why on earth should ARVN fight? The Americans were not going to leave, so the Communists could never win. Any leader of South Vietnam would have reached the conclusion Thieu reached: that it was much more profitable to continue the war than to even consider peace.

Johnson and Nixon concluded the inevitable, that the United States would have to force ARVN to expand and take up more of the burden, while Thieu would have to broaden his government and assume real responsibility. The public reaction to Tet forced the politicians to realize that American casualties had to be reduced. Another conclusion forced on both Nixon and Johnson was that the United States had to enter into serious negotiations, which implied making at least some concessions to the Communists.

It was at this point, the last day of March 1968, that America reversed its policy in Asia. Ever since 1898, the American presence in Asia had expanded, sometimes rapidly, sometimes hardly at all, but at the end of each decade, there were more American troops in Asia than there had been ten years earlier. Since 1964, the rise had been spectacular. Now the decision was to begin withdrawing.

This meant that America was abandoning victory as the goal in Vietnam, and was now seeking a face-saving formula that would allow withdrawal without humiliation. That decision has since been much criticized, as Americans have adopted their own version of the German "stab in the back" myth of 1919: that it was the politicians at home who lost the war, not the soldiers in the field. The argument carries with it the implication that if only the politicians had not turned chicken, America could have won.

Whatever the merits of the charge that the politicians lost a war that the military was winning, the charge puts the spotlight directly on the two leading politicians in the nation, Lyndon Johnson and Richard Nixon. As the heads of their respective parties, they were more sensitive than anyone else to all the tugs and pulls of American politics. And their conclusion, reached simultaneously, to the point that had not Nixon canceled his speech they would have made the announcement simultaneously, was that America could not win.

Stalemate was unacceptable, for obvious reasons. Therefore there must be negotiations. But there could be no humiliation. Insistence on those points created a dilemma. In seeking an honorable peace through negotiations, the policy of Johnson and Nixon ran into this difficulty: how could the United States negotiate a satisfactory peace agreement with North Vietnam while at the same time disengaging from the fighting and eliminating the base of military power in the field that made credible negotiating possible?

If the Americans were going to leave anyway, why on earth should the North Vietnamese negotiate?[32]

On national television, Sunday evening, March 31, 1968, Johnson announced that he was de-escalating the war. He said he had ordered a halt to the bombing of North Vietnam, except for an area immediately north of the DMZ. He was going to launch a peace offensive, indeed had already begun by dispatching former ambassador Averell Harriman to Paris to begin talks with the North Vietnamese. Then he made the stunning announcement that he was not a candidate for re-election. Nixon heard about it from Pat Buchanan, who met him at La Guardia Airport—Nixon had been flying in from Milwaukee as Johnson spoke. Reporters demanded a statement. Nixon gave them one.

"This is the year of the dropouts," he said. "First Romney, then Rockefeller, now Johnson." He admitted that he was surprised by Johnson's announcement; he rated Kennedy the new Democratic favorite; he said Humphrey would move in as Johnson's candidate; he declared, "I'd be very surprised if President Johnson lets Bobby Kennedy have it on a platter"; he speculated that Rockefeller might now reconsider.

He said not one word about Vietnam, or Johnson's policy change, or what he had been prepared to say that evening.

The next day, he issued a statement saying that he was declaring a self-imposed "moratorium" on comment on Vietnam. This included delaying a "comprehensive statement on Vietnam which I had planned this week." He explained that he assumed Johnson would not have halted the bombing unless he was acting "on private diplomatic information available only to the Government. I further assume that intensive and delicate diplomatic moves are now under way, possibly involving the Soviet Union. . . . As I have often said, I believe that the key to peace in Vietnam probably lies in Moscow."

Nixon said that he would withhold any criticism of Johnson for "two or three weeks" in order to see what the North Vietnamese did, rather than said, about the bombing halt. He refused a request from newsmen for a general press conference, and walked away.[33]

So Nixon's comment was no comment. He neither criticized Johnson nor supported him. This was good politics, but bad policy. Had Nixon thrown his weight behind Johnson's peace efforts, it is possible (but admittedly highly improbable) that Johnson could have ended the war sometime between the election and January 1969. It staggers the imagination to even begin to think about what a difference this would have made to the Nixon Presidency.

But if Nixon had supported Johnson, he might well have lost the Republican nomination. Keeping quiet allowed hawks to think that he was one of them, while doves could take solace in the thought that Dick was Ike's boy, and thus would know how to get us out of Vietnam. Nixon figured that keeping quiet had an additional advantage; it would give him a free hand when he took power. Actually, his decision put him in a bind that he never escaped, a bind brought on by the basic dilemma of trying to negotiate an honorable peace while withdrawing.

The Tet offensive not only caused Nixon to rethink the Vietnam War, but also the emerging balance of power in Asia. In March 1968, he told Teddy White, in an exclusive interview for the book White was writing on the 1968 campaign, that "if he were elected President, the very first thing he'd do would be to try to get in touch with Red China. There had to be an understanding with Red China. In ten or fifteen years it would be impossible to run the world if Red China weren't part of it."

Nixon had also told White five months earlier, "I've always thought this country could run itself domestically without a President; all you need is a competent Cabinet to run the country at home. You need a President for foreign policy; no Secretary of State is really important; the President makes foreign policy." [34]

ON APRIL 4, in Memphis, an assassin shot Martin Luther King, Jr. Within hours, rioters were looting and burning Washington, D.C.; by that evening, riots were in progress in New York's Harlem and Bedford-Stuyvesant areas. Soon they spread across the land.

For Nixon, the immediate problem was whether to go to King's funeral or not. Safire urged him to do so, and reminded him of the incident in 1960 when King had been arrested and Nixon had declined to telephone him, because that would be "grandstanding." Safire reminded him that some observers thought that one incident had cost him the election.

Nixon nodded. "Failing to go would present some serious problems," he said. He dialed a call himself (to John Mitchell, Safire thought).

Since the beginning of the year, Nixon had dispensed with "Hello" when he got on the telephone. So on this occasion: "I'm sitting here with Safire, Garment, and all the libs," he began, "talking about the King funeral. What do you think?"

The person at the other end opposed going. Nixon hung up, with no good-bye. "There's some feeling that we should not let ourselves become prisoners of the moment," Nixon told Safire, Garment, and the libs. "In the long run, politicians who try to capitalize on this could be hurt."

But having repeated the argument, he rejected it. Perhaps it was true that he had lost in '60 because of his refusal to call King. Whatever his motivation, Nixon announced, "I'll go down and pay my respects to Mrs. King quietly." But, he warned, "there will be no grandstanding." [35]

On April 7, Nixon flew to Atlanta, where he paid his respects to Mrs. King and the family. Nixon talked about his first meeting with King, in Ghana in 1957, and expressed his deep admiration for the man. Two days later he returned for the funeral. To avoid grandstanding, he did not march in the procession.

THERE WERE many consequences for Nixon from Johnson's withdrawal, but the most immediate was that he did not have Johnson to kick around anymore. As Ray Price put it in a memo to Nixon the morning after Johnson's speech, "New leadership becomes a foregone conclusion." Price continued, "We should now be laying whatever groundwork we can for enlisting at least his [Johnson's] tacit support in November if the Democratic nominee should turn out to be Kennedy." [36]

Nixon liked the idea, and in his first appearance after King's funeral he got started on it. The date was April 19; the place was Washington; the audience was the American Society of Newspaper Editors; the format was a question-and-answer session. Nixon had been scheduled to make a speech, but had come to like the Hillsboro approach so much that he insisted on using it before the ASNE. What Nixon liked best about it was the feeling it gave him; he stood alone, with no podium, in the center of the stage surrounded by questioners. Nixon said he felt like "the man in the arena," a feeling he enjoyed.[37] (He took the phrase from Teddy Roosevelt.)

He was a great success. He got off some quips, challenged Bobby Kennedy to a debate, and got in a dig or two at Rockefeller. Nixon said he would remain silent on the war "as long as there is hope for successful negotiation." He called on Americans to support the President, to give him "a free hand to negotiate an honorable peace.... As far as I'm concerned, I'm not going to do anything to undercut him until he's had a chance to bring it about." [38]

Nixon, in other words, was in the happy position of publicly being able to wait to see if the policy change he privately advocated and Johnson had adopted was going to work, without identifying himself with the policy, and could wrap himself in the flag while doing so. The editors, patriots all, were impressed; Nixon's staff was ecstatic.

Ike liked it too. He sent Nixon a letter of congratulations. It was warm and generous, but it did not contain that elusive endorsement that Nixon had been seeking every four years since 1956. Ike stuck to his self-imposed, and self-serving, rule—he would withhold an endorsement until the delegates had chosen the Republican nominee.

Eisenhower said he was hearing good things about Nixon and was delighted to note that his campaign was making "real progress." Then he entered a criticism, although typically he attributed it to unnamed others: "In fact, the only statement of yours that I've heard criticized was the one to the effect that you would, as President, quickly end the war. Even this seems away into the background." [39]

David Eisenhower was assuming a role of liaison between his grandfather and his father-in-law-to-be. David very much wanted a clear preconvention endorsement of Nixon. The eagerness of General and Mrs. Eisenhower for an early wedding, frequently expressed, gave David some leverage, but working against him was Ike's ambivalence about Nixon.

"Of course I have been listening over the past twelve years to some of those whiners saying 'I don't like Nixon' or 'Dick can't win,' " Eisenhower wrote his grandson. "Most of these same people will concede that Dick is the best-prepared . . . When they express this . . . attitude to me, I answer, 'Well, if you are convinced that he is the best qualified then why don't you take off your coat, roll up your sleeves, and go to work for what you believe is best for the U.S.A.' " [40]

David must have wished that Ike would tell such people, "Well, he's my candidate." But Ike would not.

David helped make up for it by joining Julie on a thirty-state campaign swing that spring. Both nineteen years of age, they concentrated on small towns, where they were smash hits. Tricia, then twenty-two, was out on her own, making appearances for her father. Pat worked the hardest of all. While her husband rested or worked in his hotel room, she went to the factories, schools, and shopping centers. At age fifty-six, she was still the woman who had told Jessamyn West a decade earlier that she never got tired, hungry, or sick. Every other weekend or so, the Nixons got together for a weekend in Key Biscayne. While her daughters relaxed, Pat wrote letters, by hand, to correspondents, fifty or so a day. The family member who least wanted to be involved ended up working the hardest.

On the campaign trail, she seldom made speeches, but occasionally she would answer questions. She told a reporter who asked about her youth, "Life was sort of sad, so I tried to cheer everybody up. I learned to be that kind of a person."

Another reporter asked, "What is your greatest contribution to your husband?"

"I don't nag him," Pat replied. "The best I can [do] is cheer him up."[41] Then she added, "I fill him in on what women think. They're thinking peace at home and peace abroad."

On one day in San Antonio she met local Republicans, the local press, and visited a hospital, spent an hour conferring awards on women achievers, another hour accepting scrolls and medals for her own achievements, and in between times shook thousands of hands, smiled for thousands of Instamatic cameras, signed autographs, and attended a fair. A reporter who spent the day with her said she went thirteen hours on two cups of coffee and a Coke.

"I don't mind," Pat said when asked about it. "Creature comforts don't matter."[42]

ON APRIL 30, Rockefeller announced that he was back in the race. Publicly, Nixon welcomed his entry. Privately, he worried not about Rockefeller but about Reagan. The California governor would certainly be tempted to join Rockefeller in a stop-Nixon movement. It was equally obvious that the right wing of the party preferred Reagan to Nixon.

Not that Nixon went into a panic; far from it. He showed a public confidence that was justified. All spring his chief delegate hunters, Bob Ellsworth and John Sears, had been lining up Nixon votes. Unlike Goldwater in '64, they did not ask the delegates for binding pledges, and they encouraged favorite-son candidates. Of course, they also made it clear that the bandwagon was under way, and that there would be a better spot on it for those who climbed aboard early.

At national headquarters, Stans kept bringing in the money, while Mitchell ran the organization, as Safire, Price, and Buchanan churned out slogans, and Haldeman kept the press away from the candidate. It all ran smoothly and efficiently. Nixon appeared to be a sure winner. A delegate count on May 4 showed that 725 of the 1,333 total votes were either committed or leaning to Nixon, with 402 for Rockefeller and 206 for Reagan.[43]

But there was Oregon to get through. In Oregon, voters could choose between Rockefeller, Reagan, and Nixon. Neither of Nixon's opponents came to the state to campaign, but both were on the ballot and both spent large sums of money on television advertisements. In the end, Nixon outspent them; he also campaigned harder in Oregon than he had in any previous primary state.

By this time he had dropped one theme from his basic speech, the call for new leadership, as either Rockefeller or Reagan could supply that ingredient as well as he could, and was putting more emphasis on others. He maintained his moratorium on comment on Vietnam, wisely enough in view of the crosscurrents in the war. On May 3, the North Vietnamese agreed to join the United States in peace talks in Paris, but in South Vietnam the post-Tet battle raged on. In the two weeks before the Oregon primary, a record one thousand GIs were killed in action.

Nixon could not escape the question: How can you ask us to vote for you when you won't tell us what you want to do in Vietnam?

Nixon's standard reply was "If there is a chance we can get the war over before this election, that is much more important than anything I might wish to say to get you to vote for me." [44]

He did not mean it, as his actions in the last weeks of the campaign showed, but he insisted on it. So rather than talk about the violence in Vietnam, he talked about the violence in the United States. He made law and order his central theme, and played it hard to enthusiastic audiences who greeted his punch line with vigorous applause: "Some of our courts have gone too far in weakening the peace forces as against the criminal forces."

He denounced the *Escobedo* and *Miranda* decisions and called for new legislation to permit a case to come to trial and let judge and jury decide whether a confession was voluntary and valid. He strongly endorsed wiretapping against criminals and described as "puzzling and astonishing" the Administration's "adamant opposition to the use against organized crime of the same wiretap and electronic surveillance the Government employs to safeguard the national security." [45]

The role of poverty as a cause of crime had been "grossly exaggerated" by the Democrats, Nixon asserted. Besides, "the economic crisis of 1968 has ruled out any massive new transfusion of Federal funds into programs for the poor." [46]

What then did Nixon have to offer the poor? It was "black capitalism." The federal government, through tax write-offs and other inducements, should encourage the development of locally owned businesses within the ghettos of America. Nixon had not yet worked out many of the details of bringing the benefits of free enterprise to the inner cities, but it was an idea he had adopted enthusiastically, and one that he would stick with.

That theme got a strong enough response for Nixon to reveal another, even broader one. In a May 16 speech entitled "A New Alignment for American Unity," Nixon said there was a "new majority" coming into being. "The new majority is not a grouping of power blocs, but an alliance of ideas. . . . Many of these men and women belong to the same blocs that formed the old coalitions. But now, thinking independently, they have all reached a new conclusion about the direction of our nation." It should be toward decentralization, a decrease in federal power, more local control, more personal freedom.

Nixon singled out one group for special praise: "That is the silent center, the millions of people in the middle of the American political spectrum who do not demonstrate, who do not picket or protest loudly. . . . As this silent center has become a part of the new alignment, it has transformed it from a minority into a majority." [47]

The night before the Oregon primary, Nixon bought two hours of network television time to show clips from his meet-the-people panels and then answer questions called in from around the nation. Julie and Tricia were among the girls taking the phone calls. Former football coach Bud Wilkinson sorted the questions and decided which ones to ask the candidate. The coach openly marveled at Nixon's answers.

As Nixon expected, he won big in Oregon. It was Nixon's 73 percent to Reagan's 23 percent and Rockefeller's 4 percent. On the Democratic side, McCarthy upset Kennedy, 43 percent to 37 percent.

In his victory statement, Nixon declared, "The chances of my now being derailed are pretty well eliminated." That afternoon, he told reporters that he was not going to put pressure on uncommitted or favorite-son delegates. "None of that—'Get aboard, it's now or never.'" But that evening, he told the press, "I expect some phone calls tonight," and said he would tell his callers, "Now is the time to get on the train before it leaves the station." [48]

The next day, Nixon flew to Key Biscayne for rest and strategy sessions. On May 31, it was off to Atlanta for a meeting with his southern supporters. The last threat left to his nomination was a surge from the South for Reagan. Nixon spent the day with Senator Tower, Senator Thurmond (the former Democrat and Dixiecrat who had converted to Republicanism in 1964), and others. Nixon assured them that he would slow the pace of integration, especially by resisting forced busing as a solution to racial segregation in the schools, and that he would not make the South into a whipping boy for national problems. He promised Thurmond he would use tariffs against textile imports to protect South Carolina's mills, and he promised a strong national defense policy. Thurmond was on the Senate Armed Services Committee and had the Charleston Naval Yard in his state; Nixon was telling him what he wanted to hear. [49]

His southern flank secured, Nixon returned to Key Biscayne, where he pondered the meaning of McCarthy's victory in Oregon.

According to the pundits, it meant that Hubert Humphrey, the President's candidate, would win the Democratic nomination.

Nixon mused aloud about the possibilities. "If it's Bobby," he said, "it will be a contest between men and if it's Hubert, a contest between politicians. Bobby and I have been sounding pretty much alike already and we can't hold his feet to the fires of the past.

"But Hubert—Hubert can be portrayed as the helpless captive of the policies of the past." Nixon recalled 1952, when the Republicans jumped on Adlai Stevenson's comment that there was a mess in Washington. "Hubert will have to admit the mess, too. We'll hang that around him hard."[50]

CHAPTER EIGHT

THE NOMINATION
June–August 1968

IN THE PRESIDENTIAL CAMPAIGN of 1968, nothing ever stayed fixed. In January, Nixon assumed that Romney was his chief Republican opponent for the nomination, and that Johnson would be his foe in November. By April, it looked like Rockefeller followed by Mc-Carthy. By the end of May, it looked like Reagan and then Humphrey. But in Atlanta, Nixon had blocked Reagan by reinforcing his southern forces, and by June 4 it looked like Nixon versus whoever won the Democratic primary in California, Kennedy or McCarthy.

Nixon stayed up late in his New York apartment the night of June 4, watching the returns from California with Pat, Tricia, Julie, and David. Kennedy was beating McCarthy, apparently regaining the momentum he had lost in Oregon. As he went to bed, Nixon remarked, "It sure looks like we'll be going against Bobby."

Later, from his bedroom, he heard David calling his name: "Mr. Nixon. Excuse me, sir. Mr. Nixon."

"What is it?" Nixon mumbled.

"They shot Kennedy," David told him.[1]

The next morning, Nixon canceled all activities for two weeks. He went to the Kennedy funeral at St. Patrick's Cathedral; others present included Romney and Rockefeller, Humphrey and Mc-Carthy, Dean Rusk and JCS Chairman Earle Wheeler, and Lyndon Johnson.

Nixon used the time he gained from the general moratorium from politics to get started on the first responsibility he would face once he was nominated, to choose a vice-presidential candidate.

He used the selection process to solidify his support, through the time-tested technique of hinting to the various favorite sons that they were under serious consideration as a running mate. Among those who came to see him, or whom he mentioned as possibilities, were Senator Percy, Governor Romney, Governor Daniel Evans of Washington, Senator Mark Hatfield of Oregon, Governor Ray Shafer of Pennsylvania, Governor Spiro Agnew of Maryland, Governor James Rhodes of Ohio, Mayor John Lindsay of New York City, and Representative George Bush of Texas.[2] Nixon also sent a letter to some three hundred Republican leaders, soliciting their advice on the selection of his running mate.[3]

In late May, Bob Haldeman had joined the staff in New York on a full-time basis, to serve as chief of staff, while Mitchell became full-time campaign manager. Haldeman's new duties created a problem. Haldeman took his job with the utmost seriousness, and he demanded much of people. Extremely good-looking, with a winning smile that he chose to use only on the rarest of occasions, Haldeman had no soft curves; he was all sharp edges and corners. He was rough on his subordinates, but he was devoted to Nixon's interests, if not necessarily to the man himself. Though he was often praised for his efficiency, no one ever thought to praise him for his humanity, and he wanted it that way. His methods helped create a tense, overworked, increasingly cynical staff.[4]

With Haldeman's arrival, the number of staff, and of advisory groups, began to grow. Haldeman brought with him from the J. Walter Thompson advertising firm Dwight Chapin, Larry Higby, and Ron Ziegler, all young, eager, and dedicated. Murray Chotiner came on board to work for Mitchell. Alan Greenspan, an industrial economist, agreed to serve Nixon as his coordinator on domestic policy, and to oversee the work of a forty-man advisory committee on the economy. Richard Allen, a senior staff member at the Hoover Institution on War, Revolution and Peace, took a leave of absence to serve as coordinator of foreign-policy research.[5]

Aside from law and order, black capitalism, and the need to cut back on the Great Society programs, Nixon had had relatively little to say about domestic issues. In June, David Lawrence, publisher of U.S. News & World Report, urged him to come out strong for government reorganization. Nixon sent Maurice Stans a handwritten note: "Possibly the germ of a good idea here? A broad reorganization of the government is needed."[6]

In a statement later in June, Nixon called for a thorough reappraisal and substantial revamping of the federal system to help arrest "the epidemic disorder" in American society. He asserted that the alienation and discontent so widely felt by the American people came in part from a growing sense that "the power to control decisions affecting one's life is vanishing." He wanted the federal government to relinquish some of its power and responsibilities to state and local governments. To that end, he proposed a commission on government reorganization to search out "every feasible means to decentralizing government and getting it close to the people."[7]

Although Nixon's interest in government reorganization had deep roots—he had spent part of his time while Vice-President working on various reorganization proposals—and a viable future, he was much more concerned with who was going to run the government than with how it was organized. But he had to watch, more or less helplessly, as events and personal conflicts from the past combined to rob him, apparently, of one of the highest powers of the Presidency. On June 21, it was revealed that Chief Justice Earl Warren had submitted his resignation to President Johnson.

Warren had never much liked Nixon. Warren thought, with reason, that in 1952 Nixon had stolen the California delegation to the Republican Convention from him, thereby giving the nomination to Ike and depriving Warren of his chance.

By 1968, Nixon had become almost as critical of the Warren Court as he was of the Johnson Administration. He was promising, as President, to appoint judges who would reverse some of the basic decisions of the past fifteen years. When Warren resigned, reports spread quickly that he had chosen this moment to do so because he feared that Nixon would win in November and eventually have the opportunity to appoint Warren's successor. Nixon told Klein that he looked on Warren's timing as being vindictive because of the Chief Justice's known dislike for him.[8]

Other Republicans were indignant. Senators Robert Griffin of Michigan and John Tower of Texas vowed that they would fight any effort by Johnson to name a new Chief Justice in the fading months of his term.[9] Nixon, flying to Lansing, Michigan, on June 26, told reporters on the plane that because of the Court's "transcendent importance, a new President with a fresh mandate" should appoint Warren's successor.

But when Nixon got off the plane, he learned that Johnson had already announced his selection of Associate Justice Abe Fortas for the post of Chief Justice. Although Fortas was a Democrat from Tennessee and a Johnson crony, and although he was Jewish, he was a man Nixon had praised privately and publicly on several occasions. Nixon did not attack the appointment, although he did tell reporters at the airport that "I felt that it would have been wise for the President to have delayed the appointment . . . until the new President had been elected." [10]

THE POLLS, at the beginning of summer, were volatile. First McCarthy ran ahead of either Nixon or Rockefeller, then Humphrey took the lead, then Nixon drew even, then he fell back, as the lead changed daily. Rockefeller, whose only hope was to bamboozle the Republican delegates into thinking that he could lick Humphrey or McCarthy and Nixon could not, unleashed a $5 million advertising campaign, with full-page insertions in the forty-one largest newspapers in the country, citing polls (paid for by Rockefeller) that showed Rockefeller defeating Humphrey or McCarthy, and Nixon losing to both. Rockefeller challenged Nixon to a debate. He accused Nixon of hiding, of being coy at a time when forthrightness was critical. Nixon, wisely and coolly, ignored him. [11]

Nixon still wanted Eisenhower's preconvention endorsement. To get it he had Bryce Harlow, a former White House aide to the general and now working for Nixon, and a man the general liked very much, write to Ike to urge him to announce his support for Nixon.

No reply was forthcoming.

Nixon then persuaded Admiral Lewis Strauss, an old friend of Ike's, to go to Gettysburg to solicit an endorsement. Eisenhower had been having more heart problems, so Nixon told Strauss to get the endorsement before the old man died. Strauss tried, without success. A week or so later, Ike had his fifth heart attack.

On July 15, Nixon went to Walter Reed Hospital in Washington, where Eisenhower was recuperating, to solicit directly. The seventy-seven-year-old Eisenhower was little more than skin and bones by now, and tired easily. Nixon knew his time was short, so he got right to the point.

Eisenhower immediately put his mind at rest: "Dick, I don't want there to be any more question about this. You're my choice, period." [12]

Ike promised that he would call in the press and make a public endorsement on the opening day of the convention, Monday, August 5. Nixon thanked him, and left.

So there it was, finally, after all those years, a preconvention endorsement. But would it be too late to help? Nixon's mind raced through a possible sequence of events, and he started to worry. What if, he wondered, Eisenhower's announcement were preceded by preconvention endorsements from favorite-son candidates, coming in such numbers as to guarantee Nixon's nomination on the first ballot? What if Ike died before giving the endorsement?

Nixon fretted over the problem. Having finally received Ike's blessing, he naturally wanted to get the most out of it that he could. That meant he would have to go back to Eisenhower, hat in hand, one more time.

He did. A few hours after his meeting at Walter Reed with Eisenhower, Nixon wrote him a long letter. He said Governors Agnew and Rhodes and Senator Percy might all publicly endorse him the week before the convention. Thus, "we face the distinct possibility that in the public mind the decision would have been made before your endorsement was announced." These possibilities, Nixon said, "bear on the critical question of the timing of your announcement and the relationship of that timing to the effect your announcement will have on the voters in November."[13]

Thus prodded, Eisenhower moved quickly. A day after reading Nixon's plea, Ike called in the cameras and reporters. Dressed in a bathrobe, seated in a wheelchair, painfully thin, intense and serious, he read a statement in a low voice. He said he was supporting Dick Nixon for President, and cited as his principal reason "my admiration of his personal qualities: his intellect, acuity, decisiveness, warmth, and above all, his integrity."

When he finished, the old general took a few questions from the half-dozen reporters allowed into his room. In response to one, he said he hoped he had laid to rest the persistent speculation that he had never particularly admired Nixon. "This is a mere misapprehension. I just want the country to know that I have admired and respected this man and liked the man ever since I met him in 1952."

A newsman asked whether his grandson, David, and Julie Nixon had influenced his decision. Ike flashed his world-famous grin. "I think," he said with a twinkle in his eye, "they tried to."

Whatever his motivation, his pronouncement was a warm, generous, fulsome tribute to Nixon's character. Nixon, obviously elated, told reporters the Eisenhower endorsement would give his preconvention drive a "great lift."[14]

DESPITE THE straightforwardness of Eisenhower's praise, he had failed to dispel the misapprehension. Twenty years later, people were still asking, What did Ike really think of Nixon?

His thoughts were complex and ambivalent. How could they have been otherwise?

Leaving aside their personal relationship, was Nixon really Eisenhower's choice for the Presidency in 1960 and in 1968, or would he have picked someone else had events not forced his hand? The answer is both no and yes. There were a half-dozen men Eisenhower thought more qualified for the Presidency than Nixon, but none of them had any chance of winning a Republican Party nomination, and from among the real choices Nixon was far and away Eisenhower's first choice.

Did Eisenhower believe that Nixon was qualified to be President (as opposed to "more qualified")? The answer is no, but to it one must immediately add that Eisenhower did not believe that *anybody* except himself was so qualified. The real question should be, Was Eisenhower prepared to turn over the governmental affairs of the country he loved and had served all his life to Richard Nixon? Here the answer is a resounding yes.

Eisenhower demonstrated this truth in a most dramatic fashion in 1956. He had agreed to run for re-election, despite a heart attack in 1955. There was a real possibility that he would not survive a second term; if he died or were incapacitated, his running mate would replace him as the nation's leader. His own popularity was immense, to the point that it hardly mattered, from the standpoint of the election, whom he chose as Vice-President. He would have won with Harold Stassen. Indeed, the polls in the spring of 1956 showed that the only Republican who would cost him votes was Nixon.

Still Eisenhower chose Nixon. It was the ultimate endorsement, the symbolic anointing of his successor, the final answer to the question, What did Ike really think of Nixon?

BY THE TIME Nixon received that long-sought Eisenhower endorsement, he didn't really need it. The Nixon campaign had become a juggernaut. Rockefeller was still putting millions of his own dollars into newspaper advertisements, and Reagan was on a heavily scheduled cross-country speaking tour, but no matter—the Nixon campaign, reflecting the ruthless efficiency of Mitchell and Haldeman, was unstoppable. Every delegate had been contacted, Nixon had wooed state party leaders and congressional delegations, nothing had been left to chance.

So, on the day Ike made his announcement, Nixon got to work on selecting his running mate. He dined that evening in Annapolis with John Mitchell and Governor Spiro Agnew.

Both Nixon and Mitchell were impressed; Nixon later said he admired the governor's "inner strength." [15] But Agnew's real appeal to Mitchell and Nixon lay in his recent actions. Elected in 1966 as a moderate Republican, he had been a leading Rockefeller supporter. Although he was hardly a national figure, Agnew had managed to seize a moment on the national stage in the aftermath of King's assassination.

When rioting broke out in Baltimore, Agnew had called the black leadership of the city to a conference in Annapolis. About one hundred came, ministers and lawyers and politicians and others, expecting the governor to ask their help in working together to save the inner city.

To their astonishment, Agnew had blamed them for the riots. They had listened aghast as the governor called them "circuit-riding, Hanoi-visiting . . . caterwauling, riot-inciting, burn-America-down type of leader[s]," and accused them of "breaking and running" when they should have been on the streets stopping the riots. Eighty of the black leaders walked out.[16]

Buchanan thought Agnew's harangue was right on the mark, and he made sure that Nixon heard about it, in detail. Nixon listened, and said, "That guy Agnew is really an impressive fellow. He's got guts. He's got a good attitude."[17]

Agnew also appealed to Nixon because, like Nixon, he had risen from humble beginnings: son of a Greek immigrant, hard times in the Depression, diligent law student, company commander in Europe in World War II, hardworking insurance claims adjuster, manager of a chain of food stores, trial lawyer, Baltimore county executive, Kiwanian, Legionnaire, governor.

At the dinner in Annapolis, Mitchell asked Agnew if he would place Nixon's name in nomination at the convention, with the implication that if he did a good job he would be considered seriously for the vice-presidential spot. Agnew accepted. After they left, Mitchell and Nixon conferred and agreed that Agnew would make an excellent running mate.[18]

About this time, Nixon told Haldeman, among others, that no one could add any strength to his ticket, and that he would have to make his final choice on a defensive basis: Who would cost him the least?[19] Nixon told another aide, "The Vice President can't help you. He can only hurt you." A third aide expressed the sentiment in the Nixon camp: "Actually, we wanted to run without a Vice President."[20]

Nixon was far too intelligent to believe this nonsense. He knew perfectly well that Agnew could bring in voters whom he could not attract himself. Thanks to Maryland's permanent status of geographical confusion—Is Baltimore a southern city or an eastern city?—Agnew was acceptable in both the South and the East. Much more important, Agnew's tough talk to the black leaders and his tough response to the Baltimore riots made him the ideal foil for warding off the danger on Nixon's right, the Wallace campaign.

Nixon never mentioned Wallace, but he could never stop thinking about Wallace's campaign, which was eliciting an extraordinary response from voters across the nation, most especially in the border states and in the South.

Nixon's southern regional campaign director was Howard Callaway, a textile manufacturer who had nearly beaten Lester Maddox in 1966 in the race for governor of Georgia. Herb Klein said Callaway "exemplified to us the new spirit of Republicanism in the South." He exemplified it a bit too well. In Jackson, Mississippi, Callaway said, "Perhaps we can get George Wallace on our side. That's where he belongs."

Rockefeller jumped on that one. He cited Nixon's support from Senators Thurmond and Tower, said that there were racist overtones in the Nixon campaign, and implied that Callaway was right, that there was little or no difference between Nixon's views and those of Wallace.

Nixon managed the affair adroitly: he repudiated Callaway's statement but not Callaway. Nixon told the press he had been "in politics for 22 years and never had a racist in my organization, and I don't have any now." He said the Wallace appeal was "in the direction of the racist element . . . such an appeal wouldn't be made by either of the two national parties. We will be able to present the American people a choice, but we will not divide the country on a race basis."

Then he explained that Callaway meant a vote for Wallace would be wasted and might help a liberal Democrat win. As the election drew near, Wallace voters would realize that truth and come over to Nixon.[21]

There was a multitude of Wallace voters. The July polls indicated that no matter who ran for the major parties, George Wallace was going to get 20 percent of the vote.[22]

The persistence of Wallace's strength would make the contest for the Wallace vote one of the chief battles in the November election. Nixon had to win a substantial portion of it to have any chance at victory, as he was running five points behind Humphrey (35 percent to 40 percent) and four points behind McCarthy in the polls.[23]

There was more to the Wallace phenomenon than racism. Wallace had a slogan—"Send Them a Message"—that seemed to sum up perfectly the sentiments of his supporters, and was even catchier than "Nixon's the One." And Wallace's quip that there wasn't a dime's worth of difference between the Republicans and the Democrats was another dandy. That one hurt Nixon more than Humphrey, because it denied that Nixon's election would bring any change in Washington.

Change was what Wallace's supporters wanted. They resented

deeply what had happened in Washington the past seven years, they hated the civil rights acts of the mid-sixties, and they hated even more the actions of the federal government in enforcing those laws. They envied the apparent success of many blacks that resulted from that enforcement, success that had been achieved, so far as they could tell, at their expense.

The nightly television news brought into their living rooms scenes of pampered college students at expensive, elite universities occupying the administration buildings, acting like crazed anarchists, followed by scenes of black Americans looting and burning in riots across the land. The same TV program then showed them their sons, husbands, lovers, and brothers walking the point through the rice paddies of South Vietnam, followed by close-ups of New Left longhairs burning the American flag.

No wonder their indignation had passed the boiling point. Anger, a terrible, red-hot anger, was the result. And that anger led to fear—a fear that the government was going to continue to grow, to meddle, to dictate, to force a social and economic revolution, all at their expense.

Who better than Nixon to appeal to resentment and fear? They had been his stock-in-trade for twenty-two years.

But politics is never simple. Nixon's critics, led by Rockefeller, charged that Nixon's increasing emphasis on law and order was a subtle appeal to the racist vote. That may have been true, but it was equally true that to millions of Americans, by no means all racists, law and order was a legitimate issue, and Nixon was saying what they wanted to hear.

Further, by no means would Nixon get all the Wallace votes if the former governor dropped out or if his supporters were persuaded that they would throw away their vote if they gave it to Wallace. A majority of Wallace's southern supporters had voted Democrat or Dixiecrat all their lives, and were as likely to go to Humphrey as to Nixon. Up north, too, most Wallace voters were lifelong Democrats. If they did not vote for Wallace, they were more likely to go home to Humphrey than off the reservation with Nixon.

So, for Nixon, although it really was impossible to say for certain, it was probably better if Wallace stayed in the race. In any event, there was little Nixon could do about Wallace's decision to run. What he could do was chip away at Wallace's strength by emphasizing law and order, hoping that those voters who abandoned Wallace would come to him.

On the Democratic side, meanwhile, RFK's troops had thrown their support to Senator George McGovern of South Dakota, rather than to Gene McCarthy, meaning that the Democratic Left was as divided as its Right. The antiwar liberals were furious with Humphrey; they were taunting and heckling him at his rallies.

ON JULY 21, with the Republican Convention only two weeks away, Nixon showed how confident he was of winning the nomination by disappearing from public view. He flew out to Los Angeles and stayed in a private oceanside home at Newport Beach. Haldeman told the press he was working on his acceptance speech. He was really working on the Vietnam plank for the Republican platform.

It was a complex and divisive subject. Nixon had so far managed to hide behind Johnson, continuing to say that he did not want to undermine the Paris peace talks by "sniping from the sidelines" or by doing anything to give the North Vietnamese the impression that a new President would "give them a better deal." But the Republicans were clearly going to have to say something specific in their platform about Vietnam, the central issue in the campaign, and it had to come from the candidate himself. Nixon would have to say whether he planned to end the war by winning it or by withdrawing.

On July 26, Nixon flew to Washington, at the President's request, for a briefing on Vietnam from Johnson, Rusk, and Walt Rostow. Johnson said he would not stop the bombing north of the DMZ until Hanoi agreed to accept the South Vietnamese at the peace table, and made other concessions; Rusk said that all of Asia would be in a "panic" if the United States withdrew from Vietnam without an honorable peace settlement; Rostow said China would "dominate Asia if the United States pulled out." [24] Johnson spoke bitterly about North Vietnam's refusal to respond to earlier bombing halts, and assured Nixon that he planned no halt at that time. He would continue to bomb until the Communists agreed to "reasonable terms."

Nixon promised Johnson he would continue to support his goals, although he would be critical of tactics. "I also pledged," Nixon recorded in his memoirs, "not to undercut our negotiating position just in case the Communists came around and agreed to the conditions Johnson would insist upon in return for a bombing halt." [25]

From Washington, Nixon flew on to New York, then drove out to the eastern tip of Long Island, where he sequestered himself in a five-room cottage at Montauk Point. There he went to work on his legal pads, creating a Republican platform. On his walks along the beach, he thought about his acceptance speech. Most of it he already had in hand—like many of his predecessors, he planned to use the punch lines that got the most response in his earlier campaign speeches. But he wanted an ending that would uplift and inspire, and be fresh and new. With Price's help, the ending began to take form.

While Nixon secluded himself at Montauk Point, Rockefeller and Reagan managed to create some anxiety and thus provide some badly needed suspense to the convention. Rumors ran rampant—Reagan was supposed to have swayed this or that southern delegation, Rockefeller to have hidden strength here and there. Senator Percy, to Nixon's surprise, endorsed Rockefeller.

Nixon stayed on Long Island. He relied on Mitchell and Mitchell's political staff to keep his delegates in line. Meanwhile Price told reporters that Nixon was devoting his time to his acceptance speech, which was described as "the most important address of his life." [26]

On August 3, Nixon sent down to the GOP platform panel in Miami his proposed planks on violence at home, and on Vietnam. He said that the chief deterrent to crime was respect for law and the rights of others. "But when the homes and schools and churches of a free society fail in their role as commissioned watchmen of those standards," he continued, "then the people must fall back for their safety upon police and prosecutors and courts." He pronounced this "the last line of defense of a free people."

His Vietnam statement was much longer and far more complex. "The war must be ended," he declared flatly at the outset, and for the first time in years he did not refer to Vietnam as "essential" or "vital" to America's strategic interests. He expressed himself as ready to seek a "negotiated settlement." But, he warned, "it must be ended honorably, consistent with America's limited aims and with the long-term requirements of peace in Asia."

Until that honorable peace could be found, Nixon insisted that the war "must be waged more effectively." Not through an escalation on the military front, but through "a dramatic escalation of our efforts on the economic, political, diplomatic and psychological fronts." This required a new strategy, one that recognized that Vietnam was a new kind of war. It "requires a fuller enlistment of our Vietnamese allies in their own defense."

Without mentioning his own advocacy of more American military pressure over the past four years, Nixon dealt with it and explained his changed position: "The swift, overwhelming blow that would have been decisive two or three years ago is no longer possible today." Johnson had "done far too little, too late, to train and equip the South Vietnamese." Johnson had also "failed in candor at home and in leadership abroad." Nixon refused to make specific comments on the Paris peace talks, because American negotiators "should be free from partisan interference. . . . The pursuit of peace is too important for politics as usual."

Nixon was more specific on how he would wage the war while waiting for the enemy to agree to an honorable peace. He proposed to greatly expand the arming and training of ARVN troops. "As they are phased in," Nixon said, "American troops can—and should be —phased out. This phasing-out will save American lives and cut American costs."[27]

That was a fairly clear and relatively accurate description of what the platform committee called "a progressive de-Americanization of the war." It contained no details as to how Nixon proposed to convince Hanoi to abandon its goals while the Americans retreated, and it hardly differed from the policies Johnson had put into effect on March 31, but it was Nixon's plan "to end the war and win the peace," finally revealed.

In seeking peace, Nixon said the U.S. should enter into "searching conversations" with the Soviet Union, and pointed out that "Vietnam does not exist in isolation." In a press conference a few days later, he expounded on that theme. He said he had "revised" some of his views on Communism, not because he had changed, but because the Communist world had changed. In 1960, Nixon said, "the Communist world was a monolithic world. Today it is a split world, schizophrenic, with very great diversity." Therefore, the "era of confrontation" had ended; as President, he would replace it with a "new era of negotiations."

Nixon was almost calling for an end to the Cold War, and was taking risks in doing so, because if either the right-wing Republicans or the Wallace voters paid attention, it would cost him votes. What he was saying was not at all what they wanted to hear about the Communist enemy.

He said it anyway, and although the press did not pick up on the significance of his statement, and although three years later almost everyone was astonished when he announced that he was going to China, he could not have been clearer. "Whoever is President," he said, "whether it is President Johnson or Humphrey or Nixon, whoever is President in the next four years must proceed on the assumption that negotiations with the leaders of the Soviet world, negotiations eventually with the leaders of the next superpower, Communist China, must take place."

But as with Nixon's statement to Teddy White that his first act as President would be to open up to Red China, this one went relatively unnoticed. What did attract attention was Nixon's position on the controversy putting the Paris peace talks on hold, the demand of the National Liberation Front (NLF, the political arm of the Vietcong) for a place at the peace table, matched by a demand from the United States for a place for the Saigon government. "I will only say," Nixon declared, "that I believe the negotiating table must be big enough and the issues broad enough so that we can reach a negotiated settlement of the war on an honorable basis."

He matched that hint to the doves with a promise to the hawks, that the war was still "winnable" in the sense of achieving an honorable settlement: "I should state further that I certainly do not seek the Presidency for the purpose of presiding over the destruction of the credibility of the American power throughout the world."[28]

To no one's surprise, on August 5 Reagan flew into Miami to announce that he had dropped his favorite-son status to become an avowed contender for the nomination. Playing the role of drafted candidate, Reagan summoned up all his onstage shyness as he professed to have been bowled over by the spontaneous and unsolicited support he had received.

Some of Nixon's supporters were fearful that Reagan would steal the South at the last minute, and grumbled that Nixon's absence at a time when he should have been leading the fight might cost him the nomination.

Nixon stayed calm. When he arrived in Miami later that day, he was smiling and confident, and the confidence was justified. The Nixon juggernaut was functioning smoothly. Richard Kleindienst, a former chief strategist for Goldwater, who had joined the Nixon forces as field coordinator, together with Mitchell, Haldeman, and the others were holding the line.

When Nixon got to his penthouse suite in the Hilton Plaza Hotel, he called Mitchell.

"John, what's the count?" he asked.

Mitchell chuckled and replied, "I told you you didn't need to worry, Dick. We've got everything under control."[29]

Nixon spent the next day visiting various delegations, especially southern ones. The Miami *Herald* planted a tape recorder in one caucus room, and later printed parts of the transcript. The secret recording was relatively harmless, as Nixon told the southern delegates in private what he had already said in public, that he would not pick as a running mate anyone who "is going to divide this party," meaning he would not pick Lindsay or Rockefeller. Asked if he favored busing for the sole purpose of racial integration, he said, "I think that busing the child . . . into a strange community —I think you destroy that child. The purpose of a school is to educate." On the Supreme Court and civil rights, he used one of his favorite lines: "I think it is the job of the courts to interpret the law and not make the law."[30]

Meanwhile, Strom Thurmond met with other southern delegates to assure them that Nixon "will not ram anything down our throats," again meaning that the vice-presidential candidate would not be a northern liberal.

On August 7, Pat, Tricia and her boyfriend, Ed Cox, Julie and David, Rose Woods, Haldeman, Pat Buchanan, Dwight Chapin, Ray Price, and Len Garment joined Nixon in his suite to watch the nominating speeches. Agnew, placing Nixon's name in nomination, looked terrific. Big, square-shouldered and square-jawed, he exuded strength and sincerity. His powerful voice added to the positive impression.

What he said was less impressive. He got off to a good enough start, but, in a convoluted concluding passage, ended with a dangling climax. "When a nation is in crisis and history speaks firmly to that nation," Agnew said, "it needs a man to match the time. You don't create such a man; you don't discover such a man—you recognize such a man."[31]

Shortly after midnight, the roll call of the states began. Nixon agreed to allow a CBS film crew into his suite to record the moment for posterity. (The footage was later presented on the very first showing of a television program that became hugely successful, "60 Minutes.") Nixon sat alone in the center of the room, watching the television set. The others were on the sofas, around and behind him. He kept score on a yellow legal pad, with running commentary to David.

The voting proceeded smoothly. The South stayed with Nixon. Wisconsin put him over the top. Pat rose from the sofa behind her husband, walked over to him, patted him on the shoulder two or three times, and walked off.

The telephone rang. It was Nelson Rockefeller, to congratulate him. "You're good to call," Nixon said.

When he hung up, Nixon told his entourage it was "nice of him to call. . . . He couldn't have been nicer. . . . He said he gave me a good run. . . . He said Ron [Reagan] didn't come through as good as he thought he would." Nixon allowed himself a little shiver of delight. He lifted his eyes to the ceiling, brought them down, and broke into a mischievous grin.[32]

WELL MIGHT he grin. He had climbed back from the political depths to achieve once again his personal pinnacle, Republican nominee for the Presidency.

Nixon, like the nation, had changed considerably since his nomination in 1960. For Nixon, on the positive side, it had been a time of growth. His foreign travels in the fifties, when he was Vice-President, had been long on drama and short on learning; his foreign travels in the sixties, when he was out of office, were the opposite. So he knew more in 1968 than he did in 1960.

And he thought about it harder. In 1960, he had vied with Jack Kennedy for the title of the nation's number-one anti-Communist. In his acceptance speech in 1960, he had vowed eternal resistance to the Communist threat; in 1968, he told reporters when he arrived in Miami that his 1960 acceptance speech would be "irrelevant to the problems of 1968."

"As the facts change," Nixon explained, "any intelligent man does change his approaches to the problems. It does not mean that he is an opportunist. It means only that he is a pragmatist." [33]

By 1968, Nixon was a supreme pragmatist. His thinking on America's position in the world was more sophisticated than it had been, and more sophisticated than that of any of his rivals. Nixon saw the broader significance of the Vietnam War, the rise of modern China, the Soviet achievement of nuclear equality, and the emergence of an industrialized Asia clearly and realistically. He struggled with the implications, with how these events related, what they meant for America. His response was bold, imaginative, and sensible.

It was called détente.

Détente, not just with the Soviets, but with the Chinese as well. Nixon had decided that as President he would have to turn American foreign policy away from the knee-jerk anti-Communism of the forties, fifties, and sixties. He would replace confrontation with détente.

The details of Nixon's détente will appear in their appropriate places in the following chapters. The point to stress here is that Nixon went into the general election campaign with a world view in place. He knew what he wanted to do. [34]

He was perfectly clear about it—he was going to launch a "new era of negotiations" with the Russians and the Chinese.

In sum, Nixon in 1968 was far more capable of taking command of America's foreign policy than he had been in 1960.

On the domestic side, Nixon was in a better position in 1968 than he had been in 1960. Then he had been forced to defend a record when the general sentiment was for change. In 1968, he could attack a record when there was overwhelming demand for change. In 1960, the issues had been unemployment, recession, and civil rights. In 1968, they were crime, inflation, and civil rights.

What linked the two elections was Nixon's relative indifference in both to domestic affairs (save crime, where his indignation was very great). His view, often expressed, was that the Cabinet could run the country on the domestic side. The President's job was to take charge in foreign affairs.

What was most different in 1968 was the staff. The dominant insiders were new men, Mitchell, Haldeman, and, increasingly, Ehrlichman. They made a disparate trio; what they had in common was fierce, unquestioning loyalty to Nixon, and the fact that not one of them had ever stood for elective office or ever engaged in the give-and-take of legislative activity. They all were cynics who ascribed to their political enemies the worst imaginable motives. The lesser members of the 1968 staff could be characterized as young, inexperienced, energetic, and ruthless.

From top to bottom, the staff consisted of men who were vindictive. For Nixon, this was highly dangerous, because he was also a vindictive man, with a long memory and a deep capacity to hate. By surrounding himself with vindictive types, Nixon encouraged in himself one of his worst and most self-harmful characteristics.

In addition, a great deal had happened to him since 1960 to encourage his vindictiveness. The Kennedy Administration had harassed him with an extensive IRS audit, and with an investigation into the Hughes loan to Donald Nixon, an investigation whose purpose was to indict Nixon. Nixon believed his own phone had been tapped, and he knew that the Kennedy Administration had wiretapped and otherwise illegally spied on and harassed its perceived enemies, including Otto Otepka, Victor Lasky, Drew Middleton, and Martin Luther King, Jr. The Johnson Administration was equally ruthless and lawless in dealing with its enemies.

Rather than abhorring their methods, Nixon appreciated the precedent, and could hardly wait until he got his hands on the power to go after his political enemies in the same way.

IN MIAMI, it was time for the newly nominated candidate to go to work on selecting a running mate to help him get that power. Nixon spent what remained of the nomination night and a good part of the next morning in a series of meetings with various staff and politicians, trying to form a consensus. Eight years earlier, Nixon had made a bad mistake when he chose Henry Cabot Lodge, Jr. Already trailing Humphrey in polls, he could not afford to make a mistake at this time.

Whether he already had his mind made up on his choice is impossible to say. In all his meetings, he was the only one to bring up Agnew's name as a possibility. Agnew was Mitchell's first, second, and last choice, but no one else wanted him. Agnew was hardly known nationally, had never held a federal post, had less than two years' experience in Annapolis, came from a small state, and was not terribly smart. Still, Nixon liked him.

Nevertheless, in the course of the discussion, Nixon offered the nomination to someone else. Whether he meant it or not, whether he anticipated a refusal or not, cannot be said. But he did make the offer, to Bob Finch.

Finch was one of his oldest political friends, and one of the very few politicians who was close to Nixon personally; indeed, Finch was sometimes described as "almost a son" to Nixon.

Nixon made the offer toward the end of his last meeting. "Well," he asked no one in particular, "who should I take?"

"I think it should be Finch," one of his aides replied. "You know him, you know you can trust him, you know he can handle himself."

But Mitchell cut in. "You can't do it," he said. "It's nepotism." (He meant cronyism.)[35]

Nixon asked to talk to Finch alone. Finch then made a series of points that could hardly have been overlooked by Nixon: that the jump from lieutenant governor to Vice-President was too big, too soon; that Mitchell was right to fear charges of cronyism; that he and Reagan were rivals in California, so his nomination would irritate Reagan's people.

Nixon persisted. He said Finch had "youth and freshness, and . . . would have great appeal to the party and to independent voters."

Nixon sounded persuasive, and eager to have Finch. But Finch turned him down. Finch had a large and growing family, ranging from three young girls to a high-school-age boy. Already he was bothered by the taunts his kids were getting from antiwar students in school. He knew what was involved in a national campaign; he understood the price his family would have to pay. He said no.[36]

It was one of those innumerable "what if" turning points in Richard Nixon's life. What if Finch had said yes? It certainly would have made a difference in the campaign, and, assuming that the Nixon/Finch ticket won, in the ensuing Administration.

Big, sandy-haired, casual and relaxed, good-looking and easygoing, Finch was the opposite of Agnew. Finch's instinct was to bring people together, not drive them apart. Finch's method of operation was to study a problem thoroughly before speaking on it, not shoot from the hip. Finch had a broad sense of humor and often laughed at himself. Finch distrusted ideology; he was a pragmatist who sought progress through compromise and negotiation. Finch combined a warm human sympathy with a basic common sense. And the biggest differences of all between Finch and Agnew were these: Finch was sensitive to the feelings of others and not at all vindictive.

Aside from these personality differences, there was another important one: Nixon liked and trusted Finch, and would listen to him. Not necessarily respond, but at least listen.

But Finch said no, so there is no point in speculating on what if he had said yes. All we can be sure of is that things would have been different had Finch instead of Agnew been Nixon's Vice-President.

When Nixon emerged from his meeting with Finch, he consulted with Mitchell, then told Congressman Rogers Morton of Maryland to call Agnew and inform him that he had been picked as the running mate. Astonishingly, in view of Nixon's troubles with his "secret fund" when he became the Republican vice-presidential nominee in 1952, Nixon did not ask Agnew any questions about his finances, or whether he had any skeletons in his closet. Nor did Nixon make any attempt to conduct a private investigation of Agnew's actions as governor of Maryland (when he had been taking bribes on a regular basis).

Nixon went down to the ballroom at about 1 P.M., August 8, to make his announcement. When he said his choice was "Governor Agnew of Maryland," there were gasps of incredulity. Immediately, there were cries of "Spiro who?" Nixon strode out without taking any questions.

Nixon may have hoped that his choice would be seen as a moderate one; if so, the press reaction was discouraging. When Agnew appeared at the microphone, the press bombarded him with questions about his recent hard-line tactics in the Baltimore riots. Most interpreted his selection as a sop to the South, a view reinforced by some Agnew remarks about law and order.

"The name of Spiro Agnew," he readily acknowledged, "is not a household name. I certainly hope that it will become one within the next couple of months."[37]

It hardly took that long. Republican liberals revolted, creating the first Agnew controversy. They did not want Agnew and decided to challenge Nixon's choice on the floor of the convention. Mayor Lindsay agreed to place George Romney's name in nomination.

The revolt made Nixon angry. He asked Mitchell for suggestions on what to do to crush it.

"Ah, screw 'em, Dick," Mitchell replied. "It'll blow over."

Nixon shook his head. "I'm not going to stand for this kind of revolt," he said. "If the sore losers get away with something like this now, they'll do the same damn thing during my Presidency."

Saying it was "a test of my leadership," he instructed Mitchell to go to work to keep the Romney vote as low as possible. In the roll-call vote that afternoon, Agnew got 1,128 votes to Romney's 186.[38]

At 11 P.M., August 8, Nixon appeared before the convention to accept the nomination. As wave after wave of wild applause broke over him, he lifted and spread his arms. His smile lit the place up, and the roar became deafening.

When he could finally speak, Nixon began with a reference to his nomination in 1960. He said the difference this time was "We're going to win." Pandemonium.

Growing serious, dropping his voice, Nixon cited a personal reason: "General Eisenhower, as you know, lies critically ill in the Walter Reed Hospital tonight. I have talked, however, with Mrs. Eisenhower on the telephone.

"She tells me that his heart is with us. She says that there is nothing that he lives more for, and there is nothing that would lift him more than for us to win in November.

"And I say let's win this one for Ike." Double pandemonium. Tears dropping down the faces of strong men, flowing down the faces of deeply moved women.

Nixon followed with the revised version of his basic campaign speech. He would make ending the war in Vietnam his first order of business. He would offer the hand of friendship to the nation's Cold War adversaries. "After an era of confrontation the time has come for an era of negotiations with the leaders of Communist China and the Soviet Union." He stressed law and order. He mentioned black capitalism. He supported civil rights but opposed busing. He used his "it's time for change" paragraph exactly as he had first delivered it in New Hampshire, and many times since.

As he moved toward his climax, he became more and more original. This was fresh, new material, the fruits of his labors on the seaside in California and Montauk Point.

"Tonight, I see the face of a child," he said. The child was black, white, Mexican, Italian, Polish. He lived in a great city. He was a poet, or a scientist, a teacher or craftsman. "He is America." He dreamed the dreams of a child, but when he awoke, it was "to a living nightmare of poverty, neglect, and despair." The child failed in school, ended up on welfare. "For him the American system is one that feeds his stomach and starves his soul. It breaks his heart."

Fortunately, that was only one part of what Nixon saw in America. "I see another child tonight. He hears a train go by at night and he dreams of far away places where he'd like to go. It seems like an impossible dream.

"But he is helped on his journey through life. A father who

had to go to work before he finished the sixth grade, sacrificed everything he had so that his sons could go to college. A gentle, Quaker mother, with a passionate concern for peace, quietly wept when he went to war but she understood why he had to go."

Nixon went on to mention his teacher, his football coach, his minister, his wife, and his children—all had helped him on his way. "And tonight he stands before you—nominated for President of the United States of America."

So, Nixon explained, "You can see why I believe so deeply in the American dream." He asked the delegates to "help me make that dream come true for millions to whom it's an impossible dream today. . . .

"My fellow Americans," Nixon concluded, "the dark long night for America is about to end.

"The time has come for us to leave the valley of despair and climb the mountain so that we may see the glory of the dawn of a new day for peace and freedom to the world." [39]

CHAPTER NINE

THE NINTH CAMPAIGN

PART ONE
August 9–October 14, 1968

THE MIAMI CONVENTION had been a great success for Nixon. He had won the nomination and in the process broadened his appeal to conservative Democrats and independents. Polls taken a few days before the convention had shown him slightly ahead of Humphrey for the first time (40 percent for Nixon, 38 percent for Humphrey, 16 percent for Wallace, 6 percent undecided). The Gallup poll taken after the Republican and before the Democratic Convention gave Nixon 45 percent to 29 percent for Humphrey and 18 percent for Wallace.[1]

A sixteen-point lead was twelve or more points better than Nixon had ever done in a national poll, and was certainly confidence-inspiring. Still, Nixon did have some immediate problems, of which the chief was the reaction to his selection of Agnew as his running mate. There was an outcry from the liberals so great that Agnew, the day after the convention, felt compelled to deny that he was a bigot, and Nixon was forced to spend most of his time at his first news conference as the Republican candidate defending his running mate.

Agnew, according to Nixon, had poise under pressure. "When it comes to carrying the attack and resisting the attack," Nixon went on, "he's got it. You can look him in the eye and you know that this guy has got it."[2]

Whatever it was that Agnew had, from that moment on, until election night, Nixon almost never again mentioned his name in public. He appeared with Agnew only once. That did not necessarily mean that he thought he had made a mistake, or that Agnew was

177

a liability, although others quickly jumped to that conclusion. James Reston, for example, wrote that "by this single decision [picking Agnew] Nixon chose to go with the conservative minority of the country and defy the liberal majority, and in the process helped reunite the Democrats and divide the Republicans."

Nixon did not agree that the majority was liberal; as he said in his press conference in Miami, he intended to put together a "new coalition" composed of traditional Republicans, the New South, black militants (sic), new liberals, and the silent millions in the middle of the political spectrum. What united this odd collection of "strange bedfellows," Nixon explained to the reporters, was that "they are all unhappy about something, all protesting against centralized government, and all calling for greater individual freedom."[3]

Put another way, Nixon wanted everyone who was unhappy to vote Nixon/Agnew; his assumption was that there were more unhappy people than the other way around. It was the politics of resentment and outrage, which made good sense in a year in which there was plenty to resent and much to be outraged about.

Following the press conference, Nixon flew to California for strategy sessions and a rest. Along the way he stopped in at the LBJ Ranch in the Texas hill country for a pro forma briefing from the President, the Secretary of State, and the head of the CIA (Richard Helms). Nixon wanted to pacify Johnson, to keep him on the sidelines, so the first thing he told the President was "I am not going to undercut the [Paris] negotiations."

Johnson assured Nixon once again that he would not halt the bombing north of the DMZ until Hanoi made concessions. At the end of the briefing, Nixon made informal remarks to the press: "The President should have the respect of all American citizens, and I will do nothing to destroy that respect." He thought the first priority of the Vietnam War was not to stop the bombing, as the doves were insisting, but "to stop the killing of American boys."

Johnson took Nixon for a tour of the ranch, then drove him to the helicopter pad. As Nixon climbed aboard the helicopter, Johnson's dog Yuki darted between his legs and into the cabin. Johnson shouted, "Dick, here you've got my helicopter, you're after my job, and now you're gonna take my dog."

Nixon laughed and replied that Johnson could have the dog back, as two out of three was enough.[4]

IN THE United States, politics starts with money. In his postconvention hideaway in Mission Bay, California, Nixon began his campaign with a review of the financial situation. Stans reported that he had spent $9 million to win the nomination, that he had no debts, and that he planned to raise $24 million to meet the budget for the fall campaign (four years earlier, Goldwater had spent a record $21 million).

Stans's major device for fund-raising was a series of $1,000-a-plate dinners. Using the miracles of modern technology, he scheduled one such event in twenty-two cities for the night of September 16, and had Nixon speak from New York to each of them via closed-circuit television. Stans also sent out ten thousand letters to wealthy Republicans, asking for an immediate $1,000 contribution to get the campaign started. Stans later recalled that he and Nixon met daily in Mission Bay, "and when I left, we had the . . . program ready to go. This gave us a terrific edge over the Democrats. . . . My approach . . . was to free the candidate from any money worries whatsoever. Ours was by far the most expensive campaign ever, and I never once had to go to him to ask him to do anything." The relative ease with which such large sums of money were raised was an indication not so much of the donors' liking for Nixon as of how badly they wanted to get the Democrats out of the White House.[5]

Free of money problems, Nixon turned next to party unity. He had been stressing the theme through the preconvention period by refraining from any criticism of either Rockefeller or Reagan, and by repeating over and over that "a party that cannot unite itself cannot unite the nation." He got on the telephone, and stayed on it, until he had talked to every prominent progressive Republican in the country. One by one he brought them around; first Romney pledged his full support, then Ohio Governor James Rhodes, then Governor Raymond Shafer and former governor William Scranton of Pennsylvania. Governors John Love of Colorado and Dan Evans of Washington joined up. So did Senator Percy. Finally the four most prominent holdouts came in: Senator Jacob Javits of New York, Governor Rockefeller, Mayor Lindsay, and, best of all, Senator Edward Brooke of Massachusetts, the only black man in the Senate. In every case, Nixon only had to remind them of the obvious, that their refusal to endorse Goldwater in 1964 had almost destroyed the Republican Party, and that no matter what they thought of Agnew, they simply had to get aboard this time. Every one of them did.[6]

When he was not on the telephone, Nixon discussed strategy with Mitchell, Haldeman, Safire, Buchanan, and the rest of the staff. He made or reaffirmed some basic decisions. One was that in contrast to 1960, when he had campaigned in all fifty states, in 1968 he would concentrate on the Big Seven—New York, Pennsylvania,

California, Texas, Illinois, Ohio, and Michigan. Between them, these states had 210 of the 270 electoral votes needed for victory. In 1960, Nixon had carried only California and Ohio; in 1968, he figured he would have to take at least four of the Big Seven in order to win.

As to issues, there was no question as to what they were: Vietnam, crime and violence, and inflation. Senator John Tower, chairman of Nixon's "key issues" committee, flew out to California, conferred with Nixon, then met the press to announce the obvious, that the Nixon campaign would concentrate on the "growing crime rate, growing civil disobedience . . . the growing deterioration of buying power, inflation . . . and of course the involvement in Southeast Asia." What Tower did not say was how Nixon proposed to deal with these issues, for the good reason that Nixon's strategy was not to spell out his position in detail, but just to denounce crime, inflation, and the Democrats' conduct of the war.

On Vietnam, Nixon was determined to remain as silent as he had been ever since March 31. His platform statement about "de-Americanization" of the war was as specific as he proposed to get. There was good reason for this, because, as an aide explained, "There was always the uncertainty of what Hanoi would do on the war, and there was Johnson. Nixon always was concerned that he'd pull a rabbit out of the hat. We knew he couldn't end the war, but we knew too he'd try a gesture sooner or later that might be interpreted that way."[7]

As to the tactics of the campaign, Nixon spelled them out in detail to Haldeman, who passed them on to the staff in a confidential three-page memorandum. It was essential, Nixon insisted, to "maintain the initiative." This would be done by emphasizing certain themes. The first was "The Come-Back Theme." Haldeman, using words dictated to him by Nixon (who increasingly referred to himself in the third person), pointed out that "this has an immense appeal and RN does not believe it has adequately been covered." The way to "get it out" was to point up "the obvious, that RN accomplished this [his comeback] despite the overwhelming opposition of the financial establishment and the press establishment and without . . . PR gimmicks, etc."

Other themes Nixon stressed included "The Calibre of the Nixon Team," "The Youth of the RN Organization," and "RN, 'the man for the times.'" This last, Nixon felt, was "perhaps most important of all. . . . The Churchill analogy is probably appropriate." It was of "vital importance" that "we . . . play the confident line from now until November. . . . We are on the offensive and we must stay on the offensive. . . . We should exude confidence, not cockiness."[8]

The tactics, like the strategy, like the fund-raising, were all geared to a single point, that "Nixon's the One." And not just "the one," but the only one. There was almost no mention of the Republican Party (and absolutely no mention of Spiro Agnew). Issues would be brought up not to propose solutions or to promote dialogue but to denounce the Democrats and to insist that only Nixon had a solution. Both Wallace and Humphrey were also promising change, necessarily so in a year in which almost everyone wanted things changed; Nixon's argument was that Wallace could not win and that Humphrey was too closely tied to the politics of the Johnson Administration to bring about any effective change, so—"Nixon's the One."

In the three weeks between the end of the Republican Convention and the opening of the Democratic Convention, Nixon carefully kept himself out of the public eye. He told reporters at Mission Bay that he would have no comment on the Democrats until they had chosen their candidate. It was clearly in his interest to keep the spotlight on the upcoming convention, because the divisions within the party, as expressed in the preconvention quotes and maneuvers of the major candidates, Humphrey, McCarthy, and McGovern, made it likely that television exposure was going to hurt, not help, the Democrats. Chicago promised to be divisive and perhaps even disastrous for the Democrats. As Nixon told Republican leaders, "They're going to split that party at the convention, whichever way they go. Let's get those that they leave behind."[9]

Nixon was exactly on the mark, but even he could not have anticipated just how lucky he was, as the events at the end of August in Chicago were valuable to him beyond any measure. As the nation looked on, aghast, the world's oldest political party tore itself apart. Inside the convention hall the delegates, tightly controlled by Lyndon Johnson, nominated Hubert Humphrey, who had not won a single primary; outside the hall the Chicago police, stirred up and encouraged by Mayor Richard Daley, went on a rampage against the youthful demonstrators of the New Left, who for their part were engaged in provoking the cops in every imaginable way, including calling them "pigs" and worse, blowing marijuana smoke in their faces, giving them the finger, fornicating in Grant Park, and otherwise behaving in an infantile and inexcusable way.

It was a shameful disgrace for all concerned—the city of Chicago, the Democratic Party, the New Left, the television cameramen and commentators, the United States of America. The only winner was Richard Nixon, whose election now seemed a certainty.

A major result of the 1968 Democratic Convention was that the doves, representing nearly half the American people and an obvious majority within the Democratic Party, were left without a candidate. This was dangerous not only to the Democratic Party, but to democracy in America, as it left the doves feeling helpless, disillusioned, and frustrated. The number-one political issue of 1968 was the war in Vietnam, and more specifically the continued bombing of North Vietnam, but when the Democratic Party turned back a "stop the bombing" resolution and endorsed Johnson's policy, the American people had no chance to vote on that number-one issue.

Meanwhile, Humphrey was trapped. He could not break with Johnson, and thus he could not attack Nixon on Vietnam. This allowed Nixon to support Johnson on the bombing, while criticizing him on his conduct of the war. The only alternative for the voter was George Wallace, whose policy was to increase the bombing. This situation contributed heavily to the extreme bitterness of the presidential campaign. It was not Nixon's fault, but it worked very much to his benefit.

Had Bobby Kennedy lived and won the nomination, or had McCarthy or McGovern prevailed over Humphrey, the nominee would have forced Nixon to say how he proposed to end the war, and in the process converted the election into a clear referendum on Vietnam. But it was not to be.

Nixon moved quickly to take direct advantage of the Democratic debacle in Chicago. The day the convention ended, he announced that he would begin his campaign the following week with a motorcade through the Loop in downtown Chicago. There was a risk involved, of course, as the city was reeling and tense, as well as resentful of the intense criticism the media were directing at the mayor and the police force. But if Nixon could manage a successful appearance, he would score a psychological and symbolic victory, underscoring his law-and-order theme and cultivating his reputation as a champion of domestic tranquillity, while contrasting himself in the best possible way with Humphrey.

It worked beautifully. More than 400,000 turned out, many of them city workers given the afternoon off by Mayor Daley. His Honor also told his police force to make certain everything went smoothly, and everything did. The crowds were not necessarily enthusiastic, but they were respectful and the atmosphere was one of decorum. Irony of ironies, the man who had stolen the Presidency from Nixon in 1960, Richard Daley, got him off to the best possible start in 1968.

Pat rode beside Nixon in the lead; Julie and David were in the next car, followed by Senator Brooke. David got a laugh when he said that he had just visited his grandfather in Walter Reed Hospital, and Ike had finally stopped telling him to cut his hair. Instead, David told the reporters, Ike had said "that the most important thing I could do this fall would be to help elect Richard Nixon." Brooke made his contribution: he stepped forward to say of Nixon, "He'll do everything he can to bring an end to the war in Vietnam. ... He's going to unite the country, black and white as well." [10] Polls released that day showed Nixon with a twelve-point lead (Nixon 43 percent, Humphrey 31 percent, Wallace 19 percent), an indication of just how badly Chicago had hurt Humphrey.

The motorcade was all symbol and image. On the issues, Nixon continued to use his self-imposed "moratoriums" to avoid comment. He absolutely refused to discuss Vietnam, as that would undercut the President. He also refused to comment on the confirmation hearings of Justice Fortas. Republican opposition to Fortas's appointment to the Chief Justice post was strong and growing. Some of Fortas's supporters suggested that Nixon could single-handedly destroy that opposition, but Nixon would say only that he wished Johnson had let the next President choose the Chief Justice, and that he admired Fortas personally and as a jurist. But, he insisted, he would not intervene because he felt he had no business interfering with the deliberative processes of the Senate.

Nixon also used the calculated moratorium to avoid comment on Mayor Daley and his police force. Reporters pressed him for some statement, but Johnson saved him from having to comment when he appointed a committee to investigate the violence in Grant Park and at the convention hall. Nixon promptly announced that he would withhold any statement on the grounds that "political figures should not make partisan comments from the sidelines" during the investigation.[11]

Two days later, September 8, a Sunday, Nixon made certain that Johnson was aware of how much Nixon was doing on his behalf, by spelling it out in detail for his friend Billy Graham, with explicit instructions to Graham to pass it along to Johnson. As Graham made notes, Nixon said, "I (Nixon) promise never to embarrass him (Johnson) after the election.

"I respect him as a man and as a President.

"He is the hardest working and most dedicated President in 140 years.

"I want a working relationship with him, and will seek his advice continually."

Nixon said he would send Johnson on "special assignments after the elections, to foreign countries." He would be forced to "point out some of the weaknesses and failures of the administration, but I will never reflect on Mr. Johnson personally." He promised that when Vietnam "is settled I will give you (Johnson) a major share of the credit, because you deserve it."

In conclusion, "I will do everything to make you (Johnson) a place in History because you deserve it."

Graham flew to Washington the following week for a private meeting with Johnson. He read his notes, "point by point." Johnson was "touched and appreciative, and asked me [Graham] to read them twice." The President told Graham that "I intend to loyally support Mr. Humphrey but if Mr. Nixon becomes the President-elect, I will do all in my power to cooperate with him."

Nixon then called Graham on the telephone to ask Johnson's reaction. Graham assured him that the President was appropriately grateful for "his generous gesture," which Graham personally characterized as "unprecedented in History." [12]

Along with telling Johnson what he wanted to hear, Nixon went to Houston to tell Texans what they wanted to hear. He promised a roaring throng of thirty thousand in the Miller Memorial Amphitheater that he would never, ever, reduce the oil depletion allowance or oppose the Texas right-to-work law.

Texas was not only oil country, but also Wallace country. Nixon was careful not to mention Wallace by name, but he did steal one of Wallace's favorite lines, twist it a bit, and make it work for him. "There is not a dime's worth of difference," Nixon said, "between the policies of Hubert Humphrey and what we've had for the past four years."

He then turned around Humphrey's demand for a debate. Nixon charged that his rival had been on "both sides" of every important issue, and concluded, "In fact, my friends, it appears that the Great Debate this year is going to be Humphrey versus Humphrey, and I'm going to have to ask for equal time." [13]

Humphrey could use fear and ridicule too. In Humphrey's case, the fear he stressed was simple and straightforward, the fear that Richard Nixon would become President of the United States. Asked if there really was a "new Nixon," Humphrey responded, "I think Mr. Nixon has exposed the same Nixon, the real Nixon that we knew before." When Nixon refused to debate, Humphrey called him "Richard the Chicken-hearted."

As to Nixon's basic theme, Humphrey declared, "When you play fast and loose with law and order, you've got to expect to get rapped on the knuckles. . . . For every jail Mr. Nixon wants to build I'd like to build a house for a family. And for every policeman he wants to hire I'd like to hire another good teacher." [14]

Lyndon Johnson had told Bill Moyers, back in 1966, that he would rather run against Nixon than any other Republican, because no one else would drive Democratic doves back into the fold quicker than Nixon. Humphrey had felt the same way in 1968. But he was discovering, in the first weeks of the campaign, that no matter how much he lambasted Nixon, the doves were not coming to the Democratic roost. Bobby Kennedy and Gene McCarthy supporters were so furious about the tactics used against them in Chicago that they not only refused to come home, they actively went after Humphrey.

It was a mark of how much the doves detested the Vietnam War that they forgot how much they detested Nixon. Wherever Humphrey went, he was met by organized demonstrators chanting "End the War" or similar slogans, disrupting his meetings, making it impossible for him to deliver a speech, and clearly causing him great personal embarrassment and deep humiliation.

The demonstrations were also a mark of the political ignorance of the demonstrators, and of their penchant for self-indulgence. (Senator McCarthy did not help any; he refused to endorse Humphrey.) When interviewed by reporters, most hecklers said that they would probably end up voting for Humphrey (where else could they possibly go?) but that they hoped to "push him toward the left." What they were really doing was pushing him toward a disastrous defeat.

"I don't enjoy chanting in unison," one demonstrator, a graduate student, told a reporter. "But when the best candidate on the horizon is a man who can talk in 1968—1968!—about the politics of joy, he's out of touch. For us it represents total frustration." [15]

Hecklers also went after Wallace, but unlike Humphrey, Wallace used them to his advantage. "Pointy-headed liberals," he called them, or "anarchists, the kind of people we don't want in America," or "bums and jerks." His audiences loved it. If any demonstrator ever tried to stop his motorcade by lying down in front of his car, Wallace vowed, he would run right over him—and his supporters roared their approval.

The passions aroused in the 1968 presidential campaign were unprecedented in America's twentieth-century political history—one had to go back to 1860 for a comparison—and of course Nixon could no more escape those passions than he could resist the temptation to use them. But Nixon hecklers were not so obvious as those who went after Humphrey, nor so numerous as those who went after Wallace. Still they were there, more than he had ever seen before. Nixon deplored the heckling; throughout his career he had consistently denounced any attempt to keep a politician from saying his piece. Demonstrators made him furious, but he was much more effective than Humphrey in dealing with hecklers, without goading them on the way Wallace loved to do.

Nixon's most effective technique was to screen out the hecklers from his rallies and speeches. He was able to do so because his staff was so much larger than Humphrey's or Wallace's. Admission to a Nixon rally was by ticket only. Ten times as many tickets as seats were handed out, to insure an overflow audience. There were Nixon aides at every entrance to make certain it was a sympathetic audience. The aides would send long-haired youngsters off to the left, down a hallway to an exit door that led back out to the street, while sending clean-cut youngsters to the right, down to the front-row seats. Or they would simply turn away long-haired ticket holders, telling them the tickets were counterfeit.

Some hecklers still got through; when they did, Nixon ordered John Ehrlichman to have the Secret Service detail rough them up. Ehrlichman told Nixon the Secret Service would not do it. So Nixon told him to create a flying goon squad to rough up the hecklers, take down their signs, and silence them. Usually Ehrlichman found that the local police were happy to do that work for him; occasionally he had to pay cash to off-duty police for such tactics.[16]

Nixon told his staff to conduct the campaign as if it were an all-out war. That was a terrible way to regard a political contest in a democracy, but then the jeering, heckling, and obscene signs the demonstrators thrust into the candidates' faces were disgraceful, disruptive, and undemocratic too. Few participants in the 1968 campaign, at whatever level, had anything to be proud of, and all had much to be ashamed about.

Although Nixon seethed inwardly whenever confronted by hecklers, he managed to stay cool outwardly. In sharp contrast to 1960, he ran a relaxed, evenly paced, smooth-functioning operation. He gave every indication of inner ease, quiet self-confidence, and an above-the-battle posture. Harrison Salisbury, who interviewed Nixon in mid-September, came away convinced that Nixon's mind was "ranging far beyond November to the great problems he will confront as the next President."

With a twenty-point lead in the polls, Nixon—according to Salisbury—"was thinking more in terms of what kind of victory he will win in November, or what kind of a mandate he will receive. . . . He could win the election with 2 percent of the negro vote, but he could not expect to govern the country on such a divided basis. Domestic questions would be so sharpened as to beggar solution." To be an effective President, Nixon told Salisbury, he had to win at least 12 percent of the black vote; to achieve that goal, he kept Senator Brooke close by his side in his travels through the country.

It was not enough. In Cleveland, Salisbury reported, a black reporter said, "To be perfectly honest, Mr. Nixon, the negroes are a little afraid of you." Nixon asked him why this attitude existed.

"I don't know," the reporter replied. "I want you to tell me why and what are you going to do about it."

Nixon replied that blacks were the chief victims of crime in the United States, and that his law-and-order message was designed to help them, a reply that did not satisfy the reporter, but was all that he got.[17]

That Nixon tried to play both sides of the fence on the explosive race issue was as obvious as it was inevitable. He firmly upheld the Supreme Court's school-desegregation decision, and stated unequivocally that segregation should not be perpetuated. But he went on to describe as "dangerous" the Johnson Administration policy of withholding federal funds from school districts that refused to integrate public schools, despite the fact that the power to withhold funds was the only effective weapon available to the federal government in its efforts to enforce *Brown* v. *Topeka*.

Nixon could be maddeningly convoluted on the subject. "I believe that the decision [*Brown* v. *Topeka*] was a correct one," he said on a television interview shown throughout the South, "but while that decision dealt with segregation and said that we would not have segregation, when you go beyond that and say that it is the responsibility of the Federal Government, and the Federal courts, to, in effect, act as local school districts in determining how we carry that out, and then to use the power of the Federal Treasury, to withhold funds or give funds in order to carry it out, then I think we are going too far.

"In my view, that kind of activity should be very scrupulously examined and in many cases I think should be rescinded."[18]

In Philadelphia, on September 21, Nixon spoke to both white and black audiences. He told prosperous white suburbanites in a shopping center, "You are fortunate people, but you know that in the great cities of America there is terrible poverty. There are poor people. There are people who haven't had a chance, the chance that you've had.

"You can't be an island in the world. You can't live in your comfortable houses and say, well, just as long as I get mine, I don't have to worry about the others." Having affirmed his commitment to social justice, Nixon turned back to his law-and-order theme, adding to it his program for black capitalism, which seemed to indicate that the folks in the shopping center really did not have to worry about their little island, because Nixon was not going to overwhelm them with black citizens moving out from the inner-city ghetto; rather, he was going to uplift the ghetto. He made this explicit later in the day in a black area of North Philadelphia, when he campaigned in the only black-owned shopping center in the country. At his side was the Reverend Leon Sullivan, a black leader with a reputation as someone who could get local businessmen to provide jobs and government agencies to provide technical and financial help for black entrepreneurs. Nixon expressed boundless enthusiasm for the Reverend Sullivan and his efforts.[19]

Humphrey continued his efforts to frighten voters by reminding them of who Nixon was and what the Republican Party stood for. He asserted that the American people "have never had it so good," and warned that Nixon and the Republicans "will take it away." He recalled the Great Depression, and Herbert Hoover, and Franklin Roosevelt, as every Democrat had done for the preceding thirty-two years.

Nixon was scornful in his reply. "The American worker knows that is not the truth," he said with reference to the "you never had it so good" theme. "You know it when your wife goes to the grocery store. You know it when you pay your taxes." He charged that every raise the workingman had received over the last four years had been wiped out by increased prices and taxes, and said that "the United States cannot afford Hubert Humphrey as President." Attacking Humphrey's record as a senator, Nixon claimed that "the difference between what Hubert recommended that the country spend from 1949 to 1961 and what Congress actually spent is nearly $100 billion." Nixon promised to balance the budget to stop inflation and restore the purchasing power of the dollar.[20]

He made other promises. In Florida, late in September, he proposed an increase in Social Security benefits with an automatic increase in pensions whenever the cost of living went up (in so doing, he was following Humphrey's lead; Humphrey had made an identical proposal a few days earlier).[21]

In Chicago, Nixon stressed his commitment to Israel, in the process going much further than Ike had ever done. The Eisenhower Administration had refused to sell arms to Israel, but after the Six-Day War in 1967, the Johnson Administration had sold some tanks and fighter aircraft to the Israelis. Still, Israel wanted more, especially Phantom F-4s (supersonic fighter-bombers).

Johnson, so far, had hesitated. Nixon told the B'nai B'rith triennial convention that the "balance of power in the Middle East must be tipped in Israel's favor," and pledged, if elected, to "support a policy that would give Israel a technological military margin to more than offset her hostile neighbors' numerical superiority. If maintaining that margin should require that the U.S. supply Israel with Phantom F-4s, we should supply them."[22] (In late December, Johnson made the sale.)

In New York, Nixon revealed one of his new ideas, revenue and power sharing with the states. "For a period of 40 years," he declared, "we have had power flowing from the people and from local and state government to Washington, D.C. I think it's time for a change. Let's have power flow back from Washington to the states and local government and the people of this country."[23]

The 1968 election was the first for the initial wave of the Baby Boom. Thousands of people born in 1946 and 1947 participated in the campaign, whether as volunteers, hecklers, demonstrators, or just plain voters. Naturally the politicians—like Hollywood, the radio stations and television producers, the pop-music industry, and Madison Avenue advertisers—went after them. This was no simple task for middle-aged men, set in their ways, because the youth of 1968 were so rebellious. Their hair styles, like their clothes and music and literature, reflected their rejection of traditional mores, and gave their elders the impression that in their nonconformity those kids were part of the most conformist generation ever.

But there was diversity among the Baby Boomers. There were plenty of youngsters around who were square, subdued, and solidly Republican. The most prominent of these were David Eisenhower and Julie Nixon. The couple was immensely popular, and not just with Republican parents. Reporter Charlotte Curtis noted that when David arrived at the St. Louis airport, there was a throng to meet him, composed of teenaged girls. One ebullient blonde, fourteen years old, bolted forward when her idol arrived, clutched at his brown tweed sleeve, and squealed delightedly. "I touched him," she cried. "I actually touched him."

David, lanky, freckle-faced, jug-eared, with a grin that reminded older observers of his grandfather, handled such adulation with the aplomb of a rock star. So did Julie, who also got touched, hugged, and patted wherever she went. Together, they were America's newest celebrity sweethearts. Young Republicans, according to Curtis, were "hanging on their every word."

David was good at grinning; Julie, pert, attractive, carefully groomed, and full of spirit, was good at answering questions. "What about Vietnam?" hecklers would shout at her.

"Daddy wants the peace talks to succeed so much he thinks he shouldn't talk about the war," she would answer. "When he becomes President, he'll put the pressure on the Soviet Union. Remember, Daddy was with the Eisenhower Administration and they got us out of one war."[24]

David and Julie were tireless in their campaigning. Nixon made up their schedule for them. He instructed Haldeman at length and in detail about where they should appear, how they should be introduced, what they should wear and talk about. Special aides and advance men were recruited for them, as Nixon, in Ehrlichman's words, "didn't miss a single opportunity to employ them to advantage." The campaign had three chartered jets, one for Nixon and his family and staff, the others for the press. Nixon named them the *Tricia,* the *Julie,* and the *David.*[25]

David was head of Youth for Nixon. He announced the formation of a student coalition to advise Nixon on how to develop proposals to meet "the new issues and new concerns that will confront young America." David declared that this entailed, first of all, "the involvement and support of this new generation to translate into action the fresh and bold ideas that the burgeoning social problems of our era demand."[26]

Nixon played the youth theme hard. At David's suggestion, instead of running down the Baby Boomers, he praised them, extolling the virtues of this generation of American youth and beckoning it to join him in his quest for "a new America." In Anaheim, California, facing perhaps his most conservative audience of the campaign, ten thousand residents of Orange County, he asked those in their twenties to hold up their hands. When they did so, he said, "What we are seeing here you see all over America. I want to say something. Today, too often we get the impression that the young people are going to the dogs. Today, too often, flashing across our television screen, we see the seamy side of American youth. Remember, I believe in young people. They are great. Give them a chance. That's what we want."[27]

Nixon had a specific promise for youth. He said that as soon as he ended the war in Vietnam, he would abolish the draft and create an all-volunteer army. He explained that in the future there would be no more large conventional wars, only nuclear wars or guerrilla struggles. The first would not require large armies and the second would require special skills.[28] To a generation to whom the biggest single concern was the draft, that sounded awfully good.

Of course, the trick was to end the war. Nixon swore that he would do it. His basic line, one that got by far the most applause of any that he used throughout the campaign, was: "If on November 5 this war is still going on, if after all the power and the support the Administration has had, then they've had their chance, now give us our chance.

"We will end the war on an honorable basis."[29]

It was something of a surprise and a bit of an embarrassment to Nixon that this line generated more real enthusiasm than any other. His punch lines on law and order, or inflation, his jokes about Hubert, were usually well received, but it was the "end the war" line that brought them to their feet, cheering madly. So he used it more and more, to the point that by late September he was talking almost exclusively about ending the war. In addition, he quietly dropped from his standard speech that section in which he described the struggle in Vietnam as "vital to America's strategic interest."[30]

What was in America's strategic interests, Nixon did not say. One of the sharpest contrasts with the 1960 campaign was his refusal to discuss foreign policy in any detail, and hardly even in general terms. He scarcely mentioned the Soviet Union, except to hint occasionally that he would pressure the Kremlin to help achieve peace in Vietnam. He mentioned China only once, in his interview with Harrison Salisbury, when he said he was looking forward to "the inevitable negotiations with China. The China problem cannot be indefinitely swept under the table."[31] He never mentioned Cuba.

It was the oddest thing. He had spent half or more of his time over the past five years building his reputation as an expert on foreign policy. During the primaries, he had put forth new ideas on negotiating with the Russians, on relating to America's NATO allies, on opening to China, on responding to the new forces throughout Asia, and most of all on new approaches to ending the Vietnam War. But during the campaign, he all but ignored foreign policy.

Insofar as he could, he also ignored the Republican Party, his own running mate, and George Wallace.

As to his fellow Republicans, if Nixon ever mentioned one of them it escaped the notice of the reporters for *The New York Times*, the Los Angeles *Times*, and the Chicago *Tribune*.

Meanwhile, Agnew unleashed was proving to be almost as much an embarrassment to Nixon as Nixon unleashed had been to Eisenhower back in 1952. Agnew accused Humphrey of being "squishy soft, soft on inflation, soft on Communism and soft on law and order over the years." Referring to the appeasement of Hitler at the Munich Conference thirty years earlier, Agnew said that Humphrey "begins to look a lot like Neville Chamberlain . . . maybe that makes Mr. Nixon look more like Winston Churchill."

In Chicago, in mid-September, Agnew observed that "when I look out at a crowd, I don't see there a Negro, there an Italian, there a Polack . . ." In Tennessee, when asked why he was not campaigning in more ghetto areas, Agnew snapped back, "When you've seen one slum, you've seen them all." On a plane ride to Hawaii, Agnew spotted Gene Oishi, a Maryland reporter, snoozing in his seat. "What's wrong with the fat Jap?" Agnew asked.[32]

When Agnew explained that Oishi was an old friend, Nixon sent his running mate a note: "Dear Ted: When news is concerned, nobody in the press is a friend—they are all enemies." [33]

Nixon said nothing in public about Agnew, who may have looked like a stumblebum and a clown to sophisticated reporters from the big cities, but who was drawing large and enthusiastic crowds. He had an undoubted appeal to Wallace voters. Nixon claimed years later that exit polls revealed that most Wallace voters would have come to him, Nixon, had Wallace dropped out of the race. [34] That may have been true; if it was, Agnew was a big part of the reason. In any event, Nixon was extremely careful never to attack Wallace by name, and certainly did nothing to pressure him to drop out.

Instead, Nixon used Wallace as another way of attacking Humphrey. In mid-September, he said that he had received reports of collusion between Humphrey and Wallace, the purpose of which was to block a Nixon victory. The reports indicated that there was a conspiracy to insure a sizable Wallace victory in enough Deep South states to prevent a clear Nixon triumph in the electoral college. [35] Two weeks later, in Tampa, Nixon called Wallace the "secret weapon" of the Democrats and warned that a vote for Wallace would only result in "four more years of the same." He pleaded with "angry Americans" not to "throw away their votes on a third-party fling" and charged that Humphrey was attempting to "build up Mr. Wallace to defeat the Republicans where he himself cannot do so."

Humphrey, on September 26, had sent a telegram to Nixon proposing, for about the twentieth time, a debate. Nixon brushed aside the proposal with some sharp words of contempt. He said Humphrey was just "thrashing in the wind." The Democrats knew that a three-man debate would undermine the two-party system and that a two-man debate was not possible until Congress suspended the equal-time rule that required participation by all contenders.

"This is the sort of kid stuff that somebody goes through when he's behind," Nixon declared, and he added that Humphrey "apparently needs the debate exposure for Mr. Wallace.... He's trying to use Wallace to beat Nixon in the South." Nixon charged that Humphrey was injuring the two-party system and risking a constitutional crisis. The Republicans in the Senate, meanwhile, were filibustering against any change in the equal-time rule.

But clearly Humphrey was getting to Nixon with his "Richard the Silent" and "Richard the Chicken-hearted" slogans. A reporter asked Nixon if he was afraid to debate. His face flushed, Nixon snapped back, "I'm not afraid of anybody. So that's the way it's going to be and don't plant any words in my mouth to the effect that I'm afraid to debate Mr. Humphrey. I've done it [debate] before and I'll do it again and we'll win next time."[36]

The reporters, delighted to have the old Nixon back after weeks of blandness, made headlines out of his temper display. But on October 3, Nixon got a great break when Wallace announced that he had chosen General Curtis LeMay as his running mate, and LeMay, in his first press conference, said that he would use nuclear weapons immediately in Vietnam. Nixon said he "disagreed completely" and accused the American Independent Party of irresponsible and excessively hawkish attitudes on foreign affairs.[37] Nixon, by inference, and without saying what he would do in Vietnam, was responsible and moderate.

At the end of the first week in October, with a month to go in the campaign, the polls still showed Nixon fifteen or more points ahead. *The New York Times*, after a telephone poll of several hundred political leaders of both parties around the country, predicted that Nixon would win thirty-four states, Wallace seven, and Humphrey but four, with five states too close to call.[38]

Nixon, in these circumstances, was acting more and more like a President-elect, rather than a candidate. Reporters said they had rarely seen him in a better mood. He appeared relaxed and radiantly happy. Arriving at Miami's airport at 2:30 A.M., he spent several minutes under the floodlights tossing a football back and forth with a newsman before departing for Bebe Rebozo's place for a weekend of rest and relaxation.[39]

Surely here was a new Nixon. And apparently a new Humphrey too, as the Vice-President gave the impression that he was desperate and angry. Where Nixon never mentioned a fellow Republican, past or present (except for an occasional reference to General Eisenhower), Humphrey clutched the coattails of FDR, HST, JFK, and even LBJ. Where Nixon ignored Agnew, Humphrey talked increasingly about what a great man Senator Edmund Muskie, his running mate, was. Where Nixon took no chances at all, Humphrey increasingly took risks.

Humphrey was no Adlai Stevenson when it came to quips, nor could his speech writers come up with the one-liners the way Safire and Buchanan could. Still, he had his moments. "Some people say there's a new Nixon," Humphrey said in one speech, "and there may be. Some people say there's an old Nixon. I'm not unkind. I just say there's the real Nixon, and that's trouble enough."[40]

To a New York Liberal Party audience, Humphrey opened thus: "I want you to think as I say it—President Agnew and President LeMay." When the groans ended, Humphrey said that Nixon and Wallace "have no right to play with our country's destiny like that."[41]

But no matter how much Humphrey managed to frighten people with the specter of a Nixon Presidency, no matter how many times he invoked the glories of the Democratic past, he could not move up in the polls. In 1968, people wanted change, which meant, first and foremost and above all else, something different from Lyndon Johnson. If Humphrey was going to make any progress in bringing Democrats back home, he was going to have to break with the President, most of all with Johnson's policies in Vietnam.

Ever since March 31, when Johnson had announced that he was stopping the bombing of Hanoi but continuing to bomb north of the DMZ, Nixon and Humphrey had refused to discuss the war. It was as if Johnson had built a dam designed to hold back the potential floodwaters of public debate on the war. Neither Nixon nor Humphrey could find a way around the dam; more correctly, they never sought one, as they realized they could no more control the flood than Johnson could, or direct it, or escape it. So the water backed up, and rose ever higher. By mid-September, it threatened to either overflow Johnson's dam or burst it.

As the waters rose, there were whirlpools of deceit building behind the dam, and eddies of discontent. Currents of passion were rising that had to find an outlet. The longer the politicians allowed the waters to rise, the worse the catastrophe that would follow the bursting of the dam threatened to be.

Nixon was a major contributor to this growing danger, but he was by no means the only one. There was scarcely a politician in America who was not involved. Nearly every one of them could clearly see the threat, but hardly a one of them was willing or able to offer a workable solution.

The doves cried, "Stop the bombing," as if that would solve the problem. This grossly exaggerated the importance of the bombing campaign (just as the hawks were doing) and obscured the real issue. The doves claimed that when the bombing ended, Hanoi would negotiate. Negotiate what? The doves said that negotiations would lead to a coalition government in Saigon that could bring peace and reconciliation to Vietnam. The hawks were absolutely correct in their scornful rejection of such a position. As Nixon told Safire, "If you give 'em [the Communists] the bombing pause and a coalition government, you give 'em the whole goddam country."[42] The doves were guilty of gross pretenses, that there could be peace without surrender and that the Communists would share power with President Thieu.

In Paris, the peace talks were bogged down over the issue of who should be talking to whom. The North Vietnamese insisted on direct negotiations with the Americans, excluding the South Vietnamese government, which according to the Communists had no legitimacy. In addition, Hanoi wanted to bring the Vietcong's political arm, the NFL, into the talks. Saigon would not agree to its own exclusion, nor to the inclusion of the NLF, which it insisted had no legitimacy. The United States wanted to include Saigon but exclude the NLF. The positions taken by Washington and Hanoi were based on a fundamental fact, that neither side was willing to surrender.

These were not complicated points. It took no great genius to recognize them. The issue of the war, from start to finish, was who was going to rule in Saigon.

There was another simple fact, obvious to the most casual observer. That was that the United States was not prepared to pay the price required to win the war. That did not mean, however, that the country was ready to accept the logical conclusion and admit defeat. As noted, the doves were as guilty as the hawks in maintaining the illusion that there could be peace with General Thieu still in power.

"I am not going to be the first President to lose a war," Johnson insisted. Why not, he never said, nor did the American people ask. Doves and hawks alike accepted Johnson's simpleminded proposition as if the logic behind it were obvious. Never did American hubris show itself more clearly, or more destructively. Every other nation in the world had lost a war, or wars, at one time or another. In many cases it was the best thing that could have happened to them. Think of Germany and Japan in 1945, or France in Algeria, or—come to that—the Confederate States of America.

Nixon said he would end the war, with honor. But what did peace with honor mean? It meant he would accept nothing short of the continuation in power of the military government in Saigon, which meant the total frustration of Hanoi's war aims, which meant surrender by Hanoi, which meant that Nixon's peace with honor really meant peace with victory.

But America had already lost the war, and Nixon knew it, even if he would not admit it. But then, neither would any other major politician, nor would the American people, who were unwilling to hear it.

Nixon claimed that he could not speak out on the war because he did not want to undercut the President. What he was in fact afraid of was that Johnson would undercut him; what he hoped was that Johnson's intransigence would prevent Humphrey from speaking out too. Through September, Humphrey kept quiet.

Meanwhile the swirls and eddies and whirlpools and crosscurrents building behind Johnson's dam grew larger, so much so that, as Nixon later put it, "I was no longer sure of anything."

In mid-September, Rockefeller's foreign-policy adviser, Henry Kissinger, approached John Mitchell, offering his assistance. Kissinger claimed that he was privy to the innermost circles of the Johnson Administration, and said he was eager to pass on information to the Nixon camp, if his role could be kept confidential. (Kissinger insisted on secrecy because he was simultaneously attempting to insert himself into the Humphrey inner circle; whoever won the election, Kissinger wanted to be the foreign-policy adviser.) Nixon agreed to open communication with Kissinger.

Two weeks later, Kissinger called Mitchell again. He said he was just back from Paris, where he had learned that something big was about to happen. He did not know what, but he advised Nixon to avoid making any new proposals (as if there were the slightest chance of that happening!). At the end of September, Kissinger reported that "there is a better than even chance that Johnson will order a bombing halt at approximately mid-October."[43]

This was less inside information than it was common sense—with Humphrey still almost twenty points behind in the polls, and with the doves insisting that a bombing halt would bring about genuine negotiations and a coalition government and finally peace with honor, it was obvious that Johnson would bend heaven and earth to have a bombing halt.

On September 24, Representative Melvin Laird of Wisconsin added to the rumors. Laird was chairman of the House Republican Conference. He said he had learned that Johnson intended to reduce American forces by roughly ninety thousand men by June 30, 1969. He said the reduction would take place without an outright withdrawal, but rather by not sending replacements when one-year tours of duty ended.[44] Nixon, who was with Laird at the time he made the announcement, could hardly have been taken by surprise; what Laird had described as Johnson's policy was exactly what Nixon had promised in his "de-Americanization" plank in the Republican platform.

Nevertheless, Nixon jumped on it. He charged that the Administration was "so intent on ending the war that it will impair the negotiating position of the United States [in Paris] by promising to cut back combat forces in Vietnam."[45]

The dissembling among the politicians continued. Defense Secretary Clifford, who behind the scenes was the leading advocate of a reduction in the American effort, which was in fact Johnson's new policy, just as Laird said, told the press that the Administration had "no intention" of lowering the level of American troops in Vietnam "either by next June or at any time in the foreseeable future."

Humphrey, however, said that "it would be my policy to move toward a systematic reduction in American forces. I think we can do it. I am determined to do it."

Nixon replied, "I think it would be very unfortunate if any implication was left in the minds of the American people that we were able to bring home our forces now because suddenly the war was at an end."

Piously, he went on: "I don't want to pull the rug out from under our negotiations in Paris. . . . The military presence that the United States has in Vietnam should remain at its present level." [46]

Five days later, Nixon said the opposite. Humphrey had announced a major speech on Vietnam for the evening of September 30. Nixon, with good reason, suspected that Humphrey, after a month of hinting that he would turn into a dove as soon as he escaped Johnson's nest, was going to advocate a bombing halt. So Nixon turned dovish himself, earlier that day.

Nixon declared himself "pleased" at the emphasis Clifford was placing on speeding up the training and equipping of South Vietnamese forces. Nixon said he had long since advocated such a program, and called it "the best route of hope for reduction of American military units." He pledged his support of the Administration and promised that "after my election to the Presidency, I intend to advance this program far more vigorously than has the present Administration." He said it was possible for the South Vietnamese to assume a much larger share of the fighting in a relatively short time—and then criticized Humphrey once again for raising "false hopes of parents of men in Vietnam by suggesting that the combat forces would be cut."

That night, in Salt Lake City, Humphrey came out for a bombing halt. He said he would take a "risk for peace" if Hanoi gave some sign of being willing to engage in serious peace talks. [47] This was the first crack in Johnson's dam, and it had manifold consequences, of which the most important, to Nixon as well as to Humphrey, was that the doves suddenly found Humphrey acceptable. From that moment on, he was free of hecklers. Senator McCarthy endorsed him. Democrats by the tens, by the hundreds, by the thousands, by the tens of thousands, rallied behind their nominee.

Hanoi, for its part, stated the obvious: a spokesman called Humphrey's pledge a campaign maneuver that contained "nothing new." White House spokesmen added the same obvious observation, that what Humphrey had said did not represent a break with the Administration, as Johnson had all along said that he would stop the bombing when the North Vietnamese agreed to negotiate seriously. Nixon held a press conference, where he said he wanted to make his own position perfectly clear. It was that "the trump card" of American negotiators was a bombing halt. "Now, if that trump card is played by either of the Presidential candidates by indicating that we in January [1969] might do something that the negotiators have refused to do in Paris, it means that all chance for those negotiations to succeed will evaporate.

"I would respectfully submit that the risk is not his [Humphrey's]. The risk that is taken is to the thousands of Americans in the DMZ whose lives would be threatened in the event that a bombing halt occurred and the North Vietnamese forces were able to attack them in greater numbers than presently is the case."

Nixon accused Humphrey of playing both sides of the street. He said no one could tell what Humphrey's real position was, as this was the "fourth and possibly fifth different position [he has taken] on a bombing halt."

Larry O'Brien, the Democratic national chairman, delightedly leaped on that one: "If Mr. Nixon really needs a 'clarification,' there would be no more effective way than for him to pose his questions in a series of televised debates."[48]

Nixon brushed O'Brien aside, but what he could not brush aside was the deep and widespread reaction Humphrey was getting to his call for a bombing halt. Nixon's lead in the polls was ebbing away as Johnson's dam crumbled.

So, on October 7, in Washington, before the UPI editors and publishers, Nixon explained in a bit more detail how he proposed to end the war. He hinted that as the South Vietnamese shouldered more of the burden, a Nixon Administration might be able to agree to peace terms that the Johnson Administration could not accept. He provided an analogy to make his point. He recalled that in 1952, Eisenhower had not been explicit about what he would do in Korea, but the voters had chosen him because he was so much better prepared to carry on negotiations than Stevenson was. Nixon reminded the editors that Republicans had always acknowledged that President Eisenhower was able to accept a settlement in Korea on terms that President Truman could not possibly have accepted without opening himself to Republican charges that he, Truman, had sold cheap the sacrifice of American lives.

Nixon said that he favored a "generous" peace, that he had no wish to destroy North Vietnam or conquer it, and that he was, in fact, willing to help rebuild it.[49]

The American public, meanwhile, was as confused and divided as were its politicians. A Louis Harris poll of October 7 showed that 48 percent wanted some form of de-escalation, while 43 percent was opposed. Only 13 percent favored a complete withdrawal. Given the contradictions of their political leaders, it was small wonder the people were confused and divided.[50]

IN THE SENATE, Republicans were using the filibuster not only to prevent any suspension of the equal-time rule, thereby blocking a debate between the presidential candidates, but also to block Abe Fortas's confirmation as Chief Justice. Fortas's foes charged that he was lacking judicial propriety because he had accepted a $15,000 lecturer's fee, and because he had continued to advise President Johnson while serving on the high court. The Republicans were also using his confirmation hearings to criticize both Fortas and the Warren Court for *Miranda* and other decisions on criminal defendants' rights.

On October 2, to halt what he called "destructive and extreme assaults upon the Court," Fortas abandoned his fight. A week after Fortas withdrew his name, Johnson announced that he would not make another appointment; instead, he would allow the next President to place a nominee to succeed Warren before the Senate. The rejection of Fortas made the selection of the next President just that much more critical.

WITH THREE WEEKS to go in the campaign, Nixon gave every appearance of complete confidence that he would be the man to name the new Chief Justice. At this stage in 1960, he had been in near continuous motion; in 1968, on October 12 he flew to Miami to spend three days at Key Biscayne, partly to talk strategy with Mitchell, Ellsworth, Garment, and his speech writers, mainly to rest and relax and keep up his tan.[51]

He had good reason to be confident. Humphrey had hardly made a dent in his lead in the polls, despite the Salt Lake City speech promising a bombing halt. Nixon had more money in his campaign treasury than he could spend. He was pouring hundreds of thousands of dollars into the most massive broadcast campaign in history, with ten national radio speeches for the next ten days and an hour-long nationally televised rally at Madison Square Garden in October.

In fact, he was acting as if the election were over. He told the press he hoped for bipartisan support on the great diplomatic issues, especially Vietnam, and actually praised Humphrey's character in a bid for the Vice-President's cooperation. Nixon pledged to include Democrats in his Cabinet, and said he would seek President Johnson's assistance to end the war in Vietnam.[52]

The only thing Nixon had to fear was a dramatic move toward peace by Johnson. That had always been a great danger, but it seemed unlikely. Johnson had so far stayed out of the campaign, in some part because of Nixon's careful cultivation of the President's ego, and at the end of September, Secretary of State Rusk assured the Nixon people that there were no new developments in the Paris talks and that the Administration would not "cut our legs off" with a dramatic announcement.[53]

On October 8, less than a week after the humiliation of his old friend Abe Fortas (which Johnson described in his memoirs as "the final blow to an unhappy, frustrating year"),[54] Johnson broke the silence on presidential politics that he had maintained since March 31. In a thirteen-and-a-half-minute radio talk, he praised Humphrey ("few men that I have ever known have understood our urgent national needs so well") and derided Nixon as the man who said that Medicare "would do more harm than good" and who had opposed "so much vital and progressive legislation." Johnson also raised the possibility of Spiro Agnew becoming President, noting that one out of three twentieth-century Presidents had died in office.[55]

Even taking into account Nixon's careful cultivation of Johnson's ego, that was mild stuff. But Nixon knew that there was much more Johnson could say; more frightening, there was much more that the President, if aroused, could do to deny Nixon the prize. As one of Nixon's aides at Key Biscayne put it, on October 14, "I wish the elections were tomorrow instead of three weeks away."[56]

CHAPTER TEN

THE NINTH CAMPAIGN

PART TWO
October 15–November 6, 1968

IN MID-OCTOBER, following the Fortas withdrawal, Nixon went after the law-and-order issue harder than ever. He stepped up his criticism of the Supreme Court and promised that he would name to the Court only strict constructionists. He called Humphrey a "do-nothing candidate on law-and-order" and recalled a two-year-old Humphrey statement that had he lived in a ghetto as a youth, "I might have led a pretty good revolt." Humphrey's remark, Nixon said, constituted "adult delinquency.... There is no cause that justifies breaking the law." (That last was a typical flat categorical statement of principle that Nixon could not possibly have meant.)

"Whenever I begin to discuss the Supreme Court," Nixon said, "Mr. Humphrey acts like we're in church. Mr. Humphrey's respectful silence [on controversial Supreme Court decisions on law enforcement] may stem from the fact that he has spent four years in [Lyndon Johnson's] Obedience School."

Another favorite line in the last weeks of the campaign was "In the [past] forty-five minutes . . . this is what has happened in America: There has been one murder, two rapes, forty-five major crimes of violence, countless robberies and auto thefts . . ."

Nixon told an Ohio audience it could choose between "Nixon with money in your pocket or Humphrey with his hand in your pocket." He criticized Senator Muskie for "grinning while free scofflaws burned their draft cards." He said Humphrey sat on his hands "while watching the United States become a nation where 50 per cent of American women are frightened to walk within a mile of their homes at night."

After promising that he would not indulge in "personal charges" against his opponents in the last days of the campaign, Nixon told an El Paso audience that Humphrey had "a personal attitude of indulgence and permissiveness toward the lawless." He charged that Muskie was "giving aid and comfort to those who are tearing down respect for law across the country." He claimed that Humphrey showed his sympathy for the criminals when the Vice-President cited poverty as the root cause of crime.[1]

Still insisting that he would not indulge in "personal charges," Nixon told an Ohio audience, "Mr. Humphrey's public record gives no indication that he believes there is a bottom to the well of the United States Treasury. He has built a public career of buying the people's votes with the people's money."[2] In Michigan, he accused the Vice-President of "the fastest switch of position ever seen in American politics. . . . Week after week [he] shows on every issue that he would rather switch than fight, rather spend than save, rather talk than mind his tongue."[3]

In Pennsylvania, Nixon spoke truthfully when he said, "You know politicians are in trouble when they start to name call, when they start to panic, to hit below the belt." Of course, he was referring to Humphrey, not himself. Making great circling motions with his arms, he went on: "We can't be led into the seventies by the same men who stumbled their way through the sixties."[4]

In the 1964 campaign, the Republicans had been outraged when the Democrats ran a television commercial that showed a little girl playing in a field of flowers. An atomic bomb went off in the background, and as a mushroom-shaped cloud filled the TV screen, a voice-over asked whose finger the voter wanted on the nuclear trigger.

In 1968 the Republicans struck back. At the end of October (and thus too late in the campaign for the Democrats to mount a reply), on the popular Rowan and Martin "Laugh-In" TV show, the Republicans ran a commercial that showed battle scenes in Vietnam, black rioters in a burning American city, and a frail starving child interspersed with scenes of Humphrey laughing and smiling and promoting the politics of joy.[5]

The Democrats in 1968 had a good one of their own: A radio spot that opened in silence; then came a soft, steady "thump, thump . . . thump, thump . . . thump, thump . . ." Then, above the thumping, a voice asked incredulously: "Spiro Agnew? A heartbeat away from the Presidency?"[6]

In the 1960 campaign, the Democrats had falsely charged that the Republicans had allowed the Russians to catch up and pass the United States in weaponry, thereby creating a "missile gap." In

1968, Nixon struck back. In Pennsylvania, on October 24, Nixon pledged that as President he would restore "clear-cut" American military superiority. He charged that "the present state of our defenses is much too close to the peril point, and our future prospects are in some respects downright alarming." He accused the Kennedy and Johnson Administrations of having fostered "a gravely serious security gap."

Nixon explicitly rejected "the peculiar, unprecedented doctrine called 'parity,' because this parity concept means superiority for potential enemies." He warned that "by 1970 or 1971 we could find ourselves with a 'survival gap.' " He gave no facts or figures, nor did he cite any sources.[7] As he showed in his actions three months later, Nixon did not believe one word of this.

Humphrey pounced on Nixon's statements, labeling them "ill-tempered, ill-considered, and irresponsible." He charged that Nixon's concern was not for national security but "only for votes." He castigated Nixon's call for nuclear "superiority" as an attempt to promote "an increasing militarization of American life and American foreign policy." Clark Clifford issued a statement in which he insisted that the United States still maintained "substantial military superiority" (eight months earlier, Clifford's predecessor, Robert McNamara, had said the opposite). Clifford's statement included a barrage of facts and figures.[8] They were about as accurate as Nixon's charges, which is to say, not at all.

The following day, apparently disturbed by Humphrey's portrayal of him as irresponsible on the arms race, Nixon pledged that if elected he would seek "meaningful arms control agreements with our adversaries."[9] But four days after that, in Texas, Nixon called Humphrey one of those "fuzzy thinkers and false prophets who profess to believe that keeping America strong is somehow against peace." He went on: "They will, if they have their way, get America into war, not because they want war but because they don't understand how to keep the peace. . . . Let me tell you that I am the one who stands for a stronger United States and Mr. Humphrey who stands for a weaker one."

Nixon did a bit of psychoanalyzing (something he hated when it was applied to him) to explain Humphrey's "piteous outcry" over the charge of a security gap. The reason, according to Nixon, was that Humphrey had "a long-harbored guilt feeling over Mr. Kennedy's trumped-up charge of a missile gap in the Eisenhower Administration."[10]

That same week, General Eisenhower wrote Nixon from Walter Reed Hospital. He apologized for not being able to campaign for Nixon, but said he was proud that his wife, his son, John, and his grandson, David, were all out on the campaign trail for Nixon and his cause, "in which they fervently believe." Eisenhower then praised Nixon for the way, in which he had conducted his campaign: "You have stood steady and talked straight, despite what must have been heavy pressures and temptations to reach for popular support through irresponsibility. I commend you especially for this; it befits you and befits our country." [11]

General Eisenhower was old and dying and eager for the Julie Nixon–David Eisenhower wedding to take place as soon as possible in a time of triumph. Still, to many of Ike's admirers, it was distressing to see him endorse Nixon's cynical use of the "survival gap," as it amounted to a rejection of everything Ike had stood for on defense policy for eight years.

Nixon, elated by the former President's "extremely flattering and generous statements," replied that he had "instructed my people who are experts in this promotion business to make maximum use of your letter, in order to show the American people that the man they admire the most thinks well of me." [12]

The experts, Haldeman and press secretary Ron Ziegler, thought the best way to make the letter public was to have David Eisenhower read it on television, which was done.

ADLAI STEVENSON in 1952 and Jack Kennedy in 1960 had managed to inject a bit of badly needed comic relief into the campaigns, but in 1968 Humphrey's sense of humor was almost as deficient as Nixon's, while Wallace's frequent attempts at jokes were always cruel and often vicious. What humor there was came from an improbable source, Lyndon Johnson.

On October 16, Johnson showed up unexpectedly at the twenty-third annual dinner of the Alfred E. Smith Memorial Foundation at the Waldorf-Astoria Hotel in New York. Nixon and Humphrey were already there; this was their only meeting of the campaign. Johnson told the surprised and appreciative audience, "Pretty soon you won't have Lyndon Johnson to kick around any more." He described himself as "the resident prisoner of a big white jailhouse." Glancing at Humphrey and Nixon, he said, "I can just see Al Smith sitting up there with St. Peter—maybe even with Herbert Hoover—chuckling at all the secret thoughts at this head table."

Humphrey's contribution to the banter was "In my present position I take heart from Harry Truman's campaign of 1948. I have to."

Nixon's contribution was a comment on Humphrey and himself: "Regardless of what others may call us, he's a son of a druggist and I'm the son of a grocer." Nixon praised Johnson as "the hardest working President we have had in this century. He is a President who is devoted to peace." Many of LBJ's critics would have regarded that last sentence as a joke, but Nixon was not joking. Referring to Vietnam, he said, "We have one President at a time. Let none of us say anything that will undercut his chance to bring that war to a conclusion."[13]

Two weeks later, in a luncheon speech at the same New York hotel, Johnson said, "One of my daughters asked me coming up here today, 'Tell me, Daddy, how was it that after losing a national election in 1960 to President Kennedy and then after losing a state election as Governor in California in 1962 to Pat Brown, how does it happen that Richard Nixon has been able to win his party's nomination for the Presidency in 1968?'"

Johnson, with a puzzled expression on his face, let the audience anticipation grow for a moment or two. Then he said, "I told her that if she would give me a week or two I would try to think of some reason." The ballroom exploded in laughter.[14]

THE DEMOCRATS had cause to be happy. Despite Nixon's name-calling and unsubstantiated but frightening allegations about Humphrey's neglect of the national defense and his softness on law and order and his willingness to spend the country into bankruptcy, or perhaps because of the wildness of Nixon's charges, Humphrey was creeping up in the polls.

In large part, this was because Wallace supporters in the North were coming to agree with Nixon's observation that a vote for Wallace was a wasted vote, while ignoring his advice to vote Republican. Try as he might, Nixon could never get above 43 percent in the polls. Wallace, meanwhile, slipped from 22 percent at the beginning of October to 18 percent by October 20. On that same day, Nixon had fallen back to 40 percent, while Humphrey had moved up to 35 percent (7 percent undecided).[15]

As the gap narrowed, the specter of a constitutional crisis grew. Wallace was an almost certain winner in Arkansas, Louisiana, Mississippi, Alabama, and Georgia, with a total of forty-five electoral votes. If Humphrey could split the remainder of the states with Nixon, or just come close to doing so, the election would go to the Democratic-dominated House of Representatives. Nixon, facing the prospect of having another national election stolen from him, called on Humphrey to agree that the winner of the popular vote be declared the next President.

Humphrey refused. He piously said he would "stand by the Constitution." He insisted that the members of the House of Representatives would vote not as partisan politicians but as "free-thinking citizens selecting the man they regarded as the best President." (Maybe Humphrey had a better sense of humor than the author has given him credit for.) He said he would be able to govern effectively, even if he got fewer votes than Nixon, because of his "good rapport" with blacks, Congress, and young people.[16]

Nixon, stung by Humphrey's continuing charge that he was "Richard the Chicken-hearted" because of his refusal to debate, kept Humphrey on the defensive on this one. "I do not fear the voice of the people," Nixon said on October 30. "Does Hubert Humphrey?

"I want to spare our nation from the possibility of an administration that owes its existence to a third party—does Hubert Humphrey?

"If Hubert Humphrey turns away from this moment of truth for democracy; if he shrinks from this challenge to let the American people select their own President, if he fails to put the future of his country ahead of his own ambition—then America will need no further proof of the depth of his desperation."

Nixon predicted that he would win the popular vote by three million to five million.

Humphrey stood by the Constitution.[17]

George Wallace announced that he would require a public espousal of his own views to be broadcast on national television by anyone hoping to gain his support in the electoral college.[18] But his electors from the Deep South were required by state law to vote for him; he could not hand them over to Nixon or Humphrey; if the election went to the House of Representatives, Wallace would have no control over the way the delegations from Louisiana and the other states voted; so what he said was pure bombast.

Not that he was alone.

ON OCTOBER 16, Nixon was campaigning in Missouri. An aide told him that President Johnson had placed a conference call to all three candidates. Nixon took the call in a tiny room in Kansas City's Union Station; it was a poor connection and he had trouble hearing. Johnson told the candidates there had been a breakthrough. Hanoi had agreed to allow the government of Vietnam (GVN, President Thieu's government in Saigon) to participate in the peace talks if Johnson stopped the bombing. Acting under Johnson's instructions, Ambassador Harriman in Paris had told the North Vietnamese delegates that they would also have to agree to respect the DMZ and to refrain from attacking cities in South Vietnam. According to Johnson, Thieu said he would not oppose a bombing halt if

Hanoi met those conditions. Johnson also told the three candidates that the U.S. Joint Chiefs of Staff had agreed to a bombing halt if Hanoi accepted Harriman's terms.[19]

That night, Johnson made his surprise visit to New York, where he saw Nixon and Humphrey at the Al Smith dinner. The President took Nixon aside to assure him that there would be no bombing halt without reciprocity, i.e., Hanoi's agreement to Harriman's terms.[20]

For some weeks, Nixon had been anticipating a bombing halt. He both feared and welcomed it. Much depended on the timing; even more depended on the immediate reaction in the two Vietnams.

This was high-stakes politics. If Johnson could pull off a bombing halt, get Hanoi to a peace table with promises to behave, bring the GVN into the talks, make it appear that a coalition government was about to be formed, and be able to claim that peace and reconciliation were just around the corner, why then Humphrey, already closing fast, would be a sure winner.

But if anything slipped, if the GVN refused to sit down with the Communists, or if Hanoi took advantage of a bombing halt to send more men and weapons across the DMZ and down the Ho Chi Minh Trail, it would appear that LBJ had played politics with peace, and then it was Nixon who would be an almost certain winner.

Nixon's first public move was to prepare his followers for the possibility of a bombing halt. Speaking in Johnstown, Pennsylvania, the morning after Johnson had personally urged him to be careful about what he said on Vietnam, and asked him not to reveal the breakthrough until Hanoi had responded to Harriman's terms, Nixon told a rally: "If a bombing pause can be agreed to in Vietnam, one which will not endanger American lives, and one which increases the chances for bringing a peaceful and honorable solution to the war, then we are for it. And the one who can make that determination is the President of the United States."

He concluded, "We do not want to play politics with peace." But of course, as he wrote in his memoirs, "that was inevitably what was happening."[21]

In private, Nixon made contact with President Thieu in an effort to scuttle the peace prospects. His connection was Mrs. Anna Chan Chennault, the Chinese widow of the wartime hero General Claire Chennault. Mrs. Chennault was president of Flying Tiger Airline and a frequent traveler throughout Asia. She had close ties with Chiang Kai-shek, and with Nixon and his friends in the China Lobby. She was cochair of the Republican Women for Nixon

(Mamie Eisenhower was her partner) and had raised $250,000 for Nixon's campaign. Most important of all, she was close to President Thieu and his aides.

Through Mrs. Chennault, Nixon had earlier met with the South Vietnamese ambassador to the United States, Bui Diem. Nixon had told him to pass on anything he had to Mrs. Chennault, who would in turn pass it on to John Mitchell. Nixon had promised Bui Diem that he would make Vietnam his top priority and "see that Vietnam gets better treatment from me than under the Democrats." [22]

At the end of October, with Johnson apparently ready to call a bombing halt, Nixon had Mitchell call Mrs. Chennault.

"Anna," Mitchell said, "I'm speaking on behalf of Mr. Nixon. It's very important that our Vietnamese friends understand our Republican position and I hope you have made that clear to them." He said that if Mrs. Chennault could persuade Thieu to refuse to go to the peace table, Johnson's bombing halt would look unwise at best, cynical at worst, and would therefore backfire on the Democrats. Mitchell used guarded language to convey this message, because he knew that Mrs. Chennault's telephone was tapped by the FBI and that J. Edgar Hoover would make sure that Johnson heard about the Chennault-Mitchell conversation. [23]

While Johnson spied on Nixon and his friends, Nixon had his own mole within the Johnson inner circle. On October 22, Bryce Harlow, one of Nixon's closest aides, passed along in a memorandum information he had received from the mole. "The President is driving exceedingly hard for a deal with North Vietnam," Harlow reported. "He is becoming almost pathologically eager for an excuse to order a bombing halt."

Harlow added that Clark Clifford, Joseph Califano, Llewellyn Thompson, and George Ball were the Johnson people pushing hardest for a halt, and that careful plans were being made "to help HHH exploit whatever happens. . . . White Housers still think they can pull the election out for HHH with this ploy; that's what is being attempted." [24]

In a poker analogy, Nixon and Humphrey, Johnson and Thieu, and the North Vietnamese were playing the last and biggest hand of the evening, placing and calling bets recklessly, under intense pressure.

Nixon had Mitchell call Kissinger to check on Johnson's plans. Kissinger knew nothing.

Nixon told Senator Everett Dirksen to call Johnson to tell the President that the Republicans were on to his plans. Johnson vehemently denied any forthcoming bombing halt. [25] (The President was not, in this case, dissembling; Hanoi had not yet agreed to

Harriman's terms, indeed was continuing to demand a bombing halt without conditions other than its agreement to accept the GVN at the peace talks.)[26]

On October 23, Nixon threw another bet into the pot. In an attempt to reduce in advance the political impact of a move toward peace, he accused Humphrey of having the "fastest, loosest tongue in American politics. On this great issue of war and peace, on the great issue particularly of whether or not we should have a bombing pause, he's been for it unconditionally, and then he said we should have conditions." (When or where Humphrey ever said he was "unconditionally" for a bombing halt, Nixon did not say, for the good reason that Humphrey never said it.)

"He has been unable to mind his tongue when negotiations are going on," Nixon continued. "In this terribly important function of keeping the peace, you must remember that when there is miscalculation, when a potential enemy is not sure what you stand for—that's when the danger of war escalates."[27]

The following day, October 24, Harlow reported that his source said an agreement had been reached with Hanoi (which was not true). Nixon "immediately decided," as he wrote in his memoirs, "that the only way to prevent Johnson from totally undercutting my candidacy at the eleventh hour was for me to make public the fact that a bombing halt was imminent."

In other words, after having gone seven months without comment on Vietnam, using the excuse that he did not want to undercut the President, Nixon decided to undercut the President. In his own words, "I wanted to plant the impression . . . that his motives and his timing" were political.[28]

Nixon had Harlow draft a statement, which he then revised extensively, and released on October 26. He praised Johnson for resisting pressure to contrive a "fake peace." He said Johnson had told him, often and convincingly, that "he will not play politics with this war." However, "in the last thirty-six hours I have been advised of a flurry of meetings in the White House and elsewhere on Vietnam. I am told that top officials in the administration have been driving very hard for an agreement on a bombing halt, accompanied possibly by a cease-fire, in the immediate future." He said he had learned that "these reports are true." (They were not, as documents in the LBJ Library make clear. In addition, Harlow had *not* written a word about a cease-fire, and had *not* stated categorically that "these reports are true.")

"I am also told that this spurt of activity is a cynical, last-minute attempt by President Johnson to salvage the candidacy of Mr. Humphrey," Nixon went on. "This I do not believe."[29]

Johnson called Nixon's bet, and raised him. At a luncheon

speech in New York the next day, October 27, the President portrayed Nixon as the shallow and deceitful man the Democrats had always said he was. Johnson charged that Nixon's statement contained "ugly and unfair charges," and he called Nixon "a man who distorts the history of his time." [30]

Nixon called and raised. Speaking that evening on CBS radio, Nixon warned that a coalition government in South Vietnam would constitute a "thinly disguised surrender. . . . Far from ending the war, it would only insure its resumption under conditions that would guarantee Communist victory." Neither Johnson nor Humphrey had said one word about a coalition government.

According to Nixon, Humphrey "has provided a classic example of what a President must not do. . . . He has talked too much and too loosely about Vietnam. By trying to please every audience and appease every faction, he can only have sown consternation among our friends and confusion among our adversaries. He seems bewildered and straddling."

Nixon went on to pledge that he would "do nothing that might interfere" with the Paris negotiations.[31]

That same day, October 27, Hanoi made its bet: the North Vietnamese agreed to respect the DMZ and refrain from attacking South Vietnamese cities, and to accept the GVN at the peace table, in return for a place at that table for the Vietcong and for a bombing halt.[32]

Johnson immediately summoned his military commander in Vietnam, General Creighton Abrams, to Washington for consultation. At 2:30 A.M., October 29, Johnson met the just-arrived Abrams in the Cabinet Room. After a review of the military situation, Johnson asked Abrams if he had any reluctance or hesitancy about a bombing halt. Abrams had no reservations; he said it was the right thing to do.[33]

At 6:15 A.M., Johnson called another meeting, to discuss Mrs. Chennault's activities on Nixon's behalf. Thieu had already indicated that whatever Abrams thought, the GVN was not ready to accept a bombing halt or to sit down with the Vietcong at the peace table. Clifford was outraged at the Nixon/Chennault/Thieu intrigue, calling it "reprehensible." But to denounce Nixon publicly for interfering with the peace process was to admit that the FBI had been tapping Mrs. Chennault's telephone, so nothing was done. Instead, Johnson sent word to the American ambassador in Saigon, Ellsworth Bunker, to put every pressure he could on Thieu to cooperate.

The betting had come around to Thieu, who was—like all the other players—taking tremendous risks. If Thieu refused to go along with Johnson and Humphrey won anyway, he would be in big trouble with the new President. Nevertheless, Thieu refused to go to Paris, whatever Johnson did.[34]

Meanwhile Nixon appeared on CBS's "Face the Nation" television show, his first network confrontation with reporters in two years. The questioning centered around his statement on the "rumors" about a bombing halt, and Johnson's angry response.

"I think President Johnson wants to bring this war to an end," Nixon explained. "I think he'd like to have a bombing pause provided it isn't going to cost American lives. . . . I made [my] statement and I would think that the President would be thanking, not attacking me."

Martin Agronsky asked Nixon why, if he really thought the rumor about a bombing halt was false, he had raised it at all.

"Because," Nixon replied, "it seemed to me that with all the speculation that was going on, the speculation that there was about to be a bombing pause, and that it would be negotiated for political reasons, that it was important . . . for me to nail it once and for all [sic]." He insisted that he was backing the President all the way, that it was Humphrey who was advocating a bombing halt without preconditions. "Who has backed the President? . . . I back him up and I only wish that Hubert Humphrey now would button up his lip and stick with the President on this."[35]

Johnson continued to pressure Ambassador Bunker to pressure Thieu to accept a bombing halt and a place at the peace table, without success. After two days of fruitless effort, on October 31, with the election five days away, Johnson either had to fold his hand and leave the game or bet everything he had.

That evening, he threw all his chips into the pot. On national television, he announced a breakthrough in Paris. He said Hanoi had agreed to expanded peace talks, to respect the DMZ, and to refrain from attacking South Vietnamese cities in return for an end to the bombing north of the DMZ. Johnson announced that he had therefore ordered a bombing halt, and that the expanded Paris talks would resume on Wednesday, November 6. He added that both the GVN and the Vietcong were "free" to participate in the peace talks.[36]

A giant wave of relief swept across the nation. Finally, at last, after all those years, there was an end in sight. Polls taken the next day showed a 55–28 approval for the bombing halt. Humphrey, according to the Washington Post, made "clear in public and private his belief that an enormous burden had now been lifted from his candidacy."[37]

The hoopla that surrounded the bombing halt generated the

falsest of hopes. The Democrats were inflating the prospects for peace beyond any reasonable expectation. Nixon, who had good reason to suspect that Thieu was not going to go along with Johnson (he noted immediately that Johnson had said the GVN was "free" to attend, not that it would), wisely kept his thoughts to himself. "I'm not going to say anything to undercut [Johnson]," Nixon declared the following morning in Texas. "Peace is too important for politics, and that's the way we're going to play it." [38]

Nixon let the euphoria build. Even as Humphrey passed him in the polls, he kept quiet. On November 2, Humphrey went ahead of Nixon in the Lou Harris poll, 43 percent to 40 percent, with Wallace down to 13 percent and 4 percent undecided. But Nixon believed Johnson was bluffing, that he could not deliver Thieu, that Thieu would call the bluff, and that the Democrats would then lose. He was exactly right.

On November 2 in Saigon, Thieu announced that "the government of South Vietnam deeply regrets not being able to participate in the [peace] talks." He said the GVN would not sit down with the Vietcong. [39]

With Thieu's announcement, the air started to leak out of the balloon. Suddenly peace seemed not so much at hand as more elusive than ever.

Nixon moved quickly. Although he still refused extended comment, and still insisted he would not undercut the President, he said, "In view of the early reports that we've had this morning [from Saigon], the prospects for peace are not as bright as we would have hoped a few days ago." [40]

On Sunday morning, November 3, en route from Texas to California for the final rally of the campaign, Nixon had Bob Finch brief two wire-service reporters, Bill Boyarsky of AP and Dan Rapoport of UPI. Finch said the Nixon camp had been "surprised" by Thieu's refusal to go to Paris, because "we had the impression that all the diplomatic ducks were in a row." Finch implied that Johnson had acted hastily in order to help Humphrey.

In Los Angeles, Nixon went to a TV studio to tape a "Meet the Press" program. Boyarsky and Rapoport had spread the news of Finch's charge. On the TV panel, Herbert Kaplow of NBC News made it his first question: "Mr. Nixon, some of your close aides have been trying to spread the word that President Johnson timed the Vietnam bombing pause to help Vice President Humphrey in Tuesday's election. Do you agree with them?"

Nixon: "No, I don't make that charge. I must say that many of my aides and many of the people supporting my candidacy around the country seem to share that view. They share it, I suppose, because the pause came at that time so late in the campaign. But

President Johnson has been very candid with me throughout these discussions, and I do not make such a charge."

The dissembling left Kaplow in disarray. He recovered sufficiently to ask if it was conceivable that Nixon's aides would speak out in disagreement with Nixon.

Nixon: "Oh, altogether conceivable. I know, for example, one of my aides who—so-called aides who made this statement is Lieutenant Governor Robert Finch. He completely disagrees with my appraisal of this. His appraisal of the situation around the country is that many people believe that the bombing pause was politically motivated and was timed to affect the election. I don't agree with him, but he is a man in his own right and has made this statement."

Nixon had moved from the inconceivable through the unimaginable to the absolutely impossible without a hint of a smile; indeed his face and his body language exuded sincerity.

Things got worse. Nixon went on to say he wanted to "make it very clear" that if he won on Tuesday, "I will be willing to cooperate with the President in any way that . . . [he] would deem helpful. If he, for example . . . would consider it helpful for me to go to Paris or to go to Saigon in order to get the negotiations off dead center, I would be glad to do so."

Nixon's pledge, with its implicit reminder of Ike's 1952 promise that if elected "I shall go to Korea," was as bold and brazen as anything he had done in a career marked by boldness and brazen effrontery. Here he was, the direct beneficiary of Thieu's refusal to cooperate, which he had secretly encouraged, saying that he was willing to go to Saigon to get Thieu to cooperate!

Nixon went on: "Let me make one thing clear. I don't suggest this as a grandstand stunt. . . . The key point, of course, is to get the South Vietnamese to that conference table. I believe they ought to go to the conference table. . . . If my influence could be helpful, I will be helpful." [41]

Nixon's grandstand stunt, inviting himself to be the negotiator for the Johnson Administration with Thieu, seemed to the President to be about the same as asking the fox to guard the henhouse. Furious with Nixon already because of Finch's remarks on the plane, he called Nixon on the telephone.

"Who's this guy Fink?" Johnson bellowed. "Why is he taking out after me?"

"Mr. President," Nixon replied calmly, "that's Finch, not Fink." [42]

The President demanded to know what Mrs. Chennault was up to, thus letting Nixon know that the Democrats had the goods on the Nixon/Mitchell/Chennault/Thieu connection.

Nixon told Johnson that Mrs. Chennault represented no one

but herself, that she was acting on her own, and that Nixon's only wish was to help Johnson achieve peace.[43]

There are so many lies told by American politicians that it is a common practice for the politician who is being lied to (in this instance Johnson, a master liar himself) to, in effect, shrug and say to himself, "Well, if that's his line, even when he knows that I know that he is lying, I'll just pretend to accept it." Johnson did so in this case. He signed off by complaining some more about "Fink," then hung up.

Despite Nixon's denial, the Chennault story was a potential bombshell. It was widely known among the reporters covering the campaign, but it was up to Humphrey or Johnson to make it public, as none of the reporters had any hard information. As Teddy White later wrote, if the Democrats had made "an open charge that the Nixon leaders were saboteurs of the peace," Humphrey "might have won the Presidency." But, according to White (who was a great admirer of the American political system and its practitioners), "the good instinct of that small-town boy Hubert Humphrey prevailed," and Humphrey refused to break the story.

White was nearly struck dumb by his admiration for Humphrey at this moment: "I know of no more essentially decent story in American politics than Humphrey's refusal to [break the story]."

White was almost as impressed by Nixon, who was, according to White, perfectly innocent. White wrote that when the Nixon camp first heard the story, Nixon's aides investigated, found out about Mrs. Chennault's activities, and were "appalled." White gave the Nixon people his personal clean bill of health: "The fury and dismay at Nixon's headquarters when his aides discovered the [Chennault] report were so intense that they could not have been feigned simply for the benefit of this reporter."[44]

The Humphrey people were also capable of dissembling. They put out the word that if they broke the story, and Nixon still won the election, it would make it impossible for Nixon to govern. So they held the story back for the good of the country.[45]

In another version, Johnson would not let Humphrey break the story because he would have had to reveal the illegal telephone tap on Mrs. Chennault. Further, according to an unnamed official in the Johnson White House interviewed by Seymour Hersh, Johnson was angry at Humphrey for breaking with him on the war, and thus "had no interest in defeating Nixon. He wasn't going to do anything for the purpose of seeing Nixon discredited."[46]

Over the years, as the details of the Chennault story began to emerge in the memoirs of the participants, it became one of the favorites of the Nixon bashers. They charged that he was so utterly

cynical, so completely self-serving, so absolutely lacking in principle of any kind, that he deliberately sabotaged peace just to win
the election.

Insofar as the charges imply that Nixon prevented peace in
November 1968, they are false.

Not that Nixon did not want to, or try to, but he did not
have to.

Nixon did not need Mrs. Chennault to persuade Thieu to refuse to go to Paris. Thieu had no trouble figuring that one out for
himself, as the Johnson people well knew. In an unsigned, undated
memorandum in the LBJ Library in Austin, with no salutation or
other indication as to whom it was directed, Clark Clifford wrote
by hand: "Reason why Saigon has not moved and does not want to
move [on peace talks]. A). Saigon does not want peace.

1. Make better political settlement later.
2. In no danger because of U.S. troops.
3. No compulsion to help ARVN.
4. Wealth in country.
5. Personal corruption."[47]

Clifford was absolutely right.

The GVN was a government without a country or a people. Its
sole support was the U.S. government. Its sole *raison d'être* was
the war. For the GVN to agree to peace would be to sign its own
death warrant. The 550,000 American soldiers in South Vietnam,
plus the U.S. Navy offshore, plus the American Air Force stationed
in Thailand, the Philippines, Guam, and elsewhere, meant exactly
what Clifford said, that the GVN was "in no danger."

There was no need to improve ARVN when the Americans
insisted on doing all the fighting anyway. Almost the only wealth
in the country, almost the only source of employment, was the U.S.
Army and the American Embassy. The personal corruption in the
GVN was as bad as any in the world.

Under these conditions, why on earth should Thieu go to a
peace table? He had everything to lose, nothing to gain.

And who created these conditions? Not Richard Nixon.

It is true that he had contributed, with his hawkish statements
from 1954 right on through to 1968, but so had the Kennedy Administration and before that the Eisenhower Administration and after
that the Johnson Administration. The GVN of 1968 was an all-
American creation.

The big lie in 1968 was that there was a way to peace through
a coalition government, one that could be achieved in four-power

talks (U.S., GVN, North Vietnam, and NLF) in Paris. That implied that the GVN really was a government that really did represent something more than itself and a handful of corrupt high-ranking ARVN officers.

Nixon knew that Thieu would not go to Paris, with or without that rather silly woman whispering in his ear the promises John Mitchell was passing along from Richard Nixon. Being Nixon, he worried, and could not keep himself from trying to influence Thieu through Chennault, so he was guilty in his motives and his actions, but he was not decisive. It was not Nixon who prevented an outbreak of peace in November 1968. He merely exploited a situation he did not create.

He did so by mounting a calculated campaign to convince the American people that their President had sold out the people of South Vietnam, tried a tricky political deal and failed, capitulated to the Communists, deceived the GVN, and played politics with peace.

He kept it up, right to the end. On Monday, November 4, in an unscheduled visit to party workers in Los Angeles, and again that evening in a nationwide telethon, he pounded home the point that the "high hopes for peace of three days ago" had dwindled. He said he would not criticize Johnson's motives; indeed, he credited the President with stopping the bombing with "the best of intentions."

"But when we consider the fact that it was only three days ago that the hopes for peace were tremendously high as a result of the bombing pause, and that now those hopes are quite discouraging because of the developments since then, it is clear that if we are going to avoid what could be a diplomatic disaster, it is going to be necessary to get some new men and a united front in the United States."

As President-elect, he promised he would "work with President Johnson to put together these fragile hopes of peace that now seem to be hopelessly apart." [48]

The polls had shut down on Friday evening, showing that the Humphrey surge following the bombing halt had put him over the top. Nixon and his people believed that had the election come on Saturday or Sunday (or had Johnson waited two or three days before making his announcement, thus preventing Thieu from undercutting him before Tuesday), Humphrey would have been the almost certain winner. But with their adroit handling of Thieu's refusal to go to Paris, by Monday night hopes ran high among the Nixon people. [49]

On his nationwide television broadcast that evening, Nixon

seized his final opportunity to drive home the point that the bombing halt was a political decision taken at the expense of American boys fighting in Vietnam. He said that at first Johnson's order had appeared to offer real hope, "but then the negotiations came apart at the seams."

Nixon said he had heard "a very disturbing report" that in the past two days "the North Vietnamese are moving thousands of tons of supplies down the Ho Chi Minh Trail, and our bombers are not able to stop them."[50]

He had heard no such report. He simply made that up.

The Democrats were monitoring the Nixon show. Humphrey was told about what Nixon had said. He immediately replied, telling his audience "there is no indication of increased infiltration." His aides had checked with the Pentagon, he said, and no one there had heard any such thing. "And let me say that it does not help the negotiations to falsely accuse anyone at this particular time."[51] Of course, it also did not help the negotiations for the Democrats to pretend that serious peace talks were going to begin on Wednesday.

THERE WAS a remarkable similarity between the last days of the 1968 campaign and the last days of the 1972 campaign. In the first case, the Administration implied that peace was at hand. In the second case, the Administration said explicitly that peace was at hand. In each case, the President knew that the GVN had *not* agreed to the proposed peace formula, and that the North Vietnamese had *not* agreed to settle for something short of victory. In each case, in its quest for votes, the Administration treated the American people with cynical contempt.

In 1968, American politics had sunk to depths not reached since the Civil War and Reconstruction. America's political leaders, Johnson and Humphrey, Nixon and Agnew, and most of the others, were just playing with people. The image they conjure up for this author is one of Charlie Chaplin acting the mad dictator, kicking around the globe as if it were a balloon. If they had the slightest feeling for the death and destruction that was devouring Vietnam, if they had any concern for the lives of the American soldiers in Vietnam, if they had the least commitment to a decent respect for the opinion of mankind, if they had the vaguest concern to meet their constitutional obligation to promote domestic tranquillity, if it ever even occurred to them to strive to provide the conditions that would allow the American people to pursue happiness, they managed to ignore it all in their single-minded pursuit of personal political victory at any cost.

It would take years, and many violent storms with hurricane-force winds, to clear the air of the loathsome stench of the last week of the 1968 campaign.

ON MONDAY NIGHT, from Los Angeles television studios, Nixon and Humphrey staged telethons, two hours for Humphrey, four for Nixon. Nixon appeared alone, sitting in the middle of a stage in a contoured swivel chair. Humphrey had Senator Muskie by his side. Both presidential candidates answered call-in questions, which came in at an astonishing rate of 130,000 per hour.[52]

Humphrey made much of Agnew's absence and Muskie's presence. He had been pushing Agnew's name all week; the last-minute Democratic TV commercial showed Agnew accompanied by uproarious canned laughter. On live TV, Humphrey said, "My co-pilot, Ed Muskie, is ready to take over at any time." It got so bad that James Doyle of the Boston *Globe* composed a make-believe lead for his Election Day story that read, "Vice President Hubert H. Humphrey pledged today that if elected, he will resign immediately and let Senator Edmund S. Muskie become President."[53]

Both candidates paraded an array of Hollywood stars, top billing going to Frank Sinatra and Paul Newman for Humphrey, Jackie Gleason for Nixon. A high point for Humphrey came when the cameras switched to Hyannis Port to show Larry O'Brien and Senator Edward Kennedy, the last of the Kennedy brothers, walking along the beach. Nixon countered nicely; he brought David Eisenhower, all freckles and arms and legs and awkwardness and grin, to his side to report that Granddad wanted Mr. Nixon elected.

As his show ended, Nixon threw his hands over his head, spread them, and extended his first two fingers on each hand in the V-for-Victory sign first made popular by Winston Churchill, then used as a trademark by Dwight Eisenhower, and now adopted by Richard Nixon as his own. He executed a brief Jackie Gleason shuffle, joked, "And away we go," and strode out of the studio.[54]

The following morning, Tuesday, November 5, Election Day, Nixon (who had already voted by absentee ballot) boarded the *Tricia* with his family and staff to fly to New York. He settled down in his private compartment, as he had done all through the campaign, and summoned people forward. He thanked his speech writers, thanked the advance men, thanked the managers. He told his family he expected to win, but it was quite possible that he would lose, because of the bombing halt, which he estimated had cost him from three to five million votes. He gave Pat a present of a diamond-and-pearl pin with earrings to match.[55]

By 7 P.M., Eastern time, he was settled in his suite on the thirty-fifth floor of the Waldorf Towers. Pat and the girls had their own suite; before retiring to his room, Nixon told them that unlike 1960, this one would be settled by midnight or 1 A.M., Eastern time. He took a hot bath, tried to nap, failed, and by 8:20 P.M. was drinking coffee and watching the early returns. From time to time, Haldeman would pop in with a piece of information, or Dwight Chapin with more coffee or cigars, but until nearly midnight Nixon was alone. It must have been pure agony for him, with who could ever guess how much *déjà vu.*

At 9 P.M. he had 41 percent to Humphrey's 38 percent.

At 9:30 P.M. he had 41 percent to Humphrey's 39 percent.

At 10 P.M. the two men were dead even.

At 10:30 P.M. they were still even.

At 11 P.M. Humphrey had moved into a slight lead.

Nixon, on his yellow legal pad, played with the nearly infinite number of possibilities. If he carried California, Ohio, Illinois, Missouri, and Maryland, all still too close to call, and added them to the states he had surely won, he would have 288 electoral votes (270 needed to win). There were other toss-up states that might come his way, Texas, for example, but Haldeman had brought word that there was some chicanery going on in Dallas, and of course every Republican in the nation was worried about what Mayor Daley might do in Cook County.

By midnight, Humphrey was leading Nixon in the popular vote by 600,000, or 43.5 percent to 42.6 percent. Nevertheless, after checking with Murray Chotiner, Nixon was confident that he had 231 solid electoral votes and a better than fighting chance for at least 70 more.

At this point, Nixon should have sent a silent prayer of thanks to the gods of political fortune for Humphrey's insistence that he would "stand by the Constitution." Had Humphrey agreed to Nixon's demand that he support whoever got the most popular votes, regardless of what happened in the electoral college, and if the current trend continued, with Nixon winning in the electoral college while Humphrey won the popular vote, Nixon would have been embarrassed at best, challenged by Humphrey to live up to his own stipulation at worst. But since Humphrey had not agreed, that was one possibility Nixon need not worry about.

At 2:30 A.M. Nixon summoned Finch, Haldeman, Mitchell, and Chotiner to his suite. They waited in his living room until 3 A.M., when Nixon emerged from his bedroom, clutching his legal pad. He went over the totals, the projections, the trends, the figures, and announced that his calculation was that he was a winner.

"Any objections?" he asked. Everyone agreed.

Nixon telephoned Agnew: "Well, Ted, we've won." He called Nelson Rockefeller to thank him for his help. Then he summoned his speech writers and inner staff for a get-together. Nixon sipped a beer, smoked a cigar, and unwound. He asserted and reasserted his belief that Agnew had been the right choice. The man had capacity, brains, energy, and quality. Someone quipped, "Well, we sure concealed that from the American people during the campaign." Safire prepared a victory statement.[56]

A few doors down the hall, the confidence surging through the Nixon suite was not felt at all. In Pat's room, all was tension. At 6 A.M., television commentators reported that Mayor Daley was holding back the Cook County vote. Pat experienced a wave of agonizing memories of 1960. Julie, Tricia, and Helene Drown watched her disappear into the bathroom: "We could hear that she was sick to her stomach."[57]

By 8 A.M. the television networks had conceded victory to Nixon. He went to bed, tried to sleep, could not, and was up at nine. He went to the suite where Pat and the girls were staying; Julie presented him with the gift she had been sewing for him on the airplane throughout the campaign, the presidential seal, done in crewel. She had stitched at the bottom, "To RN—JN."

"Daddy," Julie said as she gave it to him, "I never had any doubt you would win. I just wanted something to be ready right away to prove it."[58]

Pat asked, "But, Dick, are we sure of Illinois? Are we completely sure?" Nixon assured her that Daley had released the Cook County votes and he had carried the state, and the nation, and was now President-elect. Pat cried with relief and happiness.[59]

At 11:30 A.M. Humphrey called from Minneapolis to concede and to wish Nixon luck.

Nixon had 31,770,237 votes (43.4 percent), which was 2,338,345 fewer votes than he had won in 1960, despite a 4.5 million vote increase in the total number cast. Humphrey had 31,270,533 votes (42.7 percent), and George Wallace, 9,906,141 (13.5 percent). Minor-party candidates, all on the Left, had 239,908 (.35 percent). If the minor-party votes had gone to Humphrey, plus 2.5 percent of Wallace's votes, Humphrey would have won the popular vote. But in the electoral college, Nixon had a solid victory, 301 votes to Humphrey's 191 and Wallace's 46.

Of the Big Seven states on which Nixon had concentrated, he carried California, Illinois, and Ohio, while losing New York, Michigan, Pennsylvania, and Texas. Except for Washington and Texas, he had carried all the Great Plains, Rocky Mountain, and Far West states. The South had brutally rejected the Democrats;

Wallace took Arkansas, Louisiana, Mississippi, Alabama, and Georgia, and the rest went to Nixon. But the Northeast had rallied to Humphrey; Nixon carried New Jersey, Vermont, and New Hampshire, with the remainder going to Humphrey. In the Midwest, Humphrey won his home state of Minnesota, plus Michigan, with Nixon taking all the others.

Nixon was the first candidate since Zachary Taylor in 1848 to win the Presidency while his party failed to carry either House or Senate. In 1968, the Democrats lost five Senate seats but retained a 58–42 majority; in the House of Representatives, the Republicans gained but four seats (after predicting gains of thirty-five to forty seats), leaving the Democrats with a 243–192 majority.

In his own analysis, Nixon stressed that 57 percent of the voters had chosen either him or Wallace, which he interpreted to mean that a majority wanted change across the board. The congressional figures indicated that what the voters wanted was change at the top. The negative side, for Nixon, included the embarrassing fact that he ran 367,000 votes behind the total Republican vote for the House of Representatives, as opposed to 1960, when he ran 5,483,000 votes ahead of the Republican candidates for the House. (In 1960, Kennedy ran 3,000 votes ahead of the Democratic Party; in 1968, Humphrey was 1,069,000 behind his party.)

In sum, despite the clear-cut victory in the electoral college, Nixon's mandate to govern in 1968 was no clearer than Kennedy's in 1960.

At noon, November 6, Nixon went to the ballroom of the Waldorf-Astoria to meet his deliriously happy supporters.

"Having lost a close one eight years ago and having won a close one this year, I can say this—winning's a lot more fun." Cheers and applause.

"A great philosophy is never one without defeat. It is always one without fear. What is important is that a man or a woman engage in battle, be in the arena." More cheers.

Then he turned to the material Safire had prepared. "I saw many signs in this campaign," Nixon said. "Some of them were not friendly and some were very friendly. But the one that touched me the most was the one that I saw in Deshler, Ohio, at the end of a long day of whistle-stopping. . . . A teenager held up a sign, 'Bring Us Together.'

"And that will be the great objective of this administration at the outset, to bring the American people together." [60]

No one could deny that the American people very badly needed to be brought back together. Less clear was whether Nixon was the man who could do it. His campaign had been almost totally bereft of any reaching out to blacks, the counterculture, the doves, or the poor. Instead, he had run a sophisticated campaign to capitalize on the polarization among the nation's people, its races, and its regions. He made it into an "us versus them" contest, the "us" being the Silent Majority, Middle America, the white, comfortable, patriotic, hawkish "forgotten Americans." By his actions in the last week, he had given Thieu a veto power over his Vietnam policy. He had urged the American people to lower their voices, while he and Agnew raised theirs.

His tactics, whether cynical or sincere, had worked. He had won. But now he had to govern, and his tactics had so badly divided further the already badly divided nation that it was going to be difficult at best for him to do so.

CHAPTER ELEVEN

TRANSITION AND INAUGURATION
November 6, 1968– January 20, 1969

AT AGE FIFTY-FIVE, after twenty-two years in politics, Richard Nixon was about to take command. It would be a new experience for him. He had been a campaigner all his career, which had allowed him to concentrate exclusively on what was wrong with the Democrats. Criticism, not constructive comment, was his stock-in-trade. As a critic, he could pick and choose the issues on which the Democrats were most vulnerable, ignoring or sidestepping all others.

As President, he would not have that luxury. He would have to deal with all the issues, attempt to solve all the problems, take responsibility for his actions and words. His viewpoint on America's problems and policies was 180 degrees different on November 6 from what it had been on November 4. Now they were his problems, where they had been his opportunities; soon they would be his policies, where they had been Johnson's; in ten weeks, he could no longer criticize, but must command.

As he had stressed for the past eight years, the problems were immense. First of all, there was Vietnam. Peace in Vietnam was his number-one priority, a clear-cut goal. What was not so clear was how to achieve it. He could not gain peace through victory—an invasion of North Vietnam, the destruction of the NVA, the occupation of Hanoi, on the model of Germany in World War II, was out of the question because of the strength of the antiwar opposition within the United States. So was the use of atomic weapons, on the model of Japan in World War II.

Peace through unilateral and immediate withdrawal was

equally out of the question, at least to Nixon. He insisted on peace with honor, meaning peace with Thieu still in power (at least in South Vietnam's cities) and ARVN still in action.

Nixon's model was Korea, 1953. He would get peace not through victory, or withdrawal, or surrender, but through an armistice, one that would keep Vietnam divided on an indefinite basis, like Korea, and through the improvement of ARVN, so that it could defend South Vietnam.

As with Korea in 1953, Nixon saw the key to peace in Vietnam in 1969 in Moscow and Peking. In 1953, Ike had forced the Chinese to accept an armistice by threatening them with a wider war if they did not. He had also made it clear to the Russians that any easing of tension elsewhere in the world depended on their restraining the North Koreans. As Nixon knew, Ike had not been explicit in making these threats. He let his reputation do it for him (he was, after all, the man who had pulverized Germany just eight years earlier).

Nixon had a reputation too, and he thought it would speak for itself. As he explained to Haldeman during the campaign, "I call it the Madman Theory, Bob. I want the North Vietnamese to believe . . . I might do *anything*. . . . We'll just slip the word to them that, 'for God's sake, you know Nixon is obsessed about Communism. We can't restrain him when he's angry—and he has his hand on the nuclear button'—and Ho Chi Minh himself will be in Paris in two days begging for peace." [1]

Back in August, Nixon had responded to a question from one of the southern delegates to the Miami convention—"How do you bring the war to a conclusion?"—by citing the Korean example and Eisenhower's use of threat. "I'll tell you one thing," Nixon had continued. "I played a little poker when I was in the Navy. . . . I learned this—when a guy didn't have the cards, he talked awfully big. But when he had the cards, he just sat there—had that cold look in his eyes. Now, we've got the cards. . . . What we've got to do is walk softly and carry a big stick." [2]

The flaw in Nixon's reasoning was that he did not hold the winning cards. As McNamara had made clear earlier that year, the Soviets could match the United States bomb for bomb, which was why the atomic option was not a real option. Nixon thought he could threaten the North Vietnamese into accepting an armistice (really, a cease-fire in place). But any implied threat to destroy Hanoi immediately raised the counterthreat, that the Soviets would destroy Saigon. Nixon was not the only madman in a position to make threats.

What Nixon did have, and was counting on, was a carrot to

offer Peking and another for Moscow. For the Chinese, a normalization of relations. For Moscow, arms control, trade, and an easing of tension. To Nixon, these seemed such reasonable deals that he was almost certain of success; he thought that within six months of his inaugural, a year at the outside, he would have peace with honor in Vietnam.

PEACE IN VIETNAM would solve many of his other problems and lessen all of them. Most obviously and most immediately, peace in Vietnam would bring peace to the campuses and an end to the antiwar movement. The generation gap, if not bridged, would at least be narrowed. No more violence in Vietnam would mean much less violence at home.

Abroad, Nixon's entire concept of a "new era of negotiations" to replace the preceding era of confrontation would be enhanced, in China, Russia, the Middle East, and around the world, if the peace talks in Paris were successful. The Soviets had already indicated that they were eager for a new start. The Johnson Administration had been committed to Strategic Arms Limitation Talks (SALT) with the Soviets, but had canceled the initial meetings following the Soviet invasion and occupation of Czechoslovakia in August. In a speech on November 6, First Deputy Premier Kirill Mazurov called for the "normalization of relations" and noted that Soviet proposals for mutual limitations on nuclear weapons were still on the table. He urged Nixon to pick them up.[3]

The potential benefit of peace in Vietnam and arms control for the American economy was very great. During the campaign, Humphrey had told voters that they had never had it so good, and in many ways that was true, but the wartime prosperity had been purchased, in large part, at the expense of the future. Not until June 1968 had Congress raised taxes to pay for the war (through a one-year 10 percent surtax). Meanwhile the Johnson Administration had resisted demands for a slowdown in spending while the Federal Reserve Board pumped out excessive supplies of money. Unrestrained spending in the public and private sectors had created a massive federal deficit and a pervasive inflationary psychosis.

Nixon was inheriting an economy in which the inflation rate, at 4.7 percent, was the highest since the Korean War. Wage increases of 6.5 percent in 1968 showed no signs of slowing. With only 3.3 percent of the labor force without jobs, the country was suffering from overemployment. Interest rates were at their highest levels since the Civil War (the prime rate jumped from 5.75 percent in October to 6.5 percent in late November). The overheated American economy had generated a flood of imported goods, which had inflicted a serious toll on America's traditionally favorable trade balance, reducing it to only $1 billion.

Nixon's job was to cut the inflation rate. There were many ways for him to do that, but much the quickest and most effective was to end the war.

All this Nixon knew perfectly well, and he was more than ready to give Hanoi peace and security in return for peace and security for the Thieu government in Saigon, just as Ike had given the North Koreans their peace and security in return for peace and security for the Syngman Rhee regime in Seoul. It struck Nixon as a fair and reasonable offer. Whether Ho Chi Minh would see it that way, he would have to find out.

ON NOVEMBER 6, late in the afternoon, Nixon, his aides, and his family flew on an Air Force jet to Key Biscayne, where Nixon had rented a three-bedroom bungalow on Biscayne Bay from Senator Smathers, next door to Bebe Rebozo's home. The first night there, Nixon slept nine hours straight, a near-record for him.[4]

For the family, Key Biscayne provided a badly needed opportunity to rest. Life was slow and quiet there. Only two relatively small resort hotels dotted the beach. Nixon's aides stayed at villas of the Key Biscayne Hotel, a few blocks away. Half the island was wild mango groves. The garish high-rise hotels of Miami Beach were far away; the homes on Key Biscayne were modest one-story affairs, not to be compared to the mansions of Palm Beach.

The Nixons had been coming to the place for seventeen years; it was one of the few spots in the world where Nixon could relax, just as Bebe Rebozo was one of the few people in the world with whom Nixon felt entirely comfortable. Only in Key Biscayne would Nixon drive a car. He would rent one at the airport, and drive with Bebe to the small shopping center for groceries or sun-tan lotion. Nixon and Rebozo especially enjoyed going to the drugstore to pick up humorous birthday and anniversary cards.[5]

But in November of 1968, President-elect Nixon discovered that such simple human pleasures were no longer possible. The Secret Service had moved in on him, along with the national press corps and a horde of curious tourists. Whatever he wanted from the shopping center, he had to send someone out to get it for him. Driving a car himself was out of the question. If he wanted privacy outside his living quarters, he could get it only by going off on Rebozo's boat, and even then the Coast Guard and Secret Service kept a close watch.[6] He could get away for a day by flying by helicopter to Grand Cay in the Bahamas, about 140 miles off the Florida coast, where his friend Bob Abplanalp owned the island.

NOVEMBER 6, 1968–JANUARY 20, 1969 | 227

Rebozo handled Nixon's personal finances. During the campaign, Nixon had listed his total worth at $515,830. The great bulk of that money, $401,382, was invested in Fisher Island, a 220-acre island off Miami Beach being developed by Rebozo. Immediately after the election, Nixon decided to sell his apartment in New York and to purchase two bungalows in Key Biscayne, the one belonging to Senator Smathers and the one beside it. The two homes, along with Rebozo's, were to be brought into a single compound by enclosing the three structures behind an eleven-foot-high hibiscus hedge. Together, Nixon's two homes cost him a quarter of a million.[7]

For the family, according to Julie, "a perfect day was reading in deck chairs . . . occasionally looking out over the glassy calm toward the city of Miami. . . . If it was warm enough, we took a morning and afternoon swim, always a walk on the beach, and finished the day with one of Bebe's delicious steak and Cuban black-bean dinners."[8]

Nixon often said that he wished he had more time for reading, that he envied the professors their contemplative lives, so one might have thought he would seize the opportunity to do as his family did in the Florida sunshine. But that was not at all his style; he was much too restless for such a life.

"What do we do with him?" Haldeman asked rhetorically one day in December 1968. "He knows he needs to relax, so he comes down to Florida. He likes to swim, so he swims for ten minutes. Then that's over. He doesn't paint, he doesn't horseback-ride, he doesn't have a hobby. His best relaxation is talking shop, but he knows he should not be doing that, because that doesn't seem to be relaxing. So what do we do with him?"[9]

The obvious answer was, talk shop, which was what was done beginning on November 7. After his long sleep, Nixon ate his regular breakfast of orange juice, half a grapefruit, cold cereal and skim milk, and coffee, took a short swim, and went to work. His aides came over, and they began the process of creating a Nixon Administration.

NIXON HAD no practice in this sort of thing, and he proved to be no good at it. He kept people dangling and in suspense far longer than he needed to, subjected them to anxieties they should not have had to deal with, gave them feelings of insecurity that hampered their effectiveness and curtailed their willingness to tell the boss something they guessed he didn't want to hear—and all this with men who had served him loyally and well since the 1960 campaign (Haldeman and Ehrlichman), or in the fifties (Harlow), or even back to the forties (Finch, Klein, and Chotiner). The single aide who had his immediate and wholehearted backing, and knew it, was John Mitchell, whom he first met in 1964.

It was characteristic of Nixon that he inspired and got far more loyalty than he ever gave.

Nixon took weeks to choose his White House staff because, as Safire wrote, he did not want anyone to assume that just because he or she had been prominent in the campaign, and was widely respected, and had been loyal, he or she was entitled to a job. Safire said of Nixon's technique, "Everybody was to sweat a little." [10]

Nixon's first staff appointment was Rose Mary Woods as his personal secretary. It was an inevitable choice, and a perfect one, as she had everything a President could want in a secretary. She was marvelously competent, she knew Nixon as well as any living person outside his family, she got along easily with Pat and the girls, she never gossiped, and her loyalty was, rightly, legendary.

His second appointment was Bob Haldeman as his chief of staff. That was not so inevitable, but it was a good one, as Haldeman had many of the qualities any President wants in a chief of staff. He was intelligent, hardworking, efficient, ruthless, loyal, and tough enough to stand up to the slurs and pounding that went with the job of being the President's son of a bitch, the man who would have to say no to requests to see the President or for other favors far more often than he would be able to say yes.

Haldeman's job, as Nixon described it, was "administrative rather than substantive. . . . He would be a funnel rather than a filter . . . the gatekeeper of the Oval Office." [11]

Haldeman was, in many respects, like Ike's chief of staff, Sherman Adams. Both men were humorless and essentially friendless. Ike's relationship with Adams was entirely professional; so too Nixon's with Haldeman. After more than a decade of the most intimate association, Nixon did not know how many children Haldeman had. [12]

Haldeman and Woods were at loggerheads from day one. Each wanted to be the first person Nixon saw in the morning, and the last at night. The evidence indicates that Nixon wanted it that way, as it kept them struggling against each other, rather than combining against him.

Herb Klein went all the way back to 1946 with Nixon; in that year, as an editor of the Alhambra *Post-Advocate,* Klein had been one of the first to endorse Nixon in his campaign against Jerry Voorhis. Like Nixon, Klein had risen in the world since those days, to become editor of the San Diego *Union.* He had served continuously as unofficial Nixon adviser, and in 1960 and 1962 as press secretary. He directed the press operation in the 1968 campaign. He anticipated that he would be one of the first named by Nixon to the White House staff, and the obvious post for him was press secretary.[13]

Klein was widely respected by the working press, from the giants at the top like James Reston of *The New York Times* and Hugh Sidey of *Time* magazine down to the local reporters. The common expectation was that he would be the James Hagerty of the Nixon Administration. Hagerty, as Ike's press secretary, was generally regarded as the best at that job since World War II. More than just a spokesman, he had been a prominent and influential member of Eisenhower's White House staff.

But whatever the media, and Klein, expected, Nixon wanted no part of a Hagerty-type press secretary on his team. The President-elect had a quite incredible view of the media and their relationship to the White House, and an equally incredible view of the relationship of the President to news events. No one could ever describe those views better than Nixon himself, in his memoirs: "In the modern presidency, concern for image must rank with concern for substance."

Nixon believed there was a continuous war going on between the President and the press corps. He was, he wrote, "prepared to have to do combat with the media in order to get my views and my programs to the people," but he complained that it would not be a fair fight, because "the media are far more powerful than the President in creating public awareness and shaping public opinion."[14]

This was a profound misjudgment on Nixon's part. The truth is the opposite. It is the President, not the press, who decides what is news. It is the President, not the press, who can make an event into a crisis or downplay it so that it disappears.

For a realistic view of the relationship between the President and the media, consider Eisenhower's answer to a question at his last press conference, in January of 1961. Robert Spivack asked him if he felt the reporters had been fair to him over the years.

"Well," Ike replied, "when you come down to it, I don't see what a reporter could do much to a President, do you?"[15]

But although Ike downplayed the importance of the press, he nevertheless wooed it, primarily through Hagerty. Nixon grossly exaggerated the importance of the press, then went to war with it. One tactic Nixon used was to insult the press by appointing as his press secretary a totally inexperienced and completely unprepared young man, twenty-nine-year-old Ron Ziegler, late of J. Walter Thompson and before that a barker at Disneyland, while shunting aside the potential Hagerty on his team, Klein. After a long and painful delay, Nixon finally named Klein his director of communications. It was a new post with no clearly defined duties.[16]

For Nixon, this convoluted arrangement had two advantages. It put Ziegler and Klein in competition with each other, and it prevented either man from emerging as the Hagerty of the Nixon White House. This meant, in practice, that Nixon would be his own press secretary.

NIXON ALSO INTENDED to be his own foreign secretary. He showed this determination decisively when he left Key Biscayne, on November 11, to return to New York, stopping en route in Washington for a foreign-policy briefing from Johnson, Rusk, Clifford, Helms, and Rostow. Nixon's foreign-policy adviser during the campaign had been Richard Allen, a thirty-two-year-old fellow at the Hoover Institution and a minor figure at best in the Republican Party (by way of contrast, Eisenhower's foreign-policy adviser during his 1952 campaign had been sixty-four-year-old John Foster Dulles, easily the most prominent Republican in foreign affairs). Allen's importance to Nixon could be measured most accurately by Nixon's decision to go to his briefing from Johnson and the high command of American foreign policy without Allen.

The briefing, not surprisingly, revealed that there were no significant differences between Nixon's views and those of the Administration. For the most part, Nixon listened while Rusk described in some detail the steps that had led to the bombing halt. All those present agreed that the United States had to see the war through to a successful conclusion.

How to achieve that goal? Clifford offered three alternatives. First, continue fighting without talking. Second, hold private, secret negotiations with Hanoi. Third, pressure Thieu to come to Paris. Clifford recommended the third course, to be implemented by having Johnson tell Thieu that the talks would go ahead with or without him. Simultaneously, Clifford recommended that Johnson begin to reduce the level of combat and begin a troop withdrawal. This, Clifford said, would be "a major step to end the war." Nixon could "clean up the details" after his inaugural.[17]

Nixon gave both public and private support to Clifford's program for pressuring Thieu to come to Paris. When he emerged from the meeting, he told reporters that the Johnson Administration would speak for his Administration in foreign affairs during the following two months, and suggested that this one-voice policy might lead to "some very significant action and progress toward peace." This was widely interpreted as being directed toward getting Thieu to Paris.[18]

In private, Nixon had Mitchell call Mrs. Chennault to ask her to tell Thieu that he should go to Paris. That one did not work: an indignant Mrs. Chennault reminded Mitchell that just two weeks earlier he had called the talks "phony" and urged her to tell Thieu not to go. Now Nixon had completely reversed his position.[19]

Mrs. Chennault's refusal forced Nixon to act himself, and he wrote Thieu to tell him to go to Paris, or else. Clifford added to the pressure by publicly threatening to go forward with the talks without Thieu, which the South Vietnamese leader took to be a threat to overthrow him if he did not cooperate.[20]

By concentrating on the problem of getting Thieu to Paris, meanwhile ignoring Clifford's suggestion that a major withdrawal of American troops from Vietnam begin immediately, a great opportunity was lost.

No law prevented Johnson from accepting the onus of abandoning South Vietnam and pulling the fighting troops out before Nixon took office. The United States would have survived, and Nixon would have begun his Presidency with a clean slate. He could have muted his criticism of Johnson, just as he muted his criticism of Eisenhower fourteen years earlier, when Ike had abandoned the northern half of Vietnam.

Of course it borders on madness to even suggest that either Johnson or Nixon could have done such a thing. Each man swore, publicly and with deeply felt emotion, "I'm not going to be the first President to lose a war."

Still, it is nearly impossible to avoid the temptation to wonder, What if Johnson had brought the boys home in December 1968?

THE DAY AFTER the White House meeting, on November 12, Henry Kissinger sent one of his secret, back-channel messages to Nixon. His conduit was William F. Buckley, who in turn relayed the message via Frank Shakespeare of CBS. The message was that Clifford had decided, "probably," to "depose Thieu before Nixon is inaugurated." Kissinger either hinted at or charged directly that assassination was a real possibility. He wanted Nixon to know that "if Thieu meets the same fate as Diem, the word will go out to the nations of the world that it may be dangerous to be America's enemy, but to be America's friend is fatal."[21]

Thus did the relationship between Nixon and Kissinger get started on a basis of secrecy, rumor, intrigue, and circuitous communication, all covered by a veneer of concern for high principle (America must stick by its friends) and highlighted by Kissinger's dramatic phraseology.

Two weeks later, Nixon called Kissinger to his transition headquarters in the Hotel Pierre in New York. It was the first real meeting between two men destined to have a thousand and more meetings, some of which would change the world, and nearly all of which each man would describe in his memoirs in overwhelming detail that was designed not so much to elucidate and enlighten as to confuse and contradict.

So it was with this first meeting. According to Kissinger, Nixon was "painfully shy. Meeting new people filled him with vague dread." The President-elect put on "a show of jauntiness that failed to hide an extraordinary nervousness." There was a noticeable (at least to Kissinger) lack of self-confidence; Kissinger wrote that at a follow-up meeting two days later, Nixon "rather touchingly" gave him the names of some of his professors at Duke University who could vouch for Nixon's intelligence!

Kissinger claimed that Nixon's purpose at the initial meeting was to bash the foreign-affairs bureaucracy of the U.S. government. To this perfect stranger, who still worked for Nixon's political rival Nelson Rockefeller and who had done nothing to help Nixon win office, Nixon opened his heart as he had never done before (except possibly to Bebe Rebozo, in private). Nixon said he did not trust the State Department, that "its personnel had no loyalty to him." He charged that the Foreign Service "had disdained him as Vice President and ignored him the moment he was out of office." He intended to "exclude the CIA from the formulation of policy" because "it was staffed by Ivy League liberals who . . . had always opposed him politically."[22]

In Nixon's recollection, the meeting centered around the great issues of foreign policy. Nixon said he would avoid the trap Johnson had fallen into of devoting too much time and energy to Vietnam, "which was really a short-term problem." Nixon wanted to concentrate on problems vital to America's "security and survival," such as the Middle East, the Soviet Union, Japan, and NATO. He told Kissinger he wished to "re-evaluate our policy toward Communist China," and urged Kissinger to read his *Foreign Affairs* article on Asia after Vietnam.

In Nixon's account, the two men went on to discuss structure. Nixon wanted to be his own Secretary of State, and to revitalize the National Security Council (NSC), which had fallen into disuse since Eisenhower's day. Kissinger was in hearty agreement.

Nixon recalled that he felt a "strong intuition about Henry Kissinger, and I decided on the spot that he should be my National Security Adviser."[23] Two days later, at the follow-up meeting, Kissinger agreed.

They made an odd couple, the California-born WASP and the

NOVEMBER 6, 1968–JANUARY 20, 1969 | 233

German-born Jewish refugee, the lifelong politician and the Harvard professor, the hard-core Old Guard Republican and the intellectual guru of the liberal Eastern Establishment. In part, their coupling was an expression of the physical principle that opposites attract. In part, it was shrewd politics on Nixon's part, demonstrating his ability to co-opt the number-one man on the Rockefeller payroll.

But for all their differences, there was an affinity that ran very deep. They sensed in each other, in their first meeting, a shared love of secrecy and surprise, a strong sense of contempt for the bureaucracy, for established methods, for regular procedure. They were born conspirators.

No one has caught this better than Raymond Garthoff, himself a former Foreign Service officer and ambassador, and author of one of the two or three best books ever written on the Cold War, *Détente and Confrontation*. Garthoff writes, "[Nixon] wanted a foreign policy which would place America in a central and manipulative position of power in the world, just as he sought to consolidate a central, manipulative position of power at home within the White House" by excluding the State Department from policy making through the device of making Kissinger his National Security Adviser with offices in the White House.[24]

The most immediate proof of Garthoff's assertion is one of timing. Nixon appointed Kissinger to his post *before* he selected his Secretary of State. This from the man who claimed to admire John Foster Dulles above all his contemporaries, save only Eisenhower himself. It is unimaginable that Dulles would have accepted under such conditions.

Not only style but also substance brought Nixon and Kissinger together. They were as one on setting priority. As Garthoff puts it, "The dominant foreign policy preoccupation of Nixon and Kissinger in 1969, and indeed for the entire period through 1972, was not a détente . . . with Moscow, but finding an honorable exit from Vietnam. Improvement of relations with the Soviet Union, and a possible parallel rapprochement with China, were . . . seen as much as means to that end as they were ends in themselves."[25]

THE FIRST TASK Nixon gave Kissinger was to assess William Rogers' suitability for "a senior foreign policy post." Then, as if to show Kissinger who was in charge, Nixon made his appointment of Rogers as Secretary of State without waiting for Kissinger's assessment.

Rogers had been Nixon's friend and supporter for twenty years. He was the man Nixon had turned to for advice in critical moments, as at the time of the fund crisis in 1952. During the tense days following Eisenhower's 1955 heart attack, it was Rogers on whom Nixon had leaned. But Nixon did not choose Rogers as his Secretary of State on the basis of old friendship; indeed over the past few years the two men had drifted apart, even becoming competitors for the same clients in New York legal affairs.

Nixon, according to Kissinger, described Rogers as "one of the toughest, most cold-eyed, self-centered, and ambitious men he had ever met." Rogers would make "the little boys in the State Department" behave. Rogers knew almost nothing about foreign policy, but Nixon told Kissinger that was an asset because it guaranteed that policy direction would be in the White House. As Kissinger comments, "Few Secretaries of State can have been selected because of their President's confidence in their ignorance of foreign policy." Or, as Garthoff puts it, "Nixon's choice of . . . Rogers was, to be blunt, predicated on an ability to use him as a front man, rather than as a partner or even participant in foreign policy-making."[26]

In announcing Kissinger's appointment to the press, Nixon said the opposite of what he had told Kissinger in private. "Dr. Kissinger," the President-elect declared, "is keenly aware of the necessity not to set himself up as a wall between the President and the Secretary of State."[27]

Kissinger, at that news conference, told reporters that despite his reputation for toughness and arrogance, he had tried for fifteen years "to avoid labels like 'hard' and 'soft.' "

Nixon stressed that Kissinger would present a spectrum of attitudes toward foreign policy. "I am one who likes to get a broad range of viewpoints expressed," Nixon explained, "and Dr. Kissinger [will] see to it that the President does not just hear what he wants to hear, which is always a temptation for White House staffers."[28]

FOLLOWING HIS MEETINGS with Kissinger, Nixon called the director of the FBI, Edgar Hoover, to the Hotel Pierre for a talk. Nixon and Hoover went back a long way, to the Hiss case of 1948, when they had been, if not quite antagonists, at least on opposite sides. Each man had been, in private, critical of the other.

But over the years they had come together, primarily around their shared views on the dangers of internal Communism to the Republic. Nixon estimated that they had been at the same dinner parties on at least a hundred occasions, a high figure considering that neither man much enjoyed socializing and kept it at a minimum. They attended Washington Senators baseball games together, and got together in Florida.[29]

Like almost every other politician in America, Nixon had reason to fear Hoover. The FBI had files on just about everyone of any importance, and Hoover ran the FBI more as a dictator than a director. Only he decided what information or rumor to release, and when, and to whom. He did not have to threaten; his control of the raw files was in itself a sufficient threat. Thus one of President-elect Kennedy's first acts in 1961 had been to announce that he had asked Mr. Hoover to stay on the job.

With his seventieth birthday, on January 1, 1965, Hoover had become vulnerable himself, because he had reached the compulsory retirement age for federal employees. He was doggedly determined to hang on, and by engaging in a series of illegal activities for Johnson (as he had also done for Kennedy), he was able to persuade Johnson to sign an executive order waiving the rule. These activities included the wiretapping and bugging of Martin Luther King, Jr., and of the Mississippi Freedom Democratic Party at the 1964 Democratic Convention, and the Congress of Racial Equality (CORE) and other civil rights groups.

At one of their transition meetings, Johnson told Nixon, "If it hadn't been for Edgar Hoover, I couldn't have carried out my responsibilities as Commander in Chief. Period. Dick, you will come to depend on Edgar. He is a pillar of strength in a city of weak men. You will rely on him time and time again to maintain security. He's the only one you can put your complete trust in."[30]

No wonder then, that at the meeting at the Pierre, Nixon opened by saying, "Edgar, you are one of the few people who is to have direct access to me at all times." Hoover nodded; he obviously expected no less.[31] Nixon said that, like Johnson, he intended to waive the mandatory retirement rule for Hoover. The director was pleased.

Then Hoover began to deliver. He said that Johnson had ordered the FBI to wiretap Nixon during the campaign, and that the FBI had successfully planted a bug on Nixon's campaign airplane. He said the FBI had wiretapped Mrs. Chennault's telephone, something Nixon already knew. He surprised Nixon with the information that the FBI had also bugged Humphrey during the campaign for Johnson.

"When you get into the White House," Hoover continued, "don't make any calls through the switchboard. Johnson has it rigged, and little men you don't know will be listening." He said Johnson had set up taping facilities to record his Oval Office conversations whenever he chose to flip on the switch; the system also allowed his aides in nearby offices to secretly monitor the conversations, live.[32]

When Hoover left, Nixon turned to Haldeman, who had attended the meeting, and said, "We'll get that Goddamn bugging crap out of the White House in a hurry." (In January 1969, Haldeman saw to it that Nixon's instructions were carried out.) Then Nixon made a remark that surprised Haldeman, who expected anger at Hoover's revelations of Johnson's bugging and wiretapping.

"Well," said Nixon, "I don't blame him. He's been under such pressure because of the damn war, he'd do anything. I'm not going to end up like LBJ, Bob . . . I'm going to stop that war. Fast. I mean it!"[33]

DURING THE second half of November, Nixon divided his time between Grand Cay, Key Biscayne, and the Hotel Pierre. He devoted most of his working hours to selecting his Cabinet.

He wanted a moderate, middle-of-the-road Cabinet, and even talked about a national-unity government to meet the crisis the country faced. But his efforts to reach out to Democrats were not very energetic and generally unsuccessful. Humphrey turned down his invitation to be ambassador to the United Nations. Senator Henry Jackson (D., Wash.) refused an invitation to become Secretary of Defense. Attempts to bring aboard some black leaders also failed. Senator Brooke refused the U.N. post; Whitney Young, executive director of the Urban League, turned down an offer to be Secretary of Housing and Urban Development (HUD).[34]

The one Democrat who did join up was Daniel Patrick Moynihan, a Harvard professor and sub-Cabinet member in the Kennedy and Johnson Administrations. Nixon did not know the man, but he was aware of some of Moynihan's writings, and Price recommended him strongly as the antibureaucratic "new liberal" who would make something of a reality of Nixon's "new alignment" of American politics.

Nixon's first question about Moynihan was characteristic. "But could we count on him to be loyal?" Nixon wanted to know. "I don't mean Republican. I mean—you know—one of us." Reassured, Nixon met with Moynihan. They were as opposite as Nixon and Kissinger; Moynihan, the tough Irish Catholic kid who grew up on the streets of New York and became one of the country's leading intellectuals, was passionately opposed to the Vietnam War. He let Nixon know that at once. Yet the two men hit it off. Nixon, like most people, was drawn by Moynihan's gift for gab, by the brilliance of his mind, by his uncompromising honesty, by his pixie qualities, and by the originality of his thought. Finally, Moynihan had a fondness for handing out flattery that was unusual for a Harvard professor and quite welcome to Nixon.

They talked about the welfare system. Although Moynihan, as an Assistant Secretary of Labor, had helped design some of the Great Society poverty programs, he told Nixon that the current welfare system had failed and needed to be completely reformed. Nixon could not have agreed more. He told Moynihan he intended to establish an Urban Affairs Council, which he described as the domestic-policy equivalent of the NSC.

"That's a capital idea!" Moynihan exclaimed.

Nixon offered him the directorship. Moynihan accepted.[35]

He never regretted it, despite his later break with Nixon over Vietnam and other issues, and remained a great admirer of Nixon.[36] And Nixon, despite those later disagreements, remained an admirer of Moynihan.

Nixon did not intend to make Moynihan his domestic-policy czar. Instead, he created conflicting centers of power. On one side of Moynihan, he made Ehrlichman the White House counsel, with primarily domestic responsibilities. On the other side, he created a new Cabinet-level position of Counsellor to the President and named economist Arthur Burns to fill it. Nixon reasoned that Burns's conservatism would be a useful and creative counterweight to Moynihan's liberalism.[37] Steve Hess, who went to work for Moynihan, thought Nixon had done well, creating an atmosphere for an honest conflict of ideas for domestic affairs.[38]

There was a fourth man who would be intimately involved in domestic policy, Bob Finch. Nixon persuaded him to accept the post of Secretary of Health, Education and Welfare. Other appointments included George Shultz as Secretary of Labor. Nixon could not remember Shultz's first name, and could not spell his last; describing Shultz, Nixon wrote, "Dr. _____ Schultz has earned the respect of management and labor as one of the nation's outstanding mediators."[39] (Nixon could not spell Ehrlichman's name, either; he consistently left out the first *h* and often the second. Nor could he remember Ehrlichman's first name, frequently calling him Bob.)[40]

Maurice Stans became Secretary of Commerce; David Kennedy, head of the Continental Illinois National Bank and Trust Company of Chicago, the Secretary of the Treasury (Nixon wanted someone from outside the New York banking community); George Romney, Secretary of HUD. Other appointments included Winton Blount as Postmaster General, Governor Walter Hickel of Alaska as Secretary of the Interior, John Volpe for Transportation, and Clifford Hardin for Agriculture.

Next to the post of Secretary of State, the two most important appointments were Secretary of Defense and Attorney General. For DOD, there had been some talk about retaining Clifford, but

Clifford was much too partisan for Nixon. Nor did Nixon want one of the Detroit automobile people, like McNamara or Charlie Wilson. Instead, he turned to Representative Melvin Laird of Wisconsin, an expert on defense appropriations and, in Nixon's view, "a strong man and a shrewd politician," widely respected in Congress.[41]

Nixon initially offered the post of Attorney General to John Mitchell. Mitchell said no, because of his problems with his wife's health. Nixon turned to Ehrlichman, who said, rightly, that he was not qualified. Nixon then returned to Mitchell and persuaded him to accept.

In a memo dated December 9, 1968, Nixon described Mitchell as "the strong man in the campaign team and its leader, not because he was named as such but because he earned that place due to his immense competence . . . he will provide leadership far beyond the technical problems of his department."[42] In his memoirs, Nixon explained further that Mitchell was "tough, intelligent, and fair. Moreover, I counted him my most trusted friend and adviser, and I wanted to have his advice available, not just on legal matters but on the whole range of presidential decision-making."[43]

It must be noted that Nixon had known Mitchell for only five years; it was quite remarkable to describe him as "my most trusted friend." Further, Mitchell's whole life until the 1968 campaign had been in the narrow world of bond issues and financing; he had no preparation for offering advice on the "whole range of presidential decision-making." But, as will be seen, Nixon meant it, and Mitchell did so advise.

Overall, the Cabinet appointments—which were announced simultaneously on December 11—met with general approval. Although there were no blacks, no women, no Jews, no Democrats, and no Rockefellers (Nixon had explained to Nelson Rockefeller that he could do his best service for the nation by staying in Albany), the Cabinet was praised as moderate and middle-of-the-road. The members were self-made men, highly successful either in business or politics. It expressed Republican confidence and experience. The business community found it reassuring, especially so when Nixon announced that Paul McCracken, a conservative economist at the University of Michigan, would be chairman of the Council of Economic Advisers.[44]

The businessmen would have been less approving had they known Nixon's thoughts on the place and function of the Cabinet. Just as there was an unspoken but widely held assumption that Nixon would somehow manage to follow Eisenhower's lead and get the country out of the Vietnam War as Ike had gotten it out of the Korean War, so was there a sense that Nixon would emulate Ike and emphasize teamwork and the importance of the Cabinet. But Nixon had no such intention.

"I had attended hundreds of Cabinet meetings as Vice President," Nixon declared, "and I felt that most of them were unnecessary and boring." He was determined to keep Cabinet meetings to a bare minimum, and to prevent the rise in the Cabinet of "members who were too strong-willed."[45]

Nixon drew another negative lesson from the Eisenhower years; in his view, Ike had been much too lax on getting rid of Democrats in government. He told his Cabinet to act quickly to remove the entrenched bureaucrats. "If we don't get rid of those people," he said, "they will either sabotage us from within, or they'll just sit back on their well-paid asses and wait for the next election to bring back their old bosses."[46]

The larger Eisenhower example Nixon rejected was this: it was Eisenhower's method to unite to rule. He wanted to bring people together, to talk. Nixon's method was to divide to rule. He kept people apart. Ike wanted a team of well-informed men who understood one another's problems and were working together on solutions. Nixon compartmentalized knowledge and power, and set people at odds with one another.

Of course Eisenhower, when he became President, had a self-confidence unmatched by any of his predecessors, save only Washington and Grant. As commander of Operation Overlord, he had nothing to prove. It gave him a certain serenity. Nixon had everything to prove. It gave him great anxiety.

Inside the Oval Office, Nixon had created a situation of conflict between Haldeman and Woods. In dealing with the press, Nixon had set up a situation of competition and even antagonism between Klein and Ziegler. In foreign policy, it was Kissinger versus Rogers. In domestic policy, it was Burns versus Moynihan versus Ehrlichman versus Finch. The only unifying element was Nixon himself.

FOR THE FAMILY, the excitement of closing down the New York apartment and preparing to move into the White House was all but overshadowed by the excitement of Julie's wedding, scheduled for December 22. The preparations were nearly endless; as one example, the wedding rehearsal took four hours, and the President-elect had to stay through every minute of it, including repeated walks down the aisle with Julie.

At Julie's first bridal shower, in late November, held at Mrs. Elmer Bobst's East Side apartment, she received ruffly nightgowns and long, flowing princess robes, silver bookends, and so forth.

Mrs. Henry Clay Frick gave her a black tray inlaid in gold with pictures of all thirty-six men elected President, including her father and David's grandfather. Rose Woods was rather more practical; her gift was a new steam iron.[47]

The father of the bride had big bills to pay, and not just those to cover the wedding and reception. Pat got a new Persian lamb coat for the occasion ($1,700, from Blum & Fink); Tricia got a white lamb with a moiré curl and silver filigree buttons ($1,100, from Fur and Sport); Julie, a black curly lamb with frog closings ($600, also from Fur and Sport).

The fashion pages of the big-city papers could not get enough detail. Bribes were paid for inside information, and of course the designers made sure their creations got a mention, and everyone was in something of a dither. Priscilla of Boston was the envy of her competitors; she had designed Luci Johnson Nugent's bridal gown, and now had the plum of designing Julie's as well, plus Pat's, plus the bridesmaids'.[48]

Julie and David wanted the wedding to be as personal and nonpolitical as possible, which was why she insisted on getting married before the inauguration, even though her father urged her to wait and have the ceremony in the White House. But whatever their wishes, Ike's grandson and Nixon's daughter could hardly get married in private, and in the end this most political of couples chose for the site of the wedding one of the most prominent churches in America, the Marble Collegiate Church in New York. Presiding was the Reverend Dr. Norman Vincent Peale, a minister who rivaled Billy Graham himself in celebrity status.

The 114-year-old church, with its scarlet, gold, and white sanctuary, cranberry-red carpeting, huge green balsam wreaths and masses of red and white poinsettias, was about as traditional and handsome a setting for a wedding as could be imagined.

Julie's slightly Victorian silk peau d'ange and Belgian lace dress had a high collar with pearl embroidery at the yoke, short puffed sleeves, and a flared skirt with a chapel-length train. Her illusion veil was appliquéd with lace and held in place by a lace-and-pearl headband. She carried lilies of the valley, narcissus, sweetheart roses, and bouvardia. She looked marvelous, her smile lighting up the place.

Pat wore a jeweled aquamarine lace dress; the bridesmaids wore pink gowns. Nixon, who was fighting a touch of the flu, could not stop smiling, not that he tried. The only sad note was the absence of General and Mrs. Eisenhower. They were in Walter Reed Hospital. They were supposed to see the ceremony, thanks to NBC-TV, which arranged to televise it exclusively for them on a closed circuit, but the picture failed and all they got was the sound.

The lead item in the papers describing the ceremony came when Nixon stepped forward to give away the bride. On an impulse, Julie turned to her father and kissed him on the cheek. It brought tears to many eyes, including his.

The guests included Elmer Bobst ("Uncle Elmer" to Julie), Bebe Rebozo ("Uncle Bebe"), Mr. and Mrs. Manuel Sanchez, the Nixons' live-in servants, Tom Dewey, Mrs. Clare Boothe Luce, Jack and Helene Drown, Rose Woods, the Agnews, most of Nixon's aides, all his newly appointed Cabinet, and some five hundred others.[49]

The reception was held at the Plaza Hotel. The young Eisenhower couple chose "Edelweiss" as their first dance. Halfway through, Nixon tapped David on the shoulder and cut in. He remarked later that he never felt lighter on his feet.[50] Not light enough, however, to dance with Pat.

Immediately after the wedding, Dick, Pat, and Tricia, along with Bebe Rebozo, flew down to Florida. So did Julie and David, for their honeymoon, which they spent at the mansion of Ellis Slater, an old friend of Ike's, on the ocean in Palm Beach. On Christmas Day, the newlyweds drove down to Key Biscayne for dinner; the following day, the entire party flew by Coast Guard helicopter to Grand Cay for a swim.

Altogether it was a grand and wonderful wedding, followed by a relaxing vacation, just the right thing to help Nixon get ready physically and mentally to assume his awesome duties and responsibilities.

THE WAR WENT ON. Nearly three hundred GIs died each week in Vietnam in the two and a half months between the election and Nixon's inauguration. With regard to the peace talks in Paris, Thieu had finally indicated that the GVN would participate. This set off another controversy, over the shape of the negotiating table. A four-sided table would imply equal status for the four parties—Hanoi, the United States, the GVN, and the NLF. This was unacceptable to the NLF and to the GVN. Finally, in mid-January, a Russian-suggested compromise was accepted: the negotiators would sit around a circular table without nameplates, flags, or markings.

President Johnson, at a second transition meeting in the White House, held on December 12, urged Nixon to stay the course. Nixon promised that he would, and promised further that when he finally achieved peace with honor he would see to it that Johnson received the credit he deserved.

Staying the course meant continuing the bombing. Johnson's late-October bombing halt applied only to the area of North Vietnam just beyond the DMZ. In South Vietnam, the B-52s and American fighter-bombers continued to pound away at enemy positions. In addition, the Air Force was hitting Communist-held areas in Laos (a total of 3,377 missions in 1968). As the bombers were called off North Vietnam, the missions in South Vietnam and in Laos increased.[51]

Nixon approved, indeed was considering extending the bombing. In early January, he sent Kissinger a note: "In making your study of Vietnam I want a precise report on what the enemy has in Cambodia and what, if anything, we are doing to destroy the buildup there. I think a very definite change of policy toward Cambodia probably should be one of the first orders of business when we get in."[52]

At the second transition meeting, Johnson urged Nixon to be as secretive as possible in making and executing policy. Never discuss major decisions before the Cabinet or the NSC, Johnson advised. "Everybody there's got their damned deputies and note-takers with them sitting along the wall. I will warn you now, the leaks can kill you." Johnson said he even excluded Humphrey from important meetings, yet "even with all the precautions I take, things still leak."[53]

The other side of leaking was knowing what the opposition was doing. The narrow margin of victory in 1968 and Democratic control of Congress meant that winning re-election in 1972 was no sure thing. Therefore, Nixon decided, "we must begin immediately keeping track of everything the leading Democrats did. Information would be our first line of defense."[54] To gather that intelligence, he intended to use every bit of power available to him.

AT THE END of December, the Nixons flew to California to attend a "Welcome Home, Pat and Dick" reception in the Anaheim convention center. On New Year's Day, they went to the Rose Bowl game between Ohio State and Southern Cal. Nixon gave the Ohio State coach, Woody Hayes, some tips on how to contain the star halfback of Southern Cal, O. J. Simpson. Whatever Nixon's advice, it did not hurt Ohio State, whose team won the game, 27–16.[55]

For his fifty-sixth birthday party, Nixon, Pat, and Bebe went to the Eisenhowers' student apartment in Northampton, Massachusetts. Julie had returned to Smith College after taking the fall semester off to campaign, and David was commuting to Amherst College. Julie prepared the dinner (when asked by the press about Julie's abilities as a cook, Tricia broke into giggles), a chicken casserole with broccoli topped with cheese, and Jell-O.[56] Nixon returned to New York refreshed and happy, ready to fly to Key Biscayne to put the final touches on his Inaugural Address.

• •

NIXON WORKED HARD on his speech. He read every previous Inaugural Address, an impressive feat in itself. He concluded, wisely, that the short ones were the longest remembered. His competition was Kennedy, with his "ask not" and his "pay any price, bear any burden," which, as Nixon noted, "caught the mood and caught himself." Of course, Nixon had already decided, as had Johnson before him, that the country would not pay any price or bear any burden, that there were definite limits. But then Inaugural Addresses almost demand rhetorical hyperbole.

Nixon had a heavy volume of unsolicited advice on what to say; he asked for suggestions from only two men. Both were former Harvard professors with a gift for overblown rhetoric, Henry Kissinger and Pat Moynihan. Even Ray Price, hardly one to restrain himself in stringing together catchy phrases, found the Kissinger draft to be "mostly standard boiler-plate rhetoric." Nixon used little of it.

Moynihan urged Nixon to reassure the black community, telling him that "the rumor is widespread that the new government is planning to build concentration camps."[57]

On Inauguration Day, January 20, 1969, the Nixons drove to the White House. Sixteen years earlier, Eisenhower had refused to go in and sit down with Truman; instead he waited in his car for Truman to join him for the drive to the Capitol. Nixon's relationship with Johnson was much better than that. Johnson greeted Pat with a kiss. Together with their wives and with the Humphreys, Nixon and Johnson chatted easily over coffee and rolls.

During the drive to the Capitol in 1953, Eisenhower and Truman had sat side by side in a frosty silence. In 1969, Johnson talked freely. He told Nixon that at dinner the previous evening, people had been telling him how much Muskie had contributed to the campaign. Johnson snorted that although the press had "slobbered over Muskie," the senator had delivered only Maine, while Agnew had brought home five southern states for Nixon.[58]

There had been some speculation in the press that Nixon might not want Chief Justice Warren to administer the oath of office, because of Warren's attempt to resign before Nixon became President, or that Warren might not want to swear in Nixon. But Nixon graciously asked Warren to do it, and Warren just as graciously agreed.

Pat held two Milhous family Bibles for the swearing in, the same ones she had held in 1953 and 1957. At Nixon's request, she opened them to Isaiah 2:4: ". . . they shall beat their swords into plowshares, and their spears into pruninghooks: nation shall not lift up sword against nation, neither shall they learn war any more."

Back in 1953, Eisenhower had opened with a prayer, one he had composed only a couple of hours before the ceremony began. Nixon too had a last-minute idea for his opening, and it was an inspired one. "I ask you to share with me today the majesty of this moment," he said. "In the orderly transfer of power, we celebrate the unity that keeps us free."[59]

In the body of the speech, he reached out to assuage the blacks' fears, of which Moynihan had warned: "No man can be fully free while his neighbor is not. To go forward at all is to go forward together. This means black and white together, as one nation, not two."

He gave a "sacred commitment: I shall consecrate my office, my energies, and all the wisdom I can summon to the cause of peace among nations."

He set his priority: "The greatest honor history can bestow is the title of peacemaker. This honor now beckons America—the chance to help lead the world at last out of the valley of turmoil and onto that high ground of peace that man has dreamed of since the dawn of civilization. . . . This is our summons to greatness."

The most quoted lines came from Price, and they spoke to the divisiveness that was separating the American people, the divisiveness that Nixon had used to help win the election but that had now become his responsibility to cure. The words themselves were thoughtful and conciliatory.

"The simple things are the ones most needed today," Nixon said, "if we are to surmount what divides us, and cement what unites us.

"To lower our voices would be a simple thing.

"In these difficult years, America has suffered from a fever of words: from inflated rhetoric that promises more than it can deliver; from angry rhetoric that fans discontents into hatreds; from bombastic rhetoric that postures instead of persuading."

Former Vice-President Humphrey, sitting behind Nixon, could hardly have helped wincing at the irony of those words coming from that man after the 1968 campaign. But he also could not have helped but agree with what followed.

"We cannot learn from one another until we stop shouting at one another."[60]

AFTER THE SPEECH, Nixon patted his wife affectionately on the shoulder (reporters asked later why he didn't kiss her; he explained that he didn't do that in public, although he did kiss Mamie Eisenhower as she left the reviewing stand later that day).

For the inaugural parade, from the Capitol back to the White

On November 7, 1962, the morning after his loss in the race for Governor of California, Richard Nixon warned reporters, "You won't have Nixon to kick around anymore, because, gentlemen, this is my last press conference. . . ." Actually, he used the occasion to begin his next bid for the Presidency.

At Key Biscayne, Florida, Nixon sets out for a round of golf with his friend Charles "Bebe" Rebozo. Although Nixon had hundreds of associates, he had only a handful of friends. Rebozo was one of the few with whom he could completely relax.

UPI/BETTMANN NEWSPHOTOS

WIDE WORLD

Nixon's law office in New York City was a museum to his Vice-Presidency. His abilities as a lawyer were such that, had he stuck to his practice, he would have gone to the very top.

Nixon with the Barry Goldwaters at the 1964 Republican Convention. Nixon had tried and failed to outmaneuver Goldwater for the nomination, but during the campaign he was one of the few prominent Republicans who supported the ticket.

Eighteen-year-old Patricia Nixon and her escort, Edward Finch Cox, at the International Debutante Ball in New York, December 29, 1964. Her parents looked on with pride from the balcony.

Two bright and able young speech writers who worked for Nixon, Bill Safire (upper) and Pat Buchanan (lower). When Nixon wanted a moderate speech, he turned to Safire; when he wanted a hard-hitting, right-wing talk, he called on Buchanan.

Nixon visits with ARVN troops in Vietnam, September 5, 1965. He told the press he was opposed to a negotiated settlement because it would lead to more war, not peace. Nixon was consistently critical of the American war effort through the year, calling it too little and too late.

Nixon with his daughter Julie and her boyfriend, David Eisenhower. He could not have been happier with the romance, which delighted Republicans everywhere and filled society pages across the nation.

Two Nixon aides, John Ehrlichman (upper) and Maurice Stans (lower). During Nixon's drive to the Presidency, Ehrlichman did the advance work, while Stans raised the money.

Nixon, at a Republican fund-raiser in Atlanta in 1966, pounds the table as he calls for stronger action in Vietnam. The clenched fist was a trademark, as was his demand for victory in Southeast Asia.

Nixon with fellow Republican hopefuls, Governors Ronald Reagan and George Romney, at a Republican fund-raiser in Washington, in 1967. Nixon easily outmaneuvered his rivals.

Governor George Wallace of Alabama. Wallace's campaign for the Presidency on an independent ticket in 1968 played a central role in the way Nixon structured and carried out his own campaign.

Another rival, Governor Nelson Rockefeller, arrives in Miami on the eve of the 1968 Republican Convention. Rocky had the money to pay for signs and polls but neither the support nor the skill to wrest the nomination from Nixon.

Presidential hopefuls Hubert Humphrey and Eugene McCarthy meet on August 27, 1968, during the tumultuous Democratic Convention. The split in the party between hawks and doves worked to Nixon's benefit.

President Lyndon B. Johnson, March 31, 1968, just before announcing that he would not be a candidate for re-election. Nixon and Johnson had been antagonists for two decades, but after Nixon became President, the two men became all but allies.

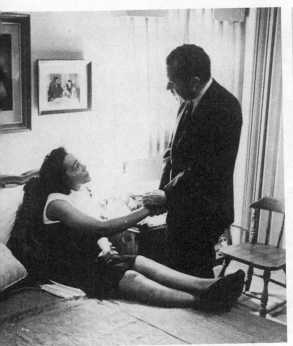

WIDE WORLD

Nixon visiting Coretta King in Atlanta, April 10, 1968, following her husband's assassination. In 1960, when King had been arrested during the campaign, Nixon had refused to intervene on his behalf. Some of his aides convinced him that his refusal to come to King's aid had cost him the election, and so he decided on this occasion to pay his respects and express his sympathy.

President Nguyen Van Thieu of South Vietnam, seated in front of a mural of Vietnam's first king. Thieu cooperated with Nixon in the last week of the 1968 campaign by helping to sabotage President Johnson's peace proposal. In the last week of the 1972 campaign, he tried to undercut Nixon's armistice plans.

Former President Dwight Eisenhower, July 18, 1968. Ike was in Walter Reed Army Hospital recuperating from his fifth heart attack. He called in reporters to endorse Nixon for the Republican nomination. Nixon had worked hard for that endorsement and was justly proud of it.

The 1968 election was one of the most divisive in American history. All three candidates faced hecklers at every stop. Here Nixon, in Atlanta, reacts to some anti-Nixon signs he has just spotted.

Nixon and his running mate, Governor Spiro Agnew of Maryland, at the Republican Convention in Miami, August 9, 1968. Nixon hardly knew Agnew, but he approved of Agnew's hard line with rioters in Baltimore and felt Agnew would help him win over George Wallace's supporters.

The winner. Nixon and his family, plus Julie's fiancé, David Eisenhower, meet the press on November 6, 1968, shortly after Nixon's narrow victory over Humphrey.

As a freshman Congressman in 1947, Nixon was one of the first supporters of the Marshall Plan, and later of NATO. As President, he made his first overseas trip to Europe, in February 1969, to emphasize the importance of the Alliance. Here he meets with NATO leaders in Brussels. Secretary of State William Rogers is at his right, National Security Adviser Henry Kissinger behind him.

Nixon and J. Edgar Hoover exchange private remarks at a meeting of the board of directors of the Boys' Clubs of America, 1969. Their association went back to the 1948 Alger Hiss case; between them they knew almost every secret in Washington.

Nixon with Warren Burger, May 21, 1969, just after nominating Burger for the post of Chief Justice of the United States. Burger was Nixon's first Supreme Court nominee.

In July 1969, Nixon visited with combat troops from the 1st Infantry Division at Di An, ten miles northeast of Saigon. That summer, he announced that he was beginning the withdrawal of American troops and starting a new policy of Vietnamization.

On April 30, 1970, Nixon went on national television to announce that American and South Vietnamese troops were making an incursion into Cambodia. On the map, he pointed to the "Parrot's Beak" and the "Fishhook," areas of Communist buildup and targets in the offensive.

The Cambodian incursion brought a storm of protest. It reached its peak following the May 4, 1970, shooting of students by the Ohio National Guard at Kent State University.

On June 12, 1971, Tricia Nixon and Edward Cox were married in the White House Rose Garden. In the reception in the East Room, Cox danced with the First Lady while the President danced with the bride.

Henry Kissinger in Paris, July 12, 1971, with the chief of the American delegation to the Paris peace talks, David Bruce. Kissinger was in and out of Paris on a regular basis, for both public and secret talks with the North Vietnamese.

Charles Colson, Nixon aide and hatchet man. "That Colson," Nixon said, "he'll do anything." Colson said of himself that he would walk over his grandmother to insure Nixon's re-election.

Attorney General John Mitchell and his wife Martha. She was the most outspoken and colorful of the Cabinet wives; he was Nixon's former law partner, close friend, and strong supporter.

Two Nixon antagonists who provoked the President into illegal break-ins. Daniel Ellsberg was the man who released the classified Pentagon Papers; Nixon set out to discredit him by, among other things, breaking into his doctor's office. Lawrence O'Brien was the Democratic National Chairman whose office was in the Watergate complex. O'Brien had a close connection with Howard Hughes; Nixon wanted to know what O'Brien knew about the Nixon-Hughes relationship.

On February 17, 1972, Nixon flew to Peking, where he met Chou En-lai and Chairman Mao Tse-tung. His announcement of his trip to China came as a complete surprise. For two decades, Nixon had been Mao's most severe critic; in February 1972, he became one of Mao's great admirers, and developed a deep appreciation for Chou.

In May 1972, three months after his visit to China, Nixon flew to Moscow for a summit meeting with the Soviet leaders. Here he drinks a toast to the SALT I agreement with Premier Aleksei Kosygin and Chairman Leonid Brezhnev. Together, the China trip and the Moscow summit marked the high point of the Nixon Presidency, as he established his policy of détente.

In his 1972 re-election campaign, Nixon found support in the oddest places. Not only Mao and Brezhnev rooted for their old enemy, but so did much of organized labor. Here Nixon meets with Frank Fitzsimmons, the president of his favorite union, the Teamsters, on July 17, in San Clemente. Fitzsimmons had just announced that the Teamsters were backing Nixon.

H. R. "Bob" Haldeman, Nixon's chief of staff and closest working associate, here seen with Nixon on their way to the White House from Nixon's EOB office, December 20, 1969. Through turmoil and triumph, at home and abroad, Nixon and Haldeman walked in step.

Senator George McGovern accepts the nomination of the Democratic party at the 1972 Convention in Miami. Despite the display of Democratic greats on the wall, McGovern faced a party that was disastrously divided.

TWO PHOTOS: UPI/BETTMANN NEWSPHOTOS

First Lady Pat Nixon gives her husband a hug as they celebrate the 1972 election victory in Washington. Despite Nixon's broad smile, he was in a depressed and angry mood, as he showed the following morning, when he abruptly demanded the immediate written resignations of all his aides and Cabinet members.

Nixon's official Presidential portrait, taken by Phillipe Halsman on Nixon's 56th birthday, January 9, 1969, at the Pierre Hotel in New York City.

Nixon, in a characteristic pose in the Oval Office, 1971, ponders his problems.

House, the Secret Service insisted on putting up the top on the presidential limousine. An agent explained to Nixon that there were demonstrators along Pennsylvania Avenue.

It was a gray, ugly day with a northeast wind that cut to the bone. The city was the color of wet cement. Russell Baker wrote that what should have been a joyous, hopeful occasion was not; that the only happy person in town was Lady Bird Johnson. Baker heard a black man and a white man exchange angry racial epithets when the crush of the crowd pressed them together. Even worse were the hundreds of young antiwar demonstrators.

"Four more years of death!" they chanted, or "Ho, Ho, Ho Chi Minh, the NLF is going to win." One poster proclaimed, "Nixon's the One—The No. 1 War Criminal." All along Pennsylvania Avenue, demonstrators burned the small American flags distributed by Boy Scouts. They spat at police.

"Communist swine!" a middle-aged man in a lumber jacket shouted at the youths. Others matched the demonstrators, obscenity for obscenity.

This was the first disruption of an inaugural parade or ceremony in the 180 years of the American Presidency. Not even in 1861 had anything like this occurred.

It was a national disgrace. It was so bad that when the Nixons' limousine got to 13th Street, a barrage of sticks, stones, beer cans, bottles, and obscenities hit the vehicle.

When the parade rounded the corner onto 15th Street, it finally left the demonstrators behind. A cheer went up. Nixon ordered the sun roof opened and he and Pat stood up.[61]

There were the usual balls that night, four of them altogether. There was a heavy rain, cold and depressing.

The Nixon party, after visiting all the balls, went to the White House at about 1:30 A.M. David Eisenhower led the way to the second-floor family quarters. He showed the family the hidden door to the passageway linking the second floor with the third, then led a tour of the third floor. He lifted a rug and pulled out a note he had hidden there eight years earlier: "I will return." Nixon played the piano, ending with a song he had composed when courting Pat. The lights on the first floor were all off; Johnson had ordered them off years earlier to save electricity.

"Dick," Pat said, "let's turn on all the lights in the White House and make it cheery."

"It's done," he responded. He called the usher's office, and the lights went on.[62]

CHAPTER TWELVE

GETTING STARTED
January–June 1969

"WATERGATE, WHERE REPUBLICANS GATHER."

So read the headline on a story by Myra MacPherson in the "Style" section of the Washington *Post* shortly after the inaugural. MacPherson noted that three Cabinet members—Volpe, Mitchell, and Stans—and their wives had moved into the apartment-office complex, while another Cabinet couple, the Hickels, were looking at an apartment. Rose Mary Woods had taken up residence, as had a number of Republican congressmen.

The Watergate complex, begun five years earlier and not yet completed, was located in a former slum and swamp area of Foggy Bottom. It was owned by Societa Generale Immobiliare of Italy; the Vatican held 20 percent of SGI's stock. The real-estate agents for the place were ecstatic that the Republicans had come to town, according to MacPherson, because the Democrats could not afford the prices. The only Democratic client was the Democratic National Committee, which had leased a suite in the office building. With the arrival of the Republicans, one agent bragged, "We could have a Cabinet meeting here." A major selling point was the tight security throughout the buildings, featuring TV-monitored elevators and private guards patrolling the halls at night.[1]

After eight years of the Democrats, there were going to be lots of other changes in Washington. White tie for state dinners, for example, replacing the black tie Johnson had preferred, and a large, formal U-shaped table in place of the intimate round tables for ten that Jackie Kennedy had used. Nixon set up his working office in the old Executive Office Building, next to the White

House, reserving the Oval Office for more formal occasions. And, on the first Sunday after the inaugural, Nixon held a worship service in the East Room of the White House, with Billy Graham doing the preaching. Although unprecedented, this became a regular practice.

The services were ecumenical. Among others, those who conducted them included Terence Cardinal Cooke, Dr. Norman Vincent Peale, and Rabbi Louis Finkelstein ("One of the few religious leaders," Nixon pointed out proudly to the press, "to have been on the cover of *Time* magazine"). The congregation was as mixed as the preachers; the Chief Justice, members of the Cabinet, and members of Congress were joined by the White House butlers and maids. Inevitably there were criticisms, as when the doxology was chanted during Rabbi Finkelstein's service. Of course there were charges that the Nixons were more interested in publicity than piety; Nixon responded hotly that he sponsored services in the White House, rather than worshiping in a Washington church as all his predecessors had done, so as to avoid publicity. He also instructed Haldeman to arrange to broadcast the services on the radio.[2]

Initially, at least, life in the most public house in America gave the Nixons more family time together. Pat told a reporter that at the end of their first week, she and Dick had sat down to dinner "together every night—which is a record in the history of our marriage." Tricia lived in the White House, and Julie and David moved in after their final exams.

From the start, the Nixons suffered at the hands of the Washington society-page reporters, who called them staid and even dull and compared their parties and state dinners unfavorably to those of the Kennedys. Nixon professed to be unconcerned, but he also managed to top the Kennedys when, at the end of April, he hosted a history-making event, a seventieth birthday party for Duke Ellington. He got the guest list from Ellington, and it included dozens of famous black musicians. The result, as MacPherson reported in the *Post,* was "a jam session such as that old mansion has never known. It lasted until the early hours."

One black musician commented, "Nixon did something no one else has ever done—this is the first time an American black man was honored in the White House." Another said he was from Los Angeles and had voted against Nixon seven times, "but if he ran for Grand Dragon of the Ku Klux Klan I'd vote for him after tonight!"[3]

Two weeks later, Ehrlichman and Haldeman convinced the President it would be a good idea for him to see Ralph Abernathy and other black political leaders. But after the White House meeting, Abernathy told reporters that it was "disappointing and fruitless." Nixon scribbled at the bottom of a report: "E–H, This shows that my judgment about *not* seeing such people is right. *No More of This!*"⁴

Pat did lots of entertaining, held receptions for congressmen's wives, handed out awards, sponsored Girl Scout cookies, and in general, as always, was indefatigable in her public appearances. But she did not have Jackie Kennedy's charm, looks, flair, or sophistication, nor did she have a cause, as Lady Bird Johnson had. *Newsweek* wrote that "if there is one thing Mrs. Nixon needs, it's humanizing." Nixon's scribbled comment was "R.N. does *not* agree—I would just as soon keep the society reporters away altogether (if we could get away with it)."⁵

When the Nixons moved into the White House, they found scores of gadgets and electronic equipment. There were, for example, microphones and tape recorders hidden in the Oval Office and various other rooms. Nixon ordered them removed. There was an electronic push-button device installed by Johnson to open a window in the bedroom; Nixon ordered that removed too, explaining, "I took it out because I was afraid if I pushed the button I'd blow up the world."⁶

Johnson, as Nixon noted, "felt a constant need to know what was being said about him in the press and on television." Johnson had installed two wire-service ticker tapes in the Oval Office, along with three color TV sets that he could run with a remote-control device. He had a similar setup in another office, and a third in the President's bedroom. Nixon ordered all but one of the nine sets removed.⁷

Nevertheless, Nixon was obsessed with his image at least as much as Johnson, if possible more so. From his first day in office until his last, he insisted on a "News Summary'" that told him what had been said about him, his Administration, and world events during the past twenty-four hours. Mort Allin, recruited by Buchanan, was the editor. Buchanan often helped out. The daily effort ran from twenty to fifty typed pages. Nixon read it avidly, frequently scribbling comments.

Nixon hardly ever watched television himself. Allin and Buchanan fed him their own impressions of how he was faring on TV; in so doing they indulged their own prejudices and fed his. Reading the summaries with whatever objectivity twenty years can bring, one is struck by the antipathy felt by Allin and Buchanan toward virtually all the big names in TV broadcasting, but most especially Dan Rather and Walter Cronkite of CBS News. They fed

Nixon's *idée fixe* that the television newsmen, like the newspaper reporters, were all his bitter enemies, men who hated him and would do anything to hurt him.

It was not true, as Herb Klein kept trying to tell him. But Allin's shop operated independently of the director of communications, and Nixon very much liked what Allin was producing. He could not get enough of it.[8]

Although Allin was a recent graduate of the University of Wisconsin, his analysis of the television news was more or less identical to that heard at cocktail parties in Orange County. Here is an example from the last week in February. The principals are Deputy Defense Secretary David Packard and Senators J. William Fulbright (D., Ark.) and Albert Gore (D., Tenn.). The issue was the antiballistic missile (ABM).

"The soft-spoken Deputy Defense Secretary was filmed by ABC on the Hill being badgered by a testy Fulbright who wanted to know why we weren't talking with the Russians right now instead of building ABM's.

"NBC did nothing for Secretary Packard today. Fulbright and Gore received most of the footage and Packard's presentation of his charts was pretty well negated by Gore presenting some of his own.

"CBS opened with film of Packard 'moving through his charts as the Pentagon chart-turners stood stiffly at attention and snapped the charts with military precision,' etc., etc., etc. Then there was Gore apologizing for his 'amateurish' charts, asking if he could borrow Secretary Packard's 'wand' to use as a pointer. All in all, CBS had a great time turning the entire proceeding into one giant joke."

Nixon's handwritten comment was "Give me a report by noon today on what we are doing to raise hell with NBC and CBS on this."[9]

Nixon used the News Summaries as a way to send instructions to his staff. On a report that bureaucrats in the Office of Economic Opportunity had given a "chilly response" to the idea of black capitalism, Nixon wrote: "H—I want some action taken to clean up this outfit (Moynihan objects but Burns thinks it is essential and I agree)."

Nixon's obsession with leaks is rightly legendary. Allin made certain every one came to his attention. He quoted John Osborne of *The New Republic*, who had written in his column, "The Nixon Watch," that White House staffers were saying the President was "troubled and frustrated." Nixon wrote: "E & H: Here we go again. Certainly we should be able to find out who on our staff talks to this character."

When the St. Louis *Post-Dispatch* reported on a dispute among "high Administration officials," Nixon wrote: "H—I have told Zeigler [*sic*] *not* to have our people talk to *Post Dispatch*—or *N.Y. Times* or Washington *Post. Knock It Off!!!*" On another report, the President commented: "H & E, Note. *Newsweek* is loaded against us. Cut them like we cut *Times*."[10]

Another Nixon obsession was Teddy Kennedy. Allin fed that one too, by noting every Kennedy appearance on television. After a couple of months of this, Nixon ordered Klein to go over the network news since the inaugural and report back "as to the total time Ted Kennedy has received." He instructed Klein to then use the figures to demand equal time. He concluded, "We need to get on the networks and give them more hell."[11]

The Kennedys were always Nixon's touchstone. As Safire put it, the Nixon White House wondered "how . . . could so much legend be made out of so little accomplishment?"[12] To find out, Nixon ordered his staff to study the Kennedys and to emulate them. When Nixon saw a memo praising him, from the Israeli ambassador, he wrote: "Erlichman [*sic*]: You might pass this to some of the press. Why can't we get some of this kind of reaction out publicly? The Kennedy's [*sic*] *always* did so."[13]

Less than two weeks after his inaugural, Nixon demanded action on printing and disseminating his Inaugural Address. He noted to "Erlichman" that "Kennedy had his sent by U.S.I.A. in classy slick production job with appropriate pictures" all around the world. Nixon wanted the same.[14]

"The press is the enemy." Nixon made that categorical statement dozens, if not hundreds, of times. Yet he wanted to use the press to get more publicity and praise for himself and to build his base with public opinion. "The President feels that we have not adequately moved to merchandise the favorable reaction to his Inaugural address," Haldeman told Klein on February 5. Nixon wanted Klein to "collect one-line reactions and comments from across the country and the world and have these mailed to editors of dailies and weeklies"—and he wanted it done by the end of the week.[15]

Over the years, Nixon had put together a list of ten thousand names of editors, reporters, broadcasters, professors, and other opinion makers. Whenever something favorable appeared on him in the News Summaries, Nixon would instruct Klein to "get it out to our 10,000 list! Today!"[16]

Nixon was forever trying to manipulate the news—"getting our story out," he called it. At the end of the first week, he asked on the News Summary: "E—Have we done adequate job on RN at work? (Begins in office at 7:45—non stop to 6:30 or 7:00)—Let me know." [17]

On an end-of-January News Summary, Allin had an item from UPI. An Egyptian girl had written the President, reminding him that her father had been his pilot on a trip on the Nile River in 1965, and reporting that he had been killed in the 1967 war. She asked him to stop selling arms to the Israelis. Nixon scribbled: "E. —This is a great human interest story. 1. Get a letter off to girl— invite her to visit RN's in DC. Publish it. 2. Set up better procedure for RN to react to such stories. 3. *Above all* see that Mort *flags* such material." As to the substance of the letter—arms sales to Israel—Nixon was blunt: "Ignore it." [18]

From the beginning, Nixon compiled lists of his friends and enemies among the reporters. His favorites were Buckley, Earl Mazo, and Victor Lasky. After his first few news conferences, Nixon sent a memo to Ehrlichman demanding "on an urgent basis" a list of those in the White House press corps who were against him. He said he intended in the future to call only on his friends. "Ziegler and Klein will disagree with this," Nixon noted, so "I don't want you to consult with them. This is my decision and I intend to follow it up." He swore he would cut those "who are definitely out to get us." [19] Ehrlichman had the list in his hands later that day.

Nixon spent hours, every day, studying the press, manipulating the press, warning his associates about the press, threatening the press—and then declaring himself indifferent to the press. In Safire's view, Nixon wanted the press "to be hated and beaten" because it was "another power center . . . unelected and unrepresentative." Safire believed that "in his indulgence of his most combative and abrasive instincts against [the press] . . . lay Nixon's greatest personal and political weakness and the cause of his downfall." [20] Only a newsman could have reached such a sweeping conclusion, but surely there was some truth in Safire's judgment. Nixon's war with the press went back to the Hiss case, but it was in his Presidency, from the first day, that it reached levels of vengeance and vindictiveness previously unimagined, and stayed there right on through to his last day in the White House.

"HIS ROLE," Walter Lippman told a Washington *Post* interviewer in 1973, at the beginning of Nixon's second term, "has been that of a man who had to liquidate, defuse, deflate the exaggerations of the romantic period of American imperialism and American inflation. Inflation of promises, inflation of hopes, the Great Society, American supremacy—all that had to be deflated because it was all beyond our power."

When Nixon saw those remarks in the News Summary, he wrote, "A wise observation." [21]

Four years earlier, an item in the News Summary began, "The U.S. has lost 'the desire and ability' to be the dominant power in the world, Britain's Institute for Strategic Studies said." Nixon commented, "H.K. [Henry Kissinger]. Very important and accurate." [22]

It was Richard Nixon's fate that he had to preside over the retreat of American power. He hated it. Every instinct in him rebelled against it. For twenty years, in every crisis, at every turning point, his advice had been to take the offensive against the Communists. Attack, with more firepower, now—that was his policy.

Yet in 1969, when he finally came to power, he had to retreat. He knew it, he accepted the fact, and he did it. The process began at his first news conference, January 27, 1969, in answering, as President, his first questions on foreign policy.

With regard to Vietnam, he said he would propose to the other side "mutual withdrawal, guaranteed withdrawal, of forces . . ." During the campaign just completed, Nixon had never mentioned the possibility of American withdrawal.

With regard to SALT, Nixon used a familiar pattern of speech, laying out two alternative courses of action, both of which he rejected. One called for arms control "apart from any progress on political settlement," the other for no SALT agreement until there was some progress on political settlements, for example, in Vietnam.

Nixon then gave his own middle course: "What I want to do is to see to it that we have strategic arms talks in a way and at a time that will promote, if possible, progress on outstanding political problems at the same time." This was a policy of linkage, of obtaining Soviet concessions in other areas as the price for American participation in SALT, which Nixon assumed the Soviets needed more than Americans did.

With regard to China, although Nixon rejected any immediate change in policy, he said he looked forward to "what the Chinese Communist representatives may have to say . . . whether any changes of attitude on their part on major issues may have occurred." [23] In itself, this represented a major change from the two previous Administrations. Kennedy's and Johnson's hostility toward the Chinese was so great that both men actually considered, seriously, dropping nuclear weapons on the Chinese nuclear production facilities, in combination with the Soviet Union. It was the Soviet reluctance, not American, that led to the quiet demise of that harebrained scheme. [24] Nixon had privately told General Vernon Walters that one of the first things he wanted to do was establish contact with the Chinese. This at a time when Kissinger was dubious at best about opening to China, and at a time when the Chinese press characterized Nixon as the "newest puppet of the monopoly bourgeois clique." One of Nixon's News Summaries had quoted the Chinese Ninth Party Congress as denouncing Nixon as a "hypocritic priest, a gangster wielding a blood-dripping butcher's knife." Nixon's only comment had been "H.K.—pretty colorful!"[25]

With regard to the nuclear arsenal, Nixon—quietly, without fanfare—turned Democratic policy on its head. Kennedy and Johnson had labored mightily, and expensively, for a clear-cut superiority in strategic forces. Kennedy had even dreamed of achieving a first-strike capability. Reporters asked Nixon what his policy would be: would he seek superiority or accept parity?

"I think 'sufficiency' is a better term, actually, than either 'superiority' or 'parity.' "[26] During the campaign just completed, Nixon had charged that Humphrey advocated parity, which he then denounced as the same as surrender. Now he was adopting parity, although calling it by a different name.

The news conference was a *tour de force*. Nixon was attempting to turn around American foreign policy in a badly needed and highly realistic way. Raymond Garthoff comments that "Nixon deserves considerable credit for his readiness to accept the idea of strategic parity," and adds that it "reflected a certain maturity of judgment and recognition of the basically defensive orientation of American interests in the world."[27] It also showed that he was a much more serious statesman than he was responsible campaigner.

Nixon's decisions on these and other foreign and defense policy issues were not based on intuition, or gut feeling, or Kissinger's whispered advice, but rather on his knowledge and self-confidence. As one small example, a few days after the news conference, Nixon attended an NSC meeting. The discussion centered on the Nigerian civil war with secessionist Biafra. The question was whether the United States should recognize Biafra, as a few other nations had done.

Richard Helms, head of the CIA, opened the meeting by listing the countries that had recognized Biafra. Nixon stopped him and said, "Look, Dick, you've left out a couple of countries—Zambia and the Ivory Coast." Helms, somewhat shaken, got going again, this time about tribal rivalries being part of the problem.

Nixon stopped him again. "Yes. And this is a problem which really goes back to the history of that country. The British colonial policy favored the Moslem Hausas in the north and that aggravated the tensions and there's cultural as well as economic and political factors here. It's a very, very tragic problem." One Foreign Service officer present was "absolutely astonished at the level of knowledge of Nixon."[28]

Nixon showed his boldness and risk-taking proclivities when he announced new policies in his first news conference; he followed that up on his first overseas trip, which he undertook one month after his inaugural, against the advice of the State Department, Dean Acheson, the newspaper columnists, and the Senate Foreign Relations Committee.

The trip was to Europe. The objections were that no crisis required a special visit to the NATO countries, that there had been no time to prepare for high-level talks, that it was provocative to the Russians, and that it was just grandstanding on Nixon's part, all headlines with no substance.

Although he did not bother to explain them, Nixon had good reasons for going. He intended to enter into serious discussions with the Russians, with the North Vietnamese, perhaps even with the Chinese, so he thought it best to begin by establishing the principle that "we would consult with our allies before negotiating with our potential adversaries." He wanted to "show the world" that he was "not completely obsessed with Vietnam," even while taking advantage of the trip to seek General de Gaulle's advice on Vietnam and China. He wanted to assure the Europeans that NATO remained America's number-one commitment. Finally, as he explained in his memoirs, he wanted to "dramatize for Americans at home that, despite opposition to the war, their President could still be received abroad with respect and even enthusiasm."[29]

It was a good idea, well executed. In Brussels, London, Paris, Bonn, Berlin, and Rome, Nixon got gratifying receptions. He had long talks with de Gaulle, who urged him to get out of Vietnam and to seek détente with Russia and to open up to China. He accomplished all his objectives. On Nixon's return, Dean Acheson led the critics in admitting that Nixon had been right while they were wrong.[30]

Kissinger described Nixon as "exuberant; he adored the vestigial ceremonies and was new enough to it to be thrilled. . . . To land with *Air Force One* on foreign soil, to be greeted by a King and then a Prime Minister, to review honor guards . . . all this was the culmination of his youthful dreams . . . seemingly unattainable for a poor, somewhat resentful young man from a little town in California. It all produced one of the few occasions of nearly spontaneous joy I witnessed in my acquaintance with this withdrawn and elusive man." Kissinger adds that Nixon continually turned to him for reassurance that he had done well.[31]

Perhaps Kissinger has it right; perhaps it did happen this way. But his supercilious condescension, his portrait of this awestruck small-town boy, ignores the obvious fact that Nixon had been through similar ceremonies dozens, if not hundreds, of times, with kings and shahs and Russian dictators and governors-general and every other kind and type of world leader. It was Kissinger who was doing it for the first time; perhaps he was the one who was awed.

Certainly it was Nixon who showed the nicest diplomatic touch of the trip. The British ambassador to the United States, appointed in the spring of 1968, was John Freeman, former editor of the left-wing *New Statesman*. Back in 1962, Freeman had described Nixon as "a man of no principle whatsoever except a willingness to sacrifice everything in the cause of Dick Nixon."

In London, Prime Minister Harold Wilson held a small dinner party at 10 Downing Street for Nixon. The President's advance team saw Freeman's name on the guest list and asked that it be removed. Wilson refused. There was tension in the air. Nixon handled the situation smoothly. In his toast, he said that American journalists had written far worse things about him than had the British ambassador. Looking directly at Freeman, he went on: "Some say there's a new Nixon. And they wonder if there's a new Freeman. I would like to think that that's all behind us. After all, he's the new diplomat and I'm the new statesman."

Cries of "Hear, hear" went up. When Nixon sat down, Wilson slid his menu to him. On the back, he had written, "That was one of the kindest and most generous acts I have known in a quarter of a century in politics." [32]

NIXON COULD BE one of the most graceful of men. He could also be one of the most awkward. Herb Klein reports that "on at least fifty occasions he warmly greeted my wife by her first name, Marge, and then spoiled the effect with the same line: 'What a pretty dress. How can Herb afford it?' " [33]

And Haldeman tells of Nixon's line when giving a guest in the Oval Office a memento, such as cuff links or a tiepin. Nixon would thrust the gift at his surprised guest "and tell his standard Nixon joke that never, in my memory, drew a laugh: 'Give this to your wife *or* your secretary, whichever you prefer.' " [34]

He could not carry on small talk; equally, he seemed never to know what to do with his hands when he was on a stage or before a camera. His awkwardness created a mood; dozens of those who had private meetings with him have testified that they felt ill at ease because of the vibrations he sent out.

Yet this same man could be magnificent in the most difficult situations. On March 19, he was scheduled to present a Medal of Honor to Mr. and Mrs. Joseph Newlin of Wellesville, Ohio, whose son, Marine Pfc. Melvin Newlin, had been killed in Vietnam at the age of eighteen. Before the ceremony, Nixon read the citation and broke down himself. He said he couldn't possibly go through with it. But when the Newlins came into the Oval Office, he pulled himself together.

The President read the citation, then added impromptu remarks. "This kind of remarkable courage never occurs as an accident," Nixon said, "but only when a young man has a fine family behind him." In a sense, he went on, he was presenting the medal to Newlin's parents, because they had "contributed so much to this fine young man." Mrs. Newlin burst into tears and buried her head on her husband's shoulder. Nixon reached out in a spontaneous gesture and gave her a comforting hug.[35]

WHEN NIXON came to power, he realized that the great American air offensive, February 1965 to March 31, 1968, code name Rolling Thunder, had failed to break the will of the North Vietnamese, while adding greatly to the numbers in the antiwar movement at home. He knew further that the great American ground offensive, from the summer of 1966 to the Tet offensive of 1968, had failed to destroy the NVA. So he wanted to try a third option, an offensive against the Ho Chi Minh Trail in Cambodia. By interdicting the supply lines, he hoped he could sever the enemy forces in the South from North Vietnam, making it possible for him to withdraw the American troops from the South while simultaneously reinforcing his "madman" image as the man who might do anything, thereby encouraging the enemy to agree to an armistice.

On January 8, Nixon had ordered Kissinger to prepare a report on what the enemy was doing in Cambodia. On February 18, Kissinger informed Nixon that not only were the Communists making effective use of the Ho Chi Minh Trail through Cambodia, but that they had located their headquarters there (the Central Office for South Vietnam, or COSVN), and were using it to prepare for an offensive in South Vietnam.

Four days later, on February 22, the Communists launched a countrywide offensive. Not so great as Tet one year earlier, nevertheless the offensive was a challenge, and it did appear to violate the "understanding" President Johnson had reached with Hanoi when he called off the bombing. American casualties in the first week of the offensive were 453, and 336 in the second week.

Nixon left for Europe on February 23. En route, he suddenly ordered the bombing of the Cambodian sanctuaries, something the

Joint Chiefs had been urging him to do for a couple of weeks, with COSVN as the main target. Before the order could be executed, Secretary of Defense Laird cabled his reservations from Washington. He feared the bombing could not be kept secret, and that the press and Congress would be furious at such an escalation. Rogers agreed with Laird. Nixon, from Bonn, rescinded the order.[36]

When Nixon returned from Europe, he was seething. His instincts were to respond violently to the Communist offensive; his frustration at having to call off the bombing because of the possible outcry from the doves was very high. But he stayed calm as he answered a March 4 news conference question about the Communist challenge: "We have not moved in a precipitate fashion, but the fact that we have shown patience and forbearance should not be considered as a sign of weakness. We will not tolerate a continuation of a violation of an understanding. But more than that, we will not tolerate attacks which result in heavier casualties to our men at a time that we are honestly trying to seek peace at the conference table in Paris. An appropriate response to these attacks will be made if they continue."

Later in the news conference, Nixon was asked if he would resume bombing North Vietnam. He replied, "I believe that it is far more effective in international policy to use deeds, rather than words threatening deeds, in order to accomplish our objectives. . . . I am not going to threaten—I don't think that would be helpful."[37]

President Thieu had recently hinted that it might be possible to withdraw fifty thousand American troops in the immediate future. Asked about this, Nixon said, "There are no plans to withdraw any troops at this time, or in the near future," but he added that as the ARVN improved, and the level of fighting decreased, "it may be possible to withdraw."

"Do you feel," another reporter asked, "that you could keep American public opinion in line if this war were to go on for months and even years?"

That question got to the point, because by this stage the struggle was essentially one for the hearts and minds of the American people. Nixon needed time to bring the boys home without surrendering South Vietnam to the enemy, time to train and equip ARVN, time to cut the Ho Chi Minh Trail and so isolate the NVA. To buy time, he needed public support.

"Well," Nixon replied to the question, "I trust that I am not confronted with that problem, when you speak of years. Our objective is to get this war over as soon as we can. . . . I think that the American people will support a President if they are told by the President why we are there, what our objectives are, what the costs will be, and what the consequences would be if we took another course of action." He said he thought he could be effective in explaining "why we are there." [38]

Ten days later, on March 14, Nixon held another news conference. The enemy offensive in Vietnam continued. Merriman Smith wondered if Nixon's patience wasn't wearing a little thin.

Nixon replied that what he had said on March 4 had been widely interpreted as a warning. "It will be my policy as President to issue a warning only once, and I will not repeat it now. Anything in the future that is done will be done. There will be no additional warning." He said that his response had been "measured, deliberate, and, some think, too cautious. But it will continue to be that way, because I am thinking of those peace talks every time I think of a military operation in Vietnam." [39]

The following day, at 3:35 P.M., Nixon called Kissinger on the telephone. He said he was ordering an immediate B-52 attack on COSVN. "State is to be notified only after the point of no return," Nixon declared. "The order is not appealable." But Kissinger convinced him to at least give Laird and Rogers an opportunity to express their views, so he agreed to a meeting the next day, Sunday, March 16, in the Oval Office.

At the meeting, Nixon employed a favorite technique, pretending to canvass opinion on a decision on which he had already made up his mind. Rogers was opposed, because of public opinion. Laird was ready to go ahead, but favored "going public right away," as he thought it could not be kept secret.

Nixon concluded the meeting: "I have decided to order the bombing to begin as soon as possible. Tomorrow, if the weather is good enough." The weather was suitable, and on March 17, B-52 bombers hit COSVN. Elaborate procedures were used to keep the raid—code name Breakfast—a secret, obviously not from the Cambodians or Vietcong or North Vietnamese, but from the American people. The Air Force judged Breakfast a success. [40]

SOFT WORDS and tough deeds, keeping the enemy guessing, reinforcing the madman image—all this appealed to Nixon's sense of the dramatic and satisfied his need to feel that *something* was happening. He also rather liked the idea of sending out mixed signals.

That same week, at his March 14 press conference, he sent a complex signal to the Russians. Funding for the ABM system was a subject of hot debate in Congress, with Senator Kennedy leading the opposition, supported by Fulbright and Gore. Nixon had stayed away from the controversy during the campaign. Now he announced that he was supporting a modified version of Johnson's Sentinel ABM program.

Nixon called his proposal Safeguard. It differed from Sentinel in a number of ways, most importantly in that it did not attempt to defend American cities. Instead, Safeguard was designed to protect the intercontinental ballistic missile (ICBM) launch sites, which meant America could get by with far fewer ABMs. Safeguard's primary purpose, Nixon said, was to defend "against any attack by the Chinese Communists that we can foresee over the next ten years." In addition, it was a safeguard against "any irrational or accidental attack that might occur." What it did not do, Nixon said, was "provide defense for our cities," because "there is no way that we can adequately defend our cities without an unacceptable loss of life." Further, moving to a massive city defense system "tends to be more provocative in terms of making credible a first-strike capability against the Soviet Union. I want no provocation which might deter arms talks . . . and escalate an arms race."

Nixon had adroitly managed to come down on the side of the ABM while reassuring the Soviets that he wanted to curb the arms race. Herb Kaplow of NBC News missed the point. He asked Nixon how the Russians could regard his ABM decision "as not being an escalating move in the arms race." Nixon carefully explained to him the difference between Johnson's attempt to protect the cities and his program to protect launch sites. He then pointed out what he called "an interesting thing about Soviet military and diplomatic history: They have always thought in defensive terms, and if you read not only their political leaders, but their military leaders, the emphasis is on defense." [41]

Nixon's realism and sound historical judgment must have been reassuring to the Soviets, even if American reporters failed to get his point. To make it easier for them, Nixon added that Secretary Laird would soon present a defense budget that would cut $2.5 billion from the Johnson budget.

Nixon the mad bomber. Nixon the builder of an ABM system. Nixon the arms-control advocate. Nixon the first President to cut the DOD budget in eight years. Which was the real Nixon?

ON MARCH 19, at 10:30 A.M., Nixon met with one of his oldest and bitterest adversaries, Dean Acheson. Back in the late forties, and through the 1952 campaign, Nixon had said the most awful things about Acheson (the classic was the crack that Adlai Stevenson was a "graduate of Dean Acheson's Cowardly College of Communist Containment"). But by 1969 Acheson was ready to forgive and forget, and Nixon was eager for his advice.

Nixon opened with a gracious remark: he had always considered the Marshall Plan, in which Acheson had played such a vital part, to have been one of the great acts of statesmanship in

American history. Then down to business. Nixon said he realized that the "overwhelming opinion of the business, finance, and legal world in New York [was] in favor of scuttling Vietnam at any price." He said he was "dead-opposed to this," but admitted that he found "the whole situation frustrating and puzzling." What did Acheson think?

Acheson's advice, as always, was to keep the powder dry, make no concessions, enter into no negotiations, and dig in for the long haul. He said the fighting in Korea ended only when the Chinese realized "they could not defeat Ridgway . . . and simply stopped fighting." He pointed out that there was no political settlement in Korea, and he doubted that there ever would be one.

Acheson later wrote a long memorandum on the meeting. One part read, "I thought American policy had been very sensible until the Johnson decision in '65 to put in substantial troops. Although I had supported this, I now thought I had been wrong. Here the President interjected that he had also supported it and also thought that we had been wrong."

These confessions of converted Cold Warriors were of course completely private. Neither man would have dreamed of admitting in public that he had been wrong, nor did the realization lead Acheson to wonder if perhaps he had been wrong in his consistent refusal to ever negotiate with the Soviets (from the time of Potsdam, July 1945, until he left office, in January 1953, Truman had held not one meeting with the Soviet leader).

Nixon asked hopefully if Acheson "thought the present was a good time to initiate discussions with the Russians." He pointed out that they were having trouble, including border clashes and terrible name-calling, with the Chinese.

"I replied that I did not think it was a good time to negotiate." Indeed, in Acheson's view, it was never a good time.

Acheson was more impressed by Nixon than the other way around. He wrote a friend after the meeting that he "got a feeling of orderliness and concentration rather than a Napoleonic drive and scattered attention." He backed Nixon's ABM decision in a speech a month later before the American Society of Newspaper Editors, and began lobbying intensively for the Safeguard system. For his part, Nixon was grateful for the support, but he did not again ask Acheson's advice on how to deal with the Russians.[42]

"CITY OF FEAR AND CRIME" read *The New York Times* headline the day after Nixon's inaugural. The Washington *Daily News* had a full-page, front-page editorial, addressed "Dear Mr. President." It welcomed Nixon back to the city, then asked him to personally intervene to root out the "fear that stalks the streets of Washington."

Nixon wrote on the News Summary: "John Mitchell and John E—Let's get going with an announcement in 48 hours of *some* action. It is of highest priority to do something meaningful on D.C. crime *now*."[43]

Mitchell immediately held a news conference, where he pledged a "vigorous" law enforcement. He said he and his key assistants were committed to getting tough with criminals and with "activists" who demonstrated against the war or disrupted college campuses. Those assistants included Richard Kleindienst, Deputy Attorney General; William Ruckelshaus, Assistant Attorney General in charge of the Civil Rights Division; and William Rehnquist, head of the Office of Legal Counsel.[44]

Nixon asked Congress for more police and judges for the District and sent to the Hill a crime bill for Washington that included provisions empowering judges to jail criminal suspects for sixty days before trial and allowing police to break into homes without a knock. These came to be known as "preventive detention" and "no-knock" and were attacked as unconstitutional. Congress, whose members lived and worked in the city, eventually passed the bill anyway.

On January 27, Nixon announced that he was turning on the lights on the White House lawn as a contribution to making the streets safer. A White House secretary had been robbed the previous evening, by a purse snatcher, just outside the East Gate. The lights had been off since Johnson's inaugural in 1965, to save a few thousand dollars each month. The Washington press corps was 100 percent behind Nixon on this one; even Mary McGrory, usually a critic, applauded his anticrime program—she invited him to drop by her apartment for some of the cheesecake she had been serving to policemen who had been investigating her neighbors' burglaries.[45]

Of course, there was no quick fix possible. In early March, when the Nixon party returned from Europe, Rose Mary Woods discovered that her apartment in the Watergate had been burgled. She was robbed of some $7,000 worth of jewelry. Obviously, security at the Watergate was not up to the skills of Washington's criminals.[46]

Beyond street crime, Nixon's law-and-order constituency was concerned about antiwar demonstrations and campus disorder. These were primarily youthful movements, and sparked a widespread concern about where America's young people were headed. In 1968 and earlier, such actions as "occupations" of the administration offices, massive antiwar rallies, disruption of classrooms, and so forth, had been mainly at elite universities. By early 1969, they were just as likely to be happening at state colleges out in the sticks. In the same way, marijuana and free speech and dirty clothes and long hair and free sex were moving from the trend-setting universities out to the teacher-training institutes.

There was a feature to this widespread rebellion of the young against their society little noticed by commentators in the United States, but one that Richard Nixon saw clearly. It was this: the youthful rebellion was a worldwide phenomenon. It was happening in Paris and Prague almost as much as it was in Pittsburgh. Students taking to the streets, students defying their parents, students rejecting the society they were inheriting. Only in Moscow and Warsaw, evidently, were the forces of law and order strong enough to suppress the phenomenon. In China, the young were on a rampage, as they were in Mexico and Peru and West Germany and Italy.

There was no simple explanation. Older Americans blamed the rebellion on Vietnam, but clearly there was more involved, as Vietnam hardly touched student life in Bonn or London. The students of the late sixties had been born just after World War II. Some of them came into a world of devastation and death; others, into a world entering an unprecedented economic boom. But whether their parents were among the winners or the losers didn't seem to matter; either way, the kids went into revolt as soon as they were old enough to leave home.

One of Nixon's first acts as President was to order the NSC to undertake a study of the worldwide student revolt. The following day, January 24, his News Summary quoted ABC-TV as saying there were student uprisings in Pakistan, Spain, Czechoslovakia, Paris, and—worst and most ominous—Tokyo. Nixon wrote, "Kissinger—this shows pertinence and urgency of my student insurrection study. I want to have a C.I.A. analysis in depth of communist factors in youth disturbance."[47]

To suspect that the Communists were behind the whole thing was to grant them an influence they only wished they had, and indeed Nixon's approach to the problem was not as simpleminded as his instructions to Kissinger suggest. On March 22, as the good weather for rioting season began, he made a much-anticipated statement on campus disorders. Antiwar leaders had convinced themselves that Nixon equaled Hitler, that jackbooted storm troopers were about to descend on the campuses, but in fact the President in his speech was moderate and conciliatory, considering the provocation and what was at stake.

Nixon asked for no new legislation. He did insist that the provisions of the 1968 Higher Education Act would be enforced; the law said that a student convicted of a crime in court, or one judged by the college administration to have committed a "serious" violation of campus regulations, would be ineligible for two years for federal scholarships or loans. With regard to action, that was it, and surely it was a long way short of SS guards replacing the campus cops.

In his rhetoric, Nixon was somewhat tougher. He warned that if violence continued, "cultural calamity" loomed. Noting that physical violence and intimidation were apparently becoming acceptable on campus, he commented, "It is not too strong a statement to declare that this is the way civilizations begin to die. . . . As Yeats foresaw: 'Things fall apart; the center cannot hold.' None of us has the right to suppose it cannot happen here."

He urged university officials to enforce their own rules, and reminded that "from time immemorial expulsion has been the primary instrument of university discipline." He thought those who refused to abide by the rules "should simply be required to leave."

But he made it clear it was up to the schools themselves. "The Federal Government cannot, should not—must not—enforce" or attempt to guarantee campus peace.[48]

His hortatory effort had little if any effect. Antiwar leaders acted as if his threat to enforce the law on federal scholarships and loans was depriving them of a basic human right; university officials could not find the strength to actually expel students guilty of "serious" disruption; riots and protests spread as the warm sunshine made its way north. The great gathering place during Easter break in 1969 was not Fort Lauderdale, but the local administration building. By the end of April, daily scorecards were being printed listing the campuses "on strike," the administration buildings "occupied," and so forth. There were literally hundreds involved.

Nixon tried again. On April 29, in a twenty-minute impromptu speech to the U.S. Chamber of Commerce, he asserted that there could be "no compromise with lawlessness" and urged university officials to display some "backbone" against campus revolutionaries. He conceded that students should be awarded a strong voice in university affairs (based on more than a quarter century in the classroom, this author has to say that Nixon was badly wrong on that one), and agreed that "peaceful dissent" was essential to the vitality of any institution. Without it, he admitted, "the educational system becomes in-grown, stultified, loses the ability to develop the new ideas to keep pace with change . . ."

But, he concluded, "when we find situations in numbers of colleges and universities which reach the point where students in the name of dissent and in the name of change terrorize other students and faculty members, when they rifle files, when they engage in violence, when they carry guns and knives in the class-rooms, then I say it is time for [the authorities] to have the back-bone to stand up against this kind of situation." [49]

Again, he had little effect. As graduations approached, disruptions continued. Things had gotten so bad that it was widely believed the President of the United States could not safely appear on a college campus in the United States. Lyndon Johnson had stopped trying some years earlier, and in his first four months in office Nixon had not set foot on a campus.

On June 3, Nixon went to General Beadle State College, in Madison, South Dakota, to speak at the dedication of the Karl E. Mundt Library. He had chosen well; there were no demonstrators, no hecklers. His message oscillated between lyrical defense of American democracy and sharp criticism of those who caused and condoned disruptions. He said that student revolutionaries, propelled by a "self-righteous moral arrogance" and abetted by "permissive" faculties, were subjecting fundamental democratic values to their sharpest challenge in the life of the nation. "It should be self-evident," he said, that faculty who supported student demands should "know better." [50]

No doubt they should have known better, but then Nixon should have known better, too, than to look to Communist influence, rather than the violence going on in Vietnam, as the cause of the disruptions. Two days after his speech at General Beadle, Nixon got a memorandum from Ehrlichman on "Communist Financial Support of Campus Disorders." This was the culmination of the various studies Nixon had ordered from the CIA, the NSC, the FBI, and others. Sadly, Ehrlichman reported that "the intelligence community conclusion is that our Government does not have specific information or 'ironclad proof' that Red China or Cuba is funding campus disorders." More hopefully, he went on, "this is not to say that it could not be concluded from the evidence that such funding is taking place."

Nixon wrote at the bottom, "1. Keep after this; 2. give Huston [Tom Charles Huston, former Defense Intelligence Agency aide currently working on special projects in the White House] (or someone of his toughness and brains) the job of developing hard evidence on this; 3. pass info to Karl Mundt." [51] Mundt, on the Senate Internal Security Subcommittee, had been Nixon's associate in Communist hunting on HUAC back in the late forties.

Nixon judged, rightly if cynically, that the heart of the antiwar movement was male college students threatened with the draft. He believed the demonstrators were not idealists but only frightened young men out to save their own skins. Next to ending the war, the best way to undercut the antiwar movement was to end the draft. On March 27, Nixon announced the creation of a commission to help him "achieve the goal of an all-volunteer force."[52]

On May 19, he sent a special message to Congress on the changes he was asking for in the Selective Service System. They included going from an oldest-first to a youngest-first order of call, meaning nineteen-year-olds first, along with a reduction in the period of prime draft vulnerability from seven years to one year. The net effect was that twenty-year-olds and up were no longer threatened by the draft, and, just as Nixon hoped and expected, most of them stopped marching for peace and started getting on with their lives.

For the nineteen-year-olds, a lottery system would let them know where they stood, so that they too could make plans. Nixon continued the undergraduate student deferment, with the understanding that the year of maximum vulnerability would come whenever the deferment expired.[53] Taken together, these changes were popular with America's young men.

The stick that went with this carrot in the Nixon Administration's offensive against the antiwar movement was provided by Mitchell's Justice Department. It consisted of a program of harassment of antiwar groups, including infiltration of student groups by FBI agents, disruptive tactics, sabotage, and the like. Mitchell hauled protesters into court on charges that were never sustained by any jury anywhere but that did have the effect of keeping such organizations as the Vietnam Veterans Against the War tied up in court, spending their energy and time and money defending themselves. One of the early moves in this direction came on March 20, in Chicago, when a federal grand jury indicted leaders of the demonstrations at the Democratic Convention; the charge was that the accused had violated a law recently passed by Congress that made it illegal to cross state lines to incite a riot. The "Chicago Seven" soon became a *cause célèbre*.

That same spring, Nixon set young Tom Huston to work on "getting the IRS to take a close look at the activities of left-wing organizations which are operating with tax-exempt funds." Huston reported to Nixon that the IRS "does not fully appreciate the extent of our concern" and was not fully cooperating. Huston wanted to get going, at once: "Certainly we ought to act in time to keep the Ford Foundation from again financing Carl Stokes' mayoralty campaign in Cleveland."

Nixon wrote on Huston's memorandum, "1. Good.—2. But I want *action*.—3. Huston, Follow up *hard* on this."[54]

That same week, Arthur Burns sent Nixon a memorandum

warning him that Congress was proposing to put a $5,000 limitation on individual contributions to political campaigns, as a part of so-called Clean Elections Legislation. Burns feared it would be impossible to stop the bill. His best advice was for the Administration to send to the Hill its own bill, limiting not only individuals but corporations, trade associations, and political action committees as well. Nixon commented, "Unless this [the PAC limits] is included, forget it. The stupid Congressmen are only thinking of themselves. They don't get contributions over 5 g. Let's be sure a contributor can give 5 g. to *each* candidate and *no* limitation before nomination."[55]

For himself, Nixon on March 27 took a whopping tax deduction. Acting on advice from Lyndon Johnson, Nixon gave to the National Archives the second installment of his personal papers, some 600,000 documents, appraised by Ralph Newman of the Abraham Lincoln Book Store in Chicago at $576,000, giving Nixon a tax deduction worth nearly a quarter of a million dollars.

Nixon's "gift" was hardly free and clear. Only Nixon could decide who had right of access so long as he was President (later he extended this censorship to 1985), and even when the papers were made available to scholars, Nixon retained the right (which in the event he exercised vigorously) to remove any documents that might be personally embarrassing, to him or other living people, as well as his correspondence with famous men (Eisenhower, Johnson, Kennedy, foreign heads of state or government, and so forth).

That the papers were worth what Newman said they were there can be little doubt; the autographs alone on the incoming correspondence made them valuable. That they were his personal property was well established by precedent. Johnson, among many others, had done what Nixon did. That the precedent was a bad one is also clear; after all, the bulk of the papers came from Nixon's period as Vice-President, when he was a public employee, engaged in correspondence that was public business, for which the public provided him with an office and a staff and a salary. To those of us who labor in the archives in an attempt to discover and then describe what our public officials have done when carrying out the public's business, it is infuriating that these politicians, years and even decades after they have run in their last campaign, can still control and censor the record of their actions.[56]

SHORTLY AFTER NOON on Friday, March 28, Nixon was talking in the Oval Office with Kissinger and Laird. Haldeman brought in a message from Dr. Walter Tkach, the White House physician. "Mr.

President," Haldeman said, "President Eisenhower just died."[57] Nixon broke down and cried.

Eisenhower, who had made many of the arrangements himself for his state funeral, down to details, had chosen Nixon to deliver the eulogy. Nixon went to Camp David to prepare it.

Ray Price, who was helping with the eulogy, mentioned that one thing that set Ike apart was that he was truly loved throughout the world. That got Nixon started on a series of insightful remarks.

"Everybody loved Ike," he told Price. "But the reverse of that was that Ike loved everybody." That was exactly right, as all those who knew Ike would agree. What came next is not so certain, although Nixon was just as categorical about it.

"In politics," Nixon said, "the normal reactions are to have strong hatreds one way or the other."

To this author, who has spent much of his career reading and researching and thinking and writing about Ike and Dick, the biggest single difference between them is right here: Eisenhower was a man full of love, for life and for people, while Nixon, sadly, was a man who all too often gave in to an impulse to hate.

No one ever pointed this out more clearly than Nixon himself, up at Camp David, talking to Price on that highly emotional occasion.

"Ike didn't hate anybody," Nixon said. "He was *puzzled* by that sort of thing. He was puzzled by the kids in these recent years. He was puzzled by Joe McCarthy. He would disagree with people and he'd take a strong stand for principle—but . . . he never allowed those arguments to get him *emotionally* involved. . . . He didn't think of people who disagreed with him as being the 'enemy.' He just thought: 'They don't agree with me.' "[58]

Delivering the eulogy, on Sunday, March 30, Nixon was magnificent. Standing before the coffin in the Capitol Rotunda, he praised Eisenhower as "one of the giants of our time," a man who was "loved by more people in more parts of the world than any President America has ever had." His voice brimming with emotion, he never broke down. He called Eisenhower "a good and gentle and kind man" who "made us proud of America." He cited as the source of Eisenhower's strength a line Ike himself had used, in his Guildhall Address shortly after V-E Day: "I come from the heart of America."

Turning to Mamie, who was openly weeping, Nixon said he was sure she would not take it amiss if he related Ike's last words to her, which she had repeated to Nixon: "I've always loved my wife. I've always loved my children. I've always loved my grandchildren. And I have always loved my country."

Nixon concluded, "We salute Dwight David Eisenhower standing there in our memories—first in war, first in peace and, wherever freedom is cherished, first in the hearts of his fellow men."[59]

NIXON WAS relatively uninterested in domestic policy, as he frequently said, but there was one area in which current policy got him so angry that he took an interest and insisted on some action. It was welfare.

The system, in Nixon's view, was an inexcusable, even criminal, mess. Started in the New Deal, Aid to Families with Dependent Children (AFDC) had been based on the assumption that the taboo on illegitimacy and the ethic of paternal responsibility were too strong to be affected by financial incentives. That proved to be a big mistake. In 1940, 2 percent of America's children were on welfare. By 1969, the figure was 11 percent. Eight out of ten welfare children were on the rolls not because their fathers were dead or disabled, as AFDC had presumed, but because the fathers had deserted. And if the father did not desert, but had no job, or only a pathetically low-paying job, his children were not eligible for welfare.[60]

Meanwhile, a vast bureaucracy had sprung up to administer AFDC. These social workers were paid middle-class wages. Johnson's War on Poverty had added immeasurably to the numbers of bureaucrats, but not noticeably to the income of poor people. The Johnson program had assumed that what poor people needed was skills; it proposed to teach them through new government agencies. What the poor people really needed was money, or so at least HEW Secretary Finch believed, as did Moynihan. What the nation needed was to get the poor to work at decent wages, and to get out of the welfare business, which was becoming horrendously expensive. It was also grossly unfair, because each state set its own levels. At the extremes, a mother and three children with no means of support in Mississippi got a maximum of $50 a month, of which the federal government paid $41.75. In New York, a mother and three children received $278 per month, of which $139 came from Uncle Sam.[61]

On January 15, Nixon had sent a memorandum to Finch and Moynihan, asking for an investigation of welfare. He noted, quite correctly, that "the American people are outraged, and, in my view, they should be. . . . I do not want this swept under the rug or put aside. . . . This whole thing smells to high heaven and we should get charging on it immediately."[62]

Moynihan was pleased and excited. He went to work, and

along with Finch and others came up with a Family Security System proposal designed to help the working poor, to stop discriminating against low-income fathers who stayed with their families, and to provide incentives for those on welfare to go to work. It was, in essence, a negative income tax. It would require, initially, adding millions of working poor to the welfare rolls, but it promised, eventually, to reduce dramatically the numbers on welfare. It would also cut back sharply on the bureaucracy.

Arthur Burns was dead set against it, because of the initial cost. But when Nixon called a meeting with Burns, Finch, and Moynihan at Key Biscayne during the Easter weekend (April 4–5), Burns was astonished to discover that Nixon rather favored it. Burns thought this wholly out of character.

"You would add seven million persons to the welfare rolls!" Burns exclaimed.

"What's wrong with Republicans providing income maintenance for seven million people?" Finch asked.

Nixon broke in. "I understand, Arthur, that you don't like it; and I understand your reasons. But I have a problem. If you don't like it, give me another solution."

Turning to Moynihan, Nixon asked, "Will FSS get rid of social workers?"

"It will wipe them out!" Moynihan enthused.

Nixon told him to keep at it.[63]

AT FIRST LIGHT on the morning of April 15, Kissinger called Nixon on the telephone to inform the President the North Koreans had shot down a Navy EC-121 reconnaissance aircraft. The plane, on a routine mission off the North Korean coast, was unarmed. It carried electronic equipment and a crew of thirty-one men. The barbaric act was one of those erratic cases of gratuitous violence in which North Korea indulges from time to time, apparently in this case as a birthday present to Kim Il Sung.

Nixon's instinctive reaction was that he was being tested, and that he must meet force with force. He called an NSC meeting in the Cabinet Room.

Nixon opened. "We're going to show them," he said.

Secretary Rogers reminded him, "That's what Lyndon Johnson said about Vietnam, and we're stilll there."

Secretary Laird wondered what the United States would or could do if the North Koreans responded to an aggressive retaliation by invading South Korea. At a minimum, Laird pointed out, a second ground war in Asia would require a maximum mobilization in the United States.

William Porter, American ambassador to South Korea, sent a cable warning that a strong American reaction would be taken by the South Koreans as a signal, and they might well invade North Korea.

Attorney General Mitchell wanted to charge.

Vice-President Agnew, equally bellicose, responded to Rogers' and Laird's advice to go slow until all the facts were in by asking, "Why do we always take the other guy's position?"[64]

Why indeed? Kissinger was, if anything, even more eager than Mitchell, Agnew, and Nixon. He was engaged in a behind-the-scenes but tense winner-take-all struggle with Rogers for possession of Nixon's heart and mind. He knew the President liked to hear tough talk, liked to indulge in mad-bomber fantasies, liked to be told he was being tested and was strong enough to meet the test.

This was a test, Kissinger said. The Soviets, the North Vietnamese, and the Chinese "would all be watching" (there is no evidence that any outside power was involved in the incident, and, in fact, the Russians, at that moment, were helping in the search for survivors).[65]

"If we strike back, even though it's risky," declared the National Security Adviser, "they will say, 'This guy [Nixon] is becoming irrational—we'd better settle with him.' But if we back down, they'll say, 'This guy is the same as his predecessor, and if we wait he'll come to the same end.' "[66]

Kissinger wanted an air strike against a North Korean airfield, destroying every plane on it. He spoke of the possible necessity of using nuclear weapons.[67] But Nixon hesitated. Rogers and Laird had, between them, decades of experience in government; Kissinger had three months' experience. Unquestionably the campuses of America, already in turmoil, would explode. A second ground war in Asia was unthinkable.

Nixon chose a milder response. He announced that the reconnaissance flights would continue, to be covered by American fighter aircraft (in this Nixon was frustrated by the bureaucracy; in response to the EC-121 incident, Laird ordered all such flights canceled for a period of weeks). Nixon also ordered another secret bombing mission over Cambodia, on Kissinger's insistence that this would send a strong signal to North Korea.

Kissinger was disgusted with his boss's hesitant and halting reaction. He blamed it on Nixon's personality. According to Kissinger, the key factor was a previously scheduled news conference (for April 18). The anticipation of such conferences, Kissinger said, "was an experience that usually filled him with such a combination of dread and exhilaration as to leave no energy for other reflection." Nixon's passivity continued after the conference, Kissinger believed, because the experience "left him so drained that he sought to avoid stress for days afterward."[68]

Kissinger wrote this stuff about a man who, with Ike dead and Johnson in retirement, had undoubtedly held more news conferences than any other active politician in the world.

Aside from the bombing of Cambodia, Nixon had chosen the safe, sane, sensible response to the provocation. He hated himself for doing so. As Kissinger knew so well, Nixon preferred his own vengeful and vindictive side to his reasonable, intelligent, let's-take-everything-into-account side. Talking to Kissinger later about EC-121, Nixon made a vow: "They got away with it this time, but they'll never get away with it again."[69]

Some years later, Nixon remarked that the failure to respond quickly and strongly to the North Korean attack "was the most serious misjudgment of my Presidency, including Watergate."[70]

NIXON HATED to appear weak. He also hated leaks. But he loved to leak himself, and to threaten. On a News Summary item at the end of March, which reported that ABC-TV had said, "The Administration 'at the highest levels' is considering an air strike on North Vietnam," Nixon wrote, "*Good!!* K—tell them RN is for this."[71]

Actually, he had no intention of bombing North Vietnam. At his April 18 news conference, he also said the opposite of what his policy was. Even while preparations were going forward in DOD to begin bringing the boys home, Nixon told reporters, "If we are to have a negotiating position at the Paris peace talks, it must be a position in which we can negotiate from strength, and . . . a unilateral withdrawal does not help that position. . . . I have not ordered and do not intend to order any reduction of our own activities."[72]

Simultaneously with those remarks about the Paris peace talks, Nixon was moving to undercut the talks. He had Kissinger send a message to Russian ambassador Anatoly Dobrynin proposing secret meetings between "American and North Vietnamese negotiators," to be held separately from the Paris talks.[73]

Such an arrangement appealed to Nixon and Kissinger because it cut out the State Department, because the public posturing in Paris was getting nowhere, and just because they enjoyed operating secretly, in peace talks as in bombing Cambodia. Evidently neither man saw the irony here; for years, the North Vietnamese had insisted that the only meaningful peace talks would have to be between Hanoi and Washington, one to one, while the United States had insisted that Saigon had to be included. Nixon's offer to

Dobrynin was giving the Communists what they had always demanded. Dobrynin said he would send the proposal on to Hanoi.[74]

AT THE END of April, in pursuance of sending a signal to North Vietnam in response to North Korea's shooting down of the EC-121, Nixon ordered a second bombing raid on Cambodia. The first, it turned out, had been unsuccessful, both in the sense that it failed to destroy COSVN or slow traffic on the Ho Chi Minh Trail and in the sense that it failed to wring concessions from Hanoi in the Paris talks. So the next raid was twice as large.[75]

As after the first raid, Cambodia's leader, Prince Norodom Sihanouk, who was trying to keep his country out of the war, made no protest, no public announcement that the United States Air Force was dropping bombs on his country. But on May 9, William Beecher broke the story of the first raid in *The New York Times*. Nixon was in Key Biscayne that morning; Kissinger was there too, and brought the story to him after breakfast, shaking with rage. Nixon was equally enraged. They determined to find and destroy the leaker (actually, Beecher's story was based on an on-site report from a British correspondent in Cambodia, not on a leak).

Nixon had Kissinger call J. Edgar Hoover. The three men had already had a discussion about leaks; Hoover had told the President back in April that the only way to find a leaker was through telephone taps, and that his predecessors had used that method. They had agreed that Kissinger would supply Hoover's assistant, William Sullivan, with the names of those whose phones Nixon and Kissinger wanted tapped.[76] The Beecher story so outraged Nixon that he ordered the taps installed, even though there had been some hesitancy on his part, because he realized what previous Presidents had done about wiretapping "would matter little if the press and the antiwar activists found out about what Nixon was doing."[77]

Hoover, the complete bureaucrat, wasn't about to tap the phones of White House and NSC staff, much less reporters, without protection in the form of written orders signed by the Attorney General. So Kissinger supplied the names and Mitchell signed the papers. The chief suspect was Morton Halperin, a former Harvard professor and member of Kissinger's staff. Although he was a hawk on Vietnam, Halperin was thought by Hoover to be one of those "arrogant Harvard-type Kennedy men"; Kissinger himself described Halperin as "philosophically in disagreement" with the President. Another apparent Halperin shortcoming was his Jewishness; as Ehrlichman later recalled, "Nixon would talk about Jewish traitors, and the Eastern Jewish Establishment—Jews at Harvard.

And he'd play off Kissinger. 'Isn't that right, Henry? Don't you agree?' And Henry would respond, 'Well, Mr. President, there are Jews and Jews.' "[78]

So the FBI put a tap on Halperin's phone, and on those of other Kissinger staffers. Kissinger also had taps placed on the phones of the closest aides of the Secretary of State and the Secretary of Defense. How much Nixon knew of this is unclear; in early June, another Kissinger assistant, Colonel Alexander Haig, indicated Nixon was having second thoughts. Haig urged Kissinger, in a memorandum, to ask Hoover if it was necessary to prolong the taps, and to make it "clear that the President wishes to terminate them as soon as possible." (Nevertheless the tap stayed on Halperin for twenty-one months.)[79]

The initial taps turned up no usable information. At Kissinger's request, they were extended to four newspapermen. At Nixon's request, two of his closest aides were added: John Sears, formerly of Nixon, Mudge, currently a deputy to Ehrlichman, and Bill Safire. The reason, so Safire was later told, was that they had been heard talking to a reporter.[80]

Nixon also ordered his brother Don's phone tapped, and put the Secret Service on his tail after the FBI and the CIA both refused to spy on the President's brother.[81] Don was not suspected of leaking, but of shooting off his mouth, getting favors by making promises in his brother's name, and so forth.

Nixon assumed that the taps, seventeen in all, requested by the President, ordered in writing by the Attorney General, carried out by the FBI (except in Don's case), were authorized by the Crime Control Act of 1968, and thus legal (in 1972 the Supreme Court ruled that they were not).

But Nixon also ordered what he knew to be illegal. When columnist Joseph Kraft wrote a critical piece on Nixon, the President ordered the FBI to tap his phone. There was no hint of a leak in this case, and Hoover refused. Nixon turned to Haldeman, who turned to Jack Caulfield, a retired New York City policeman, now a private investigator. Caulfield placed the tap.[82]

The upshot of all this activity was nothing. The leaker was never found, for the good reason that, at least with regard to the Cambodian bombing, he did not exist. As Nixon said some years later, referring to the taps on Halperin and another NSC staffer, W. Anthony Lake, "I know that he [Kissinger] asked that it be done. And I assumed that it was. Lake and Halperin. They're both bad. But the taps were, too. They never helped us. Just gobs and gobs of material: gossip and bullshitting—the tapping was a very, very unproductive thing."[83]

• •

HOWEVER LITTLE or much Nixon worried about the law with regard to tapping his own aides, NSC staffers, reporters, and his brother, he was insistent that the next Chief Justice be a strict construction-ist in interpreting the Constitution, and he took the appointment with the utmost seriousness.

After Justice Fortas had withdrawn his name for confirmation as Chief Justice, Earl Warren had agreed to stay on until the end of the next term of the Court, in June 1969. This gave Nixon time to consider carefully his nominee; it also gave other politicians time to make recommendations.

Eisenhower, on December 13, 1968, had recommended his own Attorney General, Herb Brownell. As Ike put it, "There's no need for me to extol his record or for me to bore you with my high opinion." [84] In fact, as Nixon did indeed know full well, Eisenhow-er's admiration for Brownell was unbounded. So was Nixon's. But there was a drawback: Nixon's southern supporters did not like Brownell. He had delivered a brilliant brief against segregation in *Brown* v. *Topeka*, and he had been the chief law-enforcement offi-cer at the time of the Little Rock school crisis, when Eisenhower had used federal troops to enforce integration.

For those reasons, Brownell was out.

Nixon next approached Tom Dewey, but Dewey ruled himself out because of his age, sixty-six.

Nixon considered Justice Potter Stewart, also recommended by Ike, but Stewart asked not to be considered, because he felt the Chief had to exercise leadership and it would be difficult for a sitting judge to suddenly elevate himself above his peers. [85]

Nixon asked Mitchell if he wanted the job; Mitchell declined. He thought it was a bad idea to appoint a political friend.

In the midst of the process, on April 24, in the White House, Nixon held a formal dinner party to honor Warren. He invited all of Warren's family. The two men had been hostile toward each other since the 1952 campaign for the Republican nomination, and Nixon had been sharply, even cruelly critical of the Warren Court during the 1968 campaign, but on this occasion they left their ani-mosities behind and had a splendid evening.

The next day, Warren wrote by hand to Nixon to express his thanks for "the wonderful party you had for us." His family would never forget, Warren said, while "for me it was the most thrilling social event of my half century of public life." [86]

Judge Warren E. Burger, of the U.S. Court of Appeals, an Ei-senhower appointee from Minnesota who had played a prominent pro-Ike part in the 1952 Republican Convention, meanwhile came to Nixon's attention. Nixon had read an article by Burger on the role of law and order in a democratic society reprinted in *U.S. News & World Report*, and was much impressed. He had Burger swear in some of his minor appointees in January, and talked to him afterward, and was even more impressed. He sent Mitchell to sound out Burger on his views on constitutional issues, and liked what he heard.[87]

Justice Fortas, meanwhile, was in further trouble. It developed that he was on a $20,000-per-year retainer from convicted financier Louis E. Wolfson. It was a delicate case, to say the least. Nixon arranged for Mitchell to keep Warren informed of new charges as they emerged from the Justice Department's ongoing investigation. Burger wrote Nixon that he was dismayed at the way Republican politicians were jumping on Fortas. He praised Nixon for staying above the fracas, and reminded him that "the American system gives every man the benefit of the presumption of innocence in the face of any charge and that everyone should suspend judgment. Time, then,—and the facts—will carry this crisis of the Court to its inevitable conclusion."[88]

A few days later, in mid-May, Fortas resigned. Nixon called him the day of the resignation to express his sympathy.[89]

On May 21, Nixon nominated Burger for the post of Chief Justice. In making the announcement, Nixon said that the Fortas affair had played a major role in his thinking; he did not want to get burned as Johnson had been appointing a personal friend, and he wanted to be certain that his appointee was above suspicion and would be quickly confirmed by the Senate.[90]

Burger was so confirmed, and he proved to be one of Nixon's better appointees. Here at least was one place where nearly all agreed that President Nixon did good service for the nation.

AMBASSADOR DOBRYNIN had passed on to Hanoi Nixon's offer to begin secret, two-party peace negotiations, but Hanoi had not responded. So on May 14 Nixon went on national television to report to the American people on the war and to make in public the offer he had intended to make in private. Up to then, the American negotiating position had been Johnson's "Manila formula," which went back to 1966 and offered to withdraw American troops from South Vietnam six months after the NVA withdrew. Nixon, on May 14, offered a simultaneous withdrawal, to be followed by an exchange of POWs and free elections in South Vietnam. He also hinted that American withdrawal would soon begin, with or without an agreement: "The time is approaching when the South Vietnamese forces will be able to take over some of the fighting fronts now being manned by Americans." He balanced that with some tough talk: "Let me be quite blunt. Our fighting men are not going to be worn down; our mediators are not going to be talked down; and our allies are not going to be let down." [91]

Hanoi replied the following day: "The plan of the Nixon Administration is not to end the war but to replace the war of aggression fought by U.S. troops with a war of aggression fought by the puppet army of the United States." [92] It was ridiculous, in Hanoi's view, to put their soldiers on the same basis as American troops in South Vietnam. Anyway, why should the North Vietnamese agree to withdraw in return for an American withdrawal that was going to take place anyway?

Nixon felt that he had made a major concession, and he was furious with the North Vietnamese. He took out his anger on the doves in the U.S. Congress.

Nixon's ABM proposal was in deep trouble in the Senate, despite an intense lobbying effort on Nixon's part personally (and this was just about the only domestic issue on which he spent some of his time and called in chits with the Senate). In his scribbles on the News Summary items that showed the ABM doing badly with the Senate, Nixon breathed fire, he bristled, he threatened, he cajoled. "E & H, There must be *no* talk of Compromise on Safeguard." "K, play a *Hard* line publicly—& a very careful calculating line privately." "Harlow—on a completely top-secret basis talk with Stennis—see what he advises." [93]

A parallel issue was the testing of multiple independently targeted reentry vehicles (MIRVs). This was an area in which the United States had stolen a march on the Soviets; the Americans had completed the research and were ready for the testing and development stages (the Russians had stolen a march on ABMs, which they had in place, while the Americans had yet to complete the research). MIRVs gave each ICBM three to ten separately targeted nuclear warheads, and represented a quantum leap in offensive power comparable to the switch from conventional to nuclear weaponry.

Inevitably, there was a split in the government on whether or not to proceed with this next step in the arms race. Nixon's talk of "sufficiency" in his first news conference gave hope to the opposition, which was led by Secretary Rogers, who opposed testing. Laird and the Pentagon wanted to move ahead. The Senate doves opposed.

Nixon sent his instructions on this critical matter in the most casual of ways, via a marginal comment on his News Summary of May 19. It read, "State and Defense: I have decided to move ahead on MIRV Testing regardless of Senatorial opposition. Inform all hands so that there will be one Adm. line."[94]

Nixon's action helps answer the question of why it is so difficult for the U.S.S.R. and the U.S. to achieve meaningful arms control. A major part of the problem is the asymmetry of weapons development. In mid-1969, the Russians had not got going on MIRV; the Americans had not got going on ABM. It should have been the simplest thing in the world to swap—the Russians give up ABM, the Americans give up MIRV. But the hawks on both sides were aghast at such a suggestion. Give it up after spending all that money? Give it up when we have such a lead over the enemy? Never. The irresistible impulse was to hold to what had been achieved and strive to catch up in other areas.

In a graduation speech at the Air Force Academy on June 4, Nixon went after his critics on ABM and MIRV. He called them the "new isolationists" who would have the United States "turn its back on the world." He declared, "We must rule out unilateral disarmament because in the real world it won't work," without naming any critics who advocated unilateral disarmament.

He insulted his political foes: "My disagreement with the skeptics and the isolationists is fundamental," he said. "They have lost the vision indispensable to great leadership. They observe the problems that confront us, they measure our resources, and then they despair. When the first vessel set out from Europe for the New World, these men would have weighed the risks and they would have stayed behind."[95]

The speech infuriated the Democrats. "It sounded like the old Nixon I used to know," said Senator Gore. "It was a form of demagoguery that was very fashionable in the time of his old colleague, Joe McCarthy," said Senator Fulbright. "A technique of setting up straw men and then knocking them down," said Senator Alan Cranston of California.[96]

THE SPEECH was hardly consistent with Nixon's inaugural plea for a lowering of voices, and hardly seemed designed to win votes for his programs in the Senate. But it certainly made Bill Buckley and his friends happy, something Nixon very much wanted to do, since what was coming next was going to make them distinctly unhappy.

After leaving Colorado Springs, Nixon flew on to Midway Island for a meeting with President Thieu. Nixon's purpose was to make public what he had already decided on in private, to institute a program called "Vietnamization" (the word was created by Laird back in March, because Laird did not like "de-Americanization").[97] It meant the beginning of the American withdrawal and was the logical consequence of the decision Johnson had made in the wake of the Tet offensive to not reinforce Westmoreland's victory.

Thieu was opposed; General Abrams was opposed; Kissinger was opposed; Johnson had resisted the move; Nixon hated doing it; but the American political system imposed it on the President. He could not escalate on the ground; stalemate was unacceptable; withdrawal was the only choice.

Having decided to retreat, Nixon might have gone about it with dispatch. Instead, he went about it with agonizing slowness. At Midway, he announced that he was pulling out twenty-five thousand men, and that at "regular intervals" thereafter he would pull out more. The pace of withdrawal would depend on three factors: progress in training and equipping ARVN (Vietnamization); progress in the Paris peace talks; the level of enemy activity.[98]

He had obtained no concessions from Hanoi for his action. In his memoirs, he was brutally honest in stating that he had begun "an irreversible process, the conclusion of which would be the departure of all Americans from Vietnam."[99] He had made it impossible for America to extract concessions in negotiations from the North Vietnamese. He had made it difficult, if not impossible, for the military commanders in Vietnam to maintain morale among the fighting men.

The phased, slow-motion retreat was the worst mistake of his Presidency. Because the war went on, tension and division filled the land, and the Nixon haters went into a frenzy. It was the continuation of the Vietnam War that prepared the ground and provided the nourishment for the Watergate seed, which without the Vietnam War would never have sprouted.

Of course, Nixon did not see it that way at all. At the conclusion of the Midway meeting, Kissinger reports that "Nixon was jubilant. He considered the announcement a political triumph. He thought it would buy him the time necessary for developing our strategy."[100]

When Nixon returned to Washington, he held a news conference. He was asked about an article in the current issue of *Foreign Affairs* in which Clark Clifford had suggested that 100,000 troops should be pulled out in 1969 and that all troops be brought home before the end of 1970.

Nixon could not resist pointing out that Clifford had been Secretary of Defense and thus had had his opportunity to withdraw, and that instead he had presided over an escalation. In short, "He did have a chance in this particular respect, and did not move on it then."

But "we have changed that policy," Nixon went on. "As far as how many will be withdrawn by the end of this year, or the end of next year, I would hope that we could beat Mr. Clifford's timetable." [101]

Nixon was certainly bold in setting his goal—America out of Vietnam by the end of 1970.

CHAPTER THIRTEEN

"DON'T GET RATTLED—
DON'T WAVER—
DON'T REACT"
July 1–October 15, 1969

On July 14, Roscoe Drummond wrote in the Philadelphia *Inquirer* that "politicians, press, professors and others" were warning the President that unless he got out of Vietnam "popular opinion will roll over him as it did LBJ."

Mort Allin highlighted that remark in the News Summary. Nixon commented: "E & K—see Drummond and tell him (1) that RN is less affected by press criticism and opinion than any President in recent memory. (2) *Regardless* of public opinion and polls —RN will do what his long experience and conviction tells him is right."[1]

WITH THE BEGINNING of summer, there was a lull in the fighting in South Vietnam. Whether this meant Hanoi was exhausted, or biding its time while the Americans withdrew, or was ready for negotiations, was unclear. On July 7, Nixon held a meeting on the presidential yacht *Sequoia* to discuss the options. Present were Laird, Wheeler, Mitchell, General Robert Cushman (a marine officer who was deputy CIA director and former military aide to Vice-President Nixon), and Kissinger.

Everyone at the meeting agreed to respond to the lull with a reciprocal slowdown, and to make a basic change in General Abrams' "mission statement." To date, Abrams had been operating under the same orders Westmoreland had received, to "defeat" the enemy and "force" its withdrawal to North Vietnam. The new statement ordered Abrams to provide "maximum assistance" to ARVN, to support pacification efforts, and to reduce the flow of supplies down the Ho Chi Minh Trail.[2]

A major effort to interdict enemy supply lines in Cambodia was already under way. The secret bombing, begun in March, expanded in June, as Nixon ordered a series of attacks under the code name Menu (chosen because the individual raids were called Breakfast, Dinner, Supper, Dessert, Lunch, and so forth). Individual missions were specifically approved by Nixon. The elaborate precautions taken to keep the raids secret (from the American people and most of the American government and armed forces) continued. When Nixon asked for an assessment of the effectiveness of the raids, Laird and Abrams assured him that they "have been effective and can continue to be so with acceptable risks."[3]

But reducing the flow of supplies was not going to bring peace; at best it would bring stalemate. And as Drummond noted, Nixon was up against a time problem. He knew it better than anyone else. In September, Congress would return to Washington and the students to their campuses; Nixon recognized this would mean that "a massive new antiwar tide would sweep the country." Then Hanoi would, probably, launch a new offensive in February 1970. With congressional elections coming up in November 1970, Nixon expected, in his words, that political demands "for more troop withdrawals [would be] impossible to stop and difficult to ignore."

Through July, he discussed the problem in a series of conversations with Kissinger. He decided, as he later wrote, to "go for broke." He would "end the war one way or the other—either by negotiated agreement or by an increased use of force." Together with Kissinger, he developed "an elaborate orchestration of diplomatic, military, and publicity pressures."

He decided on an ultimatum to Hanoi. He set a date, November 1, as a deadline. That would be the first anniversary of the bombing halt.[4]

Nixon set Kissinger to work to prepare the details of a military escalation. The preparation of options took place in a section of the NSC, without Laird's participation or even knowledge (increasingly, it was characteristic of the Nixon Administration that the right hand did not know what the left was doing). Kissinger's assistant, Colonel Haig, was the driving force in the planning.

Meanwhile, Nixon held out a sort of olive branch to Ho Chi Minh. On July 15, he wrote a letter to the North Vietnamese President.

"I realize that it is difficult to communicate meaningfully across the gulf of four years of war," Nixon began, but "I wanted . . . to reaffirm in all solemnity my desire to work for a just peace."

He said the time had come "to move forward . . . toward an early resolution of this tragic war," and promised to be "forthcoming and open-minded" in negotiations. He concluded, "Let history record that at this critical juncture, both sides turned their face toward peace rather than toward conflict and war."[5] As to specifics, Nixon mentioned only his May 14 speech, already denounced by Hanoi.

As the letter was being delivered, Haig and his staff completed a new war plan, code-named Duck Hook. It called for massive bombing of Hanoi, Haiphong, and other key areas in North Vietnam, as well as mining harbors and rivers, destruction of the dike system to bring on extensive flooding, a possible invasion of North Vietnam, and an optional use of nuclear weapons against the Ho Chi Minh Trail. In short, all-out war, on the model of Germany and Japan, 1945.[6]

The North Vietnamese, meanwhile, had agreed to secret talks in Paris between Kissinger and their representatives, Xuan Thuy and Mai Van Bo. The first meeting took place in French diplomat Jean Sainteny's Paris apartment on the Rue de Rivoli. Nixon was not optimistic. He told Kissinger he did not believe negotiations, whether public or secret, would amount to anything until there was a fundamental change in the military situation. As Kissinger put it (as if this were some great insight on his part), "The North Vietnamese were less interested in stopping the fighting than in winning it."[7]

Nixon's instructions to Kissinger, therefore, were to threaten, not to negotiate. He said he wanted the North Vietnamese delegates reminded that November 1 was the first anniversary of the bombing halt. Kissinger should tell them what they already knew, that American troops were being withdrawn and that the United States was prepared to accept the result of free elections. If Hanoi was not prepared to respond by withdrawing its troops and agreeing to participate in elections, then Kissinger should tell the delegates that Nixon would "be compelled—with great reluctance—to take measures of the greatest consequences." November 1 was the deadline.

Finally, Nixon told Kissinger to say that he had noted Hanoi's attempt to make this into "Mr. Nixon's war." Tell them, Nixon concluded, "We do not believe that this is in your interest, because if it is Mr. Nixon's war, then he cannot afford not to win it."[8]

Kissinger did as he was instructed. The North Vietnamese response was that there were no NVA troops in South Vietnam [sic] and that no agreement was possible until Thieu had given up his power, yielding to a coalition government that would oversee elections. Kissinger had been quite right—Hanoi wanted victory more than it wanted peace. And Nixon's ultimatum didn't seem to frighten the enemy at all.

• •

BACK IN 1968, Nixon, through Billy Graham, had promised Lyndon Johnson that he could rest assured that if Nixon became President, Johnson would be honored in his retirement. In so promising, Nixon was following Johnson's lead; when Johnson was in the White House, his flattery of former President Eisenhower had verged on nauseating. Nixon's motive was the same as Johnson's; neither man wanted the ex-President criticizing his policies.

Once in the White House, Nixon did all he could to make Johnson happy. Cards and letters, small favors and big (appointments, IRS questions, and the like), flowed from Washington to Johnson City, Texas, in a steady stream. Nixon kept Johnson informed, frequently calling himself to brief LBJ before a speech or an announcement, or sometimes just to chat. In a call in July, Nixon invited LBJ and Lady Bird to Redwood National Park, in California, for the late August dedication of a portion of the park to Lady Bird. The date happened to coincide with LBJ's birthday, an especially nice touch.[9]

On July 16, Johnson was present at Cape Kennedy, Florida, for the lift-off of the Apollo XI moon shot. His presence on the occasion highlighted a delicate situation. It had been President Kennedy who had dedicated the nation to the goal of putting a man on the moon before the end of the decade. Many Republicans were critical, as were many scientists, of the public-relations aspects of this technological stunt, so costly in money, so meager in scientific results, so popular with Walter Cronkite and the media generally. President Johnson had kept the funds flowing into the Apollo program.

And now it was President Nixon who stood to gain the greatest PR benefits. It made the Democrats gnash their teeth.

History is irony. Even as the spacecraft sped on its way to the moon, the younger brother and heir to the political following of the man who had set the whole thing in motion drove off a bridge on tiny Chappaquiddick Island in Massachusetts late on the evening of July 19, only hours before the lunar module landed on the moon. The passenger in Teddy Kennedy's car, twenty-eight-year-old Mary Jo Kopechne, drowned, in circumstances that were somewhat obscure but obviously did not reflect well on Senator Kennedy.

Indeed, from Chappaquiddick on, Nixon and his supporters could answer the question, often asked of Nixon, "Would you buy a used car from this man?" with a question of their own, "Would you go for a ride with this man?"

Nixon's first comment was "It'll be hard to hush this one up; too many reporters want to win a Pulitzer Prize."[10] He could have added that he himself wanted to be rid of the Kennedys, once and for all, and that he intended to do whatever he could to find out and then broadcast what had happened. Soon he had private investigators on the case. Meanwhile, two weeks after the incident, he sent a memo to Ehrlichman: "Talk to Kissinger on a very confidential basis with regard to a talk he had with J. K. Galbraith as to what really happened in the EMK matter. It is a fascinating story. I'm sure HAK will tell you the story and then you of course will know how to check it out and get it properly exploited."

Ehrlichman did as instructed, only to discover that "Henry's hot tip turned out to be unverifiable gossip."[11]

Sometime later, Ehrlichman sent Kissinger, who was in and out of Paris on a regular basis, another memo: "Can you discreetly determine through your sources whether Sergeant [sic] Shriver and the Kennedy family have been speculating in foreign exchange in Paris within the last year?" Nothing came of that one, either.[12]

The intensity of Nixon's feelings about Teddy Kennedy, obvious in so many ways, had a counterpoint in the emotions of this strange and complex man, which was a certain empathy Nixon felt for Kennedy. In the aftermath of Chappaquiddick, Kennedy's career was, apparently, shattered, just as Nixon's had been in '52 and '60 and '62. So Nixon, in preparing for a possible news conference question about Kennedy's future, wrote a note for himself: "Defeat —doesn't finish a man—quit—does—A man is not finished when he's defeated. He's finished when he quits."[13]

ON JULY 20, the day after Chappaquiddick, Apollo landed on the moon. *The New York Times* had run a nasty editorial, criticizing Nixon for his having arranged to speak by telephone to the astronauts. Kennedy and Johnson deserved the credit, the *Times* declared, and it "appears to us rather unseemly" for Nixon to jump in at the last minute and take the spotlight. "Apart from objections on grounds of taste," the newspaper said, it objected because talking to the President, even for only a moment, would cut into the astronauts' time to carry out scientific activities on the moon. The *Times* concluded, in words that many thought would have been better directed against President Kennedy and the entire Project Apollo, that Nixon's phone call "looks suspiciously like a publicity stunt of the type Khrushchev used to indulge in."[14]

Nixon made the call anyway. He talked to Neil Armstrong and Edwin Aldrin, whose image, standing in front of a small camera beside a flag, with the spacecraft in the background, appeared on television sets around the world. Nixon on the phone in the Oval Office appeared superimposed on a corner of the screen.

"This certainly has to be the most historic telephone call ever made from the White House," Nixon began. He told the astronauts how proud he and all Americans and all people everywhere were of them: "For one priceless moment in the whole history of man all the people on this earth are truly one."

Armstrong said in reply what an honor it was "to be here representing not only the United States, but men of peaceable nations . . ." [15]

Three days later, Nixon flew to the South Pacific for the splashdown of Apollo XI. He was on the flight deck of the carrier *Hornet* as the astronauts came aboard, and talked to them through the window of their quarantine chamber.

He opened with one of his awful jokes: he said the toll for a call he had made the day before to the astronauts' wives "wasn't as great as the one I made to you fellows on the moon. I made that collect, incidentally, in case you didn't know."

Nixon was no good at small talk at all; on this occasion he set some sort of record for inappropriateness as he asked the astronauts if they had been able to keep up with events back on earth while they were up in space. For example, did they know about the All-Star baseball game? And who were they for, the National League or the American League?

"Neither one," Armstrong replied.

"There is the politician in the group," said Nixon.

Then Nixon, whose euphoria was running very high, and whose penchant for hyperbole and weakness for gross exaggeration were already well known, came out with the all-time Nixonism: "This is the greatest week in the history of the world since the Creation, because as a result of what happened in this week, the world is bigger, infinitely [*sic*] . . ." [16]

A few days later, Billy Graham took issue with his good friend. He said there were three greater days: Christ's birth, Christ's death, and Christ's resurrection.

When Nixon saw the Graham remark in a News Summary, he scribbled in the margin, "H—tell Billy RN referred to a *week* not a *day*." [17]

FOLLOWING THE SPLASHDOWN, Nixon and his wife and entourage set off on a round-the-world trip, with stops in Guam, the Philippines, Indonesia, Thailand, South Vietnam, India, Pakistan, Romania, and Britain. To celebrate the Apollo success, the trip was code-named Moonglow. It was a typical Nixon whirlwind extravaganza, complete with meetings with the various leaders, handshaking excursions into marketplaces, and state dinners.

In his public statements, he stressed statistics—this was his third visit to Indonesia, his sixth to the Philippines, his eighth to Saigon, and so on. He liked to ad-lib, even though it got him into trouble. In Jakarta, for example, he began boldly enough, but then stumbled: "I realize that the position I am in is a unique one—one that will never come again—because since I am the first American President ever to pay a state visit to Indonesia, the next American President who comes here will not be in the position I presently find myself in."

He continued to use sports in an attempt to establish a link with those he met. He asked nearly every serviceman he shook hands with in Vietnam about his favorite football or baseball team. When he addressed the employees of the U.S. Embassy in Bangkok he hauled out a baseball cap and announced that while you can take American boys out of the United States, "you can never take baseball out of an American boy." [18]

In Manila, at a state dinner, Nixon talked to eight-year-old Bong Bong Marcos, son of his host, President Ferdinand Marcos. The boy was keenly interested in the space program. In his toast, Nixon said he had an announcement to make: "On the first vehicle that carries passengers that go to the moon, Bong Bong will be on that space vehicle." [19]

Pat also followed her typical routine in visiting foreign countries. In Lahore, Pakistan, in 100-degree heat, she visited a school, a hospital, a rehabilitation center, and so forth. Panting reporters asked her how she stood up to the heat: "Oh, well, I'm used to it," she replied. "I've been here before." [20]

In Saigon, she spent an afternoon at the 24th Evacuation Hospital. The administration wanted to give her a briefing; she said no, she wanted to talk to patients, and she did, to thirty-nine men. She sat by their beds, shook hands, patted their shoulders, listened to their troubles, and generally tried to comfort them.

At one bed, she picked up a book on the floor and asked if it was a war novel. Before the embarrassed patient could reply, she glanced at the cover, then dropped the book in some confusion.

She insisted on going to an orphanage. Dozens of reporters followed her, along with a horde of Secret Service men who were terrified by the possibility of an incident. The result was unhappy. The children, some 774 of them gathered to meet her, were frightened by the incessant chatter of army helicopters whirring overhead. Jet fighters crisscrossing above the helicopters added their nerve-grating whine to the sounds. The children hid their faces in their hands in fear. Pat remained cool and composed, but she was furious, and vowed never to subject children to such an ordeal again. [21]

Moonglow was a public-relations triumph. Every stop brought out huge crowds, and later headlines back home. Nixon was delighted, even euphoric, especially at being the first President to visit a war zone since Franklin Roosevelt journeyed to North Africa in January 1943. He talked to the troops of the 1st Infantry Division at Di Am, twelve miles north of Saigon. He said the war was being fought in a worthy cause, to allow the South Vietnamese "to choose their own way" and to "reduce the chances of more wars in the future." [22]

When he got home, Nixon cashed in on the publicity. The Gallup poll, he told Haldeman and Ehrlichman in a memo, was likely to show his approval rating above 60 percent, thus proving that "RN is riding high." He wanted the poll results sent to those congressmen "who may have thought that it will now be safe to give in to their deepest desires and kick us in the teeth." [23]

There was one major news story. In Guam, Nixon talked informally with reporters. To Kissinger's great surprise, he said, more or less casually, that in Asia, "as far as the problems of military defense, except for the threat of a major power involving nuclear weapons, that the United States is going to encourage and has a right to expect that this problem will be increasingly handled by, and the responsibility for it taken by, the Asian nations themselves." [24]

This was little more than a clarification of Vietnamization, but the press treated it as a major change in policy, to the point of immediately putting on it the label the "Guam Doctrine." When he saw that, Nixon went to some lengths to get it changed to the "Nixon Doctrine." [25]

There was another surprise for Kissinger. On *Air Force One,* Nixon had a long talk with Haldeman. Later, Haldeman sat next to Kissinger. "You know," he said, "he actually seriously intends to visit China before the end of the second term."

Kissinger smiled. "Fat chance," he declared. [26]

A month earlier, Nixon had seen an item about a tumultuous greeting given American astronaut Frank Borman in Czechoslovakia. Nixon had scribbled on it, "K, I believe we could needle our Moscow friends by arranging more visits to the Eastern Europe countries. The people . . . will welcome our Cabinet officers and others with great enthusiasm." [27]

Then Nixon had a better idea. On August 2, he became the first American President to make a visit to a Communist country when his plane landed in Bucharest, Romania. Aside from the uniqueness of the event, Nixon's motives were to thank the Romanians for the warm reception they had given him back in 1967, when the Russians had snubbed him, and to get the Russians to thinking about the possibility of America changing its relationship with China.

It was one of the oddities of world politics that Nixon's path to Peking led through Bucharest; it did so because President Nicolae Ceauşescu cultivated good relations with China, which made him unique among European Communists. As Nixon told Kissinger, "By the time we get through with this trip they [the Russians] are going to be out of their minds that we are playing a Chinese game." [28]

Nixon was reaching out to China in a variety of low-key ways. Just before he began the trip, the State Department announced an easing of trade and travel restrictions with China. In Indonesia, Thailand, and Pakistan, he said Asia could not advance so long as China remained isolated. He stressed that he would not participate in any condominium designed to isolate China. In Bucharest, Nixon told Ceauşescu that he hoped Romania would act as a channel of communication to establish good relations between the United States and China. [29]

Nixon also used Ceauşescu to repeat his ultimatum to North Vietnam. "We cannot indefinitely continue to have two hundred deaths a week in Vietnam and no progress in Paris," Nixon said. "On November 1 this year . . . if there is no progress, we must reevaluate our policy." He counted on the Romanians to pass the word. [30]

On August 5, Nixon returned to Washington to face three momentous, closely related issues: funding for ABM, testing of MIRV, and the start of the SALT talks. The Senate would vote on ABM on August 6. Testing of MIRV was under way, but there was a move in Congress to call for a moratorium, and *The New York Times* had recently editorialized, "Continued testing . . . threatens to take the world past a point of no return into an expensive and dangerous new round in the missile race." [31] Meanwhile the SALT talks, first agreed to by Johnson and then postponed, were up in the air; the Nixon Administration had proposed to begin in mid-August, but the Soviets had backed away, asking for more time to prepare.

Taken together, these were by far the most important issues in American-Russian relations. Between them, the two nations were spending almost uncountable sums of money on more and more unbelievably destructive weapons. ABM and MIRV were quantum leaps forward in weaponry; SALT held out a hope for some sort of lid on the madness.

The United States faced these issues with some sobering realizations, chief of which was that the days of unchallenged American superiority were over. When Nixon took office, the United States had 1,054 ICBMs, 656 submarine-launched nuclear-tipped missiles, and 540 B-52s. The Russians had, approximately, 1,200 ICBMs, 200 submarine-launched missiles, and 200 bombers. In short, each side could destroy the other many times over, and neither side could hope to gain a first-strike capability, no matter how many weapons it built. As Morton Halperin noted in a staff study, "It was impossible to escape the conclusion that no conceivable American strategic program would give you the kind of superiority that you had in the 1950s."[32]

Nixon wanted SALT to succeed, for obvious reasons: it made sense, it would save money, it would make the world safer, it would confound his liberal critics, it would be historic, it would open the way to further easing of tensions in other areas, it would inaugurate his era of negotiations, in place of the era of confrontation.

Nixon was afraid of SALT, for obvious reasons: Bill Buckley and the right wing would howl betrayal and charge the President with neglecting the nation's defenses, the Russians would cheat, American scientists would move out of arms development into other projects, the Pentagon and right-wing senators would take out their unhappiness in other areas, it was taking a risk in the strategic power game.

Nixon responded to the conflicting pressures by yielding to all of them. He pushed hard for ABM, and for MIRV testing, and for SALT. His idea was to use ABM as a "bargaining chip" in SALT. He would build new weapons, the ABM, so that the United States would not have to build new weapons after the SALT agreements were reached. Simultaneously, he would push ahead with MIRV, which unlike ABM would not be a subject for discussion in SALT.

There was something for everyone: SALT for the liberals, the doves, and the fiscal conservatives; ABM and MIRV for the conservatives, the hawks, and the Pentagon. This was smart politics. Whether it was good policy was less clear.

Nixon put more effort, and more of his prestige, into ABM than any other issue in his first year in office. As the vote approached, he told Bryce Harlow, "Make sure that all our guys are there [to vote]. Don't let anyone get sick. Don't even let anyone go to the bathroom until it's all over."[33]

Harlow sent Nixon a memorandum saying that Senator William Saxbe of Ohio, who was opposed to ABM, had a $250,000 campaign debt. The Ohio Republican Party was ready to pay it, in the process letting Saxbe know that he "was wrong in opposing the President on the ABM." The party leaders thought the message would get through "loud and clear" and felt that holding up the money until

Saxbe publicly promised support for ABM would be counterproductive.

On the memo, Nixon wrote, "I disagree—make the deal tougher with Saxbe—he doesn't understand anything else." [34]

Other liberal Republicans, led by Senator Margaret Chase Smith of Maine, remained opposed. In a memo to Harlow, Nixon instructed him to pressure them by "getting across the idea that a no vote would weaken our SALT negotiating position." [35]

Senator Muskie said that "the illusion of national security offered by the ABM offers no sanctuary against hunger, poverty and ignorance. Hunger and poverty are more dangerous than Communism." Nixon told Kissinger that this was "unbelievable nonsense from a national 'leader'! "[36]

On August 6, the Senate voted on an amendment that would have prohibited spending on ABM. The outcome was a 50–50 tie, which under Senate rules meant the amendment was defeated. Nixon wanted a more symbolic victory, and made certain Agnew was present to cast a tie-breaking vote, so ABM won, 51–50.[37]

Because he had invested so much in the contest, Nixon was elated by the result. But precisely because he had invested so much, and then won such a narrow victory, he knew ABM was in trouble. The long-term prospect for sustaining political support was poor. This made Nixon even more eager to trade or limit ABM as the centerpiece of SALT, if he could ever get a date to begin the talks from the Soviets. Meanwhile, MIRV testing went on.

A MAJOR FACTOR in the opposition to ABM (aside from serious doubts by serious people that it would work; General Eisenhower, for example, had opposed it on those grounds) was the huge cost involved. Nixon, who had made a commitment to a balanced budget, and who was trying to cut spending across the board, including a proposed $5 billion reduction in the Pentagon's budget, was sensitive to the deficit implications of ABM.

In addition, Nixon wanted to cut taxes, although not until he had balanced the budget. For 1969, he had proposed a series of tax-reform measures, which were being considered by Congress. They included a minimum income tax to ensure that high rollers would pay at least some tax, the removal of some poverty-level people from the tax rolls, and a repeal of the 7 percent investment credit.

Simultaneously, Nixon asked Congress to extend the 10 percent surtax, put on by Johnson in the summer of 1968. Congress squealed. Nixon turned the screws. Congress finally gave him the bill. David Brinkley commented on his NBC-TV News program that it seemed to him that in threatening to withhold federal projects from recalcitrant congressmen, the Nixon Administration was using public money to influence public servants to raise more public money for a war in Vietnam that the public did not want.

Nixon was furious. He scribbled at the bottom of the News Summary, "Klein, arrange quietly for *at least* ten phone calls of outrage, and as many letters, to get to Brinkley *right away*."[38]

Nixon's major domestic concern, aside from raising enough money to run the government, was welfare reform. Finch and Moynihan had persuaded him to support the Family Security System, or negative income tax. Typically, Nixon wanted to keep his decision secret. On a memo from Moynihan, warning the President that there were bound to be leaks, Nixon wrote, "E—*in confidence*—I have decided to go ahead on FSS. *Don't* tell Finch & Moynihan."[39]

The great danger in FSS was the cost. In conversation with Ehrlichman, Nixon agreed that "it will be expensive," but pointed out that "in the long run the present system will be more expensive if we don't change."[40] He instructed Ehrlichman to draw up guidelines; the resulting ten-point memorandum began, "1. The system should eliminate social workers' snooping which is essentially berating [*sic*]. 2. A work package is necessary." The most important point was number five: "The program should include a federal floor of income, much work incentive, provisions that if there is an opportunity to work the recipients must work and the scheme must lead the recipient to be better off if in training than if he were idle and better off working than if he were training."

Nixon wanted the system to provide day care for working women, because "children should not just sit around the house since this leads to their becoming non-workers."[41]

Nixon felt a strong draw toward FSS. He liked the idea of helping the working poor, neglected under the current system, and liked even better the idea of making welfare recipients work. He thought of himself as coming from a working-poor family, and at times identified with that class. So did his wife. When a welfare worker suggested, at a White House conference, that Pat put the First Family on a nineteen-cent-a-meal per person welfare budget diet to see what poverty in America was like, Pat snapped back, "I worked my way through college. I've known hunger. When we were growing up we didn't have anything. I've known what poverty is."[42]

Nixon was also drawn by Moynihan's enthusiasm. FSS, Moynihan assured him, was "a genuinely new, unmistakably Nixon program . . . [that was] likely to reverberate through the society for generations."[43]

In fact, FSS pulled Nixon in all directions at once. He enjoyed the thought of outdoing the liberals on welfare, but he feared the reaction of conservative Republicans. He relished the possibility of getting rid of the social workers, but he dreaded the cost. As Arthur Burns reminded him in a July 12 memo, "To get the surtax adopted, you have just made a firm commitment to keep the budget down. Can you come forward now . . . with the costly FSS and still maintain . . . credibility?"[44]

What Nixon wanted most was credit for boldness and innovation, without the cost. He managed to achieve those apparently conflicting goals by dramatically announcing the program while simultaneously making certain it would never be adopted.

On July 28, Harlow (who knew Congress and its workings better than any living man) sent Ehrlichman a memorandum on FSS and Congress. He said he knew that Nixon intended to unveil FSS on August 8, without any previous consultation with congressional leaders. Harlow commented: "If it is the President's object to loft this program without regard to (1) Republican resentment or (2) likelihood of Congressional approval, I of course understand and readily acquiesce.

"If however the President hopes for the maximum favorable response from the Republican Party, and if he desires to *enact* the FSS rather than merely propose it, then I consider the present plans inadequate." Harlow went on to recommend various forms of prior consultation with congressmen. He warned that without it, "I anticipate an almost violent reaction from large numbers of President's followers in the Congress and across the country."[45]

Nixon ignored Harlow. He also waited until the last possible minute to inform his own Cabinet.

At noon, on August 6, Nixon presided at a luncheon meeting of the Cabinet at Camp David. After a briefing from HEW, Nixon asked the men gathered around the table, "What do you think?"

Except for Finch, nearly all were opposed, skeptical, shocked, or sat in stunned silence.

Budget Director Robert Mayo raised a series of objections. Nixon answered them, one by one. Still Mayo persisted. It got embarrassing. Treasury Secretary David Kennedy tried to get Mayo to shut up, but he would not. The new budget would be unbalanced with FSS, he said, despite cutbacks in Vietnam War spending.

"You don't know all I know about Vietnam," Nixon replied. Mayo finally fell silent.

Another protest: FSS would help poor blacks and poor whites, who would never vote for Nixon, whatever he did for them.

"We're doing it because we can't go on with the present system," Nixon responded.

How could he be sure FSS would work?

He couldn't, Nixon admitted, but he pointed out that the current system was "a social disaster, and I'm not going to take one more step down that road." He indicated there had been enough debate, that his mind was made up.

At this moment, Agnew decided to jump in. He said FSS would be a "political tragedy." Conservatives would assail it as a guaranteed income, Democrats would ridicule the $1,600 floor as a pittance, workers would turn into loafers, and so on.

Nixon cut him off. "We don't know whether this will work, but we can't go on with the present system."

Laird broke the tension. "This name . . . sounds New Dealish to me," he said. "I think we should get a new name." And so FSS got changed to the Family Assistance Plan, or FAP, which wasn't much of an improvement.

Agnew had to go; he needed to get down to Washington to preside over the Senate, voting that afternoon on ABM.

"I guess we can count on your vote," Nixon called out to Agnew as he was leaving.

"Mr. President," Agnew replied, "if there's a tie I may call you to see if you've changed your mind about FSS!"[46]

Although Nixon had not said so during the debate, he did not agree that there were no votes for him among the working poor. One of his News Summaries around that time quoted Richard Scammon of *Newsweek* as saying that there was great potential for the GOP in blue-collar workers, who were markedly attracted by Nixon. The President commented, "H & E, It is the weakness of virtually all our programs that we keep talking to the minorities (urged on by the Establishment) and overlook our greatest potential. Let's have a study to see what we can do, program and image wise, to appeal to this group."[47]

A day and a half after the Camp David meeting, Nixon dropped his bombshell in a nationwide television and radio address. He blasted the current welfare system. "Benefit levels are grossly unequal." It "creates an incentive for desertion." It meant that the child born into a welfare family "starts life in an atmosphere of handout and dependency" and "receives little preparation for work and less inspiration . . . To put it bluntly and simply any system which makes it more profitable for a man not to work than to work, and which encourages a man to desert his family, is wrong and indefensible."

His conclusion was inescapable; the current system must be "done away with completely."

In its place, Nixon proposed FAP, which he said rested on three principles: equality of treatment, a work requirement, and a work incentive. "Its benefits would go to the working poor, as well as the non-working; to families with dependent children headed by a father, as well as to those headed by a mother; and a basic Federal minimum would be provided, the same in every State." That last clause was the closest he came to confessing that he was proposing a negative income tax, or a guaranteed income.[48]

Nixon, according to Moynihan, was "euphoric" about the speech. It made banner headlines across the nation. Conservative newspapers like the Chicago *Tribune* praised it for its "workfare" features (the word was Nixon's), while *The New York Times* praised it for the negative income tax feature. The initial Gallup poll found an astonishing 65 percent favorable opinion, only 20 percent unfavorable.

A few days after the speech, Nixon called Moynihan on the phone. "Do the people still like it?" the President asked.

"Like it!" exclaimed Moynihan. "Why, there are more telegrams coming in than at any time since Johnson announced he was quitting!"

They chatted a bit longer. Then Moynihan rang off with a piece of advice: "Enjoy it while you can, Mr. President. The criticism will soon start." [49]

Nixon already knew that, thanks to Harlow's prediction. He didn't mind. He had what he wanted out of FAP, a great PR triumph. He wasn't all that sure he wanted it passed, anyway. After all, what kind of a Republican President would he be if he added six or seven million people to the welfare rolls?

FOLLOWING THE FAP speech, the Nixons flew out to California for a summer vacation. It was their first in a house on the ocean they had purchased back in March. Located just south of Laguna Beach, near the then-tiny resort community of San Clemente, the five acres of grounds and forty-three-year-old Spanish-style house cost Nixon $340,000. He had paid for it with money realized from the sale of his stock in the Fisher Island development in Florida. In a financial statement issued by the White House after the sale, Nixon showed assets of $980,400 and liabilities of $383,500, or a net worth of $596,900.[50]

FDR had once played poker in the house, built by onetime Democratic finance chairman Hamilton Cotton. When Pat picked it out, the girls were unhappy; the rooms were dark and musty, tall hedges and canvas awnings reduced the sunlight and blocked most of the views. "The house had such a strong personality," Tricia later said to Julie, "that I wondered if we could ever make it our own."

She should have trusted her mother; Pat had moved almost as many times as an army wife, and was an expert in making a place over to her satisfaction. In what Julie described as "one long, incredibly busy day," Pat worked with decorators in Los Angeles on carpeting, draperies, furniture, wallpaper, and paint. She made each room "light and beautiful," and delighted the girls. Nixon named the place La Casa Pacifica.[51]

The centerpiece was a square courtyard on which all fourteen rooms, except Nixon's second-floor study, opened. In the center of the courtyard a cupid sat atop a pyramid fountain decorated with Spanish tiles. Four green frogs sprayed jets of water. Golds and yellows dominated the inside walls.

Laguna Beach was something of a hippie hangout, but San Clemente was far too expensive for the long-hair crowd. Just south of San Clemente was Camp Pendleton. The Nixons could hear artillery and small arms from the base, where marines were being trained for Vietnam. Occasionally, troopships would line up in the Pacific in front of La Casa Pacifica, for miles up and down the coast, for predeparture maneuvers before sailing to Vietnam.[52]

Except for those reminders of the war, Julie wrote later, the three weeks in August 1969, in San Clemente, were "the last calm period in the Presidency."[53] Nixon, savoring the triumphs of Apollo, the trip, the ABM victory, and the FAP speech, actually relaxed. Julie and David persuaded him to go bowling, swimming, and to play golf every day.[54]

OF COURSE, he worked too. Aside from reading reports and papers and talking on the telephone, he concentrated on his second Supreme Court appointment.

Abe Fortas's resignation, under threat of possible impeachment proceedings against him because of conflict of interest and other ugly charges, left a seat open on the Court. Nixon had done well in his first appointment; Judge Burger had gone through the confirmation process with no difficulty, and Nixon had been generally praised for his selection. But that very success carried with it the possibility of difficulties the next time around. The Democrats would have had to be saints not to want revenge for the way the Republicans first turned Fortas back as Chief Justice, then exposed him and drove him from the Court altogether—and no one had never thought of the Democrats as saints. Common sense and the least political wisdom dictated that Nixon be just as careful, just as wise, in his next nomination as he had been in his first.

Nixon directed Mitchell to conduct the search, with the general guidelines that he wanted a strict constructionist from the

South. "With this one," Ehrlichman later wrote, Nixon exulted that "we'd stick it to the liberal, Ivy League clique who thought the Court was their own private playground."[55] Translated, that meant no Jews (with Fortas gone, the so-called Jewish seat on the Court was vacant), no Harvards.

On August 18, Nixon announced his choice. It was Judge Clement F. Haynsworth of South Carolina, chief judge of the Fourth Circuit Court of Appeals. This delighted the Democrats, North and South. The southerners were pleased to have one of their own named to the Court; the northerners anticipated with glee what they could do to this southern gentleman in the confirmation hearings. Haynsworth had a segregationist background, as did virtually every southerner of that time; he belonged to exclusive clubs; he was a wealthy man.

When the Senate went into session in September, Birch Bayh (D., Ind.) unleashed a barrage of charges against Haynsworth, centering on an allegation that he had adjudicated cases in which he had a financial interest. The Washington *Post* and the television news programs added innuendo and rumor of their own. Nixon complained, with some justice, that no rich man would ever be able to meet the standards demanded of Haynsworth. But by the end of September, Harlow knew Haynsworth could not make it. He advised withdrawing the nomination.

Nixon would have none of that. He told Mitchell to tell Republican senators, "The President is on the line for Haynsworth. This is his first big issue in the Senate. You can't let him down."[56]

After the successes of the summer, the troubles over Haynsworth indicated a more difficult fall. Nixon returned to Washington in a combative mood, ready to tighten up his staff, make it more responsive to his needs, and to do battle with the Republicans, the Congress, the Russians, the Vietcong, and the North Vietnamese.

NIXON'S STAFF had caught on quickly to his basic domestic theme, that style was more important than substance, PR more important than action. Thus it was Bill Safire, who came out of the PR world, who supplied the memorandums on economics that Nixon read most closely, although Safire's memorandums were on ideas and slogans, not programs. In July, he sent Nixon a five-page, single-spaced paper on how to establish "in the public mind" the program of the Nixon Administration for the economy. He called it "growth economics," and had twenty-three different approaches to selling it (get the Cabinet involved, get the NSC involved, have the President make a series of radio speeches, etc.). Nowhere, however, did he suggest what "it" would be.

Nixon was enthusiastic. He wrote "Good!" beside nearly every point, and on page one, he scribbled, "E—An excellent idea—one of best I've seen in Administration. We need more like this. I believe we should follow thru—Don't let it get submerged in 'study.' Why don't Price and Moynihan develop a similar P.R. plan for Urban?"[57]

By the fall, Safire was signing his memorandums "Publius" and undertaking nothing less than the production of a "New Federalist Papers." The purpose was to sell Nixon's proposal for revenue sharing, whereby the federal government would return some $1 billion in taxes to the states. The idea was linked to FAP. Nixon commented on one draft, "Excellent but a major change is needed on page 21 & 22. The entire emphasis is on *Negro* poor—bring out the fact that *all* poor are helped by Family Assistance."[58]

The staff in the summer and early fall of 1969 was undergoing some changes. Haldeman and Mitchell held to their top positions; Ehrlichman was moving up; Harlow was holding on, but was the object of some suspicion as he too often took the congressional rather than the presidential point of view; Kissinger, who was very tough whenever he was in Nixon's presence, was getting ahead nicely; Finch was slipping badly, mainly because he took his responsibilities at HEW seriously, especially with regard to desegregation; Agnew was barely tolerated, but was proving useful as a speech maker; Safire, Price, and Buchanan were all successful as sloganeers and speech writers; Klein, who gave Nixon the best advice he was getting on how to deal with the press, was falling back, precisely because he was too honest and too inclined to see the media's point of view.

Overall, Nixon was less than satisfied with the production he was getting from his staff. This meant in PR, not programs. On the first day of fall 1969, Nixon wrote a memo on the subject. More could be done, he said, to impress the public with the accomplishments of the Administration. "For example: hard work, dignity, staff treatment (compared with Johnson), boldness in offering new programs, world leader restoring respect for United States and the world [*sic*], RN family, and others that may come to mind. Get Garment and Safire as well as Buchanan . . . on this."[59]

In a much longer memorandum, written the same day and addressed to Haldeman, Nixon was more specific. Senator Kennedy had recently attacked the Administration on its draft policy and for the slowness of the troop withdrawals from Vietnam. Nixon thought the charges were "totally irresponsible," but felt "it was very clever for him to launch this attack. He is trying to divert attention . . . " Nixon had a long list of items to counterattack with, such as getting some loyal senators to take Kennedy on, "a major mailing-out to editors and columnists in Massachusetts . . . mailed . . . from Boston. Buchanan also should be able to get a columnist or two . . . to pick up this line."

Nixon went on: "Every Monday, I want a week's projection as to what we anticipate will be the major opposition attacks so that we can plan our own statements with those in mind." He thought friendly reporters, like Earl Mazo, could "keep us informed."

In general, Nixon wrote, he was unhappy with the reports on PR he had read in San Clemente, reports written at his request by Kissinger, Ehrlichman, and Harlow. "I think I could sum up my reaction in this way—the only area where we really came through with a better-than-average grade (and here it was considerably better than average) was on Family Assistance and Welfare." Nixon himself had done the game plan on PR for FAP. "On the Foreign Policy front, on the Nixon Big Charge front, our record [is] . . . considerably lower than average."

Nixon recognized that Kissinger, Harlow, and Ehrlichman were too busy to do the PR job properly. "I have reached the conclusion that we simply have to have that full-time PR Director, who will have no other assignments except to bulldog these three or four major issues we may select each week or each month and follow through on directives that I give but, more importantly, come up with ideas of his own." [60]

In fact, a trio of men came aboard to work full-time on PR. First was Franklin "Lyn" Nofziger, forty-five years old (which made him one of the oldest members of the White House staff), a former press secretary to Governor Reagan. Next was Jeb Stuart Magruder, thirty-four years old, head of two small cosmetics companies in Southern California, who had worked on the 1968 campaign in Los Angeles. Nofziger went into Harlow's office, Magruder into Haldeman's.

The third addition was Charles "Chuck" Colson, a Washington-based lawyer, thirty-eight years old, who had once worked for Senator Leverett Saltonstall of Massachusetts and had also been in the 1968 campaign effort. As a youngster Colson had turned down a Harvard scholarship because he thought the faculty there "too radical." He had a reputation of enjoying lashing out at his enemies and going for the jugular when he did so. When he came to the White House, Harlow—who had recommended him—commented, "Well, I warn you, we've got a tiger on our hands now; this Colson will chew some people up." [61] He immediately showed an ability to see which way Nixon was leaning, and to state brilliantly whatever the President wanted to hear. Nixon liked him at once.

• •

ON AUGUST 25, Ho Chi Minh's reply to Nixon's July letter arrived. It was, in Nixon's words, a "cold rebuff."[62] On September 4, in Hanoi, Ho died. What this meant for North Vietnam, for the war, for the world, was unclear. Doves urged Nixon to seize the moment and declare a cease-fire. Nixon would not go so far, but he did suspend military activity for the day of Ho's funeral. That step promoted even more speculation about a possible armistice.

Marvin Kalb reported on CBS-TV that South Vietnam was violating the "truce," and that Nixon was furious with Thieu for his refusal to abide by it. Kalb said that if Thieu persisted in his intransigence, Nixon was prepared to initiate a unilateral truce of his own.

When Nixon saw those comments, he exploded. "K—1. Who put this out? 2. Knock it down. 3. Deny it to Thieu. K this is a deliberate job. I want a report *today* as to who in State put it out!"[63]

When the bombing started again the day after Ho's funeral, Senator Mike Mansfield criticized Nixon for his action. Nixon responded, "Stopping the Bombing of North Vietnam did not lead to more conciliatory attitude by Hanoi—Kissinger, get a columnist to write this as my conclusion."[64]

Far from thinking about a cease-fire, armistice, or truce, Nixon was considering a major escalation of the war. On September 12, at an NSC meeting, he listened appreciatively as Kissinger declared, "We need a plan to end the war, not only to withdraw troops." He wanted to make one more appeal to the new leadership in North Vietnam. If it was refused, he recommended putting Duck Hook into operation. The target date was November 1, when Nixon's ultimatum would run out.[65]

Nixon was strongly tempted. But the tug in the other direction, toward continued de-escalation, was also powerful. The summer had been relatively calm, the antiwar protest relatively muted, thanks to the first troop withdrawal announcement. But as Laird warned the President in early September, "I believe this may be an illusory phenomenon. The actual and potential antipathy for the war is, in my judgment, significant and increasing."[66]

The signs were everywhere—in the rush of congressmen to introduce resolutions designed to disengage the United States from the war, in the new round of hearings on the war coming up in the Senate Foreign Relations Committee, and most importantly in the call from antiwar activists for a "Moratorium" on October 15, November 15, and so on until America was out of Vietnam. The activists, mainly former students and supporters of Bobby Kennedy or Eugene McCarthy in 1968, were by the fall of 1969 veteran organizers, experienced in putting together demonstrations and attracting the media's attention. Just by setting a date for demonstrations, they attracted nationwide support as local committees sprang up on campuses. In addition, the call for the Moratorium put pressure on congressional doves, who had been silent through Nixon's first eight months in office, to start speaking out again.

In an attempt to undercut the Moratorium, Nixon announced on September 16 that he was withdrawing another sixty thousand troops from Vietnam by December 15. Three days later he said that because of the withdrawal, draft calls for November and December had been canceled, and that on December 1 the first draft lottery would be held.[67]

Senator Kennedy then announced that he would begin his own set of hearings on the draft. Nixon scribbled on the News Summary, "E—we *must* keep the offensive on this. Don't let Teddy grab it. Get some of our guys to talk *daily* about the draft."[68]

On September 26, Nixon held a news conference. He intended it to pacify the dissidents, but ended up making them angrier than ever. Asked about legislation proposed by Senator Charles Goodell (R., N.Y.) that would require the withdrawal of all U.S. troops from Vietnam by the end of 1970, Nixon said he opposed the bill because it assumed the war would still be going on at that time. The Goodell bill "inevitably leads to perpetuating and continuing the war . . . and destroys any chance to reach the objective that I am trying to achieve, of ending the war before the end of 1970."

That sounded too good to be true, so reporters kept returning to the question, prompting Nixon to twice repeat his "hope." On the third occasion, Nixon declared flatly, "Once the enemy recognizes that it is not going to win its objectives by waiting us out, then the enemy will negotiate and we will end this war before the end of 1970."[69]

That would have been the next day's headline had not Nixon responded belligerently when asked his view of the Moratorium. "As far as this kind of activity is concerned," the President said, "we expect it. However, under no circumstances will I be affected whatever by it."[70]

On September 30, Nixon held two separate meetings with Republican leaders. In the first, he made a veiled reference to Duck Hook and his ultimatum. He said the next sixty days would be crucial, and asked for support. "We are going to need unity more than we ever needed it before," he said. "I can't tell you everything that will be going on, because if there is to be any chance of success, it will have to be done in secret. All I can tell you is this: I am doing my damnedest to end the war. . . . I won't make it hard for the North Vietnamese if they genuinely want a settlement; but I will not be the first President of the United States to lose a war."

In the second meeting, with nine Republican senators, Nixon let out the Duck Hook secret. He said he was considering blockading Haiphong and invading North Vietnam.[71]

A few days later, that story appeared in a Rowland Evans and Robert Novak newspaper column. Senator Howard Baker (R., Tenn.) called Bryce Harlow to say he was quite distressed about the leak. Nixon wrote on the bottom of Harlow's memo, "No problem. No comment from W.H."[72] The President himself was the one who had leaked the story.

This was the first the Secretary of Defense and the Secretary of State had heard about Duck Hook. Laird and Rogers immediately urged the President not to implement it. In response, Nixon sent a memo of his own to Kissinger: "It would be very helpful if a propaganda offensive could be launched, constantly repeating what we have done in offering peace in Vietnam in preparation for what *we may have to do later.*"[73]

BY THE FIRST WEEK in October, Nixon's freedom of maneuver was rapidly eroding as the somnolent summer gave way to a frenetic fall. There was uproar at Berkeley, Penn, Cornell, Duke, and dozens of other campuses. Ugly racial charges were being hurled at Judge Haynsworth, and by extension at Nixon for appointing him. The Administration's go-slow policy on school integration upset Secretary Finch and his staff and infuriated black leaders. Congressional efforts to cut all funding for the war seemed to be on the verge of success. Senator Fulbright broke his prolonged silence on Vietnam; he announced new hearings on the war and said tartly that the President had been in office nine months and was not making "progress in delivering on his campaign promises to give birth to his plans to end the war."[74]

The presidents of seventy-nine colleges signed an appeal to Nixon "for a stepped-up timetable for withdrawal from Vietnam."

The White House was, figuratively, under siege; literally, there were protesters carrying signs, sometimes in large numbers, sometimes only a few, but always there, surrounding the White House. *Newsweek* carried a headline, "MR. NIXON IN TROUBLE," and *Time* devoted its National Affairs section to describing "Nixon's Worst Week."[75]

The President did have his defenders. The most prominent, somewhat surprisingly, was Hubert Humphrey. Emerging from a White House briefing, he told reporters he thought Nixon was "on the right path" in Vietnam and called for public support: "We only have one President at a time and I think the worst thing we can do is try to undermine the efforts of the President." [76]

Nixon, greatly pleased, told Haldeman to have at least a hundred telegrams sent to Humphrey, praising the former Vice-President for "his courageous stand." At the same time, Nixon wanted telegrams sent to Senators Goodell, Charles Mathias (R., Md.), and Percy, "blasting them on their consistent opposition to the President on everything he is trying to do for the country." [77]

Another surprising defender was the Washington *Post* columnist David Broder. On October 7, he wrote, "It is becoming more obvious with every passing day that the men and the movement that broke Lyndon Johnson's authority in 1968 are out to break Richard M. Nixon in 1969. The likelihood is great that they will succeed again, for breaking a President is, like most feats, easier to accomplish the second time around." Referring to Fulbright's statement, Broder went on, "The orators who remind us that Mr. Nixon has been in office for 9 months should remind themselves that he will remain there for 39 more months—unless, of course, they are willing to put their convictions to the test by moving to impeach him. Is that not, really, the proper course, rather than destroying his capacity to lead while leaving him in office?" [78]

A third surprising defender was Dean Acheson, who told *The New York Times*, "I think we're going to have a major constitutional crisis if we make a habit of destroying Presidents." [79]

Overall, however, the Republican Party did *not* rally behind its besieged President, the Establishment did *not* rally behind the besieged institution of the Presidency, the media did *not* give the President fair and objective treatment, and, most damaging of all, the hawks kept silent. As the hysteria leading up to the Moratorium grew, hardly a peep was heard from the American Legion, from the Veterans of Foreign Wars, from the active-duty armed services, from the retired admirals and generals, from Lyndon Johnson, from any of those who had taken America into the war and then insisted on escalating it.

Why this silence? Because Nixon, back in May, had ruled out a military victory in Vietnam. Up to that point, the theme of the hawks had been "Let's win or get out," by which they meant "Let's go in and win." But after Nixon announced that he had no plans to "win" the war militarily, the hawks found themselves willy-nilly going over to the dove theme of "If we are going to get out, let's get out."

The war had always been a hard sell; once Nixon began to withdraw, it was nearly an impossible one.

He did what he could to defuse the protest. On the aggressive front, he had Ehrlichman put Jack Caulfield (the private investigator who had placed the tap on Joseph Kraft's phone) to investigating who was supporting the Moratorium organizers. Caulfield reported, on October 10, that "the heaviest outlay of funds for mailing lists, leaflets and transportation has come from the Socialist Workers Party," with support from the CP-USA and the "New York underground press." Ehrlichman showed Caulfield's report to Nixon, who scribbled on it, "*Priority*, get this out to all columnists and have our people in Congress hit it." [80] But the information was rumor, not fact, and little was done.

On a more public front, Nixon unexpectedly relieved General Lewis B. Hershey, long a target of antiwar groups, from his post as director of the Selective Service System. Although Nixon praised the seventy-six-year-old Hershey, the move was widely seen as an attempt to undercut the Moratorium.

On October 13, Nixon announced that he would make a major address to the nation concerning Vietnam on Monday, November 3. This too was seen as an attempt to undercut the Moratorium.

Finally, that same day, Nixon responded to a letter from a Georgetown University student, Randy Dicks, who had written him to take exception to his statement that "under no circumstances" would he be affected by the Moratorium. Dicks said, "It has been my impression that it is not unwise for the President to take note of the will of the people; after all, these people elected you, you are their President, and your office bears certain obligations."

Nixon, in his public reply, said there was a "clear distinction" between opinion and demonstrations, and it was by no means clear that the demonstrators represented a majority. Thus, "to allow government policy to be made in the streets would destroy the democratic process. It would give the decision, not to the majority, and not to those with the strongest arguments, but to those with the loudest voices. It would reduce statecraft to slogans. It would invite anarchy."

Nixon argued that there was nothing new to be learned from demonstrations. "Others can say of Vietnam, 'Get out now'; when asked how, they can give the simple, flip answer: 'By sea.' They can ignore the consequences." But he could not, and he believed that "history would rightly condemn a President who took such a course." [81]

Nixon's counterattack failed utterly. Tens of thousands of protesters marched around the White House on October 15; across the country, in every major city, tens of thousands attended antiwar rallies. It was, by far, the largest antiwar protest in America's history. Altogether, millions were involved. There was little or no violence. Most disturbing to Nixon and his supporters, the Moratorium brought out the middle class and the middle-aged in very large numbers.

Nixon put out the word that he spent the afternoon watching a football game on television, even as the marchers encircled the White House. He called his gesture "cool contempt." This only enraged the protesters further.[82]

But something else happened. Here and there, the more radical (some would say crazy) demonstrators waved Vietcong flags, chanted "Ho, Ho, Ho Chi Minh is going to win," and even burned American flags. They numbered less than 1 percent of the demonstrators, but they were as magnets to the television cameras. And all across America, viewers by the millions, even including many who had marched earlier that day, were disgusted and/or enraged.

That evening, Nixon started work on his November 3 speech. Safire, who wanted to help, "found that the President was treating this with the seriousness of an Inaugural or an acceptance address, doing it all himself."[83]

At the top of his yellow legal pad, Nixon started to make notes. He began, "Don't get rattled—don't waver—don't react."[84]

CHAPTER FOURTEEN

THE SILENT MAJORITY
October 16–December 31, 1969

THE MORNING AFTER the Moratorium, Dwight Chapin, a twenty-nine-year-old White House staff member working under Haldeman, prepared a long memorandum entitled "The 'Peace' Movement and November 15." On October 15, Moratorium rallies had been staged all across the country, but for November 15 the organizers were calling on demonstrators to come to Washington for a single mass rally.

The purpose of Chapin's memo was to "isolate" and "expose" the radical leaders of the Moratorium, and to bring back "into the fold of national consciousness" those middle-class folks who had been duped into marching for peace on October 15. Chapin realized that the key date was November 3, when the President would make his Vietnam speech. Whether the Administration could successfully undercut the November 15 Moratorium or not would depend on what the President said and how he said it.

Chapin's problem was he had no idea what the President was going to say. Nixon might order an escalation, in a go-for-broke bid for victory, or he might announce further withdrawals, in an attempt to placate the doves. If the first, Nixon would "only fuel the November 15 movement," if the second, he would defuse it.

Chapin worked on the assumption that whatever Nixon decided would be right, and that it was his job to generate a massive display of public support for the President's decision. He suggested all sorts of techniques, ranging from "a full-fledged drive . . . against the media" to "exposing" the radical sources of support for the demonstrators.

305

Chapin's central idea was to follow up immediately after Nixon made his November 3 speech, to preempt the publicity the Moratorium organizers would be trying to generate during that week. Beginning right after the President signed off, Chapin wanted a flood of letters, telegrams, and phone calls to deluge the White House, Congress, and the networks. He recommended that on Saturday, November 15, people should be encouraged to go to football games, with patriotic displays at halftime. Nixon could help on this by announcing that he was attending a game that weekend.[1]

So much for PR as for policy. On October 17, Kissinger, evidently considerably shaken by the Moratorium, recommended against Duck Hook.[2] That same day, Nixon talked to a British guerrilla-warfare expert, Sir Robert Thompson, who had played a leading role in defeating a Communist insurrection in Malaysia in the 1950s.

"What would you think if we decided to escalate?" Nixon asked.

Thompson was opposed. He thought it would cause a world-wide furor without enhancing South Vietnam's long-term survival chances. Vietnamization, the improvement of ARVN, was the right course. The analogy was Korea, where the improvement of the ROK forces, not a massive offensive against North Korea or a political settlement, had insured the survival of South Korea.

Vietnamization meant a continuation of American involvement in the war beyond Nixon's proclaimed target date of the end of 1970 or earlier. He asked Thompson if he thought it important for the United States "to see it through."

"Absolutely," Thompson replied. "In my opinion the future of Western civilization is at stake in the way you handle yourselves in Vietnam."

That was bombast, pure and simple, but Nixon agreed with Thompson's apocalyptic view. He also accepted Thompson's judgment, and Kissinger's recommendation, about Duck Hook. He felt that "the Moratorium had undercut the credibility of the ultimatum."[3] Duck Hook was dead.

Put cynically, after having proclaimed that he would not let policy be made in the streets, Nixon let policy be made in the streets. Put positively, he had repressed his instinct to smash the enemy in favor of a more moderate course with better long-term prospects. Put objectively, he had recognized that even though he was commander in chief of the world's most powerful armed forces, there were definite limits on his power.

Almost twenty years later, in April of 1988, Nixon said on "Meet the Press" that his decision against Duck Hook was the worst of his Presidency. He said that if he had implemented the offensive, he could have had peace in 1969. He did not explain why he thought so, or how that could have happened.

At the time, after deciding to let his November 1 deadline come and go without action, Nixon escalated the rhetoric. He began on October 19 by unleashing Spiro Agnew, who called the leaders of the antiwar movement an "effete corps of impudent snobs who characterized themselves as intellectuals."[4] The following day, Nixon bombarded Ambassador Dobrynin with some of the toughest talk any Soviet ambassador ever heard from an American President.

Nixon began by holding out to Dobrynin the promise of détente, mentioning all the good things that could result, such as more trade, arms control, and less tension. But, he went on, détente was dependent on the Soviets helping end the war in Vietnam.

"You may think that you can break me," Nixon said. "You may believe that the American domestic situation is unmanageable. . . . I want you to understand that the Soviet Union is going to be stuck with me for the next three years and three months. . . . If the Soviet Union will not help us get peace, then we will have to pursue our own methods for bringing the war to an end."

Nixon threatened: "We cannot allow a talk-fight strategy to continue without taking action. . . . I can assure you, the humiliation of a defeat is absolutely unacceptable to my country. . . . We will not hold still for being diddled to death in Vietnam."[5]

Balancing the tough talk, Nixon agreed to begin the SALT talks, the centerpiece of détente, in a month. He also assured Dobrynin that the various overtures he had made toward China were "in no sense designed to embarrass the Soviet Union . . . [and are] not directed against the Soviet Union." He added, "The only beneficiary of U.S.-Soviet disagreement over Vietnam is China." Dobrynin, for his part, denied that his government had as much influence in Hanoi as Nixon seemed to think.[6]

Four days later, Nixon went to Camp David for a long weekend. He worked twelve to fourteen hours a day on his Vietnam speech. Back in Washington, he spent most of the next week at the same task.

He was getting lots of advice. Rogers wanted him to emphasize negotiations, Laird said he should stress the success of Vietnamization, while other Cabinet members, and most of the White House staff, recommended establishing clearly his sincere desire for peace. Senator Mansfield wrote him: "The continuance of the war in Vietnam, in my judgment, endangers the future of this nation." It was more than the cost in lives and money. "Most serious," Mansfield asserted, "are the deep divisions within our society."[7]

Dean Acheson wrote to suggest that Nixon explain the Administration's goals and then ask the American people for their support. Like Chapin, Acheson wanted to drown out the demonstrators with a massive show of support for the President. On October 27, Nixon arranged a meeting with Acheson. The President asked the former Secretary of State if he would advise announcing further troop withdrawals and setting a time limit. Acheson was emphatically opposed. To disclose a troop withdrawal timetable would only "indicate weakness and yielding to pressure." It would not "appease those who criticized him or reassure the great mass of people that he was in command of the situation and was operating under a definitive plan." Acheson concluded by saying that the President's policy was "sound, but that he has great trouble communicating with the great majority who really agree with him."[8] That gave Nixon an idea.

SPECULATION in the days before November 3 was intense. Most commentators agreed that Nixon would announce major new troop withdrawals; insofar as they disagreed, it was over how many troops he would bring home. There was also widespread agreement that he would propose a cease-fire, even a unilateral cease-fire.

Such speculation delighted Nixon, who loved to surprise and confound the experts.

On Monday night, November 3, at 9:32 P.M., sitting behind his desk in the Oval Office, Nixon went on national television and radio to talk about the war in Vietnam. He began by saying that when he took office, "there were some who urged that I end the war at once by ordering the immediate withdrawal of all American forces." He said that politically that would have been a "popular and easy course." He could have blamed the defeat on Johnson "and come out as the peacemaker. Some put it to me quite bluntly: This was the only way to avoid allowing Johnson's war to become Nixon's war." But, he said, he had to think about bigger things than his own popularity.

He gave a short essay on the origin of the war (North Vietnam instigated a revolution in 1954; Ike sent economic aid; then Kennedy sent sixteen thousand military personnel as advisers; then Johnson sent combat forces). He spoke of the massacres that took place in North Vietnam after the 1954 Geneva Accords, and of the massacres of civilians in Hue after Tet in 1968, and predicted that if Hanoi won, "these atrocities . . . would become the nightmare of the entire nation."

He followed with a string of unprovable predictions that he presented as fact. "For the United States, this first defeat in our

Nation's history would result in a collapse of confidence in American leadership, not only in Asia but throughout the world. . . .

"Precipitate withdrawal would thus be a disaster of immense magnitude. . . . It would not bring peace; it would bring more war." American defeat and humiliation in South Vietnam would "without question" promote more reckless aggression by the Communists elsewhere in the world.

His voice was stern, his bearing measured and calm, his expression grim. He listed the steps he had taken to bring about peace: an offer to withdraw all American forces, an offer to accept a cease-fire under international supervision, an offer to hold free elections under international supervision, and an offer to discuss these offers and any the enemy might wish to put forward. "Anything is negotiable except the right of the people of South Vietnam to determine their own future."

He revealed that secret talks had taken place, that he had asked the Soviets for their help in achieving peace, that he had written privately to Ho Chi Minh. In return, flat rejection.

The "other side" had refused to show "the least willingness to join us in seeking a just peace." He followed with another prediction, this one more accurate than his earlier efforts: Hanoi would not cooperate "while it is convinced that all it has to do is wait for our next concession, and our next concession after that one, until it gets everything it wants."

So, Nixon admitted, he could not hold out much hope for negotiations. But he had another plan to bring peace, Vietnamization, based on the Nixon Doctrine. He explained the doctrine, then reviewed his policy changes since taking office. He had altered General Abrams' orders, he had reduced bombing operations by 20 percent, he had withdrawn sixty thousand men, and he had greatly improved ARVN's equipment and training.

All this had brought results. Infiltration was down, as were American casualties. If those trends continued, so would American troop withdrawals. Nixon said he would not announce a timetable for the withdrawals, as the pace of withdrawal would be tied to the level of enemy infiltration and American casualties. If these went up, "I shall not hesitate to take strong and effective measures. . . . This is not a threat. This is a statement of policy."

After repeating that he rejected "the easy way," precipitate withdrawal, in favor of "the right way," Nixon said he wanted to address the young people of the country.

"I respect your idealism.

"I share your concern for peace.

"I want peace as much as you do."

He said he had signed eighty-three letters to mothers, fathers, wives, and loved ones of men who had died in Vietnam that week. There was nothing he wanted more than to see the day when he did not have to sign any more such letters. "But I want to end [the war] in a way which will increase the chance that their younger brothers and their sons will not have to fight in some future Vietnam some place in the world."

He said he had chosen a plan for peace that he believed would succeed. He paraphrased Lincoln, saying that if his plan worked, "what the critics say now won't matter." And if it did not, "anything I say then won't matter."

His peroration was a paraphrase of what Sir Robert Thompson had told him two weeks earlier, and as sweeping and silly: "Any hope the world has for the survival of peace and freedom will be determined by whether the American people have the moral stamina and the courage to meet the challenge. . . .

"And so tonight—to you, the great silent majority of my fellow Americans—I ask for your support. . . .

"Let us be united for peace. Let us also be united against defeat. Because let us understand: North Vietnam cannot defeat or humiliate the United States. Only Americans can do that." [9]

"VERY FEW SPEECHES actually influence the course of history," Nixon wrote in his memoirs. "The November 3 speech was one of them." [10]

That was nonsense. Had Nixon announced Duck Hook, or had he announced a complete withdrawal by the end of the year, along with a unilateral cease-fire, the speech might have changed the course of history, but by announcing that he was going to continue doing what he had been doing for nine months, all Nixon did was to divide the nation more deeply than ever. It was true that in the process he showed, at least temporarily, that support for his policies was greater than most people imagined, but as James Reston wrote in *The New York Times* the next day, "It was a speech that seemed to be designed not to persuade the opposition but to overwhelm it, and the chances are that this will merely divide and polarize the debaters in the United States, without bringing the enemy into serious negotiations." [11]

Reston's response was typical of media commentary, and it infuriated Nixon and his supporters. He wrote a note to himself, saying that he had surprised the press, and defeated the reporters, which delighted him.

It was almost as if the media, not Hanoi, were the enemy. He wrote, "The RN policy is to talk softly and to carry a big stick. That was the theme of November 3." [12] Actually, the opposite was more nearly true; he had let the ultimatum deadline come and go without action, while he inflated the rhetoric. For Nixon to say that the survival of peace and freedom in the world depended on whether the American people supported him in his policy of keeping Thieu in power was simply ridiculous.

PR, not policy, was his concern. After the speech, the Nixon Big Charge began. Colson organized supposedly spontaneous support from thousands of veterans across the nation.[13] Magruder, Chapin, and others organized a supposedly spontaneous telegram barrage of support to the White House.

The President piled them up on his desk and called in photographers. "The great silent majority," he said, "has spoken." He asserted that "this demonstration of support can have more effect on ending the war sooner than anything else." [14]

Agnew went over to the offensive against the network commentators, who had criticized the President after his speech, as "a small band of . . . self-appointed analysts." He urged people to write the networks to complain, and tens of thousands did so, some of them, at least, inspired by Colson, Magruder, Chapin, et al.

Nixon had not set out to win support, but to show that it was there; he did not aim to convince, but to clobber the opposition; he was not attempting to reach out, to bring people together, but to isolate his domestic opposition.

He certainly achieved his immediate goals. More than fifty thousand telegrams and thirty thousand letters poured in, overwhelmingly favorable. By no means were all of them manufactured. In the House of Representatives, three hundred members cosponsored a resolution of support for the President; in the Senate, fifty-eight members signed a letter of support. Nixon's approval rating in the Gallup poll soared to 68 percent.[15] The deeper meaning of all this outpouring was very little. Of course the vast majority of the American people, and their political leaders, would rally behind the President when he made a dramatic appeal for their support. What Nixon could do with that demonstration of support, however, would depend on policy, not PR.

There was a disturbing note in the incoming mail. Walt Rostow wrote that he had talked to Herb Brownell after the speech, to remind him that "the Johnson Democrats were essential to maintaining support for Nixon's policy," and therefore the passages in the speech attacking the previous Administration "were most unwise." Rostow said Brownell had agreed and admitted that he himself had "winced" when he heard Nixon. Brownell called it "bad tactics." [16]

(The paragraph in question read, in typical Nixonian prose, blaming without naming, "Many believe that President Johnson's decision to send American combat forces to South Vietnam was wrong. And many others—I among them—have been strongly critical of the way the war has been conducted.")

Nixon saw the point of Rostow's complaint. A few days later, he wrote Rogers, who was about to testify before Fulbright's committee. Nixon admitted that he had been a hawk back in the mid-sixties, although he had "consistently taken exception to the manner in which the war was waged. These phrases in my speech were carefully chosen."

Then Nixon wrote a sentence that, in a real sense, summed up all the agony and pain and frustration and difficulty of the situation he found himself in with regard to Vietnam: "We simply cannot tell the mothers of our casualties and the soldiers who have spent part of their lives in Vietnam that it was all to no purpose." [17]

There is power and truth and a beautiful simplicity in that sentence. But it poses this problem: Could Nixon supply a purpose and justify the sacrifices that had been made by sending more boys over, by continuing the war, even after he had decided it would not be won?

THE RESPONSE of the Silent Majority to the November 3 speech put Nixon on a high, but it did not last long. All too soon, it was bad news followed by more bad news. On the long weekend of November 14–16, the protesters took over Washington. Simultaneously, a story about the massacre of South Vietnamese villagers by GIs in My Lai broke.

The antiwar demonstration attracted at least a quarter of a million people to the capital. For the most part, the rally was peaceful and orderly. One sign read, "Tyranny has always depended on a silent majority," while another proclaimed, "I'm an effete intellectual snob for peace." Comedian Dick Gregory brought the crowd at the Washington Monument to its feet when he said, "The President says nothing you kids do will have any effect on him. Well, I suggest he make one long-distance call to the LBJ Ranch." [18] Overall, the antiwar movement showed that it was still there, still significant, and could behave responsibly.

The My Lai revelations seemed to indicate that at least some American troops in Vietnam had not behaved responsibly. The initial reports were shocking to a previously unimaginable degree, indicating that American boys had acted like Nazis, cold-bloodedly shooting down women and children by the hundreds.

Commentators, congressmen, college professors, and many

others expressed their shock and outrage. Nixon was critical of the critics; he said, rightly, that they had been "noticeably uncritical of North Vietnamese atrocities. . . . The calculated and continual role that terror, murder, and massacre played in the Vietcong strategy was one of the most underreported aspects of the entire Vietnam war." He also charged that those who professed outrage over My Lai were less interested in moral questions, more concerned with using the incident to discredit the war politically.[19]

The point he did not mention was this: My Lai indicated to many members of the Silent Majority, in the very month that it came into being as a body with a name, that a part of the price of supporting Nixon in Vietnam was the brutalization of eighteen-year-old American boys. For some at least, that price was too high.

NOT ALL the news was bad. On November 17, the day after My Lai hit the newspapers, the SALT talks opened in Helsinki. The chief American delegate, Gerard C. Smith, read a statement from Nixon at the formal opening ceremony promising that the United States sought "no unilateral advantage" in the talks. "We are prepared to discuss limitations on all offensive and defensive systems and to reach agreements in which both sides can have confidence," Nixon's statement continued. He added that the delegates would be engaged in "one of the most momentous negotiations ever undertaken."[20]

That was potentially true. Nixon had been less than forthright, however, in asserting that the United States was prepared to discuss limitations on both offensive and defensive weapons. In fact, Nixon was eager to put some limits on ABM, the defensive system, partly as a bargaining chip in dealing with the Soviets, mainly because he knew he would have a difficult time, at best, in getting the funds for ABM, but he would not allow the American delegation to discuss MIRV, the offensive system in which the United States had a big lead on the Soviets.[21]

Despite that limitation, the opening of SALT was a milestone in the Cold War, the first step in Nixon's program of replacing the "era of confrontation" with an "era of negotiation."

The initial talks were general only. There was a useful airing of issues and agreement on a work program. In concrete terms the Soviets made clear their desire to limit ABMs, and did not bring up MIRVs. After the opening exchanges, the two sides agreed to meet again in Vienna in April 1970.

One week after the SALT talks opened, Nixon signed the Nuclear Nonproliferation Treaty. It had been negotiated by the Johnson Administration, but had only recently been ratified by the

314 | THE SILENT MAJORITY

Senate (with Nixon's endorsement). The treaty stated that nuclear powers that signed could not give nuclear weapons to other nations, and the nonnuclear powers that signed could not make a nuclear weapon. It was another step in easing tensions.

That same week, following meetings in the White House with Japanese Premier Eisaku Sato, Nixon had another success in diplomacy. The island of Okinawa had been under American control since the bloody battles there in 1945. On November 21, 1969, Nixon and Sato agreed on the conditions for Okinawa reverting to Japanese sovereignty. The United States kept its extensive military base on the island, but in the final communiqué of Sato's visit, Nixon pledged to recognize with respect to Okinawa "the particular sentiment of the Japanese people against nuclear weapons." In other words, Okinawa would be nuclear-free. The agreement removed a sore spot in Japanese-American relations.

Also that week, Apollo XII splashed down after a successful trip to the moon. In all the excitement on earth, it had almost been ignored. Another reason for the lack of publicity was the failure of the TV camera that was supposed to beam television pictures of the moon-walking astronauts back to earth. Apollo XII did not even rate a mention in Nixon's memoirs. It was almost as if, since it was not on TV, it never happened.

Television had been a central concern for Nixon ever since his 1952 Checkers speech, and he had learned long ago that the appearance he made on the screen was as important as the policy or argument he presented. Twelve days after the Apollo XII landing on the moon, Nixon sent a memo to Haldeman on the subject of television. The President said he needed a full-time TV man to handle his appearances in a professional way. "When I think of the millions of dollars that go into one lousy 30-second television spot advertising a deodorant," Nixon wrote, "it seems to me unbelievable that we don't do a better job in seeing that Presidential appearances always have the very best professional advice."

Before his TV presentations, Nixon wanted to spend five to ten minutes with his professional adviser, "to get his suggestion as to how I should stand, where the cameras will be, etc." He gave as an example his televised telephone call to the astronauts on the moon earlier in the year: "Even the question as to whether I should have held the phone with my right hand or my left hand is quite pertinent." [22]

IT WAS NOT a good fall for Nixon up on the Hill, even leaving aside Vietnam. FAP had brought together some strange bedfellows. Conservatives denounced it as practically a Communist plot, and far too expensive, while liberals complained that the dollar amounts were insufficient and the work requirements repressive. The National Welfare Rights Organization said FAP stood for "Fuck America's Poor" and proposed its own plan, introduced in the Senate by George McGovern, to guarantee a $6,500 income to every family of four, far above the amounts in the Nixon bill.

The liberals in the Senate were also going after Judge Haynsworth with a vengeance. Nixon told newsmen that "a vicious character assassination" was under way, and reaffirmed his support.[23] The attack continued anyway. Senator Bayh contended that it was not enough that Haynsworth had not engaged in any impropriety; for a Supreme Court judge, there must be no "appearance" of impropriety. The real objection was Haynsworth's conservative philosophy, and beyond that the Democrats' desire to have some revenge for the Fortas rejection.

Labor and civil rights groups lobbied energetically against Haynsworth. When Republicans complained that for one hundred years it had been the practice of the Senate to ignore a nominee's philosophy and judge him only on technical fitness, the Democrats replied that Fortas had been upbraided by Senate conservatives for his liberal decisions. It was the Republicans who had broken the tradition.

Nixon went all out to save his nominee. He told Ehrlichman, "The President's leadership of the nation is being put in question. Haynsworth is a good product. . . . The President . . . is being challenged. . . . What they are doing to Haynsworth is grossly unfair. . . . Tell [Chief Justice] Burger to write a letter to every Federal judge, by God. . . . Say I strongly recommend they all sell all their stocks so that the courts will be above suspicion." He instructed Ehrlichman to stimulate mail, from the Farm Bureaus, the southern bar associations, the National Rifle Association, "and our other friends; they have got to be energized. Get pro-Haynsworth speeches into the record; we've got to build a wave of support for our man." [24]

When none of this worked, Nixon got tougher. "Talk to Jerry Ford now," Nixon told Ehrlichman. He wanted Ford to "move to impeach that sitting Justice who has been charged" with improprieties, William O. Douglas, generally regarded as the most liberal member of the Supreme Court. Shortly, Ford began making speeches calling for Douglas's impeachment. This transparent attempt to link Douglas's impeachment to Haynsworth's confirmation did Haynsworth no good; in fact, Senator Robert Griffin (R., Mich.) let it be known that the linkage had turned him against Haynsworth.[25]

Nixon believed that one part of the opposition sprang from his failure to name a Jew to the vacancy created by Fortas's resignation. He told Buchanan that just as it had been wrong to oppose Louis Brandeis because he was a Jew, it was also wrong to oppose Haynsworth because he was a southerner.[26]

It was all to no avail. On November 21, the Senate voted 55–45 to reject Haynsworth's nomination. Seventeen Republicans joined thirty-eight Democrats in voting no. President George Meany of the AFL-CIO, which had been strongly opposed, called his Washington secretary from New York and instructed her to tell his staff, *"Mazel tov."* The press analysis was that it was a defeat for Nixon, but not a disaster, because he strengthened himself in the South (nineteen Democrats, all from the South, voted for confirmation).[27] *The New York Times* thought that the liberals had used up their strength, and gotten their revenge, and that Nixon's next nominee, sure to be another conservative, would be confirmed easily and quickly.

In a statement saying that he deeply regretted the Senate action and deplored the nature of the attacks made upon Haynsworth, Nixon promised to appoint a conservative. His next nomination, he said, would be made on the same criteria he applied to Haynsworth.[28]

Nixon firmly believed that the Supreme Court needed some conservative balance. This was especially true, in his view, on the explosive issue of desegregation. Acting under the terms of *Brown* v. *Topeka* (1954), which required desegregation "with all deliberate speed," the Johnson Administration policy had been to withhold federal funds from school districts that delayed implementing integration. Nixon reversed that policy, despite strenuous objections from civil rights groups. At a news conference in September, the President declared that "there are those who want instant integration and those who want segregation forever. I believe that we need to have a middle course between those two extremes."[29]

But on October 29, the Burger Court ruled unanimously that every school district had to terminate segregated schools immediately (*Alexander* v. *Holmes County*). Asked at his next news conference about how he would respond, Nixon pledged to "carry out what the Supreme Court has laid down. I believe in carrying out the law even though I may have disagreed as I did in this instance. . . . But we will carry out the law."[30]

Still, he made it clear that he "did not feel obliged to do any more than the minimum the law required," and that he hoped the Court would reconsider. Meanwhile, he was "determined to ensure that the many young liberal lawyers . . . in the Justice Department's Civil Rights Division would not treat this decision as a carte blanche for them to run wild through the South enforcing compliance with extreme or punitive requirements they had formulated in Washington."[31]

As with the Haynsworth nomination, in short, Nixon had failed to have his way, but even in losing he had strengthened his political position in the South.

A PRIVATE LIFE, having some time with his family, was something Nixon often said he wished he had, but found elusive. As President, he found it almost impossible. Privacy was practically gone. Nixon, Pat, and the girls were surrounded by Secret Service agents, almost always. Nixon himself, whenever he was outside his office in the EOB or the Oval Office, had a horde of staff members, communications team, medics and doctors, and other aides swarming around him. Neither the Nixons nor David and Julie Eisenhower could go into public without attracting scores of reporters and photographers.

Fleeting moments of real privacy, being so rare, were just that much more precious, and made Camp David, Key Biscayne, and San Clemente that much more attractive. The Nixons got away to their vacation homes as often as possible.

Tricia was the Nixon who resented the prying and snooping of reporters the most. But she lived in the White House, and could not escape them. She was twenty-three years old, and her unmarried status made her the object of intense speculation. When she went to a baseball game with Barry Goldwater, Jr., a freshman member of Congress, it was a feature item in the Washington *Post*, complete with an account of their first date, how many times they had talked on the telephone, what she wore, and so forth.[32]

As for Julie, marriage had made her more bubbly, outgoing, gregarious than ever. She spent the summer of 1969 as a volunteer guide at the White House. She would select twenty-five lucky tourists at random from the crowds lining up for the public tour of the state rooms and conduct them on a private tour of the second-floor family rooms. In the Lincoln Sitting Room, her father's favorite, she would reveal that even on the hottest summer days he liked to turn on the air-conditioning full blast, then have a fire in the fireplace. David had a job that summer with the Senate Judiciary Subcommittee. They lived in the Queen's Bedroom.[33] In the fall, they returned to Smith and Amherst for their senior years.

Nixon told a reporter doing a feature story on the girls that he thought of them as "front-line troops in the battle to re-establish the traditional virtues." He said that they cared, about their country, the world, and their generation, "and each in her own way tries her best to help. It's a trait they've always had, and one that we always tried to encourage. They keep looking for things to do—positive things—to be useful.

"In this time when so many young people are in one form or another of rebellion, it's pretty satisfying for a father to have two daughters who are trying so hard to help—and doing it so well." [34]

Just as Nixon said, to many middle-aged couples Tricia and Julie and David seemed to be ideal. To many of their contemporaries, they seemed a bit unreal, and were the object of some ridicule. Pat, too, came in for more than her fair share of negative comment. Marie Smith, in a September "Profile of Pat" for the *Post*, quoted critics. One said Pat apparently had no interests of her own. Another commented, "She speaks in platitudes. It sounds like she's reading lines someone wrote for her." Smith wrote that women who met Pat on a receiving line "come away feeling that the First Lady is too thin and terribly tense."

"Is she ill?" some of them asked.

Another criticism was that Pat had not taken up a "project." Jackie Kennedy had set out to redecorate the White House; Lady Bird Johnson, to beautify America's highways. What was Pat going to do?

None of this carping bothered Pat, or if it did she kept it to herself. She said she believed her primary duty as First Lady was to serve her husband, and that was the course she had charted for herself. Feminists winced at such remarks, but as a White House PR aide noted, "To a large segment of the population, she fits exactly what they think a First Lady should be."

A Gallup poll proved the point. In the summer of 1969, Gallup asked, "Do you approve or disapprove of the way Mrs. Richard (Pat) Nixon is handling her role as First Lady?" Fifty-four percent approved, 6 percent disapproved, and 40 percent expressed no opinion. That gave Pat an amazing approval rating of 9–1, which was far higher than Jackie or Lady Bird ever achieved.

Pat no longer did the ironing, or cooked the meals, or ran the vacuum cleaner, but she did continue to work at a backbreaking pace. For one thing, she did have a project, the critics notwithstanding. It was volunteerism. She held receptions in the White House for as many national organizations of women volunteers as she could fit into her schedule. In her first year in the White House she shook the hands of more than twenty thousand women from more than forty organizations.

When one of those women told Pat she had received a letter from her, and added, "Of course I know it wasn't really your signature," Pat bristled in a rare display of her temper. She signed every letter that went out, just as she read every letter that came in. Reading and answering correspondence was her principal occupation on her airplane flights.

Smith ended her "Profile of Pat" with a quote from a veteran White House social-page reporter, who told Pat after a long trip, "You've been nicer to us reporters than any other First Lady we've covered." [35]

Although he seldom found a way to say he realized it, Nixon was lucky to have her for a wife, just as the nation was lucky to have her as First Lady.

ON DECEMBER 15, Nixon announced a further reduction of fifty thousand troops in Vietnam, the withdrawal to be completed by April of 1970. This would mean a total reduction of 115,500 men since he took office. [36]

Of course the pace was much too slow to satisfy the doves, and of course there was no end in sight to the war, and of course in his November 3 speech Nixon had done the opposite of what he had pledged, to "bring us together," and of course he had not had much of a choice about withdrawal from the moment Johnson decided not to reinforce Westmoreland's victory in Tet. Nevertheless, Nixon's de-escalation of the war, his troop withdrawal program, was a historic event of the first magnitude. He had reversed a policy that had its roots in the Spanish-American War of 1898 and the subsequent conquest of the Philippines. America was no longer on the offensive in Asia. Johnson's March 31, 1968, speech, followed by Nixon's November 1, 1969, decision to forgo Duck Hook, along with the Nixon Doctrine, meant that America was committed to a new strategy in the struggle against Communism in Asia.

At the beginning of the decade that was now coming to an end, Dwight Eisenhower had continued his commitment to the Diem regime in Saigon, as he sent in more advisers and more equipment and more money. Kennedy had increased, dramatically, the numbers of fighting men and the quantity of equipment, even as he blatantly interfered in the inner workings of the GVN. Johnson had escalated by leaps and bounds, from 16,000 to 100,000 to 250,000 to 500,000 to 550,000.

Nixon, at the end of the decade, reversed the process. For all the criticism that can be brought against his Vietnam policy—and there is much to criticize, and this author has not hesitated, and will not hesitate, to engage in such criticism—it must be recognized that Nixon's de-escalation of the war in Vietnam was one of his historic achievements. Quite possibly no one else could have pulled it off; quite obviously none of his predecessors had been able to do so.

Nixon being Nixon, much of his policy in Vietnam was convoluted. He was doing what the doves wanted, albeit not so rapidly as they wished, and rejected what the hawks wanted, Duck Hook. Yet it was the hawks to whom he appealed for support, and the doves whose anger he exacerbated.

He was asked about this by Robert Semple of *The New York Times* in an end-of-the-year news conference. Semple noted that Nixon had received the outpouring of support he had asked for in his Silent Majority speech, but wondered if the President had not "purchased this support at the cost of alienating a sizable segment of the American public and risking polarization of the country."

Nixon replied, "One of the problems of leadership is to take a position. I like to be liked. I don't like to say things that everybody doesn't agree with." But, he continued, he had to say and do what was right, rather than what was popular.[37]

Nancy Dickerson of NBC News, in a follow-up question, asked if he had any specific plans for reaching young people. Nixon replied with his idea of a joke: "I know a way not to reach them, and that is to try to pick number one as far as the football teams are concerned."[38]

He was better when he answered a question about whether he felt the press should hold him to account. He paraphrased Winston Churchill's 1914 remark: "I have always derived a great deal of benefit from criticism and I have never known when I was short of it."[39]

THERE WERE LOTS of end-of-the-decade stories in the press at the end of 1969. Almost none noticed that Nixon had reversed policy in Vietnam, so angry were most commentators at his refusal to end the war immediately, and none noticed another reversal of policy, even more important, at least potentially, than Vietnam. This was the whole new strategy for conducting the Cold War. The media could be forgiven for not seeing the importance of the various overtures Nixon had made toward China, especially as many of them were still secret, but there was no excuse for the relative ignoring of the start of the SALT talks. For the first time ever, an American President had committed the country to at least discussing arms control with the Soviets, and beyond arms control to a general lessening of tension and even to a positive development of détente.

Here, too, however, the reporters were not entirely to blame. Nixon liked to operate in secret, to keep his plans to himself. How far he hoped to go with détente, only he knew. He refused to promote, perhaps feared, a national debate on such fundamental questions as a possible change of policy toward China or the inauguration of a détente with the Soviet Union.

Not even his Secretary of State knew what he was thinking, or what he hoped to accomplish. Even his National Security Adviser had to guess.

In his own year-end summary, Nixon described the relationship that was developing between Rogers and Kissinger. Only the word "incredible" can come close to characterizing Nixon's description. Nixon wrote, "Rogers felt that Kissinger was Machiavellian, deceitful, egotistical, arrogant, and insulting. Kissinger felt that Rogers was vain, uninformed, unable to keep a secret, and hopelessly dominated by the State Department bureaucracy." Kissinger was making a habit of storming into Nixon's office and threatening to resign if Rogers was not restrained or replaced.[40]

And these were Nixon's two principal advisers on foreign policy! Obviously, he liked it that way; if he had not, he could have fired either man at any time. Divide and rule. That was Nixon's method.

ON DECEMBER 16, Nixon made some remarks before lighting the nation's Christmas tree on the Ellipse near the White House. Appropriately, he spoke of peace. "What we want for this Nation," he said, "is not only peace now but peace in the years to come, peace for all people in the years to come . . . the kind of peace that exists not just for now but that gives a chance for our children also to live in peace."[41]

In this regard, Nixon's problem was that many millions of Americans were ready to settle for just plain peace now. In their view, they could not solve their children's problems for them; the next generation would have to make its own peace. They thought Nixon's dream of a peace not just for now but for our children, and our children's children, was as messianic, as hopelessly idealistic, as Woodrow Wilson's war-to-end-all-wars dream.

CHAPTER FIFTEEN

THE CAMBODIAN
INCURSION
January–April 1970

To MILLIONS of American males of all ages, George S. Patton, Jr., is the essence of maleness. Tough, decisive, self-confident, willing to take great risks for great gains, trusting in his intuition, impatient of restraint, a student and practitioner of the art of leadership, bold and brave in his actions, often vulgar in his language, contemptuous of his critics, Patton was the model for innumerable American men and boys, including Richard Nixon.

Nixon the politician yearned to be Nixon the commander in chief, snapping out orders, outthinking and outfighting the enemies of America, defending freedom. He knew the differences between politics and war, but they made him impatient. He hated the restraint of politics, and yearned for the freedom of the soldier to act.

Politicians have to take into account the sensitivities of all their constituents, be aware of the various groups and the separate interests, be capable of compromise, be willing to accept partial solutions and long delays, be ready to cut a deal or look the other way, be prepared to negotiate with their enemies.

Soldiers take or give orders. They mean what they say. They do as they are told. They do not compromise, or cut deals, or concern themselves with the sensitivities of their men. They just go out and do their damnedest to win, and when they do, their victories are clear, sharp, and final. They accept nothing less than the unconditional surrender of their enemies.

That was Nixon's view. In fact, as Eisenhower could have told him, it was not at all like that in the Army. Politics dominates relationships in the Army as it does in all organizations and professions. Politics isn't a curse, as Nixon (like so many other politicians) often appeared to believe; politics is life. It is interchange and relationships, and thus compromise and deals—whether in the Army or on Capitol Hill or in the White House.

It was precisely because Patton had no political skills that Ike left him out of Operation Overlord, instead putting Omar Bradley in command of the American ground forces for the Battle of Normandy. Bradley could get along with the British, as Patton could not. Bradley was sensitive to the needs and morale of his men, as Patton was not. Bradley was able to engage in give-and-take, in discussion and negotiation, with his division commanders, as Patton was not.

Once Bradley had won the Battle of Normandy, Eisenhower brought Patton and his Third Army over to France and turned him loose, because there was no one in the world better at exploiting a victory, in keeping the pressure on a defeated and retreating enemy, than Patton.

Even in the pursuit, however, Patton had a weakness. His ego was such that he lusted for headlines. To get them, he would put publicity ahead of any other consideration. Thus, in Sicily, in the summer of 1943, Patton marched away from the German Army, and toward Palermo, so that he could be the first to liberate a European city, and thereby steal the headlines from the hated General B. L. Montgomery.

In early 1970, George C. Scott played Patton in a movie. His portrayal emphasized the heroic side of Patton. Nixon loved the movie. He watched it again and again. He made his inner staff watch it with him. His feelings for the movie became so well known that halfway around the world the Chinese Prime Minister, Chou En-lai, obtained a copy of the film and watched it, in an attempt to figure out this inscrutable Occidental.[1]

Another favorite Nixon movie was *True Grit*, starring John Wayne. After seeing it, Nixon wrote, by hand, a fan letter: "Dear Duke: I have been delighted to read the rave reviews . . . I saw it in the W.H. with my family and for once we agree with the critics —you were great!"[2]

Nixon's heroic fantasies were not much different from those of his fellow American males, and indeed he was probably more forthright and honest about having them than many others. What was different about Nixon, of course, was that he was the President, and it was dangerous in the extreme, as well as inappropriate, for him to identify with Patton and the Duke.

• •

FROM MID TO LATE JANUARY, Al Haig and a team of military analysts toured South Vietnam to see how Vietnamization was progressing. They reported some improvement, but warned that there was a growing pessimism among GVN leaders, who feared an overly hasty American withdrawal. Nixon scribbled on the report, "K— the psychology is enormously important. They must take responsibility if they are *ever* to gain confidence. We have to take risks on that score."[3]

At the same time, a televised "Report from Saigon" said that the ARVN "seem to have a deep psychological fear of the NVA divisions." Nixon commented, "K—the *critical* issue . . . Raise hell with our people in Vietnam so that we don't become complacent. Particularly we must keep pounding on necessity to build up ARVN strength and morale. We must also have a contingency plan to handle whatever offensive may be launched in spring and summer—by *ourselves* if necessary (and without the big strike unless the attack size merits it)."[4]

On January 15, Denis Warner wrote in the Portland *Oregonian* that ARVN, while improving, "could not hold Saigon against a heavy enemy attack without US support." Nixon commented, "K— Keep the heat on Saigon to assume more responsibility. With the enormous advantage they have logistically over the North they have no excuse for inferiority attitude."[5]

That last sentence got close to the heart of the matter. Nixon's model remained Korea. Eisenhower had managed to achieve an armistice in Korea partly by threatening the Chinese, mainly because the ROK Army by the spring of 1953 had become a formidable fighting force. Nixon's hope was that ARVN could match that accomplishment, but despite a well-orchestrated PR campaign about ARVN's progress, the truth was that the points Clark Clifford had made back in 1968 were still valid. The ARVN officer corps was rife with corruption, the GVN had no real interest either in reform or in ending the war, and South Vietnam was not remotely ready to defend itself.

American soldiers returning from Vietnam, and by the beginning of 1970 their numbers were in the hundreds of thousands, frequently expressed their contempt for ARVN. According to the veterans, the "gooks" could not fight. Often, however, these same GIs expressed admiration for the fighting qualities of the Communist enemy, who, after all, were also "gooks." To turn Nixon's statement to Kissinger into a question, How come the NVA fought so well and the ARVN so badly?

The answer was obvious: it was due to the nature of the GVN. So was the solution to the problem: change the GVN. But Nixon's rationale for continuing the war was precisely to preserve the GVN. Of course, he hoped for improvement, but he had no plan or program to bring it about.

Instead, he increased the air offensive while railing at doves. The Menu bombing of the Ho Chi Minh Trail in Cambodia continued; the bombing of the trail in southern Laos increased beyond the 1969 average of 650 missions a day; at the end of January, fighter-bombers began attacking antiaircraft bases in North Vietnam.[6] That same week, *Time* and *Newsweek* cast doubts on the success of Vietnamization. Nixon commented, "K—this shows the Establishment *is* for peace at any price and they all go together. H—Have your ltrs team give them Hell—we *must keep our Silent Majority group involved.*"[7]

IT SOMETIMES SEEMED that Nixon was more concerned about and angrier with the American press than with the North Vietnamese. His fury escalated to new heights at the end of January, when new uniforms he had had Ehrlichman design for the White House police were worn in public for the first time. Inspired by the guards at Buckingham Palace and others he had seen on Nixon's European tour a year earlier, Ehrlichman had put the White House police into white-tunicked, gold-braided, pillbox-hatted ceremonial uniforms.

The press ridiculed the result. The Chicago *Daily News* was reminded of movie characters from *The Student Prince.* The Buffalo *Evening News* thought "even ushers at old-time movie palaces were garbed with greater restraint and better taste." "Ruritania, D.C.," scoffed *The New York Times.*[8]

Mort Allin, in the News Summary, informed Nixon that *Newsweek* had used a photo from a 1925 movie, *The Merry Widow,* and that *Life* used a photo of Emperor Francis Joseph for comparison.

Nixon was defiant. He wrote on the News Summary, "H—I want our staff to take RN's position on this *regardless* of their own views—remind them of K's line—a W.H. staffer does not have independent views on W.H. matter. H—Have Klein take the offensive on the slovenly W.H. police we found."[9] Happily for the police, his defiance didn't last, and soon they were back in less colorful uniforms.

His rage against the press did last. When John Gardner criticized his budget, Nixon wrote: "H & E—He is to be completely cut off from now on. This is an *order.*"[10]

When Walter Cronkite was quoted by Allin in a critical remark, Nixon circled his name and scribbled furiously, "A *Nothing!*" He didn't much like Cronkite's competitor, either; at his insistence,

Jeb Magruder mounted a campaign to discredit David Brinkley, including such actions as having Don Kendall of Pepsi-Cola, an old Nixon friend and client, complain to the NBC corporate heads about Brinkley.[11]

Hugh Sidey was another target. "H—I'm inclined to think Sidey is under orders," Nixon wrote on one report. "*No Contact* with him for 30 days will shake him—order this to all hands." [12] When Sidey mentioned in a column Nixon's lavish private homes and his wealthy friends, Nixon commented, "Freeze him completely for 60 days." [13] He also instructed Magruder to "initiate some letters to the editor comparing RN with LBJ, Ike, and JFK on this score." [14]

The obsession with the press and PR in the Nixon White House was never ending. On February 27, after his morning conference with the President, Haldeman sent a note to the staff. He began, "There is a need for some cold, tough decisions regarding the amount of time spent being king vs. that spent as leader of the government. Perhaps we should consider a drastic shift—reducing the 'king' time to a bare minimum. We also have to recognize that some of the time has to be spent just in being a nice person."

(Ten years earlier Ann Whitman, Ike's secretary, had observed in her diary, "The Vice-President [Nixon] sometimes seems like a man who is acting like a nice man rather than being one.")

Haldeman went on to call for some "deep thinking" about the presentation of the President, "recognizing always that it actually gets down to what is the best television." [15]

Nixon loved television, especially when he could use it to speak directly to the people from the majesty of the Oval Office, with all three networks carrying his speech on prime time (after the networks caught on and began dividing up the chore, with two showing their regular programs, Nixon's ratings sank, and he cut back drastically on his TV time).

On January 26, Nixon enjoyed a historic moment on TV. Before a nationwide audience, he explained his objections to a $19.7 billion appropriation bill containing funds for health, education, and antipoverty programs, warned against the dangers of runaway inflation, and then and there, with a flourish, signed his veto message. It was a first for TV and a dramatic way to emphasize his war against inflation. He also showed his concern for the poor and for education, as he promised to sign a more reasonable bill. Indeed, the basis for a compromise had already been laid, and there was an element of charade to the whole thing. Nixon wanted a reduction of about $900 million, or 5 percent—he was not out to scuttle the Great Society—and the Democrats were ready to live with that cut.

So they passed the bill, and made their speeches, reassuring the poor that the Democratic Party was their friend, and giving Nixon a chance to speak out against inflation.

What the Democrats had not counted on was Nixon's adroit use of the prerogatives and regalia of his office to present himself and his policies in the best possible light to the voters. They demanded equal time to reply. The networks gave it to them.

Nixon was furious. He demanded a study. A staff-written reply indicated that although the "equal time doctrine" did not apply, the "fairness doctrine" did. Nixon wrote on the memo, "I am not interested in the law—I know what it is. I want a study made on what the networks did on 'fairness' when Kennedy and LBJ were in. My recollection is that we got 'equal time' only 3 times in 8 years." [16]

NIXON'S FIRST BUDGET, presented to Congress on February 2, showed a $2 billion surplus, mainly a result of a $6 billion cut in military and space-program spending. The surplus did not come about by cutting into the Great Society programs; in fact Nixon was spending more on welfare and food stamp programs than Johnson had done. He was also spending more on the entitlement programs (Social Security, Medicare, etc.), as the irreversible and uncontrollable growth of these social programs began to take an ever-increasing percentage of the national budget, threatening to quickly offset Nixon's savings on Vietnam, defense, and space.

Spending for defense was down from 45 percent of the budget in Johnson's last year to 37 percent. Space research and technology were down from $6 billion in 1966 to a projected $3.4 billion for 1971. Nixon doubled the spending on crime prevention, to $1.2 billion. The budget included $785 million for the environment.

Altogether it was a middle-of-the-road budget, leaving the right wing unhappy at the cut in military spending and the retention of the Great Society programs, and leaving the liberals with little to complain about (they did, anyway). Nixon, in presenting it, stressed "quality of life," calling special attention to his battle against inflation and against crime.

In his first State of the Union address, Nixon called controlling inflation his "highest priority." He also spoke forcefully for clean air and clean water and had good news: "The prospects for peace are far greater today than they were a year ago."

He also had a dream, one that sounded as messianic as John Kennedy's, ten years earlier. Looking ahead to the bicentennial in 1976, Nixon said, "I see an America in which we have abolished hunger, provided the means for every family in the Nation to obtain

a minimum income, made enormous progress in providing better housing, faster transportation, improved health, and superior education.

"I see an America in which we have checked inflation, and waged a winning war against crime."

He saw a clean environment, an America at peace, an America rich beyond imagination. But, he warned, "we can be the best clothed, best fed, best housed people in the world . . . [and] still be the unhappiest people in the world without . . . the lift of a driving dream which has made America, from its beginning, the hope of the world."

So, he concluded, what America needed even more than a clean environment, peace, and riches was "an example from its elected leaders in providing the spiritual and moral leadership which no programs for material progress can satisfy." [17]

The Democrats, who had demanded equal time to reply, couldn't think of anything much to say, beyond complaining that Nixon was not doing enough. They should have complained that he had stolen their slogans. What was most notable was this fact: the word "Vietnam" never came up in their rebuttal. Nixon had, apparently, thanks to his Silent Majority speech, solved his most pressing political problem. [18]

In the State of the Union, Nixon made one short reference to the need for "a total reform of our welfare system," but in the budget he had made no provision for FAP, potentially the biggest of all the social programs, presumably because he saw little or no chance of it passing in 1970. He also made a short reference to a need for governmental reform ("It is time for a New Federalism in which . . . power will begin to flow from Washington back to the States . . . ") without any specifics or providing for such reform in the budget. [19]

A couple of months later, Nixon did undertake a reorganization of the Executive Office. He created a Domestic Council to help develop policy and an Office of Management and Budget to make certain it was carried out effectively (it replaced the Bureau of the Budget). George Shultz came over from Labor to head OMB; John Ehrlichman became head of the Domestic Council.

None of this interested Nixon very much. His eyes would glaze over when the subject of government reorganization came up (as do almost everyone else's). What he enjoyed was a chance to lash out at Washington. There is a sharp contrast here between Eisenhower and Nixon. Ike spent his career in the biggest bureaucracy of all, and he seldom complained about federal employees, Washington, or the government. Nixon spent less than a year as a bu-

reaucrat, at the beginning of World War II, but he constantly railed against them. According to Safire, for Nixon the word was "damngovernment," and the people who ran it were "damnbureaucrats."

A typical Nixon comment on the government came in February, when Ehrlichman sent him a memo on a HUD program. Nixon wrote, "This kind of *paper work* is utterly useless—government at its *worst*. Fire Somebody, & get going." He thought some more, grew even angrier, turned the memo sideways, and scribbled: "Immediately fire ½ of all the men at H.U.D. who prepare such studies." Then he thought some more and called in Alexander Butterfield, one of Haldeman's aides. He told Butterfield to send an "Administratively Confidential" memo to Ehrlichman making it clear to Secretary Romney that his handwritten instructions "constitute a Presidential order." He wanted the names and titles of those persons Romney fired on his desk in the morning.[20]

Of course nothing happened. He was like Lear, roaring into the wind. Despite his anger and his orders and his directives, the bureaucracy just grew and grew.

ONE REASON Nixon found foreign affairs so much more interesting than domestic policy was that abroad he could have an impact, even handicapped as he was—in his own view, anyway—by the bureaucracy in the State Department.

In a separate, written foreign-policy report that accompanied the State of the Union, Nixon made an explicit reference to a "desire for improved relations" with China. The Chinese news agency replied several days later with a blast at Nixon's "hypocrisy." It called the report "ridiculous" and "pitiable" and characterized it as a "paper tiger." Simultaneously, however, the Chinese ambassador to Poland met with the American ambassador, Walter Stoessel, in Warsaw for previously arranged talks on matters of mutual interest. These mixed signals from the Chinese indicated that there was a severe political struggle going on in Peking, reflecting Chinese concern over its border clashes and other problems with the Russians, and concern that the opening of the SALT talks might mean Nixon was going to join with the Russians in an anti-Chinese alliance.

Nixon tried to reassure them. He reiterated that the United States had no interest in "joining any condominium or hostile coalition of great powers." And he instructed Stoessel to tell the Chinese ambassador that the United States intended to reduce its military facilities on Taiwan "as tensions in the area diminish." According to Raymond Garthoff, this concession was "perhaps crucial in the intra-Chinese struggle over foreign policy . . . in 1970."[21]

• •

WHAT A STRANGE MAN was Richard Nixon. Subtle and skillful in his approach to the Chinese, he was stubborn and spiteful in his approach to the Senate. He had vowed, when the Senate turned down his nomination of Judge Haynsworth, that he would "show them." He did. On January 19, he nominated Judge G. Harrold Carswell for the Supreme Court vacancy.

There were all sorts of guesses as to how Nixon could have made such a choice. One was that the President told Mitchell to find a southern judge who owned no stocks, and who would thus be free of any conflict-of-interest charge. In support of that guess, there is a telegram in the Nixon archives from Senator Robert Byrd (D., W.Va.) to Nixon, urging the appointment of a strict constructionist and predicting the Senate would never reject a nominee "whose personal financial matters are not open to question," no matter how conservative the man.[22]

Another guess, widely circulated, was that Nixon wanted to insult the Supreme Court. A third said he wanted to insult the Senate. In yet another version he was aiming to stir up political passions in the South (figuring the Senate would have to reject Carswell). It was also rumored that Carswell was a friend of Strom Thurmond.

Carswell had everything going against him. As a candidate for the Georgia legislature in 1948, he had said, "Segregation of the races is proper and the only practical and correct way of life. . . . I have always so believed and I shall always so act." His rulings, as a circuit judge in Florida, had reflected those views (although he renounced the statement itself). Further, his qualifications for the high court were simply nonexistent. Bryce Harlow, always one to tell the truth, informed Nixon that the senators "think Carswell's a boob, a dummy. And what counter is there to that? He is."[23]

Senator Roman Hruska (R., Neb.) nevertheless tried to counter. In a TV interview, Hruska declared that there were millions of mediocre people in America and they too deserved representation on the Supreme Court.

In March, Harlow told Nixon that Carswell was "in increasingly bad shape. His condition is critical. The situation is dangerous." Nixon wouldn't listen. He mounted an all-out campaign to save the nominee. He made calls and promises and threats. He put the heat on Mitchell and on Deputy Attorney General Richard Kleindienst. "We'll probably lose it," he acknowledged after one meeting, but—as Ehrlichman wrote—"he couldn't let the fight alone." As the senators questioned Carswell, Nixon filled his News Summary with orders to do this, do that *"immediately"* to "save our man."[24]

• •

CARSWELL WAS but one part of Nixon's Southern Strategy. In January, when the News Summary noted that Ralph Abernathy was calling for making Martin Luther King, Jr.'s birthday (January 15) a national holiday, Nixon wrote, *"No! Never!"* [25]

But the South wanted more than symbolic defiance. While Bob Finch and his people at HEW insisted on moving ahead on desegregation, George Wallace denounced him ("The Nixon Administration has done more to destroy the public school system in one year than the last Administration did in four"). Some staffers at HEW resigned to protest the undermining of their efforts to desegregate, and 125 other HEW employees signed a letter to Nixon expressing "bitter disappointment" over his policies.[26] Truly the President was caught in the middle.

"What is our answer to this?" Nixon asked Ehrlichman. "Can't we do or say something to bring some sense into the dialogue? I just disagree completely with the court's naive stupidity. I think we have a duty to explore ways to mitigate it. . . . I don't give a damn about the Southern strategy—I do care a great deal about decent education. I know this [the current system] won't work." [27]

Pat Buchanan sent Nixon a memo on segregation in northern schools. "In city after city," he wrote, "when a school reaches somewhere between 30% and 50% black—there occurs a tipping and within a few years, it is 95% or 100% black."

That roused Nixon's ire. "Why should we continue to kick the South and hypocritically ignore the same problems in the North?" he wrote on the memo. "Is de facto segregation o.k. in the North and not in the South?" [28]

In March, Nixon released a statement on civil rights. He came out against segregation, and against busing to achieve integration. He pledged to support the law but indicated that his primary reliance would be on cooperation with local authorities in the South; he called for voluntary compliance with the law rather than federal involvement and enforcement.[29]

Civil rights lawyers in Justice and in HEW complained that the ambiguities in Nixon's statement threatened to slow, or even halt, desegregation. When Nixon saw that item in his News Summary, he roared, "H—*Get their names!* Have their resignations on my desk by Monday." [30]

One resignation that was offered, only to be refused by Nixon, came from Pat Moynihan, as a result of a January 16 memo he sent the President. The subject was "the American Negro." Moynihan noted that Negroes had made great economic and political gains in the 1960s, although those in the South lagged behind in income. (Nixon noted, "Whites are also lower in the South.") According to

Moynihan, young Negro families were "achieving income parity with young white families." Negro college enrollment had risen 85 percent between 1964 and 1968.

On the discouraging side, illegitimacy among blacks was up to 30 percent and climbing. Nearly every female-headed black family lived in poverty, and those numbers were growing too. What Moynihan called "social pathology" among young black males was "extraordinarily high" and soaring. "Social alienation" was widespread, helping explain the phenomenon of the Black Panthers and other hate groups.

But it wasn't just the poor. In Moynihan's judgment, "It would be difficult to overestimate the degree to which young well-educated blacks detest white America." (Nixon commented, "Like young well educated *whites* hate blacks.")

Moynihan concluded, "The time may have come when the issue of race could benefit from a period of 'benign neglect.' The subject has been too much talked about." He suggested greater attention to Indians, Mexican-Americans, and Puerto Ricans. Nixon underlined all this and scribbled, "*I agree!*"

In passing, Moynihan suggested ignoring the Panthers. He said that they were about "defunct" until a Chicago police raid on one of their headquarters transformed them into culture heroes, and he called Nixon's attention to a cocktail party given recently by Mrs. Leonard Bernstein to raise money for the Panthers. Mrs. W. Vincent Astor, Mrs. Peter Duchin, and other celebrities were guests. Nixon commented, "K—Note! the complete decadence of the American 'upper' class intellectual elite."[31]

A couple of months later Moynihan's memo (without Nixon's comments) leaked, and Nixon's critics seized on the "benign neglect" phrase to charge that his Administration was reactionary, uncaring, brutal. Moynihan offered his resignation; Nixon refused it.

THE WHITE HOUSE, in the late winter of 1970, was a lively place. There were the Sunday-morning worship services, and regular evening musical performances, including a memorable February 22, when the entire cast of *1776* came to put on the first full-scale, full-length Broadway musical ever presented in the White House. It was a smashing success.[32]

Pat, meanwhile, was opening up the White House as no First Lady had ever done. One day she shook the hand of every member of the DAR on a tour, some 1,675 of them. The following day, she greeted 4,702 Republican women in what *The New York Times* called "the biggest White House party since Andrew Jackson's riotous inaugural brawl in 1829."[33]

On March 2, Pat set off on a week-long trip to visit college volunteer programs in Michigan, Kentucky, Ohio, Colorado, and Missouri. She was on the go from seven each morning to ten each night. She got a warm response everywhere, and, inevitably, lots of criticism from the press because she did not visit any major university campuses "where confrontations with militant student protests were most likely." Instead, she went to places like the School of the Ozarks, where there were no antiwar protests, no hippies, no rebels.[34]

A good thing, too, that Pat stayed away from the big campuses, because as the spring rioting season got under way in 1970, student protests and rallies and actions reached previously unimaginable heights of bad taste, disgraceful and inexcusable behavior, downright insanity, and pure unadulterated terrorism. Little of this activity was directed against the war in Vietnam; since Nixon's Silent Majority speech and the November 15 Moratorium, antiwar rallies had been few and sparsely attended. Some of the activity had as its presumed point the promotion of civil rights; some of it promoted the Panthers; some of it was designed to bring down the capitalist system; much of it was random violence and rebelliousness, pure and simple.

The press complained about the tight security around Pat when she visited Denver, without noting there had been five bombings in the preceding four days in nearby Boulder. The "issue" was a rather typical one in the academic world of 1970. The University of Colorado had collected a $5 fee from each student in 1969 in order to establish scholarships for blacks. But the administration had refused to distribute the money on the grounds that the policy was illegal, as disadvantaged whites were not eligible. In response, student radicals started blowing up buildings.[35]

Elsewhere: in San Diego, California, student radicals set fire to banks; at Kansas State, they burned down the ROTC building; at Ohio State, protesters demanding the admission of more black students and the abolition of ROTC got into a six-hour battle with police in which seven students were shot, thirteen others injured, and six hundred arrested before the governor called in the National Guard; at Berkeley, an arsonist tried to burn down a library and caused $320,000 in damages; at Yale, in a demonstration in support of the Panthers, books were set afire in the Law School library.

The worst came at Stanford, where an anti-ROTC group set a fire at the behavioral studies building that completely gutted the office of a visiting Indian anthropologist, M. N. Srinivas, burning his lifetime collection of notes, files, and manuscripts.

Nixon wrote a warm and sympathetic letter. He said he knew it was "small consolation" for Professor Srinivas that the American people and the American academic community "utterly reject the tactics of the person or persons who did this. To say that they are deranged, does not excuse them."[36] Nixon must have signed the letter with a sinking heart, for good as it was, he knew it could never be good enough to make up for the loss. No scholar can think of the incident, even twenty years later, without sorrow.

The madness and the terror spread. When Julie complained that she could no longer tolerate being guarded on the Smith campus, the Secret Service conferred with her and showed her dozens of threats to kidnap or kill her. Radicals in Boston were threatening to bus two hundred thousand protesters to the Smith graduation if Julie or her parents dared to attend. Also in Boston, a crowd of ten thousand joined recently acquitted Jerry Rubin and Rennie Davis (of the Chicago Seven) in a chant, "Fuck Julie, fuck David."[37]

In early March, Senator Kennedy made a trip to Ireland. When he attempted to speak at Trinity College, Dublin, he was beset by some two hundred anti-Kennedy demonstrators, shouting "Imperialist," banging on his car, and demanding that he get out of Ireland.

Nixon asked for a report. At first blush, one might have thought Nixon would be delighted at Kennedy's discomfort, especially in Dublin. But in fact, Nixon wrote on the report, "K—very disturbing. I take no comfort in this regardless of who is the target. There is a feeling of international anarchy in the air and it *began* in the U.S. (Like Coca Cola it has spread)."[38]

Not all the young people were going to hell in a hand basket. Late that winter Nixon's son-in-law joined the Navy Reserve in an informal induction ceremony at the White House. Upon graduation from Amherst College, David would report to Officer Candidate School at Newport, Rhode Island.

IN THE LATE WINTER of 1970, violence at a higher and more deadly level than in the U.S. or Ireland dominated the Middle East. Israel, having retreated not one inch from the territory it had conquered in 1967, was launching deep-penetration air raids into Egypt and Syria. Egyptian leader Gamal Nasser then persuaded the Soviets to supply him with MIG fighter aircraft and advanced SAM-3 anti-aircraft missiles. The Israelis began taking losses, and turned to Nixon in an effort to buy more airplanes.

Nixon rather liked the position the request put him in. First of all, as he said in a memorandum on the subject to Kissinger, it forced the Jews to recognize that it was Nixon, not the liberal senators, who was their real friend. "When the chips are down," he warned, the liberals "will cut and run. . . . What all this adds up to is that [Israel's leaders] must trust RN completely. He does not want to see Israel go down the drain." But to help Israel, Nixon wrote, he needed not only the support of "the Jewish constituency in [the United States] which voted 95 percent against him, but he must carry with him the 60 percent of the American people who are in what is called the silent majority."

Nixon wanted to let the doves (nearly all of whom were friendly toward Israel) know that "it is a question of all or none." If they wanted to "stand up" in the Mideast, they had to be prepared to "stand up" in Vietnam. "This is it cold turkey, and it is time that our friends in Israel understood this. . . . Unless they understand it and act as if they understood it beginning now, they are down the tubes."[39]

Of course he would never let them go down the tubes, not because he liked Jews or thought he could get any votes from the American Jewish community, but because he could not abide the thought of the Soviet Union becoming the dominant power in the Middle East. Thus on a Kissinger memo on the subject, Nixon wrote, " 'Even Handedness' is the right policy—But above all our interest is—what gives the Soviet the most trouble—Don't let Arab-Israeli conflict obscure that interest."[40]

Back in 1968, LBJ had authorized the sale of fifty Phantom F-4s to Israel, the first large-scale sale of arms from America to Israel. Nixon in early 1970 played an on-again, off-again game with Israel, but by midyear was selling arms on a wholly unprecedented scale. He was determined that Russian guns would never be allowed to prevail over American guns in the Middle East.

ON FEBRUARY 12, the long-feared North Vietnamese offensive began, but to the surprise of the Americans, it came in Laos, not Vietnam. On February 16, at an NSC meeting, Nixon ordered a B-52 strike to support the government forces, in response to a request from Laotian Premier Souvanna Phouma. The United States was already heavily involved in the fighting in Laos, not only in bombing the Ho Chi Minh Trail in southern Laos but in the ground war as well, with hundreds of cross-border operations by army and marine units. The fact was that Laos, like Cambodia, was an integral part of the war in South Vietnam, even though all the parties involved, including the United States, tried to maintain the fiction of neutrality.

The strike Nixon ordered in support of Phouma was, however, an escalation, as it was the first time American B-52s were used in northern Laos. *The New York Times* so reported on February 19; the following day Senators McCarthy, Frank Church (D., Idaho), and Mansfield attacked Nixon for widening the war. Other senators denounced the Administration for its secrecy.[41]

On March 6, from Key Biscayne, Nixon issued a statement. He characterized as "grossly inaccurate" the reports that Americans were engaged in ground fighting in Laos and that increased air activity there was escalating the conflict. "There are no American ground combat troops in Laos," he declared. "We have no plans for introducing ground combat forces in Laos. . . . No American stationed in Laos has ever been killed in ground combat operations."[42]

Two days later the Los Angeles Times published a graphic description of an American captain's death in a firefight in Laos, and the Pentagon by the end of the day had to admit that twenty-seven Americans had been killed in Laos in the past year. Nixon had been led astray by Kissinger, whose defense was that the victims were killed in fighting clearly related to Vietnam, so technically they were not "stationed" in Laos. Nixon was furious. He hated to be caught in a lie, and besides, as he put it, "No one cares about B-52 strikes in Laos. But people worry about our boys there." To punish Kissinger, Nixon inflicted a harsh penalty; for a week, the President refused to see his National Security Adviser.[43]

The tempest in Laos had hardly settled down when a new crisis erupted in Cambodia. Prince Norodom Sihanouk for years had delicately balanced between the contending parties, complaining neither about the North Vietnamese use of the Ho Chi Minh Trail through his country nor the American bombing of that trail. But as the North Vietnamese presence expanded, he began protesting. Still he tried to play both sides against the middle; in early March he set off for meetings with the Chinese and the Russians, hoping they would help him restrain the North Vietnamese.

On March 18, while Sihanouk was in Moscow, General Lon Nol overthrew him in a bloodless military coup. As always in such cases, observers blamed the CIA. In their memoirs, both Nixon and Kissinger insist that the coup came as a complete surprise. Nixon says that the CIA itself was surprised, and quotes himself as asking Bill Rogers, "What the hell do those clowns do out there in Langley?"[44] But it is also true that on a March 17 memo from Kissinger, which explained that Lon Nol had plans to expand the Cambodian Army by ten thousand men, Nixon had written, "Let's get a plan to aid the new government on this goal." And on March 19, the day after the coup, Nixon wrote on another Kissinger memo, "I want [CIA] to develop and implement a plan for maximum assistance to pro-US elements in Cambodia. Don't put this out to . . . bureaucracy. Handle like our air strike [Menu]."[45]

Rogers, Laird, and CIA Director Richard Helms all advised Nixon to hold back. If the United States rushed aid to Lon Nol, it would convince Moscow, Peking, and Hanoi that the CIA had set up the coup, and would give the North Vietnamese an excuse to send in main-line units to overrun Phnom Penh. In addition, Helms predicted that the Lon Nol government could not last long.[46] Nixon reluctantly decided to hold back, at least for a while. But he was most unhappy with himself. It was just at this time that he started watching the movie *Patton*. Patton, one could hardly doubt, would have ignored the doubters and seized the opportunity.

ON APRIL 1, Nixon received a letter from Senator Saxbe, who said that he was disturbed by recent charges of racism and mediocrity against Judge Carswell, and added that it appeared to him that Nixon's support for Carswell "is less than wholehearted."

Nixon replied that Carswell had his "total support" and denied that the judge was a racist. "What is centrally at issue," the President continued, "is the constitutional responsibility of the President to appoint members of the Court—and whether this responsibility can be frustrated by those who wish to substitute their own philosophy . . . for that of the one person entrusted by the Constitution with the power of appointment." [47]

That line stirred the senators as almost nothing else could have. From both sides of the aisle, the solons lectured the President. They pointed out that he had only the power to nominate, and that the "consent" of the Senate was necessary to "appoint." As Senator Bayh put it, Nixon was "wrong as a matter of constitutional law, wrong as a matter of history and wrong as a matter of public policy." [48] He could have added that Nixon was wrong as a matter of politics; before the President released his letter to Saxbe, the lineup was forty-five senators against Carswell, forty-four in favor. But when the Senate voted a week later, Carswell lost, 51–45.

Nixon, frustrated all that week in his attempts to let go against the Communists in Laos and Cambodia, let go against the Senate in the United States. He called in reporters and TV cameras. He used the occasion to issue a verbal blast unprecedented in the history of rejected Supreme Court nominations.

"I have reluctantly concluded that it is not possible to get confirmation for a judge on the Supreme Court of any man who believes in the strict construction of the Constitution," he said, "if he happens to come from the South." Referring back to Haynsworth, he went on, "When you strip away all the hypocrisy, the real reason for their rejection was their legal philosophy . . . and also the accident of their birth, the fact that they were born in the South." He said that so long as the Senate "is constituted the way it is today, I will not nominate another southerner and let him be subjected to the kind of malicious character assassination accorded both Judges Haynsworth and Carswell."

Nixon concluded, "I understand the bitter feeling of millions of Americans who live in the South about the act of regional discrimination that took place in the Senate yesterday." [49]

The Senate was again incensed, and not just the Democrats (thirteen Republicans had voted against Carswell). The solons felt that they had been insulted by Nixon's accusations. Actually, it was the South, more than the Senate, that had been insulted, through Nixon's implication that Judge Carswell represented the best the South had to offer, and that he had been turned down despite rather than because of his record. Senator Gore of Tennessee, who had voted against both Haynsworth and Carswell, assailed the President's statement as "an assault on the integrity of the Senate." [50]

On April 14, Nixon nominated Judge Harry Blackmun of Minnesota, an Eisenhower appointee to the Federal Circuit Court of Appeals and an old friend of Warren Burger. His record was a solid one; no charges were made against him; the Senate had had enough of battling the President; on May 12, Blackmun was unanimously confirmed.

THERE WERE more frustrations for Nixon in April. An especially bitter one was canceling plans to attend David's graduation at Amherst and Julie's from Smith. Nixon claimed that he made the decision over Julie's objections ("She tried to hold back her tears, and she pointed out that only a few small radical groups were involved . . .").[51] But it was Julie who had written to John Ehrlichman, "I truly think the day will be a disaster if he comes. Smith girls are furious at the idea of massive security precautions." [52]

In any case it certainly was painful for the President. Agnew didn't help any, indeed he goaded Nixon. "Don't let them intimidate you," he said. "You may be President, but you're her father, and a father should be able to attend his daughter's graduation." But the Secret Service advised Nixon that there certainly would be ugly protest demonstrations if he went, and he reluctantly agreed to stay away.[53]

Simultaneously, the Senate Foreign Relations Committee voted unanimously to repeal the Gulf of Tonkin Resolution of 1964, once called by the Johnson Administration the "functional equivalent" to a declaration of war. Nixon took the position that he had inherited the war and did not need the Gulf of Tonkin Resolution to justify continuing it. Still, the committee vote, especially as it was unanimous, was another blow from the Senate, another reminder that while he was President of the United States, his ability to lead the country in directions he wanted to go was sharply limited.

On April 13, three days after the Gulf of Tonkin vote, there was more bad news. Apollo XIII, nearing the end of a three-day trip to the moon, suffered an explosion in the service module that destroyed most of the oxygen and power supplies. The moon landing had to be aborted. Happily, the astronauts managed to return to earth. On April 18, Nixon flew to Hawaii to welcome them back. He made a gracious speech of thanksgiving for their safe return, but it was not at all like the greatest week since Creation.

DURING THE first half of April, the fighting in Cambodia spread. ARVN units conducted hit-and-run raids against the Ho Chi Minh Trail. This caused the NVA and their local Communist allies to push westward, raising fears that they might surround and then capture Phnom Penh itself. On April 16, Nixon ordered the CIA to establish a station in Phnom Penh, to give all-out support to Lon Nol, to turn over captured Communist arms to the Cambodian Army, and to send in more money.[54]

The President read a report of a Vietcong base in a mountain area deep inside Cambodia. He made an instant command decision and snapped out his order: hit that base with a B-52 strike within two hours! But the report was unconfirmed, no operation could be mounted in that time, and the B-52 was the least appropriate weapon for such an attack. Nothing was done.[55]

Frustrated, angry, embarrassed by the Apollo XIII debacle, Nixon on April 19 flew from Hawaii to California. At San Clemente, he met with Kissinger. His ugly mood was made worse by his recognition that he would have to announce further troop withdrawals the next day.

Nixon had decided, in his words, "that the time had come to drop a bombshell on the gathering spring storm of antiwar protest."[56] He proposed to do that by promising that 150,000 men would come home in the next year. In Kissinger's view, this "surprise announcement . . . was one of the tours de force by which we sustained our effort in Vietnam."[57]

In his speech, Nixon was upbeat. He said Vietnamization was working so well that he could announce this major withdrawal. He reviewed American offers to the enemy for negotiations. He stressed the fact that by April of 1971 he would have cut in half the numbers of American troops in Vietnam.[58]

But for all Nixon's "bombshell" and Kissinger's "tours de

force," the truth was that Nixon had slid right past his own self-imposed timetable for peace. For eight months, since the summer of 1969, he had been saying that he hoped to beat Clark Clifford's demand that all boys be back home by the end of 1970. Now he was confessing that in April of 1971 he would still have 284,000 troops in South Vietnam.

Laird was unhappy. He met with the President the next morning to urge a faster pace of withdrawal. "I want you to know you have a fiscal problem," Laird told Nixon. "You know that, don't you?" He warned that if Nixon did not pull out more men by the fall, "you might just as well forget about the [congressional] election." [59]

Matched against that political pressure was the pressure of the enemy on the battlefield. After seeing Laird, Nixon met with CIA Director Helms, who reported a general Communist offensive in Cambodia and warned that Phnom Penh might not hold out. Nixon called an NSC meeting for the next day to discuss strategy.

As always when he approached a crisis, Nixon was tense, keyed up, anxious, unable to sleep. At 5 A.M. on April 12, he was up and dictating. It was a message to Kissinger, and it began, "I think we need a bold move in Cambodia to show that we stand with Lon Nol." He thought the cause a hopeless one, but felt it was important to do something symbolic.

"We have really dropped the ball on this one," he said. He wished he had not taken counsel of the fears of State, the CIA, and Defense a month earlier, when the help he wanted to give Lon Nol might have saved his government. But "we were taken in with the line that by helping him we would destroy his 'neutrality' and give the North Vietnamese an excuse to come in. Over and over again we fail to learn that the Communists never need an excuse to come in." He cited Hungary, 1956, and Czechoslovakia, 1968, and Laos, 1970, and now Cambodia, 1970.

"They [the Communists] are romping in there, and the only government in Cambodia in the last twenty-five years that had the guts to take a pro-Western and pro-American stand is ready to fall." [60]

The NSC meeting discussed the usual three options of doing nothing, doing something, and going all out. Rogers and Laird favored a modified do-nothing approach (give American support and advice to limited cross-border raids by ARVN, something already happening). Kissinger wanted to do something (main-force operations in Cambodia, but limited to ARVN). The Joint Chiefs wanted to go all out, using American forces inside Cambodia to destroy the Communist sanctuaries.

According to the military, there were two major targets. One was the Parrot's Beak, a sliver of land that jutted into South Vietnam and reached to within thirty-three miles of Saigon. The NVA had been using it as a staging area for years. The second was an even larger base, called the Fishhook, about fifty miles northwest of Saigon. The Chiefs told Nixon that inside the Fishhook was the elusive Central Office for South Vietnam, or COSVN, which had been a target of the original Menu bombings but was still in existence. COSVN was the "nerve center" of the entire enemy effort in Indochina, or so Nixon was told.[61]

Laird and Rogers repeated their objections to any American involvement in action inside Cambodia.

Agnew spoke up. He said that either the sanctuaries were a danger or they were not. He was against pussyfooting. He wanted to go all out. His words had a big impact on Nixon, or so at least Kissinger thought, because "Nixon hated . . . to be shown up in a group as being less tough than his advisers."[62]

Nixon made no decision. He knew, he later wrote, that if he widened the war "it could mean personal and political catastrophe for me and my administration."[63]

The next day, Nixon learned that there had been a leak and his orders to supply Lon Nol with captured equipment had been reported in *The New York Times*. He also learned that his orders to get more equipment into the CIA station in Phnom Penh had not been carried out because of bureaucratic foot-dragging.

Kissinger recalled that Nixon "flew into a monumental rage." He called Kissinger at least ten times that night, often to bark out an order and immediately hang up the phone.[64]

In one call, Nixon brought up another cause of his rage. "Those senators think they can push Nixon around on Haynsworth and Carswell," he said. "Well, I'll show them who's tough."

In another call, Nixon said, "The liberals are waiting to see Nixon let Cambodia go down the drain the way Eisenhower let Cuba go down the drain."[65]

The next morning, April 24, Nixon met with the chairman of the Joint Chiefs, General Cushman, and Director Helms to discuss the feasibility of a combined U.S.-ARVN operation against the Fishhook, in conjunction with an ARVN offensive into the Parrot's Beak. The military favored the plan and told the President the destruction of COSVN and of Communist supply dumps would buy valuable time for Vietnamization. They pointed out other sanctuaries they would like to hit. Nixon kept his own counsel.[66]

Early that afternoon, Nixon took a helicopter up to Camp David. Bebe Rebozo was along. By this stage in Nixon's Presidency, it was widely rumored—at least among Kissinger's people on the NSC staff—that whenever Bebe and Dick got together, whether at Key Biscayne or Camp David, the martinis flowed. (Other Nixon insiders deny this, or at least insist that Nixon never let booze interfere with his job. Ehrlichman said in an interview that Nixon's drinking "wasn't that frequent and he had a sense of when he was on and when he was off duty.")[67]

Whatever the truth, late that Friday night, April 24, Nixon telephoned Kissinger. His voice was slurred. He told Kissinger that Rebozo had a message for him. Nixon handed the phone to Rebozo, who said, "The President wants you to know, if this doesn't work, Henry, it's your ass." Then Kissinger heard Nixon say, "Ain't that right, Bebe?"[68]

The following day, Kissinger went up to Camp David to confer with Nixon. As the President paddled in the swimming pool, Kissinger walked along the edge. Nixon, bolstered no doubt by Rebozo, was ready to take on the world.

He told Kissinger he was eager to go ahead with the Fishhook operation, and perhaps even more. Why not resume the bombing of North Vietnam? Come to that, why not mine Haiphong harbor? What the hell, the doves were going to scream anyway.[69]

Why not indeed? For all Nixon's agonizing, for all the Joint Chiefs' talk about major operations, what the proposed Cambodian incursion represented was a minor attack on the tail of the snake. It completely ignored the head, in Hanoi. In no way could temporary incursions into the Parrot's Beak and the Fishhook have a lasting effect, or shape the outcome of the war.

Nixon said he wanted a "big play." He wanted to go for "all the marbles" since he expected "a hell of an uproar at home" whatever he did.

He enjoyed talking tough; he enjoyed pretending that he was making a decision about equivalent to Caesar's to cross the Rubicon or William the Conqueror's to set off for England or Eisenhower's to launch D-Day; he wanted to think of himself as an all-or-nothing kind of guy. But Nixon shrank from the "big play," from what he sometimes called the "Nixon Big Charge." After ten minutes of fantasizing in the pool, Nixon dropped the subject.

Late on that day, Saturday, April 25, Nixon, Rebozo, and Kissinger flew back to Washington. John Mitchell joined them for a cruise down the Potomac on the *Sequoia*. There was some heavy drinking. When the *Sequoia* got to Mount Vernon, feelings of patriotism flowed through the group, and there was an awkward attempt to pay respect to George Washington by standing at attention. Not everyone managed to stay upright. When the group returned to the

White House, Nixon ordered *Patton* put on in the theater and invited his convivial colleagues to watch it with him. Kissinger, who had sat through it with the President once already, managed to escape.[70]

On Monday morning, April 27, Nixon met with Rogers, Laird, and Kissinger. Rogers remained opposed to any American involvement: "It will cost us great casualties with very little gain. And I just don't believe it will be a crippling blow to the enemy."[71] Nixon, who had already signed a Kissinger-prepared directive authorizing the attack, kept silent in the face of Rogers' logic. But when he was alone with Kissinger, Nixon ordered a twenty-four-hour delay in execution. He wanted to confer with Mitchell. The Attorney General remained firm for the plan. He urged the President to stop wavering and start acting.[72]

Tuesday morning, April 28, Nixon met with Rogers, Laird, and Mitchell in the Oval Office. Nixon began by saying that he wanted to announce his decision, which was to invade. He had reached it only after full consultation with all interested parties, and after taking into consideration the "probable adverse reaction in some Congressional circles and some segments of the public." He added that he had noted the contrary recommendations of the Secretary of State and the Secretary of Defense.

Mitchell kept the notes. They conclude, "There was no discussion of the subject matter of the meeting by others in attendance during the presence of the President."[73]

That night, sitting alone, Nixon pulled out his yellow legal pad and made a list of the pluses and minuses of the forthcoming operation. The pluses won.

Early the next morning, Nixon showed his list to Kissinger. Kissinger, amazed, said he had prepared a list of his own, and it was almost identical.

"Now that we have made the decision there must be no recriminations among us," Nixon said. "Not even if the whole thing goes wrong. In fact, *especially* if the whole thing goes wrong."[74]

ON WEDNESDAY MORNING, April 29, the wire services began to report the ARVN offensive into the Parrot's Beak. Senate doves were unhappy. They asked for assurances that Nixon did not intend to send American troops into Cambodia. The White House was silent, saying only that the President would address the nation the following night.

Nixon was worried about his daughter Julie. He asked Rose Woods to call her.

"I don't want to get her upset," he said, "but it's possible that the campuses are really going to blow up after this speech, so could you just say I asked if she and David could come down from school to be with us." [75]

Meanwhile the media began to react to the Parrot's Beak news. The overall response to the ARVN incursion was relatively mild and muted. The headline on Max Frankel's analysis in *The New York Times* read: "PRESIDENT'S GAMBLE: WIDEN WAR TO END IT MORE QUICKLY," and his conclusion was that "the short-run risks are minimal and the potential gain considerable." [76]

So while there was some tension in the air, and considerable anxiety, as people wondered what on earth Nixon might do next, the country was far from panic. After all, ARVN units had been carrying out cross-border operations for some months in Cambodia, for some years in Laos. If there were a few American advisers with them, and American aircraft overhead, why that too was not exactly new. As Nixon had said back in early March, when air raids in Laos were revealed in the press, "No one cares about B-52 strikes . . . But people worry about our boys . . ."

Nixon spent most of the day of April 30 going over his speech. The mood of the country was such that he could have downplayed what he was about to announce. He might have eliminated all bellicosity from it and stuck to a straightforward but low-key description of the operation. He could have called the move into the Fishhook what it was, a rearguard action whose only aim was to knock the enemy off balance for a brief period of time, and to give the Lon Nol government some moral support. At most a few thousand GIs would be involved, and then only for a period of weeks. The United States was not expanding the war and it had no intention of staying in Cambodia.

But Nixon was not in a conciliatory mood. If he could not act tough, he could at least talk tough. He did not want to mollify his critics; he wanted to rub their noses in it. Far from downplaying his announcement, he wanted to make it cataclysmic. Having rejected all the bold options—bombing Hanoi, mining Haiphong, invading North Vietnam, or pulling out completely, once and for all—in favor of a minor rearguard action designed to cover his agonizing, slow retreat, Nixon used the occasion to make a speech that would more appropriately have come from Franklin Roosevelt on December 8, 1941.

On Thursday night, April 30, at 9 P.M., speaking from the Oval Office, Nixon addressed the nation. He began by describing the situation in Cambodia, in the process telling some whoppers (such as his claim that the United States had "scrupulously" respected Cambodian neutrality for the past five years).

Using a large wall map, he explained the strategic significance of Cambodia to South Vietnam. Then he outlined his three options. The first was to do nothing. That would "gravely threaten" the withdrawal of American troops. A second option was massive military assistance to the Lon Nol government. Here the problem was the equipment couldn't be gotten to Phnom Penh in time.

The third choice, Nixon said, "is to go to the heart of the trouble." That would have made a good lead-in line for announcing an invasion of North Vietnam, or the bombing of Hanoi, but instead Nixon said "that means cleaning out major North Vietnamese and Vietcong occupied territories," which he pointed to on the map. They were the Parrot's Beak and the Fishhook, shown in red.

The attack on the Parrot's Beak was already being carried out by ARVN. Nixon said that in addition he had ordered a combined American-ARVN operation against the Fishhook, in order to attack "the headquarters for the entire Communist military operation in South Vietnam." This was the "key control center" called COSVN. Nixon made it sound like Hitler's East Prussian headquarters.

"This is not an invasion of Cambodia," Nixon assured the audience. The United States would not occupy the area. Once the enemy forces were driven out of the sanctuaries and their military supplies were destroyed, "we will withdraw."

Had he stopped at that point, much would have been different. Of course there would have been sharp disagreement, and some caustic criticism, and plenty of protests, but his relatively straightforward description of this relatively minor action would not have set off any avalanches.

But he plunged on. He said the action he had just announced put the men in Hanoi on notice that "we will not be humiliated. We will not be defeated."

He continued, "If, when the chips are down, the world's most powerful nation, the United States of America, acts like a pitiful, helpless giant, the forces of totalitarianism and anarchy will threaten free nations and free institutions throughout the world."

He asserted that "it is not our power but our will and character that is being tested tonight."

He said that in the room from which he was speaking, Woodrow Wilson had made the great decisions of World War I, and Franklin Roosevelt the tough decisions of World War II, and Dwight Eisenhower the decision to end the war in Korea, and John Kennedy, "in his finest hour, made the great decision which removed Soviet nuclear missiles from Cuba."

He noted that in those decisions "the American people were not assailed by counsels of doubt and defeat from . . . opinion leaders." But in his case, he had already heard senators carping and complaining and warning and whining that his decision would cost the Republican Party in the November elections, and "make me a one-term President."

He assured the audience that "no one is more aware than I am of the political consequences. . . . It is tempting to take the easy political path: to blame this war on previous administrations and to bring all our men home immediately." But "I have rejected all political considerations in making this decision."

Then he pulled out all the stops, making it sound as if he were Martin Luther: "Here I stand, I can do no other." Nixon said, "Whether I may be a one-term President is insignificant compared to whether by our failure to act in this crisis the United States proves itself to be unworthy to lead the forces of freedom in this critical period in world history. I would rather be a one-term President and do what I believe is right than to be a two-term President at the cost of seeing America become a second-rate power and to see this Nation accept the first defeat in its proud 190-year history." [77]

The immediate reaction was as upbeat as Nixon's spirits. The family, especially Julie, thought he had been wonderful. Telephone calls poured in, 80 percent favorable (of course, many of them had been manufactured by Magruder, but they bolstered the President anyway). Chief Justice Burger came by at ten-thirty. He apologized for disturbing Nixon, but said he wanted to let the President know he thought the speech "had a sense of history and destiny about it." Burger added that he knew it had taken guts. Nixon said that if the operation didn't work, or if anything else happened that made him unelectable in 1972, "I would like you to be ready . . ." [78]

Nixon made his usual round of telephone calls to supporters across the country, each of whom praised the President for his courage and character. If it was all a question of will, as Nixon said, his friends were sure he had it.

Finally, around 3 A.M., Nixon went to bed. Not to sleep, but to savor the speech.

George Patton couldn't have done it better.

CHAPTER SIXTEEN

REAPING THE WHIRLWIND
May–August 1970

EARLY IN THE MORNING of May 1 Nixon was too keyed up to sleep. He rose, dressed, ate, and set off for a spur-of-the-moment drive over the 14th Street Bridge to the Pentagon for a firsthand briefing from the Joint Chiefs on the Cambodian operation. As he was guided through the labyrinth of corridors, the early arrivals among the uniformed military personnel and civilian workers mobbed him.

"God bless you!" one cried.

"Right on!" another exulted.

"We should have done this years ago!" shouted a third.[1]

Bolstered by the enthusiasm, Nixon's spirits rose even higher in the briefing room. A huge wall map, covered with arrows and pins, showed American and ARVN forces, some ten thousand altogether, swarming through the Parrot's Beak and the Fishhook. They had come in by helicopter, after the ground had been softened by air strikes. Briefing officers reported 194 enemy killed so far, 161 of them by the air strikes. American casualties were six wounded.

The only news that was less than upbeat was the absence of any significant enemy resistance, suggesting that the NVA had slipped away in the night. Nor had COSVN been found.[2]

There is an inescapable exhilaration to combat, and to command. This was the first ground offensive Nixon had ordered, and the largest allied operation since the Tet counterattack, more than two years earlier. Nixon was swept up in the excitement.

Studying the wall map, he noticed that in addition to the Parrot's Beak and the Fishhook, there were four other areas marked as sanctuaries.

"Between the ARVN and ourselves, would we be able to mount offensives in all of those other areas?" he asked the Chiefs. "Could we take out *all* the sanctuaries?"

He wanted a "can do" answer, but the Chiefs cautioned him about the negative reaction such a move would receive in the media and Congress.

"Let me be the judge as far as the political reactions are concerned," he promptly and properly snapped back. "The fact is that we have already taken the political heat for this particular operation."

No one spoke. Nixon made an on-the-spot decision.

"I want to take out all of those sanctuaries," he declared. "Make whatever plans are necessary, and then just do it. Knock them all out so that they can't be used against us again. Ever."[3]

He marched out of the briefing room, very full of himself and his power. Employees surrounded him, full of enthusiasm themselves. A young woman thanked him on behalf of her husband, who was serving in Vietnam. Another woman said, "I loved your speech. It made me proud to be an American."[4]

Nearly overcome with emotion himself, Nixon made an impromptu comparison.

"You think of those kids out there," he began. "I say 'kids.' I have seen them. They are the greatest.

"You see these bums, you know, blowing up the campuses. Listen, the boys that are on the college campuses today are the luckiest people in the world, going to the greatest universities, and here they are burning up the books, I mean storming around about this issue—I mean you name it—get rid of the war; there will be another one."

He meant another so-called issue to riot about, not another war.

"Out there we've got kids who are just doing their duty," he continued. "I have seen them. They stand tall, and they are proud. I am sure they are scared. I was when I was there. But when it really comes down to it, they stand up and, boy, you have to talk up to those men."[5]

Back at the White House, Nixon went for a walk on the lawn with Kissinger, Ziegler, and Haldeman. Ziegler reported that the congressional leadership was rallying behind the President. Nixon, pleased, said the congressmen were "ballsy." He turned to Kissinger and said, "The line is cold steel—no give."[6]

Late that afternoon Nixon sailed down the Potomac on the *Sequoia*. As the yacht passed Mount Vernon, the President, the

First Lady, David and Julie, and Bebe Rebozo stood at attention as the *Sequoia*'s loudspeaker boomed out the national anthem. By the time the party got back to the White House, Nixon's "bums" statement was getting as much play from the media as the offensive into Cambodia.

By dividing the young males of the Baby Boom generation into bums and heroes, Nixon was entering territory as alien as the jungles of Southeast Asia. To a large extent, the bums were the offspring of the rich and affluent, natural Republicans, while the heroes were the offspring of the working class, natural Democrats. To make just a couple of obvious points: One notable difference between World War II and Vietnam was the almost complete absence in Vietnam of the sons of the powerful, whether from business or politics or the intellectual community. A second difference was the overrepresentation of black Americans in the fighting line; in World War II the Army was segregated, and blacks were kept out of combat on the grounds that they did not make good soldiers. But although it is widely believed, it is not true that blacks did most of the fighting in Vietnam; the majority of the grunts in that war were working-class whites.

In the mid-sixties, there had been a great deal of talk about the danger of the United States becoming two nations, one black, one white. In his bums and heroes remarks, Nixon had focused on another division, almost as sharp and bitter, the split between middle- and upper-class white youth and the working-class youngsters. The first group was privileged, pampered, and petted; the second felt put upon, put down, and put out. The first group grew up in the suburbs; the second, in the ethnic neighborhoods of the cities. The first went to college; the second, to Vietnam. The first smoked marijuana; the second drank beer. And the damnedest thing of all, the first group rebelled against the society that had been so good to it, while the second respected authority and was intensely patriotic. About the only thing the two groups had in common was that each was a part of the Baby Boom.

Add to this a President who, in the midst of a war, exacerbated the division among his own people, and the result was a volatile situation. Between the bums and heroes, and the pitiful helpless giant, and the rest of the rhetoric, Nixon had provided enough fuel for an unpredecented national conflagration.

THEN HE ADDED to it. As a part of the offensive, but without Laird's knowledge, Nixon ordered air attacks against North Vietnam. More than a hundred fighter-bombers were involved. They struck anti-aircraft sites and logistical support facilities. Nixon tried to keep these missions secret, using the back channel he had established for the Menu operation, but on May 2 the story broke. John Finney of *The New York Times* asked various senators for their reaction.

"Good God," Senator Fulbright gasped. Majority Leader Mike Mansfield said, "It is a difficult situation to reconcile one's mind to. . . . The outlook seems to be getting grimmer by the day."[7]

Nixon was livid about the "leak." Actually, the *Times* got the story from a radio broadcast from Hanoi. Haig, on instructions from Kissinger, asked the FBI to place wiretaps on four high officials in DOD and State; these were designed to catch Laird and Rogers as the source of the leak.[8] The Nixon White House was thus spying on the Secretaries of State and of Defense. Laird, meanwhile, without consulting Nixon, announced on May 4 that the United States was "terminating" the raids on North Vietnam.

Meanwhile, Soviet Premier Aleksei Kosygin assailed Nixon for the Cambodian incursion and said it threatened to "complicate" the SALT talks, while the Chinese denounced the United States and pledged support to North Vietnam (and, within a few days, both Communist powers announced stepped-up shipments of supplies to North Vietnam).[9]

That same day, May 4, thirty-seven college presidents signed a letter urging Nixon to "demonstrate unequivocally your determination" to promptly end the war. They said the Cambodian incursion and the renewed bombing of North Vietnam had generated "severe and widespread apprehensions on our campuses." They added, "We share these apprehensions. We implore you to consider the incalculable dangers of an unprecedented alienation of America's youth." Among others, the letter bore the signatures of the presidents of New York University, Princeton, Columbia, Notre Dame, Dartmouth, Pennsylvania, and Johns Hopkins.[10]

The fire became a roaring inferno that afternoon, when four students at Kent State University, two of them girls, were shot to death by a volley of National Guard gunfire.

This shocking event was made more shocking by later revelations that while some of the Kent State students had been involved in an antiwar rally, others were simply changing classes, and the Guard—called out earlier by the governor of Ohio in response to the burning down of the ROTC building on campus and other disturbances—was neither threatened nor provoked.

Nixon made a terrible situation worse when he had Ziegler read a statement to the White House press corps: "This should remind us all once again that when dissent turns to violence, it invites tragedy. It is my hope this tragic and unfortunate incident will strengthen the determination of all the Nation's campuses—

administrators, faculty, and students alike—to stand firmly for the right which exists in this country of peaceful dissent and just as strongly against the resort to violence as a means of such expression." [11]

Not a word of sympathy for the dead students, or their families, or the eight wounded students. The father of nineteen-year-old Allison Krause, one of the victims, did catch the attention and the heart of the American people when he told a reporter, "My child was not a bum."

The campuses went into an uproar such as had never been seen before, and pray God never will be again. Four hundred fifty colleges and universities went on strike. In California, Governor Reagan, citing "emotional turmoil," closed down the entire state university and college system (nineteen colleges, nine universities, 280,000 students). At campuses across the nation, a copy of the Constitution was buried, to the sound of taps. Antiwar rallies that had previously been sparsely attended and addressed only by bearded young radical professors were now pulling almost the entire student body, and the principal speakers were the older professors and the administrators. At Yale, President Kingman Brewster, Jr., announced that he would lead a delegation of a thousand faculty and students to Washington to lobby against the war. A group of prominent Harvard professors publicly announced their break with Nixon and their intention to go to Washington to urge their old colleague Henry Kissinger to resign. [12]

At Harvard, the Students for a Democratic Society threatened to burn down the house of another Cambridge professor, Daniel Patrick Moynihan. Nixon, informed of the threat, ordered the Secret Service to provide protection for Mrs. Moynihan and the home. [13]

There was another leak. On May 6, Max Frankel reported in *The New York Times* that Rogers and Laird "had serious misgivings about the use of American troops in Cambodia, and there are many indications that President Nixon's war decisions in the last two weeks have been reached in an atmosphere of confusion as well as dissension." That same day, Terence Smith reported in the *Times* that American troops had penetrated Cambodia in four more areas (these were the attacks Nixon had ordered during his Pentagon briefing on May 1). [14]

Nixon declared himself "shocked and disappointed" by the leaks. Laird was a good soldier; he denied everything and insisted that he had "supported fully" the Cambodian incursion. Rogers was silent. Nixon called to inform him that it was his duty to get behind the President once a decision had been made. [15]

As the campuses shut down, antiwar protest rallies sometimes turned into riots. Students marched through the streets, chanting, throwing rocks, breaking windows, all too frequently burning down buildings. The Baby Boomers were on a rampage.

These activities shocked and frightened older Americans as much as Kent State had shocked and frightened the college kids. In the view of older folks, these kids should have been grateful for their privileges; in the view of the college students, the older Americans should have been ashamed of themselves for supporting Richard Nixon.

The President, faced with unprecedented upheaval, began to back down. On May 5 he met with congressional committees and pledged that he was "firmly committed" to withdrawing American troops from Cambodia in three to seven weeks. He also promised that no American troops would go deeper than twenty-one miles into Cambodia. Now it was the military's turn to be unhappy. Nixon's pledges, limiting the time and the area of operations, made it difficult, not to say impossible, for the Army to carry out its mission of destroying the sanctuaries and COSVN.

Nixon's attempts to calm the nation were insufficient. On May 7 there were firebombings on at least ten campuses. Vandalism hit many schools, followed by police or National Guard use of tear gas and bird shot. Before the turmoil subsided, the Guard had been called out by sixteen governors for twenty-one campuses.[16]

In New York City, on May 7, it was Nixon supporters who grew violent. Construction workers, so-called hard hats, many of them Irish or Italian, nearly all of them men who had voted Democratic all their lives, strong Kennedy supporters in 1960, most of them veterans of World War II or Korea, were enraged when Mayor Lindsay, after Kent State, lowered the American flag to half-staff over City Hall. The workers stormed the building, got that flag up where they felt it belonged and beat up students and hippies, while the cops looked on.

More violence was expected the following day. Student groups planned a protest rally at City Hall; the hard hats vowed to stop them. The probable confrontation was symbolic of the madness of those days: the protesting groups were made up of students from the business schools of Harvard, NYU, Columbia, MIT, the Wharton School of Economics, and Dartmouth.[17] It was a good bet that among them were future bank presidents, corporate heads, chairmen of the Fed, and so forth. And here they were, goading lifetime Democrats into a frenzy over the policies of a Republican President.

The National Student Association called for a national day of protest in Washington, to be held on Saturday, May 9. On Friday, the eighth, students from all the eastern states began driving to the city.

Nixon decided, over the objections of some of his staff, to call a news conference in an effort to defuse the situation. He announced that he would hold it on Friday night at 10 P.M., making it possible for students driving to the capital to listen on their car radios. This was high-risk politics to a fare-thee-well. It would be absurd to say that the fate of the Republic was at stake, but it would be wrong to downplay the importance of the event. This was Nixon's severest test to date of his ability to lead the nation.

Facing the reporters, Nixon was in control, convincing, confident, conciliatory, all at once. Far from goading the students, or calling them names, he tried to reason with them, to appeal to their better judgment. To some extent, he succeeded.

The tone of the news conference, and the mood of the nation, was set in this question: "Mr. President, some Americans believe this country is heading for revolution, and others believe that dissent and violent demonstrations are leading us to an era of repression. I wonder if you would give us your view of the state of the American society and where it is headed."

Nixon's answer was calm and reassuring: "This country is not headed for revolution." He pointed to the obvious; that the safety valve of the right to dissent was open and working perfectly. With regard to repression, "That is nonsense. . . . I do not see that the critics of my policies are repressed. . . . [They] are very vigorous and sometimes quite personal. . . . I have no complaints about it."

Asked if he had been surprised by the intensity of the protest, Nixon said he had not. Herb Kaplow of NBC News asked what Nixon thought the students were trying to say in their demonstrations.

"They are trying to say that they want peace," Nixon replied. "They are trying to say that they want to stop the killing. . . . They are trying to say that we ought to get out of Vietnam. I agree with everything that they are trying to accomplish."

He asked for some understanding on their part. "I did not send these men to Vietnam," he said. There were 525,000 men there when he took command, and since then "I have been working 18 or 20 hours a day, mostly on Vietnam, trying to bring these men home."

Asked about Agnew's remark that day ("Every debate has a cadre of Jeremiahs, normally a gloomy coalition of choleric young intellectuals and tired, embittered elders"), Nixon said he was not going to tell his Vice-President what to say. He did hope that everyone in his Administration would keep in mind "a rule that I have always had, and it is a very simple one: When the action is hot, keep the rhetoric cool."

That was too much for Phil Potter of the Baltimore *Sun*, who wanted to know what had happened to that rule in the Pentagon a week earlier, when Nixon made his bums and heroes remarks. Rather than answer the question Nixon explained that he did not mean to apply the word "bums" to "those who dissent," but rather to those who "engage in violence, burn buildings, terrorize their fellow students and the faculty. . . . 'Bums' is perhaps too kind a word to apply to that kind of person."

He explained the Cambodian incursion as necessary to protect the remaining American troops in Vietnam, and called it "a decisive move." He said it was a warning to the enemy that if "he escalates while we are trying to de-escalate, we will move decisively and not step-by-step." He specifically threatened that if the NVA were to move massive forces across the DMZ, against the marines in that area, "I would certainly not allow those men to be massacred without using more force and more effective force."

As against those generalized threats, he made a specific pledge, one that went a long way toward defusing the domestic situation: "The great majority of all American units will be out by the second week of June, and all Americans of all kinds, including advisers, will be out of Cambodia by the end of June." [18]

To his critics on the right, Nixon had just let policy be made in the streets. There was no way the troops could clear out those sanctuaries, find all the hidden matériel, uncover COSVN, do their job in so short a time. The storm of protest was sure to blow itself out; for certain it could not get any worse; having endured it so far, it made no sense to the hawks for Nixon to buckle now.

To his critics on the left, Nixon had for once heeded common sense. Unless the United States was prepared to occupy Cambodia indefinitely, something not even the most extreme hawk was advocating, nothing decisive could be accomplished there. Nixon's offensive had accomplished what it was going to accomplish—the uncovering and destruction of some six months' worth of supplies. It had set the Communists back, and bought time. Meanwhile the domestic turmoil simply had to be brought to an end. Nixon's pledge, and his general demeanor, made a major contribution to that goal.

Whatever one thought of his actions, everyone could agree that the President had just put in an alarmingly inconsistent week.

AFTER THE NEWS CONFERENCE, Nixon was much too excited to sleep. Between 10:35 P.M. and 1:55 A.M. he made more than forty telephone calls to friends and supporters around the country. He slept for about an hour, then at 3:24 A.M. began another round of calls. He put a record on the turntable. Manolo Sanchez heard the music and came in to ask if the President wanted some tea or coffee.

Nixon was standing at the window, looking at the small groups of students beginning to gather on the grounds of the Washington Monument for the protest rally later that day. No, he did not want anything. Nixon remarked that the Lincoln Memorial at night was the most beautiful sight in Washington. Manolo said he had never seen it.

"Let's go look at it now," Nixon blurted out.

To the consternation of the Secret Service, the President and his valet soon appeared on the lawn. Nixon asked for a car, and told the driver to take him to the Lincoln Memorial. He climbed the steps, with Manolo at his side. After reading the inscriptions, he approached a group of eight students in the rotunda, introduced himself, and shook hands.

A couple of the students said they had not heard Nixon's news conference. He said he was sorry they had missed it because he had explained that his goals in Vietnam were the same as theirs, "to stop the killing and end the war and bring peace." His objective was not to get into Cambodia, but to get out of Vietnam. Nixon then expressed the hope that the students would not let their hatred of the war turn into a bitter hatred of the whole system. A bit dazzled by all this presidential attention, and exhausted after driving all night, the students failed to respond.

Nixon tried a new tack. "I know most of you think I'm an SOB," he said, "but I want you to know that I understand just how you feel." He recalled that when he was about their age, British Prime Minister Chamberlain had come home from Munich claiming he had peace in hand. As a good Quaker, Nixon had concluded that Chamberlain was "the greatest man alive," and that Churchill, Chamberlain's critic, "was a madman."

But events proved that Churchill was right, Chamberlain wrong.

Still no response. Nixon tried again. He urged the students to travel when they were young, to borrow the money if they had to, because if they waited until they were old, they could not enjoy it. Warming to what was one of his favorite themes, he told them where to go—out West, to start with, to see the Indians, and California. He described the beach at San Clemente, "the greatest surfing beach in the world." It had been closed to the public because of the Marine Corps base nearby, but Nixon had ordered some of it opened, as a part of "our whole 'quality of life' environmental program."

After they had seen California, Nixon went on, they should go overseas. "Europe's fine," he said, "but it's really an older version of America." It was worth seeing, but Asia was better. He said he hoped that sometime during his Administration they could go to China. They should not overlook India, and Asian Russia.

The group surrounding the President had gradually grown larger, from eight or so to perhaps thirty. One of the newcomers interrupted Nixon's travelogue to say, "I hope you realize that we are willing to die for what we believe in."

Nixon replied that he certainly did, and that when he was their age he had been willing to do the same, and still was today. But the point was to not have to die for what you believed in, rather to be able to live for it.

He returned to his world tour. Prague and Warsaw were much more beautiful than Moscow.

"We are not interested in what Prague looks like," a student interjected. "We are interested in what kind of life we build in the United States."

Nixon agreed, and returned to his environmental program. He talked about people, and the need for mutual understanding, and got going on "spiritual hunger," which, he said, "all of us have and which, of course, has been the great mystery of life from the beginning of time."

Dawn had arrived. The sun was climbing over the Washington Monument. Turning to some just-arrived students, Nixon shook some more hands and asked where they were from. One girl replied, "Syracuse University." Nixon praised the Syracuse football team. Then he descended to his car, where he said he understood the students' frustration and anger, and again expressed the hope that their opposition didn't turn into a blind hatred.

"Remember this is a great country, with all of its faults," he called out before getting into the car and driving away.[19]

He drove to the Capitol, where he gave Manolo a tour of the building. In the empty House Chamber, he told Manolo to make a speech from the Speaker's chair, as he sat in the front row. Manolo talked about how proud he was to have become an American citizen. The President, and the cleaning women present, applauded. Nixon autographed a Bible for one of the women, an aged and dignified black lady who had known Nixon when he was Vice-President. He told her, "You know, my mother was a saint."

Still keyed up, Nixon insisted on having breakfast at a restaurant. By now, the White House communications system had brought his close aides running, and he was joined by Haldeman, Ziegler, and Dwight Chapin. They went to the Rib Room of the

Mayflower Hotel, where Nixon had corned-beef hash with a poached egg on top. It was his first meal in a Washington restaurant since he became President. At 7:30 A.M. he returned to the White House, which was completely encircled by military buses, parked bumper to bumper, rather like the wagons out west preparing for an Indian attack, and for the same purpose. He had been gone about three hours.

He had enjoyed the experience, but it cannot be said that he had learned much from it (he had done almost all the talking, and had often told the students he already knew what they were thinking and feeling), or that it did him any good on the PR front. In fact, the PR was terrible. Reporters, resentful that the President had gotten out of the White House and held a public discussion without their being present, descended on the Lincoln Memorial to interview the students.

"I hope it was because he was tired," one girl told them, "but most of what he was saying was absurd. Here we had come from a university [Syracuse] that's completely uptight—on strike—and when we told him where we were from, he talked about the football team. And surfing." Another said, "He wasn't really concerned with why we were here."[20]

The press played this up, to the point that Ehrlichman a few days later told Nixon he had "created problems" by talking about sports to students who had traveled all night to protest the war. Nixon snapped back about the problems he had when even his staff believed false stories spread about him.[21]

Nixon's anger was justified. He really had not spent all that much time talking sports. But his own summary of the event, in a memo to Ray Price, was just as misleading as the press coverage. Nixon claimed that what he had done for the students at the Lincoln Memorial was "to lift them a bit out of the miserable intellectual wasteland in which they now wander aimlessly around."[22]

KISSINGER, AS ALWAYS, was playing to both sides. To Nixon he said, Be tough, stand up to the students. To the student groups that he met with, he said, Be patient. "Give me six months." To his Harvard colleagues, he said, "If you only knew what I'm staving off from the right."[23]

Nixon was not pleased with Kissinger's sudden prominence. The President told Haldeman to "get K away from the press. He talks too much." Nixon also complained that Kissinger was "not good with the Cabinet—he can't handle Rogers and Laird." He also worried about "where can K go to get ego gratification?"[24]

For his part, Kissinger was not pleased with the way Laird was thrusting himself forward, or with the praise Rogers was getting for having urged caution in Cambodia. On May 12, Laird told the Senate Armed Services Committee that several thousand American troops had already been withdrawn from Cambodia and that more would be pulled out immediately. He predicted that all ground combat in Vietnam would be taken over by ARVN by July 1971.[25] This was headline stuff, and even though it served the purpose of further calming the nation, Kissinger was jealous. Kissinger was also unhappy with the advice Laird and Rogers were giving. They were always saying no to the President's bold plans.

So Kissinger told Haldeman to tell Rogers and Laird that they "must talk affirmatively to the President, stop discouraging him. Above all, don't let them bring problems to the President."[26]

Nixon had enough problems as it was. The Senate, for example, was moving to restrict his freedom of maneuver in Southeast Asia. On May 11, the Senate Foreign Relations Committee adopted, 9–1, an amendment to a military appropriations bill that required the President to have all American troops out of Cambodia by June 30 (which was the deadline already announced by Nixon). The sponsors were Senators Frank Church and John Sherman Cooper (R., Ky.).

In addition to the Cooper-Church amendment, Senators McGovern and Hatfield were pressing for an amendment that would cut off funds for any military operation in Cambodia by June 30 and in Laos by the end of 1970, and require the withdrawal of all American forces from Vietnam by June 30, 1971.

Nixon called Cooper-Church and McGovern-Hatfield unconstitutional.[27] The arguments were nicely balanced. The Constitution says, in the plainest possible English, "The Congress shall have power to declare war." It also says, in the plainest possible English, "The President shall be Commander-in-Chief of the Army and Navy of the United States."

The controversy surrounding attempts at reconciling those two clauses will last as long as the Republic lasts. Nixon's argument was that it was not he who started the war. He inherited a situation in which more than a half million American servicemen were involved in a war, so his responsibilities as commander in chief overrode any legal or constitutional objections to his manner of conducting it.

The doves in Congress could not break that argument, so they tried to go around it. The Senate amendments were designed to deny the President his power by invoking another constitutional clause, namely that "the Congress shall have power to raise and support armies . . . [and] to provide and maintain a navy." By amending appropriations bills, the Senate Foreign Relations Committee was extending the power to raise armed forces to include the power to tell the President where, when, and how they could be used. In support of such a limitation on the powers of the commander in chief, the doves could cite yet another constitutional clause, the one that gave to Congress the sole power to appropriate money. Again, the wording could not be clearer: "No money shall be drawn from the treasury, but in consequence of appropriations made by law."

These arguments, intrinsically interesting, potentially decisive, would be settled less by learned debate, more by public attitudes toward the war. And in the area of public opinion, in the aftermath of Cambodia and Kent State, Nixon by the third week in May was doing surprisingly well, as the inevitable backlash to the demonstrations took hold.

On May 20, 100,000 or more pro-Nixon demonstrators, led by thousands of helmeted construction workers, marching under a sea of American flags, paraded to a noontime rally on Broadway opposite City Hall in New York City. There was a "jingoistic joy" in the air, according to *The New York Times*. Some of the slogans painted on signs were "Lindsay for Mayor of Hanoi," "Love It or Leave It," and "God Bless the Establishment." One marcher pointed to a flag and told a reporter, "It's me. It's part of me. I fought for it." [28]

A flood of mail had meanwhile filled the White House mail room to overflowing. Nearly a half million letters and cards had come in, an all-time record. Most were supportive. At the same time, Congress had also received a record volume of mail; some 225,000 pieces to Senator Fulbright alone, and almost as many to other doves. The congressional mail was 97 percent against Nixon, or so at least Fulbright claimed. As one of his aides put it, "The President couldn't have realized what a raw national nerve he was touching with the decision to invade Cambodia." [29]

The Gallup poll brought great satisfaction to Nixon; it showed 50 percent approved his decision to go into Cambodia, while 39 percent disapproved. Nixon called it "remarkable," [30] but there is another point of view on the poll. The traditional response of the American people in a time of crisis is to rally behind the President. That only half did so in May of 1970 would have given some Presidents pause. Back in 1956, for example, when the House of Commons supported Prime Minister Anthony Eden's incursion into Suez, 270–218, Eisenhower had commented, "I could not dream of committing this nation on such a vote." [31]

One letter Nixon received came from a former President who knew what it was to be embattled. Johnson wrote to praise Nixon and pledge his support. Nixon replied, "Only one who has had the responsibility knows the problems, and I deeply appreciate your support and understanding." [32]

On June 3, Nixon went on national radio and televison again to address the nation. He spoke from the Oval Office. He said he had conferred with Secretary Laird, General Abrams, and other senior advisers to receive a report on the Cambodian operation, and based on that meeting, "I can now state that this has been the most successful operation of this long and very difficult war." Nixon claimed that "all of our major military objectives have been achieved." As film footage from Cambodia went on the screen, the President ran through a long list of figures: 10 million rounds of ammunition captured, 15,000 rifles, 2,000 mortars, 11 million pounds of rice, and so forth.

Nixon said the meaning of these figures had been brought home to him dramatically a few days earlier, when he had been talking to a construction union leader from New York. The man's son had been killed in Vietnam in February. He told the President that "had we moved earlier in Cambodia, we might have captured the enemy weapon that killed [his] son."

Nixon took on his critics. They had charged, he said, that the incursion "would increase American casualties, that it would widen the war, that it would lengthen our involvement, that it might postpone troop withdrawals. But the operation was undertaken for precisely the opposite reasons—and it has had precisely the opposite effect."

He guaranteed to have all American troops out of Cambodia by June 30, pledged again to have another 150,000 out of Vietnam by the end of April 1971, and asked for support. He reminded his audience that "only this administration can end this war and bring peace. We have a program for peace—and the greater the support the administration receives in its efforts, the greater the opportunity to win that just peace we all desire." [33]

He said not one word about COSVN, for the good reason that it had never been found. Nor did he mention the 344 Americans killed in Cambodia, or the 1,592 wounded, or the 818 dead and 3,553 wounded ARVN, or the 130,000 Cambodian refugees. [34]

Nor did he mention the implied commitment the United States had made to the survival of the Lon Nol government. Nor did he deal with a question raised by Max Frankel in *The New York Times:* "Has the Cambodian operation really won time for the allied side or has it, by advertising the divisions in the United States and the restraints on the President, only persuaded Hanoi that the total exhaustion of American will and resources is near?" [35]

On the positive side, Nixon surely was justified in his claim that the material captured was a setback for Hanoi. Indeed, it was almost two years before Hanoi was able to mount a major offensive in South Vietnam, and then it came across the DMZ rather than out of Cambodia. But overall, there was a haunting quality to Secretary Rogers' April 27 warning to Nixon: "It will cost us great casualties with very little gain. And I just don't believe it will be a crippling blow to the enemy."

THERE WAS another price to be paid for Cambodia. At his May 8 news conference, Nixon had rejected out of hand the fear expressed by one reporter that the country was headed for "an era of repression." The fear nevertheless persisted. Chief Justice Burger spoke to it on May 19 in an address to the American Law Institute.

"Some say that we must 'crack down,' that we must 'smash' the challengers and restore tight discipline," he noted. "In periods of stress there are always some voices raised urging that we suspend fundamental guarantees and take short cuts as a matter of self-protection." He warned against such action. "In those few periods of our history when we suspended basic guarantees of the individual in times of great national stress," he reminded his audience, "we often found, in retrospect, that we had overreacted." [36]

That message would better have been delivered to the White House. According to Haldeman, May 1970 "marked a turning point for Nixon; a beginning of his downhill slide. . . . Nixon had given up on the intelligence and investigatory agencies such as the FBI to help in his battle to quell the national uproar. . . . As far as he was concerned, the FBI was a failure; it hadn't found the leakers of military secrets; it hadn't found Communist backing for the antiwar organizations which he was sure was there. . . . Of course Nixon knew very well he couldn't count on the CIA." [37]

Nixon seemed almost angrier at J. Edgar Hoover than at the antiwar protesters and the radical terrorist groups. Hoover, Nixon said, was showing "more concern for the rights of the accused than for the protection of the innocent," and he explained this amazing turnabout on Hoover's part by pointing out that "a new liberalism was fashionable." [38] Hoover's concern was to protect the FBI from congressional critics; therefore he refused to engage in any more black-bag jobs (surreptitious entries) and mail openings, and put limits on the FBI's wiretapping operations. He restricted the recruitment of campus informants to men twenty-one years of age or over. Nixon knew that earlier Presidents had had the benefit of these sources and techniques; it was galling to have Hoover turn him down, especially as he faced a far more critical domestic situation than any of his predecessors. [39]

So it was an angry Nixon who on June 5 presided over an Oval

Office meeting of Hoover, Helms of the CIA, General Donald Bennett of the Defense Intelligence Agency, Admiral Noel Gayler of the National Security Agency, Haldeman, Ehrlichman, Finch, and Tom Huston of Haldeman's staff. Nixon told the directors of the intelligence agencies that they were disorganized, inefficient, and unproductive. He wanted them reorganized into a single unit, under Hoover's chairmanship, with the staff directed by Huston.

Nixon said the problem was that the American people, "perhaps as a reaction to the excesses of the McCarthy era, are unwilling to admit the possibility that 'their children' could wish to destroy their country."

He went on: "We must develop a plan which will enable us to curtail the illegal activities of those who are determined to destroy our society." [40] Huston went to work to draft such a plan.

THE FOLLOWING DAY, June 6, David and Julie and Susan Eisenhower, and David's parents, John and Barbara, and John's uncle Milton, along with Bebe Rebozo and Rose Mary Woods, joined the Nixons at Camp David. Rebozo brought along academic robes, which he wore for a mock graduation ceremony for David, Julie, Susan, and John (Susan had just graduated from high school; June 6 was the twenty-sixth anniversary of John's graduation from West Point). Rebozo made a humorous commencement speech, written for him by Pat Buchanan, and Nixon offered several toasts. But, Julie confessed, "despite all his attempts to make the party a gala celebration, most of us were unable to forget why we were not in Massachusetts." [41]

As if the make-believe graduation was not sad enough, that same week Nixon got blasted in the press for some construction activity at his home in San Clemente. *Parade* magazine reported that Nixon had ordered the General Services Administration to pay the bill for a "wind wall" around his swimming pool. The story said the wall, all glass, was designed to cut down on the strong prevailing offshore wind, and that it cost $60,000.

The truth was much different. The wall was a bulletproof glass shield. Nixon had not wanted it put up, indeed objected strenuously, but the Secret Service insisted that it was a necessary security measure. Herb Klein demanded a retraction from *Parade*, but none appeared, and the story remained a regular item for the Nixon bashers. [42]

For their graduation present, David and Julie got a trip to Japan, where they represented Nixon at Expo '70 in Osaka. They returned in time to act as hosts for Prince Charles and Princess Anne (then twenty-one and nineteen years old, respectively). They took the young members of the royal family on a round of games, sight-seeing, and parties, with no one over thirty involved. The newspapers reported that at a White House dance with 564 young people in attendance, the men were all "short-haired and black-tied, the women full-skirted." David danced with Princess Anne; Julie, with Prince Charles.

As always, the American press could not get enough of the British royalty. From the dozens of stories, one will suffice: At the Smithsonian Space Museum, Prince Charles talked to Neil Armstrong about his trip to the moon. In a reference to Isaac Newton, Armstrong assured Prince Charles that "your countryman had a lot to do with it." [43]

Shortly after the visit, Nixon told Haldeman to have Klein "get a good feature article written on how well State visits are done by this Administration." Nixon wanted to stress "the new style and grace that the Nixons have brought to these State visits." Klein should point out such details as "the fact that the President makes his arrival statement and his toast at the State Dinner without notes."

Overall, Nixon told Haldeman to have Klein make certain the story stressed "the combination of elegant pageantry with simple, quiet charm." [44]

THE COMBINATION of pageantry and charm that Nixon felt characterized the state visits to the White House was notably absent on May 20, when the presidents of fifteen black colleges and universities met with the President in the Oval Office. The meeting was tense from the outset. A week earlier, six blacks had been shot dead at a civil rights rally in Augusta, Georgia; on May 14, two girls were killed and twelve wounded when state police opened fire on the women's dorm at Jackson State in Mississippi.

A spokesman read an opening statement to Nixon. It accused the President of adopting policies that had led to "anger, outrage and frustration" among blacks. The statement said specifically that "the 'Southern strategy' leads to the conclusion that blacks are dispensable." It went on to cite "the neglect of urban problems; insufficient support of education; your nomination of Justices to the Supreme Court; your hesitancy to support strong measures to assure the voting rights of black citizens; your failure to use your great moral influence to bring the people of this great nation together." [45]

It was a damning and bitter indictment, and it hurt. Back in the fifties, Nixon had had a better record on civil rights than any other national politician; at that time he was the only one who would go into the South and tell southerners that segregation was morally wrong. In the sixties, he had been off the firing line, more or less a bystander during the so-called Second Reconstruction. Now, in 1970, he was the chief executive officer of the government, charged with the responsibility for implementing the laws and rulings laid down in the sixties.

It made him uncomfortable, philosophically as well as politically. He later described his position in a memo to Ehrlichman: "I am convinced that while legal segregation is totally wrong, forced integration of housing or education is just as wrong."[46] In practical political terms, he saw himself as a loser whatever he did. He felt he would never get credit from blacks, no matter how vigorously he enforced the law (he told Ehrlichman, "The NAACP would say my rhetoric was poor even if I gave the Sermon on the Mount"). But it was unthinkable that he *not* enforce the law, and if he ever did indulge such thoughts, Bob Finch was there to remind him of his duty. Finch, ambitious himself, wanted to go back to California to run for the Senate. He wanted and needed a good, solid record for himself as Secretary of HEW to do so. The laws were on the books, it was his job to enforce them, and he intended to do just that.[47]

Nixon was not running for the Senate from California; he was President of all the people. And all the people included the white southerners. Nixon had sympathy for them. He told Ehrlichman, "The people are going through an agony down there and we shouldn't make it worse for them."[48]

Nixon's wants were contradictory. He wanted voluntary compliance with the court orders, which was about as likely in the Deep South as an August snowstorm in Mississippi. He wanted the confrontations over and done with in 1970, so there would be relative peace on the racial front during his re-election campaign in 1972. He wanted to expand his gains in the South, even as desegregation took place. He wanted to do what was right, without having to use force, and without having to pay a price.

As a consequence of these contradictory goals, the Nixon Administration did not have a consistent policy. Mitchell, at Nixon's urging, tried to hold back the young eager-beaver lawyers in the Justice Department; Finch, to Nixon's dismay, urged on the young eager beavers in HEW. Justice contended, with Nixon's approval, that a tax-exempt status for the private schools springing up in the South was legal; Finch persuaded Nixon to ask Congress for $1.5 billion to help finance the desegregation of southern schools and to provide incentives for northern school districts to integrate. Nixon's orders to Justice and HEW were "Do only what the law requires, not one thing more."[49]

Finch was impatient with such restraints and Nixon was unhappy with Finch's activism. On June 6, Finch stepped down, in the Administration's first Cabinet shift. Under Secretary of State Elliot Richardson replaced Finch, who stayed on as an adviser to the President with the title of Counsellor.[50] Richardson, a Harvard graduate and longtime Republican officeholder, was a charter member of the Eastern Establishment, so he brought some political strength and prestige with him.

Nixon needed help, as he was catching it from both sides. Republicans in the South were saying they had been "sold out" by "Tricky Dick." Harry Dent, Nixon's political adviser with the southerners in Congress, reported in a June 16 memo that George Wallace, who had just won the Democratic gubernatorial primary in Alabama, was charging that Nixon had destroyed the public-school system in the South. Dent said that Wallace was exploiting widely shared sentiments in the South. The view from Dixie was that "the administration is heading left in an effort" to get liberal votes. There is a feeling down there that "the squeaky wheel gets the grease."[51]

Beginning on June 24, and continuing through the summer, Nixon met with the advisory committees he had created for the seven Deep South states, to discuss ways and means to achieve peaceful desegregation. These committees were biracial, in itself a major innovation. His attempts at persuasion were sincere, if inconclusive.

On July 28, at San Clemente, he presided over a meeting of his own people. He told them to "quit bragging about school desegregation. We do what the law requires—nothing more. This is politics, and I'm the judge of the politics of schools. Only Mitchell and Richardson should be talking about schools, and they must not —they *will* not—be sucked into praising 'our great record.' "[52]

He wanted them to recognize "that we will get no credit from the blacks but a lot of heat from our own supporters. We don't win anything. . . . We have to do what's right, but we must separate that from politics and not be under the illusion that this is helping us. . . . Our approach is one of cooperation, not coercion, of doing only what is necessary, not grandstanding." He did want his people to speak out "against busing at every opportunity."[53] Above all, Nixon wanted "as low a profile as possible" on desegregation.[54]

On August 14, Nixon went to New Orleans to meet with the Louisiana advisory committee and to assure the South that he was at once firm and reasonable in his approach to desegregation. "I shall meet my responsibility," he said, "but we are not going to carry out the law in a punitive way, treating the South as a second-class part of this nation."

Nixon sat in an open car for a parade through the French Quarter at high noon. Although the mid-August sun was beating down on him, he kept his suit jacket on, his tie in place. When he spoke at Jackson Square, a small crowd of student hecklers from the University of New Orleans began chanting, "U.S. out of Vietnam." When police started moving in on them, the students changed the chant to "More pay for cops." That stopped the police, allowing the kids to begin chanting, "Free David Eisenhower."[55]

Five days later, Whitney Young, executive director of the National Urban League, called the record of the Nixon Administration uneven, indecisive, and flabby. "It's sort of like Jell-O," said Young. "You can't really get ahold of it, you know. It's what I call white magic, now you see it, now you don't."[56]

Moynihan sent Nixon a memo on Young's remarks, with the comment, "Can you believe it? Talk about class interests." Nixon scribbled on the memo, "E—I think this cooks Whitney Young. He is hopelessly partisan. H—can't some of our people who help finance the Urban League hit him?"[57]

Moynihan was most upset with Young because the Urban League was against FAP, at a time when the bill needed help. On April 16, FAP had passed the House, but since then it had been stalled in the conservative Senate Finance Committee. On July 1, Moynihan sent a memo to the President: "I fear the chances are now less than even that Family Assistance will be passed this year, and if not this year, not this decade." He warned that it was not just conservative Republicans who were the problem: "The Democrats see an opportunity to deny you this epic victory, and at the same time blame you for the defeat." Moynihan thought the bill could be saved, "but only *you* can save it by working on the Republican Senators."[58]

With the off-year elections coming up, Nixon wasn't sure he could get the bill, or that he wanted it. Through the summer he was involved in a ritual Republican President/Democratic Congress fight over the budget. He wanted to stop inflation by balancing the budget; the Democrats wanted to stop inflation by giving him power to impose wage-and-price controls, which he did not want and swore he would not use even if given to him.

So Nixon got behind FAP, as Moynihan urged, but not very enthusiastically. In August, the President suggested a compromise of allowing a year of "field tests" of FAP before it went into full operation. Still the bill languished in the Senate Finance Committee.[59]

On FAP, after his dramatic introduction of the plan, Nixon was nearly motionless. His welfare reform policy was like his civil rights policy, Jell-O. The reason there was no substance was that there was no leadership. In these areas, Nixon shrank from the leadership role he had fought so hard to win.

EVEN AS CONGRESS was trying to thrust wage-and-price-control power onto the President, the Senate was moving to curtail his power to wage war. On June 30, as the last American troops left Cambodia, the Senate passed the Cooper-Church amendment, which for the first time in American history placed restrictions on the warmaking powers of the President as commander in chief. The amendment specified that after July 1 the President, in the absence of congressional approval, could not retain U.S. troops in Cambodia, provide military advisers or hire mercenaries for the Cambodian government, or supply air support for Cambodian forces.

This was but one more instance of congressional determination to reassert the powers of Congress in foreign affairs. Earlier in the Cold War, in the days before Vietnam, Cooper-Church would have been unthinkable. Back in the late forties and the fifties, and in the first years of the sixties, Congress all but begged the President to take complete command of foreign affairs. The Truman Doctrine, the Eisenhower Doctrine, and the Gulf of Tonkin Resolution were only the most obvious examples. But on June 24, 1970, the Senate, following the recommendation of its Foreign Relations Committee, had voted to repeal the Gulf of Tonkin Resolution, and on June 30 to adopt Cooper-Church.

Congressional mistrust of the President was clearly very great; it but reflected a national mistrust. Nixon had been in office for only a year and a half; in no way could the blame be attached to him for the remarkable shift in public and congressional attitudes toward the President.

In 1960, it was all but inconceivable to Americans that their President would lie to them. Ten years later, it was all but taken for granted that the President would lie. In 1960, nearly everyone agreed that in a Cold War crisis the President had to be supported and trusted, and quite right, too, as he was uniquely qualified to make the right decision. In 1970, it was widely felt that in a Cold War crisis the President had to be questioned and restricted, and quite right, too, as his judgment was not to be trusted.

Nixon did not create this situation, just as he did not create the Vietnam War, but he had to live with it, as much as he hated it.

BY LATE JUNE, Tom Huston had his plan ready for combating the Black Panthers, the Weathermen, and other domestic terrorist groups. He recommended budget increases for the various intelligence agencies, which would then carry out a series of operations, including covert mail opening, black-bag jobs, increased electronic surveillance (wiretapping and bugging), and an increase in campus informants.

To Huston's dismay, J. Edgar Hoover opposed the whole plan. He attached a series of footnotes to the document Huston sent to the President. Electronic surveillance: "The FBI does not wish to change its present procedure of selective coverage on major internal security threats as it believes this coverage is adequate at this time." Mail coverage: "The FBI is opposed . . . because it is . . . illegal . . . if done, information would leak out of the Post Office to the press and serious damage would be done to the intelligence community." And so on down the list of techniques.

Huston also recommended a supervisory body to coordinate intelligence operations, with a head appointed by the President to "coordinate . . . in the same manner as Dr. Henry Kissinger . . . coordinates foreign intelligence on behalf of the President." Huston undoubtedly had himself in mind for this role of super–secret policeman. For that reason, among others, Hoover was dead set against it.[60]

On July 14, Huston sent his plan, along with Hoover's objections, to the President. Nixon approved it, but as the whole point of the exercise was to get the intelligence community moving against the terrorists without getting the President legally involved, he told Haldeman to pass the word to Huston that Huston should sign the order himself to put the plan into effect.

The absence of a presidential signature doomed the plan before it ever got started. One army intelligence chief concluded that Nixon "didn't have the guts" to sign it himself, and another intelligence head commented that Nixon's decision not to sign showed "what a hot potato it was."[61]

Huston sent a memo around to the ad hoc committee of intelligence heads, informing them that he would put the plan into operation on August 1. Hoover rushed to Mitchell's office to warn the Attorney General (who knew nothing about the Huston Plan; as was becoming more and more typical in the Nixon White House, he had simply been bypassed). Mitchell went to the President to say that he agreed with Hoover; the plan was much too dangerous, especially with Hoover opposed to it. So on July 28, four days before the Huston Plan was scheduled to go into effect, Nixon withdrew his approval.

It was galling to him to be denied services from the FBI that he knew had been available to his predecessors. Nor did he ever see anything wrong with the Huston Plan. In his memoirs, he wrote that "the crisis of terrorism and violence" of 1970 made the plan "justified and responsible." [62] The demise of the plan was, to Nixon, yet one more example of the way in which he was the victim of a double standard.

When the Huston Plan became public knowledge, some years later, commentators expressed shock and outrage that the chief executive who had sworn to take care that the laws were faithfully executed should give his approval to an illegal plan. Few noticed that almost exactly one month after Nixon withdrew his approval, a graduate student at the University of Wisconsin was killed by a bomb set off in the math building on campus. The bomb was placed by the Weathermen, one of the chief targets of the Huston Plan. Who can say if a wiretap on a Weatherman phone might have saved the student's life?

TO SOME OBSERVERS, it often appeared that Nixon was at war not just with young terrorists, but with the young generally. At a July 30 news conference, he was asked to comment on a report on campus unrest prepared at his request by a committee headed by Vanderbilt University Chancellor Alexander Heard. The report had put some of the blame for the unrest on the war in Vietnam, some of it on Nixon's failure to pay enough attention to student problems.

Nixon, angry, responded, "For university presidents and professors . . . to put the blame . . . on the Government is very short-sighted." He went through a list of actions the government was taking to end the war and improve the environment. "But once all those things are done," he continued, "still the emptiness and the shallowness, the superficiality that many college students find in college curricula will still be there." There was some truth in the observation, but an element of insult also, just as Nixon intended. [63]

Four days later, in Denver, Nixon gave a long, rambling statement on law and order. In the middle of it, he departed from the prepared text to say that over the weekend he had watched John Wayne in a movie entitled *Chisum*. It was an outstanding movie, he said, and "I wondered why it is that the Westerns survive year after year . . . one of the reasons is, perhaps, and this may be a square observation, the good guys come out ahead in the Westerns, the bad guys lose."

After a couple of paragraphs outlining the plot of *Chisum*, he spoke of his "concern that many of our younger people . . . tend to glorify and to make heroes out of those who engage in criminal activities. . . . I noted, for example, the Charles Manson case was front page every day in the papers and the lead in the evening news."

Manson, a hippie cultist, was on trial in California for the slaying of actress Sharon Tate and others.

Nixon went on, "Here is a man who was guilty, directly or indirectly, of eight murders without reason . . . yet who as far as the coverage was concerned, appeared to be rather a glamorous figure to the young people."[64]

There was a storm of protest that Nixon had prejudged the case, and Nixon was forced to issue a retraction. It was embarrassing and it made him angry, especially as it allowed the press to make him into the bad guy. On a memo pointing out that the media had ignored his basic point, the youth cult and the loss of older values, Nixon wrote, "This is because my point hits them where it hurts—That's why they try to divert attention from it by overemphasizing the other point."[65]

Actually, Nixon was doing quite a lot for the young. Most importantly there was his draft-reform program. In addition, that summer he signed into law a bill lowering the voting age from twenty-one to eighteen, even though he thought it unconstitutional (because the Constitution leaves the establishment of voting qualifications to the states). He had long favored lowering the voting age, and the bill he signed was part of an extension for five years of the Voting Rights Act of 1965, which Nixon said was of transcendent importance. He got some praise from black leaders; Roy Wilkins of the NAACP praised him for "safeguarding the Negro's right to vote."[66]

NIXON'S ROUTINE was to begin the day with the News Summary, then meet with Haldeman for an hour or so. Haldeman would take notes on a yellow legal pad; these became the basis for the marching orders he would send out in the form of memorandums later that morning. More often than not, the subject of those memos was the President's image.

"We have raised the point over and over," Haldeman wrote Klein on July 20. "Why can't we get out a column on how remarkable it is that the President even survives in view of the opposition? . . . The Democrats have the press, the network commentators, the Congress and all the media of communications basically on their side. . . . The point is we make points by fighting the press, and we've got to do it."[67]

Nixon conducted his war against the press on many fronts. Agnew took the point position. Ziegler was close behind, followed by Klein. Magruder, Colson, Nofziger, and others conducted guerrilla warfare, while Kissinger carried on negotiations designed to throw the enemy off guard. Nixon himself went around the flank, not confronting the press directly, but reaching out to the voters via television and personal appearances.

Travel had always been a major part of the Nixon style and image; as President, he set precedents for his peripatetic ways. Weekends he was off to Key Biscayne or Camp David; for longer breaks it was San Clemente. Those trips were only the beginning of his travels. Being Nixon, he couldn't just travel for the fun of it, or the relaxation it brought; there had to be a higher purpose, and it was essential that the public be told what that purpose was.

Arriving at El Toro Marine Air Base in early July for a brief vacation in San Clemente, Nixon told reporters, "I think that sometimes the Senate would do better to get out throughout the country and see what the country is thinking," just as he was doing. "There is sort of an intellectual incest in Washington which really reduces the level of the dialogue, and you have to go to the country now and then to get a real feeling of what people are thinking."

The senators thought this gratuitous advice rather astonishing, coming from a man who earlier that day had stopped in St. Louis for one hour to speak to fifteen thousand members of the Junior Chamber of Commerce, chatted for a few minutes with a few marine officers at El Toro, and then was last seen driving off with Haldeman on one side of him, Ehrlichman on the other, to the seclusion of San Clemente.

La Casa Pacifica, meanwhile, was being touted by Klein as the "Western White House." On Nixon's directions, Klein told reporters that Nixon was letting the people see government in action on a firsthand basis by setting up his office in California. "Government is not an exclusively Eastern institution," Klein said. "The San Clemente operation gives Westerners a symbolic share in the business of government, pulling West closer to East and unifying the nation." [68] Nixon went so frequently to his oceanfront home not to have fun but because he needed to do his duty.

There was another side to the aides' presentation of the President's travels. They insisted that there was nothing even remotely political about them. When he went to Knoxville, Tennessee, to speak to fifty thousand people gathered for a Billy Graham Crusade, he did it to encourage religion, not to promote himself. Nor was he looking for any political gain from his trip to Cincinnati for the All-Star baseball game, to Fargo, North Dakota, for a speech, to Salt Lake City for the Pioneer Days Rodeo, and so on. [69]

Nixon's image of himself was as unbelievable as were the assertions of his aides to the press. At the end of the summer, he sent Klein a long memorandum on "points . . . our people should be promoting" (Klein had not yet gotten that column written on how remarkable Nixon was). It came to Klein via Larry Higby, a White House aide, and was typically written by Nixon in the third person.

Nixon called his paper "PR POINTS TO BE MADE," and began, "To the extent that the President had *any* public support during the Cambodian venture, this was a devastating indication of the lack of credibility of the national media—especially *Time* and *Newsweek*, the Washington *Post*, the New York *Times*, and the three networks. All of them have opposed RN violently on this issue.

"This is not something new. RN is the first President in this century who came into the Presidency with the opposition of all of these major communication powers. . . . The fact that he now survives this with 55–60% approval by the people indicates not so much something about RN as it does something about the news media.

"The President has taken all this with good grace. He has never . . . called a publisher, commentator, editor, etc., for purposes of criticizing him. . . .

"The President himself has finally reached the conclusion which should be one which should cause the media some concern. He now realizes he does not have to have their support. . . .

"Along these lines also, no one has been written off more frequently than RN. . . . Obviously RN is resilient and seems to do best when the going is roughest.

"RN's effectiveness in using the television medium is remarkable. . . . Instead of trying to win the press, to cater to them, to have backgrounders with them, RN has ignored them and has talked directly to the country by TV whenever possible. He has used the press and not let the press use him. . . . This is a remarkable achievement." [70]

It was ridiculous for Nixon to claim that "all" the media were against him. It was maudlin of him to indulge in such tearful self-pity. It was pathetic for him to claim that he never called a commentator to criticize, when he had his aides doing it daily for him. It was dangerous for him to see himself as the beleaguered hero standing alone against the radio, television, newspaper, and magazine people who were out to destroy the country. And the self-imposed isolation for which he congratulated himself so heartily threatened to be expensive for the Republican Party in the upcoming elections.

CHAPTER SEVENTEEN

THE TENTH CAMPAIGN
September–December 1970

AT THE BEGINNING of the campaign season in 1970, James Reston wrote a piece on the mood of the electorate. He said that despite the passionate political minorities, a majority of the people believed that although the Vietnam War was a mess and a mistake, "after all, it is coming to an end." The majority further believed that the rebellious kids were both wrong and a menace; that more cops and tougher judges and additional laws were needed to stop crime, rather than more antipoverty programs; that "taxes are too damn high"; that the Supreme Court had assumed too much "legislative power"; that the poor were poor because they would not work and had too many kids; that education was in trouble because "they" were teaching everything but what counted, reading and writing; that blacks had rights but forced integration would leave everybody worse off; that a major national problem was "permissive parents"; that private enterprise could do anything better than government; that growth was not only inevitable but good, and that thus big business was good and bigger business was better; that big government was terrible and bigger government was dangerous.[1]

Nixon seldom agreed with Reston, but this time he was in complete accord. "H & E," he scribbled on his News Summary, "Note—even from this quarter!"

And he continued: "We'd better shape up and quit trimming the *wrong* way. It is very late—but we still have time to move away from the line of our well intentioned liberals on our staff. . . . I can't emphasize too strongly my concern that our team has been affected

373

too much by the unreal atmosphere of the D.C. press, social, and intellectual set."

Nixon offered an explanation of how such attitudes had developed: "Cambodia and Kent State led to an overreaction by our own people to prove that we were pro student, blacks, left."

Then he gave his orders: "H—E—Finch. We must get turned around on this before it is too late—Emphasize—anti-Crime—anti-Demonstrations—anti-Drug—anti-Obscenity—Get in touch with the mood of the country which is fed up with the Liberals. This stuff is dynamite politically." [2]

A week later, the News Summary reported plans for massive peace demonstrations on October 31 in twenty cities, to be organized by a coalition of student groups and the National Alliance of Postal and Federal Employees. Nixon wrote in the margin, "H— Priority! *Encourage* them." [3]

Informed that the Democrats were planning to make a campaign issue of Agnew's "words and views," Nixon commented, "Great! For us." [4]

When *Scanlan's Monthly* published a memorandum linking Agnew to a purported plan to cancel the 1972 election and repeal the Bill of Rights, Nixon furiously demanded a lawsuit, an FBI investigation, an apology, and so forth. John Dean, a thirty-one-year-old lawyer who had left the Justice Department in July of 1970 to join the White House staff as Counsel to the President, informed Nixon that there was no basis for a lawsuit, and advised the President to ignore the bogus memo.

Instead, Nixon wrote at the bottom of Dean's recommendation, "H—Have I.R.S. conduct a field investigation [on *Scanlan's*] on the tax front." [5]

The intellectual underpinning for Nixon's "political dynamite" was a book by two Democrats, Richard Scammon and Ben Wattenberg, entitled *The Real Majority*. Immensely popular with the politicians, the book described the "average American voter" as a forty-seven-year-old housewife from the outskirts of Dayton, Ohio.

Scammon and Wattenberg wrote their formulation for the benefit of the Democrats; they wanted their party to get on the right side of the so-called "Social Issue." But it was Nixon who seized it most avidly, Nixon who decided at the outset of the campaign that "we should set out to capture the vote of the . . . Dayton housewife." [6]

Not that Nixon and his friends needed guides to the electorate. In mid-September a reporter for *Women's Wear Daily* interviewed John Mitchell. The Attorney General told her that street violence and campus unrest were the biggest political issues of the campaign, and that "this country is going so far right you are not even going to recognize it."

Mitchell praised Nixon as "the best informed President there's ever been," and contrasted him with "these stupid kids" in the colleges. "And the professors are just as bad if not worse. They don't know anything. Nor do these stupid bastards who are ruining our educational institutions."

Nixon circled those lines on his News Summary and wrote in the margin, "John—*Good job*—Don't back off."[7]

Despite Mitchell's verbal fusillade, Nixon was not declaring war on college students and their professors. Going into the 1970 campaign, he said his overriding goal was the election of a Republican Congress that he could work with effectively, but his private comments made it clear he was more concerned with positioning himself for his 1972 re-election bid. In that context, he was keenly aware that in 1972 youngsters between eighteen and twenty-one would be voting for the first time in a presidential election. Through the '70 campaign, he covered his News Summaries with remarks such as "H—vitally important for '72 to set up a program to enlist our teens" and "We must do better with the youth vote in '72."[8]

Nixon knew that by no means were all America's youngsters, not even the college youngsters, radical protesters or knee-jerk Nixon haters. He consistently tried to make the point that the chic, elite students demonstrating for the environment or against the war were a tiny minority, to show that there were millions of college students who supported him.

He did so, brilliantly, on September 16, in his first major speech of the campaign. He flew to Manhattan, Kansas, to deliver the Alf Landon Lecture at Kansas State University. Because this was the first time in years that an American President had appeared on a large university campus, the networks carried his noon (Central time) speech live.

(Nixon was furious afterward when commentators indicated that he had picked Kansas State because it was a friendly, lily-white Midwestern cow college, with the implication that he would not dare speak anywhere else. Nixon pointed out, with some heat and absolute accuracy, that the media didn't make such charges in 1968 when Bobby Kennedy chose Kansas State as the site for the kickoff of his campaign.)[9]

Nevertheless, the setting *was* ideal for Nixon, and he played it like a master. He spoke in the field house, a ramshackle old basketball facility with terrible acoustics, before fifteen thousand students and faculty. The crowd greeted him with a mighty roar, followed by wave after wave of more cheering as he proudly displayed his purple tie (the school's color was purple and its slogan was "Purple Power"). He praised Kansas—another roar. Then the basketball team. Then the football team (which was attempting a comeback after a decade and more of dreary records; Nixon said that he too knew about losing and coming back). More roars.

Then he got into his theme, which was law and order. "The time has come for us to recognize that violence and terror have no place in a free society," he said. "Whatever the purported cause of the perpetrators may be. . . . No cause justifies violence."

Up in the far reaches of the balcony, to Nixon's possible delight and certain benefit, a small group of forty or so began calling out, "What about Kent State?" "Stop the war," and so forth.

Nixon plunged on. "Those who bomb universities, ambush policemen . . . share in common not only a contempt for human life, but also the contempt for those elemental decencies on which a free society rests."

From the faculty section, a couple (the author and his wife) joined the hecklers, calling out what the reporters later wrote were obscenities—"Napalm," "Free fire zones," "Body count."

Nixon began listing the characteristics of civilized society, such as self-restraint and mutual respect, and dubbed in another example: "The willingness to listen to someone else and not shout him down." The audience, which had been squirming in embarrassment at the hecklers, gave him a long standing ovation.

Encouraged, Nixon's voice rose as he denounced "those who would choose violence or intimidation to get what they wanted. Their existence is not new. What is new is their numbers, and the extent of the passive acquiescence, or even fawning approval, that in some fashionable circles has become the mark of being 'with it.' "

Another roar of approval, another standing ovation, this one punctuated by shaking fists at the hecklers.

"What corrodes a society even more deeply than violence itself is the acceptance of violence, the condoning of terror . . ." he continued, without providing any examples of who did such accepting and condoning. He pointed out that "the destructive activists of our universities and colleges are a small minority, but their voices have been allowed to drown out . . ."

He paused. He looked around. The hecklers had been silenced; a whisper could have been heard in the field house.

Nixon went on: "My text at this point reads: 'The voices of the small minority have been allowed to drown out the responsible majority.' " He looked up from his text and said, "That may be true in some places, but not at Kansas State!"

The roar this time was truly deafening; the standing ovation, truly tumultuous; he had clearly struck the most responsive possible chord.[10]

Nixon and his staff were naturally delighted. They sent out tens of thousands of copies of the speech; they came up with the money to rerun it on prime-time television; they encouraged Republican congressmen and Cabinet members to use various cheer lines from it in their own speeches. Nixon sent a fulsome letter to President James McCain ("The example set by the overwhelming majority at Kansas State will give heart and hope to those elsewhere who are equally determined to be allowed to listen"), and a copy to the press for publication.[11]

Nixon stayed with the theme of the Kansas State speech through the campaign. On September 20, he sent a form letter to some nine hundred university administrators, with copies to thousands of Republican politicians, enclosing an article written by Professor Sidney Hook of New York University. Hook, an ardent defender of academic freedom in the past, argued that college administrators had yielded too easily to the demands of campus dissidents and had thus ushered in an era of intellectual intimidation, thereby corrupting the purposes of the university. In his covering letter, Nixon said he viewed with concern the growing tendency of administrators to blame the government's foreign and domestic policies for campus disruption.[12]

A week later, Nixon sent out another article, this one by J. Edgar Hoover. In his covering letter, Nixon said that Hoover had exposed "the tactics used by extremists in their effort to promote their schemes on campus." He called Hoover's piece "a cogent and enlightening analysis of the strategy these extremists employ as they attempt to trick college students into support of lawlessness, disruption and violence."[13]

Nixon did not point out (nor did Hoover) that in at least some cases the extremists who were tricking the students into violent acts were working for the FBI as *agents provocateurs*. Small wonder Hoover could describe their tactics so accurately.[14]

ONE OF NIXON's lines at Kansas State had built on his loser, comeback theme: "There are those who protest that if the verdict of democracy goes against them, democracy itself is at fault—who say that if they don't get their own way the answer is to burn a bus or bomb a building. Yet we can maintain a free society only if we recognize that in a free society no one can win all the time."[15]

A good point, well made, but despite the implication that it was valid for all times and places, Nixon did not mean to apply it across the board. The day before he spoke those lines in Kansas, he ordered the CIA to prevent the winner of a free and democratic election in Chile from taking power.

The election, held on September 4, had given Salvador Allende, the Socialist candidate in a three-man contest, a 36.3 percent plurality. This had come as a shock to the Nixon Administration, which had supported Allende's opponents with some millions of dollars. Beginning with Harry Truman's financial support for the Christian Democrats in Italy in 1948, American Presidents had contributed to conservative political party campaigns on a regular basis (Kennedy and Johnson had both given money to Allende's foes in earlier elections), so Nixon was doing nothing new. What was new this time was that Allende was a winner, albeit with only slightly more than one-third of the total vote. American Ambassador Edward Korry reported: "Chile voted calmly to have a Marxist-Leninist state, the first nation in the world to make this choice freely and knowingly." [16]

Kissinger told Nixon that Allende's victory "was a challenge to our national interest." [17]

Nixon was furious ("beside himself," according to Kissinger) and feared being blamed for having "lost Chile." But all was not lost. According to Chile's constitution, when no candidate received a majority, the Congress would choose between the two top candidates fifty days after the election. Chile's Congress had always picked the front-runner, but perhaps the representatives might be persuaded to do otherwise to save the country from the radical Allende.

Much was made, at this time, by Bill Buckley and other conservative commentators, and by the Nixon Administration, of the fact that Allende had only 36 percent of the vote. He could not, on that basis, according to his American critics, legitimately rule. This was a strange argument to be made by people who were ruling with 43 percent of the vote.

In any event, Nixon wanted something done. His resolve was strengthened on September 14, when he met with Don Kendall, CEO of Pepsi-Cola and an old friend and major financial backer. Kendall's houseguest at this time was his newly hired vice-president of Pepsi, Agustín Edwards, a newspaper publisher and businessman in Chile who had fled the country right after the election and taken the job with Pepsi. Edwards warned Kendall of the consequences of an Allende government; at his meeting with Nixon, Kendall passed on those warnings. [18]

The next afternoon, Nixon met with Helms, Kissinger, and Mitchell. Nixon told Helms that he wanted the CIA to make a major effort to prevent Allende's accession to power, including bribes to congressmen in Chile, even if there was only one chance in ten of success. If Helms needed $10 million, Nixon would approve it. More, if necessary. The President wanted aid programs to Chile cut. He wanted Helms to "make the [Chilean] economy scream." He ordered Helms to undertake the project as a "full-time job," using the "best men we have," but keeping the embassy in the dark.[19]

Then Nixon flew off to Kansas, to scold those who would not accept the verdict of democratic elections.

WHEN NIXON returned to Washington, he found another problem with another Latin-American Marxist awaiting him. This one concerned Fidel Castro, and if Nixon's feelings about Allende were strong, they were neither so deeply rooted in the past nor as intense as his feelings toward Castro.

Nixon had first met Castro in 1959, in Washington, and immediately recognized that the man was a Communist and no friend of the United States. In 1960, Nixon had done all that he could do to persuade Eisenhower to use the CIA and/or the armed forces to overthrow Castro, but without success. It was galling for Nixon to then find himself under attack from Jack Kennedy for being soft on Castro; Nixon believed that he lost the 1960 election because of the Cuban issue. In 1962, it was once again Castro whom Nixon blamed for the loss of an election.

In the aftermath of the Bay of Pigs (1961) and the Cuban missile crisis (1962), Nixon had been intensely critical of Kennedy. If Nixon had won the 1964 Republican nomination, his public statements in the spring of that year indicated that he intended to make the Kennedy-Khrushchev agreement (an American pledge not to invade Cuba; a Russian pledge not to use Cuba as a site for offensive nuclear missiles) a major issue in the campaign. Goldwater got the nomination, and by 1968 Khrushchev was gone and forgotten, while Castro and the Russians were in a period of strained relations (because Castro was flirting with China), so Nixon did not make Cuba an issue in his presidential campaign.

But he had not put Castro out of his mind. One of his first acts in office in 1969 was to direct the CIA to intensify its covert operations against Cuba—pinprick raids, sabotage, recruiting, organizing resistance cells, and the like.[20] His friend Rebozo, well known for his passionate hatred of Castro, was a source of ideas on new covert activities, and of approval for Nixon's tough approach. Rebozo also provided a strong link for Nixon with the fiercely anti-Communist Cuban community in Miami.

Castro, well informed about Nixon and his friends, and well aware of the stepped-up CIA covert action campaign against his country, began to fear another invasion attempt. As China could be of little or no help to him if Nixon launched an attack, Castro began to express his fears to the Russians. For their part, the Russians were eager to demonstrate to Castro that they were the ones who could protect him from the Americans. And, as a part of their ongoing program to establish a worldwide presence for the Soviet fleet, they wanted to expand their naval basing facilities in Cuba.

On August 4, 1970, the Soviet chargé d'affaires in Washington called on Kissinger. After expressing satisfaction over improved relations, and the hope that there could soon be a summit meeting, he unexpectedly raised the question of reaffirming the Kennedy-Khrushchev understanding of 1962 with regard to Cuba.

Kissinger sent a long memo to the President. He noted that there was "an implicit understanding" between Kennedy and Khrushchev but "the agreement was never explicitly completed." In fact, Kennedy's "pledge" carried neither legal nor moral weight (he had no right to bind his successors to a nonintervention policy in Cuba, and the Senate never would have ratified such a treaty), and anyway the pledge was conditioned on an on-site inspection to make certain the missiles had been removed from Cuba, which condition was not met, because Castro would not allow it.

In short, there never was a deal. Kissinger did not make that clear in his memo; indeed he said the opposite, that although the Kennedy-Khrushchev deal was "never formally buttoned down," both sides had acted as if it were a formal treaty.[21]

Nixon could have responded to the Soviet request to "reaffirm" the agreement with a thunderous no, in the process denouncing the Soviets for their perfidy in failing to live up to their end of the bargain. Nixon had, after all, been Kennedy's leading critic back in 1962, when he charged that by promising not to invade, Kennedy had allowed the Communists to extend the Iron Curtain to the New World. Instead, for reasons he never explained, Nixon decided to "reaffirm" in writing the agreement, thus giving it virtually the force of a treaty, as it then had the approval of two Administrations and both political parties.

The deed was done in secret, in private exchanges of various notes and letters, beginning on August 7 and concluding on November 13. Nixon and Kissinger acted without consulting the State Department (which maintained that there was no agreement, because of the unmet on-site inspection condition) or the Defense

Department. The upshot was that the United States got a greater degree of Soviet commitment against basing offensive missiles in Cuba while the Soviets finally got an American commitment to the 1962 "pledge" not to invade Cuba.[22]

Whether this was a good deal or not is certainly debatable (Nixon, back in '62, had made a strong case for the negative). But as Raymond Garthoff comments, in what is a scathing indictment of the Nixon-Kissinger penchant for secret manipulation and ma- neuvers, "a procedure that excludes key members of an administra- tion from participation in and even knowledge of policymaking is not conducive to political discipline or practical effectiveness in policy implementation."[23]

For Nixon, Castro and campaigns went together as naturally as children and candy. In 1970, his chance to link the two began on September 16. A U-2 flight that day brought back photographs that showed construction activity in the harbor at Cienfuegos. Kissinger examined the photographs, then on September 18 burst into Halde- man's office with a demand to see the President immediately. When Haldeman hesitated, Kissinger excitedly showed him the photographs and explained that they showed soccer fields.

Haldeman wondered if Kissinger wanted to break in on a meet- ing in the Oval Office to announce that the Cubans were building soccer fields.

"Those soccer fields could mean war, Bob," Kissinger de- clared.

"Why?" Haldeman asked.

"Cubans play *baseball*. Russians play *soccer*."[24]

In his memoirs, Kissinger explained that "as an old soccer fan I knew Cubans played no soccer."[25]

Actually Kissinger was badly wrong; soccer was as popular in Cuba as in every Spanish-speaking country. But he was right about the construction activity at Cienfuegos; the Russians were improv- ing and expanding their base support facility there. A submarine tender was being installed. Kissinger told Nixon this was ominous, that it would mark "a quantum leap in the strategic capability of the Soviet Union against the United States."[26]

Nixon replied with a handwritten note. His orders were: "I want a report on a crash basis on: (1) What CIA can do to support *any* kind of action which will irritate Castro; (2) What actions we can take which we have not yet taken to boycott nations dealing with Castro; (3) Most important, what actions we can take, covert or overt, to put missiles in Turkey—or a sub base in the Black Sea —anything which will give us some trading stock."[27]

Kissinger replied that the CIA was doing all it was capable of doing already, and that points 2 and 3 would take too long and be counterproductive. Nixon then told Kissinger to play down the crisis. He said he did not want some "clown Senator" demanding a Cuban blockade in the middle of the campaign. At an NSC meeting on September 23, Nixon's caution was reinforced by Rogers. The Secretary of State wanted no announcements, no hysteria, no quickening of the public pulse before the November elections.[28]

Nixon agreed to keep quiet at least until he returned from a European trip, scheduled for September 27 to October 5. A major purpose of the trip was to publicize Nixon the world statesman inaugurating the new era of negotiations (one month before Election Day), and it would hardly do to have a second Cuban missile crisis going on while the President exchanged ceremonial toasts in Europe.

The story broke anyway. On the morning of September 25, C. L. Sulzberger in his *New York Times* column warned of a possible Soviet submarine base in Cuba. At the regular Pentagon morning briefing, a spokesman filled in the details. Cienfuegos was the lead on the evening news broadcasts and headline story in the next day's papers. A Russian delegate to the SALT talks complained to American negotiator Gerard Smith, "When one bloody little submarine goes to Cuba everyone in America goes crazy." [29]

Still Nixon kept silent in public, rejecting one obvious option, to play up the crisis as Kennedy had done almost exactly eight years earlier, on the eve of the '62 elections. The President did have Kissinger give a background briefing to the press; Kissinger reminded the reporters of the Kennedy-Khrushchev agreement (without noting that the Administration was in the process of "reaffirming" it and putting it into writing). He also told Ambassador Dobrynin, in a private meeting, that the Administration viewed the construction activity in Cienfuegos with the "utmost gravity," and made some vague threats. The next day, the President and his entourage, including Kissinger and Rogers, departed for Europe, on schedule. The trip dominated the news, and was an eloquent denial of the existence of a crisis.[30]

Nixon returned from the tour on October 5. The next morning, Dobrynin handed Kissinger a note again reaffirming the 1962 understanding and assuring the Americans that the Soviets were doing nothing in Cuba to contradict that understanding. When Nixon read the note, he said he was "tremendously relieved." To nail down the settlement, Nixon gave Dobrynin a note: "The U.S. government understands that the U.S.S.R. will not establish . . . any facility in Cuba that can be employed to support or repair Soviet naval ships capable of carrying offensive weapons . . . armed with nuclear-capable, surface-to-surface missiles."

"After some face-saving delays," Nixon wrote in his memoirs, "the Soviets abandoned Cienfuegos."[31] That was not true. The base remained, and Soviet submarines used it frequently in subsequent years. But no Soviet Y-class submarines, carrying ballistic missiles, did so.[32] Nixon had avoided a crisis while preventing the Soviets from lessening the restraints imposed by the 1962 understanding.

More often than not, Nixon would stop at nothing to win an election, but in this instance he acted with intelligent and admirable restraint, despite an obvious temptation to exploit the crisis for votes. He made his point and achieved his objective with quiet diplomacy. Unlike Kennedy, he did not challenge or confront the Soviets, but rather negotiated with them, thereby keeping the SALT talks, and improved relations with the Russians in general, on track.

AVOIDING CONFRONTATION with the Russians was a never-ending, and usually thankless, task. Still Nixon stayed with it, even when provoked, and even though he trusted the Russians not one bit. In the second installment of Khrushchev's memoirs, just published, Khrushchev said that Stalin had a great respect for Eisenhower's "decency, generosity and chivalry." Nixon circled those words and wrote in the margin, "K—note—*not* a compliment!"[33]

Nixon had no illusions about getting concessions from the Kremlin by being Mr. Nice Guy. Nor did he have any thought that American and Soviet interests ran parallel in regions torn by conflict—the Middle East, for example. The two sides were engaged in an ongoing struggle in the region. The Russians backed the so-called radical Arabs (Egypt, Syria, Iraq) while the Americans supported Israel and the so-called moderate Arabs (Jordan, Saudi Arabia). The United States and the Soviet Union had contradictory aims: to avoid at all costs a superpower confrontation in the Middle East, and to extend their own power and influence. The Russians had been doing rather better on the second aim in the aftermath of Israel's victory in the 1967 war, as Nasser had welcomed them into Egypt. Thousands of Soviet troops had moved in. They operated SAM batteries for the Egyptians, flew combat missions in their MIGs over the Sinai, trained Egyptians in the use of Soviet-built tanks, and generally threatened to become the major military power in the region.

The Soviets were also providing Syria with tanks and other weapons, and encouraging the Palestinians, displaced by the Israeli occupation of Gaza, the Sinai, and the West Bank, to carry out acts of terrorism and engage in guerrilla warfare against Israel.

Nixon's response to these developments was to authorize the

sale of more military weaponry to Israel, and to reaffirm his support for King Hussein in Jordan.

In mid-September, Palestinian forces attacked Hussein's troops, while Syrian tanks drove to the border. On the afternoon of September 17, in an interview in Chicago, Nixon told reporters that the United States would have to intervene if Syrian or Iraqi troops moved against Hussein. The following day, the Kremlin assured Nixon that the Soviets had no intention of intervening in Jordan, urged him not to do so, and suggested that he use his influence to discourage others, meaning Israel.

That same day, Nixon met with Mrs. Golda Meir, the Israeli Prime Minister. She wanted more arms, more ammunition, more support. She told Nixon that Israel's problems were not caused by the Arabs, but by Soviet guns. Nixon pledged his support, but urged her to stay out of Jordan and allow Hussein to solve the problem himself.[34]

Within a week, Hussein did, despite some cross-border raids by Syrian tanks. Hussein retained control and the fighting died down. Nixon had successfully maneuvered his way through another crisis.

Nixon was never one to hide his light under a bushel, especially not in a campaign year. Cienfuegos was an exception. In the Jordanian situation, on September 22, Nixon told Haldeman to get the word out. He was quite specific about what he wanted. In passing the President's wishes on to Klein in a memo, Haldeman was equally specific: "The Jordanian . . . crisis provides another outstanding example of how the President reacts to crises and deals with them. It gives us another chance to make the point very validly regarding his coolness in crisis, the way he works long hours, is on the phone at all hours of the night, gathers all the facts, but does not leap to conclusions or move fast. He doesn't make quickie decisions and he thereby avoids the big mistakes."[35]

IN EUROPE, early that fall, Nixon had more frustration than success. He was scheduled to visit Rome, Belgrade, and Madrid, and to observe from the flight deck of the carrier *Saratoga* a widely advertised demonstration of American firepower by the U.S. Sixth Fleet. His idea was to demonstrate on NATO's southern flank the preponderance of American strength at a time when the Soviet Navy was beginning to enlarge its presence in the Mediterranean.

The day before the scheduled demonstration, however, Nasser died. Thus Nixon lost the headlines, and had to cancel the naval maneuvers. He had been extremely bellicose, even for Nixon, in his remarks in the days preceding Nasser's death, but he toned them down afterward. Speaking to the five thousand crewmen on the *Saratoga*, Nixon said the Sixth Fleet provided "stability" in the region and called for a "generation of peace, and more."[36]

The following day, Nixon went to Belgrade, where Tito lectured him on the shortcomings of the superpowers (the United States should get out of Vietnam, the Soviets should get out of Eastern Europe, both sides should stop meddling in the Middle East). Nixon took all this with as much good grace as he could muster.

There was a four-second episode with Tito that had a funny, warm, and revealing quality about it. As Nixon and Tito finished their review of the honor guard, a line of spectators on the upper balcony of the airport broke into applause.

Nixon's reaction was instinctive (recall that Election Day back in the States was only a month away). He looked up, smiled broadly, and flashed his arms skyward to make the V-for-Victory sign. Then, again reflexively, almost as if it were a Republican candidate for the Senate at his side, Nixon patted Tito on the tummy, motioned toward the crowd, and urged him to respond. Rather shyly, the seventy-eight-year-old Tito, who did not ordinarily go in for that sort of thing, or need it politically, waved his hat at the throng.[37]

Nixon concluded his European trip with visits to Britain and Ireland. In England, Queen Elizabeth II greeted the Nixons at Chequers, the Prime Minister's country estate near Aylesbury; the photograph of the event was on the front pages of the American newspapers the next day. In Ireland, the photo opportunities were also rich and varied, as both Dick and Pat searched out their ancestors' burial sites.

The transparency of Nixon's campaign techniques in Europe aside, the trip did manage to make the point that the attitude of most Europeans toward Nixon was respectful. As a broad generalization, the Europeans certainly thought more of Nixon than they did of his immediate predecessors. And they were right to do so, as Nixon knew more about Europe and its problems than either Kennedy or Johnson, and he was far more innovative, less stuck with the clichés of the Cold War, than they had been.

The big news in Europe, relatively unnoticed by most Americans in the late sixties and the beginning of the seventies because of American preoccupation with Southeast Asia, was the development of détente. The major figure associated with this move was West German Chancellor Willy Brandt, who called it *Ostpolitik* (Eastern Policy). It climaxed in August 1970, when Brandt and Prime Minister Aleksei Kosygin signed a nonaggression pact in

Moscow that included an implicit recognition of existing boundaries in Central and Eastern Europe. Brandt followed this up in
December with a treaty with Poland, and the opening of negotiations with the East Germans.

Of those Americans paying attention to these events, some of
the best informed and most involved were deeply disturbed. On
the very day Brandt signed the Polish treaty, recognizing the postwar Oder-Neisse border, three elder statesmen from the Truman
Administration called on Nixon. They were John McCloy, Lucius
Clay, and Dean Acheson, and they were upset. They complained
about the neglect of American nuclear capabilities vis-à-vis the
Soviets, about the apparent indifference toward Europe, about the
stripping of America's NATO forces to support the war in Vietnam,
and so forth.

But mainly these original Cold Warriors came to complain
about Brandt. McCloy said he regretted the fact that West Germany, which had largely been governed by men from the Rhine-
land in the postwar era (meaning western Germans, and
specifically Konrad Adenauer, who had always opposed détente
unless and until Germany was reunified, as opposed to Brandt's
formulation of one country, two states), was now being run by
"people from eastern Germany, who are seeking to experiment
with relations with the Soviet Union."

General Clay supported McCloy vigorously. He spoke of his
distrust of Willy Brandt and his friends. Acheson added to the
chorus of criticism of *Ostpolitik*.[38]

Nixon too had been in at the beginning of the creation of America's postwar European policy, albeit in a minor role as compared
to McCloy, Clay, and Acheson. But being younger gave him more
flexibility in his thoughts; he was not so blindly wedded to a keep-
the-powder-dry and don't-change-anything policy with regard to
NATO and Europe as the three wise men. Détente in Europe was
a powerful force whose time was surely coming; the great strength
of *Ostpolitik* was that it involved the real interests of people (there
was scarcely a family in either of the two Germanys not affected by
the political division of the country) as opposed to the often fickle
political interests of leaders.[39]

Nixon was smart enough to see that détente in Europe could
not be stopped, and to see that it offered opportunities as well as
dangers. When he learned that Brandt had been greeted on a visit
to East Germany by "shouting and cheering East Germans, thousands of them," Nixon commented, "K—Good. This will scare hell
out of the Soviets. They have their problems and may now come to
us to pull them out."[40]

A new era was coming, just as Nixon said, and he was doing his best to stay on top of events, ready to create opportunities. He was as tough and cynical in his attitudes toward the Soviets as Acheson himself, but as realistic as Brandt. Unlike Kennedy, he did not force the Russians to back down in public in Cuba, but he was just as firm. And as well as any of his predecessors, he saw that the Soviets had major problems that could be exploited, for example, in Eastern Europe or with China.

THE SOVIETS might also prove to be helpful, most of all in Vietnam, where Nixon badly needed help. The war dragged on, and although he had reduced the American ground strength by almost half, Nixon was no closer to peace, with or without honor, than he had been two years earlier. Casualties were down, protests were less frequent, but dissatisfaction was rising.

One manifestation of the discontent came on September 1, when thirty-nine senators voted for the McGovern-Hatfield "amendment to end the war" by requiring Nixon to bring all the troops home by the end of 1971. Although the amendment failed, thirty-nine yeas out of the ninety-four senators voting showed how shaky Nixon's support was. Another indication of how badly he was slipping came the same day, when fourteen senators, including the majority and minority leaders, sent Nixon a letter urging him to propose a comprehensive standstill cease-fire for South Vietnam.[41]

Nixon, after almost two years in command, was more rather than less vulnerable, both at home—because of war weariness—and in Southeast Asia. His troop withdrawal program had bought him time, at the expense of firepower, even while he expanded the war into Cambodia. Despite brave words about ARVN's ability to "hack it," the discouraging truth was otherwise. The NVA and Vietcong had been hurt by the Cambodian incursion, but by no means mortally wounded. They were recovering their strength rapidly, even as the American strength dwindled.

What Nixon wanted, needed, and tried desperately to obtain was a face-saving formula that would allow him to pull America out of the war with Thieu still in power for a decent interval afterward —until, say, January of 1977. It made him furious that Hanoi would not give it to him.

In September of 1970, following yet another completely unsuccessful secret meeting with the North Vietnamese in Paris, Kissinger reported to the President that there would be no settlement so long as Thieu remained in power. Nixon wrote on the report, "This is probably the breaking point unless we can find a formula."[42] (Kissinger and Nixon loved those secret meetings, even though the

North Vietnamese said nothing there that they were not saying in the public peace talks in Paris.)

While in Europe in early October, Kissinger told Safire that "the big question is, does the other side want to settle for anything less than total victory?" That was an incredible statement; after continuous war since 1945, after driving the French out and forcing the Americans to begin withdrawing, after surviving Johnson's and Nixon's bombing campaigns, could there possibly have been any doubt about the answer?

"Their demands are absurd," Kissinger told Safire. "They want us to withdraw and on the way out to overthrow the Saigon Government. If [sic] we ever decide to withdraw, it'll be up to them to overthrow the Saigon Government—not us." [43]

To repeat what has been said before in this work, for all Nixon's twists and turns, for all Kissinger's manipulations and maneuverings, there never was anything to negotiate about in Vietnam, any more than there was anything to negotiate about in Germany in World War II. The issue was simple and straightforward: who will rule in Saigon?

Nixon's extraordinary commitment to a government that had no base, no popular support, and had never done him any favors was self-imposed. To abandon Thieu would be to lose the war, and like Johnson, Nixon swore, "I won't be the first President to lose a war." To abandon Thieu would mean peace, but without honor, or so Nixon convinced himself. It would mean an armistice that would not last, rather than peace for generations, or so Nixon insisted.

Nixon's dilemma was that he could not be re-elected if he did not continue the withdrawals, but he could not keep Thieu in power, or maintain peace, or save honor, if he did.

His one hope was Vietnamization. But for Vietnamization to have any hope of working, Nixon desperately needed much more time, to improve ARVN, to wear down the NVA, to persuade the Soviets and possibly the Chinese that if they would sell out their Communist ally, the United States could make it worth their while.

To buy time, Nixon needed more Republican supporters in the Senate. To that end, Nixon told the networks he would deliver a major prime-time speech on October 7 in order to make a new offer to the enemy.

Safire, who helped write the speech, protested to Kissinger that it "was not Nixon's way." The proposal was "grandstanding," or "showboating." It was being "presented primarily for its political impact in the States, buying Nixon some more time, with little chance of its acceptance by the North Vietnamese, but with every chance of its embrace by editorial writers who wanted a dramatic offer which they thought would break the logjam in negotiations."

Kissinger told Safire, in effect, to stick to his typewriter and leave the thinking to others.[44]

Nixon gave his speech a big buildup. On October 6, he held an impromptu news conference, where he announced that his speech the next day "will be the most comprehensive statement ever made on this subject since the beginning of this very difficult war." Anticipating criticism, he insisted that what he was going to offer was not "a propaganda gimmick."[45]

On the evening of October 7, speaking from the Oval Office on nationwide television and radio, the President offered a cease-fire in place, to be observed by international inspection teams, and to include an end to bombing and acts of terror. He also proposed an Indochina peace conference, to include Laos and Cambodia, and an immediate unconditional release of all prisoners of war held by both sides. But he insisted that the ultimate political solution must "reflect the existing relationship of political forces in South Vietnam," code words for the continuation in power of the Thieu government until free elections could be held (the Communist party was illegal in South Vietnam; the Thieu government would supervise the elections).

If Hanoi would accept this fair and generous offer, Nixon concluded, "we might then be on the threshold of a generation of peace."[46]

The initial response from within the United States was highly pleasing to Nixon. Even such antiwar stalwarts as McGovern, Hatfield, and Fulbright lent their names to a resolution of approval. *The Wall Street Journal*, usually skeptical of Nixon's plans, hailed the approach as "so appealing and so sane that only the most unreasonable critics could object to it."[47]

But then Nixon ruined the good effect with another impromptu news conference the following afternoon. What had been new in the offer was Nixon's call for a cease-fire in place, with the implication that American withdrawals would continue and that the NVA could remain. This represented a major concession by Nixon. When he took office, the American position had been Johnson's 1966 Manila formula: the United States would withdraw six months after the NVA pulled out of South Vietnam. On May 14, 1969, Nixon had offered a simultaneous pullout one year after a peace agreement was signed. Now he appeared to be offering an American withdrawal without requiring the NVA to do the same.

At his press conference, however, Nixon said that was not what he meant. He told reporters, "We offered a total withdrawal of all of our forces, something we have never offered before, if we had mutual withdrawal on the other side." He insisted this was a fair proposal and that he would not be "discouraged by rejections."

A reporter asked if he thought his peace offer would help Republican candidates in the upcoming elections.

"I don't think that it has that kind of effect," Nixon responded. "It was not, of course, intended for that."

The reporters looked dubious. Nixon went on: "If we had intended it for that, I am politically enough astute to have done it just about 4 days before the election. Then we would not have known what the result would have been and people would have voted their hopes rather than the realities." [48]

Aside from that nice dig at Johnson, Nixon had just confessed to the truth of Safire's charge, and confirmed reporters' suspicions that it was all politics. The response from Hanoi was not yet in; Nixon obviously knew it was going to be negative; what he wanted was credit for having made it, not the reality of peace.

The response was, in fact, scathing. At the Paris peace talks, Hanoi denounced the proposal as "a maneuver to deceive world opinion" and held fast to demands for unconditional American withdrawal and the overthrow of the "puppet" Thieu government. Moscow followed this up by calling Nixon's proposals "a great fraud" designed to "legalize and perpetuate the intervention of the United States in Indochina." [49]

On October 12, Nixon made another announcement that delighted Republican candidates. He said that thanks to the success of Vietnamization, he could speed up the withdrawal of forty thousand troops and have them home by Christmas. That one was transparent even by Nixon's standards. They had been scheduled to come out in early January anyway. Still, the announcement made a nice headline, and allowed Nixon to claim that together with the October 7 offer, "these two moves went so far toward removing the obstacles to a settlement that they effectively silenced the domestic antiwar movement by placing the burden squarely on the North Vietnamese to begin serious negotiations." [50]

IN THE EARLY STAGES of the 1970 campaign, Nixon had let Agnew play the role he, Nixon, had played in 1954 and 1958, spokesman for the Republican Party. For himself, Nixon said he would play Eisenhower and stay above the battle.

But Nixon could never stay out of a campaign, especially one that featured such "issues" as law and order, drugs, and pornography. Besides, the polls indicated that Agnew's efforts, though energetic, were ineffective, and the Republicans were not going to take control of the Senate (the House was hopeless for the GOP). A combination of nearly 6 percent unemployment and 6 percent inflation had led pundits to coin a new word, "stagflation," and was leading voters to favor the Democrats. Meanwhile the Democrats blunted the crime issue in early October by passing a series of Nixon Administration anticrime measures, with emotional cries in the Senate Chamber against "crime in the streets" and "terrorist bombings."

The Senate Finance Committee, at the same time, dealt Nixon a blow. His FAP had passed the House, but the Senate committee rejected the welfare reform plan, 14–1. And, of course, the Senate as a whole was coming dangerously close to legislating the United States out of Vietnam. So Nixon had good reasons, beyond his personal inclination, to get into the 1970 campaign.

He did so first of all with money. He had money left over from the 1968 campaign, and since then Stans and others had been picking up more; Bebe Rebozo, for example, had managed to get $100,000 in cash from Howard Hughes. Nixon was holding on to most of the funds for his own re-election campaign, but he was not unwilling to spend if he thought it would do some good.

Nixon's October 17 News Summary reported that in Wyoming the polls showed Republican John Wold running a close race with incumbent Democratic Senator Gale McGee. Although McGee had been one of Nixon's strongest supporters on Vietnam, for example, voting against Cooper-Church and McGovern-Hatfield, Nixon wanted him defeated.

The President wrote on the News Summary, "H—put in 200 g immediately." Then he had a thought and added, "Also Tricia." [51] This was but one of a number of cases in which Nixon more or less casually told Haldeman to put in a few hundred thousand here, a similar amount there. And he always kept a close eye on where his daughters were campaigning. (David was at Officer Candidate School in Newport, Rhode Island, and thus unable to campaign.)

The Democrats, for their part, were trying to cut into the Republican financial advantage. In early October, they passed a bill imposing a ceiling of $5 million on the amount that any political party could spend on radio and television in one campaign. In 1968, Nixon had spent more than $12 million, Humphrey about $7 million. The Democrats thought Nixon would not dare veto the bill, but he did, and they failed by four votes to override. Larry O'Brien, John Kennedy's former campaign manager who had recently assumed the duties of chairman of the Democratic National Committee, led the barrage of criticism. Nixon replied that he could not be a party to curtailing freedom of speech. [52]

(O'Brien was becoming a thorn in Nixon's side. As partisan as the President, O'Brien was getting his barbs into the papers on a regular basis. One favorite was to label the high unemployment and high inflation figures "Nixonomics.")

Ordinarily in American politics, the party in power defends its record. In 1970, however, Nixon went over to the offensive. Murray Chotiner, who had taught him way back in the 1940s that people were more likely to vote against something than for something, was now dispensing political advice from the East Wing of the White House, and that advice was to come down hard on the Social Issue. Even more central to the 1970 campaign was Chuck Colson, whose idea of a good campaign was to use innuendo to question the opponent's patriotism, intelligence, morality, manhood, anything you could get away with. Colson was so extreme that even Chotiner protested that he went too far.[53]

But not too far for Nixon, who swung into action in mid-October in one of the most ambitious political efforts of any President ever in an off-year election. Building on his Kansas State experience, the President all but encouraged hecklers, whom he then scornfully put down. In Burlington, Vermont, confronted by a small group chanting "Peace now," Nixon got a roar of approval from the audience when he pointed at the group and declared, "One vote is worth a hundred obscene slogans."

Nixon denounced those who he said mocked American institutions: "You hear them night after night on television, people shouting obscenities about America and what we stand for."

This was vintage Nixon, well laid on.

"You hear those who shout against the speakers and shout them down, who will not listen," he went on. "And then you hear those who engage in violence. You hear those, and see them, who, without reason, kill policemen and injure them, and the rest. And you wonder: Is that the voice of America?

"I say to you it is not," he shouted, his arms raised, his fists clenched. A more appropriate question might have been, Was that the voice of the Democratic Party? But Nixon managed to get across the point—whom to vote for—without mentioning the Democrats by name. The answer to those un-American voices, he said, was to vote Republican. "Let the majority of Americans speak up," the President urged, "speak up on November 3, speak up with your votes. That is the way to answer."

In Vermont, where Nixon flew to campaign for Senator Winston Prouty, one or two boys in an otherwise friendly airport crowd threw several small stones toward the President. All missed, but Colson scooped them up to show reporters. "Those rocks will mean 10,000 votes for Prouty," he said.

At other stops that day—in New Jersey, in Pennsylvania, and in Green Bay, Wisconsin—demonstrators shouted antiwar slogans, allowing Nixon to go into his own anti-obscenity speech (Robert Semple wrote that neither he nor the other reporters covering the trip heard any obscenities).

Another line Nixon used at every stop was: "As I stand before you today, I can say confidently the war in Vietnam is coming to an end, and we are going to win a just peace in Vietnam."[54]

Two days later, on a swing through Ohio, North Dakota, and Missouri, Nixon said that "a rising tide of terrorism and crime" could only be stemmed by Republican votes. Once again there were enough protesters around, carrying signs and shouting slogans, for him to object frequently and vehemently to "four-letter obscenities." In Grand Forks, North Dakota, he added a new line: "The four-letter word that is the most powerful of any in the world is 'vote.' "

In Columbus, Ohio, Nixon gestured at several hundred young people on the edge of the crowd who were shouting at him and declared, "We're not going to stand for that!"

"It is time for the great silent majority of Americans to stand up and be counted," he shouted back. "And I'll tell you how you can be counted—on November 3 in the quiet of the polling booth. If a candidate has condoned violence, lawlessness and permissiveness, then you know what to do."[55]

On October 24 Nixon seized a heaven-sent opportunity. President Johnson had appointed a National Commission on Obscenity and Pornography before he left office; the commission gave its report to Nixon in early October. Its conclusion was that pornography did not contribute to crime, delinquency, or sexual deviation. Nixon, in commenting, let out all the stops. He said, "I have evaluated that report and categorically reject its morally bankrupt conclusions and major recommendations. . . . Pornography can corrupt a society and a civilization . . . poison the wellsprings of American and Western culture. . . . Smut should not be simply contained . . . it should be outlawed in every State in the Union. . . . Pornography is to freedom of expression what anarchy is to liberty."[56]

That week, Nixon went south, where the enemy was busing. He was pushing himself at a terrific pace (he spoke in twenty-one states in the course of the last two weeks of the campaign). In Asheville, North Carolina, speaking at an outdoor rally in the rain, his voice cracking as he fought against hoarseness, he railed against those "who would bus children clear across town to achieve an arbitrary racial balance."[57]

Campaigning in Michigan, George Romney, Secretary of HUD, was boasting that the Nixon Administration was requiring integration in suburbs that accepted federal money for building projects. When Nixon read about it in his News Summary, his order was short and swift: "Stop him." [58]

Indeed, at no time in the campaign did Nixon make a point of his accomplishments. Except for his claim that peace was coming, sometime soon, and with honor, Nixon did not advertise what he had done as President. Instead, he ran against pot, permissiveness, protest, pornography, and dwindling patriotism. These were the issues, he obviously believed, that would help voters forget stagflation and vote Republican.

On October 29, Nixon went to San Jose, California, where he was appearing with Governor Reagan and Senator George Murphy. As the entourage approached the civic auditorium, about a thousand demonstrators greeted the politicians with screams, howls, and roaring chants, many obscene. Safire, who was there, called it "an orgy of generalized hate." [59]

Inside the auditorium, some five thousand supporters gave the men an enthusiastic welcome. Reagan spoke, then Murphy, finally Nixon.

He warmed up the crowd with some pleasant remarks about Southern California. He added that no matter what he had said or heard about football teams in Texas, Ohio, Indiana (Notre Dame), or Nebraska, "when I am in California, Stanford is number one." He got in plugs for Reagan, Murphy, and other Republican candidates. Then he launched into his standard 1970-style stump speech. He stressed his search for something more than just "peace now"; he wanted peace for a generation and more. "They are fighting in Vietnam so that those young men that are outside shouting their obscene slogans won't have to fight in Vietnam or anyplace else any time in the future." [60]

As he spoke, the demonstrators outside began beating on the walls of the building. When the rally ended, and Nixon walked outside to his car for a motorcade, the demonstrators on the other side of the police barricades began chanting "One, two, three, four —we don't want your fucking war." Nixon, in his own words, "could not resist showing them how little respect I had for their juvenile and mindless ranting." [61]

He climbed atop his car and thrust out his arms in the V-for-Victory sign; one reporter nearby overheard him growl, "That's what they hate to see." The gesture had the effect Nixon anticipated; a chorus of jeers and boos began.

Then the unpredictable happened: a shower of eggs began to fly, followed by rocks, some of them the size of baseballs. As Nixon hurried inside his armored car, the rocks began to bounce off. The car pulled out, followed by the staff bus, which now became the target. "Just like Caracas," Rose Woods cried out as she hit the deck.[62]

By the time the motorcade got to the airport and Nixon climbed aboard *Air Force One*, Safire had a statement ready. "The stoning at San Jose is an example of the viciousness of the lawless elements in our society," it began. "The time has come to take the gloves off and speak to this kind of behavior in a forthright way. Freedom of speech and freedom of assembly cannot exist when people who peacefully attend rallies are attacked with flying rocks."[63]

Nixon, according to Jeb Magruder, "persuaded himself that this was the last straw, that national outrage over an attack on the President would trigger a Republican landslide. The next morning Haldeman called my office with orders that we stress the San Jose incident in every possible way over the weekend."[64]

It seemed to be a natural, especially as the same day there were three bombings of police facilities in New York City, and a bomb scare at City Hall. But to the consternation of the Nixon people, the media rather downplayed San Jose. To their fury, Larry O'Brien was widely quoted as saying that Nixon was playing to people's fears.[65]

To Nixon's supporters, the relative indifference to what should have been a major story—after all, no one could think of a precedent; Nixon was the only President who ever had rocks thrown at him—proved what they had believed all along, that the press was prejudiced against their man. But to uninvolved observers, Nixon had no one to blame but himself. He had stressed his antidemonstrator position too often, had goaded too many hecklers, staged too many events, to elicit much sympathy. He had expressed himself as shocked and outraged when those emotions were an inappropriate overreaction, so that when the event really was shocking and outrageous, as San Jose most certainly was, he couldn't get the sympathy he deserved.

Nixon, of course, stayed with it. In Phoenix, Arizona, on October 31, he went after the "haters" in San Jose. The time had come, Nixon said, when "appeasement" of the "thugs and hoodlums" in American society must end.

"When a man cannot bring his child to a political rally for fear the person in the next seat will start yelling some filthy obscenity, when a man can't bring his wife to a rally . . . then I say appeasement has gone too far, and it's time to draw the line."

For himself, he said that "as long as I am President, no band of violent thugs is going to keep me from going out and speaking with the American people wherever they want to hear me and wherever I want to go. This is a free country, and I fully intend to share that freedom with my fellow Americans. This President is not going to be cooped up in the White House."

The speech was a big hit with the audience, and got a big spread in the papers (but so did Larry O'Brien's criticism, that Nixon had "hit a new low in campaign activities").[66]

Nixon liked the speech so much he spent the money to put it on national television on Monday night, November 2. This was later judged to be a big mistake. The sound track was poor, and Nixon's frenetic campaign style contrasted badly with Senator Muskie, who gave a calm, low-keyed, reasoned appeal for the Democrats.

That those last-minute shows changed many votes is doubtful at best; what is certain is that Nixon's law-and-order, sock-it-to-the-demonstrators, -to-the-Democrats, and -to-the-defenders-of-pornography campaign was a failure. The Republicans were losers in the national election. In the vote for the House of Representatives, the Democrats got 28.9 million votes (compared to 33.2 million in 1968), while the Republicans got 24.4 million (compared to 32.1 million in 1968). The Democrats had increased their margin from 1.1 million to 4.5 million, an ominous sign for 1972. The Democratic majority in the House increased by nine seats. In the Senate, despite Nixon's all-out effort, the Republicans gained but two seats, and the Democrats easily retained control. The Democrats also picked up eleven governorships (but in the two largest states, the Republicans were triumphant, with Reagan in California and Rockefeller in New York).

There was another piece of bad news that same day. In Chile, the CIA's efforts to persuade the Congress to turn back Dr. Allende had failed, and on November 3 he was sworn in as President.

The day after the election, Nixon met reporters in San Clemente to make a statement. He put the best face he could on the outcome: "When the party in power loses little or anything in an off year election, it has to be called a victory. Consequently, I would call this a victory by that standard."[67] That was thin gruel, considering that the Republicans started off as the minority party in both houses of Congress, so they were not exactly the party in power. Certainly they had failed to win over that Dayton housewife.

Nixon, nevertheless, despite what he called the "mixed success" of the Social Issue, claimed that "the basic strategy was right," and in his postmortem for Haldeman put the blame on "lackluster Republican . . . candidates."[68] Nixon also said it was "imperative" to get "politics out of the White House" by setting up a special presidential re-election committee.[69] He wanted Agnew to "de-escalate the rhetoric without de-escalating the substance of his message." He also wanted to make more use of Chuck Colson. In his view, Colson should be his "political point-man" because Colson was "positive, persuasive, smart, and aggressively partisan" with an "instinct for the political jugular." When he complained to Colson, he "felt confident that something would be done."[70]

Nixon's postmortem had been self-serving and defensive; Ray Price's critique was devastating. Price said the "bile" became counterproductive, that the President's negative approach hurt far more than it helped, that Nixon badly needed something "elevating" to talk about, "something that would speak to the hopes, to the goodness, to the elemental decency, of the American people." It was essential to "return to lowered voices, reason, bring-us-together" themes, Price said, "and identify ourselves not so much with angers and frustrations as with the desperate popular yearning for an end to bombast. This is the one really strong card that Muskie has to play; and the trick for us is to play it first, and better: to persuade the people that we can calm the passions."

Without saying so, in his conclusion Price totally rejected Nixon's 1970 approach, and urged him to change direction 180 degrees. "Looking to the future," Price wrote, "my recommendations would all center on developing and maintaining a climate of confidence in the Presidency as an institution, and in RN as President. We can go seriously astray if we think too much of 'issues,' and not enough about the Presidency itself—its aura, its mystique, the almost religious way in which Americans respond to it."[71]

Without saying so, Nixon decided Price was exactly right. That was the great lesson of the 1970 campaign.

THE ECONOMY had hurt the Republicans in the election; in the aftermath, Nixon began to work on improving it. As he prepared for 1971, he let it be known that he was willing to allow a large budget deficit in an attempt to pull the economy out of the doldrums, and hinted that he would like to see the Fed ease up and allow a more rapid expansion of the money supply.[72]

In these circumstances, Nixon was angry when his enemies in the Senate, led by William Proxmire (D., Wis.), managed to halt all spending for the development of a supersonic transport airplane (SST). In a statement, Nixon called the Senate action "a devastating mistake," especially at a time of substantial unemployment in the aerospace industry brought on by cutbacks in Defense Department spending. Nixon charged that stopping work on the two half-completed prototypes was "like stopping the construction of a house when it was time to put in the doors." He argued that "the SST is an airplane that will be built and flown. The issue is simply which nation will build them." He warned that if the Senate action was not reversed, the United States would be "relegated to second place in an area of technological capability vital to our economy and of profound importance in the future." [73]

One great friend of the SST was a former governor of Texas, John Connally. A Humphrey supporter in 1968, and longtime protégé of Lyndon Johnson, Connally had retired to a private law practice in Texas. In early 1970 Nixon had put him on the President's Advisory Council on Executive Organization, headed by Roy Ash. At a March Cabinet meeting in which Ash had bored Nixon to tears with a listless presentation of the council's recommendations, Connally had stolen the show with an impromptu and enthusiastic summary of the report. Nixon had been impressed.

Treasury Secretary David Kennedy, meanwhile, had become the obvious scapegoat for the 1970 election losses. He had insisted on a tight money policy and on waiting for a recession before undertaking any expansionary policies. In mid-December, Nixon announced that he was accepting Kennedy's resignation and appointing John Connally as his replacement. This gave a welcome "bipartisan" feel to economic policy, gave SST a boost, gave Nixon a member of the Cabinet in whom he had real confidence, gave Nixon an intimate who had some of the John F. Kennedy aura about him (Connally had been with JFK and was himself seriously wounded in Dallas on November 22, 1963), and gave Nixon a strong start for his re-election campaign (one Washington commentator stated, "To my dirty mind, this appointment means only one thing: the start of 'Democrats for Nixon in 1972' ").[74]

As a former governor, Connally also added support to Nixon's revenue-sharing plan, a plan Nixon intended to push hard in 1971. On November 30, Moynihan, who was leaving to return to Harvard, sent Nixon a memo of "final thoughts." He said revenue sharing was an idea whose time had come, but unfortunately there had been "a systematic blackout on the fact" that Nixon was the first to propose such a program. "E & H," Nixon wrote on the memo, "I want a report next week on what program we have initiated to fight this. I agree completely [with Moynihan]—an utter PR failure on our part." [75] A week or so later he announced that one of the defeated Republican senatorial candidates for whom he had campaigned hard, George Bush of Texas, would assume the post of U.S. ambassador to the United Nations. In another shake-up, he fired Interior Secretary Hickel, who had been critical of the President on the Cambodian incursion and on environmental policies.

On December 1, Nixon leaked to the press his intention to resubmit his revenue-sharing plan to Congress in January, and to expand it from $5 billion to as much as $20 billion.[76]

In the postelection period, Nixon also sent a couple of messages to Hanoi. On November 21, on Nixon's orders, a joint task force carried by helicopter landed twenty miles from Hanoi, at the Son Tay prison compound, in order to find and rescue American POWs. Unfortunately, the prisoners had recently been moved elsewhere. Still, the raid was a victory, in that the task force landed successfully, defended itself, inflicted casualties, carried out its search, and departed without losing a man. This was a sharp reminder to the NVA that the American military in Indochina still had some punch to it, that it retained sufficient firepower and mobility to carry out a raid almost within gunshot of the enemy capital.

As a cover for the raid, Nixon also ordered a two-day bombing offensive, with some of the bombers ranging more than two hundred miles north of the DMZ. These were massive operations, aimed at supply bases, warehouses, truck concentrations, and air defense emplacements, and they too reminded Hanoi of the latent American power in Indochina.

At the end-of-the-year news conference, his first in four months, Nixon made an explicit threat to Hanoi. Helen Thomas, noting that the recent air strikes had raised speculation that the policy of not bombing North Vietnam might be changing, asked, "What is our policy?"

Nixon responded, "At a time when we are withdrawing from South Vietnam, it is vitally important that the President . . . take the action that is necessary to protect our remaining forces. . . . If the North Vietnamese, by their infiltration, threaten our remaining forces . . . then I will order the bombing of military sites in North Vietnam, the passes that lead from North Vietnam into South Vietnam, the military complexes, the military supply lines. That will be the reaction that I shall take."

The doves were expressing fears that even as Nixon was withdrawing from Vietnam, he was extending American support to Lon Nol in Cambodia. He was asked, "How do you plan to keep your quarter billion dollar aid program for Cambodia from escalating into a guarantee of the survival of the Cambodian Government?"

Nixon did not answer directly; instead he defended the aid, saying it was "probably the best investment in foreign assistance that the United States has made in my political lifetime." He explained that the Cambodians "are tying down 40,000 trained North Vietnamese regulars. If those North Vietnamese weren't in Cambodia, they'd be over [in Vietnam] killing Americans. . . . The dollars we send to Cambodia saves American lives and enables us to bring Americans home."

To its supporters, the Cambodian program was a brilliant application of the Nixon Doctrine; to its detractors, it was another American commitment to defend an ally it could not possibly defend.

At the United Nations, the General Assembly was coming ever closer to seating the Chinese Communists. Asked at the news conference whether there had been an American policy change, Nixon replied, "No. . . . We have no plans to change our policy with regard to the admission of Red China to the United Nations at this time." But he went on to say that he would continue "the initiative that I have begun, an initiative of relaxing trade restrictions and travel restrictions and attempting to open channels of communication with Communist China. . . . Looking long toward the future we must have some communication and eventually relations with Communist China." [77]

Although the President did not inform the reporters, he was trying to hurry the process along. In late October, President Yahya Khan of Pakistan had paid a state visit to the United States. Nixon used the occasion to tell Yahya that he had decided to attempt to normalize relations with China, and to ask for his help. Yahya said he would try.

The following day, October 26, President Ceauşescu of Romania was Nixon's guest at a state dinner at the White House. In his toast, Nixon referred to Communist China as "the People's Republic of China," the first time any American President had used the official name, and was thus a significant diplomatic signal.[78]

A month later, in a memo to Kissinger, Nixon noted that the time was soon coming when the United States would not be able to muster the votes to block Red China's admission to the U.N. "The question we really need an answer to is how we can develop a position in which we can keep our commitments to Taiwan and yet will not be rolled by those who favor admission of Red China." [79]

On December 9, one day before the news conference in which he discussed his attempt to open channels of communication with China, Nixon heard via President Yahya that Chou En-lai had said that an American representative would be welcome in Peking for a discussion of the question of Taiwan. A week after the news conference, Mao Tse-tung told an old friend, radical American writer Edgar Snow, that he would welcome Nixon to China, whether he came as tourist or as President.[80]

As for the Soviet Union, and the SALT talks, and ongoing talks on the status of Berlin, Nixon pointed out at his news conference that "we are not going to find easy agreement, because we are two great powers that are going to continue to be competitive for our life-time. But I believe that we must continue on the path of nego-tiation."[81]

Nixon the mad bomber, ready, nay eager, to bludgeon Hanoi into accepting his peace proposals. Nixon the defender of Cambodia, ready to tie down the NVA with American guns and Cambodian troops. Nixon the seeker of a new relationship with China. Nixon the advocate of negotiation with the Soviets, hoping to find the key to peace in Vietnam in Peking and Moscow. These were his goals for 1971. To some they may have appeared contradictory, but to Nixon they seemed all of a piece.

CHAPTER EIGHTEEN

NIXON AT MIDTERM:
AN ASSESSMENT
1969–1970

AT THE END of 1970 two highly placed Irish-Americans passed judgment on Nixon's first two years in the White House. One was critical, the other friendly.

The critic, Larry O'Brien, was predictably partisan and polemical: "The Nixon Administration lacks initiative, it lacks imagination, it lacks compassion for human needs. It has established no rapport, no communication, with the people. It has given the nation no clear vision of a direction for the future."[1]

The friend, Pat Moynihan, in his farewell address to the President and the Cabinet on December 21, was surprisingly sympathetic for someone whose program, FAP, had fallen short of success. Moynihan said, "The President, on taking office, moved swiftly to endorse the profoundly important, but fundamentally unfulfilled, commitments, especially to the poor and oppressed, which the nation had made in the 1960's. . . .

"This has been a company of honorable and able men, led by a President of singular courage and compassion. . . .

"To have seen him late into the night and through the night into the next morning, struggling with the most awful complexities . . . doing so because he cared, trying to comprehend what is right, and trying to make other men see it, above all caring, working, hoping for this country that he has made great already and which he will make greater still."[2]

(Eighteen years later, Moynihan—by then Democratic senator from New York—remained a great admirer of Nixon. Commenting on his two years as a member of the Nixon Cabinet, Moynihan said that he still regarded Nixon as good and honest and decent, and that what impressed him most about Nixon's leadership was what did not happen. The country was in danger of falling into something approaching anarchy, or civil war, when Nixon took office, according to Moynihan; Nixon, provoked though he was, stayed calm and managed to ride out the crisis. Asked if he were not guilty of exaggerating the threat to the Republic, Moynihan insisted that if anything he was understating it.)[3]

Julie was almost as enthusiastic as Moynihan. In a late-December 1970 interview, Helen Thomas asked Julie how she thought her father was doing. "I really think he is doing a good job," Julie replied, "a great job. I really do and I just wish he could get legislation passed. It's so frustrating. It's terrible because how can he have a record to present to the people unless he can get his legislation passed?"

"Many people say your father is not warm and does not relate to people," Thomas said. "What do you think?"

"I don't agree," Julie replied. "He's just a very human, warm person. . . . He is such a sensitive person."

On Vietnam, Julie said it "really isn't too much of an issue anymore. . . . Just look at the casualty figures. . . . The war's coming to an end."

When Nixon saw the interview in his News Summary, he scribbled, "Julie, Great job!" and "H—you can see what a waste it was not to have this on TV."[4]

On January 4, 1971, Nixon provided his own assessment of his performance in a televised interview with four representatives from the networks. John Chancellor of NBC opened by asking Nixon how he had changed in the past two years. The President said he had learned patience, that while he was not disappointed in the record he had established, he had "great hopes for the next two years, because I think I know better how to do the job."

Eric Sevareid of CBS asked what was his greatest accomplishment and his primary failure. Nixon said his accomplishment was reducing the casualties and the troop commitment in Vietnam, and bringing in sight an end to the war. His greatest disappointment was "the failure to get welfare reform."

Nancy Dickerson wanted to know what the President planned to do to restore people's confidence in the economy. Nixon said that unemployment was high (about 5.5 percent) because of the transition from a wartime to a peacetime economy. He expressed his sympathy for the unemployed, and promised "an expansionary budget, a budget in deficit," to spur the economy.

Going to specifics, Sevareid reminded Nixon that Republicans had delighted in blaming Democrats for the loss of China. He wanted to know "Who lost Chile?"

"That was the decision of the people of Chile," Nixon replied, "and we accepted that decision. . . . For the United States to have intervened—intervened in a free election and to have turned it around, I think, would have had repercussions all over Latin America that would have been far worse than what has happened in Chile." If his statement about the sanctity of elections was brazen beyond belief, given what he had tried to do to Allende, his assessment of what the repercussions would have been had he succeeded was on the mark.

Howard K. Smith of ABC wanted to know about Vietnam. Nixon repeated his threat—if Hanoi showed signs of stockpiling supplies on the Ho Chi Minh Trail, he would not hesitate to bomb North Vietnam. But Smith wanted to go beyond that point; he wondered what would happen in 1972, when "our role is virtually eliminated, we are passive, we have few troops there, then the North Vietnamese attack and begin to come into control of the country. What is our policy then? Do we stand aside?"

Nixon was reassuring. By 1972, he said, the North Vietnamese might well launch an attack, "but I am convinced that at that time . . . the South Vietnamese, based on the watershed that occurred when they jelled and became a fighting, confident unit after the Cambodian intervention, I am convinced that they will be able to hold their own and defend themselves in 1972."

Other issues came up. Nixon reaffirmed his support for the SALT talks and expressed an interest in a summit with the Soviets. Twice he proclaimed his undying support for FAP and revenue sharing ("There is nothing I feel more strongly about"). He reiterated his willingness to unbalance the budget to help the economy.

(After the show ended, Smith expressed surprise at this. Nixon told him, "I am now a Keynesian in economics." The startled Smith said that was "a little like a Christian crusader saying, 'All things considered, I think Mohammed was right.'")

Dickerson reminded Nixon of his 1968 campaign and its call for "the lift of a driving dream." She wondered what had happened to that goal.

"Before we can really get the lift of a driving dream," Nixon replied, "we have to get rid of some of the nightmares we inherited. One of the nightmares is war without end. We are ending that war. . . .

"If we can get this country thinking not of how to fight a war, but how to win a peace—if we can get this country thinking of clean air, clean water, open spaces, of a welfare reform program that will provide a floor under the income of every family with children in America, a new form—a new approach to government, reform of education, reform of health—if those things begin to happen, people can think of these positive things, and then we will have the lift of a driving dream. But it takes some time to get rid of the nightmares. You can't be having a driving dream when you are in the midst of a nightmare."[5]

Pat Buchanan was aghast at Nixon's performance. In a memo full of fulminations, he accused Nixon of "adopting a liberal Democratic domestic program." He feared Nixon's apparent advocacy of national health insurance, of FAP, of an unbalanced budget would drive the Old Guard out of the party. Except for the speech writers, Buchanan said Nixon had no conservatives in his Administration; he thought "Ehrlichman's shop is a small group of pragmatic technicians who can teach it either way." Conservatives felt Nixon took them for granted, that they were "the niggers of the Nixon Administration." They got the rhetoric, while the liberals got the programs. There was some danger that the conservatives would go into revolt and back Reagan for the 1972 nomination.

Buchanan filled seven single-spaced pages with his complaints. Nixon, who had always been a man of the center in domestic affairs, for exactly the reason Buchanan cited (the conservatives had no place else to go, and the right wing alone was never strong enough to elect a Republican President), answered him with two short scribbled comments.

"What do they think of Cambodia, etc.?" was one, and the other was "You overlook RN's consistent hard line on foreign policy."[6]

Actually, Nixon was hardly as liberal as Buchanan's superficial analysis supposed, nor was he as tough on foreign policy as he claimed. In each area, in his first two years in office, Nixon had shown more appearance than he had delivered reality.

To take up domestic policy first. The measurement of greatness in a President is his ability to bring about permanent change that affects everyone's life: Theodore Roosevelt and conservation; Woodrow Wilson and the Federal Reserve System; Franklin Roosevelt and Social Security; Harry Truman and the integration of the armed forces; Dwight Eisenhower and the Interstate Highway System; Lyndon Johnson and the Civil Rights Act of 1964 and the Voting Rights Act of 1965 and Medicare.

Nixon's bid for greatness in this area was FAP. It truly could have been historic, just as Moynihan said, and it was to Nixon's credit that he adopted it and got it through the House. But the measure of how badly he wanted it came in 1970, when, again just as Moynihan said, it either got through the Senate or it was dead, and Nixon did practically nothing to get it through. When Nixon had announced the plan, Harlow had warned him that if he wanted to get it passed, he had better prepare the ground; if all he wanted was publicity, he could spring it as a surprise. Nixon chose to spring it as a surprise.

This was but one example of the way in which Nixon wasted a priceless asset: Bryce Harlow's congressional connections. Nixon complained that he couldn't get his bills passed, but he ignored the advice of the man who could have got them passed for him. For that reason, in December 1970, Harlow left the Administration to resume his job as lobbyist for Procter & Gamble.

Harlow's resignation left a gap that could never be filled, and it exacerbated one of Nixon's major shortcomings as President, his inability (or refusal) to work effectively with Congress. Teddy Roosevelt once said that he wished he could be President and Congress at the same time, a feeling other residents of the White House have shared. But of course it can't be, and most Presidents find ways to flatter, cajole, bribe, pressure, persuade, influence, motivate, stir, and otherwise move Congress to be cooperative. Nixon knew all the techniques, and he went through all the motions—letters of thanks to congressmen, campaigning in their districts, arm-twisting, the use of patronage, roads and other projects for the folks back home, private and small group meetings, the whole endless array—but he did it without enthusiasm, without conviction, without joy, and thus without success.

After two years in command, he had shown himself to be the least effective President in dealing with Congress since Herbert Hoover, which was why his list of legislative accomplishments was so short and unimpressive.

Nixon's rejoinder was that he was stuck with a Democratic Congress. True enough and fair enough, but the complaint ignored the willingness of the Democrats to be led in certain areas, above all in civil rights. This put Nixon in a bind, because his friends among the Democrats came from the South. Consequently, he passed on his best opportunity for greatness.

That opportunity was civil rights. Lyndon Johnson had prepared the ground and planted the seeds; it was Nixon's task to cultivate and fertilize and water the plant to make civil rights grow and prosper. Nixon could have been the President who did more for civil rights than any other, even including Johnson. He had a chance to create a genuine integrated school system within a racist-free society. Not much of a chance, to be sure, but a better one than any of his predecessors or successors had. A forthright denunciation of segregation, an enthusiastic advocacy of integration, a wholehearted acceptance of the necessity for equality of opportunity in the marketplace, a compelling commitment to decency in race relations in all areas—who can say what effect such presidential leadership in the first two years after Lyndon Johnson might have had? Who can say what might have been accomplished by a Republican President and a Democratic Congress at this critical juncture?

But it was not to be, because in this area Richard Nixon did not want to be the nation's leader. He only wished the problem would go away.

Nixon's defenders pointed out, rightly, that there was more desegregation during his Administration than under any other President. But, obviously, this was because the laws had been put on the books in 1964 and 1965 and the courts had ruled that they had to be enforced. Nixon had to be hauled kicking and screaming into desegregation on a meaningful scale, and he did what he did not because it was right but because he had no choice.

His comments on the News Summaries and in his talks with Ehrlichman, Finch, and Mitchell about civil rights, with his constant refrain of "do what the law requires and not one thing more," displayed a meanness of spirit that is embarrassing.

So whatever the appearance, it was silly of Buchanan to accuse Nixon of liberalism.

What of Nixon's boast, that he always took the hard line in foreign affairs? Here, certainly, the appearance was one of toughness and resolution. He issued ultimatums and threats and on occasion acted the mad bomber.

But the reality was far more complex, and mixed. Nixon let the November 1, 1969, deadline he had set come and go without action; he issued his Duck Hook ultimatum and did not follow through. He was back and forth on Cambodia, ordering the troops in with a tremendous fanfare, then almost immediately backing down by limiting the time and area of operation. In Vietnam, his policy of retreat without surrender, without negotiations, without concessions, was making the remaining American force in South Vietnam ever more vulnerable without satisfying the doves or ending the war. He could not win the war; he would not end the war; he refused to lose the war. He had put himself in the impossible position of fighting a war while retreating from it without attempting to win it but refusing to admit that his country had lost it.

As with civil rights, Vietnam was a problem that he wished would simply go away. Here, too, the man who had fought so hard to become the nation's leader did not want to lead.

Where he did want to lead was in the area of the world balance of power. Here his credentials, his enthusiasm, his abilities, his thoughts, and his wishes all came together. He envisioned a wholly new world order, with himself as its architect. He picked Kissinger as his adviser to help him sharpen and realize this vision. And, in his first two years in office, he had prepared the ground for just such an accomplishment, with his careful cultivation of Moscow, Peking, and the NATO allies.

Here the difficulty was that, with the exception of the well-publicized European trips and the SALT talks, he had preferred to operate secretly. This made for serious structural weaknesses.

The great Presidents in foreign affairs are those who bring about great, permanent changes: Wilson committing the United States to a decisive intervention in European affairs; Roosevelt committing the United States to a world role even in peacetime, through the United Nations; Truman committing the United States to the doctrine of containment and the Marshall Plan; Eisenhower committing the United States to the role of active honest broker in the Middle East. In each case, the President imposed a great change on American foreign policy through careful planning and detailed preparation. There were long debates, in and out of Congress, which produced a constituency for the new policy.

Not so with Nixon. He liked surprises, and back channels, and secrecy. As he showed with Cienfuegos, he excluded the State Department from the most delicate deliberations, where he needed the expertise most. So although he was moving toward détente with the Russians and a new relationship with China, he was not building support for such major policy changes. The same was true of Kissinger's secret negotiations with the North Vietnamese. Nixon was not working with the bureaucracy, but against it; he was not bringing the public along with him, but thrusting changes on it. These techniques made it questionable that Nixon's changes, if and when they came, would have the staying power of Wilson's, Roosevelt's, Truman's, and Eisenhower's.

Flawed techniques aside, Nixon's thinking about foreign policy was profound, pragmatic, and full of promise. He was more realistic about America's role in the world, and its relationship to the Communist powers, than any of his Cold War predecessors. In just two years, he had shown a potential to become a great world statesman. Whether he could realize the promise or not depended in large part on how soon, and at what cost, he managed to extricate the United States from Vietnam.

ANY COMPARISON between Nixon and his predecessors brings to mind this obvious point: that whereas Truman, Eisenhower, Kennedy, and Johnson all enjoyed life in the White House, each in his own way, Nixon, except for the ceremonial functions, seemed to take little pleasure in being President. To the contrary, he seemed to be always angry, to the point that those writing about him were driven to the thesaurus to find yet another synonym for anger. Herb Klein wrote in his memoirs, "I do not recall a moment when I saw him completely lost in happiness." [7]

His anger showed most clearly in that most revealing of sources, his scribbles on the daily News Summary. It was in these jottings that Nixon came as close as he ever did to spontaneity; his comments reveal his instinctive and impulsive response to men and events of all kinds. It is not altogether accurate to describe Nixon's emotions on the basis of his News Summary remarks, because in preparing the summaries, Mort Allin and Pat Buchanan were playing to their audience; very conservative themselves, they goaded the President with their gibes at the liberals. But out of balance though they were, Nixon devoured those summaries; he paid them the ultimate compliment of reading them through, all forty or fifty pages, every day. They were one place where he could express his real feelings.

The first thing that stands out in his commentary is his word choice; his verbs are almost always violent. "Get someone to hit him," Nixon would write about one reporter, or "fire him," or "cut him," or "freeze him," or "knock this down," or "fight him," or "dump him," or "don't back off."

In response, the staff kept a Freeze List and an Opponents List of reporters and politicians and entertainers who were never to be allowed to attend a White House function. It went further. In August 1971, John Dean sent a memo to the staff that addressed the question of "how we can maximize the fact of our incumbency in dealing with persons known to be active in their opposition to our Administration. Stated a bit more bluntly—how can we use the available federal machinery to screw our political enemies?" [8] This Enemies List mentality grew out of the sentiments Nixon expressed so directly on his News Summaries.

Another feature of the News Summary comments is the way in which he sounded like the Queen of Hearts in *Alice in Wonderland* ("Off with his head!"). He was constantly "firing" this man or that, or sometimes entire agencies, or half of a bureaucracy. These "firings" were seldom if ever carried out, partly because he almost never had the authority, partly because in the cases where he did, Haldeman would hold up the order for a few days while the boss cooled down.

Nixon was aware of what Haldeman was doing. On a June 16, 1969, memo to his chief of staff, Nixon wrote, "I have an uneasy feeling that many of the items that I send out for action are disregarded when any staff member just reaches a conclusion that it is unreasonable or unattainable." Nor was he unaware that Haldeman was doing him a favor: "I respect this kind of judgment." He did insist that he be told when no action was taken.[9]

Sometimes he found occasion to praise someone on his staff, or in his Cabinet, but not often; even rarer was praise for a Republican in Congress. He did have some favorite columnists and reporters, whose work would bring a "Good job!" or similar comment from him. Victor Lasky was one of his favorites, along with Earl Mazo and Bill Buckley. Others included John Roche, Vermont Royster, Joseph Harsch (sometimes), and C. L. Sulzberger.

Nixon's News Summary comments were revealing in another way: he governed through notes. Nixon found it difficult to give orders face-to-face, to fire someone, to express his wishes and give his commands in a meeting. Even at age fifty-seven, in short, he remained a shy Quaker boy, one who hated personal confrontation and avoided it if at all possible.

So he gave his orders via his News Summaries. "H—do this," he would write, or "E—do that." Some of Kissinger's most important marching orders came on the margins of the News Summaries. It was a most unusual way to run the government of the United States.

This method of giving orders allowed Nixon to keep power and knowledge in very few hands. Indeed, it is astonishing how few people he worked with. Overwhelmingly, his orders went out to "H," "E," or "K," and, after mid-1970, to "C" (Colson). Nixon came close to running the government through this handful, three of whom—H, K, and C—were natural conspirators themselves (and E wasn't far behind).

For the rest, Rogers and Laird hardly ever saw the President, and certainly were not taken into his confidence. Moynihan had once been an insider, but by the second half of 1970 had drifted away, and was gone by the beginning of 1971. Connally was coming on; Nixon liked him and intended big things for him. Mitchell remained a powerful figure, one of the few people Nixon turned to for advice, but as his exclusion from the formation of the Huston plan showed, he was no longer the insider's insider.

Safire, Buchanan, and Price all remained close to the President, men he turned to for help in working up slogans or writing speeches. They often provided him with analysis. They were not, however, men he turned to for advice.

For fun, relaxation, enjoyment, he turned to his daughters, David Eisenhower, sometimes Pat, often Rebozo, and one or two others. That was about it. He remained that strange creature, a politician without friends. He had thousands of acquaintances, but except for Rebozo none could be called real friends. He worked intimately, on a daily basis, with Haldeman, Ehrlichman, Kissinger, and Colson, but none of them could in any way be considered friends.

He remained what he had always been, a loner.

And he remained, as he had always been, angry. Angry with the press, with the Democrats, with most Republicans, with the professors and their students, with the blacks, with so many others. He was angry with J. Edgar Hoover, and *The New York Times*, and the Washington *Post*, and the Eastern Establishment, and the CIA, and the Supreme Court. All this showed, in one form or another almost every day, in his News Summary comments. (The amazing thing is that hundreds of his scribbled remarks were pulled from the News Summaries in the National Archives by his lawyers before scholars were allowed to see them, on the grounds that they would cause personal embarrassment. The ones quoted in this work are those that survived a screening process designed to protect Nixon from his own words.)

And what pleased him, aside from praise for himself? One searches the News Summaries in vain for an answer.

His comments often showed his cynicism, his suspicious nature, his penchant for paranoia. They never showed a sense of humor. Not once does he poke a bit of fun at himself; in this regard, he was the ultimate stuffed shirt.

"I'm not a bit thin-skinned," he told Haldeman in a May 9, 1971, memo, before going on to complain that at the annual White House Correspondents' Dinner all the awards went to "way out left-wingers. . . . Every one of the recipients was receiving an award for a vicious attack on the Administration—Carswell, wire tapping, Army surveillance, etc. I had to sit there for 20 minutes while the drunken audience laughed in derision as the award citations were read."

In the future, he continued, he wanted the staff "to protect the office of the Presidency from such insulting incidents." [10] That was certainly reasonable, and he was more correct than not in insisting that the working White House press contained few friends and many detractors. His analysis about the reason, however, was questionable. He thought the press hated him personally; he could not believe that it was his policies, rather than his personality, that caused the criticism. Could he really have expected to be praised for nominating Carswell or for wiretapping reporters?

His self-delusion, as revealed day after day in his scribbles, was monumental. Even leaving aside his absurd but fixed notion that the media hated him, he was a man full of self-pity and pretension. He saw himself as the leader of the Silent Majority of decent, honest Americans—nay, more than the leader, the embodiment of all that was good and strong and God-fearing and right about the American people. He saw himself as the defender of this Silent Majority against the wimpy, whiny liberal minority of un-Americans, those who were not good and not strong and not God-fearing enough. And he pitied himself, because the battle was so unequal, because even though he led the majority, the minority had somehow managed to take control of all the newspapers, and all the television networks, and all the radio shows, and all the college classrooms in the country.

He was beleaguered. But he was heroic.

It was so sad. He was a man of very great gifts, to whom much had been given, but he was incapable of enjoying life, or of seeing himself and his role realistically.

In this regard, Nixon stands in sharp contrast to other Presidents, most of all Eisenhower. No one could come in contact with Ike without being impressed by all sorts of things—his vitality, that grin, his intelligence, his self-confidence, his knowledge and experience, his love of life and of people, his curiosity, his bearing, among many others—but one attribute stood out above them all. It was the pleasure he took in living.

Surely this author is not alone in thinking that it must have been a wonderful thing to be Dwight Eisenhower.

Nixon's qualities were different from Ike's, and in some ways superior. In terms of pure intelligence, Nixon may well have been smarter, at least in the sense of the power of memory, or the retention of fact. His imagination too may have been greater; halfway through his first term in office, Nixon had already shown an ability to think more innovatively about the structure of world politics than Eisenhower had demonstrated. Nixon had also indicated that he was more willing to take a chance. Obviously the two men were very different: Ike's smiles, Nixon's snarls; Ike's generosity of spirit, Nixon's meanness of spirit; Ike's *joie de vivre*, Nixon's anger; and so on.

But the difference that stands out the most was Nixon's inability to take pleasure in living.

Surely this author is not alone in thinking that it must have been a terrible thing to be Richard Nixon.

CHAPTER NINETEEN

LAOS AND OTHER WOES
January–April 1971

IN THE FIRST MONTHS of 1971 the Nixon Presidency, hardly a great success to date, fell to its lowest point yet. The war in Vietnam dragged on, with no end in sight. Nixon escalated with an offensive that resulted in more controversy but brought him no closer to peace with honor. The SALT talks were apparently stalemated. Stagflation continued. Relations with Congress, already bad, worsened. The Senate ridiculed his Secretary of State, permanently killed the SST project, and came close to mandating a legislative end to the war. In the House, his revenue-sharing proposal found little support, and there was a call for his impeachment, from, of all people, a Republican congressman from California. In the Gallup poll, at the end of winter, he slipped below a 50 percent approval rating for the first time, while trial runs between Nixon and Muskie grew increasingly worrisome (in February, the Harris poll showed Senator Muskie leading 43–40; in March, it was 44–39; in May, 47–39). Nixon began to worry that he might not even be renominated, much less re-elected.[1]

There were other portents of peril. In early March, Moynihan, who was, in his own words, "picking up some consulting fees," wrote Nixon to report on his soundings among big-business men and bankers at various conventions and conferences. Moynihan said he had been "astonished—that is the word—at their hostility to the administration." Their attitude, according to Moynihan, could be summed up in the phrase, "Fascism is Here." Nixon scribbled on the letter, "H—effect of editorials and columns," which may have been an explanation of the phenomenon but hardly helped make it go away.[2]

413

In February, Gallup took a poll of students around the country. Some 60 percent felt a need for stronger national leadership (a point Nixon told "H" to "Note!"), but what hurt most was that three dead men ran ahead of Nixon in the list of most admired men (JFK got 34 percent, Martin Luther King, Jr., got 18 percent, Robert Kennedy got 15 percent, and Nixon got 9 percent). Nixon commented, "H—Result of the liberal bias in teaching and media," and complained that he did not want to be compared to ghosts; he instructed Haldeman, "Our poll of youth should be limited to potential candidates [in 1972] plus Agnew." [3]

Everywhere his enemies seemed to be on the offensive. Senator McGovern told an audience he wanted to amend the draft laws to require the President and military leaders "to spend a reasonable amount of time in the front lines in combat." Nixon asked "Coulson" (as with Ehrlichman and Shultz, Nixon never learned how to spell Colson's name), "What is McG's record in combat? I think he was in WWII." [4] He was indeed; McGovern had a distinguished combat record flying bomber missions out of Italy, and had been shot down over Yugoslavia.

Common Cause, a citizen lobbying group with such goals as depoliticizing the Justice Department, ending illegal covert police and intelligence activities, terminating the war in Vietnam, solving the problems of poverty, and halting the B-1 bomber and the SST, was growing rapidly, under the leadership of John Gardner, former Secretary of HEW under Johnson. Among others, John Chancellor and David Brinkley, along with the wives of Abe Fortas, James Reston, Arthur Goldberg, Christian Herter, and Dean Acheson, had joined the cause. "H—the old Establishment!" Nixon remarked. When Gardner said Nixon had "difficulty in sparking enthusiasm," Nixon commented, "H—note—this is a theme even among our friends in the press. Connally may have arrived too late!" [5]

Nixon tried to fight back. When he read that Ralph Nader (compared by Buchanan to Joseph McCarthy as "a demagogue who has eclipsed all visible competition") had 50 percent name recognition and an overwhelmingly favorable response to his name, Nixon instructed, "H—I want you to develop a plan for exposing him. He is an unprincipled huckster—all for power—and dangerous to the business system so essential to survival of the nation. . . . Mobilize a business group to finance an effective research and counterattack campaign." [6]

Some Hollywood stars turned against the President, to his fury. In February, Jane Fonda announced plans to tour GI bases with an antiwar show, in order to display a "different view of the war" from that offered by Bob Hope, whom she called a "superhawk who has a corner on the market on entertainers speaking to soldiers." Nixon would not stand for it: "Laird: *NO* approval to be given; H—this must *NOT* be approved."[7]

There was more bad news from California that month. Representative Paul McCloskey, a Republican from San Bernardino, called for impeaching the President "as one way of ending the war." Nixon commented, "H—get a movement calling for his recall going."[8]

Mail was always important to Nixon. He used it to generate good PR and to win votes. He sent a two-page, single-spaced memo to Haldeman on the subject of the operation of the White House mail room. "As we get near the campaign period," he began (this was seventeen months before the 1972 election), he wanted improvements. Was enough personal attention being paid to the incoming correspondence? Were the answers prompt, personal, and warm? How did the operation compare with that of the Kennedy-Johnson period? Nixon wanted the mail read carefully as a source of anecdotes for his speeches, and for those "grabbers" to which he could reply publicly and thus generate some publicity.[9]

Haldeman replied with four single-spaced pages, assuring Nixon that the incoming mail was the greatest in volume in history, that the outgoing mail surpassed all records, that every letter got a personal reply, that one person was reading the mail for the sole purpose of finding anecdotal material ("H," Nixon wrote on the margin, "step this up to maximum—4 fold"), that some 275 Republican Volunteer Women were working nearly full time analyzing the incoming mail for pro and con views on various issues, and so forth. Nevertheless, Haldeman assured the boss, "all of us share the view that we have not fully utilized the human interest, anecdotal or PR aspects of the incoming mail and that we need to improve." He promised to do so.[10]

Toward that end, Haldeman put some of the top guns on the job. Ray Price, for one, worked the President's mail. A typical effort came in April, when Price recommended a response to one B. Allen Groves, of Carbondale, Illinois, who had written to say that he was a college student who had demonstrated against the Cambodian incursion, that he had changed his mind, that he was now an enthusiastic supporter, and to inform Nixon that "part of your silent majority has long hair."

Price saw the letter as an opportunity to show that "RN recognizes that although a lot of people are turned off by hair styles, etc., the important thing is what's *in* the head, not what's *on* it," and to praise open-mindedness and willingness to change opinions. "Good," Nixon wrote on the memo, and added, "Emphasize RN's

faith in final verdict of people—and his respect for those who disagree." [11] (Especially, of course, when they saw their error and
came to agree with him.)

Nixon had an ability to cut to the heart of a matter. In April,
Bob Finch, still in Washington serving as Counsel to the President,
sent Nixon a memo on "The Role of Women in the Administration." Finch said only 3.5 percent of Nixon's appointees were
women, and commented that to make a difference with women
voters in 1972, "we must do much better." He recommended concentrating on high-level, visible appointments. (Pat was simultaneously urging her husband to put some women on the Federal
Appeals Courts, and to nominate a woman for the Supreme Court.)
Nixon's reply was blunt and direct: "Finch: I seriously doubt
if jobs in government for women make for many votes from
women." [12]

Nixon was not always the utter cynic, however, nor would it
be correct to say that everything he did was self-serving. In late
January, the official Kennedy portraits were ready to be hung in
the White House. Pat invited Jacqueline Kennedy Onassis and ten-
year-old John Kennedy and thirteen-year-old Caroline for a ceremony. Mrs. Onassis replied that an official ceremony would be
hard on her children "and not leave them with the memories of the
White House I would like them to have." Pat then suggested a
private viewing; Mrs. Onassis quickly accepted.

Pat kept it private. Only four members of the White House staff
knew of the visit, and no photographers or reporters were present.
Pat, Julie, and Tricia gave Mrs. Onassis and her children a tour of
the mansion, ending with a call on the President in the Oval Office.
Nixon showed young John where he used to play underneath his
father's desk. There were drinks, and dinner, and light talk ("I
always live in a dream world," Mrs. Onassis told Nixon). [13]

Later, the former First Lady wrote the President: "The day I
always dreaded turned out to be one of the most precious ones I
have spent with my children." Peter Flanigan, himself a highly
successful Irish-American (senior partner at Dillon, Read & Company) and a White House consultant, told Nixon that his sister
Peggy and Jackie Onassis were very close friends. "Peggy tells
me," Flanigan wrote Nixon, "that Jackie was overwhelmed with
the kindness and warmth of her reception. She went so far as to
say, when describing you, that 'I could have hugged him!' " [14]

The two living former Presidents were both Democrats, men
with whom Nixon had had tumultuous relationships. Although he
had a public reconciliation, of sorts, with Harry Truman, his feelings about the man were still strong. In March, when Tom Dewey

died, Nixon's News Summary reported that Bess Truman had told reporters her husband would have no comment. Nixon scribbled, "H—note, our Dem friends always play it partisan to the end!"[15]

With Lyndon Johnson, however, Nixon had become practically an intimate. There was an obvious empathy between the two, both embattled over Vietnam, and in addition each could do a great deal for the other. Johnson had almost become Nixon's number-one supporter, not only on Vietnam but on other issues as well; his public statements were full of praise. For his part, Nixon helped Johnson out in various ways, most importantly in the dedication of the Johnson Library in Austin. Among other favors, Nixon offered to fly down to Texas in *Air Force One* the guests from the Washington area Johnson was inviting, including the Democratic leadership in Congress, Generals Westmoreland and Wheeler, John Connally, Johnson's Supreme Court appointees, Dick Helms, and Mrs. Alice Roosevelt Longworth. Best of all, Nixon himself attended, and got a laugh with a slip of the tongue; in his speech at the dedication, Nixon said, "Just a few minutes ago, as President Johnson was throwing me around the library—I mean showing me around . . ."

Johnson, in a fulsome letter of thanks, concluded, "In the fullness of time perhaps you can throw me around the Richard M. Nixon Library at its opening!"[16]

When the JFK Center opened in Washington, the News Summary said that the reporters could "find no adjectives too lavish to describe the place." Nixon wrote, "H—Compare this orgasm over this utter architectural monstrosity with the nit picking of the poor LBJ Library!"[17] Sometime later, the News Summary reported that the Democrats were trying to get $1 million appropriated for additional furnishings for the JFK Center. Nixon's comment was "H—No! *Never.*"[18]

OF ALL the irritations and problems Nixon had to face in early 1971, the worst by far was Vietnam. And in Vietnam, aside from the obvious fact that if the war was still going on in November 1972 it could well cost him his job, Nixon's most worrisome problem was the rapid deterioration of morale. He was commander in chief of an Army that had lost the will to fight, an Army in which discipline was in danger of disappearing altogether, an Army that was being rocked to its very foundations.

It was his own fault. He was the one who kept sending half-trained, at best, eighteen-year-olds halfway around the world to engage in a war he had long since decided he could not win, to participate in a rearguard action designed to protect a corrupt and nonrepresentative government long enough to secure his own re-election. These were hardly causes likely to make a patriot's heart beat faster.

The evidence of the deterioration was overwhelming. By the spring of 1971, of the quarter million American GIs in country, some forty thousand were heroin addicts. There was a higher risk of a soldier going to Vietnam becoming hooked on heroin than becoming a war casualty. Marijuana use threatened to become universal. An entire generation of America's fighting men was being corrupted.

Nixon's response to a report on the drug abuse in Vietnam was to order Haldeman to "get our story out fast by the inspired leak route (talk to Safire). Submit a report." [19] The trouble was, the Administration had no story on this one; the facts were the facts.

A helicopter pilot reported that almost entire American units, including officers, were "doing heroin." He said, "The majority of people were high all the time. For ten dollars you could get a vial of pure heroin the size of a cigarette butt, and you could get liquid opium, speed, acid, anything you wanted. You could trade a box of Tide for a carton of prepacked, prerolled marijuana cigarettes soaked in opium." [20]

Then there was "fragging"—fragmentation-grenade attacks by enlisted men against unpopular officers. More than two hundred incidents had been reported in 1970, and the rate was increasing in early 1971. Racial tension was at an all-time high as America's most integrated Army divided itself into "bloods" and "honkies." Rednecks from the Deep South hated the California and New York liberals, and vice versa. The President who had vowed to "bring us together" was watching in apparent helplessness as even his own Army tore itself apart.

Not that Nixon didn't try to deal with the crisis. He appointed a commission to look into the problem of drug addiction among young Americans generally and servicemen specifically. He pledged to undertake a "national offensive" against drugs. He described himself as unalterably opposed to legalizing marijuana. He said he would halt drug traffic at the foreign sources, prosecute sellers, initiate a "massive" educational effort in the United States, and provide treatment facilities for addicts, especially servicemen. [21]

The follow-up failed to match the fanfare. The problem continued, indeed grew worse.

At the end of May, Nixon went to West Point to speak at graduation ceremonies. He was brutally realistic: "It is no secret," he told his newly commissioned officers, "that the discipline, integrity, patriotism and self-sacrifice, which are the very lifeblood of an effective armed force and which the corps represents, can no longer be taken for granted in the Army in which you will serve." They would be leading troops who were guilty of drug abuse and insubordination. It was up to them, Nixon said, to reaffirm "the military ethic . . . and to give it new life and meaning." He did not tell them how to accomplish that goal.[22]

THE ONLY SOLUTION was to end the war, but Nixon remained determined to avoid being the first President to lose a war, and insisted that his policies would bring peace with honor. To that end, he decided once again to go over to the offensive.

The American military had long been attracted and repelled by the prospect of operations in southern Laos, against the Ho Chi Minh Trail. It was a tempting target, but it was a long way from the American supply bases, close to those of the NVA. The terrain was unfavorable, but the potential payoff was high. Westmoreland had estimated he would need four full divisions to pull it off, however, and that was too big a commitment, even for the Americans.

But by late 1970 the high command was once again urging the President to undertake offensive operations into Laos. There was no question about using American troops; Nixon had given his word that American ground troops would not extend their activities into Laos. But Admiral Thomas Moorer, chairman of the JCS, said that ARVN could do the job if protected by American air power, on which Nixon had not imposed restrictions.

In Cambodia, back in 1970, the enemy had fallen back and waited for the American troops to withdraw; in 1971 in Laos the chances were that the NVA, closer to home, would stand and fight, especially against ARVN. Well and good, said Admiral Moorer; in that case American air power would isolate the battlefield and inflict heavy losses that would be difficult to replace. The operation would give a boost to ARVN morale, show the world that Vietnamization was working, cut the Ho Chi Minh Trail, and destroy the enemy supply buildup, thus blunting any offensive scheduled for 1971. In short, Operation Lam Son promised "decisive" results.[23]

Nixon believed all this, and went to great lengths to convince others. He attended a series of briefings as he widened the circle of those in the know. At these briefings, Kissinger later wrote, "Nixon was earning himself high marks for acting ability. He listened each time with wide-eyed interest as if he were hearing the plan for the first time. His questions—always the same—were a proper mixture of skepticism, fascination, and approval."[24]

On January 18, in a meeting with Laird, Rogers, Helms, Kissinger, Haig, and Moorer, Nixon gave the order. Some five thousand

ARVN troops, mostly marines, the best in the South Vietnamese armed forces, would spearhead a widespread search-and-destroy operation into Laos. The United States would provide artillery, helicopter and gunship, and air ferry support, plus B-52 raids.[25]

It looked grand on paper, but Rogers was not sold. He convinced Kissinger that another review was necessary. On January 27, at the final meeting, Rogers told Nixon the risks were excessive. ARVN's plans were already known in Hanoi. Nixon was sending one South Vietnamese division to do a job that Westmoreland would not touch with less than four U.S. Army divisions. An ARVN defeat would expose Vietnamization as a fraud, and undercut all the gains of the past two years. And it would add yet another country to the list of Asian nations America was committed to defend.

Nixon, according to Kissinger, "simply did not believe that his Secretary of State knew what he was talking about."[26] Kissinger was Mr. Tough Guy. He urged the President to go forward. The President did.

On February 8, Lam Son began. In its initial stages, it went well. Things soon deteriorated, as the NVA gleefully pounded the ARVN, especially with its Russian-supplied armored units, used here on an extensive scale for the first time. The Administration tried to paint the operation as a success, with upbeat briefings at the Pentagon, but the networks and the press reported ARVN bitterness and a feeling on the part of the South Vietnamese that they were being used by the United States as pawns. Marvin Kalb said on CBS that privately the Pentagon was admitting a serious underestimation of NVA firepower.

Nixon was predictably furious at the negative coverage. "Laird & K," he instructed, "Don't admit anything—say we *expected* heavy going."[27] He ordered Haldeman to "personally ride hard on the Coulson Magruder operation to start a campaign against T.V. coverage of Laos. Have Agnew blast T.V. for the distorted coverage."[28]

But within two weeks, the offensive designed to prove that Vietnamization was working had turned into a rout, made painfully visible to American television viewers by footage showing ARVN troops fighting among themselves for a place on American helicopters extracting them from Laos. Nevertheless, at a February 17 news conference, Nixon continued to try to sell Lam Son. "The operation has gone according to plan," he said. ARVN was "fighting in a superior way."[29]

The PR effort was to no avail. The images of ARVN troops hanging on the helicopter skids were too devastating. Bill Timmons, who had taken Bryce Harlow's place as congressional liaison, reported to Nixon that "in the last two days perhaps twenty hawkish Congressmen—Democrats and Republicans—have contacted me to report a swift change in their constituents' attitude toward Vietnam . . . brought on by the negative press over the Laos operation."[30] George Bush reported from the United Nations that he had met with seven top people at *Newsweek:* "They were to a man convinced that the Laos operation was a failure. I'd say totally close minded on this issue."[31] And Clark MacGregor, also working in the congressional liaison office, told Nixon that Jerry Ford, Senator Baker, and Congressman Peter Frelinghuysen (R., N.J.) were nearly distraught. Frelinghuysen had said, "Laos is one more straw —and a substantial one—on the camel's back. Most Americans— myself included—have come to feel that this war has gone on too long."[32]

Still Nixon hung tough. He wrote in his memoirs that "the net result was a military success but a psychological defeat," brought on by the TV coverage. He recorded that Kissinger told him at the end of March, when the pell-mell retreat had ended, "If I had known before it started that it was going to come out exactly the way it did, I would still have gone ahead with it."[33]

Kissinger remained foursquare for Lam Son. In his memoirs, he wrote that "the strategy Nixon and I devised . . . was carried out in essence in 1971. . . . And it worked."[34]

But the truth came from the heartland. Nixon's war was being waged for the hearts and minds of the American people, and on April 12 his News Summary recorded his failure. It quoted the mayor of Galesburg, Illinois, who said that in his once-hawkish town "virtually everybody wants out of VN." Nixon scribbled, "K —note—this is our *problem,*" as if this were some great insight.[35]

ONE OF THE REASONS Chuck Colson moved up in the White House team was his ability to supply gossip and information. Nixon and his people could not get enough of the stuff. In December 1970, Colson supplied a juicy tidbit; he reported that Howard Hughes was dropping Larry O'Brien from his payroll (as his PR man in Washington) and replacing him with Bob Bennett, currently on the staff of the Department of Transportation and the son of Republican Senator Wallace Bennett of Utah. Colson ended his memo, "Bennett is a good friend of ours and has volunteered to do anything we want at any time with the Hughes people."[36]

Nixon, meanwhile, read a story in the January 14 edition of the Los Angeles *Times* about another development in the Hughes empire. Robert Maheu, once Hughes's chief assistant, had broken with Hughes; the story reported that Maheu planned to subpoena his former boss for a $50 million lawsuit. It was unlikely that Hughes, living as a recluse in the Bahamas, would appear, but his secret memos had already been impounded by a Nevada court, and reporter Jack Anderson claimed to have seen some of them.[37]

What was in those memos, Nixon did not know. They could mean trouble for him. Hughes had been a regular contributor to his campaigns for two decades. The Hughes loan to Don Nixon back in the fifties had hurt Nixon in the 1960 and 1962 elections. In the past year, Hughes had made a $100,000 cash contribution, giving the money to Bebe Rebozo, who was holding it in a safe-deposit box in Miami. Don Nixon had ongoing business dealings with Hughes's people. There was much to fear.

But there were also some interesting and potentially profitable facts. For years, Nixon had been accused of being Howard Hughes's hired man in Washington. How sweet it would be to turn the tables and reveal that the chairman of the Democratic National Committee had been on a secret retainer (Colson said, accurately, that it amounted to $15,000 per month) for Hughes. And the man who could do the revealing and make it stick was Robert Maheu, because Maheu had handled Hughes's political affairs for years and was the one who hired O'Brien in the first place.

Immediately after reading about the Maheu-Hughes lawsuit, Nixon sent a memo to Haldeman. "It would seem that the time is approaching when Larry O'Brien is held accountable for his retainer with Hughes. Bebe has some information on this, although it is, of course, not solid. But there is no question that one of Hughes' people did have O'Brien on a very heavy retainer for 'services rendered' in the past."[38]

The next day, January 15, at their regular morning meeting in the Oval Office, Nixon told Haldeman, "We're going to nail O'Brien on this, one way or the other. O'Brien's not going to get away with it, Bob. We're going to get proof of his relationship with Hughes—and just what he's doing for the money."[39]

Haldeman put John Dean to work; Dean quickly learned how deeply the Hughes tentacles extended into American political life. There surely were scandals waiting to happen, but by no means did they all center on Larry O'Brien. If things started to blow, there were plenty of Republicans who were going to get hit too. There were CIA connections, with Maheu and Bennett, among others. Rebozo had had dealings with Hughes. And who knew what Maheu might have told O'Brien about the Nixon brothers' dealings with Hughes?

When Dean reported to Haldeman, he said Bennett would help him expose O'Brien, but it had to be done in such a way as to not embarrass Hughes. Haldeman talked to Nixon, and came back to Dean: whatever you do, he ordered, "keep Bob Bennett and Bebe out of this at all costs." But that was no more possible than keeping Hughes himself out of it, so for the time being Nixon let the O'Brien-Hughes matter drop.[40]

EARLY IN 1971, Nixon replaced, improved, and extended the taping system originally set up by Johnson. A manual switch had to be turned on in the systems utilized by Johnson (and Kennedy, and Eisenhower); Nixon's system was voice-activated. Earlier Presidents had placed microphones in the Oval Office and the Cabinet Room; Nixon did the same, and added coverage for his EOB office. In addition, Nixon had recorders placed on the telephones in the Oval and EOB offices, the Lincoln Sitting Room, and on the office phone at Camp David.[41]

His motives were varied. Johnson had told him he had been foolish to remove the taping capability in the first place, and that his own tapes were proving invaluable in preparing his memoirs. Nixon could certainly see the point. Another former President, Dwight Eisenhower, at a Cabinet meeting attended by Nixon in the mid-fifties, had advised his people to tape-record all their telephone calls. Laughing, Eisenhower had explained, "You know, boys, it's a good thing when you're talking to someone you don't trust to get a record made of it. There are some guys I just don't trust in Washington, and I want to have myself protected so that they can't later report that I said something else."[42]

Although Ike seldom used the tape recorder in the Oval Office, he always had General Andrew Goodpaster in the room with him during meetings. Goodpaster's job had been to take notes in order to provide an accurate record of everything said. Nixon, however, felt it inhibited visitors to have a notetaker present, and he rejected that system. He still needed the accurate record; tape recordings would provide the most accurate record of all.

According to Haldeman, one of Nixon's main concerns with regard to people saying one thing in the Oval Office, and something else entirely different to reporters when they emerged, was Henry Kissinger. Insofar as there are almost uncountable examples of Kissinger doing exactly that, the Haldeman observation makes good sense.[43]

Nixon ordered Haldeman to install the taping system secretly. The only people who knew it was there were Nixon, Haldeman, Alexander Butterfield (Haldeman's assistant), and the Secret Service technicians who placed the hidden microphones and operated the system. Nixon did not even inform his family that their private conversations were being taped.[44]

The system went into full operation in early February. Almost two decades later, of the thousand hours of recorded conversation, twelve and a half hours had been made public in various trials and lawsuits. Prosecutors, defense lawyers, judges, juries, and scholars have discovered that there are all sorts of problems in using the tapes. To begin with, you can't see body language, the nod of the head or the shrug of the shoulder, the grin that belies what is being said, the angry gesture that gives force to the low-key phrase. Words are often inaudible; sometimes, entire sentences. What would seem to be a simple process, transcribing the tapes, turns out to be a source of sometimes bitter controversy, as different typists hear different things. Often it is simply impossible to tell.

In addition, the men carrying on the conversation know so much more than the listener ever can. In business, sports, or almost any area, in private conversation between knowledgeable people, the assumption that the other person or persons know what you are talking about leads to all kinds of shortcuts. What would take whole paragraphs, or even pages, to describe in written form can be covered in a simple "Ya know?" followed by a nod. (Having worked extensively with both systems, this author would argue that Goodpaster's notes are not only much easier to work with but much more accurate than Nixon's tapes. Of course, the trick is to find a Goodpaster.)

So what at first glance might appear to be the perfect source on what Nixon thought, said, and did turns out to be ambiguous and misleading. Nevertheless it is a unique source (because the Kennedy and Johnson tapes remain under seal) and obviously invaluable. To make the point, just imagine what it would be like to have recordings of George Washington's intimate conversations with Alexander Hamilton and Thomas Jefferson.

But the tapes are also a dangerous source, not only because of their poor quality and ambiguities, but for an even more important reason. It is the simple fact that only Nixon and Haldeman knew that what they were saying was being recorded. Julie Eisenhower claimed that "once the decision was made to tape, my father seemed to forget that the system existed." [45] The opposite was true. Anyone who listens to the tapes quickly realizes that Nixon often is speaking for the record; as will be seen, he could be quite transparent about it.

In his memoirs, Nixon wrote that he intended to use the tapes to prepare his memoirs, and to protect himself from "revisionist histories." [46] What better way to prove his innocence should he be charged with a crime or an impure motive or whatever than to haul out a tape and say, "Here, listen to this part, here is what I said about that." Still, there were times when Nixon really did forget that the tape recorder was rolling, times when he accepted it—as he explained to his family when the secret was revealed and Pat and the girls learned that they too were on the tapes—"as part of the surroundings."[47] Haldeman, too, often forgot the system was in place; as he told this author, he certainly would not have said some of the things he did say after the Watergate break-in had he remembered.

Over the next two years, Nixon let the asset build, without once drawing on it. He had no transcripts made, nor did he listen to any of the tapes. He just continued to make them.

IN HIS "Fascism is Here" letter to Nixon in early March, Moynihan said that "really dreadful things occurred when my party was in power," things Nixon had corrected in "your brilliant first year in office." Meanwhile, those "who started it" ("it" meaning wiretapping, Army spying on private citizens, black-bag operations, and so forth) had assumed "the role of outraged and indignant defenders of liberty."[48]

It was ironic that Moynihan's letter arrived just as the President was restoring an expanded version of Johnson's taping system. It was a coincidence that a month earlier the wiretapping program that Kissinger had ordered on his NSC staff and some reporters was terminated. The taps had not turned up any useful information, and besides, J. Edgar Hoover was about to go to the Hill to testify; it was his practice to discontinue as many wiretaps as possible before his congressional appearances, so that he could truthfully report a minimum number of taps in effect.[49]

Still the congressmen pressed him, and the Democrats saw an issue they could exploit. The Justice Department was carrying out a broad range of surveillance actions against antiwar and radical groups, including wiretapping. Attorney General Mitchell insisted that the government's right to defend itself against violent attack justified the programs; the Democrats charged that the investigations of dissenters were posing a threat to individual freedom and violating privacy rights. Muskie was taking the lead for the Democrats.

On a radio interview on April 16, Nixon defended the FBI and the tapping program as necessary to preserve the nation's freedom. He said he was aware of charges being made by prominent Americans and in newspaper editorials that the country was in danger of becoming a police state.

"Let me say I have been in police states," Nixon commented, "and the idea that this is a police state is just pure nonsense." He pointed out that in a real police state, "you can't talk in your bedroom. You can't talk in your sitting room. You don't talk on the telephone. You don't talk in the bathroom. . . . You can't even talk in front of a shrub. That is the way it works."[50]

Of course he was right. The United States, during Nixon's Presidency, could in no way be described as a police state. There was absolutely more freedom to demonstrate, more freedom of expression, more freedom to work for a change in government than in any other nation on earth.

But it was also true that during Nixon's Presidency you couldn't talk without being secretly tape-recorded in the Oval Office, or in the EOB, or in the Cabinet Room, or over the White House telephones.

EXTREMISM IN political criticism was increasing, as indicated by the police-state charges. This was a reflection of the growing frustration felt by the doves. Nixon had accompanied the Lam Son operation with more bombing of North Vietnam; at the end of February, Senator McGovern let out all the stops when he charged that this was "the most barbaric act committed by any modern state since the death of Adolf Hitler." That same day Hubert Humphrey, who had been supporting Vietnamization, declared that had he become President he would have removed all American troops by now.[51] And Senator Stuart Symington (D., Mo.) characterized the Secretary of State as "an object of ridicule," because it was common knowledge that Nixon never turned to Rogers for advice, but instead went to Kissinger.

Senator Fulbright's frustration, meanwhile, was that he could not get either Rogers or Kissinger to testify before his Foreign Relations Committee. So on February 28 he submitted a bill to compel the Secretary of State and other officials (read Kissinger) to appear before Congress to explain the Administration's policies. Fulbright said it was absolutely necessary to limit the Administration's use of the doctrine of "executive privilege" as an excuse for not testifying.[52]

Nixon, preparing for a news conference, asked John Dean to work up a defense of the doctrine. This was not an easy task, as nowhere in the Constitution do the words "executive privilege" appear. Nixon himself, back in 1948, had made devastating arguments against the doctrine, when Harry Truman was trying to cover up for Alger Hiss by refusing to allow his aides to testify before HUAC. Fortunately for Nixon, since then Eisenhower had made a sweeping assertion of executive privilege, in the case of Joe McCarthy versus the U.S. Army. Because most reporters and politicians were on Ike's side on the immediate issue at hand, few noticed and fewer complained about his boldness in establishing a precedent. So, although Dean had to admit that the doctrine could only be derived by "implication" from the Constitution, the precedent was clear: "The President and his immediate advisers are absolutely immune from testimonial compulsion by a Congressional committee." [53]

At his news conference the following day (March 4), Nixon was at his brazen best. He said that "looking back in retrospect" on the Hiss case, he had decided that President Truman had been right to insist upon executive privilege. In fact, Truman had not gotten away with it; his aides did have to testify. But Nixon cited Truman's advocacy as precedent for the position "that executive privilege is essential for the orderly processes of government." [54]

Kissinger did not have to testify before the Foreign Relations Committee, and Fulbright's bill languished.

FULBRIGHT'S ATTEMPT to get Kissinger to explain and defend in public the American foreign policy was almost ludicrous, given that Kissinger would not even explain it to the Secretary of State. In early 1971, with Nixon's encouragement, Kissinger had his backchannel (meaning excluding the State Department) contacts with the Russians and the Chinese in high gear. With the Russians, he was telling Dobrynin to ignore what the official American negotiating team was presenting in the SALT talks, and pay attention only to his private communications. With China, as noted, Nixon and Kissinger had sent secret messages via the Pakistani and Romanian channels.

On January 11, Chou En-lai responded with a written message, passed on by the Romanian ambassador. Chou said that Nixon's verbal offer to exchange high-level personal representatives "is not new." He insisted that "there is only one outstanding issue between us—the U.S. occupation of Taiwan. The P.R.C. [People's Republic of China] has attempted to negotiate on this issue in good faith for fifteen years. If the U.S. has a desire to settle the issue and a proposal for its solution, the P.R.C. will be prepared to receive a U.S. special envoy in Peking." Chou added that as Nixon had visited Bucharest in 1969 and Belgrade in 1970, the President himself would be welcome in Peking. [55]

It was a good question as to who was pursuing whom the hardest. To the Chinese, Taiwan was a critical issue. To Nixon, it had been at one time, but no longer was, now that he was President. Chinese attempts to force the U.S. off Taiwan in the fifties had failed, when Eisenhower took a hard line on the Quemoy-Matsu question; Ike had been backed by Nixon, who made his willingness to risk war for the islands a major issue in the 1960 campaign. Incapable of taking control of Taiwan by military means, by 1971 the Chinese were eager to see what could be done through negotiations.

China was reaching out not only to the United States, but to the whole world, as its period of self-imposed isolation came to an end. Chou was seeking improved relations with Britain and Japan, and a renewal of diplomatic relations with a variety of countries. China was eager to get into the United Nations. The intense ideological rivalry between China and Russia, highlighted by armed clashes along their long border, was also driving the Chinese along that most ancient of diplomatic paths—the enemy of my enemy is my friend.

The potential rapprochement between China and the United States suffered a setback in early February, when Nixon launched Lam Son. Nixon engaged in damage control at his February 17 news conference, when he stressed that the operation in Laos was directed against North Vietnam only: "I do not believe that the Communist Chinese have any reason to interpret this as a threat against them or any reason therefore to react to it." [56]

Eight days later, Nixon followed up when he declared in his second annual presidential report on foreign policy that "we are prepared to establish a dialogue with Peking" and again used the designation "People's Republic of China" in place of "Red China." [57]

Perhaps more important in reviving Chinese interest was the failure of Lam Son. The ARVN retreat from Laos, and the fact that the United States had not sent its own troops into the country, could not help but be reassuring to Peking.

On March 15, Nixon sent another signal, when he announced the termination of all restrictions on American travel to mainland China. But momentum in one part of Asia was slowed by a setback in a Vietnam-related development.

On March 29, Lieutenant Calley was convicted of murdering Vietnamese civilians, and on March 31 was sentenced to life imprisonment. He refused to admit any wrongdoing. "They were all enemy," Calley declared. "They were all to be destroyed."

There was a national uproar. Thousands of telegrams poured into the White House, protesting the way in which the Army had obviously made Calley a scapegoat. Nixon reacted by releasing Calley from the stockade at Fort Benning and ordering him returned to his quarters on the base while his conviction was reviewed. This brought on another wave of protest, led by Captain Aubrey Daniel, the prosecutor in the case, who wrote Nixon that even more appalling than the massacre at My Lai itself were "the political leaders who have failed to see the moral issue or, having seen it, compromise it for political motives in the face of apparent public displeasure with the verdict."[58]

With no end to the war in sight, meanwhile, the POW issue was becoming a major one. CBS-TV interviewed the wife of a prisoner who said she was "tired of raids, etc." She thought Nixon should set a definite timetable for complete withdrawal, otherwise her husband might never come home. In his closing, Walter Cronkite noted that it was the couple's tenth anniversary.

In his News Summary, Nixon circled Cronkite's name and wrote, "K—hit him hard on why he doesn't put in just one of the P.O.W. wives who *support* RN's position."[59]

Nixon put his old friend General James "Don" Hughes at the head of an Ad Hoc Inter-Agency Group Concerning Prisoners of War and charged it with informing families of the POWs about everything the Administration was doing to get the prisoners released. On a late-February report from Hughes, Nixon wrote, "H—what we lack here is enough P.R. Put a P.R. man on this to tell what we are doing."[60]

But PR could not overcome the stark reality that the POWs were an asset to Hanoi, and that the more fuss the President and the country made about them, the more valuable that asset became. Nixon's response was to tell a news conference in mid-February, "As long as the North Vietnamese have any Americans as prisoners of war, there will be Americans in South Vietnam and enough Americans to give them an incentive to release the prisoners."[61]

Larry O'Brien replied for the Democrats. He accused the President of planning "an endless war in Indochina."[62]

On April 7, in a nationally televised report to the nation on Vietnam, Nixon moved on the PR front to improve the situation. "I can report that Vietnamization has succeeded," he declared, citing the Lam Son operation as proof. Therefore, he was increasing the rate of American withdrawals; by December 1, an additional 100,000 men would be brought home (leaving 180,000 at the end of 1971). "The American involvement in Vietnam is coming to an end," he promised, but he would not set a date for total withdrawal, because if he did that it would throw away "our principal bargaining counter to win the release of American prisoners of war [and] we would remove the enemy's strongest incentive to end the war sooner by negotiation."

Harking back to the 1968 campaign, Nixon recalled that "I pledged to end American involvement in this war." (Actually, he had pledged to end the war.) "I am keeping that pledge. And I expect to be held accountable by the American people if I fail."[63]

That same day, in Japan, there was an announcement that surprised and pleased Nixon. The president of the U.S. Table Tennis Association, traveling with a team of American Ping-Pong players, said the team had received an invitation to make a week-long tour of China. Nixon gave his approval; a week later, Chou En-lai personally received the team. He said the trip had "opened a new page in the relations of the Chinese and American people" and asked the players to extend the best wishes of the Chinese people to the American people.[64]

Simultaneously, Nixon sent out his own signal. He announced a further easing of trade and travel restrictions with the P.R.C.[65]

On April 16 Nixon told the American Society of Newspaper Editors that his long-range goals included "a normalization of the relations between the government of the United States and the government of the People's Republic of China, and the ending of the isolation of Mainland China from the world community." He also said that he had advised his daughters to travel while they were young, and that "the place to go is to Asia." He said they should go to China. "I hope they do. As a matter of fact, I hope sometime I do. I am not sure that it is going to happen while I am in office."[66]

The eagerness of both sides to get together was by now almost palpable. On April 27 Chou responded to Nixon's signals with a message sent via Pakistan that amounted to an invitation. After insisting that the problem of Taiwan had to be solved before relations could be restored, Chou said, "The Chinese government reaffirms its willingness to receive publicly in Peking a special envoy of the President . . . or even the President of the U.S. himself for a direct meeting and discussion."[67]

This was a potential breakthrough of fundamental importance. After his long winter and early spring of discontent, it gave Nixon a great lift. He had earned it, by being as realistic about the need for a new relationship with China as he was unrealistic about the war in Vietnam.

There was another foreign-policy lift in the offing, also a result of Nixonian realism. At a news conference back in March, Nixon had responded to a question on how the SALT talks were going by noting that "the two great super powers now have nuclear parity. Neither can gain an advantage over the other if the other desires to see to it that that does not occur. Now, under these circumstances, therefore, it is in the interest of both powers to negotiate some kind of limitation, limitation on offensive and defensive weapons."[68]

This was a fundamental insight on his part. He was the first Cold War President to face the reality that American security could no longer be enhanced by building more weapons. His insight held great promise for his own future, and that of his nation.

• •

NIXON WAS as bored by domestic-policy issues as he was excited by foreign policy. Discussions of budget matters or government organization would cause his eyes to glaze over. His feelings were clear, and set the tone of his Administration. There is an unsigned, undated handwritten note on White House stationery in the Nixon papers that illustrates the point well. It concerns Caspar Weinberger, Nixon's deputy director of OMB. The note reads: "This is Nixonomics 1A. You get full semester's credit if you stay awake 'till 9:00," followed by a further note at the bottom, "8:51—Weinberger didn't make it—he just fell asleep." [69]

Still, Nixon worked hard on domestic policy, not because he wanted to, but because he had to, not so much because it was his responsibility as President, but because he knew that was where the votes were. He wished people would vote their fears, or for the man with the most experience in foreign affairs, but he knew—as he said many times—that people voted their pocketbooks (which was why the Republicans took such a licking in the 1970 congressional elections). And Nixon's perennial problem, from the day he entered politics until the day he left, as he complained hundreds of times, was that the Democrats could always outpromise the Republicans on economic issues.

Nixon was not an utter cynic on economics and domestic policy. He was a strong adherent of a moderate Republican philosophy, that government is too big and too paternal and too expensive, that segregation is wrong but that forced integration, especially by busing, is wronger, that what is good for big business is good for the U.S.A., and so forth. It was just that he didn't believe in any of these propositions so strongly that he would let his beliefs stand in the way of his re-election; for example, his conversion to Keynesian economics after the 1970 campaign. So, to understand Nixon's 1971 domestic policies, it is necessary to keep always in mind that he did what he did with the 1972 re-election campaign in mind.

That was neither wrong nor bad, and hardly unique. After all, leaders in a democracy are supposed to do what the people want them to do. There was a mid-1971 cartoon that made the point succinctly. Two guys are sitting at a bar. One turns to the other and says, "Listen, Nixon's no dope. If the people wanted moral leadership, he'd give them moral leadership."

What the people wanted in 1971 was what they always want: peace and prosperity. Nixon couldn't give them peace, at least not yet, so he went to work to provide prosperity.

His budget for fiscal 1972, announced in late January, was full of the usual hocus-pocus of such documents, but this time with a new twist. Nixon called it a "full-employment budget," and explained that it would be a balanced budget if everyone in the country had a job. As everyone did not have a job, it would be $11.6 billion in the red, or so Nixon predicted (for fiscal 1971 he had predicted a $1 billion surplus, but in fact ran a $23.2 billion deficit, due to stagflation). Nixon assured the nation that his new budget was "expansionary but not inflationary."

The budget increased spending in every area: defense, the environment, agriculture, crime, even education. In large part, increases were mandatory, as a result of the New Deal and Great Society entitlement programs; Social Security was up 6 percent, Medicare and Medicaid up $1 billion, and so on. Overall, it was a budget that would prevent massive unemployment as the boys came home from Vietnam, and might even spark a boom.[70]

Much more interesting, and potentially far more important, was Nixon's proposal for revenue sharing. In his State of the Union address, he declared, "The time has now come in America to reverse the flow of power and resources from the States and communities to Washington, and start power and resources flowing back from Washington to the States and communities and, more important, to the people all across America."[71] He proposed to do this by sending $5 billion per year to the states as a kind of tax rebate, with no strings attached—the states could spend the money as they chose. More dramatic was his proposal to take $10 billion out of existing aid programs, which required spending for this or that designated purpose, usually to help the poor and minorities, and leave it to the states to decide how to spend it.

Nixon called it a revolutionary program. The Democrats called it a counterrevolution. Nixon's claim was that state and local governments, being closer to the people, could better decide how to spend the people's money. The Democrats' charge was that the middle- and upper-class whites who controlled state and local government would use the money to reduce their own property taxes, pave suburban roads, build new airports, and leave the inner cities to rot.

Whether or not it was good government was a debatable point. That it was good politics for Nixon could not be argued. Win or lose on this one with Congress, revenue sharing gave Nixon a strong domestic claim for the 1972 campaign, at least with the suburban, small-town, and rural homeowning Silent Majority. Revenue sharing appealed to their disgust with the performance of government, to their outrage that they paid high taxes to support giveaway programs for the poor, to their fear that if property taxes kept rising they would soon be driven from the ranks of homeowners.

Nixon's appeals to the suburbs were direct and unashamed. He described property taxes as the most "unfair, unpopular, and fastest-rising of all taxes," and promised that adoption of revenue sharing would lead to a 30 percent reduction in property taxes.[72] He also pledged that he would not use federal leverage to force local communities to accept low- and moderate-income housing against their wishes (by law, federally funded housing had to be integrated housing).

And, of course, he spoke out against busing at every opportunity. In mid-April, he was badly undercut when the Supreme Court unanimously approved mandatory busing to overcome racial segregation in the schools. At a news conference, Nixon said he would uphold the law, but reiterated, "I do not believe that busing to achieve racial balance is in the interests of better education," and said he would not allow busing to be used to integrate schools that were segregated not by law but by housing patterns.[73]

He was unhappy with the Supreme Court; he was also unhappy with the bureaucracy. On the day the Court made its busing decision, Nixon railed to his subordinates, "We have no discipline in this bureaucracy. We never fire anybody. . . . We always promote the sons-of-bitches that kick us in the ass. . . . When a bureaucrat deliberately thumbs his nose, we're going to get him. . . . There are many unpleasant places where civil service people can be sent."[74]

He didn't much like Congress, either.

Wilbur Mills (D., Ark.), chairman of the House Ways and Means Committee, was firmly opposed to revenue sharing, and was determined to use his power to keep the House as a whole from even considering the proposal. Nixon tried to get Mills to change his mind, or to go around him, but not very energetically, as credit for having proposed revenue sharing was almost as valuable to Nixon as actually getting the bill.

Through the first months of 1971, Congress worked on Nixon's budget. The Democrats chipped away at his requests for defense spending while putting more funds into Great Society programs. To Nixon's dismay, the Senate made its final, decisive vote to kill the SST, 51–46. This cost Boeing in Seattle some 7,000 jobs; the company had already cut its work force since the peak of the Vietnam War from 101,000 to 44,000. Nixon called the vote "distressing and disappointing."[75] In May, gall turned to wormwood when the News Summary reported that the Soviet entry in the SST field was the sensation of the Paris Air Show. Nixon commented, "E, make all environmentalists on our staff take note. The *number one Technological* Tragedy of our time."[76]

Much as Nixon wanted to pump money into the economy, he

drew the line at certain projects. When Paul McCracken, chairman of the Council of Economic Advisers, recommended establishing a foundation to study "projects with a high potential social return, e.g., in environment and mass transportation," Nixon wrote on his memo, "*NEVER!!!* Another foundation will simply be another subsidy for Universities. I want these Foundations *Cut*." [77] On a memo informing him that MIT and the University of California (all campuses) were receiving $160 million and $379 million, respectively, in federal funds, Nixon wrote, "E—I want them severely cut." [78]

Organizations with fewer intellectuals and more voters did better. On March 23, in the Oval Office, Nixon met with Connally, Ehrlichman, Secretary of Agriculture Hardin, Shultz, and others to discuss milk price supports. The tape recorder was running; the tape was later made public as a government exhibit in a federal trial. But although the transcript is the first of a kind, the discussion centered on some of the most commonplace problems of presidential politics.

Without getting too deeply into details, the issue was milk price supports. The dairy farmers were well organized, and quite skillful in their lobbying efforts. Their single objective was to keep price support levels high, and they had a majority in Congress with them. Nixon wanted to economize and he wanted to cut prices for consumers, but he also knew he could not sustain a veto and he wanted votes in the farm states.

The issue was hardly earthshaking, but the transcript is wonderfully revealing of the way in which politicians go about convincing themselves that what is good for them carries with it the added bonus of being the fair thing, the right thing, the just thing to do.

Nixon asked Connally to review the situation. Connally said he did not want to go over the economics. "How about the politics?" Nixon asked.

"Well," Connally replied, "it appears very clear to me that you're going to have to move, uh, strong in the Midwest. You're going to have to be strong in rural America."

He went on to describe the desperate plight of the farmers and he mentioned the strength of the dairy lobby, and the "enormous amounts of money they have amassed to put into political activities." Of course it was the public's money, coming back to the congressmen who appropriated it via the dairy lobby, who got it from the price supports.

"I think they've got a worthy case to begin with," he continued. Nixon suggested holding down the price in '71, then raising it in '72. Connally pointed out that "if you do something for them this year, they think you've done it because they got a good case and because you're their friend. If you wait till next year, I don't care what you do for them. They're going to say, 'Well, we put enough pressure on them this election year,' and you, you get no credit for it."

Hardin pointed out that no matter what, the dairymen had the votes in the House and the Senate. Nixon noted helplessly, "If we don't do it, they're going to do it anyway. . . . We have a damn near insoluble problem."

Connally made the obvious point that if Nixon vetoed, he would still lose the money, plus his political payoff. "You, you're infinitely worse off."

"I could not veto it," Nixon sighed. "Not because they're milk producers, but because they're farmers. And it would just be turning down the whole damn middle America. Uh, where, uh, we, uh, where we, uh, need support. And under the circumstances, I think the best thing to do is to just, uh, relax and enjoy it."

That said it all, but he wanted a better justification than political necessity. Hardin gave it to him: he said it took a terrific investment to go into the dairy business, unlike hogs. In the pork business, when the price of corn went down, a small investment could bring a big profit.

What about the consumer? Connally had an answer: "Just remember when you talk about food prices, now, and, and bleed for the consumer, that today, food prices in the United States are cheaper than they've ever been in the history of this nation. In terms of what it takes for, well, uh, hours of work to feed a family. Sixteen percent. That's the lowest in the history of the world."

Nixon was pleased. "He's my favorite secretary," the President said of Connally.

Nixon was convinced: "Well, I think you got a good game plan. You, you'd, uh, you know your friends and our friends and so on." He thought of another good reason to support the dairymen; he said he was disturbed by all the sleeping-pill advertisements he saw, and he wanted to tell the country "milk is a sedative." People should drink milk rather than take pills. He decided that for the good of the country he had better sign.

Ehrlichman quipped, "Better go get a glass of milk. (*Laughter.*) Drink it while it's cheap."[79]

The dairymen got their increased price support; grateful, they pledged $2 million to Nixon's re-election campaign.[80]

Nixon's philosophy, which he called relaxing and enjoying the inevitable, was really one of profiting from the inevitable, as in the case of the conglomerate International Telephone and Telegraph

(ITT). The company was at the cutting edge of a new wave of corporate mergers and takeovers on a grand scale, at a time when the antitrust laws dated back to Senator John Sherman in the nineteenth century and the Clayton Antitrust Act of the Wilson Administration. The laws were based on an assumption that in business big was bad. No twentieth-century Republican President agreed with that assumption, but the permanent bureaucracy in the Justice Department insured that antitrust suits were filed no matter who was President.

ITT was a target because of its aggressive acquisition activity. Richard McLaren, head of the Antitrust Division of the Justice Department, had sued in 1969 to force ITT to divest itself of three recent acquisitions, Canteen Corporation, Grinnell Corporation, and the Hartford Fire Insurance Company. When the government lost the case on Grinnell (maker of automatic sprinkler systems), McLaren announced he would appeal.

On April 19, Nixon laid down the law to Ehrlichman: "They're not going to file [an appeal]. . . . I don't know whether ITT is bad, good, or indifferent. But there is not going to be any more antitrust actions as long as I am in this chair." He then called Richard Kleindienst, Deputy Attorney General, on the phone: "I want something clearly understood, and, if it is not understood, McLaren's ass is to be out within one hour. The ITT thing—stay the hell out of it. Is that clear? That's an order. . . . I do not want McLaren to run around prosecuting people, raising hell about conglomerates, stirring things up at this point. Now you keep him the hell out of that."

John Mitchell then persuaded Nixon that it would be "political dynamite" to stop the appeal, and the President allowed Mitchell to work out a compromise whereby ITT kept the Hartford in exchange for divesting itself of Grinnell and Canteen. And ITT pledged a substantial contribution to underwrite the 1972 Republican Convention.[81]

FOR ALL his frustrations and political difficulties, Nixon was having more success on the prosperity front than he was in bringing about peace. The Chicago Sun-Times, using a football metaphor, warned him that it was "3rd and 20" for his Administration on the Vietnam War, citing a Gallup poll that reported 61 percent of the public now said the war was a mistake. Nixon commented sadly, "K—note, probably an accurate reading of public sentiment."[82]

But no matter how war weary the country was, Nixon saw it as his responsibility, and burden, to hold the people to their duty, so that they would reject the glittering prospect of "peace now" in favor of a greater goal. In describing that greater goal, he was getting more and more carried away.

In late winter, in remarks at the dedication of the Woodrow Wilson International Center for Scholars, in Washington, D.C., he recalled that Wilson had tried but failed to stem the tide of postwar isolationism, and that he had died a broken man. But later generations realized that Wilson had been right, and that if the American people had followed his lead, World War I might well have been the war to end all wars.

"Every wartime President since Woodrow Wilson has been tempted to describe the current war as the war to end wars," Nixon went on. "But they have not done so because of the derision that the phrase evoked, a reminder . . . of hopes that were raised and dashed."

Having said that, Nixon came close to identifying himself and his cause with the Wilsonian phrase: "What I am striving for above all else . . . is something that America has never experienced in this century: a full generation of peace."[83]

On April 29, he went further. Antiwar groups were preparing for a May Day demonstration in Washington; many young people had already arrived and were picketing the White House and the Capitol. Nixon at a news conference said he had seen them, and was moved by how many were teenagers. "This is the thought that passed through my mind: My responsibility is to bring peace, but not just peace in our time, but peace in their time. I want peace not just for us, but peace for our children, their children."

Later in the same news conference, however, Nixon said that a residual force of U.S. troops would remain in South Vietnam indefinitely—"no matter how long it takes"—if Hanoi refused to release American prisoners of war.[84]

To the youthful demonstrators, that sounded like permanent war. Their frustrations contributed to their irresponsible behavior on May Day, when they tried to shut down the government. The Nixon Administration responded with mass arrests, which inevitably brought on outraged protests about violations of civil liberties.

Nixon, in a subsequent news conference, defended the D.C. police. Gripping the lectern before him, and visibly agitated by reporters who were critical, the President gave his wholehearted approval to the police and the Justice Department. If there were similar situations in the future, he would have them do the same. He explained that the D.C. authorities had always defended the right of people to protest peacefully, "but when people come in and slice tires, when they block traffic, when they make a trash bin out of Georgetown and when they terrorize innocent bystanders, they are not demonstrators, they are vandals and hoodlums and lawbreakers, and they should be treated as lawbreakers. . . . This Government's going to go forward and that kind of activity is not going to be tolerated in this capital." [85]

Nixon's outrage was genuine and appropriate, but, as after the San Jose incident the previous fall, many reporters did not share his feelings. That this was so said something about the reporters, to be sure, but it also said something about how perilously close Nixon was coming to losing control of the situation. It truly was 3rd and 30, and Nixon needed a big play to extract himself if he was to avoid having to punt.

CHAPTER TWENTY

DÉTENTE WITH RUSSIA AND CHINA
May–August 1971

DÉTENTE IS a French word that means a "relaxation of tension," as with the release of a taut bowstring. The meaning is considerably different from that of another French word used in diplomacy, *entente,* which signifies a close and cooperative relationship.

Nixon wanted détente with both Russia and China for overwhelming and obvious reasons. Nixon loved drama, surprise, and confounding his enemies. What could be more dramatic or surprising than for the world's number-one anti-Communist for two decades to open to China and to sign an arms-control agreement with Russia? What could be more confounding to Nixon's Vietnam critics than for the warmonger to suddenly become the peacemaker?

Nixon prided himself on his realism, and by mid-1971 the patterns established early in the Cold War were no longer realistic. America could not maintain a nuclear monopoly; it could not even maintain a nuclear superiority. The United States military forces could not defend the country; they could only retaliate. The damnedest paradox had developed; the more bombs and missiles America built, the less secure it became, because the Soviets could and would match the effort, and the Chinese were starting to come on strong.

American strategy in the fifties and sixties had been to stay strong and wait. The thought (hope) was that sooner or later the internal contradictions of Communism would bring about the collapse of the regimes in Moscow and Peking. By 1971, it was clear that was not going to happen anytime soon.

439

America could not destroy the Communists, as it had destroyed the Nazis. The Communists were not going to self-destruct, as the Spanish Empire had in the Philippines and Cuba.

Another development: the Communists were no more able to stick together as a monolithic force than the Christians had been. By 1971 Russia and China had become the bitterest of enemies, hurling their worst invective at each other rather than at the Americans, engaging in acts of war on their border and anxiously seeking allies for the struggle.

As the Sino-Soviet split deepened and widened, each side found itself impelled toward détente with the United States. There were monumental and apparently unconquerable obstacles, including the decades of hostility and the entrenched interests that had been built up in support of the status quo of Cold War, and such issues as the American presence on Taiwan or Russian control of Poland. But the structure of world politics in 1971 led toward détente, if only the imagination and the will could be summoned to achieve bold breakthroughs.

It took no great insight or stunning brilliance to see these rather simple truths or to recognize the opportunities that were opened by them. It did take courage, political skills, diplomatic sensitivity, and dogged determination to respond appropriately, because the men and forces in all three great powers who were opposed to détente were numerous, cunning, and powerful.

In promoting détente, Nixon had strengths of his own, many of them equally obvious. First, as he often pointed out, he was the one, the only one, who could pull it off. It was not just that his anti-Communist credentials were impeccable; it was that he did not have to deal with Nixon. That is, had anyone but Nixon tried to promote détente, Nixon would have been the leading, and devastating, critic who would have rallied the right wing to kill the initiative.

Second, the Russians and the Chinese were pursuing him as avidly as he was pursuing them. He could make overtures without risking rebuff or ridicule.

Third, the timing was perfect. The American people were weary of war. For the first time in the Cold War, there was a constituency for peace. Not all, by any means, but surely a majority was saying, "Give peace a chance."

Fourth, there was an election coming up. Back in 1962, the Democrats had forced Nixon to repudiate the Far Right (the John Birch Society), and it had hurt him. In 1972, through the boldness of détente, he would not have to repudiate the extremists by name; he could do it by policy. They could rant and rave, but they had nowhere to go in a national election except to Nixon, which would force them to mute their criticisms. Meanwhile, he could pick up the votes of moderates and even liberals, and strip the Democrats of what they anticipated would be one of their best issues.

There was an obvious, even ideal, path available to Nixon to begin the journey to détente, the SALT talks. They dealt with a problem of fundamental importance. Arms control commanded public support. The Johnson Administration had proposed the talks, which had the effect of committing the Democrats to them, while leaving Nixon free to claim that any agreement reached was his achievement.

The Soviets were ready, indeed eager. This in turn gave Nixon an added inducement to negotiate. By linking SALT to Vietnam, he hoped to be able to give in the arms-control area to get Soviet cooperation in Vietnam.

Typically, Nixon had begun the process by apparently moving in the opposite direction, when he announced (March 1969) his Safeguard (ABM) program to defend American ICBM launch sites. Then he told Dobrynin (June 1969) that the U.S. was prepared to begin the SALT talks. After some Soviet stalling, the talks began in Helsinki (November) and continued in Vienna (April 1970).

The Soviets wanted to limit or even eliminate ABMs, a position supported by Senate liberals and doves. The Soviets were not interested in placing limits on ICBMs. Nixon insisted that ABMs were vital as a "bargaining chip," to be traded for limits on ICBMs and SLBMs (submarine launched ballistic missiles). The Soviets were increasing their ICBM and SLBM arsenals, while the Americans were not; American improvements were qualitative (MIRV), not quantitative. Thus the Americans were asking for a unilateral freeze by the expanding Soviets, while accepting no limits on their own MIRV program.

Nixon's position was weak because he was trying to trade something he probably would never get anyway (ABM) for something he could not prevent (Soviet expansion of ICBMs). In Vienna, therefore, the chief American negotiator, Gerard Smith, proposed limiting ABM to the defense of National Command Authorities (NCAs), i.e., Washington and Moscow. The Soviets quickly accepted. They proposed (December 1970) to decouple the defensive (ABM) and offensive (ICBM and SLBM) issues, and by March of 1971 a draft treaty was ready, limiting both sides to two ABMs to defend NCAs. But the American officials continued to insist on linking limits on ICBMs as well as ABMs.

Kissinger, meanwhile, carried on back-channel negotiations with Dobrynin. He told the Soviet ambassador to ignore the official

American position in Vienna; Dobrynin responded with an offer Nixon could hardly refuse—a summit meeting in Moscow to complete an ABM agreement with an "understanding" that there would be certain limits on ICBM construction, with the exact limits to be determined in future talks.

Nixon's eagerness to accept that offer revealed another linkage in the whole complex process—the linkage between arms control, a summit, and the upcoming American election. But then what Kissinger called "a bizarre incident" intruded; at Vienna, the Soviets made the Dobrynin offer public and official. If the breakthrough came in Vienna, Gerard Smith, not Nixon, would get the credit. If that happened, Kissinger warned Dobrynin, "the President's anger at what he could only construe as a deliberate maneuver to deprive him of credit would be massive."

To convince the Soviets that they should deal only through the back channel, Kissinger—on Nixon's instruction—made some secret offers to Dobrynin. In return for a summit, an ABM treaty, and a short-term constraint on Soviet ICBM construction, the United States would not insist on SLBM limits (on which the delegation in Vienna had been insisting). The Soviets accepted.[1]

At noon on May 20, in the Briefing Room at the White House, Nixon went on nationwide radio and television to read a statement (released simultaneously in Moscow). It said the U.S. and the U.S.S.R. had agreed to a limitation on ABMs. "They have also agreed that . . . they will agree on certain measures with respect to the limitation of offensive strategic weapons." The statement said both sides were convinced that this course "will create more favorable conditions for further negotiations to limit all strategic arms. These negotiations will be actively pursued."

Nixon called the agreement "a major step," which, if fully successful, "may be remembered as the beginning of a new era."[2]

FOR ONCE, he was not indulging in hyperbole. Although there was (and is) much to criticize in his methods and the results, this was a historic achievement, the first positive movement toward real arms control since the onset of the atomic age. Not even Eisenhower, by far the Cold War President most committed to putting a cap on the arms race, had been able to get anything remotely as concrete as Nixon had achieved.

Of course, there were critics. The right wing said what it was expected to say, that the Soviets could not be trusted. The arms-control experts were furious at the way Kissinger and Nixon had operated behind their backs, and highly critical of Kissinger for excluding the SLBMs from the deal, and for failing to nail down limits on offensive weapons in general. Garthoff was especially critical of Kissinger's failure to include limits on MIRVs, and charged that Nixon had pursued "agreements that were politically the most easy to reach in internal negotiations in Washington, rather than to the agreements that would be most effective in curbing the arms competition between the two powers."[3]

Nixon anticipated such criticism, and he was embarrassed at having to inform his Secretary of State that a major deal had been struck with the Russians not only without State Department participation but without it even knowing such negotiations had been going on.[4] But he continued to insist on secrecy. After making the announcement, he held a Cabinet meeting. "Don't tell the bureaucracy anything," he declared. "Close down the curtain. Don't speculate on where the negotiations are going. The less said regarding what is going on the better. The more we talk, the less chance of an agreement."

Nixon also anticipated, correctly, an enthusiastic response to the announcement, but he warned the Cabinet to play it down, not up. He described the breakthrough as "a significant first step which could be decisive," but warned that there was a long way to go and "this is not a time for euphoria."[5]

John Scali, a former ABC-TV correspondent, had joined the White House staff in April as senior consultant on foreign affairs information policy. On May 26, he sent Nixon a memo analyzing the "avalanche of favorable comment that has been unleashed since the . . . SALT announcement." Scali said he feared Nixon was being "overly praised" by the very commentators who, just a few days earlier, had been critical of his arms-control policy. He expected that this praise would multiply, because it was coming from the "opinion molders." Among others, he named James Reston, Max Frankel, Harrison Salisbury, Chalmers Roberts, and Peter Lisagor.

"After months of enduring criticism," Scali wrote, "I would not blame you for sitting back for a period to savor the sweet success your efforts have wrought," but he warned that there was a danger. "A national euphoria is developing that will backfire if, as seems likely, the slow pace of developments fails to keep step with the rosy expectations." Nixon underlined the sentence and wrote in the margin, "K—note. Right!"

Scali recommended that Nixon "cool off the great expectations by stressing the enormously difficult negotiations that lie ahead," that he give notice that "secrecy is indispensable to a successful result," and that he tell his spokesmen to take a "low-key approach." Beside each sentence Nixon wrote "O.K."[6]

Nixon had told the Cabinet, "We can't say the Soviets gave all and we gave nothing." The right wing was charging the opposite, with some justification. Senator Thurmond said Nixon had yielded to the Soviet demand that a limitation on ABMs be negotiated prior to offensive weapons: "The Soviets have won their point, for all practical purposes."

"K—straighten him out," Nixon ordered.[7]

National Review charged that Nixon had acted more out of election concern than anything else. "The U.S. has knuckled under to what has been the consistent Soviet demand, a limitation on ABMs." Nixon read the remarks in his News Summary and wrote, "K—talk to Buckley *soonest*—He can keep them from getting on wrong track."[8]

So some of Nixon's oldest supporters were on his back, while some of his oldest critics were hoisting him on their shoulders. Democratic presidential hopefuls could but applaud. The bureaucrats were furious at their exclusion from policy formulation. The American people, overwhelmingly, were relieved and happy. In every foreign capital, diplomats asked each other, "What next?"

And the man himself sat in the catbird seat, grinning.

NIXON'S SUCCESS notwithstanding, Congress remained difficult. The prospect of a SALT agreement made no apparent contribution to peace in Vietnam, where the war, fought by the Vietnamese for the most part, with Chinese, American, and Russian weapons, went on. A Republican dove, Representative John Anderson of Illinois, called for a congressional investigation into allegations that the big oil companies were behind the American commitment, with the aim of exploiting supposedly huge oil deposits off the Vietnamese coast. An exasperated Nixon wrote on his News Summary, "K— this is totally ridiculous and should be immediately nailed."[9]

In the Senate, Mike Mansfield had attached an amendment to the selective service bill that would assure troop reductions in Europe as a quid pro quo for draft extension. Nixon turned to Harry Truman's old crowd for help in defeating it. On May 13 he gathered Lucius Clay, John McCloy, and Dean Acheson, among others, in the Cabinet Room to ask them to lobby the Senate against Mansfield. All did, and on May 19 the Senate responded. In what had been expected to be a close vote, it turned down the Mansfield amendment, 61–36. A few days later a delighted Nixon sent a note of thanks to Acheson: "You were among [those] at the Cabinet Room who could truly claim to have been 'Present at the Creation.' All can now proudly look back to the events of the past few days and with some degree of truth say that they were 'Present at the Resurrection.' "[10]

• •

NIXON HAD another reason to grin that spring. On June 12, in the social event of the season in Washington, Tricia got married in the Rose Garden.

The groom was Edward F. Cox, a Princeton graduate who was a second-year law student at Harvard. He and Tricia had been dating for years, and denying that they were serious for almost as long. Julie described them as "intelligent, opinionated, and strong-willed." Although Cox was a Republican, he frequently disagreed with Nixon's policies, which Tricia vigorously defended. In the summer of 1968, following his graduation, Cox had worked for Ralph Nader as a "Nader Raider," while Tricia had campaigned for her father. Love overcame politics, and in November 1970, Cox asked Nixon's permission to marry Tricia. He said yes, and on Pat's birthday, March 16, the couple made the announcement.

The wedding was the eighth of a presidential daughter at the White House but the first in the Rose Garden, and the interest it aroused can be seen in one fact: some sixteen hundred reporters requested White House credentials to cover the ceremony.[11]

The guest list set tongues to wagging all through Washington. J. Edgar Hoover was there, along with Billy Graham, Norman Vincent Peale, Red Skelton, Art Linkletter, Bebe Rebozo, Hobart Lewis, Warren Burger, members of the Cabinet, and Ralph Nader. Notable by their absence were the chairman of the RNC, Senator Robert Dole of Kansas, Gerald Ford and Hugh Scott (minority leaders in the House and Senate), and in fact every representative and senator—not a single member of Congress was invited.[12]

The wedding was set for 4 P.M., but at 2:45 P.M. it was raining. Nixon strolled over to the press tent to announce that he had advised Tricia to "play it safe" and move the ceremony indoors. He then took refuge in his EOB office, where he spent his time on the telephone, alternately talking to Tricia and Air Force meteorologists.

Tricia wanted to wait, hoping for a letup.

At 4:15 P.M., the weathermen predicted a fifteen-minute pause in the rain, starting at 4:30.

Nixon told Haldeman to get the ushers moving. By 4:30, the guests were seated, and as promised, the rain halted. At 4:48, in a dainty white garden pavilion covered with flowers, Tricia and Ed were pronounced man and wife. Within minutes, the rain started up again, and everyone hustled inside.

The reception was in the East Room. Nixon danced with Tricia while Ed danced with Pat. This was the first time Nixon had ever danced in the White House, in fact the first time he had ever danced in Washington. The startled guests broke into delighted applause when he danced with Pat. His face showed his complete delight; this was one time at least when he was genuinely happy, having fun, enjoying himself. He danced with Julie (David was not present; he was on sea duty in the Mediterranean), then with others. He spotted Lynda Bird Johnson standing alone (her husband, Chuck Robb, was also in the service), and danced with her.[13]

ON SUNDAY MORNING, June 13, Nixon read the front-page account of Tricia's wedding in *The New York Times*, then glanced at the story beside it. He looked again. The headline read, "VIETNAM ARCHIVE: PENTAGON STUDY TRACES 3 DECADES OF GROWING U.S. INVOLVEMENT."

These were the so-called Pentagon Papers, a rather poorly done and woefully incomplete narrative of American involvement in Vietnam from the end of World War II until the mid-sixties. The study contained documents from Defense, State, the CIA, the White House, and the JCS, many of them classified top secret. Despite the classification, the *Times* indicated it planned to publish some of those documents.

Nixon read the story with interest but without outrage or excitement. And why not? In the first place, it was history. It did not concern his Administration. Better yet, it was history about Democrats, and deliberately written to embarrass Kennedy and Johnson. It showed how both Presidents had lied to and deceived the public about their intentions and policies in Vietnam. Nixon's initial reaction was, let Larry O'Brien complain, if he dared.

This business of leaking classified documents was disturbing, but hardly unique. Back in 1963, Nixon had been the leading defender of Otto Otepka, the State Department employee who had leaked classified documents to the Republican senators who were trying to block the confirmation of Walt Rostow for the NSC. Otepka had been roundly criticized by *The New York Times* and the Washington *Post* for violating security procedures; Nixon had defended him (and, when he became President, Nixon restored Otepka to a government post), so he was not in a good position to make a big fuss over violations of security procedures.

Four days later, Nixon met with Kissinger, Haldeman, and Ehrlichman to discuss the situation. Kissinger came into the meeting with a couple of items foremost in his mind.

First, there was secrecy. He was convinced that if he had not been able to keep his back-channel negotiations with Dobrynin a secret, there never would have been a breakthrough on SALT. The back-channel talks with the Chinese were on the verge of success; again, Kissinger was convinced, because they were secret. If the newspapers continued to publish the Pentagon Papers, the Communist governments might well conclude that the U.S. government was incapable of keeping a secret, and break off negotiations.

Second, there was the embarrassing fact that the man who had given the Pentagon Papers to the newspapers was Dr. Daniel Ellsberg, who had once lectured to Kissinger's Harvard seminar. In 1969 Kissinger had brought Ellsberg onto the NSC staff as a consultant.[14]

So in the Oval Office, Kissinger proceeded to put on a performance that Haldeman characterized as "beyond belief." He was enraged. His paranoia poured out of him. It was "one of his most passionate tirades."[15] Kissinger said Ellsberg was a "genius," one of the "brightest student[s]" at Harvard, but a man fatally flawed. He was a sexual pervert who made love with his wife in front of his children. He was a drug abuser. He had once been a hawk who enjoyed shooting Vietnamese peasants from helicopters in Vietnam, but had gone from "hawk to peacenik." He had in his possession critical defense secrets of current validity, such as nuclear targeting. Kissinger described Ellsberg as "the most dangerous man in America today," who "must be stopped at all costs."[16]

(Reporter Stanley Karnow confirms at least one part of this diatribe: "When our paths first crossed in 1966 in Saigon," he writes of Ellsberg, "where he belonged to a special counterinsurgency team headed by Edward Lansdale, he was a fervent believer in the war who hotly disputed my lack of enthusiasm.")[17]

Nixon enjoyed gossip as much as anyone, but his taste ran much more toward political stuff than sexual sensations; in this, as in so much else, he was the opposite of Kissinger. What Nixon wanted to know was, Who took the money? or Who is going to run? or Who made the payoff?—not Who slept with her? or Is he really gay? So Nixon was relatively unmoved by Kissinger's avalanche of accusations against Ellsberg. What got him to take bold and dramatic and illegal action was Kissinger's argument that the President did not understand how dangerous the release of the Pentagon Papers was. "The fact that some idiot can publish all of the diplomatic secrets of this country . . . is damaging to your image . . . and it could destroy our ability to conduct foreign policy." Then, the absolute clincher: "It shows you're a weakling, Mr. President."[18]

That line propelled Nixon into action, on numerous fronts. The Justice Department sought an injunction against the publication of any more of the Pentagon Papers (on June 30, the Supreme Court ruled against the government, 6–3). Excited by Kissinger's gossip,

Nixon tried to get the FBI to undertake a full investigation of Ellsberg. He snapped out orders on his News Summary: "H—C—Be *sure* [McGeorge] Bundy and *no* foundation people have clearances —I want a full report on *all* non-government people who have clearances on my desk Wednesday A.M. in San Clemente."[19] He ordered Haldeman to "confront personally every single Cabinet officer and agency head, brutally chew them out and threaten them with extinction if they didn't stop all leaks in the future."

The President told Haldeman, "You're going to be my Lord High Executioner from now on." He told him to start by giving a lie detector test to every employee in the State Department who might have had access to the Pentagon Papers.[20]

Nixon wanted to smash the Brookings Institution. He recalled that back in 1969 he had asked Haldeman to get him a copy of the Pentagon file on the events of October 1968, leading up to Johnson's bombing halt; he had wanted the information to use as political leverage against Clark Clifford and others who were opposing his Vietnam policy. Haldeman had reported that the material had been taken from the Pentagon to Brookings. Now, in June 1971, Nixon asked for it again, and was again told that it was at Brookings and the Institution would not give it up.

"I was furious and frustrated," Nixon later confessed. He could not get his hands on top-secret material because it was being held by antiwar Democrats in a private think tank. "It seemed absurd. . . . I saw absolutely no reason for that report to be at Brookings." He told Haldeman, "I want that goddamn . . . material and I don't care how you get it," and made it clear that included surreptitious operations.[21]

But nothing came of this order, nor would the FBI get moving, which only increased Nixon's frustrations. Ehrlichman told him that Robert Mardian, one of Mitchell's assistant attorneys general, had managed to lift ("smuggle" was the word Ehrlichman used) the internal FBI report on Ellsberg, and it showed foot-dragging. Ehrlichman added that Mitchell had told him the reason: Ellsberg's father-in-law, a toy manufacturer named Louis Marx, was a close friend of Hoover's (and, Nixon must have known, a friend of Ike's as well). Hoover had attempted to stop an FBI interview with Marx, then suppressed the report when the interview was done anyway, and demoted the official who approved it.[22]

Shortly thereafter, on July 12, Mardian flew to San Clemente to tell Nixon that Hoover was threatening to use the seventeen wiretaps placed on Kissinger's aides and on reporters back in 1969 as blackmail in order to retain his post (rumors were rife in Washington that Nixon wanted to get rid of the seventy-six-year-old Hoover). Nixon said he had often heard that Hoover used such blackmail to keep his job, but he never believed it, and did not now. But he also did not fire Hoover, or demand his resignation.[23]

What he did do was order Haldeman to destroy the logs from the wiretaps, and issue instructions that all such activities cease. Haldeman, Mitchell, and Ehrlichman discussed Ellsberg's various appearances on the tapes made from the taps (Ellsberg knew almost everyone on Kissinger's NSC staff), and what could be done with that evidence. Nixon, perhaps aware that his own secret tape recorder was running, said of the logs and transcripts, "I naturally never saw any of that stuff." [24]

Meanwhile, Nixon was being goaded almost beyond bearing, as Ellsberg became the darling of the doves. CBS News gave him a half-hour show of his own, with Walter Cronkite asking the questions and Ellsberg warning that he feared "a replay of 1964," meaning a campaign promising peace followed by a postelection escalation.[25]

If the FBI would not act, Nixon would. He gave Ehrlichman the marching orders: "If we can't get anyone in this damn government to do something about [leaks], then, by God, we'll do it ourselves. I want you to set up a little group right here in the White House. Have them get off their tails and find out what's going on and figure out how to stop it." On July 17, Ehrlichman gave the job to Egil "Bud" Krogh, one of his assistants, and David Young, from the NSC staff.[26] Young set up an office in the EOB and put a sign on the door, "Plumbers," signifying that he was going to stop the leaks.

The whole setup was irresistible to Colson, who within days got in on the act with a long memo for Ehrlichman. He recommended that Krogh hire a former FBI agent, G. Gordon Liddy, and a former CIA agent, E. Howard Hunt ("Liddy is an excellent man," Colson wrote, and "Hunt can be very useful").

Turning to policy, Colson went on: "The question is where the political punch line is. . . . To paint Ellsberg black is probably a good thing; to link him into a conspiracy which suggests treasonous conduct is also a good thing, but the real political payoff will come only if we can establish that there is . . . a 'counter government' which is deliberately trying to undermine U.S. foreign policy . . . and that it is the President who stands against this 'counter government,' who conquers them and who rescues the nation from the subversion of these unsavory characters. We must be certain we can direct this effort in a way that gives us the political positions we need and ties our political opposition into the enemy camp." He said he was putting Hunt to work on exposing "the Harrimans, the Warnkes, the Cliffords, the Vances, the McGeorge Bundys, and McNamaras, etc." [27]

And where did Colson get such ideas? According to Colson, from the President himself, who told him, "We've got a counter-government here and we've got to fight it. I don't give a damn how it is done, do whatever has to be done. . . . I don't want to be told why it can't be done. I want the most complete investigation that can be conducted. . . . I don't want excuses. I want results. I want it done; whatever the cost." [28]

Hunt went to work, and the plot began to thicken. It turned out that Hunt had a friend, Bob Bennett, the man who had replaced Larry O'Brien as Howard Hughes's man in Washington. And Bennett's firm, Robert R. Mullen Company, was a CIA cover agency. [29]

IN THE MIDST of this flurry of activity, Kissinger, who had set it all in motion, went on a Far Eastern trip. The announced purpose was consultations in Vietnam, with a stop in Pakistan on the way back. The real purpose involved China.

By the spring of 1971, Nixon and Chou were practically exchanging semaphore messages in their eagerness to get together. Chou's late-April message that Nixon would be "welcome" in Peking, along with the Ping-Pong tour, prompted Nixon to have Kissinger tell the Pakistani ambassador to tell President Yahya to tell Chou that the President was prepared to accept Chou's invitation. He proposed that Kissinger visit China first, secretly, to arrange an agenda.

At a June 1 news conference, Nixon said that he would soon announce further easing of restrictions on trade with "Mainland China." He continued, "There is a Chinese proverb to the effect that a journey of a thousand miles begins with a single step. . . . We have started the journey toward a more normal relationship with Mainland China." [30]

The next evening, after a state dinner for President Somoza of Nicaragua, Nixon was reading in the Lincoln Sitting Room. Kissinger burst in, out of breath. He handed Nixon a note.

"This just arrived in the Pakistani Embassy pouch," he gasped, excited and beaming.

The message was from Chou. It said that Mao was looking forward to discussions with Nixon to settle in a concrete way "the withdrawal of all the U.S. Armed Forces from Taiwan" and that the Chinese welcomed Kissinger "as the U.S. representative who will come in advance for a preliminary secret meeting with high level Chinese officials to prepare and make necessary arrangements for President Nixon's visit to Peking."

Kissinger, no more averse to hyperbole than Nixon himself, declared, "This is the most important communication that has come to an American President since the end of World War II."[31]

On June 10, Nixon made his promised announcement, as he ended a twenty-one-year embargo on trade with China and lifted all controls on imports from China. There was another part to the new policy, hardly noticed by the press, and not connected to China. It was a further sweetener to the Russians in anticipation of a SALT agreement and a summit in Moscow: Nixon ended the requirement, in force since 1963, that called for half of all grain shipments to the Soviet Union to be carried on American flag vessels.[32] This opened the door to a grain deal with the Soviets, secretly promised by Kissinger in his back-channel talks with Dobrynin.

"We have done it now," Kissinger said. "We have got it all hooked together."[33]

In early July, Kissinger flew off to Asia. On July 9, in Pakistan, the reporters accompanying him were told he had a stomachache and would stay in bed. He went out a back door and to the airport, where a Pakistani jet waited to fly him over the mountains into China; code name for his trip was Polo. If all went well, he had a code word to flash to Nixon when he returned to Islamabad—Eureka.

On July 11, Al Haig telephoned Nixon. A cable from Kissinger had arrived. It read, "Eureka."[34]

This was the high point of the Nixon Administration to date. He had turned the tide, and put the woes of the first half of 1971 behind him. He made the most of it, beginning with his debriefing of Kissinger.

In his memoirs, Nixon wrote that Kissinger's report on his trip was "fascinating," but he barely mentioned the substance of Kissinger's talks with Chou. Kissinger, in his memoirs, devotes a fifty-five-page chapter to loving detail about the trip, mainly emphasizing what a great man Chou was and how remarkable a man the author was to deal with him as an equal. But, like Nixon, Kissinger spares us the drudgery of assimilating information on the substance of the talks.

So the Polo journey remains shrouded in mystery, and given the obsession of both Nixon and Kissinger in their retirements to continue the cover-up by using every means possible to keep the basic documents under seal, it is likely to remain shrouded. The men who have worked hardest to penetrate the mystery are reporter Seymour Hersh and diplomat Raymond Garthoff. Their sources are interviews with men close to Kissinger and Nixon; such sources are always unsatisfactory and unreliable unless grounded in the contemporary documentary record, but until Nixon chooses to reveal that record, interviews are all that are available.

The main outline of the story that Hersh and Garthoff got from their informants is as follows: even before Polo, Kissinger had privately let the Chinese know that in return for receiving Nixon in Peking for a summit early in the election year of 1972, the U.S. was prepared to make a public commitment to withdraw all American troops from Taiwan.

Lest that appear too cynical, consider the words of one of Hersh's unnamed informants: Nixon "recognized right from the start that you couldn't even begin to negotiate until you got that out of the way. We couldn't quibble over that." [35] Quite right, too, and to Nixon's credit he got something from the Chinese in return for accepting the inevitable.

He got more than the summit, in fact, as the Chinese also had to betray an ally. Nixon's quid pro quo for Taiwan was North Vietnam. The Chinese had to accept, in principle, the role of mediator; i.e., they made an implied promise that they would urge the North Vietnamese to allow the U.S. to withdraw before the election and without overthrowing the Thieu government.

This was not, however, much of a concession on China's part. Once the United States got out of Southeast Asia, China's main competitor for power and influence in the region would be Vietnam. Thus, when Kissinger told Chou that if North Vietnam launched an offensive in 1972, Nixon would strike back furiously and expect the Chinese to acquiesce, Chou evidently agreed.

Kissinger let Chou know that the U.S. would no longer attempt to block Chinese entry into the United Nations (the vote was scheduled for October), but that was no concession, as China already had the votes for entry.

It is often true in diplomacy that what is central to an alliance, a rapprochement, or a détente does not have to be discussed, precisely because it is central. It was fear of the Soviet Union that had brought China and the United States together, yet the Soviet Union was a subject that was hardly discussed. Just the thought of the Soviet reaction to the announcement of their meeting was enough to cause shivers of pleasure and hours of delight for both Kissinger and Chou, who did not need to discuss it to know it.

Kissinger did bring a gift, a not-very-subtle reminder to Chou of the sophistication of American technology and of what could be in it for China should the normalization of relations lead to a closer collaboration. It was a series of highly classified American satellite reconnaissance photographs and communications intelligence concerning the Soviet buildup on the Chinese borders. Chou was polite enough not to ask how they had been obtained; Nixon was smart enough to announce, two weeks after Kissinger returned, the suspension of previously unacknowledged aerial reconnaissance flights over China.

Kissinger got another concession from China. Chou knew enough about American politics to be aware that Nixon was trailing Muskie in the polls, and that within a year and a half the Democrats might well be in the White House. He therefore had indicated he intended to issue visas to Senators Muskie and Kennedy, and that they might possibly visit China before Nixon did. Nixon told Haldeman, "Never," and instructed Kissinger to make certain it did not happen. In Peking, evidently, Chou agreed that Nixon would come first.[36]

At 7:31 P.M., July 15, 1971, from the NBC studios in Burbank, California, Nixon spoke to the nation over radio and on television. He was on for only a moment, but what he said astonished the nation and the world. He read an announcement that was being issued simultaneously in Peking. It referred to Kissinger's trip, Nixon's "expressed desire to visit the People's Republic of China," the Chinese invitation, and Nixon's acceptance. "The meeting between the leaders of China and the United States is to seek the normalization of relations between the two countries and also to exchange views of concern to the two sides."

In a nicely written paragraph, Nixon added a bit of explanation, aimed at Taiwan and the Soviet Union, as well as the right wing in the United States: "Our action in seeking a new relationship with the People's Republic of China will not be at the expense of our old friends. It is not directed against any other nation." He insisted that "all nations will gain from a reduction of tensions and a better relationship between the United States and the People's Republic of China." He concluded with a hope that had by now become his favorite theme: "I will undertake . . . a journey for peace, peace not just for our generation but for future generations on this earth we share together."[37]

Despite the scores of signals Nixon had sent up on this subject, beginning with his "Asia After Viet Nam" article in *Foreign Affairs* back in 1967, the American media were taken by complete surprise. "Stunning," "unbelievable," "incredible," were some of the words used in the newspaper reports. Nor were the world capitals at all prepared: Taiwan reacted initially "with disbelief, then dismay"; in Moscow, the news came "with stunning surprise"; in London, diplomats agreed that Nixon's move "had suddenly and vastly altered the world political scene." In Warsaw, the development was described in a newspaper as "a shocking somersault"; in Paris, *Le Monde* called it "a great turning point in world politics."[38]

At home, the response was favorable, although not overwhelmingly so. Mansfield said he was "flabbergasted, delighted and happy," a line most of the Democrats followed. But Nixon's right-wing supporters were flabbergasted and unhappy. Representative John Schmitz (R., Cal.) charged Nixon with "surrendering to international communism." The Young Americans for Freedom, a Republican Party youth organization, denounced Nixon's policies. At their convention in Houston in early September, amidst shouts of "Dump Nixon," they endorsed Spiro Agnew for President in 1972. Barry Goldwater commented, "Nothing Nixon did surprised me anymore. He had contradicted himself so often that I was beginning to expect it."[39]

Haldeman, on Nixon's orders, put the White House PR team into high gear selling Nixon the world statesman. There was more than a little irritation on the President's part because of the sudden emergence of Kissinger, heretofore relatively unknown to the general public, now the object of a tremendous outpouring of articles that featured the National Security Adviser, rather than Nixon, as the key player in the epic poem. Most embarrassed was the Secretary of State, who read about the opening to China in the newspapers.

Generally, however, Nixon was all but overwhelmed by good feelings brought on by his triumph. This was even better than the greatest week since Creation. Like Kissinger, he saw Chou and Mao as two of the genuinely great men of the century (an odd twist for this charter member of the old China Lobby, but there it was). He gave Kissinger detailed instructions on what to tell the press; the main point was to urge reporters to note the resemblance between Chou and Nixon. In a July 19 memo to Kissinger, Nixon instructed him to point out to the press some of those "ironic similar character characteristics" the President and the Premier shared, such as "at his best in a crisis. Cool. Unflappable. . . . Never concerned about tomorrow's headlines but about how the policy will look years from now . . . steely but subtle."[40]

On August 2, Nixon found an even better line; his News Summary reported that the Washington *Daily News* had a feature on "the deep similarities between the lives of RN and Mao." The delighted Nixon scribbled in the margin, "K—Note!"

On August 4, at a news conference, Nixon was asked when he would make the trip. He said it would be before May of 1972, because he did not want his journey to get mixed up in partisan politics during the re-election campaign.[41]

• •

DESPITE ALL the favorable press coverage and editorial comment Nixon got that summer, on SALT and on the China opening, his war with the media went on. He met with Mitchell and Ehrlichman to plan a campaign against the networks, in which the chief assault would be an antitrust action. That offensive, arranged in detail some months earlier, had been delayed because of the Pentagon Papers controversy. Nixon had feared that an antitrust suit at that time would be "misconstrued." By late summer, however, he was ready to go ahead.

Ehrlichman warned him to expect the networks to "counterattack vigorously." Nixon noted that it was "vitally important to plan the P.R. aspects—get Coulson [sic] in on this phase of it." [42]

It was not only the commercial networks that roused Nixon's ire; he was more or less permanently angry with PBS as well. When the News Summary reported that Robert MacNeil and Sander Vanocur would be anchoring a weekly political program on PBS in 1972, Nixon exploded. He circled Vanocur's name and scribbled, "Flanagin [sic]—This is the last straw. Cut all funds for Public broadcasting immediately. Work it out with the House Appropriations Comm." [43]

Walter Cronkite's name was guaranteed to bring forth a strong negative reaction from Nixon, so Allin and Buchanan goaded their boss with little Cronkite items from time to time. After a long piece in September on the Washington Senators deserting the nation's capital (with a loud protest from Nixon but relative silence from Congress), the News Summary went on: "Cronkite noted the report by 2 psychologists who studied 15,000 athletes and found sports has virtually nothing to do with building character, win or lose." Nixon, scarcely able to believe his eyes, scribbled: "Coulson [sic] —he should be banged by our sports enthusiasts—This is typical left-wing hogwash."

When a Long Island newspaper began a series on Rebozo's finances, Nixon ordered Haldeman to get the IRS to go after the paper: "Figure out a plan . . . to harass. . . . Use the power we have." A bit later that summer, Nixon told Haldeman to get the "names of the big Democratic contributors. Get them investigated. Also the Democratic celebrities." [44]

"COLSON ENCOURAGED the dark impulses in Nixon's mind," according to Bob Haldeman, "and acted on those impulses instead of ignoring them and letting them die." [45] A midsummer gratuitous insult to the personal honor of Arthur Burns illustrates the point.

The sixty-seven-year-old Burns, a professor of economics who had been in and out of government for decades, and served in 1969 as Counsellor to the President, became chairman of the board of the Federal Reserve System in January 1970. In appointing Burns, whom he claimed as an old friend (Burns had been his economic adviser in the 1960 campaign), Nixon lauded his "independence," but added his hope that Burns would "independently conclude that my views are the ones that should be followed." [46]

Burns nevertheless followed his own course, to Nixon's irritation. A crisis of sorts came in July, when Burns stated that there had been "very little progress" in the fight against inflation and called for wage-and-price controls (a policy also being urged by the Democrats in Congress, who were getting close to having enough votes to force it on Nixon). The President, furious and exasperated, unleashed Treasury Secretary Connally, who declared that "very substantial progress" had been made in the war on inflation.[47]

Nixon, meanwhile, assured Burns in various ways that he still admired and trusted him. "You're sitting next to Arthur?" he asked Safire over the telephone, having called Safire out of a meeting. "You know, Arthur is a fine man. Really, a fine man. Tell him I said that." [48]

Just about this time, Colson joined Nixon for a cruise on the *Sequoia*. Henry Kissinger and Caspar Weinberger were along. Nixon, with a smile and a chuckle, had an idea on how to fix Burns. He told Colson to plant a rumor to the effect that while Burns was demanding monetary restraint, he was hypocritically seeking a $20,000 raise in his own salary.

That was meat and potatoes for Colson, who planted the story through Herb Klein's office (but without Klein's knowledge). It got a big play, and caused Burns considerable anguish (actually, Burns had proposed, and Nixon rejected, a 10 percent pay cut for all Administration officials). Burns had to deny the story, which caused an even bigger play.[49]

Nixon's little intrigue had worked, but it backfired. Burns had friends and admirers. They were outraged by the leak, which they correctly traced to Colson, never suspecting the President himself had been the prime mover. Klein, Safire, *The Wall Street Journal*, and many others protested. Nixon was forced to then issue a statement "to set the record straight." He denied that Burns had ever maneuvered for a salary increase, said that in fact he had turned one down, and praised Burns as "the most responsible and statesmanlike" Fed chairman in memory.[50]

His real favorite was Connally. "Big Jawn" had quite swept Nixon off his feet; the President's White House aides said "the

Boss is in love." For a while Nixon's favorite had been John Mitchell, then Pat Moynihan; by mid-1971 it was Connally.[51]

On July 20, in the Cabinet Room, Nixon told Ehrlichman he was fed up with Agnew (who had just said he opposed the opening to China), and wanted Ehrlichman and Haldeman to meet with Connally and Bryce Harlow "to figure out how the hell we can get Agnew to resign early." Nixon continued, "I talked to John Connally for three hours yesterday. I offered him the Vice Presidency or, if that's not possible, then Secretary of State. I want to position him as my logical successor."[52]

That was all fantasy, of course; the Republican Party was never going to accept a turncoat Democrat from Texas, a protégé of LBJ, as its leader. Nixon knew that, but he also had unbounded admiration for Connally. It was a case, Safire thought, of opposites attracting: Nixon the loner, Connally the extrovert. In Kissinger's view, "Connally's swaggering self-assurance was Nixon's Walter Mitty image of himself. He was one person whom Nixon never denigrated behind his back."[53] (Which was one more than the number on Kissinger's list.) Whatever the cause of Nixon's feelings toward Connally, they led the President to put Connally first among all the courtiers. Nixon told Bill Gulley, head of the Military Office in the White House, which among other duties was responsible for *Air Force One* and Camp David, "I want this guy [Connally] to have anything he wants. He can use my plane. He can have Camp David. . . . I want him to have anything he wants."[54]

Connally was a politician with no experience in banking or economics. When a reporter asked him his qualifications to be Secretary of the Treasury, he quipped, "I can add." What he could add was not so much money as votes, which was one reason Nixon liked him so much—he put first things first.

By August 1971, the economy came first. Nixon's Big Charge on SALT and China was going along swimmingly, but the economy was drowning. The causes were continued inflation, continued high unemployment, a looming trade imbalance, and an international monetary crisis, featuring a dollar under attack by speculators because of the inflation, unemployment, and trade imbalance. Nixon blamed the messenger for the bad news. He ordered Frederick Malek, a White House aide, to root out what he called the "Jewish cabal" at the Bureau of Labor Statistics. The President was convinced that these liberal Jewish bureaucrats were using selected statistics to make his Administration's economic record look bad.

On Friday, August 13, Nixon convened an economic summit at Camp David. Connally was there, and Burns, and Shultz, and the other heavy hitters. Nixon opened with a classic line: "Circumstances change. In this discussion, nobody is bound by past positions."[55]

Especially not the President, whose opposition to wage-and-price controls was as legendary as his devotion to free trade and defense of the dollar. But Burns and the Democrats had built up an unstoppable momentum on wage-and-price controls, something had to be done to stem the inflow of imports, and the dollar could no longer be defended.

Nixon was better than any politician in America at bowing to the inevitable; he was also a man who, as he often said, when he changed policy, liked to leapfrog the next position in line, as in the China opening. He conducted the meeting like a maestro, leading the participants to his foreordained conclusion.

On Sunday night, August 15, Nixon went on nationwide radio and television from the Oval Office to announce the decisions. "We are going to take . . . action," he declared, "not timidly, not half-heartedly, and not in piecemeal fashion. . . . The time has come for a new economic policy for the United States." Although the phrase was Lenin's, Nixon was not trying to bury capitalism, but to shore it up. To create jobs, he instituted a 10 percent Job Development Credit for investment in new equipment. He also repealed the 7 percent excise tax on automobiles to stimulate the American car industry. He added a small tax break for individuals to boost the economy in general and employment in particular. To offset the loss of revenue, he ordered a $4.7 billion cut in federal spending (and in the process abandoned most of his revenue-sharing proposals). He imposed a temporary additional tax of 10 percent on imported goods.

These were all more or less the kind of tinkering-with-the-economy measures most Administrations indulge themselves in when an election looms and the economy is in trouble. There was nothing earthshaking or dramatic about them. Nixon's next announcement was most certainly dramatic, however, although hardly as decisive as he said it was: "I am today ordering a freeze on all prices and wages throughout the United States for 90 days." He also announced that he was appointing a Cost of Living Council within the government to work with labor and business after the ninety-day freeze in order to achieve continued wage-and-price stability.

As had been made clear in the Camp David arguments between Burns (who favored) and Connally (who opposed), no one could tell what long-term effect, if any, Nixon's action would have. The controls stopped inflation for ninety days, but a year later it was hard to tell what, if anything, they had accomplished. But it surely made him look like the man in command, a bold and flexible leader willing to abandon a lifetime position when the reality demanded it.

Nixon's final announcement did have substantial (if hard to define) long-term consequences. "I have directed Secretary Connally to suspend temporarily the convertibility of the dollar into gold." He thus closed the gold window, established by the Allies at the end of World War II, when the United States had agreed to establish the dollar as the standard against which all other currencies would be matched by buying gold at $35 an ounce (the fixed price had made the dollar "as good as gold"). From that moment on, the dollar floated, like other currencies, requiring the creation of a whole new world monetary order.[56]

The initial reception was overwhelmingly favorable. On Monday, the New York Stock Exchange set a record for the number of shares traded (31 million) and the Dow Jones industrial average registered a record one-day advance of 32.9 points, closing at 888.95.[57] Republican skeptics (there were many) held their tongues, while the Democrats were confounded, except for George McGovern, the only announced Democratic candidate, who denounced the entire speech as "sheer bunk, irrelevancy and mystery." McGovern said the wage-price freeze was four years overdue, the Job Development Credit was "a handout to big business," and closing the gold window "a disgrace [that] amounts to a backdoor devaluation."[58]

Businessmen and bankers were generally favorable, if wary; George Meany, president of the AFL-CIO, was strongly critical. Meany called the freeze "patently discriminatory" against working men and women. Overseas, the West Germans and the Japanese were confused and anxious; in their view, the mark and the yen were the targets. The yen was thought to be undervalued as against the dollar by as much as 25 percent, giving the Japanese a terrific advantage in selling their products to the American market.[59]

For all the noise, the actual impact, even short term, was minimal. By the end of the year, the annual inflation rate had dropped about a point, to around 4 percent, while unemployment fell from 6.1 percent to 5.1 percent, and the dollar was off by about 10 percent against the mark and the yen. Nixon had created a big splash without making many big waves.

International speculators, the undervalued mark and yen, and big labor with its big wage demands were among Nixon's villains, but there were others, for example, the environmentalists. In early August, Ehrlichman sent Nixon a memo on the economic impact of pollution control, requested earlier by the President and written by Paul McCracken, that pointed out the "negative economic impact of . . . the environmental movement." Nixon wrote on it, "I completely agree—We have gone overboard on the environment—& are going to reap the whirlwind for our excesses—get me a plan for cooling off the excesses."[60]

Another villain was the welfare system, which Nixon was still trying, albeit halfheartedly, to reform. In July, Safire tried to revive the word "workfare," which he admitted had been received "with some scorn" back in 1969 when Nixon introduced it, but which he said had now "crossed that mysterious line from gimmick to accepted label of a concept." Who was Nixon to argue with the acknowledged master of political verbiage? "E & H & C," he scribbled on the memo, "this is a good idea. Regardless of the Libs' objections I want *all* admin. spokesmen to use this term—see what Safire can do to get it used broadly—give me a report on the *plan*."[61]

Buchanan found a good item in an Indiana newspaper for the President's News Summary. It seemed that an Indiana welfare couple, fed up with Indiana's stingy payments, packed up their $10,000 air-conditioned trailer and their four TVs to head for California, "where they know how to take care of folks on welfare." In California, they would get more than $500 per month, compared to $325 in Indiana. Nixon wrote in the margin, "Pat, pass this one on to Reagan!"[62]

THE UNANIMOUS Supreme Court decision in April that mandatory busing was one of the acceptable tools for achieving court-ordered desegregation had led by July to some HEW and Justice Department plans for Austin, Dallas, and Richmond for the fall. Herb Klein, alarmed, sent a memo to the President warning him that "the laws are being over enforced." That was as sure to rouse Nixon's ire as the Indiana welfare couple's move was to rouse Reagan's. Nixon's penciled marching orders were explicit: "E—I want you personally to jump Richardson and Justice and tell them to *Knock off this Crap*. I hold them personally accountable to keep their left wingers in step with my express policy—Do what the law requires and not *one bit more*."[63]

In the first week in August, with schools soon to open across the nation, Nixon suddenly and dramatically reaffirmed his 1968 campaign stand against "the busing of students to achieve racial balance in the schools." He said he had instructed HEW and Justice "to work with individual school districts to hold busing to the minimum required by law," and he disavowed the plans already put forward by his Administration for busing in Austin. He urged Congress to amend his earlier request for a $1.5 billion appropriation for school desegregation assistance to "expressly prohibit the expenditure of any of those funds for busing."[64] With these statements, he firmly established himself as the nation's number-one opponent of busing.

In so doing, he was occupying ground that George Wallace claimed as his own. The next week, Wallace made some scornful remarks about Nixon being all mouth, that the reality was that Nixon's HEW and Justice Departments were shot through with liberals bent on enforcing busing. Nixon responded through Ziegler, who emerged from a half-hour conference with the President to tell reporters that any federal officials who pushed busing "will find themselves involved in other assignments or quite possibly an assignment other than the Federal Government."[65]

Haldeman, meanwhile, had put in motion a program to disrupt, ridicule, and harass the Democratic candidates. His assistant, Gordon Strachan, a twenty-eight-year-old USC graduate, joined by his fellow USC graduates Dwight Chapin and Donald Segretti, was in charge. A major objective was simple political intelligence, i.e., monitoring the Democrats. At the end of the summer, the team came up with a dandy: Senator Muskie had told a group of black leaders in a private meeting in Los Angeles that for him to select a black man as his running mate would set back the cause of civil rights, because the ticket would not be "electable."

Nixon jumped on that one. He made Muskie's remarks public, in an impromptu news conference, and accused the senator of a "libel on the American people." The President pontificated, "It is very important for those of us in positions of leadership not to tell a large number of people in America, whoever they are, that because of the accident of their birth they don't have a chance to go to the top."[66]

BETWEEN APRIL 1 and July 1 of 1971, there were seventeen House or Senate votes seeking to restrict Nixon's authority to conduct the war or to fix a date for unilateral American withdrawal. *The New York Times* called Vietnamization a "cruel delusion."[67] The Vietnam Veterans Against the War staged a series of protests in the capital. The Milwaukee *Journal* spoke from the heartland: "The South Vietnamese will rely on us as long as we are there. They have one of the world's biggest armies. If they can't stand on their own feet now it is too late."[68]

Hanoi, too, was feeling some pressure to reach an agreement to end the war. Although there is no evidence that the Nixon-

Kissinger attempt to link progress in reaching a settlement in Vietnam with détente with the Soviet Union ever paid off in any direct way, such as a reduction of the flow of arms from Russia to Vietnam, evidently the Kremlin was urging Hanoi to be more reasonable (i.e., to accept a cease-fire and return the POWs for an American withdrawal, without insisting on the overthrow of the Thieu government). The Chinese, too, pressed their allies to be reasonable; following Polo, and again later in 1971, they suggested that Hanoi accept a compromise (although, like the Russians, they did not reduce the flow of supplies).[69]

Years later, the Americans and the North Vietnamese each claimed that they had responded to these pressures. According to Nixon and Kissinger, on the last day of May 1971, they made a "final offer" that incorporated new proposals. It consisted of seven points (each side made a fetish of producing multipoint offers): the U.S. would set a date for total withdrawal; the U.S. would abandon its demand for mutual withdrawal; Hanoi would agree to send no additional troops or supplies into South Vietnam; there would be a cease-fire throughout Indochina; Hanoi would guarantee the territorial integrity and neutrality of Laos and Cambodia.

This appeared to the Americans to be reasonable and generous; it appeared to the Communists to be the opposite. If accepted it would leave Thieu in command in Saigon. It would prevent a Communist takeover of Laos and Cambodia, just when they were on the verge of victory in both countries.

It really was an absurd bargaining position. Kissinger had made no mention of American air strength (and Nixon had publicly insisted that U.S. air power would remain in Southeast Asia until a final settlement was reached). So in return for an American withdrawal of U.S. ground troops, which was already happening and could not be stopped, Hanoi was being asked to abandon its war in South Vietnam, Laos, and Cambodia, and to return the American POWs.

There is some evidence that Nixon was aware that he and Kissinger were just toying with the North Vietnamese, that he did not expect them to take American offers seriously. In his memoirs, Kissinger complained that "on almost all the [secret] negotiations I conducted I was faced by this ambivalence on his [Nixon's] part. He usually had to be persuaded to enter them at all; each new visit to Paris was preceded by a more or less protracted internal debate. . . . When I was under way, he would deluge me with tough-sounding directives. . . . The reason may have been his unease with the process of compromise."[70]

Nixon had a goal—to get out before November 1972, with

Thieu and Lon Nol and Prince Souvanna Phouma in power and the POWs returned—but he did not have a policy. He had nothing to offer the North Vietnamese in return for their cooperation, except the negative—that he would not become Nixon the mad bomber.

The alternative, always there, was highly tempting. That would have been a policy, to bomb Hanoi into accepting Nixon's goals. From time to time Nixon indulged himself in fantasy thoughts about doing just that. On July 10, Haig sent Kissinger (in Peking) a cable that indicated Nixon was thinking about a sudden announcement of a total ground-troop withdrawal coupled with an all-out air assault, a modified version of the old Duck Hook option. Haig's cable began: "You should be aware that he [Nixon] is seriously considering the alternative plan which he has mentioned previously of moving out precipitously and concurrently undertaking major air effort against North."[71]

But without provocation from the North, such a spasm would have brought an outburst from the Senate, the newspapers, and the people much greater than anything that had gone before. And far from being provocative, the North Vietnamese were offering—or so they later claimed—an easy exit for Nixon. In Paris, Le Duc Tho told Kissinger, in effect, that if Nixon would not overthrow Thieu, let the people of South Vietnam do it. Let them do it in a constitutional and democratic way, by voting him out of power.[72]

The opportunity was there. It came about because back in 1967 Lyndon Johnson, in one of his PR ploys, had forced the government in Saigon to accept an American-written constitution; that constitution called for presidential elections in October 1971. Le Duc Tho was calling the Nixon-Kissinger bluff; they had proclaimed since coming to office that they would abide by the results of democratic elections (except they said these would be held *after* the NVA withdrew from South Vietnam and the VC laid down their arms). Now Le Duc Tho was saying that Hanoi would abide by the results of the election, if it was fair and honest (meaning, if Thieu lost).

But Thieu would not cooperate. He rigged the conditions for the election in such a way that he ran without opposition. This made a mockery of the entire process, but it did guarantee that Thieu stayed in power. Thieu reasoned, evidently, and if so certainly correctly, that Nixon had too much invested in him to pull the plug now. What he misjudged was the effect on the American people of an "election" with only one candidate. This was his worst and fatal mistake.

At a news conference at the end of the summer, Nixon was

asked to comment on attempts in the Senate to cut all aid to South Vietnam unless Thieu held a contested election. The President replied that the United States was providing military and/or economic aid to ninety-one countries in the world, and only thirty of them were democracies. Why single out South Vietnam?

That answer did not satisfy, and the reporters pressed harder. Did not the U.S. have some leverage it could use to force Thieu to hold real elections?

Well, Nixon replied, if what was being suggested was "that the United States should use its leverage now to overthrow Thieu, I would remind all concerned that the way we got into Vietnam was through overthrowing Diem."

It was all very frustrating. The U.S. had been fighting for years to help the people of South Vietnam establish a genuine democracy, and now, just look. Was the President satisfied with these conditions?

"No," Nixon snapped. He admitted that it might be "several generations" before democracy came to Saigon. "But at least we will be on the road." He asked reporters to recall that it took the British "500 years to get to the place where they had . . . a democratic system." He lectured the impatient reporters: "You cannot expect that American-style democracy, meeting our standards, will apply in other parts of the world." It would take time.[73]

ONE APPARENTLY insoluble problem was solved in the summer of 1971, and although Nixon had little to do with it, his policy of détente was one of the beneficiaries.

Since 1945, divided and occupied Berlin had been one of the most dangerous tinderboxes of the Cold War. Three times the city had almost been the site of the outbreak of World War III: in 1948, when Stalin imposed a blockade; in 1959, when Khrushchev issued an ultimatum for a separate peace treaty for East Germany (that turned out to be a bluff); and in 1961, when another Khrushchev ultimatum led to the Berlin Wall. Easing tensions in Berlin and making movement from West Germany to West Berlin and from West Berlin into East Germany easier and more secure were some of Chancellor Willy Brandt's major goals in his *Ostpolitik*.

The German-born Kissinger was suspicious of Brandt and *Ostpolitik*, but his boss saw a bigger picture. Nixon instructed Kissinger to facilitate the negotiations; Kissinger, more by habit than necessity, did so in a back channel, excluding the State Department, and made an important contribution to the successful outcome of the talks. Still, the central players were Brandt and Erich Honecker of East Germany. The agreement they reached guaranteed access to West Berlin matched by a promise never to seek to incorporate West Berlin as an integral part of the Federal Republic of Germany. The result was hailed around the world and contributed to the easing of tensions, thus facilitating Nixon's journey toward détente.[74]

EVER SINCE the publication of the Pentagon Papers in June, Nixon had been pressing for action. Spurred especially by Kissinger's vivid description of Ellsberg's weird habits, Nixon wanted the Special Investigations Unit (Krogh's Plumbers) in the White House to discredit and/or disgrace Ellsberg. They undertook various investigations, but came up empty. Ehrlichman kept Nixon up to date on their activities. He later declared, "Invariably when they made recommendations, jointly or severally, the President concurred. His only criticism of their effort was that it was not vigorous enough."

Nixon told Ehrlichman that "Krogh should, of course, do whatever he considered necessary to get to the bottom of the matter—to learn what Ellsberg's motives and potential further harmful action might be."[75]

On August 11, Krogh and his partner David Young sent a memo to Ehrlichman: "We would recommend that a covert operation be undertaken to examine all the medical files still held by Ellsberg's psychoanalyst." Ehrlichman approved.[76]

Was Nixon behind this? Did he give Krogh the order, then tell Krogh to get Ehrlichman's approval as a way of protecting himself? Nixon's continuing cover-up of the basic documents in his presidential papers in the National Archives makes such questions impossible to answer. In his memoirs, Nixon has a tantalizing, self-serving line: "I do not believe I was told about the break-in [at Ellsberg's doctor's office] at the time, but it is clear that it was at least in part an outgrowth of my sense of urgency about discrediting what Ellsberg had done and finding out what he might do next."[77]

Haldeman has written that five years later Nixon said to him, "I was so damn mad at Ellsberg in those days. And Henry was jumping up and down. I've been thinking—and maybe I did order that break-in." And John Dean testified that Krogh told him that the orders for the break-in came directly from the Oval Office. If true, that meant it would be on the tapes, which makes this small mystery easy enough to solve, except that Nixon has so far managed to keep the tapes under seal.

If Nixon did order the break-in (Ehrlichman says he did), his performance with Haldeman and others in the Oval Office afterward illustrated once again what a great actor he was. The surprise and chagrin he displayed when told of the break-in was absolutely convincing.[78]

Whatever the truth in this sordid matter, J. Anthony Lukas is on the mark when he points out that the break-in represented "a quantum leap in White House tactics. . . . The White House moved across the line from jittery prodding of other agencies into direct operations more appropriate to a secret-police force. It was, indeed, the ultimate step in applying the techniques developed for foreign intelligence operations to the domestic political scene."[79]

On Labor Day weekend, Howard Hunt and G. Gordon Liddy, heading a team of three Cuban-American burglars and acting as a part of the White House Special Investigations Unit, broke into the office of Ellsberg's psychiatrist, Dr. Lewis J. Fielding, in Los Angeles. They found nothing that could be used to discredit Ellsberg.

CHAPTER TWENTY-ONE

TILTING AT WINDMILLS
September–December 1971

IN MID-SEPTEMBER, Nixon's never-ending battle with Congress escalated, as the doves in both parties tried to use the need to extend the selective service bill to force Nixon to withdraw altogether from Vietnam. The Universal Military Training and Service Act of 1951 had been extended every four years since it first passed, the last time in 1967. Nixon had pledged an all-volunteer Army in the '68 campaign, and again when he introduced the lottery system in 1969, but made it contingent on the ending of the war. The bill before Congress in September 1971 called for a two-year extension of the draft, but it included increased military pay and benefits as a first step toward an all-volunteer Army.

Politics creates odd situations. The liberals, who said they wanted an all-volunteer Army, were opposed to the bill, because it would give Nixon sufficient troops to stay in Vietnam with a sizable ground force. The conservatives, who strongly opposed an all-volunteer Army, favored the bill, because they did not want to undercut the President on Vietnam.

The Nixon Administration, represented by Clark MacGregor, by now the White House's chief congressional lobbyist, worked hard to get the bill passed, with the usual promises and threats.[1] The President himself, at a September 16 news conference, used strong language in support of the bill, saying that if it was defeated, "I think this would be one of the most irresponsible acts on the part of the United States Senate that I could possibly think of. . . . A vote against the draft, in my opinion, would be a vote that seriously jeopardizes peace initiatives of the United States around the world, and without question it is a vote that will make the United States the second strongest nation in the world, with all the implications that has insofar as the ability of the United States to keep the peace and to negotiate for peace in this critical period."[2]

The bill passed, thanks in large part to presidential pressure.

With the third branch of government, the judiciary, Nixon had little or no ability to threaten, cajole, or bribe the judges into complying with his wishes. But, unlike his relationship with the legislative branch, he did have one ultimate authority—he was the sole source of nominees for the federal bench. Thus in 1971, although he was jolted by the Supreme Court's approval of busing, he was encouraged by the prospect of creating a "Nixon Court" because of the advanced age of some of the members.

On September 17, Nixon received Justice Hugo Black's letter of retirement. Six days later, Justice John Harlan also retired. With two nominations to put forward, Nixon wanted to take his time, make no more mistakes, as with Haynsworth and Carswell. He wanted young men, so that his influence would extend far beyond his own Presidency; he wanted at least one southerner; he wanted strict constructionists. By custom and tradition, the Attorney General would present him with a short list of recommendations, but after his experiences in 1969, Nixon had reason to doubt John Mitchell's judgment in such matters, and he wanted time to have the Plumbers check out Mitchell's recommendations.

Pat Buchanan, however, urged Nixon to hurry, "to head off mounting lobbies of women, blacks and labor. To delay is to allow them more time to build public support to work the Senate." Buchanan wanted Nixon to send up the name of the strictest constructionist he could find in the South as the first nominee, thus holding Senators Kennedy's, Humphrey's, McGovern's, and Muskie's feet to the fire: "It is a bitterly divisive issue for Democratic candidates —either they kick their black friends in the teeth [by voting yes], or they kick the South in the teeth [by voting no]." For the second choice, Buchanan wanted the strictest constructionist Italian-American to be found. "Play up his Italian background—and let the Democrats chop him up, if they want."[3]

Len Garment thought Buchanan was wrong to put politics ahead of policy, and wrong to pressure Nixon for an early decision. Further, he thought Buchanan's first choice, Congressman Richard Poff (R., Va.), ranking minority member of the House Judiciary Committee, a bad one. Poff had signed two "Southern Manifestoes," he had opposed all civil rights legislation, and he had little legal experience. Garment pointed out the obvious, that civil rights, church, ethnic, and women's rights groups would mount a concerted opposition, and what Nixon needed to avoid above all else was another divisive confirmation controversy.[4] Garment was right about Poff; when his name leaked, Poff found that reporters were digging into his past, and he asked John Mitchell to withdraw his name from consideration.[5]

Mitchell's next nominee was Herschel Friday, an Arkansas lawyer who had represented the Little Rock school board in opposing the integration of Central High. Nixon sent the Plumbers to check him out; David Young asked John Dean to join him in investigating; they reported he was too much like Carswell to stand much of a chance in the Senate.[6]

Nixon thought about appointing Agnew; it had the advantage of letting him then appoint John Connally as Vice-President. But when Ehrlichman said the obvious—"the Senate would clobber him"—Nixon backed off. He next considered Senator Robert Byrd of West Virginia. Although he told Ehrlichman that Byrd was "a very vain man, of limited ability," he leaked Byrd's name to gauge the reaction.[7] It had the advantage of causing the Democrats considerable discomfort. Initially McGovern, for example, said he would support his fellow Democrat, but then issued a statement: "I cannot accept a man who is mediocre, who is a racist and who is unethical for membership on the U.S. Supreme Court." Nixon commented, "H—Muskie, Hubert, now McGovern—total flip flop on issue after issue. The Press would murder any Republican who did that."[8]

Pat Nixon, who had been urging her husband to appoint a woman to the Court ever since his election, thought that with two nominations available, he surely could find one woman. She felt so strongly about it that she made an uncharacteristic public statement. En route to Newport News, Virginia, to dedicate a nuclear-powered aircraft carrier, Pat granted an interview, urging a woman for the Court. "Don't you worry," she told the press, "I'm talking it up."[9] Nixon yielded to the point of asking Mitchell to see if he could find one; Mitchell recommended a Los Angeles judge, Mildred Lilley. Nixon had his Plumbers check on her; they had no objection. But the American Bar Association thought her unqualified, and although Chief Justice Burger was one of her supporters, Nixon turned her down.

Pat was furious. When Nixon did make his nominations, and no woman was among them, she let her husband know how she felt. At dinner on October 21, she repeated again and again her reasons why one of the nominees should have been a woman. Her husband finally cut her off, saying with exaggerated weariness, "We tried to do the best we could, Pat."[10]

(Nixon had shown his attitude toward women in politics a week earlier, when the League of Women Voters criticized him for his "growing ransom list of demands made of our trading partners." Nixon commented, "H—My god! Can't they stay out of subjects they know *nothing* about." Shortly thereafter, in a veto message on a bill creating comprehensive child-care services, including day care for working mothers, he indicated his idea of the proper place for women. In a passionate message, he stressed his distaste for "communal approaches" to child rearing and charged that the bill would "sovietize" the nation's youth. "Good public policy," he said, "requires that we enhance rather than diminish . . . parental involvement with children.")[11]

There were calls for a Jewish nomination. When it was clear that Nixon was considering no Jews, Clayton Fritchey asked in *The New Republic* if "the Administration is touched with anti-Semitism." Nixon commented, "C!!—with Kissinger, Garment [*sic*], Safire and Burns? Someone should really crack him for this inexcusable innuendo."[12]

Mitchell suggested others, including Governor Reagan's counsel and friend, William French Smith. The ABA rejected them all, on the grounds that they lacked stature. Nixon, furious, instructed, "E—never again do they [the ABA] get a shot at *any* judges after this performance." A week later Mitchell informed the ABA that the Administration was terminating its agreement to check the judicial qualifications of potential Supreme Court nominees with the association.[13]

Four days later, on October 25, the current president of the ABA, Houston lawyer Leon Jaworski, moved to patch things up. He sent Nixon a copy of an article he had written for the ABA *Journal* praising Chief Justice Burger for "the high qualities of leadership he has demonstrated. . . . I wanted to bring the article to your attention because I felt it would be a matter of personal interest to you."[14] Nixon replied with a warm and gracious letter drafted by John Dean. He praised Jaworski for recognizing the "striking parallels" between Burger on the one hand and John Marshall, William Howard Taft, and Charles Evans Hughes on the other.[15]

Eventually, to Mitchell's chagrin and embarrassment, Nixon went elsewhere for his recommendations. White House Special Counsel Richard Moore suggested Assistant Attorney General William Rehnquist and Virginia attorney Lewis Powell. Rehnquist, who had been in law school with Ehrlichman (Stanford, '52), had been a leading Barry Goldwater supporter in 1964. In the Justice Department, he had been strong for Nixon's law-and-order measures, including the right to wiretap citizens when national security was involved. Powell, a former president of the ABA, was widely respected. Nixon announced their nominations on October 21. Rehnquist was confirmed, 68–26; Powell was confirmed, 89–1. The former went on to become Chief Justice; the latter had a distinguished career, often being compared to Justice John Marshall Harlan.

NIXON'S INFLUENCE on Congress was limited to what he could get through promises and threats; his influence on the courts was limited to his power to nominate; his influence on the third branch of government, the executive, should have been unlimited, as he was the boss. But it doesn't work like that at all.

By the fall of 1971, the seventy-six-year-old director of the FBI, J. Edgar Hoover, had become a liability and a problem to the President. Nixon had a long string of complaints, including Hoover's refusal to work with the CIA, Hoover's refusal to extend the government's wiretapping program, Hoover's refusal to approve the Huston plan, Hoover's refusal to go hard after Daniel Ellsberg. On the other hand, Hoover had a political base of his own, the millions of Americans who saw him as the symbol of anti-Communism and anticrime crusades. Further, if Hoover were forced out, he knew enough to bring a lot of men down with him.

But Hoover was becoming more dictatorial than ever, and more unreasonable. The number of his critics and their complaints were growing constantly, and for the first time top men inside the FBI, division heads, were among their number. Hoover had responded to the internal dissent by firing those who dared to speak out, but that only led to resignations—and then denunciations—by others.

In September, John Ehrlichman warned Nixon that things were getting worse, that two of the top four people under Hoover were about to quit, that there was a threat of a congressional investigation of the FBI, and that a conference at Princeton University on the FBI was going to be "very rough on Hoover." [16]

A month later, on October 23, Ehrlichman responded to Nixon's request for a prognosis on the FBI and Hoover. He said that William Sullivan, once the number-two man at the FBI, was about to blast Hoover with attacks "which could literally destroy him." He said that Hoover was still dragging on the Ellsberg case. And he attached a memorandum that analyzed in detail the problems caused by Hoover's long tenure; it concluded with a recommendation that Hoover should be asked to resign. The author of the memo was G. Gordon Liddy, former FBI agent, currently one of the Plumbers. [17]

Ten days later, Nixon met with Ehrlichman to discuss the

problem. Hoover had been described innumerable times as a man of "bulldog tenacity" (no one who wrote on Hoover could resist the cliché, because it was so apt and because it fit Hoover's physical appearance so perfectly); Nixon knew the old man wanted to die in office and would resist resignation resolutely. He had told Mitchell to ask for Hoover's resignation, but Mitchell ducked, saying that Hoover would respond only to the President. The purpose of the meeting with Ehrlichman was to help Nixon work out arguments to present to Hoover to persuade him to resign.

Nixon hated—and always resisted—firing people. It was a characteristic he shared with Eisenhower. In part this was just good manners, in part it was his Quaker shyness, in part it was fear of confrontation. He could say the most awful things about people behind their backs, but he found it difficult to make even the slightest criticism to their faces.

What he did like to do was make up speeches, casting himself in the third person. Thus, with Ehrlichman on this occasion, it was "suppose the President said this," "what if RN pointed out that." He wandered over the landscape, searching for arguments that would convince Hoover to resign. After an hour or so of this, he asked Ehrlichman to use what he had said to prepare talking notes for a meeting with Hoover. He said the meeting would be at breakfast, in the residence, the next morning.[18]

The notes show Nixon at his most devious and manipulative. The purpose was to persuade Hoover that he should resign for his own good, for the good of the FBI, for the good of the country, and that the good of Richard Nixon had nothing to do with it.

The reason for the breakfast meeting was the fierce public attacks on Hoover recently, from his own people, from Congress, from the press, from Princeton. But Nixon not only denied that these attacks had anything to do with the meeting, he congratulated Hoover on how well he was doing in his PR recently. Nixon approached the subject of resignation on tiptoes, and from behind. "In thinking about your future," he said, "I have concluded that you must stay as Director of the Bureau through November of 1972. I hope you will agree [to stay on] because I think it's very unrealistic to even contemplate your replacement in the meantime." Nixon said he wanted to keep the Bureau out of the political cross fire in an election year, "and the best way to do this is for you to say right now, publicly, that you have decided to serve one more year, until just after the Inauguration in January."

There was a promise and a warning: "Obviously, if I am reelected, your replacement would be someone who would carry on your tradition. On the other hand, if the Democrats were to prevail, the Bureau would be subject to some Director that neither of us would like." The last thing Nixon wanted to do, he said, was give the Democrats access to FBI records and investigative powers to use against the Republicans.

Hoover sat there, impassive. He had outlasted every President since Woodrow Wilson. Back in the days of the Hiss case, some twenty-three years earlier, he had read a memo from an agent saying that young Congressman Nixon, while critical of the Justice Department, "had nothing but praise for the Director and the Bureau." Hoover had scribbled on the memo, "This fellow Nixon blows hot & cold."

So in 1971 Hoover sat over his eggs and bacon, waiting to see which way Nixon would blow next. Nixon, desperate, tried turning around his opening point; the President said that as an "astute politician" Hoover must recognize that the vicious attacks on him were only going to get worse. It would be a "tragedy" if his career ended under a cloud.

Hoover's response was classic. He assured Nixon he wanted to see him re-elected "more than anything else." As to the attacks on the Bureau, "they don't make any difference to me. I think you know that the tougher the attacks get, the tougher I get." [19]

To prove his point, Hoover then made a request of his own. He wanted to be permitted to install FBI agents in more U.S. embassies abroad. These "legal attachés" could send back news and gossip (Hoover hated having to rely on the CIA for foreign news). State and Justice had refused the request. Nixon now approved.

The following day, Ehrlichman asked Haldeman what happened in the Hoover-Nixon meeting. "Don't ask," Haldeman replied. "He doesn't want to talk about it."

Not until a year later could Ehrlichman get Nixon to tell him about the meeting; the President confessed that it was "a total strikeout." [20]

GEORGE MEANY, head of the AFL-CIO, was another national figure of bulldog tenacity and appearance who also had a power base of his own and who caused Nixon considerable anguish. But Meany also gave the President significant help. Their relationship, as with Nixon's more general relationship with organized labor, was complex and complicated.

In his first campaign, in 1946, Nixon had made organized labor in general, and the CIO specifically, his target. As a freshman congressman, he had been a leading supporter of the Taft-Hartley bill, anathema to organized labor. As Vice-President, he had been a leading critic of the AFL-CIO. And as President, his advocacy of the so-called Philadelphia Plan, designed to get blacks into the white construction unions, had alarmed the unions.

In a March 8, 1971, memo to Colson, Nixon wrote, "RN has no use for the UAW leadership at the top or the left wing people who are head of the Garment Workers Union. They are basically not only hopeless Democrats, but also hopeless pacifists, as distinguished from Meany who is an all out Democrat, but a great patriot." [21]

Nixon had been ecstatic over the support the hard hats had given him at the time of the Cambodian incursion. He always identified himself with the working class; he always expressed a preference for working stiffs over the idle rich; but after Cambodia, he became rhapsodic when he described those who worked with their hands for a living.

By 1971, Nixon saw a "crisis of character" in America. He believed that it was the working class, not the leadership class, that had "whatever is left of the character of this country." When it came to standing up for America when it counted, it was the working class who "offer their backs and their brawn," in contrast to "the elite, which has been showing signs of decadence and weakness. The more that people are educated, it seems, the more likely they are to become brighter in the head but weaker in the spine." [22]

According to Nixon, Meany, at age seventy-six, had "backbone, guts, and all the things a lot of our businessmen lost years ago." In his retirement, Nixon frequently asserted that he would much rather have a labor union leader negotiating with the Russians than the most successful businessman.

All this romanticism about workingmen sounded more like Jack London or Woody Guthrie than Dick Nixon, and it must be noted that for all his love for working people, Nixon spent precious little time with them, in contrast to his big-business pals. His anti-elite, anti-intellectual, antiwealth talk was mostly rhetoric; it made him feel good to rant and rave about the loss of character among the leadership class, but he seldom meant it seriously enough to do anything about it.

There were exceptions. On August 1, 1971, the News Summary quoted a teacher who said parents had been misled about a college education as the only road to success and suggested wider use of technical schools. Nixon commented, "E—she's absolutely right—we have far too much subsidy for higher education. Give me a plan for cutting it & putting more into elementary and technical." [23] But there was no follow-up.

What Nixon did do was impose a wage freeze, with no freeze on corporate profits. Colson warned the President in a memo,

"Meany thinks . . . we are trying to destroy the building trades through wage controls and especially through minority hiring practice requirements."[24] Meany's anger grew in mid-September, when Nixon promised that in Phase 2 of his economic program, when the freeze ended, he would restrain wage increases. There would be teeth in the program to insure it.[25]

As Phase 2 approached (it was a complicated program, centering on a wage-price control board), the unions became increasingly apprehensive that their old nemesis Dick Nixon was going to control inflation at their expense. Nixon's News Summaries were full of reports that the economy "won't be all that bullish in '72," and that Meany and his cohorts in the Democratic Party were going to make the economy the major issue of the campaign. Nixon commented, "C—much of the negative talk on the economy is stimulated by politically motivated people," and "H-C—Note—They *must not* be allowed to get away with this—Int'l Affairs is *our* issue; Economy is theirs regardless of what happens to it because Libs can *always* promise more."[26]

Still, Nixon was not altogether unhappy to have Meany as a political foe. On October 7, the President told Safire, "We may have a good villain in Meany. You see that picture on both the covers of *Time* and *Newsweek*, with the cigar and the scowl? I like Meany—as a man, I'd take him to most businessmen, but he's the perfect symbol of the old politics."[27]

In November, the unions mandated their representatives on the control board to adopt a policy of "noncooperation." Nixon decided on one of his bold strokes. The AFL-CIO was holding its biennial convention in Bal Harbour, Florida. Nixon told the leaders he wanted to address the convention. Meany could hardly refuse, although he did turn down Nixon's request to speak on the opening day. "Who the hell does he think he is?" Meany boomed over the telephone.

"Class" was all Haldeman could say to that.

When Nixon got to Bal Harbour, Meany found other little ways to insult him, such as putting him in a seat in the second row on the platform and banishing the band just before Nixon's entrance so "Hail to the Chief" would not be played. There was but light applause as the President entered.

Nixon, smiling, praised labor for its support of his Vietnam and defense policies. No response. He promised to seek a lessening of tensions in the world. No response. He promised to fight inflation. The delegates sat on their hands.

Nixon tried patriotism again: "When the chips are down, organized labor's for America." The delegates wanted none of that;

like Meany, they were suspicious of Nixon's upcoming China trip and hostile to détente with the Soviets.[28] Applause finally rang through the hall when Meany, as Nixon was departing, turned to the agenda and announced, "Now we start Act Two."

Nixon felt that he had at least succeeded in going over the heads of the union bosses to reach the rank and file, people he felt were with him on the need to curb inflation and ease tensions. He was put out when the newspaper and television commentaries stressed how nervous he looked; the AP said he appeared to be "rattled." Nixon responded, "H-C—Note—we didn't get across! The Press failed to take the only honest line, RN's guts in going and effectiveness of speech." [29]

Herb Klein gathered together some of the editorials on Nixon's appearance at the convention. They showed strong support for the President, but the President was not satisfied. He remarked, "H & C—the theme of Editorial Comment is that Meany & Labor looked bad," which was not good enough for Nixon, who went on, "The idea of a strong gutsy President standing up for all the people is what *we* want to get across." [30]

Other Presidents might have wanted to get support for their policies, but not Nixon. He just wanted good PR for himself.

It was about the same in religion as in politics. In December, Ray Price sent Nixon a draft preface to be signed by the President for a book Hobart Lewis of *Reader's Digest* was publishing. It was a collection of the sermons delivered at the White House Sunday-morning services. Price said a preface from Nixon was important to the success of the book.

Nixon scribbled his reaction: "Ray—fine job—Possibly you might add a paragraph to effect that a compelling reason for the W.H. services was my intense dislike for 'going to Church for show.' Worship has always been a very private matter in our family." [31]

NIXON'S FREQUENT PRAISE of workingmen and snide remarks about the softness of businessmen did not keep him from convivial evenings with rich Republicans who were eager to contribute to his re-election campaign. In November, the Republicans held a fund-raising dinner ($500 per plate) in twenty-one cities, with Nixon appearing on closed-circuit TV in what was called a Salute to the President. Bob Hope told the jokes, Bob Dole declared that "GOP" stood for "Generation of Peace," and Dick Nixon ate his hors d'oeuvres in New York (2,500 dinners), then flew to Chicago for his dessert (1,900). Total attendance around the country was ten thousand, with plentiful supplies of bourbon, Scotch, and wine. One

Republican in New York said with glee, "This is really a fat cat dinner." [32]

The Republicans had cause to exult. The polls indicated that Nixon's slump was over; China, SALT, and the wage-price freeze had lifted Nixon from nearly ten points behind Muskie in May to a 43–35 lead in November. Still, Nixon could not keep from fretting.

He knew he was vulnerable, and if he ever lost sight of that fact, the Democrats were quick to remind him. At the AFL-CIO convention, Senator McGovern had followed him to the platform and received a rousing ovation as he damned Nixon's economic policies. A couple of weeks later, Senator Muskie referred to Nixon as "Tricky Dick." That red flag brought a Nixon comment: "C—we *must* crack him if he gets in this line." [33]

In the fall of 1971 Dwight Chapin, one of the three USC alumni on Haldeman's staff, joined a dirty-tricks operation designed to throw Democratic candidates into disarray. Chapin worked with yet another USC graduate, Donald Segretti. In October, Segretti set up his headquarters outside Los Angeles, taking care that there was no visible connection between his operation and the White House or the Republican Party. Soon he had twenty-eight people in seventeen states forging letters and distributing them under the Democratic candidates' letterheads, leaking false statements, manufacturing items for the press, throwing schedules into confusion by phoning ahead to cancel appearances, and so forth. Chapin told Segretti to concentrate on Muskie, whom Nixon considered his most formidable rival. [34]

All this Nixon activity stirred Larry O'Brien. As chairman of a party some $9 million in debt, he could only watch with dismay as Nixon raised big sums from big-business men. But the Democrats had an asset, and O'Brien had an idea. The asset was control of Congress; the idea was to make the American people pay for the 1972 Democratic campaign. O'Brien's scheme was this: the Democrats would attach an amendment to a tax-cut bill they felt Nixon could not afford to veto; the amendment would let any major party (read Democratic Party) draw up to $20.4 million from the public treasury to finance its presidential campaign. There were two conditions: (1) the party could not spend more than that amount and (2) enough taxpayers would have to earmark $1 of their 1972 payment for that purpose. The amendment also allowed any major party (read Republican) to refuse these public funds, put the arm on as many wealthy contributors as possible, and spend as much as it pleased.

The amendment sailed through the Senate, but Nixon threatened to veto the entire bill. He also made some private deals with

Wilbur Mills, who in conference committee then pushed through a compromise that approved the public funding plan, except that it would not become effective before 1976.[35]

There was another worry, however. Congress was attempting to write new law to replace the Federal Corrupt Practices Act of 1925, which Lyndon Johnson had characterized as "more loophole than law." But as the new bill moved through congressional committees in the fall of 1971, Clark MacGregor worked to slow it down. What the Republicans feared was the more stringent reporting requirement. Congress eventually passed the bill on January 26, 1972; Nixon signed it on February 7. It would not take effect for sixty days, creating a window of opportunity between the expiration of the old law, on March 10, and the effective date of the new one, April 7. In those four weeks, no disclosure of contributors' names was required at all. During that time the money, mostly cash, poured in, millions and millions of dollars. No public record was kept, but Rose Mary Woods kept a list of the pre–April 7 contributions. "Rose Mary's Baby," it was called.[36]

"INTERNATIONAL AFFAIRS is *our* issue," Nixon had told Colson. In the fall of 1971 he moved aggressively to make it a winning one.

He got started on October 12, when he announced that he would be going to Moscow in May 1972 for a summit meeting to conclude the SALT talks. Asked how the Moscow summit related to the Peking summit, Nixon insisted that "the two are independent trips. . . . Neither trip is being taken for the purpose of exploiting what differences may exist between the two nations; neither is being taken at the expense of any other nation."[37]

The announcement was headline news around the world, and added new luster to Nixon's already bright image. Behind the scenes, meanwhile, he was acting to give some economic substance to détente, just as the Soviets were striving to give the policy some human-rights significance.

The Soviets, due to their incredibly inept agricultural system, made even worse by some recent crop failures, were desperately in need of grain. The United States, due to its incredibly efficient agricultural system, made even more profitable by subsidies for crops already in surplus, had government silos groaning with grain and was desperate to find buyers. Seldom have the needs of the two superpowers meshed so perfectly. In June 1971, Nixon had cleared the way for massive grain sales when he announced an end to the policy that required half of all grain trade with Communist nations be carried on American flag vessels. Shortly after his October announcement of the forthcoming summit, the Soviets moved into the American grain market, quietly buying up almost four million tons of barley, corn, and oats.

A problem emerged down in Bal Harbour. Nixon praised the labor unions for their patriotism. Sometimes, however, he wished they would not take it quite so seriously. Thomas "Teddy" Gleason and Jesse Calhoon, leaders of the maritime unions movement, were like George Meany. They thought all Communists were swine to be avoided when they were not being attacked. They refused to load Soviet ships. Kissinger tried to reason with Gleason, who told him to "go fuck yourself." Nixon decided that this sort of negotiation was more in Colson's line, and sent him to see Gleason and Calhoon.

Colson told Calhoon that "the whole Soviet SALT agreement hinged on the trade agreement." Calhoon yawned; he didn't much like SALT anyway. "He was tough," Colson later remarked. "No liberal."

"We've got to make a deal," Colson said.

"What's in it for us?" Calhoon asked.

Quite a bit, it turned out. Colson promised the Nixon Administration would free up funds for construction of more merchant ships, and otherwise act favorably on legislation important to the maritime unions. The deal went through. Ten months later, Gleason became the first member of the AFL-CIO's executive committee to endorse Nixon's re-election.[38]

The Soviets, on their side, were seeking to ease, if not remove, a source of aggravation in Soviet-American relations. It was the difficulty Jews in Russia had in obtaining exit documents in order to emigrate to Israel. In 1969, only two thousand were allowed to leave; in 1970, even that small number was cut in half. Then in the first nine months of 1971 the number went above ten thousand. But although the percentage jump was huge, that still left hundreds of thousands who wanted to get out but could not. Nevertheless, it clearly showed that one of the benefits of détente would be relaxed Soviet emigration policies. On November 5, in Washington, an announcement was made about Soviet grain purchases; that same day, in Moscow, an announcement was made about a new surge in Jewish emigration.[39]

Two WEEKS after Nixon announced the Moscow summit, Kissinger returned to Washington from Peking, where he had made another secret trip to prepare for the Peking summit. This time it was Kissinger, not Nixon, whose name was in the headlines. Kissinger also got his picture on the front page of *The New York Times*, sitting with Chou En-lai at a banquet in his (Kissinger's) honor. Nixon was getting a bit irritated and jealous. His News Summary informed him of a *Parade* magazine feature that ended by asking "if one man should have so much power." Nixon wrote, "H—*Again* the theme of K's power—Not helpful!"[40]

While Kissinger was in Peking, the United Nations voted on admitting the P.R.C. With the upcoming Peking summit, Nixon obviously could not oppose, and in any case the P.R.C. now had the votes whatever the United States did. Nixon sent Kissinger to Peking when he did so that Kissinger would be out of the country when the vote was taken. The President's policy was to mount no opposition to seating the P.R.C., while pursuing a "two Chinas" policy that would allow Chiang Kai-shek's China (Taiwan) to stay in the General Assembly. In his memoirs, Nixon said it was not easy for him to take a position "so disappointing to our old friend and loyal ally, Chiang," but he did it anyway.[41]

On October 25 the U.N. voted to admit the P.R.C. and expel Taiwan. There was cheering, handclapping, and dancing in the aisles of the General Assembly. Nixon expressed his "shock and dismay" at such goings-on; Senator Teddy Kennedy said it was the President's fault and accused him of playing on "the worst instincts in his party and the nation." Kennedy wanted to know if Nixon's forthcoming China trip "is to be a fixed star on the road to peace instead of a passing comet in an American election year."[42]

There were other critics, coming from different directions. George Meany reacted to the announcement of the Soviet summit by suggesting that Nixon also visit Castro in Cuba. "If he's going to visit the louses of the world," Meany remarked, "why doesn't he visit them all?"[43] And actor John Wayne wrote his friend in the White House to deplore the China trip, which he said was "a real shocker." Wayne enclosed some reading for the President, including a spurious "Communist rules for revolution" pamphlet that was enjoying a right-wing vogue, and a hate piece "fact sheet" on "that Jew, Kissinger."[44]

Nixon was able to ignore the puppies nipping at his heels. He had seized the imagination of the nation, indeed of the world, and his momentum was unstoppable. On November 12, at a news conference, he captured the headlines again with another welcome announcement: he was going to withdraw forty-five thousand more Americans from Vietnam before the end of the year. He added that withdrawals in 1972 would depend on the level of enemy activity, progress in Vietnamization, and progress in obtaining a cease-fire throughout Southeast Asia and in gaining the release of all American POWs.

Asked when he intended to begin withdrawing American air

power, Nixon made it clear it would not be soon. Indeed, he threatened: "If we see any substantial step-up in infiltration in the passes, for example, which lead from North Vietnam into Laos [and] through Cambodia into South Vietnam—if we see that, we will have to not only continue our airstrikes; we will have to step them up."

In fact, even as he spoke, the Air Force was carrying out a series of strikes on strategic targets in southern North Vietnam and along the Ho Chi Minh Trail.

Asked to comment on his three-year-old pledge to "end the war," Nixon said he wanted to be judged on that one on Election Day, 1972. He added, "Every promise that I have made I have kept to this date, and that is usually a pretty good example of what you might do with regard to future promises."

If he was unable to get a negotiated settlement with Hanoi, would he leave a residual force of forty thousand or fifty thousand men in Vietnam until the POW issue was settled?

In a long, wandering, complex reply, Nixon said yes.

Did he foresee ever granting amnesty to the young men who fled the country to avoid fighting in Vietnam? In a one-word, simple, to-the-point reply, Nixon said, "No."

Asked about the recently triumphantly re-elected President Thieu and Vietnam, Nixon said Thieu was "enormously impressed with the speed of the training program," which he asserted "has gone faster than we had thought." Further, "the level of enemy activity has not been as great as it was, due to the fact that the enemy doesn't have the punch that it had."[45]

Altogether it was a wonderfully upbeat report, one satisfying to all but the most extreme dove. It showed Nixon in the best possible light, as the total realist, the consummate statesman, carefully calculating his way through the shoals, guided by the principle of what was good for America. No wonder Nixon wanted to make foreign affairs *our* issue.

THE EMOTIONS of all Presidents tend to be like a yo-yo, going up and down in response to actions and events they cannot control. As in so many other areas, in this regard Nixon was the extreme example. In the first quarter of 1971, he had been at a low point, almost in despair, under attack from many quarters, unable to get the ARVN to fight effectively in Laos, unwilling to accept the Supreme Court's dictum that busing to achieve racial balance in the schools was permissible, incapable of halting inflation or bringing down unemployment, unloved by the Establishment and by the students. Then came the Big Charge, on China, on SALT, on wage-

and-price controls, and he began to move up in the polls. His spirits rose. Although there was a setback with the publication of the Pentagon Papers and the resulting troubles with the FBI and Hoover, his Supreme Court appointments and his confrontation with Meany brought him up again. So did the successful fund-raising efforts.

But in December, as he began to concentrate more single-mindedly than ever on the '72 re-election campaign, he sank once more, as a crisis in East Asia nearly overwhelmed him.

In 1947, when Britain granted independence to India, it also divided the subcontinent, uniting a large part of the Muslim population in Pakistan. But Pakistan was divided into East and West, separated by a thousand miles, with India in between. This was an impossible situation, and over the next two decades severe political problems developed between East and West Pakistan. A free election in December 1970 showed that 97 percent of the people of East Pakistan wanted autonomy. President Yahya responded by arresting the leader of East Pakistan and, on March 25, 1971, sending in the Army to impose martial law and, in fact, begin a civil war.

West Pakistan's repression was cruel and bloody almost beyond belief, even in this most bloody of centuries. The Hindu minority of East Pakistan were special targets. Refugees by the hundreds of thousands crossed over the border into India, creating serious problems for the government. The State Department, responding to congressional and public pressure, but even more to the logic of the situation, wanted to shut down economic and military aid to West Pakistan, to force Yahya to end the repression. But on a May 2 note to that effect, Nixon wrote, "To all hands. Don't squeeze Yahya at this time. RN." [46]

Nixon wanted to reward Yahya for his help in communicating with China, and he had an intense personal dislike for Indian Prime Minister Indira Gandhi. Further, he saw Pakistan as a friend of China, India as a friend of the Soviet Union. In addition, Kissinger was being fed information by an enemy of Gandhi's, inside her government, to the effect that India was plotting an aggressive war designed to extinguish West Pakistan.[47]

Nixon believed these tales of Kissinger's (no one else involved in any way in the crisis ever did), and by July issued instructions "to tilt toward Pakistan." [48] By then there were ten million refugees. East Pakistan and India were becoming ever more desperate; world public opinion ever more outraged. But Nixon stuck with Yahya, among other reasons because Kissinger said Yahya provided the only link to China (which was not even remotely true; Yahya had provided an airplane for Polo, but after Nixon's July 15 announcement that he would go to China, the United States and China were in direct, open communication via a variety of channels).

Nixon's triangular diplomacy was just coming into play in the summer of 1971, and already it was getting terribly complicated as the number of actors grew beyond the original three, the U.S., China, and Russia. India, fearful of the emerging U.S.-China-Pakistan alignment, and rebuffed by a hostile Nixon Administration, sought friendship in Moscow. On August 9, as Kissinger put it, "came the bombshell of the Soviet-Indian Friendship Treaty." [49]

It was not a military alliance, but Nixon and Kissinger acted as if it were a veritable Pact of Steel between Axis aggressors. In complete contradiction to the assessments of the State Department, the CIA, the British press and Foreign Service officials, and indeed every other informed observer in the world, the President and his National Security Adviser insisted that India's aim was to destroy West Pakistan, that the Soviets were a part of this conspiracy, and that the danger of an Indian strike was imminent. Both Nixon and Kissinger expressed this view repeatedly; it was an *idée fixe* of theirs.[50]

Thus did Nixon and Kissinger elevate what was really a problem left over from British rule in India into a Cold War confrontation of the first magnitude.

By October, both India and West Pakistan were sending troops to their border. Kissinger convened a meeting of the Washington Special Action Group (WSAG), composed of representatives from State, Defense, CIA, and NSC. Everyone but Kissinger thought that independence for East Pakistan was inevitable and desirable, and that India had no designs on West Pakistan. Kissinger's expressed fears of a Chinese intervention on Pakistan's side were considered unrealistic. State wanted to sit back, stay calm, and let the inevitable happen.[51]

Kissinger wanted to get tough, with both India and the Soviets. So did Nixon. On October 19, Nixon instructed Haig (Kissinger was on his way to Peking) to "hit the Indians again on this," by threatening to cut off American aid to India, already under great stress because of recent droughts, followed by major floods and a cyclone, on top of the problem of feeding ten million refugees.[52]

On November 4, Prime Minister Gandhi came to Washington. She met with Nixon. Seldom in the annals of diplomacy have two more mismatched leaders attempted to negotiate a peaceful settlement. She was supercilious and condescending and pacifist; he was sullen and suspicious and contemptuous. She assured Nixon,

"India has never wished the destruction of Pakistan or its permanent crippling. Above all, India seeks the restoration of stability. We want to eliminate chaos at all costs." He gave her a blunt warning: "It would be impossible to calculate precisely the steps which other great powers might take if India were to initiate hostilities."[53]

Later, Gandhi commented, "It was not so much Mr. Nixon talking as Mr. Kissinger, because Mr. Nixon would talk for a few minutes and would then say, 'Isn't that right, Henry?' and from then on Henry would talk on for quite a while and then Nixon would say two words and then he would say, 'Wouldn't you say so, Henry?' "[54]

Nixon also commented later, in his diary. He called Gandhi "hypocritical" and "duplicitous," and indulged himself in a little moralism: "Those who resort to force, without making excuses, are bad enough—but those who resort to force while preaching to others about their use of force deserve no sympathy whatever."[55]

On November 22, Yahya claimed in a radio broadcast that India had invaded West Pakistan in an "all-out offensive." The report was not true, but Nixon and Kissinger believed it anyway. Nixon was determined to stop what he perceived as Indian aggression and Soviet adventurism. He ordered a suspension of export licenses for military goods for India and a cutoff in economic aid.

On November 29, Nixon announced that he would make his trip to Peking in February 1972. On December 3, war broke out in earnest in the subcontinent, but it was Yahya, not Gandhi, who started it. The Pakistani Air Force launched a surprise attack on Indian airfields. This proved to be a great mistake; the strikes did little damage, but they provoked India. Mrs. Gandhi ordered a full-scale offensive into East Pakistan and a limited offensive in West Pakistan.

The Soviets, from day one, urged restraint on India. Mrs. Gandhi, for her part, announced that she would accept a U.N. call for a cease-fire as soon as Bangladesh (East Pakistan) was independent. Nixon escalated.

On December 3, the day the war began, Kissinger convened the WSAG. "I've been catching unshirted hell every half-hour from the President, who says we're not tough enough," he said. "He really doesn't believe we're carrying out his wishes. He wants to tilt toward Pakistan."[56]

On December 6, Nixon sent a letter to Brezhnev in which he bluntly charged that India was out to "dismember the sovereign state of Pakistan," and accused the Russians of being an accomplice. He warned Brezhnev to restrain India, on pain of sacrificing the upcoming Moscow summit. Brezhnev replied that Russia was already urging restraint and acceptance of the call for a cease-fire.[57]

Although the fighting was already dying down, and the Indian offensive in West Pakistan had halted, Nixon continued to believe Gandhi's objective was total victory. In some respects, he was engaged in what Seymour Hersh called "a personal vendetta against Indira Gandhi," [58] but he was also—in his own mind, and as goaded by Kissinger—trying to protect the opening to China. Kissinger told him at the height of the crisis, "We don't really have any choice. We can't allow a friend of ours [Pakistan] and China's to get screwed in a conflict with a friend of Russia's." [59]

On December 8, Nixon told Kissinger that perhaps they should cancel the Moscow summit. The next day, beside himself over press stories that senior U.S. diplomats were opposing his "anti-Indian bias," Nixon called in the principal officials of the WSAG. As Kissinger recorded it, "He told them that while he did not insist on the State Department's being loyal to the President, it should be loyal to the United States." [60]

The following day, December 10, Nixon sent two warnings to Brezhnev. One was relatively innocuous—another threatening letter. The other was serious in the extreme; he ordered the U.S. Navy to send the aircraft carrier *Enterprise* (nuclear capable), nine accompanying warships, and two thousand combat-ready marines from Vietnam to the Bay of Bengal. It was called Task Force 74. Nixon later declared that by this act America "had threatened to go to nuclear war with the Russians." [61]

Nixon ordered this action without an NSC meeting, or a WSAG meeting, or any consultation whatsoever with the Secretary of Defense, or the Secretary of State, or the JCS, or the Navy. Neither Admiral Moorer, chairman of the JCS, nor Admiral Elmo Zumwalt, Chief of Naval Operations, was told the purpose of the move.

Thus did a shockingly misguided policy, based on stubborn ignorance and refusal to face the most elementary facts, cross over to sheer folly, creating about as dangerous a situation as could be imagined for goals that were vague at best and self-serving at worst.

Kissinger later commented that here "the first decision to risk war in the triangular Soviet-Chinese-American relationship was taken." He also noted, "Nixon had many faults, but in crises he was conspicuously courageous." [62]

The courage consisted of more threats, via the hot line to Moscow, but actually the crisis was already over. Even as the U.S. fleet moved into the Bay of Bengal, a cease-fire went into effect as Bangladesh was born and the Indian Army began to pull out of West Pakistan.

Nixon and Kissinger congratulated themselves. They were convinced that they had curbed Soviet adventurism and saved Pakistan while cementing the U.S.–Chinese relationship.

In his memoirs, Kissinger let out all stops in his praise of his master: "Nixon understood immediately that if the Soviet Union succeeded in humiliating China, all prospects for world equilibrium would disappear." He spoke of Nixon's "lonely and brave decision," and of "his courage and patriotism in making such a decision, at risk to his immediate political interest, to preserve the world balance of power for the ultimate safety of all free peoples." [63] Thus was the world saved by the far-seeing geopolitical comprehension, statesmanship, and courage of two beleaguered figures, Nixon and Kissinger, isolated even within the American government.

Garthoff's conclusion brings us back to reality: "When all of Kissinger's frenetic crisis fever, histrionic signals, threats, attempted pressures, and the meanderings of the American fleet are set aside, the course of events actually unfolded in a way entirely consistent with the expressed positions taken by India, Pakistan, the Soviet Union, and China . . . before the movement of the fleet, the hot line communication, or the misplaced alarm over a possible eruption in Sino-Soviet hostilities. . . . [By December 9] *all* those participants had expressed support for a settlement along the lines finally agreed to: independence of Bangladesh, a return to the status quo in the West, and complete cessation of hostilities." [64]

Nixon never saw the Indo-Pakistani War of 1971 as a regional conflict caused by local conditions; to him it was a global struggle between the superpowers. It was almost as if it *had* to be that way for Nixon for him to justify his actions to himself. On December 20, he told British Prime Minister Edward Heath that there was a "lesson" in the crisis for the world: "The Soviets have tested us . . ." [65] Nixon, always eager to be tested, made it sound as if it were his manhood, not his statesmanship, that had been tested. He had played it tough and, in his view, won.

At the height of the crisis, Kissinger told a Russian official, "It is not President Nixon's style to threaten." [66] That statement had about the same relationship to the truth as the Nixon-Kissinger policy in South Asia had to reality in December 1971.

THE MINUTES of the December 3 WSAG meeting, the one in which Kissinger relayed Nixon's orders to "tilt toward Pakistan," were stolen by a spy from the NSC staff. The spy was Navy Yeoman Charles Radford; his clients were the Joint Chiefs of Staff. Radford had stolen much more than the minutes of one WSAG meeting; he had taken the minutes of all of them, plus many other documents, including the contents of Kissinger's briefcase from his Polo trip. Radford was secretary to Admiral Robert O. Welander, the JCS liaison to the NSC. For some time past, Yeoman Radford's superiors had encouraged him to bring them copies of everything he saw, but most especially memorandums of Nixon's conversations with Kissinger and Kissinger's comments about Nixon to others. Radford had done so with skill and enthusiasm; it is not an exaggeration to say he was one of the most accomplished spies in history.

Jack Anderson got copies of the WSAG memos, possibly from Radford, who was a fellow Mormon and a friend. When Anderson began printing them on December 13, a Plumbers' investigation of the source of the leak quickly revealed some of Radford's activities, and under questioning he confessed to the rest (except he insisted he did not give the memos to Anderson).

When Nixon found out about Radford's spying, he wrote in his diary that he was "not particularly ... surprised ... although I don't think it's a healthy practice." [67]

But despite Nixon's rather ho-hum, it's-all-part-of-the-bureaucratic-game response, this was really incredible. If there is an analogy for the top military command spying on the commander in chief, it is Nazi Germany, and even there it was not so systematic or successful.

Perhaps the reason Nixon was not shocked was that he realized it was his own fault. The absence of any coordination at all, the absolute refusal of the commander in chief to consult with the defense establishment before undertaking long-range moves of the greatest possible military significance (the opening to China) or his ordering specific military moves full of a high level of risk (Task Force 74 into the Bay of Bengal), without even informing the officers in charge of the movement about its purpose or objective, forced the JCS, in self-defense and in order to meet their responsibilities, to spy on the President.

When the investigation of Radford turned up Admiral Welander's name, Nixon ordered Ehrlichman to interview Welander. The admiral confirmed everything to which Radford had confessed. Ehrlichman took a tape recording of Welander's remarks to Nixon's EOB office, where the President, the Attorney General, and the President's chief of staff listened to it.

Were they outraged? Did they swear to punish the guilty, to see to it that nothing like this ever happened again?

Not a bit of it. Nixon was paralyzed because of his own Byzantine arrangement of the command system. He explained to his cohorts that many of his orders for action in Vietnam were transmitted through Admiral Moorer and the JCS because he could not be sure Secretary Laird would follow his orders. Nixon said he and Kissinger had "invested much confidence in Moorer," meaning that Moorer had the goods on them and was thus untouchable. Nixon admitted that if he disciplined Moorer for spying on the White House, it would impair the vital back channel to the Air Force and Navy in Vietnam. And if he disciplined Moorer, he mused, "it would give Laird a whip hand over the Joint Chiefs."[68]

So Nixon did nothing about Moorer. To stay on top of things, he ordered a tap on Radford's telephones at home and at work (Radford had been quietly transferred from his NSC duties to a remote post in Oregon). Nixon refused to authorize a tap that Mitchell wanted to place on Jack Anderson.[69]

Nixon sent Mitchell to interview Moorer, who said he thought the memos he was getting from Welander were routine liaison material sent to him for information. He denied any knowledge of Radford's activities. That was plenty good enough for Nixon, who breathed a sigh of relief and ordered a halt to any further investigation into the Radford-Welander spying case.

Instead of an inquiry, Nixon sent Mitchell to see Moorer again, this time "to let him know that we had the goods." At the same time, Nixon renominated Moorer to serve a second two-year tour as chairman of the Joint Chiefs. When Ehrlichman was asked in an interview why Nixon did that, Ehrlichman smiled and said, "After this, the admiral was preshrunk."[70]

The point being that with the SALT agreements coming up in five months at the Moscow summit, Nixon could not afford to have the JCS criticizing his arms-control deal. And with the China summit coming in February, Nixon could not afford to have the JCS criticizing the concessions he was going to have to make on reducing the American military presence on Taiwan.

Yeoman Radford had rendered his President a great service by making it possible for the commander in chief to blackmail his military high command into supporting his policies.

IN THE AFTERMATH of the Indo-Pakistani War, Nixon had another problem, in the form of his National Security Adviser. There were far too many leaks, for one thing, and Nixon blamed Kissinger for failing to keep a tight control on his NSC staff. Further, Jack Anderson's revelation of the tilt toward Pakistan had brought down an avalanche of criticism on Nixon's head, generally in the form of a question: How could he support Pakistan, when Pakistan was so clearly in the wrong?

Kissinger compounded that problem on December 14, the day after Anderson's first column appeared. He gave a background briefing to the press. He said, "Soviet conduct on the subcontinent was not compatible with the mutual restraint required by genuine co-existence. If it continued, we would have to re-evaluate our entire relationship, including the summit."[71]

Kissinger had not cleared this threat with Nixon, and with the crisis over by then, it made no sense to make it. Nixon was angry. In addition, he was growing increasingly jealous of all the attention the press gave to Kissinger, and the way the press fawned on the man. Nixon wanted Kissinger's services, and he was as one with Kissinger in his love of intrigue and conspiracy and surprises, but he also wanted the spotlight exclusively on himself.

Nixon was suspicious, and rightly so, that Kissinger used his briefings of the press to build himself up. In November, Nixon wrote on a News Summary, "H—I think it would be well to cut backgrounders for awhile—They really do more harm than good on balance—& these guys [the press] have asked for it. Particularly —*No* K backgrounds for next 3 months."[72]

But within the month, Kissinger had held at least a dozen backgrounders, in which the theme was, as always, the way in which Kissinger the reasonable statesman kept Nixon the mad bomber from running amok. But, also as always, Nixon had no one to blame but himself, because along with his orders to cut all Kissinger backgrounders, he filled the News Summaries with such comments as "K—knock this down" and "K—nip this fast."[73]

When Ted Lewis wrote in the New York *Daily News* that the accomplishments of most summits never equaled the great expectations, Nixon scribbled, "K—set him right on why these trips [to Peking and Moscow] are totally different."[74]

Nixon's contradictory instructions fed the jealousy, backbiting, and intrigue that were increasingly dominating the atmosphere in the White House. The two central participants were Haldeman and Kissinger (aside from Nixon himself). Kissinger charged, with regard to the Plumbers' investigations into the NSC staff as a source of leaks, that "Haldeman wanted to prove that [my] people were unreliable and that only people hired by Haldeman were reliable."[75] For his part, Haldeman told Ehrlichman that Kissinger was mounting daily tirades against Bill Rogers and that the President was "nearly to the point of firing Henry, just to end the wear and tear."[76]

During Christmas week of 1971, things almost blew apart. On December 23, Nixon told Ehrlichman to brief Kissinger on the Radford-Welander spy ring. This was the first Kissinger knew about it. Kissinger was dubious, so Ehrlichman played the recording of Welander's confession for him.

Kissinger, who so often described Nixon as being "beside himself," was beside himself. When the tapes ended, he began striding up and down, shouting: "He [Nixon] won't fire Moorer! They can spy on him and spy on me and betray us and he won't fire them! If he won't fire Rogers—impose some discipline in this Administration—there is no reason to believe he'll fire Moorer. I assure you all this tolerance will lead to very serious consequences for this Administration!"

Two hours later, Kissinger burst unbidden into Nixon's EOB office. Ehrlichman was there. Kissinger wanted to talk about Moorer. "I tell you, Mr. President, this is very serious," he said. "We cannot survive the kinds of internal weaknesses we are seeing." Nixon tried to reassure him, without success.

When Kissinger left, Nixon told Ehrlichman he was worried about "Henry's mood swings." Ehrlichman later wrote, "Nixon wondered aloud if Henry needed psychiatric care." [77]

Kissinger, meanwhile, told Bernard and Marvin Kalb, reporters who were writing his biography, that "Haldeman and Ehrlichman, always on the lookout for an anti-Kissinger opportunity, were ... engaged in an intensive effort to undermine [my] position in the White House." Three years later, Kissinger was still complaining; referring to the events of December 1971, he told a group of *Time* editors, "For four weeks I was not allowed to have a press conference and Ziegler said not a word to defend me. . . . I debated for several weeks at that time whether I should go on, and decided to." [78]

Nixon, meanwhile, made a decision not to prosecute Radford. Instead, he told the Justice Department to stay after and speed up the prosecution of Ellsberg.

He also continued to fret about Kissinger's mental health. He repeated to Ehrlichman his wish that Kissinger see a psychiatrist. "Talk to him, John," the President instructed. "And talk to Al Haig. He will listen to Al."

Ehrlichman wrote later that he "could think of no way to talk to Henry about psychiatric care." He did talk with Haig. Haig's response was "The President needs Henry. You've got to realize that the President isn't doing his homework these days. It's only Henry who pulls us through." [79] So nothing was done, and soon enough Kissinger was back in favor.

Joan Hoff-Wilson, the only professional historian to whom Nixon gave interviews in his retirement, points out that the relationship of Nixon and Kissinger was an unhealthy one. Different though they were (Quaker and Jew, Whittier and Harvard, politician and professor), they shared a love of eavesdropping on others (the taps and the tapes), of secrecy, of surprises, of conspiracy, of backbiting, of power plays. They were alike in their utter cynicism, and in their contempt for everyone else, including each other. Yet they spent enormous amounts of time together, three or four meetings nearly every day, interspersed with innumerable phone calls. They spent more time together than was good for them.[80]

NIXON DID NOT let his problems with Kissinger ruin his holiday season. A few days before Christmas, he and Pat went up to New York, where they met Ed and Tricia Cox and David and Julie Eisenhower. David was home on leave from the Navy and looked quite dashing in his uniform. On Saturday night, the eighteenth, they went to the St. James Theatre to see *Two Gentlemen of Verona*, and on Sunday morning Nixon and his family, trailed by threescore photographers, went to Norman Vincent Peale's Marble Collegiate Church. Christmas in the White House was a quiet family day.[81]

In between the New York weekend and Christmas Day, Nixon worked in the EOB. On the twenty-third he had his tumultuous meeting with Kissinger. That same day, he dealt with a problem that had been on his mind for a long time.

Back in 1961, Attorney General Robert Kennedy had organized a "Get Hoffa" task force in the Justice Department. James "Jimmy" Hoffa was president of the Teamsters Union; Kennedy charged that he had links to organized crime. In 1964, Hoffa was convicted of jury tampering. In 1967 he began to serve a thirteen-year prison term. He remained president of the union, coordinating contract negotiations and investing the huge pension fund from his cell. He remained popular with the rank and file among the Teamsters. A rumor went around that the Teamsters had contributed $100,000 to Nixon's 1968 campaign, with the understanding that this would secure Hoffa's pardon.

Shortly after Nixon became President, Ehrlichman began pressing him for the pardon. It made good political sense and was a nice way to stick it to the hated Kennedys. But Colson, a close friend of Teamster Vice-President Frank Fitzsimmons, convinced Nixon to put a hold on Hoffa's pardon until after the union elections in 1971, so that Hoffa could not challenge Fitzsimmons for the presidency. Hoffa evidently got wind of this; in any event, on June 3, 1971, he said he would not be a candidate in the July election. Still no pardon. On June 20, therefore, as the executive board of the Teamsters gathered at the Playboy Plaza Hotel in Miami Beach for preconvention meetings, Hoffa sent a telegram announcing his resignation.

The next morning, the board swore in Fitzsimmons as Hoffa's

successor. At noon, who should show up at the hotel but the President of the United States himself, who had driven up from Key Biscayne. He asked for a twenty-minute private meeting with the board. According to Ziegler's later briefing of reporters, Nixon never mentioned Hoffa. His theme was best expressed in his opening sentence, "My door is always open to President Fitzsimmons and that is the way it should be."

Still no pardon for Hoffa. Meanwhile Fitzsimmons became a golfing partner of the President's, and the Teamsters pledged financial support and an endorsement for Nixon in '72. Also, Fitzsimmons and Hoffa were quarreling, evidently because Fitzsimmons kept up the contacts with organized crime while Hoffa reportedly wanted the Teamsters to go straight. Indications were that Hoffa, once free, would challenge for the leadership, and he remained popular with the members.

Nixon wanted to please the members and Fitzsimmons. On December 23 he found a way to do both when he finally granted Hoffa a commutation. It was not a full and clear pardon; Nixon barred Hoffa from engaging in union activity for eight years, and he ordered Hoffa placed under constant surveillance.[82]

Thus the spirit of Christmas at the Nixon White House.

CHAPTER TWENTY-TWO

POLITICS, HANOI, PEKING, AND BUSING
January–March 1972

ON JANUARY 2, 1972, Nixon had a televised interview with Dan Rather of CBS. He opened by saying that he had not yet decided whether he would be a candidate, but indicated that if he decided to run, Agnew would stay on the ticket. Back in 1956, Eisenhower had put Nixon through a season of agony. The President had resisted tremendous pressure to say that Nixon was his choice as running mate, and not until the delegates selected Nixon at the convention did Ike welcome him on the team.

When his turn came, Nixon did it differently: he told Rather that "the Vice President has handled his difficult assignments with dignity, with courage." Admitting that Agnew "has been a man of controversy," Nixon nevertheless gave him an unambiguous endorsement: "When a man has done a good job in a position, when he has been part of a winning team, I believe that he should stay on the team." The statement had the advantage of settling the question of the second spot on the ticket, thus depriving the reporters and columnists of one of their favorite subjects for speculation, and therefore keeping the spotlight on Nixon.

Nixon followed up with a ritual and meaningless promise: "I will engage in no public partisan activities until after the Republican Convention." He explained that the problems he had to deal with were so great that "it will not be possible to take time off for partisan politics."

Rather went immediately to the most serious problem, Vietnam. Would the President explain why the U.S. Air Force was currently carrying out bombing raids on North Vietnam?

493

Because of North Vietnamese provocation, Nixon replied. The enemy had stepped up the infiltration and "violated the understanding of 1968, when the bombing halt was agreed to, with regard to firing on our unarmed reconnaissance planes." Further, "they shelled Saigon on December 19." Under those circumstances, "I had no other choice but to bomb."

Rather quoted a comment Nixon had made to *Time* magazine three days earlier: "The issue of Vietnam will not be an issue in the campaign . . . because we will have brought the American involvement to an end." He asked if that meant there would be no American forces anywhere in Indochina by Election Day.

Nixon said that depended on the enemy. The North Vietnamese held four hundred POWs. Slipping into the third person, Nixon posed his own question: "Can the President . . . withdraw all of our forces as long as the enemy holds one American as a prisoner of war? The answer is no." So if Hanoi did not free the prisoners, "we will have to continue the possibility of air strikes on the North Vietnamese."

"Then how can you campaign saying you have ended the American involvement?" Rather asked.

"Well," Nixon replied, "the important thing is whether the American people are convinced that the President of the United States had done everything that he can to bring this desperately difficult war to an end." He went on to recite the statistics on the reduction of casualties and number of troops in Vietnam.

Rather observed that "everything seems to have been pointed in the direction of climaxing in this election year: besides your ultimate goals in the war, victory over inflation, driving down unemployment, agreement for the strategic arms limitations, trips to Peking and Moscow." He wondered "if all of this is coincidental," or was "the timing politically motivated?"

Nixon acknowledged that was a legitimate question, and cited a recent example to show why he understood such suspicion: "After all, when you look at the bombing halt of 1968, I know many on our side felt that that was politically motivated, at least the timing of it. I, of course, never made such a charge, and would not."

So the answer was that the timing was coincidental. The developments Rather had listed all had a long history. For example, Nixon said, he had written about an opening to China as far back as 1967, in an article in *Foreign Affairs*. Although Rather and the rest of the media had missed the point, "in that article, I raised the lid on what many think was the biggest surprise in history when I made the 90-second announcement that we were going to China."[1]

Who but Nixon could make such an absurd claim?

But his bravado and exaggerations notwithstanding, the President was worried, with good reason. In 1968, he had promised to end the war; by 1971 that had become a promise to end American involvement in the war; by 1972 he was admitting that he would not even accomplish that if Hanoi held the prisoners, and there was no indication that Hanoi would release them until it ruled over all of Vietnam. He was below a 50 percent approval rating in the polls, he had no domestic programs that he could point to with pride, he was trapped into enforcing busing, and in three years he had failed to shake the Tricky Dick image. Most of all because of his record in Vietnam, but for other reasons as well, people just did not trust President Nixon.

The day after the Rather interview, Doug Hallett of Colson's staff prepared for Colson and Nixon an analysis of a recent series by David Broder in the Washington *Post* on "The Politicians and the People." Hallett said Broder's major points were that Nixon "seemed more unpredictable, more mysterious, more inconsistent" to the people after three years in office than he did when he entered, that the big issue in 1972 was going to be "trust and confidence," and that people were "alienated."

Hallett then delivered a devastating critique of his own. He pointed out that despite the Nixon Big Charge of the past six months, the President had gained only two or three points in the polls. He said this was "our fault. We have done virtually everything imaginable to undermine our own credibility and consistency." In 1969, the Administration had promised to "go forward together." In 1970, it was a "New Federalism." In 1971, it was a "New American Revolution." What next? "The Second Coming, perhaps?"

Nixon, far from being offended, scribbled in the margin of the memo, "Very perceptive. Absolutely correct. Too much rhetoric!"

"P.R.-wise," Hallett went on, "we have behaved as village burghers, testing the wind, dragged into every reform." Nixon commented, "E—note! Too *many programs.*"

Hallett was specific: "The welfare program is pronounced the greatest domestic program since the New Deal, but we expend far more effort trying to place G. Harrold Carswell on the Supreme Court. We start off with a very exciting and challenging commitment to the first five years of life, but denounce day-care (no, middle-class day-care) as committing the government to communal living. . . . It is no wonder that today we find the public doubting anything we do, seeing in us instability when their greatest want is for just the opposite."

Nixon underscored that passage.

As to Broder's point about the psychological issue of trust and confidence, Hallett asserted that FDR, Truman, Eisenhower, and Johnson all came across as leaders. "Richard Nixon? Man on the make; ashamed of and constantly running away from his past; manipulator; unsure of his convictions; tactician instead of strategist; Grand Vizier of all Rotarians, substituting pomposity for eloquence. That is the public impression."

Nixon commented, "H—he may be a good analyst in pointing this out—This is probably the attitude of most of the intellectuals."

Hallett thought Nixon's problem was "trying to reassure the left, which cares everything about words, with substance; trying to reassure the right, which cares everything about substance, with words." Nixon underscored the sentence and scribbled, "H & E—Note! A very legitimate criticism."

Hallett had some specific suggestions, beginning with calming down the PR. He wanted the President to present himself as the first occupant of the White House "to realize that the hyper-individualistic—'We're No. 1'—frontier American philosophy is bankrupt and outdated." Nixon was having none of that: he wrote, "Wrong on this—Typical Ivy League." Nixon did approve of the next suggestion: "Stop displaying the President as if he had a stick up his ass. Put him in gutsy, colorful, photographic situations with people."

"H—Good!" Nixon wrote.[2]

Three days later, Colson sent in his own analysis of the Hallett memo. He thought the most important point was playing to the Left with substance while trying to appease the Right with rhetoric, and Hallett's biggest error was failing to see how remarkable it was that Nixon had survived at all in view of the Pentagon Papers, Calley, the expulsion of Taiwan from the U.N., Laos, and the sluggish economy.

Hallett wanted Nixon to appeal to the broad public and ignore the special-interest groups; Colson thought he was badly wrong. He told the President that the key to the election "is the cultivation of important voting blocs; in short, exploiting the advantages of incumbency." Nixon noted, "Correct (a weakness in the Hallett memo)."[3]

One bloc Nixon had no hope of winning was the university vote. Straw polls at Stanford and Dartmouth showed McGovern far out in front, followed by Muskie, with Nixon trailing badly. Nixon had no illusions about being able to turn that around, but he did want to improve his standing. He pointed out to Haldeman that "we must make a greater effort in University oriented communities, especially California: This is a Republican liberal defection."[4]

The vote he had to have was on the right. His major problem here was George Wallace, but there were others, including Congressman John Ashbrook of Ohio, who along with antiwar Republican Paul McCloskey was challenging Nixon in the primaries. Ashbrook was claiming his candidacy was forcing Nixon to the right; he cited the veto of the day-care bill and Nixon's praise for Agnew in the Rather interview as proof. Nixon commented, "H— this is such blatant nonsense. It should be knocked down—if let stand it's a 'little lie' which contributes to myth RN is totally political." [5]

Elliot Richardson, Secretary of HEW, also had advice for the re-election campaign. He thought the major theme ought to be the way Nixon "deals with the process of coming to terms with change. It concerns the hard, wrenching actions necessary to align perception with reality, commitment with capacity, and promise with performance." Key points included the way in which the Nixon Doctrine adapted American policy to the realities of a multipolar world, the SALT success, the China opening, the New Economic Policy, government reorganization, revenue sharing, and welfare reform. Although Richardson's approach was the opposite of Hallett's, and although Nixon had stressed to H and E that the Administration had "too many programs," Nixon nevertheless was most enthusiastic about Richardson's suggestions. "Correct," he wrote, and "Right!" and "Good!" He concluded: "H—our PR group should take this up as our major theme. . . . Use for thought pieces in prestige mags and columns—for TV—talk shows—for staffers to feed out as RN's basic philosophy and—2 or 3 radio talks around Easter time by RN, with Big *build up*. Put one of your best men on this to develop a program and follow through." [6]

DESPITE THE OBVIOUS confusion over what the President stood for and believed in, and over how he should present himself as a candidate for re-election, the Nixon campaign gave the appearance of being well organized, well managed, and on track. On January 5, Nixon made his formal entry into the race when he agreed to leave his name on the ballot for the New Hampshire primary. John Mitchell was in the process of resigning as Attorney General to take up the post of campaign manager. Already the staff had set up the Committee to Re-elect the President (the title was created by Safire; to his annoyance, instead of becoming CRP, it became CREEP) at 1701 Pennsylvania Avenue, just down the street from the White House.

The use of "the President" rather than "Nixon" was a nice touch that emphasized a major decision, to disassociate Nixon from the Republican Party. That decision seemed wise, there being so many more Democrats than Republicans. To the party faithful and Republican candidates who complained about it, and about the way the Nixon people grabbed all the political contributions for CREEP, leaving little or nothing for congressional and state candidates, CREEP replied that the President's coattails would be long and broad enough to bring them to Washington too.

The decision was Nixon's, as were most of the others in the campaign, as had been the case in all his previous campaigns. His control frequently extended down to the smallest detail. It was Nixon, for example, who decided to make the maximum possible use of Julie. He also wanted David Eisenhower heavily involved, which posed a bit of a problem, because as an officer of the U.S. Navy, David was prohibited by law to engage in political activities. Nixon got around that one easily enough; the law, he pointed out, did not preclude David's accompanying Julie and attending, in uniform, the innumerable "affairs" that were a part of her campaigning.[7]

Nixon also adopted a policy, used by every incumbent seeking re-election, of ordering his department heads to speed up spending in order to stimulate the economy. On January 5, he personally intervened when he rejected the advice of his science advisers. They had told him it would be unwise and indeed harmful to attempt to put people into space with a space shuttle program. But Nixon knew that the same thing had been said about Kennedy's program to put a man on the moon, and that whatever the scientific community thought about this "stunt," it had paid off politically for Kennedy. So Nixon announced a six-year $5.5 billion space shuttle project, which he said would "help transform the space frontier of the 1970's into familiar territory, easily accessible for human endeavor in the 1980's and '90's." He also pointed out that the program would create fifty thousand jobs.[8]

In New Hampshire, as the Democratic candidates slogged through the snow, Nixon stayed aloof. He did send in some of his big guns to campaign for him, including most of the Cabinet, Governor Rockefeller, four senators and five representatives. He gave the Cabinet members their instructions at a private dinner.

"This is January 20, 1972," he said in impromptu remarks, "and tonight the fourth quarter begins. The football analogy tells us that the fourth quarter really determines the game." He went on to give a pep talk full of praise of himself, most of all for his foreign-policy achievements and for restoring decency to public life. In his peroration, he waved the flag in classic political rhetoric: "I simply want to say, as one who has seen government for 25 years, who has no illusions, who is considered to be totally pragmatic and by many totally political, I make an admission, I say it very unashamedly. You see, I happen to believe very deeply in this country. I think it is a great country. . . . I know that if America fails, peace and freedom in this world will not survive. . . . [We in this room] have the opportunity to see that America succeeds—succeeds in making this difficult problem of representative government work in America; succeeds in the field of foreign policy; succeeds not in the sense of a phony idealism, but with a pragmatic view toward the problems in the world. I realize that because we were here for these four years, America is a better place in which to live, the world is a safer place in which to live, and whatever happens after that, whatever happens in the election, really doesn't matter. We can all be very proud, and I am very proud of everybody in this room." [9]

The audience was quite swept off its feet. Safire was awe-struck. What was missing was the slightest hint as to what Nixon stood for, other than his own re-election. All he said on the number-one issue, Vietnam, for example, was "we think we have done very well and we will bring it to an end." How, he did not say, as he did not know, just as he did not know whether he would follow Richardson's advice and point with pride to specific programs, or Colson's advice to go after the bloc votes, or Hallett's advice to make general appeals to the broad public.

Not knowing what to stress did not bother him. He knew, from his experiences in the 1956 campaign, that an incumbent presidential candidate could stay above the fray. Far more important than any of the issues, or than his own campaign, was his opponent. Using CREEP as his principal tool, Nixon set out to manipulate the Democratic Party into nominating its weakest candidate.

THE MEN he most feared were Muskie and Wallace. Hallett had written that "Muskie's public image is everything the President's is not: strong, reflective, prudent, even wise," and warned that he would take on a presidential aura once he was nominated.

The Wallace threat was different. Nixon feared he would again run as a third-party candidate, and although there had been some doubt as to whom he had hurt the most in 1968, Humphrey or Nixon, there was none in 1972: Wallace's strength was with disgruntled Democrats who would vote for Nixon if they could not vote for Wallace.

Nixon had tried to knock Wallace off back in 1970 in the Alabama Democratic primary for governor. Wallace's wife, Lurleen, serving as stand-in governor for George, who was denied a third term by the Alabama constitution, had died of cancer in 1968. She had been succeeded as governor by Albert Brewer. In February

1970, Wallace had entered the primary against the incumbent. Nixon had sent $400,000 of leftover campaign funds down to Alabama to support Governor Brewer, but Wallace won anyway.[10]

As governor, the feisty little Wallace became a big problem for Nixon. He hammered away at the President to deliver on his "two-year-old unfulfilled pledges to stop busings and school closings and to re-establish freedom of choice," and he pointedly declared that "the Republican Party knows it cannot win without the South in the next election." He made a big show of ordering Alabama school boards to disregard court-ordered integration plans (although, in the event, he failed to stop them). But ineffective though his actions were, his words were what his constituency wanted to hear, and no matter how often Nixon declared himself to be against busing, Wallace always countered that Nixon's big mouth was belied by the actions of his Administration.[11]

Nixon then tried another tack, designed to get Wallace to run in the Democratic primaries in 1972, in order to disrupt the party and preclude his running as an independent. The IRS undertook an investigation into irregularities in the taxes of the governor's brother and former law partner, Gerald Wallace. Jack Anderson reported on the audit, claiming it involved kickbacks, illegal campaign contributions, and the other usual questionable items that make most politicians vulnerable to that kind of investigation. Gerald Wallace complained that there were forty-seven agents on his tail. "You all are trying to beat George Wallace," he said. "You're not interested in my tax returns."

In mid-1971, Nixon asked Wallace to fly with him from Mobile to Birmingham. What they talked about on that brief flight is not known. On January 12, 1972, the IRS announced that it was dropping its investigation of Gerald Wallace. The next day, George Wallace announced that he was entering the Democratic primaries.[12] The Democrats were disconcerted and alarmed. Larry O'Brien disavowed the Wallace candidacy; George Meany denounced Wallace as a "bigot and racist."[13] Nixon kept his reaction to himself.

As for Muskie, Nixon sicced Segretti and his dirty tricks on the senator. Segretti turned out bumper stickers that read, "Help Muskie in Busing More Children," and so forth. Nixon told Haldeman that Muskie "may have an emotional problem," and instructed him to go after it; Segretti then began casting aspersions on Muskie's wife and implied that the senator made racist remarks about "Canucks" (New Hampshire had a large Franco-American minority).[14] The President also directed Agnew to concentrate his attacks on Muskie.[15]

Nixon had his own problems, among them that old perennial, Howard Hughes. The McGraw-Hill Book Company had recently announced a forthcoming "autobiography" of Hughes, written by expatriate author Clifford Irving, who claimed to have had meetings with Hughes. The publishers handed out tantalizing tidbits from the book, including new material on the Hughes-Nixon loan back in 1956, of which the most sensational was that Clark Clifford had arranged the loan for Don Nixon. Hughes, then living in seclusion in the Bahamas, held a telephone press conference; the reporters who listened in said the voice sounded authentic. He denied that the book was an autobiography or that he had ever met with Irving.[16]

Hughes's denial notwithstanding, obviously Irving must have had some inside information from somewhere, enough to convince McGraw-Hill (and *Life*, which was scheduled to run excerpts) that the manuscript was basically accurate. Robert Maheu, for example, Hughes's closest confidant, now his archenemy, reportedly had stolen Hughes documents. Those documents were rumored to be in the safe of Maheu's friend Hank Greenspun, publisher of the Las Vegas *Sun*, and Greenspun was thought to be close to Jack Anderson. Worse, Greenspun knew about the $100,000 cash contribution Hughes had made to Nixon via Rebozo, and Nixon knew that because Greenspun had told Herb Klein, who had told Ehrlichman.[17] Worst of all, Maheu was a friend of Larry O'Brien's, so presumably whatever Maheu knew about the Hughes-Nixon dealings, O'Brien knew.

Nixon told Haldeman to have Colson and Dean find out what was in the Irving manuscript. Dean checked with Robert Bennett, the Hughes lobbyist in Washington who had CIA connections and had volunteered to help Colson and the Administration in whatever way he could.

"Is the book hard on Nixon?" Dean asked.

"Yes," Bennett replied, "*very* hard on Nixon." He urged Dean to get the Justice Department to investigate Irving. Dean refused.[18]

The White House did manage to get a copy of the manuscript. Irving claimed that Hughes had passed $400,000 to Nixon when he was Vice-President, to fix a Justice Department case against his airline, TWA. Irving also claimed that Hughes had told him that he, Hughes, was the one who in 1960 leaked the story of the Hughes loan to Don Nixon to Jack Anderson, as an act of revenge for Nixon's failure to come through on the TWA affair. By 1972, Hughes had another reason to be angry at Nixon; he had tried desperately to get Nixon to carry out atomic bomb tests someplace other than Nevada (Hughes had been living in a penthouse in Las

Vegas at the time and feared for his health), but Nixon had gone ahead with the tests anyway.[19]

In fact, so far as this author can tell, Haldeman is right when he claims that Nixon never did anything for Hughes.[20] Nixon was innocent in the Hughes–Don Nixon loan affair[21] and had refused repeated Hughes demands that he move those bomb tests. But Nixon had taken big money from Hughes in secret cash contributions; given the publicity that surrounded anything Hughes did, along with his unsavory reputation, that made Nixon vulnerable.

On January 24, *The New York Times* revealed that back in 1961 Attorney General Robert Kennedy had secretly started an investigation of the Hughes–Don Nixon loan, and considered prosecuting Nixon and his family (Hannah Nixon had put up the security for the loan).

An angry Nixon characterized Kennedy as "a ruthless little bastard. He wanted to bring criminal charges against my *mother!*"[22]

That same day Jack Anderson charged in his column that Nixon had taken $100,000 from Hughes through Rebozo, and that he had documentary evidence to back the charge.

On February 3, *The New York Times* reported that Greenspun had some two hundred Hughes documents in his safe, many of them handwritten memos from Hughes himself.

The following morning, Gordon Liddy met with Mitchell, Dean, and the deputy campaign chief at CREEP, Jeb Stuart Magruder, in Mitchell's office. Liddy presented a scaled-down version of an espionage plan code-named Gemstone. Mitchell was leery of the proposal—he had turned it down once—and did not approve. But he did suggest that Liddy consider breaking into Greenspun's office, cracking the safe, and finding out what he had. Mitchell also suggested making Larry O'Brien a target, for the same purpose.[23]

When the Plumbers unit was broken up in 1971, Liddy and Hunt had gone to work for CREEP. Among other assignments, they were responsible for espionage. For some time past, Nixon had been pressing Haldeman: "When are they going to *do* something over there?"[24] Now, apparently, the President was going to get some action.

Nixon's fear of and anger at O'Brien increased in late February, when Jack Anderson began a series charging that Nixon had killed an antitrust suit against ITT in return for a donation of $400,000 to the Republican Convention. Anderson had documents that seemed to prove the case, but the truth was much more complicated than he implied, the story much less sensational.

The Justice Department settlement of the antitrust suit had not been all that favorable to ITT. Most of the money ITT had pledged was due to go to the city of San Diego to help defray expenses in hosting the 1972 Republican Convention, and at least a part of it was to promote a new hotel being built in the city by ITT's subsidiary, Sheraton. Further, the sum soon slipped to $100,000. Finally, Nixon had opposed the site selection; he told RNC Chairman Dole and his campaign manager, Mitchell, that he preferred Chicago or Denver (in March of 1972 the embarrassed Republicans shifted the site to Miami).[25]

But the Anderson charges were a natural for the Democrats— big business getting hugely profitable settlements for handing money to the Republicans—and led by O'Brien they went after it with a vengeance. The Administration inadvertently helped. Richard Kleindienst had been Assistant Attorney General and in charge of the ITT case. In January 1972, Nixon nominated him to replace Mitchell. His confirmation hearings already had cleared the Senate Judiciary Committee when the Anderson series began, but Kleindienst insisted that the hearings be reopened so that he could clear his name.

In Nixon's words, that decision turned out to be a "tactical disaster." Goaded by O'Brien, the press made the hearings a major event. Nixon complained bitterly in his diary; in his view, the press let the Democrats get away with "outlandish procedures that it would immediately condemn if the investigation were being aimed at subversives" instead of at the Administration. He wrote that "fair procedures" should be followed in such congressional investigations, "something I have always insisted upon. It bugs the press that I have done so. . . . They just don't like to admit they had a double standard."[26]

Nixon put Colson and Dean to work on the case. One of their tasks was to prove that a key document, a copy of which was in Anderson's possession, was a forgery (a claim ITT's lawyers were making). They sent it to J. Edgar Hoover; to their dismay, the FBI came back with a report that said no definite finding was possible.

When Colson told Nixon, he later related, the President was as angry as he had ever seen him. Nixon wrote a note to Hoover, asking him to "cooperate," and sent Ehrlichman to the director's office to turn him around. Hoover stood firm. When Ehrlichman reported, Nixon mused, "I don't understand Edgar sometimes. He hates Anderson."[27]

At the Kleindienst confirmation hearings, meanwhile, Brit Hume, one of Anderson's investigators, told the committee that Nixon had personally told Mitchell to "make a reasonable settlement" in the ITT case, causing another sensation. The same day,

Clifford Irving was indicted by a federal grand jury for committing a fraud. That hardly helped Nixon, because Greenspun still had those Hughes documents, and O'Brien still knew whatever Maheu had told him.

The ITT case bothered Nixon considerably, and obsessed Colson. Haldeman had advised the President to stay calm, lay the facts on the table, and be done with it—obviously wise advice. But Nixon rejected it. He wrote in his diary that Colson was trying to shake up the staff to get results, and that he encouraged that approach to the Democratic attack. "I told him this is only the beginning of a much greater assault at a later point—for us to stand firm.

"I think we have got to find tougher language to throw at some of our Democratic friends. Instead of doing the nation's business, they are spending all their time in smears." [28]

Nixon wanted to counterattack by getting the goods on O'Brien's retainer from Hughes. He told Haldeman, "O'Brien's not going to get away with it, Bob. We're going to get proof of his relationship with Hughes—and just what he's doing for the money." [29] He told Colson it was an "outrage" that O'Brien, of all people, was making a fuss about ITT underwriting the Republican Convention, when Hughes was underwriting the DNC. [30]

Colson called Magruder. "Why don't you guys get off the stick and get Liddy's budget approved?" he demanded. "We need the information, particularly on O'Brien."

Magruder explained that Mitchell was all tied up by the Kleindienst hearings, but promised action soon. [31]

Kleindienst, meanwhile, told the Senate Judiciary Committee flatly, "I was not interfered with by anybody at the White House [on the ITT case]. I was not importuned. I was not pressured. I was not directed." [32] That was not true (see page 436 for the Nixon-Kleindienst conversation).

Colson suggested dropping Kleindienst, but instead Nixon defended him. At a March 24 news conference, the President responded to a question from Helen Thomas of UPI. He said he had "noted that you ladies and gentlemen of the press have been pressing on this matter, as you should, because it is a matter of very great interest in the Senate and in the Nation." He reaffirmed his faith and confidence in Kleindienst: "I believe that he should be confirmed and I believe that he will be confirmed." (He was—and two years later pleaded guilty to a charge of failing to testify fully and accurately under oath before a Senate committee.)

Later in the news conference, Nixon defended the Justice Department's handling of the ITT case, and got in some digs at the Democrats in the process: "It is significant to note that ITT became the great conglomerate that it was, in the two previous Administrations primarily. It grew and it grew and it grew, and nothing was done to stop it.

"In this Administration we moved on ITT . . . effectively. We required the greatest divestiture in the history of the antitrust law. If we wanted to do a favor for ITT, we could just continue to do what the two previous administrations had done, and that is nothing, let ITT continue to grow. . . . [We are] very proud of [our] record." [33]

A week later, at a meeting with Magruder in Key Biscayne, Mitchell approved Liddy's Gemstone plan. The initial targets were Greenspun's safe in Las Vegas and O'Brien's office at the Watergate in Washington. [34]

NIXON'S PROBLEM in Vietnam was to find justifications for continuing the war. He provided a number of them. Elections in South Vietnam allowed him to claim that the country was on the road to democracy. The ARVN was bigger and better armed than it had been in 1969. Both in the public and in the secret negotiations, the Americans had been more forthcoming in their offers. America did not abandon its allies and commitments.

The air offensive had certainly hurt the enemy, but it had also increased the number of POWs. The bombing raids on North Vietnam at the beginning of January had been costly to the NVA, but they had also cost Nixon and the Air Force. The raids inflamed the antiwar movement in the States. Further, the Russians, in their own version of Vietnamization, had dramatically increased the number of surface-to-air missiles (SAMs) in North Vietnam; they were taking their toll. By the end of the week, Hanoi held another score of POWs.

Those POWs were an increasingly valuable asset to Hanoi. This was partly because Nixon stressed the POWs so strongly, partly because of the inherent emotional quality of the issue. It led to an impasse: Nixon would not give up the bombing raids so long as Hanoi held a single prisoner, while Hanoi would not give up the prisoners so long as any American armed forces remained in Indochina.

To most Americans, the South Vietnamese "elections" were a farce, a hoax, an insult. One-man military rule in Saigon was a long way from democracy. ARVN might be bigger and better armed, but its performance in Laos had convinced millions that it would never be able to defend the country without the American Air Force.

By the beginning of 1972, Nixon's presumed policy, to end American involvement in the war, would have satisfied a large majority of the voters. That was exactly what the congressmen who voted for "set a withdrawal date in return for the prisoners" resolutions wanted. But what they refused to face, or admit, was that such a policy would abandon South Vietnam and end Vietnamization. Nixon's Vietnamization policy meant an end to a ground combat role for Americans, and possibly, someday, an end to the air role, but it did *not* mean an end to American involvement. If Nixon ever did manage to withdraw all American armed forces, the logic of the situation was that he would have to increase the flow of arms, ammunition, supplies, and equipment to the ARVN. That was why Hanoi would not agree to exchange the POWs for American withdrawal.

Nixon's ultimate justification for his policy, other than the demand for the return of the POWs, was that the United States did not go back on its word. If America walked away from its commitments, he insisted, American credibility would never recover. But he had already promised Chou En-lai, secretly, that America would walk away from its commitment to Taiwan. Taiwan had been thrown out of the U.N. without a significant protest from the United States. Soon Nixon would be making a public pledge to withdraw American forces from Taiwan.

As to the American negotiating position, Nixon had indeed made concessions. Lyndon Johnson had promised to withdraw six months after the NVA left South Vietnam. In 1969, Nixon had softened that to a promise to withdraw simultaneously. But he refused to even consider Hanoi's demand that he promise to stop supplying the Saigon government with the tools of war (although he was demanding the Russians stop supplying Hanoi), much less that he "overthrow" the Thieu regime. Meanwhile, the doves kept up their drumbeat—set a firm withdrawal date in return for the prisoners—without facing the reality that Hanoi would not agree to release those prisoners until *all* American involvement ended. In their own way, the doves were as unrealistic as Nixon, as unwilling to explain to the people the logical consequences of their proposed policy.

For Nixon, it was all terribly frustrating. He felt he had gone as far as he possibly could go, that what he was offering Hanoi, while dangerous, at least gave Thieu a chance, but his public support was slipping with each passing day. In September 1971, Senator McGovern had met with North Vietnamese delegates in Paris. He returned to announce that they were willing to return all the POWs as soon as Nixon agreed to set a date for complete American withdrawal. That seemed so simple, and was so appealing, that the senator got a big play in the press and more votes in Congress.

McGovern's action infuriated Nixon. He believed he had already made such an offer, through Kissinger in the secret talks in Paris, and that Hanoi had rejected it.[35] Actually, the American offer was by no means so simple: Kissinger had numerous additional points in his presentation, including a cease-fire throughout Indochina, and he made it clear that Nixon would never stop supporting the Thieu government.[36]

The doves were unfair to Nixon when they charged that all he cared about was his re-election, but they were less than candid with the American people when they refused to deal with the question of what would happen to South Vietnam if the Americans did withdraw completely (meaning not only the Air Force but also future support). Nixon was right to charge that the doves had become advocates of peace at any price, and right to assert that Hanoi was demanding nothing short of total victory, but he was less than candid in pretending that his policies would end American involvement in the war.

Hanoi had its own problems, including the not-so-subtle Russian and Chinese pressure to be reasonable, to let Nixon withdraw with honor, and then settle with President Thieu and his clique. But that would leave the Communists with a numerically large and fabulously equipped ARVN to deal with, backed by an unending flow of supplies from the United States. The NVA had recovered from Cambodia and Laos; it had built up its strength along the DMZ and the Ho Chi Minh Trail (American intelligence had seen this buildup, which was the proximate cause of the January bombing offensive, which, so typical of the Vietnam War, had been enough to rouse the doves but was not sustained long enough to really hurt the enemy). America no longer had division-sized units in Vietnam; the ARVN was presumably improving and certainly growing; NVA strength was at its peak; Nixon refused to give in the negotiations. Taken together, these facts all but dictated a go-for-broke NVA offensive in early 1972.

Nixon had to do something. His re-election depended on what he did about Vietnam; as he told Rather, he had to convince the voters he had done all that could be done to end the war. The polls indicated that he had not been convincing: the Harris poll in the first week in January reported Nixon and Muskie even at 42 percent each, with Wallace at 11 percent. Those were not reassuring figures.

Nixon decided to move on the PR front on Vietnam. He scheduled a televised report to the nation for January 25; he intended to reveal the secret Kissinger–Le Duc Tho talks in Paris, so that he could claim that he *had* offered a fixed withdrawal date in return for the POWs, only to be rejected. That would undercut the doves.

Nixon put Safire to work on the speech. Kissinger explained to

Safire that "the purpose is to give decent people a chance to come over to our side. We will be hit with a military offensive from the North in March or April, and it pays for us to be very conciliatory early. If we have to counterattack, then we'll be attacking a truculent enemy who chose to make war and not peace."

Nixon, in written instructions to Safire, was more explicit: "If the enemy's answer to our peace offer is to step up their attacks, I shall . . . [order] air strikes against the enemy's military installations in Laos, Cambodia, South Vietnam and North Vietnam." [37]

There was a big White House buildup to the speech, including a Nixon announcement in mid-January that he would pull seventy thousand more combat troops out of Vietnam by May 1, reducing the total in country to sixty-nine thousand. And Secretary Laird declared in a news conference that "we no longer . . . have . . . any active U.S. military divisions in Vietnam." He added that all combat responsibilities (read ground combat) had been turned over to the South Vietnamese. [38]

In his memoirs, Nixon explained that he decided to reveal the secret talks because he feared news of them would leak anyway. What difference that made, he did not say, but it was true that his obsession with leaks was greater than ever. Jack Anderson had recently goaded him by telling *The New York Times*, "I don't get my information out of a Daniel Ellsberg, who belonged to another Administration. . . . I get my information from some of Nixon's own boys." [39] When Walter Cronkite had an early story on Nixon's entry into the New Hampshire primary, Nixon wrote, "H—who in the hell would be so stupid to put this out—It absolutely serves no purpose whatever except to give C.B.S. a scoop—Stop filling in the staff on *any* political tactics." [40]

Kissinger remained suspect; when press reports said Robert McNamara was going to be reappointed to a second five-year term at the World Bank, and that it was a Kissinger intervention with the President that had made the reappointment possible, Nixon wrote, "H—*no one* but K could have put this out. It is in violation of my orders." [41]

But with regard to the secret talks, Nixon himself intended to do the leaking, on national TV. The internal contradictions of his relationship with Kissinger created a problem: Nixon wanted the full PR value of revealing Kissinger's exotic role in secret diplomacy, but he also wanted all credit for himself. On Safire's draft of the speech, which in its turn was done on a previously prepared Kissinger draft, the President changed "we" to "I" several times, and whenever "I asked Dr. Kissinger" appeared, Nixon changed it to "I directed." [42]

In going over the draft with Safire, Nixon mused aloud about the conflict between his National Security Adviser and his Secretary of State. "I'm sorry about how Henry and Bill go at each other," Nixon said. "It's really deep-seated. Henry thinks Bill isn't very deep, and Bill thinks Henry is power-crazy.

"And in a sense," he went on, "they're both right. Ego is something we all have, and either you grow out of it or it takes you over. I've grown out of it.

"It's really a compensation for an inferiority complex. Henry has that, of course—and Bill has it too." [43]

On January 25, Nixon made his long-awaited statement. He opened by saying he had a new peace proposal for Hanoi: he would withdraw six months after an agreement was reached. He said President Thieu had offered to step down one month before new presidential elections, to be held following a cease-fire throughout Indochina.

Then he revealed that such an offer had already been made, secretly, by Kissinger in the last of twelve talks with Le Duc Tho and Xuan Thuy in Paris, only to be rejected. In a reference to McGovern's charge that the United States had never offered to set a date for complete withdrawal in return for the POWs, Nixon said, "We are being asked publicly to set a terminal date for our withdrawals when we already offered one in private."

"The only thing this [American peace] plan does not do is to join our enemy to overthrow our ally," Nixon said, "which the United States of America will never do. If the enemy wants peace, it will have to recognize the important difference between settlement and surrender."

In the peroration, the President spoke directly to the point of the whole enterprise: "Some of our citizens have become accustomed to thinking that whatever our Government says must be false, and whatever our enemies say must be true, as far as this war is concerned. Well, the record I have revealed tonight proves the contrary." He signed off with a call for national unity. [44]

The initial response was mixed, but mainly positive. Most of the press accepted Nixon's claim that he had done everything possible to achieve a negotiated settlement of the war, while concentrating on the puzzle of how supersecret agent Kissinger had managed to elude reporters for those meetings. Senator Mansfield hailed the proposal as "a long step forward." Senator Church said it was "fair and generous." Senator Humphrey said, "So what? There are lots of other issues." Senator McGovern complained that he had been double-crossed: "At the same time Mr. Nixon was bitterly opposed to the McGovern-Hatfield proposal to end the war, he was at the very same time offering it to the other side." [45]

Senator Fulbright was not impressed. He returned the discussion to the central point when he said the question remained: "Is the United States willing to get out and leave the Thieu Government to its own devices?" [46]

Reston did a critical analysis. "It has become a cliché that President Nixon always deals more effectively with the politics of his problems than he deals with the problems themselves," he began. He acknowledged that Nixon "has temporarily stunned the Democratic opposition, dominated the news and thus changed the politics of the issue." But, he went on, "The hard facts are these: The United States is getting its troops out fast. . . . The enemy has recaptured the Plaines des Jarres in Laos and is gaining steadily on the capital of Cambodia. Enemy forces are mounting what seems to be another major Lunar New Year offensive . . . despite the recent massive bombings by the U.S. Air Force." Thus, just when the enemy was regaining the military initiative, "Mr. Nixon calls for a cease-fire. He asks for the withdrawal of all forces—the enemy's as well as the allied forces—and asks the enemy to rely on elections that they don't even understand. This is not likely to appear to the enemy to be a reasonable proposition."

Reston charged that in dealing with the politics instead of the reality of the issue, Nixon "may have made it worse and committed himself to more fighting and more bombing if an offensive occurs." [47]

Nixon did not ignore Reston, Fulbright, and his other critics; rather, he went after them. Two days after the speech, he sent a four-page memorandum to Haldeman and Colson outlining a campaign "to sustain a massive counterattack on the partisan critics of our peace proposals." He wanted his aides to repeat "over and over again . . . that those who got us into the war are now trying to sabotage Nixon's efforts to get us out." He wanted Safire and Buchanan to work on a "line." One suggestion: "'Now his proposal has been made and has so clearly shown that the United States has offered everything that any honorable government could offer, they [his critics] are consciously giving aid and comfort to the enemy. They want the enemy to win and the United States to lose. They want the United States to surrender. . . . I cannot emphasize too strongly . . . that the attack line will be more effective than the positive line. . . . It will tend to keep the critics from getting out too far and also because it simply makes more news." He wanted Muskie made a "particular target." [48]

A week later, on February 2, Muskie made a major speech on Vietnam. He called for unilateral American withdrawal and a clear requirement that the Thieu government be compelled to seek a political accommodation with the Communists or face the loss of all American military support after the withdrawal.

Haldeman sprang into action. Relatively unknown to this time, he made his first television appearance, in an interview with Barbara Walters of the "Today Show" on NBC-TV. He caused a furor when he said that before Nixon had made his peace plan public "you could say that his critics . . . were unconsciously echoing the line that the enemy wanted echoed.

"Now, after this explanation—after the whole activity is on the record and is known, the only conclusion you can draw is that the critics now are consciously aiding and abetting the enemy of the United States."

Walters protested; she said she did not think Senate critics were helping the enemy. Haldeman insisted, "In this particular posture, I think they are consciously aiding and abetting the enemy."[49] There was a predictable uproar. (Haldeman told this author he used those words "on the direct and explicit orders of the President.")

Three days later, Nixon held a news conference of his own. Reporters wanted to know why Muskie's counterproposals were characterized by Haldeman as near treason, when Nixon himself in 1968 had said he would end the war. Nixon replied that the Muskie proposal "has the effect of having the government in Hanoi consider at least that they might be well advised to wait until after the election rather than negotiate." He said that in 1968 he had had the right to criticize Johnson when he was a candidate, but had not done so. As to Muskie and other critics of his peace plan, "they have to consult their own consciences." Pressed on the point, he declared that his critics "may feel that we should make one [a proposal] that would overthrow the Government of South Vietnam, or some other proposal that will satisfy the enemy. They have a right to say that. The American people will have to judge."[50]

In their immediate judgment, if the polls were accurate, the people made Nixon the winner. An early-February Harris poll had Nixon opening up a four-point lead, 44–40, over Muskie.[51] Gallup, a week later, showed a five-point surge in Nixon's overall approval rating, from 49 percent at the beginning of January to 54 percent. On Vietnam, 52 percent approved the manner in which he was handling the war, while 39 percent disapproved.[52]

A later Harris poll showed that although Nixon's January 25 peace-plan proposals had strong approval, and that 54 percent would support continued bombing to get the POWs back, by 46–20 the public would not feel Nixon had fulfilled his pledge to end American involvement unless there was a cease-fire by November.

Nixon underscored the 46–20 figure and scribbled the obvious point, "K—note—The problem."[53]

ON THE MORNING of February 17, a crowd of thousands, including congressmen, Cabinet officers, and other big shots, gathered at Andrews Air Force Base to give Nixon a send-off to Peking. The President was ebullient. "He knew," Max Frankel wrote in *The New York Times,* "that for this flight, no matter what else occurred, he would always be remembered." Speaking without notes, Nixon said that the United States and China must "find a way to see that we can have differences without being enemies in war.

"If we can make progress toward that goal on this trip, the world will be a much safer world."

He compared his trip to the moon flights and suggested that a postscript for his journey should be the words on the plaque left on the moon by the first astronauts who landed there: "We came in peace for all mankind."[54]

An army of newsmen accompanied the presidential party. Haldeman, on Nixon's instructions, made certain it was heavily weighted toward television personnel, sweet revenge on the print journalists who so bedeviled Nixon, and a good way to take full advantage of the PR aspects of the spectacular visual opportunities the trip afforded. Best of all, thanks to the time difference, morning events in China could appear live on American prime-time evening shows, while evening events could be broadcast live on the breakfast news programs. The combination of the timing, the breathtaking scenes, the twenty-year absence of any pictures at all out of China, and the nature of the event—Richard Nixon, a charter member of the China Lobby, meeting with Chou En-lai and Mao Tsetung—made it a historic week on television.

Nixon's instinct for the dramatic served him well. He knew that when his old friend John Foster Dulles had refused to shake the hand of Chou En-lai in Geneva in 1954, Chou had felt insulted. He knew too that American television cameras would be at the Peking airport to film his arrival. A dozen times on the way to Peking, Nixon told Kissinger and Rogers that they were to stay on the plane until he had descended the gangway and shaken Chou's hand. In the event, a Secret Service agent blocked the aisle of *Air Force One* to make certain the President emerged alone.

Chou had his own sense of the dramatic; he awaited Nixon standing alone. It was 11:30 A.M. in Peking, 10:30 P.M. Sunday night Eastern standard time back in the States, a prime television hour.[55]

When Nixon reached the bottom step, he extended his hand as

he walked toward Chou. As the handshake took place, Nixon later wrote, "one era ended and another began." [56]

They drove into the city, past empty streets. After lunch, there was an unexpected summons: Chairman Mao himself would receive Nixon. The President set off, accompanied by Kissinger but, at Nixon's insistence, without Rogers (and without a State Department interpreter, again at Nixon's insistence, as he feared an interpreter from State would leak—i.e., tell his boss what had been said).

The American party was ushered into Mao's study. The juxtaposition was almost too much for Kissinger; here was the unquestioned head of the world's most populous nation, and he was a sick old man, barely able to stand, in a study that "looked more the retreat of a scholar" than anything else. Books surrounded Mao's easy chair. But even Chou treated him with exceptional deference. Nixon thought him "remarkable." Kissinger went further; he wrote that Mao "dominated the room . . . by exuding in almost tangible form the overwhelming drive to prevail." [57]

Nixon had known and worked with many of the great, the powerful, the famous of the world, but none held him in such thrall as Mao. It certainly was not Mao's physical presence, nor the surroundings, that so moved Nixon. Part of it was, obviously, Mao's historic accomplishments, but one can speculate that there was more. All that power. Nixon could snap his fingers, as he did thousands of times on his News Summaries and in his meetings with his aides, and nothing happened. Mao could snap his fingers, and tens of thousands died.

Nixon expressed a bit of this feeling in a later report to the Cabinet. Rogers told the group he had seen Chou going over the galleys of the next day's newspaper, rearranging the front page.

Nixon muttered, "I'd like to rearrange a front page now and then." [58]

The Nixon-Mao conversation lasted an hour, half the time taken up with translation. They spoke in generalities and banalities, but both Kissinger and Nixon were awestruck by the Chairman's wisdom and wit. In their memoirs, they quoted him extensively.

Some examples:

Kissinger said he had assigned Mao's writings to his classes at Harvard. Mao said, "These writings of mine aren't anything. There is nothing instructive in what I wrote."

Nixon: "The Chairman's writings moved a nation and have changed the world."

Mao: "I haven't been able to change it. I've only been able to change a few places in the vicinity of Peking."

Nixon thought that although Mao spoke with difficulty, "it was clear that his mind was moving like lightning."

Mao: "Our common old friend Generalissimo Chiang Kai-shek doesn't approve of this. He calls us Communist bandits."

Nixon: "What does the Chairman call Chiang Kai-shek?"

Chou: "Generally speaking, we call them 'Chiang Kai-shek's clique.'"

More banter followed. Finally Nixon got serious, telling the Chinese leaders what they already knew, that the Soviets had more troops on the Chinese border than they had in Eastern Europe.

Chou started glancing at his watch. Nixon sped it up. He said he realized Mao had taken a risk in inviting him to China, "but having read some of your statements, I know that you are one who sees when an opportunity comes, and then knows that you must seize the hour and seize the day."

Mao beamed at this quotation of his own words.

"I would also like to say in a personal sense . . ." Nixon went on, "you do not know me. Since you do not know me, you shouldn't trust me. You will find I never say something I cannot do. And I always will do more than I can say."

As they parted, after Nixon said that like Mao he came from a poor family to become head of a great nation, Mao remarked, "Your book, *Six Crises*, is not a bad book."

Nixon looked at Chou, smiled, shook his head, and said, "He reads too much." [59]

The remainder of the week was taken up with a multitude of banquets and an orgy of sight-seeing, all beamed back to a fascinated audience in the States. Nixon was overwhelmed by what he saw, as anyone would be, and unable to find appropriate words to express his feelings, as anyone would be. Unfortunately for Nixon, unlike the ordinary tourist, the national press corps was there to write down his every word. What he saw was so grand, what he said was so trivial, it made him a figure of ridicule. "This is a great wall," Nixon said on his tour of the Great Wall of China. (Reporters did *not* quote the rest of the sentence, which was "and it had to be built by a great people.") In Hangchow, one of the world's most beautiful cities, Nixon remarked that the scene "looks like a postcard." [60]

Nixon did have meetings with Chou, where they explained to each other their positions on various issues. They did not mince words, but neither did they say much that was new, or change each other's mind. After the handshake at the airport and the audience with Mao, all that followed was anticlimax. Anyway, the deal had already been struck: Nixon got photographed in Peking, while the Chinese got his promise to withdraw American forces from Taiwan. Beyond that, it was the fact of the meeting, rather than anything that was done during it, that mattered. And the audience was not just the American television viewing public, which was important to Nixon but not to Chou. The unseen, unmentioned audience was in Moscow. To impress that audience, Nixon and Chou did not have to agree to anything; just the fact of the meeting was enough to shake the men in the Kremlin.

The hard work was preparing a final communiqué. There had to be one, and there was no point to pretending that they had resolved their differences, so they made the commonsense decision to simply state their views in separate paragraphs. The formula was to begin one paragraph, "The Chinese side stated." For example, on Vietnam, the U.S. side reaffirmed its support for Nixon's latest peace proposal, while the Chinese expressed support for the Communist position. The U.S. side said it intended to maintain close ties with South Korea, while the Chinese endorsed North Korea's plan for unification.

There were two important areas of agreement. The first concerned the Soviet Union, and it was easily reached, naturally enough, since it was fear of the Soviet Union that had brought Nixon and Chou together in the first place. Nixon promised Chou he was ready to "turn like a cobra on the Russians" if provoked, or if the Red Army marched either west or south. These sentiments were expressed in the final communiqué with a provision that neither nation "should seek hegemony in the Asia Pacific region and each is opposed to efforts by any other country or group of countries to establish such hegemony." As the Chinese were daily accusing the Soviets of seeking hegemony, all the world understood the slightly veiled language.

The second agreement was on Taiwan, and was much more difficult to reach. The Chinese regarded the presence of American armed forces on the island as an occupation, which was intolerable. So long as the American troops were there, no improvement in U.S.–Chinese relations was possible. For his part, Nixon had been one of Chiang's foremost American supporters for twenty-three years; he could not simply walk away and casually sacrifice the Nationalist Chinese. Further, Chiang's most fervent allies in the United States came from the heart of Nixon's constituency.

Chou wanted to express the Chinese position in a forthright manner. Nixon told him that if that were done, "I would come under murderous cross fire from any or all the various pro-Taiwan,

anti-Nixon, and anti-P.R.C. lobbies and interest groups at home."
If that happened, he continued, he might well lose the election,
and "my successor might not be able to continue developing the
relationship between Washington and Peking."

The logic was unanswerable. Chou's paragraph on Taiwan
was, considering the strength of his feelings, relatively mild: he
stated the Communist claim to be the sole legitimate government
of China and that Taiwan was a part of China. He demanded the
withdrawal of all American military forces from Taiwan, and expressed his firm opposition to any "two Chinas" formula.

"The U. S. side declared: The United States acknowledges
that all Chinese on either side of the Taiwan Strait maintain there
is but one China and that Taiwan is a part of China. The United
States Government does not challenge that position. It reaffirms its
interest in a peaceful settlement of the Taiwan question by the
Chinese themselves. With this prospect in mind, it affirms the ultimate objective of the withdrawal of all U.S. forces and military
installations from Taiwan. In the meantime, it will progressively
reduce its forces and military installations on Taiwan as the tension
in the area diminishes."

That carefully phrased promise was acceptable to Chou. The
last seven words represented a major victory for Nixon, as they gave
the Chinese side a stake in ending the war in Vietnam.[61]

On February 26, the presidential party left Peking for
Hangchow. There, for the first time, Rogers and his aides got to see
the communiqué. "I thought it was disastrous," one of the State
Department people said, because it did not mention America's
treaty obligations with Taiwan, made during the Eisenhower Administration, an omission all the more glaring because the communiqué did cite America's continued support for South Vietnam,
South Korea, and Japan. It made it appear that Nixon had agreed to
isolate and even abandon Taiwan in return for television coverage
of his trip, and for highly problematical Chinese help in ending the
war in Vietnam. There was a real danger that the right wing back
home would charge that Nixon was cutting off Taiwan to save
South Vietnam.

Rogers told Nixon that the question of America's treaty commitment to Chiang had to be addressed. Kissinger accused Rogers
of "poormouthing" the communiqué after the fact. Nixon was even
angrier. According to Kissinger, the President "was beside himself" at the "trivial" list of amendments submitted by Rogers and
his people. Nixon "recognized his political dilemma. He was already edgy about the reaction of his conservative supporters to the
trip; he dreaded a right-wing assault on the communiqué. . . . He

was so exercised that he started storming about the beautiful guest house in Hangchow in his underwear."

The President swore he would "do something" about State at the first opportunity. He called John Mitchell in Washington. According to Mitchell, "Nixon said, 'Get rid of him.' "

Mitchell was soothing. He pointed out that firing the Secretary of State over some words in a communiqué at the beginning of an election year would be a mistake. "We'll talk about it when you get back," he concluded.

Kissinger broke the impasse. Although no change was made in the text, at a news conference in Shanghai, on the last day, he orally reaffirmed the American commitment to Taiwan.[62]

On February 27, Nixon attended the farewell dinner in Shanghai, hosted by the Shanghai Municipal Revolutionary Committee. In his toast, he opened with one of his unforgettable Nixonisms: "This magnificent banquet marks the end of our stay in the People's Republic of China. We have been here a week. This was the week that changed the world."[63]

IT WAS NOTHING of the sort. It was a recognition of reality. It had brought little in the way of change, even to Asia. The American retreat from mainland Southeast Asia was already under way, indeed almost completed. Nixon's negotiations with Chou over the Taiwan paragraph in the communiqué, and Kissinger's oral statement, made it clear the United States was not abandoning Taiwan. The United States specifically reaffirmed its intention to remain in South Korea and Japan, and unstated but understood, in the Philippines.

In one sense, Nixon's China opening was but another chapter in the long history of ever-shifting realignments in the world balance of power; by no means did it mark a permanent change. These shifts, so often bewildering, are a constant factor in world politics. Consider that just three decades earlier, the United States was allied with both Nationalist and Communist China against Japan, and with the Soviet Union against Germany, while in 1972 America's closest allies were Japan and Germany. Nixon had not established diplomatic relations with China (although he did so in all but name, and formal recognition came in 1978, by which time, not incidentally, China was at war with Communist Cambodia and Communist Vietnam), much less entered into a military alliance directed against the Soviets. No provisions had been made for new trade agreements between the United States and China.

Further, Nixon's claim that he was the only man who could have done what he did brings up the unstated fact that for more than twenty years he was one of the major obstacles to establishing normal relations with China. Without saying so, he had done what the critics of America's China policy had been recommending for two decades, recommendations he had violently opposed.

But such carping should not obscure the reality: the China opening was certainly Nixon's greatest triumph, and he certainly deserved the credit for it. If the immediate payoff was slight at best, except for disturbing the sleep of the men in the Kremlin, the long-term opportunities Nixon had made possible were vast. If in part the trip was self-serving (the television coverage at the beginning of his re-election campaign), it also showed Nixon to be a man of courage, intelligence, and imagination. Sometimes, in world diplomacy, the hardest things to do are those that cry out most for doing.

For Nixon personally, he said it best in his report to the Cabinet: "This was an experience which perhaps will not be exceeded in my lifetime."[64]

NIXON BEING NIXON, he could not let the thing just stand by itself, and reap the credit he so fully deserved, but rather he had to manipulate in every way possible in order to get more credit than he deserved. The process began with the report to the Cabinet.

"There is no leader I have met who exceeds Chou En-lai's ability to conduct a conversation at the highest level," he said, meaning with himself. He called the attention of the Cabinet to the many things he and Chou had in common; for example, like RN, "whenever [Chou] said anything particularly tough, he became much cooler."[65]

He expressed similar sentiments to the congressional leadership. At the conclusion of the meeting, he grabbed Senator Fulbright by the arm and urged him to stop criticizing the Vietnam policy, because it was a delicate issue and the "string could break" if disagreement continued. Pointing his finger at the startled Fulbright, Nixon said, "OK, Bill, agreed?" Fulbright was speechless.[66]

He showed his usual extraordinary sensitivity to whatever the press said. The judgment of the Washington *Post*, that "the Chinese got the better of the bargain," angered him.[67] Joseph Kraft wrote in *The New Yorker* that Nixon was "overtrained" for the trip, and self-conscious in his courting of the press. Nixon commented, "H—a prime example of press reaching for anything to criticize!"

The least praise delighted him. Underscoring a phrase in the Chicago *Tribune*—"Nixon is a card player as smooth as that inveterate sharpster, Chou"—Nixon scribbled in the margin, "H & K— a good line to talk up." Howard K. Smith was nearly as euphoric as Nixon; reading a summary of Smith's remarks, Nixon wrote,

"Chuck—tell him RN thought his analysis was *Excellent*, brilliantly concise & perceptive."[68]

To Kissinger, Nixon "seemed obsessed by the fear that he was not receiving adequate credit." (It is remarkable how many times in his memoirs Kissinger attributes to Nixon motives and fears that other observers felt best described Kissinger.) On March 9, Nixon sent Kissinger a memorandum instructing him to make clear to the press the deep thought and analysis that lay behind his "decision" to state the American position moderately. In this regard, he urged Kissinger to read *Six Crises* (advice Nixon frequently gave to his aides; Colson claimed to have read the book fourteen times). He wanted Kissinger to tell the press that it was his idea to issue separate and conflicting statements in the communiqué (Kissinger thought the idea was Chou's). Five days later, Haldeman followed up with his own memo to Kissinger, written on Nixon's orders, telling him he would serve the President better by stressing the great personal qualities Nixon had displayed.[69]

PAT WAS an important asset to Nixon on his China trip. In Julie Eisenhower's words, "Millions of people saw China through Pat Nixon's eyes." The television cameras followed her to communes, zoos, palaces, farms, factories, and schools. At one of the banquets, Pat talked with Chou about her visit to the Peking Zoo to see the giant pandas. "Aren't they cute?" Pat said. "I love them."

"I'll give you some," Chou replied, and he did, two giant pandas for the Washington National Zoo.[70]

She was her unfailingly warm, gracious self, and was a big hit, especially with women and children. At the Shanghai banquet, the wives of some of the Chinese leaders hugged her and told her to return. She was realistic about that experience: "I've traveled so much," she told reporters. "I know they could not have done that unless it was inspired from the top." Still, she added, "I felt they were very friendly."[71]

She was almost as much a world traveler as her husband (who is certainly in the running for the title of most-traveled politician of all time) and almost as accustomed to cameras and reporters. She loved the travel and hated the publicity. But, in her own quiet way, she was developing a bit of humor. Asked to assess the state of the Union in one word, she replied, "Mess." Then she added, "But if you're going to quote me, just say that things are so much better now than they were." Asked for some inside information about a trip to Africa in January 1972, where she represented her husband at the inauguration of a new president of Liberia, she declined, saying, "I want to cash in on my diary when I write it."[72]

Of course she had no intention of publishing a diary. She

would not even cooperate with a biographer selected by the White House PR people, who wanted a biography published in time for the re-election campaign. The chosen writer was Gloria Seelye, who had been one of Pat's students in Whittier; Mrs. Seelye was also a close friend of Helene Drown, so she seemed a natural. But Pat said she was too busy to give interviews, and protested that she had an aversion to talking into a tape recorder, so the project was dropped.[73]

What she wanted most in the world, time with her husband and her daughters, she could seldom have. Nor could she get much privacy. "I think the most difficult task of all" in being First Lady, she told a television interviewer, "is to be so guarded and to be surrounded all the time. You don't have enough of what I call blessed aloneness." She explained that was why she loved San Clemente so much: "It is the only place in the world where we can sit unguarded. There may be a few people outside, but we don't see them, so when we [go there], it's just heaven without anybody around."[74]

IT IS ONE of the innumerable ironies of American history that the original desegregation case, *Brown* v. *Topeka* (1954), was a decision against forced busing. The plaintiff, Brown, lived across the street from an all-white school in Topeka, but was forced to ride a bus halfway across town to attend an all-black school. The point of her suit was to allow her to attend her neighborhood school; the Warren Court used the case to rule that she had the right to do so, not because busing was wrong, but because segregation by race was a denial of the equal protection of the laws.

In their attempts to implement the Supreme Court's mandate that desegregation of the nation's public school system be carried out "with all deliberate speed," the lower courts had run into the problem that most segregation in schools occurred as a result of segregated housing patterns. By the late sixties, the judges had turned to court-ordered busing as the only means available to overcome segregation in the schools. When blacks had been bused to preserve segregation, hardly a single white voice had been raised in protest; when whites were bused to break down segregation, there were precious few white politicians in America ready to speak out in support of the policy.

Nixon, despite his record of support for civil rights in the fifties and sixties, was dead set against busing. Only the judges and the bureaucrats in HEW and Justice, none of whom had to stand for election, supported it. This put him in the happy position of being in agreement with the vast majority of voters on one of the most explosive issues of the day. His problem was that his Administration was constitutionally required to enforce the court orders. His solution, to go slow, to do not one bit more than the law required, left him vulnerable to Wallace and others who charged that while he talked against busing, the government of which he was the head required and enforced it.

The issue threatened to become almost as big as Vietnam in the 1972 election. Nixon wished it would go away. On January 3, Professor Moynihan sent the President a suggestion, that he create a presidential commission on equality of educational opportunity. Moynihan thought "it would be a truly Nixonian gesture to ask Earl Warren to be chairman." Nixon had a one-word response to that idea: "No!" [75]

But the President could not avoid the issue. Later that month, a federal district court ordered busing in Richmond, Virginia. Worse, it required the buses to carry inner-city kids out to the suburbs to school, and vice versa. Nixon's advisers feared "a national outcry that will make the present anti-busing sentiment seem mild." Nixon himself commented, "H & E—on the *highest* priority basis I need to know what our plan is to handle this political hot potato." As a starter, he wanted them to put out the word that the judge in the case "was *not* appointed by RN." [76]

But before he could act, he got whiplashed again, by a Denver case that also ordered busing from the city to the suburbs, and which included Mexican-Americans as well as blacks. Nixon gave his orders: "E—Get legislation or a Const. Amendment ready as an option as soon as possible. I reject the advice of Richardson, Garment et al to relax & enjoy it." [77]

On January 28, Nixon set forth his philosophy in a long, detailed memorandum to Ehrlichman. "Legally segregated education," he declared, "legally segregated housing, legal obstructions to equal employment must be totally removed.

"On the other hand I am convinced that while legal segregation is totally wrong, forced integration of housing or education is just as wrong. . . . I believe there may be some doubt as to the validity of the Brown philosophy that integrating education will pull up the blacks and not pull down the whites. But while there may be some doubt as to whether segregated education is inferior there is no doubt whatever on another point—that education requiring excessive transportation for students is definitely inferior. I come down hard and unequivocally against busing for the purpose of racial balance."

There was another point, one that Nixon told Ehrlichman was "absolutely overriding." It was, "This country is not ready at this time for either forcibly integrated housing or forcibly integrated education."

There can be no doubt that he was absolutely right about that one. Of course, who can say what effect a little presidential leadership might have had?

Nixon concluded that he wanted Ehrlichman to make an attempt to draw up a constitutional amendment that would ban busing for racial balance.[78]

On February 16, the day before Nixon left for China, Ehrlichman sent Nixon a memo of talking points for a meeting that afternoon with Attorney General–designate Kleindienst. The purpose of the meeting, Ehrlichman declared, was to "discuss anti-trust and civil rights policy, especially busing, to be certain Mr. Kleindienst 'is aboard,' " and to "establish Ehrlichman as Kleindienst's conduit to and from the President on these issues."[79]

While Nixon was in China, Ehrlichman worked on a constitutional amendment. He found it impossible to draw up a satisfactory version, and so informed the President on his return.

The primary season, meanwhile, had begun. In New Hampshire, Nixon got a big break. Senator Muskie had been expected to do well in his native New England, but on a televised broadcast shortly before the voting, he had defended his wife's reputation, and answered charges that he had made racist remarks about Franco-Americans, and in the process broke down and cried. This scene evidently hurt him badly; although he defeated McGovern, 46–37, the press interpreted the results as a serious setback for Muskie.

One week later, in Florida, with little organization and only modest media expenditures, but with a vote-winning emphasis on all-out opposition to busing, George Wallace won a stunning victory in the Democratic primary. He carried all sixty-seven counties in the state and gathered 41 percent of the total vote. Humphrey was second, Senator Henry Jackson, also an outspoken foe of busing, was third. Muskie ran a dismal fourth, with only 9 percent of the vote. It was the effective end of the Muskie campaign, and thus freed Nixon of fears about the Democrat he thought had the best chance of beating him.[80]

Richard Nixon never got anything for free. Welcome as Wallace's elimination of Muskie was, it added to the Wallace problem. Wallace was never going to get the Democratic nomination, and it was a bonus to the Republicans that he could so embarrass their opponents in the primaries, but it added to the danger that in the end Wallace might again run as an independent, and on the strength of the antibusing sentiment alone attract enough votes to deny Nixon's re-election.

Even before the Florida primary, Nixon had decided to make a move against busing, frustrated though he was in finding himself unable to propose a constitutional amendment. After Florida, he decided to make his move in a dramatic speech on television, even though Ziegler had earlier said that the President would never make an antibusing speech on television because the issue was "too complex and emotional."[81]

On March 16, in a nationwide television and radio address, Nixon boldly called on Congress to impose a "moratorium" on the federal courts to prevent them from ordering any new busing to achieve racial balance. He also called for a companion measure, to be called the Equal Educational Opportunities Act of 1972, to improve the education of minority children in the central cities without busing them to the suburbs. The act, he said, would direct $2.5 billion in federal aid for this purpose.

He spoke for only ten minutes, and gave no details. The follow-up written message to Congress revealed that the proposed legislation would have the effect of making permanent the temporary "moratorium," and that the $2.5 billion earmarked for poor children would consist of $1 billion in funds already appropriated under the Elementary and Secondary Education Act of 1965 plus $1.5 billion in as yet unauthorized funds that Nixon had asked from Congress in 1969 to ease the desegregation process.[82]

In short, it was all done with mirrors. Nixon had reaffirmed his opposition to segregation while rejecting again the only available means to achieve its destruction. He was asking that a Democratic Congress countermand two decades of legal tradition and challenge an underlying premise of *Brown* v. *Topeka*, that the courts had the basic responsibility for deciding how equal education opportunity was to be achieved.

Southerners, led by Senator Sam Ervin (D., N.C.), were not satisfied. They wanted legislation not only to prevent future busing, but to turn back busing already in effect. On the Senate floor, Ervin spat out his contempt. "If it is wrong," he shouted, "it ought to be uprooted forever and thrown on the scrap heap of history. . . . It ought to be ended once and forever."

The NAACP and other civil rights groups were also critical, from the opposite point of view, but from among the Democratic presidential candidates, only McGovern spoke out against the President; he charged that Nixon had launched a "back door attack" on the equal protection clause of the Constitution and ducked his responsibilities for moral leadership. McGovern accused the President of engaging in "a frantic effort to capitalize on this emotional issue" in an attempt to distract voters' attention from Vietnam. But Senator Jackson called for a constitutional amendment banning busing, and Hubert Humphrey sighed in relief. "Thank goodness," Humphrey said, "that at long last the President has been able to get his finger up in the air and sense what's going on and has decided that he would say amen to some of the things that some of the rest of us have been trying to do." [83]

Nixon never got his "moratorium," but he surely won the PR battle. As Ehrlichman put it, "Whether Congress passed the busing moratorium was not as important as that the American people understood that Richard Nixon opposed busing as much as they did." [84]

CHAPTER TWENTY-THREE

BOMBING HANOI,
MINING HAIPHONG,
TOASTING IN MOSCOW
April–June 1972

WITH THE OPENING to China behind him, Nixon's next move in establishing triangular diplomacy was his upcoming journey to Moscow. The summit, scheduled for the third week in May, would be the culmination of his diplomacy, marking the completion of his creation of a new era of world power politics. The trip to Peking had been more symbol than reality, the meeting marked by flowery speeches and generalizations rather than direct, specific deals. The trip to Moscow would be just the opposite. And it would be more important, for the simple reason that the U.S.S.R. was incomparably more powerful than the P.R.C. China could be an irritant to the United States in various parts of Asia; the U.S.S.R. could destroy the United States in a flash.

Since 1969, Nixon had moved carefully, cautiously, but steadily toward an arms-control agreement. The obstacles were great: ingrained suspicions of the Soviets, the clamor of the hawks, the economic needs of the military-industrial complex, the war in Vietnam, tension in the Middle East and South Asia, and so forth. But Nixon had persevered, and by the spring of 1972 he was on the verge of prevailing.

He had not created the possibilities all by himself. Kissinger's academic brilliance and Metternich-like conceptions had certainly played some role, but more important was the confluence of events and needs. The first of these was the necessity felt by both superpowers to reduce the cost and dangers of the arms race. More specifically, the Soviets had some critical interests at stake. They needed to offset Nixon's Peking trip, for fear of a Sino-American

525

alliance (the beauty of Nixon's triangular diplomacy was that only he could talk to the other two sides of the triangle). Further, the Soviets wanted to promote détente in Europe, which, while progressing, was still in a delicate formative stage. They also wanted expanded trade relations with the United States; indeed they were almost desperate for American grain. In addition, they had long sought a recognition of parity and a compact of equality with the United States.

Nixon was eager to sell the grain and willing to accept détente in Europe. Already playing off the Chinese against the Russians, he now wanted to play off the Russians against the Chinese. But most of all, what he wanted from the summit was credit for an arms-control agreement and progress toward peace in Vietnam. He had already warned Chou that if the North Vietnamese launched a spring offensive, he would react with the full fury of the mad bomber. Now he wanted to let Brezhnev and his pals know that the price for détente was help in ending the war in Vietnam.

For all Nixon's acceptance of the new realities of the world balance of power, however, other more personal things mattered more to him.

As to SALT, Nixon's own words made it clear that he was more concerned with getting credit for an arms-control agreement than he was in reaching an arms-control agreement. He wanted both, of course, but if he had to choose, credit came before reality.

In early March 1972, it appeared that Gerard Smith and the American negotiating team in Vienna were on the verge of completing the SALT treaty, so that when Nixon went to Moscow it would be not to negotiate anything but simply to indulge in a ceremonial signing. Nixon responded with a March 11 memorandum to Haldeman.

"What I am concerned about," he began, "is not that we will fail to achieve the various goals . . . but that when we do make the formal agreements there will be no real news value to them." Nixon insisted that it was "vitally important that no final agreements be entered into until we arrive in Moscow." He instructed Haldeman to "begin a line of pessimism" about progress on SALT, and explained that otherwise "our critics will make it appear that all of this could have been achieved without any summit whatever, and that all we did was to go to Moscow for a grandstand play to put the final signature on an agreement that was worked out by Gerry Smith, State, etc." [1]

As to the policy of détente in general, Nixon was ready to sacrifice it if necessary to avoid what he regarded as humiliation in

Vietnam, as his actions in April and May showed, when he came exceedingly close to doing just that in response to a North Vietnamese challenge.

On March 30, the NVA launched the first phase of an offensive against South Vietnam. Using tanks and artillery in numbers never before seen in the war, the Communist forces crossed the DMZ and headed toward Quang Tri. The area had once been defended by U.S. Marines; now it was held by ARVN units that, after some initial resistance, cracked.

On his News Summary for April 3, Nixon underscored the lines that hurt the most: " 'Rout,' 'disarray,' 'crushing,' are terms used to describe ARVN retreat in first test of Vietnamization." "GIs quoted by UPI see little chance of ARVN holding at Quang Tri. And several voice strong opposition to the war itself." (The second sentence got a double underscoring plus a marginal order: "K— note!") "CBS and NBC film of thousands of refugees fleeing as enemy uses artillery more intensively than at any time in war. . . . DOD feels ARVN was taken by surprise. Situation is expected to get worse."[2]

A catastrophe loomed. It did no good to say that the offensive, after the two-year lull in the fighting in South Vietnam, had long since been anticipated. Nixon had to react. Any hesitation, and he might well face personal as well as national disaster. If the North Vietnamese won the war through force of arms, Nixon's three-year-old policy of Vietnamization would be exposed as a fraud, he would be humiliated and lose the election, and the United States would be disgraced.

Nixon did react, instinctively and immediately. Brushing aside bureaucratic opposition and counsels of moderation, he ordered an all-out counterattack by sea and air power. He sent in B-52s, more fighter-bombers, more aircraft carriers, more cruisers; he took off all budgetary restraints on air sorties; he ordered tactical air strikes up to the eighteenth parallel in North Vietnam; he ordered naval attacks twenty-five miles up the coast of North Vietnam.

In short, he counterattacked with almost everything he had available. What he did not do was launch a counteroffensive. He did not send in troops; he did not even slow the pace of ground forces withdrawal; he did not invade North Vietnam; he did not bomb Hanoi or Haiphong. His relative restraint was all the more remarkable because his anger was boundless. He thought the Communists had played with him for years, using negotiations as a smoke screen to prepare for a massive invasion. He was furious with the Soviets, whose tanks and artillery made the offensive possible. He felt that everything he had worked to achieve was threatened.

But his anger was more understandable than it was justified. In 1970 and 1971 he had been the one to launch offensives in Cambodia and in Laos. Even after they failed, his negotiating stance remained: give back the POWs, pull back your forces to North Vietnam, abandon your gains in Cambodia and Laos, and some months later the United States will complete its withdrawal (although he was never explicit on whether this withdrawal would include American air and sea power). Meanwhile Thieu would still be in power in Saigon (the promise that he would step down one month before elections was meaningless, as all his appointees would remain in charge and would be the ones to conduct the election).

Nixon, in other words, was demanding that Hanoi surrender its war aims, even as he withdrew American ground forces. How could he have expected the NVA not to attack when its leaders judged the moment to be right?

With regard to the Soviets, Nixon's complaints that they made the offensive possible were certainly true, but he ignored other relevant points. The United States was supplying more material to Saigon than the Soviets were to Hanoi. Soviet control of the actions of the men in Hanoi was never as complete as Nixon assumed it was. The Soviets had not sped the shipment of arms in the winter of '71–'72, nor had they ordered the offensive. The NVA had accumulated the arsenal thanks to the two-year lull on the battlefield, and decided on its own when and how to strike.

Nor did Nixon pay sufficient attention to what the Soviets did *not* do. While they gave Hanoi MIGs and SAMs to defend their airspace, they did not give the NVA fighter-bombers with which to attack the American air bases in Thailand, nor submarines with which to attack the American aircraft carriers in the Gulf of Tonkin. Like Nixon, they exercised some degree of restraint.

Nixon nevertheless had Kissinger tell Dobrynin on April 3 that Soviet complicity in Hanoi's attack was jeopardizing the summit.[3]

Kissinger was not happy with the assignment. He knew that "Nixon was determined on a showdown," that "he saw no point in further diplomacy until a military decision had been reached."[4] Kissinger, encouraged by Dobrynin to believe that the North Vietnamese would be forthcoming in a scheduled secret meeting between Kissinger and Le Duc Tho on April 24, was not so ready to abandon diplomacy, although he was as one with his boss on the need for an all-out counterattack.

To Nixon's extreme frustration, that attack was slow to get

going. According to the Pentagon, bad weather was the cause. Nixon had his doubts. At an afternoon meeting on April 4 with Mitchell and Haldeman, the President said, "Damn it, if you know any prayers say them. . . . Let's get that weather cleared up. The bastards have never been bombed like they're going to be bombed this time, but you've got to have weather."

"Is the weather still bad?" Mitchell inquired.

"Huh!" Nixon answered. "It isn't bad. The Air Force isn't worth a—I mean, they won't fly." He wished he had George Patton.[5]

On April 7, the NVA moved into the second phase of its offensive, attacking from Cambodia to the northwest of Saigon, toward Tay Ninh and An Loc. By then, the American counterattack was under way, as B-52s struck 145 miles north of the DMZ (the first use of B-52s in North Vietnam since early 1968), inflicting heavy casualties. Still the NVA came on; still ARVN failed to do its duty. Nixon had Kissinger's assistant, Al Haig, prepare a contingency plan; if all else failed, it called for bombing all military targets throughout North Vietnam and the mining of North Vietnamese ports.

For all his bellicosity, Nixon was downcast by events. Kissinger told him that even if the worst happened and the remaining American troops pulled out as the NVA won the war, he would still be able to claim credit for ending the war. Nixon said that prospect was "too bleak even to contemplate." He told Kissinger defeat was "simply not an option." But it was certainly a possibility. He expressed his depression in his diary: "If we fail it will be because the American way simply isn't as effective as the Communist way. . . . I have an uneasy feeling that this may be the case. We give them the most modern arms, we emphasize the material to the exclusion of the spiritual and the Spartan life, and it may be that we soften them up rather than harden them up for the battle."

Nixon was also unhappy with Kissinger: "Henry, with all of his many virtues, does seem too often to be concerned about preparing the way for negotiations with the Soviets. . . . Both Haldeman and Henry seem to have an idea—which I think is mistaken —that even if we fail in Vietnam we can still survive politically. I have no illusions whatever on that score, however. The U.S. will not have a credible foreign policy if we fail, and I will have to assume the responsibility for that development."[6]

On April 10, Nixon increased the pressure on the Soviets. Speaking at a State Department ceremony for the signing of an international convention for the banning of biological warfare, with Dobrynin in the audience, he said that every "great power" must follow the principle that it should not encourage "directly or indirectly, other nations to use force or armed aggression against its neighbors."[7]

On the battlefield, meanwhile, the B-52s were dropping hundreds of tons of bombs on the enemy around An Loc, but still ARVN was unable to push back the NVA. Nixon railed at the Pentagon. Why couldn't more be done? He wanted more B-52s sent north, to hit targets that were strategic and diplomatic, as well as tactical targets in the south.

Laird dissented. He feared that the relatively slow and not very maneuverable eight-jet bombers would be easy targets for Hanoi's SAMs. He also feared the congressional uproar that would follow. Rogers feared that such an escalation would endanger the summit.

Nixon insisted. He ordered B-52 raids against the oil depots around Hanoi and Haiphong; he even announced them in advance. On April 14, the President said that 150 B-52s, each one carrying thirty tons of bombs (ten times the capacity of the F-4 Phantom fighter-bombers), would hit North Vietnam the following day. It was obvious that such raids would have no effect on the battles around An Loc and Quang Tri; a Pentagon spokesman explained that the purposes were to slow the flow of supplies south, to demonstrate to President Thieu that he could count on Nixon, and to create a bargaining chip.[8]

The next day, April 15, the bombers moved in. They struck inside and outside Hanoi and Haiphong. They caused extensive damage, but the NVA claimed that eleven American planes had been shot down. Still, Nixon was pleased. He told Haldeman, "Well, we really left them our calling card this weekend."[9]

But that same day the North Vietnamese canceled the Paris meeting scheduled for April 24; as this was the meeting at which Dobrynin had hinted the enemy would be forthcoming, the cancellation was a blow. "Henry obviously considered this a crisis of the first magnitude," Nixon wrote in his diary. "I laid down the law hard to him that under these circumstances he could not go to Moscow." Kissinger had been slated to make a secret presummit trip to Moscow to prepare the way for Nixon. The President felt that the Soviets wanted Kissinger to come to discuss SALT, trade arrangements, and the like, when what needed to be discussed was Vietnam.

Nixon realized that his decision to keep Kissinger home "shook him because he desperately wants to get to Moscow one way or the other." But Nixon did not want to discuss SALT; he wanted to "consider our option with regard to imposing a blockade."[10]

On the afternoon of April 15, Nixon had "a pretty candid talk with Henry." The President was depressed. He told Kissinger that if he had to cancel the summit and impose a blockade, "I had an obligation to look for a successor." Nixon speculated on who might replace him; he mentioned Rockefeller, Burger, Reagan, and Connally.

Kissinger threw up his hands. He said that "none of them would do," and added that any Democrat was out of the question.

Nixon mused that if Kissinger would stay on, "we could get continuity in foreign policy." Kissinger, not averse to a little flattery himself, "became very emotional." He said Nixon "shouldn't be thinking this way or talking this way. . . . He made his pitch that the North Vietnamese should not be allowed to destroy two Presidents."

Later that evening, Kissinger called Nixon to inform him that Dobrynin was "desperate" to have him come to Moscow, and had promised that Vietnam would be the first item on the agenda. Nixon then reconsidered. He said Kissinger could go to Moscow.[11]

The following day, American bombers hit four Soviet merchant ships at anchor in Haiphong harbor. The Soviets protested, but in a relatively low-key manner, indicating their desire to go ahead with the summit.

Still Nixon had third and fourth thoughts about the wisdom of the Kissinger trip. Kissinger reassured him and Nixon again agreed to let him go. That left the problem of how to inform the Secretary of State. A month earlier Rogers had sent a memo to Nixon saying that he intended to "take personal charge" of the Moscow summit preparations. That was not Nixon's plan at all. He had Haldeman tell Rogers that all communications with the Soviets by the State Department had to be cleared in advance by the White House.[12]

Nixon decided to use a bit of subterfuge in informing Rogers. After Kissinger left for Moscow, Nixon would call Rogers to Camp David to tell him that Kissinger had received a sudden and unexpected summons from Brezhnev to discuss Vietnam. Nixon would assure Rogers that the only subject of discussion would be Vietnam (in the event, when Rogers learned that Kissinger talked about the full range of summit issues, he was "highly indignant." To complete the exclusion of the State Department from this most fundamental of all foreign-policy issues, Kissinger slipped into and out of Moscow without the American ambassador even knowing that he was there. Never before had an American President so personalized basic diplomacy, or so insulted the Department of State).[13]

It was not entirely Nixon's fault. He gave clear oral instructions to Kissinger: Vietnam was to be the first item discussed, and if the

Soviets proved "recalcitrant on this point, he should just pack up and come home." [14]

Nixon told Kissinger that while the summit had the potential of being the most important diplomatic encounter "of this century," it was "indispensable" to have "progress" on Vietnam *"by the time of the summit."* The President instructed his National Security Adviser to insist on a withdrawal of the NVA across the DMZ; he said that action was a "precondition of our ending the bombing of North Vietnam."

Nixon also told Kissinger how to describe the President to Brezhnev: "direct, honest, strong . . . fatalistic—to him election [is] not key. Will not be affected one iota by public opinion. No other President could make SALT agreement while war is still going on." [15]

Kissinger got around this set of orders by the simple expedient of ignoring them. While Kissinger was in Moscow (April 21–24), Nixon was at Camp David with Rebozo ("a conjunction that did not usually make for the calmest reflection," Kissinger noted).[16] Haig was also at Camp David. Nixon bombarded Kissinger with instructions to hang tough, to keep Vietnam up front, and so on. Kissinger in fact brushed past Vietnam, rightly expecting no progress, and plunged into the summit issues. It was the Soviets who insisted on some progress on Vietnam, and Kissinger gave it to them with hints that the United States, for the first time, might be willing to discuss a coalition government, and would not insist on the withdrawal of the NVA from South Vietnam.

Nixon, rightly suspecting that Kissinger was making unauthorized deals, demanded explanations. Kissinger sent a wire: "Brezhnev wants a summit at almost any cost." He told Haig to tell the President, "He must trust me. I have not exactly let him down on other missions." But Nixon feared Brezhnev would cancel the summit, which would be embarrassing; if it was going to be canceled, he wanted to be the one to do it. Further, Haig informed Kissinger, Nixon was in a "starchy mood" because polls indicated his popularity had risen thanks to the bombing campaign. Haig, who to Kissinger's discomfort was becoming one of the Nixon insiders, told Kissinger that the President had telephoned him and said "he views Soviet positions on South Vietnam as frenzied and frivolous and, therefore, is determined to go forward with additional strikes on Hanoi and Haiphong." [17]

In a message of his own to Kissinger, Nixon asserted that SALT was of concern only to "a few sophisticates." The main issue was Vietnam. The President wanted to go all out against the North Vietnamese and was willing to cancel the summit rather than forgo that option. Then, despite the way in which Kissinger had changed the basis of American foreign policy making, from a two-man team to a one-man show, in direct contradiction of clear orders, Nixon praised Kissinger for his "skill, resourcefulness, and determination," and concluded his message, "However it all comes out, just remember we all know we couldn't have a better man in Moscow at this time than Kissinger. Rebozo joins us in sending our regards." [18]

Kissinger speculated that a lot of drinking was going on that weekend at Camp David. Whatever the cause, the result was a set of contradictory presidential messages and orders. Apparently the chief executive of the United States did not know what he wanted, and left it to the National Security Adviser to sort out.

Kissinger returned on April 24. He justified his actions in a long memorandum; in his oral report he made the clinching argument: "If the summit meeting takes place, you will be able to sign the most important arms control agreement ever concluded." [19] Nixon decided not to hold Kissinger to account, perhaps a reflection of the independent power base Kissinger had managed to build, thanks in no small part to the enormously favorable publicity he had received in the past six months. Nixon now needed Kissinger almost as much as Kissinger needed him.

While Kissinger was in Moscow, the North Vietnamese launched the third phase of their offensive, attacking out of Laos and Cambodia into the Central Highlands, toward Kontum and Pleiku. Nixon responded with a televised speech in which he described the NVA attacks as "a clear case of naked and unprovoked aggression across an international border. There is only one word for it—invasion." He "flatly rejected" proposals from dovish senators that he stop the bombing in order to get the enemy back to the negotiating table. "They sold that package to the United States once before, in 1968, and we are not going to buy it again in 1972." He concluded with a bit of Nixonian hyperbole: "If the United States betrays the millions of people who have relied on us in Vietnam . . . it would amount to a renunciation of our morality, an abdication of our leadership among nations, and an invitation for the mighty to prey upon the weak all around the world."

He balanced his bellicosity with some encouraging words. Although Kontum and Quang Tri were surrounded, he asserted that the ARVN was doing well, so well that he could announce a further withdrawal of twenty thousand troops. And he held out hope for negotiations; despite what he said about the bombing, he announced that the canceled April 24 meeting with the North Vietnamese would be held on May 2. There was a further conflicting signal; he greeted a Chinese Ping-Pong team in the Rose Garden. [20]

On the morning of April 30, he called Kissinger on the telephone. He warned again that he intended to cancel the summit "unless the situation militarily and diplomatically substantially improves by May 15. . . . We have crossed the Rubicon and now we must win." He said Hanoi could not be trusted, "they will break every understanding." When Kissinger talked to the North Vietnamese in Paris, he should be "brutally frank from the beginning —particularly in tone." Tell them, he said, "the President has had enough and now you have only one message to give them—Settle or else!"[21]

Later that morning, Nixon flew down to Floresville, Texas, for a barbecue hosted by John Connally on his ranch, and attended by some two hundred Texas moneymen. George Brown, head of the state's largest construction company, Brown & Root, and LBJ's original backer, was there, as were John Murchison, Dallas oilman, and former Democratic governor Allan Shivers, along with the other key supporters of LBJ throughout his career. These were the same men, Democrats all, who had backed Lloyd Bentsen in his winning senatorial race against George Bush in 1970, and had made Connally governor.

Nixon, delighted to be the guest of honor in a gathering of his old political foes (these were the men who, some thought, had stolen Texas from Nixon for Kennedy in 1960), bubbled over. "I think that I have learned more about Texas on this brief visit than at any other time," he declared. Connally commented, "I have never learned much in politics, but I have learned that you have to fish with live bait. And we are not without some in this gathering this evening."

After the drinks, the beef tenderloin, and the corn on the cob, Nixon answered questions. The Texans wanted to know if he had thought about bombing the dikes in North Vietnam. He said he had, but pointed out that it would cause heavy civilian casualties. Then he added, "We are prepared to use our military and naval strength against military targets throughout North Vietnam, and we believe that the North Vietnamese are taking a very great risk if they continue their offensive in the South." To do less, he said, would insure a "Communist take-over," which would weaken the office of the Presidency, damage respect for the United States around the world, "destroy the confidence of the American people," and lead to further Communist adventures elsewhere.[22]

Those words, in that setting, gave reporters present a sense of déjà vu. They had heard it all before, from another President, on another Texas ranch, but before the same audience, between 1965 and 1968. The similarities between LBJ in '68 and Nixon in '72 were growing in size and in number.

Back in Washington, the sense of *déjà vu* increased. Headlines proclaimed that Quang Tri had fallen to the enemy. Nixon had a report on his desk from General Abrams saying that ARVN had evidently lost its will to fight. Adding to Nixon's woes, the newspapers proclaimed that *The New York Times* had won the Pulitzer Prize for the Pentagon Papers.[23]

Kissinger was in the Oval Office on the afternoon of May 1, for last-minute instructions before flying to Paris to meet Le Duc Tho. Don't give an inch, Nixon told him. "No nonsense. No niceness. No accommodations." He also wanted Kissinger to let Dobrynin know that "under no circumstances will I go to the summit if we're still in trouble in Vietnam."[24]

Kissinger flew to Paris, where he found Le Duc Tho "icy and snide." After three fruitless hours, he broke off the talks and headed home.

Nixon was not surprised. He wrote in his diary that Kissinger was so "obsessed with the idea that there *should* be a negotiated settlement" that he failed to see "there really isn't enough in it for the enemy to negotiate at this time."

Nixon recorded that he had a long talk with Haig, who like Kissinger knew that the way to the President's heart was to talk tough. On this occasion, Haig urged Nixon to take stronger action than Kissinger recommended. Nixon further steeled himself in his diary entry: "I must make whatever hard choices have to be made, and take whatever risks need to be taken."

Haig presented the President with an irresistible argument: he "emphasized that even more important than how Vietnam comes out is for us to handle these matters in a way that I can survive in office." That was putting first things first, and moved Haig up even higher in Nixon's esteem. So high, in fact, that the President told Colson later that day that Haig and Connally "are the only two men around here qualified to fill this job when I step down."[25]

Haig was as good as Kissinger himself at telling one man one thing, another man another, at backbiting, and at manipulating Nixon. He told Admiral Elmo Zumwalt (Chief of Naval Operations), for example, "that he [Haig] had to exercise considerable dexterity to stiffen the President's backbone when the President was in a bug-out mood, and that he lived in dread that some day the President would be with Henry instead of him when the bug-out mood came on and Henry would be unable to handle it."[26]

Kissinger returned to Washington the evening of May 2. Nixon had a helicopter waiting for him, to bring him to the Washington Navy Yard for a cruise on the *Sequoia*. Haig was also along.

Nixon wanted to launch B-52 strikes against Hanoi and Haiphong on May 5. Kissinger urged caution. He reminded the President that General Abrams wanted to use B-52s inside South Vietnam, to break up the enemy attacks at the point of contact, not hundreds of miles behind the lines, where the effect of the raids would not be felt on the battlefield for months. And he warned Nixon that he could not bomb and have the summit too, that the Soviets would have to cancel, blaming Nixon and the bombing. Then Nixon would really catch it from the doves, who would go after him over the bombing and over the cancellation of the summit.

Nixon acknowledged that "it was hard to see how I could go to the summit and be clinking glasses with Brezhnev while Soviet tanks were rumbling through [South Vietnam]." But he wanted to bomb so badly. But he wanted to go to Moscow so badly. He was in an agony of indecision.

He decided to postpone a decision on Hanoi-Haiphong and the summit until the following week. Meanwhile he ordered plans prepared and told Kissinger to get ready to cancel the summit. If he decided on all-out action, he wanted to preempt the Soviets by canceling first.[27]

Whatever he decided about Hanoi-Haiphong, he was determined to escalate the air war to teach the enemy a lesson. On May 4 he ordered fifty additional fighter-bombers to Southeast Asia, and ordered the fleet brought up to six aircraft carriers on active-duty station. This meant that in the past month he had increased the B-52 force in the war from 80 to 140, the number of fighter-bombers from 400 to 900, the number of carriers from three to six, and the air-navy personnel from 47,000 to 77,000. Meanwhile, he had reduced the number of ground troops from 95,000 to 68,100.[28] None of those figures include the ARVN air force, by 1972 the fourth-largest in the world.

But the enemy could escalate too. On the day Nixon sent in the carriers and the fifty fighter-bombers, the Vietcong announced the establishment of a "provisional revolutionary administration" in Quang Tri City. It was the first time in the war the Communists had succeeded in setting up a government on a provincial level in South Vietnam.[29]

"What will he do, they ask," Max Frankel wrote in *The New York Times*. "What will he do if the North Vietnamese keep coming, the South Vietnamese keep crumbling, the Russians keep stalling and the political risks keep mounting?" Noting Nixon's "propensity for psychic rage and for diplomacy by thunderclap," Frankel reviewed the options. Nixon could hardly increase the air counterattack in the South, as he had already put almost everything available into the battle. He might bomb the dikes, or use nuclear weapons, or invade North Vietnam with marines, but none of that seemed likely. He could pressure the Russians by bombing or mining Haiphong harbor, at a risk to the summit. Or he might make some concessions to the enemy in the hope of achieving a negotiated settlement. But, Frankel concluded lamely, "no one really does know what he might do." [30]

Not even Nixon knew. He continued to waver. He badly wanted and desperately needed advice, not from Kissinger or Haig (he knew their views), not from the Joint Chiefs or the State Department (he saw them as tools, not advisers), but from someone he trusted and respected (and there was almost no one he did).

He decided to turn to John Connally. Connally had once had some military experience; he had served for a few months as Kennedy's Secretary of the Navy. Nixon respected him; he constantly indulged himself in the fantasy that Connally could follow him into the White House. Kissinger acknowledged that Connally had "the best political brain in the Administration." [31] Nixon ordered Haldeman and Kissinger to go to Connally to find out what to do.

Big Jawn did not duck or shirk the responsibility. He was decisive. Haldeman reported to the President that Connally emphatically said, "Most important—the President must not lose the war! And he should not cancel the summit. He's got to show his guts and leadership on this one. Caution be damned—if they cancel, and I don't think they will, we'll ram it right down their throats." [32]

That was what Nixon wanted to hear. Once he knew Connally's views, he asked Connally to join him, Haig, Haldeman, and Kissinger in his EOB office for a council of war.

They reviewed the options, including the possibility of declaring a blockade. They decided a blockade would be too risky, as it carried the danger of having to confront the Soviet Navy. Mining was better.

Nixon pumped himself up. "As far as I'm concerned," he declared, "the only real mistakes I've made were the times when I didn't follow my own instincts." He wished he had bombed North Korea in 1969 after the EC-121 was shot down. He wished he had bombed the hell out of North Vietnam in 1970, when he went into Cambodia. "If we'd done that then, the damned war would be over now. . . . The summit isn't worth a damn if the price for it is losing in Vietnam. My instinct tells me that the country can take losing the summit, but it can't take losing the war." [33]

Kissinger described the commander in chief at this critical moment: "The only symptom of his excitement was that instead of slouching in an easy chair with his feet on a settee as usual, he was pacing up and down, gesticulating with a pipe on which he was occasionally puffing . . . he was playing MacArthur. . . .

"Nixon then and there decided upon the mining," Kissinger wrote. "It was one of the finest hours of Nixon's Presidency."[34]

Still he needed reassurance. He went up to Camp David for the weekend. Ed and Tricia Cox joined him, as did Julie Eisenhower. He told his daughters of his decision. Julie was worried: would it work? Nixon told her that if he did not do it, "the United States would cease to be a respected great power." She assured him that David would "totally agree." Tricia, Nixon wrote in his diary, "was immediately positive because she felt we had to do something, and frankly didn't know what else we could do to avoid a continued deterioration in the battle areas."

Nixon called John Mitchell. He thoroughly approved.[35]

That left the congressional leadership, the JCS, the DOD, the State Department, and the NSC. None had been consulted; all had to be informed. On Monday morning, May 8, Nixon told the NSC. The meeting lasted more than three hours and the President found it "pretty tough." Laird opposed the decision, Rogers was hesitant, Helms warned that mining Haiphong would not be decisive because the enemy had alternate supply routes available, and the professional military were more interested in fighting the battle in South Vietnam than engaging in strategic projects of dubious immediate benefit in North Vietnam.

Nixon defended his decision. "The real question is whether the Americans give a damn anymore," he said. He warned that if he followed the lead of *Time* magazine, the Washington *Post, The New York Times,* and the networks and just pulled out, "The U.S. would cease to be a military and diplomatic power. If that happened, then the U.S. would look inward towards itself and would remove itself from the world." But if the United States stayed strong and willing to act, "then the world will remain half-Communist rather than becoming entirely Communist."

With nearly ten thousand atomic weapons, plus all its additional firepower, plus its unrivaled economic strength, it is difficult to see how the United States would have ceased to be a great power if it failed to mine Haiphong harbor, but evidently no one at the NSC protested against Nixon's statement.

The President himself, however, appeared to backtrack later that day. In an afternoon meeting in the EOB with Haldeman and Kissinger, he told Kissinger that Haldeman had raised new questions. Haldeman then described the dire impact that mining Haiphong would have on public opinion; it might lead to Nixon's defeat in November. Kissinger "passionately defended the decision."

Nixon excused himself to go to the bathroom. Kissinger whirled on Haldeman and castigated him for interfering at such a moment. Haldeman, Kissinger later wrote, "grinned shamefacedly, making clear by his bearing that Nixon had put him up to his little speech." When Nixon returned from the bathroom, he signed the order without another word.

Kissinger confessed that he was unable to comprehend why Nixon had played this little game, until a year later when he learned of the taping system. "[This] suggested a possible motive: Nixon wanted me unambiguously on record as supporting the operation." (According to Haldeman, Nixon's motive was to test Kissinger's degree of conviction.)[36]

At 8 P.M., May 8, Nixon met with the joint congressional leadership. He knew what the politicians' advice would be—don't risk the summit, don't escalate—so he did not ask for it. Instead, he told them what he was going to do, and then concluded, "If you can give me your support, I would appreciate it. If you cannot, I will understand." He then walked out of the room.

At 9 P.M., he went on nationwide radio and television. He opened with a review of the military situation. "There is only one way to stop the killing," he said. "That is to keep the weapons of war out of the hands of the international outlaws of North Vietnam." To that end, "all entrances to North Vietnamese ports will be mined. . . . Rail and all other communications will be cut off to the maximum extent possible. Air and naval strikes against military targets in North Vietnam will continue."

He held out one carrot to the North Vietnamese. He would stop the bombing and remove the mines when the POWs were released and there was a cease-fire throughout Indochina. "At that time we will proceed with a complete withdrawal of all American forces from Vietnam within 4 months." Although it was ambiguous, the promise seemed to indicate that, (1) "all" included air and naval forces, and (2) by implication, the NVA could hold on to its recent gains and would not be required to simultaneously withdraw from South Vietnam. If that was what he meant, it represented a significant concession on Nixon's part.

To the Soviets, Nixon directed some carefully worded paragraphs: "We respect the Soviet Union as a great power. We recognize the right of the Soviet Union to defend its interests when they are threatened. The Soviet Union in turn must recognize our right to defend our interests.

"No Soviet soldiers are threatened in Vietnam. Sixty thousand Americans are threatened. We expect you to help your allies, and you cannot expect us to do other than to continue to help our allies, but let us, and let all great powers, help our allies only for the purpose of their defense, not for the purpose of launching invasions against their neighbors."

He noted the progress that had been made on arms limitation, trade, and other issues. "Let us not slide back toward the dark shadows of a previous age." He said the United States and the Soviet Union were on the threshold of a new relationship. "We are prepared to continue to build this relationship. The responsibility is yours if we fail to do so." [37]

The following morning Nixon, quite full of himself, went after the Pentagon. He regarded the additional bombing proposals the military had put forward as "timid" at best. He sent a memorandum to Kissinger (who had somehow become his executive officer for implementing military decisions). He told Kissinger he was determined to "go for broke. . . . Our greatest failure now would be to do too little too late. . . . I intend to stop at nothing to bring the enemy to his knees. . . . I want the military to get off its backside. . . . We have the power to destroy [the enemy's] war-making capacity. The only question is whether we have the *will* to use that power. What distinguishes me from Johnson is that I have the *will* in spades. . . . For once, I want the military . . . to come up with some ideas on their own which will recommend *action* which is very *strong, threatening,* and *effective.*" [38]

He never meant any of that; he was just puffing himself up. He had already ruled out any truly decisive action, such as reintroducing American ground troops, or invading North Vietnam, or bombing the dikes, or using nuclear weapons. He was making war by temper tantrum; his rage had no sustaining power to it. Mining Haiphong and bombing Hanoi were not decisive acts; they were irritants, major irritants to be sure, but hardly enough to turn back an enemy so determined as the North Vietnamese.

What Nixon had done was demonstrate his determination not to be humiliated. He was hurting Hanoi, not destroying it: he had, in effect, conceded Hanoi's right to keep troops in South Vietnam; what he had not done was agree to abandon Thieu, and made it clear he never would do that. He would even risk the summit, détente, his whole new era of peace, to preserve the government of South Vietnam. He had given Hanoi and Moscow much to think about; he had not changed the course of the war.

The political reaction was predictable. Representative Ford was in full support, as were most Republicans. Senator McGovern called the action "reckless, unnecessary and unworkable, a flirtation with World War III. The only purpose of this dangerous new course is to keep General Thieu in power a little longer, and perhaps to save Mr. Nixon's face a little longer."

Senator Kennedy called the mining of Haiphong "a futile military gesture that demonstrates the desperation of the President's Indochina policy. I think his decision is ominous and I think it is folly." [39]

Nixon ignored them. The reaction that mattered was Moscow's. It came quickly enough. The Soviets protested, they demanded, they made accusations—but they never mentioned the summit. Kissinger saw Dobrynin. He wondered why there was no mention of the summit.

"We have not been asked any questions about the summit," Dobrynin replied, "and therefore my government sees no need to make a new decision."

"I think we have passed the crisis," Kissinger reported to Nixon exuberantly. "I think we are going to be able to have our mining and bombing and have our summit too." [40]

Nixon had pulled off one of his great triumphs. Now, if only ARVN could hold on the battlefield, everything had fallen into place, at a perfect time to sustain his re-election bid.

IN THE UNITED STATES, elections cannot be suspended because of a crisis. Simultaneously with the crisis in Southeast Asia, the primary season went forward. On the Republican side, Nixon had no difficulty in turning back his challengers. On the Democratic side, there was near chaos, brought on by Wallace's presence on the ballot. Wallace had followed up his Florida victory with triumphs in Tennessee and North Carolina, and strong second places in Wisconsin, Indiana, and Pennsylvania. McGovern won in Wisconsin, Massachusetts, and Nebraska, and was doing well in the delegate selection process in nonprimary states. Muskie had dropped out. Humphrey had come on to challenge McGovern. Senator Kennedy waited in the wings. "To me," Nixon wrote of McGovern, "his steady climb was as welcome to watch as it was almost unbelievable to behold." [41]

Wallace was his problem, not as a Democrat, but as an independent. Wallace's unexpectedly strong showing in the northern primaries made it probable that when the Democrats turned him back at their convention, he would bolt. By the second week in May, a Wallace third-party candidacy was the major threat to Nixon's re-election.

May 16 was primary day in Michigan and Maryland. These primaries, especially in industrial Michigan, were regarded as important tests of the broadness of Wallace's appeal, and he was expected to do well. On May 15, Arthur Herman Bremer shot and badly wounded Wallace, who was campaigning in Laurel, Maryland. Although the doctors saved his life, they feared he would not regain the use of his legs.

In the primaries the following day, Wallace won big. In Michigan, he got 50 percent, to McGovern's 26 percent and Humphrey's 17 percent; he did even better in Maryland. Exit polls indicated that his showing was not due to a "sympathy vote," but to an "angry vote." Crime and busing were the reasons voters cited for supporting Wallace. A *New York Times* study showed that Wallace would cut far more sharply into Nixon's vote than into that of the Democratic candidate, even in the North.[42]

Colson talked to Richard Scammon, then sent Nixon a memo analyzing the Democratic primaries. Busing wasn't just the most important issue, he said, it was "virtually the only issue." Democrats who were never going to accept McGovern's position on the Vietnam War were more eager to vote for Wallace as an alternative than for Nixon, because of busing.

Colson reported that Scammon thought the Administration was "embarrassed" to push the busing issue because it "runs against the mainstream of Georgetown thought." Nixon scribbled in the margin, "E—he is right. Tell *all* to quit paying attention to the N.Y. Times, Post—Georgetown clique." He told "H" to "prohibit any members of the Administration from attending any Washington dinner parties until after the elections," and ordered "E" to go back to work on proposing a constitutional amendment to stop busing.[43]

There were other political developments. On May 16, Nixon made a surprise announcement: John Connally had resigned as Secretary of the Treasury. Nixon named George Shultz as his successor, with Caspar Weinberger taking Shultz's place as director of OMB. Nixon was unrestrained in his praise of Connally, describing him as the "dynamic and skilled" architect of the Administration's new economic policy and a wise and courageous counselor on matters of national security. He said he would call on Connally to undertake special foreign-affairs assignments. Reporters speculated that his real future was the number-two spot on the Republican ticket; actually, Connally had resigned in order to get started on organizing "Democrats for Nixon."

Two days after Connally's resignation, Nixon sent a memo on executive appointments to Haldeman. Nixon instructed his chief of staff to "quit recruiting from any of the Ivy League schools or any other universities where either the president or faculty have taken action condemning our efforts to bring the war in Vietnam to an end." Nixon said he felt "totally justified" in setting such a policy because "the government simply has too many Ivy League people in relationship to the percentage of Ivy League graduates compared to the total number of college graduates in the country." The President instructed Haldeman to give first priority in hiring to graduates of schools whose president or faculty had sent wires of support for the Vietnam policy, and to schools in the Midwest, the South, "and even possibly some in the far West (not, of course, including Stanford or Cal)."

The funny thing was, for all Nixon's anger at the Ivy League, more than one-half his appointees to Cabinet-level posts were from the Ivy League (four from Harvard, two from Yale, one each from Columbia and Princeton). There were three from the Big Ten, none from the West, and with the departure of Connally (University of Texas), none from the South.

In that same memo, Nixon also instructed Haldeman to shake up the CIA. "I want a study made immediately as to how many people in the CIA could be removed by Presidential action," Nixon declared. "I assume that they have themselves frozen in just as is the case with State. If that is the case I want action begun immediately . . . for a reduction in force of all positions in the CIA in the executive groups of 50 percent."[44]

Six months earlier, Nixon had tried, unsuccessfully, to persuade J. Edgar Hoover to resign. On May 2, Hoover died. In his diary, Nixon wrote, "He died at the right time; fortunately, he died in office. It would have killed him had he been forced out of office or had he resigned even voluntarily. . . . I am particularly glad that I did not force him out."[45]

In his eulogy at the funeral services at the National Presbyterian Church, Nixon said that the "bureau he built to last" would be Hoover's real memorial. Nixon used the opportunity to make a political point: "The American people today are tired of disorder, disruption and disrespect for law. America wants to come back to the law as a way of life."[46]

Nixon named L. Patrick Gray acting director of the FBI. Gray had been a Nixon supporter in 1960, an aide to Bob Finch in HEW, and an Assistant Attorney General responsible for handling antiwar demonstrations on federal property. He was known as a strong Nixon loyalist. He told reporters that he had instructions from Nixon to operate the FBI in "a totally nonpolitical way." He said Nixon felt so strongly about this that he had ordered Gray's wife, Beatrice, to resign from her position at CREEP.[47]

At CREEP, meanwhile, Liddy and Hunt were putting Gemstone into operation. Their efforts to break into Greenspun's safe in Las Vegas evidently failed, but by mid-May they had sufficient funds from CREEP to bring a team of Cuban burglars up to Washington from Miami. They attempted to place a bug in McGovern's

Washington headquarters, but that too failed. Finally, toward the end of May, they managed to break into the DNC offices in the Watergate, where they photographed some documents, and placed bugs on the phones of O'Brien's secretary and R. Spencer Oliver, executive director of the Association of State Democratic Chairmen. But the O'Brien tap was faulty, and the Oliver tap yielded nothing of value.[48]

ON MAY 20, the presidential party set off for Moscow. Nixon was exuberant. So was Kissinger, who told him en route, "This has to be one of the great diplomatic coups of all times!"[49]

It was not just that Nixon had gotten away with the mining and bombing. He was the first American President to go to Moscow and the second to go to the Soviet Union (FDR had gone to the Crimea in February 1945). It was Nixon's third trip; he had gone in 1959, when his Kitchen Debate with Khrushchev had become a major news story, and as a private citizen in 1967, when the Soviet leaders, to his intense irritation, had coldly snubbed him. Beyond the satisfaction of revenge, he was pleased to be accomplishing something that had eluded all his Cold War predecessors. Ike had been eager to go to Moscow, but Khrushchev had withdrawn the invitation after the 1960 U-2 incident. Kennedy had hoped to go, but died too soon; LBJ's proposed trip had been postponed, then canceled. There were solid agreements waiting to be signed, which guaranteed that Nixon would dominate the news back in the States even as the Democrats entered the final phase of their nominating process, and there was serious negotiating to be done, which freed him from the charge that the only purpose of the summit was to give him the headlines. He had good cause to be exuberant.

Air Force One landed in Moscow at 4 P.M., May 22. Soviet President Nikolai Podgorny, Premier Aleksei Kosygin, and Foreign Minister Andrei Gromyko were there to meet him. The party drove through empty streets to the Kremlin, where the Nixons were given an entire floor of rooms in the Grand Palace. Within the hour, Kissinger arrived with the news that Chairman Brezhnev wanted to receive Nixon in his office.

It was the same office in which Nixon had first met Khrushchev, thirteen years earlier. Although Brezhnev had been present at the Kitchen Debate, Nixon had hardly noticed him; this was in practice their first meeting.

In his diary, Nixon later wrote that Brezhnev gave him the impression of "a big Irish labor boss," or a Mayor Daley. "He has what it takes," Nixon noted, "and we can make no greater mistake than to rate him either as a fool or simply an unintelligent brute."

Still, Nixon compared him unfavorably with Chou En-lai, who combined "elegance and toughness." Brezhnev had only toughness. Nixon thought Kosygin, "by Communist terms," an aristocrat, while Podgorny struck him as "like a Midwestern senator."[50]

Nixon and Brezhnev talked about the World War II alliance. Nixon set the tone for the entire summit when he said he would like to recover the relationship that had existed between Churchill, Roosevelt, and Stalin, who managed to overcome differences between subordinates by agreement at the top level.

"If we leave all the decisions to the bureaucrats, we will never achieve any progress," Nixon said.

"They would simply bury us in paper!" Brezhnev replied, laughing heartily.[51]

Over the next few days there were talks, both general and specific, and sight-seeing and banquets, although nothing to compare to China. The Soviet leaders subjected Nixon to a three-hour diatribe about Vietnam; he gave back some tough talk of his own. At the end of each day, there were news-making agreements to sign. The agreements covered scientific and technological cooperation, including a joint orbital mission in space, trade, cultural matters, and the like.

There was also a joint statement on the "Basic Principles of Relations," which was important to Brezhnev, but a throwaway concession to Nixon. It recognized the reality of the relationship, that the Soviets had reached parity with the Americans in nuclear affairs. The two sides agreed that "there is no alternative to conducting their mutual relations on the basis of peaceful coexistence," and forswore "efforts to obtain unilateral advantage at the expense of the other." They pledged to "seek to promote conditions in which all countries will live in peace and security and will not be subject to outside interference in their internal affairs."[52]

Some issues could not be resolved, such as Most Favored Nation (MFN) status for the Soviets, or the Soviet repayment of the World War II debt, which was important to Congress but not to Nixon, and the details of the grain deal. Nixon and Brezhnev did agree to establish a commission to work on these questions.

The main outlines of an arms-control agreement had already been completed, with the major breakthrough being a treaty to limit each side to two ABMs that would protect the national capitals, not ICBM launch pads. But there were problems, created for the most part by Kissinger's meddling in the back channel, where he worked at cross-purpose with the American negotiating team in the SALT talks. Nixon shared some of the responsibility, because of his refusal or inability to master the technical details of SALT.

This failure, in turn, resulted from Nixon's overreliance on Kissinger, who was playing his usual double and even triple game, telling each player—the Soviet leadership, the American SALT delegation, and the President—what he thought they wanted to hear. It was Kissinger, for example, who privately told the Soviets they did not have to include SLBMs in the final count, then told the SALT delegation to put them in because of congressional opposition if they were not counted, then told Nixon he had obtained a Soviet concession when in fact he had made one himself. But then it was Nixon who excluded the SALT delegation from the Moscow talks and who encouraged Kissinger's intrigues.

All this naturally infuriated the professional arms-control negotiators. Raymond Garthoff, Gerard Smith's key aide on the SALT delegation, complained of Nixon, "It's not that he just didn't know the details, but he didn't even realize what proposal we had on the table. He didn't even know what anyone reading the newspapers would know. He really was so removed from the substance of SALT."[53] Smith himself, in a presummit NSC meeting on SLBMs, had complained that Kissinger had removed from a draft paper an important reservation. When he tried to explain the issue to Nixon, the President dismissed his objection with one word, "Bullshit."[54]

Smith entitled his memoir about his experience *Doubletalk*, and in it wrote, "I was flabbergasted that Kissinger once again had gone off on his own and by-passed the delegation and other government officials with SALT responsibilities. I was surprised by the President's harsh reaction to my efforts to keep some maneuvering room for the American position."[55]

The result of Nixon's relative indifference and Kissinger's active manipulation was a flawed agreement. SALT I was a five-year interim agreement that set upper limits on SLBMs and ICBMs, but these "limits" represented the planned production already under way. No limits were put on MIRV, which encouraged each side to MIRV its existing ICBMs. Thus overall SALT was about as meaningful as freezing the cavalry of the European nations in 1938, but not the tanks. And the Soviets got what they wanted from Kissinger with regard to the size ("throw weight") of their ICBMs.

(There is a revealing item in the Nixon archives that illustrates how jealously Kissinger guarded his sole access to Nixon as an adviser on Soviet relations. In a postsummit memorandum, Nixon told Kissinger he had been thinking about bringing in some of the leading academic Kremlinologists for a talk. "Consider the matter and if you think well of it have them in. I was just thinking it might be of use to us to get their views as to where we go from here."

Kissinger took two months to reply, and when he did it was

through a memo from one of his aides to Haldeman, attached to Nixon's memo. It read: "Re the attached. HAK decided it was not a good idea and that it should be dropped.")[56]

It is easy to be critical of Nixon and Kissinger on the subject of SALT. Seymour Hersh has a devastating chapter on the negotiations, of which the theme is, "They cheated their way to a summit, accepting less than what could have been achieved in the bargaining, and then lied to the press and public about what they had accomplished."[57] Garthoff, writing about the SLBM deal, notes that Kissinger "was proposing an offer the Soviet leaders could not refuse. . . . He made the terms palatable to the Soviets by permitting them to fulfill their planned programs." He also charges that Nixon and Kissinger "were moved more by domestic political-bureaucratic pressures than by arms control considerations."[58]

But this was exactly the kind of criticism Nixon anticipated, what he had in mind when he told Brezhnev at their initial meeting that they would have to go over the heads of their bureaucrats and subordinates to reach an agreement. It was not just that details bored him. Arms-control negotiations are as esoteric as medieval theology, as impossible for an outsider to master as nuclear technology. The experts always have an objection to any attempt to reach an accord. So do the politicians, who don't know what they are talking about but do know what appeals to the voters (which is, never trust the Russians).

The American nonexperts in Moscow, led by Safire, whose adulation of Nixon was as great as Colson's, knew nothing about the details, but Safire felt he understood the larger issues involved. In his memoir of the Nixon Presidency, he described a scene that Nixon and Kissinger also regarded as about equal to Lincoln's famous Cabinet meeting where he decided to issue the Emancipation Proclamation.

Except that this scene took place in Nixon's Kremlin apartment, at 1 A.M., with Nixon stretched out naked on a rubbing table, having his back massaged. Kissinger came in with bad news. The Pentagon was in almost open rebellion on such issues as SLBM and throw weight. If the Joint Chiefs did not support the agreement, hawkish senators and the right wing generally would feel free to attack and probably destroy it.

"The hell with the political consequences," Nixon quotes himself as saying. "We are going to make an agreement on *our* terms regardless of the political consequences if the Pentagon won't go along." He told Kissinger to proceed. Then he gave out a typical Nixon statement that said the opposite of what he meant: "Remember that as far as I'm concerned, we don't have to settle this week."[59]

Kissinger regarded this as "one of the more courageous decisions of his Presidency." Nixon, he said, "took a heroic position from a decidedly unheroic posture."[60]

Safire, whose penchant for exaggeration rivaled that of his boss, wrote: "He took one of the most fateful decisions of his Presidency, and of the postwar generation, there on the massage table."[61]

But the ludicrous scene, the absurd words of praise, and the false sense of drama (was Nixon suddenly going to rise up from the rubbing table to proclaim, "To hell with it then, let's go home"?) should not obscure the importance of what he had done. For all the flaws, for all that he could have driven a harder bargain, for all that he had failed to freeze, much less reduce, nuclear arsenals and delivery systems, Nixon had achieved a symbolic breakthrough, namely that the two sides could set limits on their destructive capability. And he fully intended, in his second term, to move from that position to a treaty that would lead to reductions.

Even more important, he had established a wholly new basis for the arms race. The ABM Treaty signified the acceptance by both sides of the concept of deterrence through "mutual terror." In Nixon's words, "By giving up missile defenses, each side was leaving its population and territory hostage to a strategic missile attack. Each side therefore had an ultimate interest in preventing a war that could only be mutually destructive."[62]

More than any other individual, Nixon was responsible for that breakthrough. But—and there is always a "but" with Nixon—although he claimed the ABM Treaty made this breakthrough "permanent," it had not. He had failed to include a ban on antisatellite (ASAT) weapons, which Garthoff believed could have been easily achieved.[63] Because of his ruthless rejection of State Department and SALT delegations' participation in Moscow, because of his refusal to involve congressional leaders and the Pentagon in his presummit preparations, because of his penchant for secrecy and intrigue, because of the way in which he allowed Kissinger to lie and cheat, he had failed to build a domestic constituency for his program. Whether or not as a lame-duck President he could get a SALT II treaty was more an open question than an established fact; whether or not détente in general could outlast a Nixon Presidency was problematical at best.

All that said, it remains that with the ABM Treaty specifically, and détente generally, Nixon had done what none of his predecessors had been able to do. The Moscow summit was a great achievement.

• •

NIXON RETURNED to the States on June 1. He landed at Andrews Air Force Base, then took a helicopter to Capitol Hill, where the leadership took him into the House Chamber to address a joint session of Congress. There he began the process he should have started months earlier, that of selling arms control to the politicians and beyond them to the public. In the process, he badly oversold.

"Three-fifths of all the people alive in the world today have spent their whole lifetimes under the shadow of a nuclear war which could be touched off by the arms race," he began. "Last Friday in Moscow we witnessed the beginning of the end of that era which began in 1945. We took the first step toward a new era of mutually agreed restraint and arms limitation." He claimed that "we have begun to check the wasteful and dangerous spiral of nuclear arms which has dominated relations ... for a generation." [64]

Nixon made it sound as if the arms race, if not the Cold War itself, was over. He created expectations of big savings in defense. For the most part, doves hailed his achievements, while the hawks expressed skepticism.

The truth was not long in emerging. Secretary Laird, on June 6, told the Senate Armed Services Committee that Pentagon support for the SALT agreement was conditioned on congressional approval of a number of new strategic programs, including a B-1 bomber, the MX missile, the cruise missile, and the Trident submarine-missile system. "This dose of cold water," as Gerard Smith called it, "coming so soon after the President's jubilant rhetoric, began a somewhat bittersweet legacy." One senator told Kissinger that the United States could not afford another arms-control agreement; Laurence Martin, director of war studies at the University of London, pointed out that SALT was doing "more to accelerate than to restrain strategic arms procurement on both sides." [65] Admiral Zumwalt was blunt: "The fact was that it was the unconscionable numbers in the SALT agreements themselves that virtually froze us into five more years of high spending on U.S. strategic forces." [66]

To Nixon's critics, it appeared that he had given the doves the rhetoric, with the SALT agreement, and the hawks the reality, with the Administration's new arms-procurement program. Nixon replied in a News Summary comment: "Al—when Henry gets back tell him we must build a backfire against this developing line—we must stay right on the tightrope—hold the hawks by continuing adequate defense—Hold doves by pointing out that *without* SALT the arms budget would be *much larger* because of an all out race —*and* no hope for permanent offensive limit talks." [67]

In a news conference on June 29, Nixon stayed with that line.

A number of reporters used words like "deception" and "fooling the public" in asking what was the point to an arms-limitation agreement that spurred the arms race. Nixon explained that once Congress approved the interim agreement, new negotiations would begin to achieve a permanent agreement of "far greater significance."

SALT I, he said, was "phase one, the break-through, and phase two is the culmination." Why then put all that money into the B-1 bomber? Because, Nixon patiently explained, he could only negotiate with the Soviets from a position of strength. In other words, he was building new weapons so that his successors wouldn't have to build new weapons.[68]

It was a strange way to control the arms race, and all very confusing.

And what of Vietnam? What of the President's determination to make no deals with the Soviets until and unless they restrained the North Vietnamese? In his address to Congress, Nixon hinted that he had made some progress toward ending the war while in Moscow. "The problem of ending the Vietnam war, which engages the hopes of all Americans, was one of the most extensively discussed subjects of our agenda," Nixon said. "It would only jeopardize the search for peace if I have to review here all that was said on that subject."[69]

Whether he spoke the truth or not must await an opening of the diplomatic archives, which seventeen years later Kissinger and Nixon were doing everything possible to keep closed. Garthoff and Hersh believe that Kissinger, possibly without Nixon's knowledge, made some concessions while in Moscow. Brezhnev offered to send Podgorny to Hanoi to talk to the North Vietnamese; to give him something to talk about, Kissinger evidently indicated that the United States was ready to include political as well as military elements in a settlement, although not to overthrow the Thieu government. He may have also said that the United States was willing to allow the NVA to stay in the South, and the Vietcong to retain the areas it had captured. The last was an important point, because in defending against the North Vietnamese offensive, Saigon had pulled troops out of the rich Mekong Delta region, which allowed the local Vietcong to regain control of areas liberated in General Westmoreland's 1966–1967 offensives.

While Nixon was in Moscow, the bombing offensive in the North continued. Nixon kept it up (with a single pause, while Podgorny was in Hanoi) right through to the fall; between May 9 and October 23, the United States made 41,500 attack sorties on North Vietnam.

There were other pressures on the men in Hanoi, pressures put on them as a result of Nixon's triangular diplomacy. Although neither China nor Russia was stopping the flow of supplies to the North Vietnamese, both were urging them to accept a cease-fire and to release the prisoners in return for a role in the political life of South Vietnam and the right to hold the territory they had captured. Unstated but understood was that they would have to agree to allow Thieu to remain in Saigon, in power.

The North Vietnamese resisted this approach; the official organ of the Communist Party in Hanoi chastised both China and the Soviet Union for urging a compromise. Hanoi accused Peking and Moscow of giving preference to "peaceful coexistence over proletarian internationalism, serving their own immediate interests at the expense of the [world] revolutionary movement." [70]

On the battlefield, meanwhile, the immense American air effort was taking its toll. The NVA was suffering horrendous casualties, and had been unable to capture Hue, Kontum, or An Loc. Still, although ARVN was holding, its counterattack was not driving the enemy back. Nixon was impatient. Informed that a relief unit sent to break the siege of An Loc had failed to get through, Nixon ordered, "Al, wire Abrams—this is becoming an issue—even a joke by critics of Admin. Unless there's a *strong* military reason, Have Abrams *Tell* Thieu to get off his tail & punch this outfit in there." [71]

Overall, however, the news from Vietnam in June could hardly have been better, nor come at a better time. At the end of the month, Nixon was able to announce that from that moment on, no draftees would be sent to Vietnam unless they volunteered for duty there, and that he was reducing American ground strength by ten thousand to a total of thirty-nine thousand by September 1. [72]

Taken altogether, the events of May–June 1972 were propelling the North Vietnamese toward a settlement with which Nixon could live. The failure of their offensive to take the big cities (except Quang Tri), the pressure from their allies, the destruction of much of their country by the B-52s, and the concurrent political developments within the United States, developments that indicated Nixon was going to win in November, all pointed in the direction of negotiation. Nixon, in the biggest poker game of his life, had put all his chips in the pot while simultaneously drawing to an inside straight and bluffing. He was about to rake in his biggest pot.

CHAPTER TWENTY-FOUR

POLITICS
AND THE BREAK-IN
June–July 1972

MEETING WITH MAO in Peking and negotiating with Brezhnev in Moscow had been new experiences for Nixon. When he returned to Washington, he was back in a milieu that he knew better than anything else, and that he knew more about than anyone else, that of presidential electoral politics. He never let his associates, whether Haldeman and Ehrlichman and Colson and the rest in the White House, or Mitchell and Magruder and the rest at CREEP, forget that he was *the* expert, that this was *his* campaign, that he would make *all* the major decisions.

In early June, Nixon saw a comment from one of his California campaign workers: "Contrived or real, McGovern is projecting an impression of freshness, seriousness of purpose and candor, building himself for a direct confrontation with the old politics in November." The President commented, "H—It is good to run scared —but it is *stupid* to put out *their* line." [1]

Informed that voters were saying the economy was the major issue, Nixon instructed, "H–C—it is our job to get *our* issue at the top of their concerns." [2]

That issue was Nixon the world statesman. When the Washington *Post* remarked that Nixon was the symbol of "the politics of stalemate and rhetoric," Nixon wrote, "H—here is where our people should be talking about our bold foreign policy initiatives— *never* undertaken by JFK et al." [3]

He followed political commentary with a fierce concentration, and sent out an unending flow of instructions to counter or manipulate or undercut his critics. When UPI reported from Moscow that Soviet leaders saw McGovern as a man who "recognizes the depth of America's crisis and surged to the fore with a clear, simple program," Nixon responded, "K—you should warn Dobrynin on interfering in American politics."[4] When McGovern promised that he would eliminate the foreign-policy apparatus in the White House and restore the preeminence of the State Department, Nixon remarked, "K—*if* the foreign service types needed any other reason to oppose us—they have it now!"[5]

Through the spring, Nixon took positions on various issues that were at variance with his own government but popular with the voters. Despite four years of badgering from the White House, HEW and Justice lawyers continued to bring desegregation cases to the courts. Ehrlichman told the President, "Elliot Richardson [Secretary of HEW] doesn't know how to take a hard line with the Congress on anything. He'll give away the store."

"Get him in!" Nixon replied. "I'll see the son-of-a-bitch and give him some backbone!"

The President remained hopeful that he could find a constitutional amendment to promote that would prohibit busing. "Find out when school starts next fall," he told Ehrlichman. "We'll be ready to go with a Constitutional amendment between then and the election."[6]

Nixon almost never found anything he approved of in the press, but when informed that a recent study charged the reporters were representing blacks "as throwers of Molotov cocktails, thieves, killers, rapists, and lazy good-for-nothings who do nothing but pump for more welfare," he had a one-word comment: "*Good!*"[7]

The President vetoed a clean-water bill as too costly. When William Ruckelshaus, head of the EPA, announced that his agency was banning virtually all uses of DDT, a decision the DDT producers and users immediately appealed, Nixon wrote, "E—I *totally* disagree with this decision. I want plenty of effort put in to get it reversed on appeal."[8]

Whatever the country might need, Nixon knew what a majority of the voters wanted, and he put their wishes first. McGovern, his probable opponent in November, knew what he stood for, and what a majority of the younger activists in the Democratic Party wanted, and he put that first. Thus McGovern was for clean water, whatever the cost, and against DDT, whatever the cost. He endorsed busing, and higher taxes for the rich, and a guaranteed income for every American. He wanted to cut the defense budget drastically and favored amnesty for young men who had gone to Canada to avoid the draft. Most of all, McGovern wanted to end the Vietnam War, immediately and without conditions.

Nixon hoped with all his heart that McGovern would get the

nomination. When a federal judge ruled that the McGovern-sponsored reform guidelines on delegates for the Democratic Convention, which required a certain percentage to be black, young, and women, were unconstitutional, McGovern announced that he would file an immediate appeal. Nixon commented, "C—Let's hope he wins!"[9] (He did; the U.S. Court of Appeals overturned the decision the next day.)

But Nixon did not have to manipulate the Democrats; he could let them do the damage to themselves. In debates before the California primary election, Humphrey vigorously went after McGovern. He called McGovern's tax proposals "confiscatory" and "a lot of bunk," and heaped scorn on other positions. McGovern had enjoyed a twenty-point lead in the polls, but Humphrey cut into that lead sharply. Still, on primary day, June 6, McGovern won by 5.4 percent, and with his California victory he had sufficient delegates to carry the convention.

That same day, Nixon sent a memo to Mitchell. The President said his chief fear now was that McGovern would start "clarifying" his stand on such issues as amnesty, marijuana, abortion, and welfare in an effort to move toward the center. Nixon knew that Buchanan and others were convinced that McGovern "can't get away with it any more than Goldwater was able to get away with it [in 1964]." But Nixon saw two significant differences: "McGovern is more clever and less principled than Goldwater and will say anything in order to win," and while the press went after Goldwater, the reporters were giving McGovern "about 100 percent support." Nixon's conclusion was that it was not he who should attack McGovern's record; instead, Democrats and independents should be sought out to "nail McGovern on the left side of the road."[10]

That was where John Connally came in. As one of LBJ's closest associates, as the man who had been shot sitting in front of JFK in Dallas, he was ideal for the task. Connally would not make any public move until after the Democratic Convention; meanwhile, to build him up, Nixon sent him on an ambassadorial mission to fourteen countries in South America and Asia. Nixon also built him up by refusing to comment on White House–inspired rumors that Connally would replace Agnew on the ticket. That device had the added advantage of building some suspense for the convention. The speculation got a boost from the treatment Connally received before departing on his trip; it included a three-hour briefing from Kissinger, a round of photographs with Nixon, and a weekend in Key Biscayne. Agnew, furious, commented that it was beyond imagination that a convention hall full of loyal Republicans would nominate a Democrat to replace him, but admitted that Nixon had not yet told him he would be on the ticket.[11]

Nixon looked for and seized any edge he could get. On June 14 Ray Price sent him a memo; he said he had learned a fascinating fact, that on the day the Democratic Convention opened in Miami, July 10, there would be an eclipse of the sun. Price thought it rather funny—"they even made the sun not to shine!" was his comment —but Nixon, serious as always, remarked, "C—Your people should be able to do something with this." [12]

Moving from the ridiculous to the real, Nixon's biggest worry remained that George Wallace might recover sufficiently to mount a third-party campaign. On June 19, Nixon talked to his friend Billy Graham, then met with Haldeman. It seemed that Graham had a "line" to Wallace and would be willing to talk to him to persuade him to stay in the Democratic Party. According to Haldeman's notes, Nixon wanted Graham to make the point that "W has to decide if he's to be used as spoiler (then McG will get in). Essential to keep this a 2 way race." [13]

But a week or so later, Wallace's campaign manager said that the American Independent Party saw the possibility of putting its slate on the ballot in forty-five states. Nixon commented, "H & C, note. This is probably what he will do with insured financial help from McGovern people." [14]

With the Wallace threat still alive, Nixon was taking no chances on the busing issue. On June 23 he signed a bill that brought about major innovations in federal aid to higher education: it provided money to colleges and universities with no strings attached, it provided for student loans and financial help from the federal government for disadvantaged youth, and it took away federal assistance from schools that discriminated against women. Nixon was unhappy with the bill, and used the signing ceremony to blast it for going too far in some areas, not far enough in others. In a later comment filmed for television, he charged that the bill "contains a wholesale retreat by the Congress from responsibility on school busing." He had wanted Congress to forbid busing of children under twelve years of age, and to turn back busing orders already in effect, but the "92d Congress has apparently determined that the better part of valor is to dump the matter into the lap of the 93d."

Then he stated his own position, in what amounted to a campaign speech: "Cross-city and cross-county busing is wrong; it is harmful to education; it does not unite races and communities; it divides them. If the Congress continues to refuse to act on the proposal I have made to solve this problem—moratorium on all busing orders—we will have no choice but to seek a constitutional amendment." [15]

Although Nixon signed the bill, and although Pat spent three hours signing autographs at a National Education Association reception in Washington ("every time she signs her name, she wins one more vote for Nixon," an aide commented), the president of the NEA blasted the Administration for doing "nothing" to support education. She said the only way to meet the educational needs of all children was with "raw political power." Nixon told Ehrlichman to "build a backfire against NEA," and asked, "What good did our signing the Higher Education Bill do with *any* of the professional educators?" [16]

McGovern bothered Nixon even more than the teachers. The senator was being described in the press as a "prairie populist." When Nixon saw a News Summary item that said McGovern "emanates decency, compassion, and old-fashioned goodness," Nixon scribbled, "H & Buchanan—*Urp*!!!" [17] Another item said McGovern was "not mean." Nixon wrote, "H & C, we must knock down this line," and "C—note—we must knock down the myth more." [18] There were at least seventeen other occasions in late June when Nixon instructed H or C or E to "knock this down." On the twenty-seventh, after McGovern had said he would take "an Ike approach to defense," i.e., hold down the cost, Nixon scribbled, "C & H—*Essential* to Knock this down." [19]

McGovern was getting to Nixon. When the President renewed his call for a moratorium on busing, McGovern charged that he was "playing on the racist emotion in this country." The President instructed Colson to "hit him for this smear." [20] McGovern compared the ongoing bombing campaign in Vietnam "to Hitler's campaign to exterminate Jews." Nixon told Buchanan to "hit this hard." [21]

Nixon struck back at McGovern. He gave Ehrlichman a set of marching orders. He told his aide to develop "savage attack lines," such as hitting McGovern for advocating amnesty for draft dodgers: "Put in there that it may cost a billion dollars just to buy enough white flags for this country." He warned against letting McGovern change his positions. As Nixon saw it, "The conservative cares about consistency. . . . Liberals have idealism, but they are pragmatic. They want to win. A conservative would rather lose than change his position." Ehrlichman should keep portraying McGovern as "a fanatical, dedicated leftist extremist." He should hang Abbie Hoffman, Jerry Rubin, and Angela Davis around McGovern's neck.

Summing up, Nixon said: "The issues are radicalism; peace-at-any-price; a second-rate United States; running down the United States; square America versus radical America."[22]

McGOVERN'S STRENGTHS included his opportunities to attack an Administration that was vulnerable on many fronts, his corps of enthusiastic volunteers, and his position as probable candidate of the majority party. Nixon's strengths included being the incumbent, his recent triumphs in foreign policy, and McGovern's apparent radicalism. This last point gave Nixon access to the big-money contributors, and thus one of his greatest advantages over McGovern was that he had almost unlimited money to spend, while McGovern had to watch every dollar.

The Nixon fund-raising effort was the most professional and effective ever seen in American politics. Maurice Stans headed it. He knew his way around with the heavy hitters, he was innovative, he was energetic, he was imaginative. When he read in *The Wall Street Journal* an article quoting a Midwestern businessman as saying, "If McGovern gets to the White House I'd probably want to go out and commit suicide," Stans went immediately to see him. He was working to save the businessman's life, Stans told him, and came away with $250,000.

Thanks to Nixon's adroit handling of the campaign reform bill, there had been a window of opportunity in March and the first week of April when campaign contributions could be made without being disclosed. Maurice Stans urged contributions during that period, and they came in cash. Altogether, $60 million was raised. Some $56 million was eventually spent; this contrasts with the previous high, Nixon's 1968 campaign, when he spent $36.5 million.[23]

Republican candidates around the country complained that Stans had sucked up all the money in the spring, so that nothing was available to them in the summer and fall. In truth, Stans sent only $1 million out to congressional candidates.[24] Nixon told Clark MacGregor, his liaison with Congress, to tell the candidates that the head of the ticket would produce a sweep of such magnitude that they would be pulled along with it. "In other words," as a disgruntled Safire remarked, "the local candidate would benefit more from not being helped financially." Further, Nixon refused to oppose any Democrat who was supporting him on Vietnam.[25] Once as partisan a politician as Harry Truman, Nixon in 1972 had decided to run independently of his party. Nowhere in his literature, or at CREEP, or in his speeches did the word "Republican" occur. This was in response to Nixon's direct orders.

• •

IN EARLY JUNE, Liddy brought to Magruder the transcripts taken from telephone conversations picked up by the bugs in the DNC. Mitchell read through them, then called for Liddy. When he appeared, Mitchell told him, "This stuff isn't worth the paper it's printed on." Liddy explained that the bug on O'Brien's phone was not working, and promised to straighten it out. Mitchell nodded.[26]

The Liddy-Hunt team of Miami-based Cubans went back to the DNC to replace the bug. There were four of them plus their leader, James McCord, chief of security for CREEP. At 2 A.M. on Saturday, June 17, in the Watergate office of the DNC, they were caught and arrested. They were carrying walkie-talkies, canisters of Mace, electronic equipment, burglar tools, and fifty-three sequentially numbered $100 bills.

Thus began the political story of the century.

The story is of such a magnitude, and so much has been written about it, that it is necessary here to outline what will and will not be attempted in this narrative, based on what sources, and guided by what assumptions and principles.

As this is a biography and not a history of the Watergate affair, the concentration will be on Richard Nixon, what he did and said and attempted, with what results. The method is taken from Samuel Johnson, who once said, "We cannot look into the hearts of men, but their actions are open to observation."

In Nixon's tumultuous four-decade-long political career, no event is so well documented as Watergate. His own account begins on page 625 of his memoirs and dominates to the virtual exclusion of everything else to the last page, 1090. Except for Mitchell, Nixon's closest aides, led by Haldeman, Ehrlichman, Magruder, and Dean, have written memoirs of varying length on their involvement. The Senate Select Committee, the House Judiciary Committee, and the two Special Prosecutors gathered documents and testimony, creating enough written material to fill entire stacks of major libraries. Investigative reporters and later historians have conducted interviews and done original research, then written enough books to fill additional stacks.

Despite this massive effort by so many able men and women, the basic documentary record of the internal workings of the Nixon Administration with regard to Watergate remains sealed. This is a result of Nixon's highly successful effort to continue the cover-up. In 1974 the 93d Congress passed the Presidential Records and Materials Preservation Act, which made the Nixon presidential papers government property and ordered the National Archives to process and open the records to scholars "at the earliest reasonable date." Nixon challenged the constitutionality of the act all the way to the Supreme Court, where he lost. After examining 1.5 million pages of Nixon documents in the White House Central Files, archivists blocked the release of more than ninety thousand documents, 6 percent of the total they reviewed, on the grounds of national security or to preserve the rights of individuals. (By comparison, the archivists blocked .5 percent of the Carter Papers, 2 percent of the Ford Papers.)

In an unprecedented action, Nixon rejected the findings of the archivists. In April 1987, less than a month before the scheduled opening of the papers, his lawyers demanded that an additional 150,000 documents be withheld. Although the National Archives protested and challenged, the documents in question did remain under seal. They consist of Nixon's own memos and written orders, Haldeman's notes of his meetings with Nixon, Colson's notes, CREEP documents, and so forth.

In addition, four thousand hours of White House tapes, although processed by the Archives (that is, national-security matters and items that would cause personal embarrassment have been removed), which is ready to release them, also remain under seal, as a result of legal objections by Nixon's lawyers.[27]

For the scholar, who never wants to commit himself to a conclusion until he has seen all the record, this is a frustrating situation.

Still, dozens of transcripts of tape recordings of Oval Office and EOB meetings, and of telephone conversations, are available. These include the highly edited versions released by Nixon himself on April 29, 1974, in response to persistent demands by the Special Prosecutor, plus more complete transcripts of those same meetings and conversations prepared by the National Archives, plus others used in the various trials of Nixon's associates. Taken altogether, they constitute a rich and unique source. They form the bedrock basis for all inquiries into Nixon's personal role in the cover-up.

As noted (see page 424), there are serious problems involved in using these tapes. Beyond tone of voice, unseen body language, garbled words, inexplicable pauses, and so on, there is a fundamental difficulty, which is simply stated: only Nixon and Haldeman knew that a tape recorder was running. By definition, this forces the scholar to suspect everything they said, to wonder if they were speaking the truth, or for the record.

A further problem: the man at the top, the President himself, while he did not know everything, knew more than anyone else. He used his knowledge to confuse his associates, and the record. On innumerable occasions, Nixon would ask questions to which it is perfectly clear he already knew the answers. Here his genuine if too often unappreciated acting ability came into play. He could pretend to an innocence that was not there, to a curiosity that he did not have, to an ignorance that hid a perfect knowledge, in a manner that was entirely convincing. He dissembled even with Haldeman, leaving his chief of staff thoroughly confused. The man who knew almost everything managed to make his subordinates believe that he knew almost nothing.

In sum, until the complete record is made available, no one can weave his or her way through the maze of lies, half-truths, innuendos, cover-ups, and deliberate attempts to obfuscate to present the full and accurate story of Richard Nixon and Watergate. What follows here, then, is by way of a preliminary report that concentrates on what is known and avoids speculation, with the emphasis on Nixon's own words and deeds.

NIXON WAS in Key Biscayne on Sunday morning, June 18, when he read about the arrests at the Watergate. In his memoirs, he claims that his first reaction was "It sounded preposterous," and that he "dismissed it as some sort of prank."[28] Later that morning, on the telephone, he expressed similar sentiments to Haldeman: "It has to be some crazies over at CRP, Bob," the President said. "That's what it was. And what does it matter? The American people will see it for what it was: a political prank. Hell, they can't take a break-in at the *DNC seriously*. There's nothing there." Nixon also told Haldeman to "get it as confused as possible." Further, he wanted Colson kept away from the press, and from him: "Don't let him give me any details."[29]

The following day, Nixon scribbled some comments on a press briefing memo prepared by Pat Buchanan. The memo noted that Ziegler had characterized the break-in as a "third-rate burglary." Nixon wrote: "He understated. *Attempt* at burglary. Bizarre business," and "There was no involvement whatever by W H personnel."

Thus did the cover-up begin, and to this day those words constitute Nixon's basic defense: *he* knew nothing about it and he could not for the life of him figure out *why* anyone would want to break into the DNC.

In a lifetime of bold and brazen acts, this was the boldest and most brazen, as well as the most successful. A decade and a half later, Nixon's query still dominated discussion and investigation of Watergate. Why break into the DNC? Who on earth ordered such a fool thing?

That students, scholars, and the general public continue to ask these questions, as if they were legitimate, as if there were some unsolved mystery here, constitutes a triumph for Nixon. He had been after Larry O'Brien ever since the 1960 campaign; by 1972 he was obsessed with O'Brien, and what he might know about the Nixon-Hughes relationship; O'Brien, the most outspoken of the Democrats (except for McGovern), was at the top of his list of enemies; tapping telephones was standard operating procedure for Nixon; any information picked up from the DNC, such as who was contributing money, or campaign plans, and the like, would be invaluable to Nixon.

Nixon wanted O'Brien so badly that some seven weeks after the break-in, when it was obviously dangerous for Nixon to continue to go after him, the President nevertheless was still at it. On August 9, he ordered Haldeman to use the IRS to embarrass O'Brien, whose name had popped up in an IRS investigation of the Hughes Tool Company. Nixon told Haldeman that Connally had informed him that the DNC had $9 million in unpaid bills after the 1968 Humphrey campaign, that these bills had been paid, and that it appeared that Hughes had done the paying. It was certain that O'Brien had been on the Hughes payroll. There is "some real pay dirt" here, Nixon said, and he wanted it "put out" at once.

There was something else. Nixon had made some money for himself by selling property he had invested in around Key Biscayne, land he had purchased at a bargain price from Bebe Rebozo. Evidently Hughes had some involvement in this operation, and Nixon was afraid O'Brien knew about the whole scheme. When Haldeman was trying to piece together the puzzle of who ordered the break-in and why, he had a discussion with Jeb Magruder. Haldeman's handwritten notes begin: "Plan hatched here—Hunt, Liddy & Cols[on]. Cols[on] called Jeb twice—to get going on this thing. Specifically L. O'Brien info re Fla dlgs." [30]

Yet Nixon pretended, at the time and ever since, that he could not for the life of him understand why his people bugged the DNC.

Nixon argued that even the most sophomoric political operative would know that if you were going to place a bug, you would place it on the candidate, not the DNC chairman. Ergo, none of the sophisticated men in the White House, much less the President himself, could have been involved, because no bug was placed on McGovern. This argument, too, remains alive. It ignores the simple fact that Liddy and Hunt did try to bug McGovern, but failed.

Another Nixon defense that relies on the public's short and faulty memory is this oft-posed question: Why should Nixon take chances when he *knew* he was a sure-thing winner in the 1972 election? That question also ignores some obvious points. Liddy got the go-ahead on Gemstone in February 1972, at a time when Muskie was leading Nixon in the polls. This was pre-Peking. Wallace was still a major factor. The first break-in at the DNC took place while Nixon was in Moscow, before he knew if the summit would be a success or not. Nixon's huge lead in the polls did not come until mid-July, after McGovern's nomination. At a comparable time in the 1968 campaign, Nixon had enjoyed a huge lead over Humphrey. He almost got beaten anyway. Nixon had been ahead of Kennedy in the early stages of the 1960 campaign, and ahead of Pat Brown in the 1962 campaign. To sum up, in the spring of 1972 Nixon was by no means a certain winner, and he wanted every edge he could get.

"To this day," Haldeman said at a 1987 conference at Hofstra University, "no one knows who ordered the break-in." That too remains a fundamental defense of Nixon and his associates. They have thrown out all sorts of dark possibilities: that it was a CIA and JCS operation designed to undercut the author of détente, that the Democrats themselves set it up, and so forth. The strength of the argument lies in the fact that to date no one has uncovered a memo that says, "Break into the Watergate and bug Larry O'Brien," signed "Richard Nixon."

Despite the millions of dollars and hours that have been spent trying to prove who ordered the break-in, no clear-cut legal answer has been found. No one has gone to jail for ordering the break-in (they have gone to jail for participating in it, or attempting to cover up). But John Dean had no doubts; he gave his version to Haldeman in a telephone conversation on March 27, 1973. Haldeman's notes on that conversation read: "Jeb [Magruder] believes whole Liddy plan was put together by us before presented [to Mitchell]. Dean cooked this up—probly at H[aldeman] instruc. (the idea of a super intell operation). M[itchell] bought it—was accomp fact in Dec when Liddy arrived at Comm[ittee to Re-elect]. Cols[on] got into act—pushing to do something.

"Final step: G[ordon] S[trachan] [an aide to Haldeman] called Mag[ruder]. H[aldeman] told him get this going & P[resident] wanted it. Mag[ruder] told M[itchell] this—& M[itchell] signed off on it. M[itchell] called Liddy in & read riot act re poor qual. of stuff they were getting."

It is this author's opinion that John Mitchell ordered the break-in, and that his principal agent was Jeb Magruder, whose operatives in turn were the men hired by Chuck Colson, Liddy and Hunt. All these men were responding to unrelenting pressure from Nixon to find out what O'Brien knew.

On Monday, June 19, after assuring Haldeman that this was a minor affair that would quickly blow over, nothing to worry about,

Nixon began frantically telephoning Colson. What was said is unknown, but the President was so upset he threw an ashtray across the room. Then Nixon flew up to Washington on *Air Force One*, accompanied by Haldeman. When Haldeman brought up the Watergate arrest, Nixon shrugged. "Silly damn thing," he said. He struck Haldeman as "calm, cool, even amused." Haldeman later reflected, "What an effort that facade must have cost him."[31]

The following morning, June 20, Howard Hunt's name surfaced (it was in the address books of two of the burglars). He was identified as one of the planners of the Bay of Pigs (code name Eduardo) and the apparent head of the burglary team. His connection with the White House and CREEP was not noted. Hunt himself had disappeared.

This development immediately brings to the fore another supposed Watergate mystery. Why did not Nixon just admit that his people had attempted to bug the DNC and got caught? Could he not have accepted the responsibility, defended himself by pointing out that Kennedy and Johnson regularly bugged their political opponents, apologized, and with that be done with Watergate?

Despite the persistence with which that question is asked, that option did not exist. In such a politically charged atmosphere, no judge was going to accept the claim that this was just a boys-will-be-boys prank, and even the most cursory examination into the break-in would have led to the whole Liddy-Hunt operation, thus to the Plumbers, thus to the break-in at Dr. Fielding's office in the Ellsberg affair, thus to all the other black-bag operations. The cover-up had to cover not only the Watergate break-in, but all the other illegal activities. To admit to one could lead to all.

On June 20, the DNC filed a $1 million suit against CREEP for invasion of privacy and violation of civil rights. If that case came to trial before the election, the Democrats could call as witnesses and depose under oath the leading figures at CREEP and on the White House staff. They would have to answer questions about Liddy and Hunt, where they came from, who they worked for, what they did. It was imperative for Nixon to delay the trial.

Complicating everything, the previous day the Supreme Court had rejected in a unanimous opinion written by Nixon-appointee Justice Powell the Justice Department claim of inherent power to wiretap without warrant domestic groups suspected of being subversive as a reasonable exercise of the President's power to protect national security. Justice Rehnquist had recused himself, because he had ordered some of the taps when he was in the Justice Department; Nixon's other appointees, Burger and Blackmun, had joined Powell in voting against the government.

Nixon's enemies were on the offensive. At 11:30 A.M. on June

10, Nixon met with Haldeman (whose assistants were already going through the files, removing and destroying documents that might be subject to subpoena in the DNC suit) to plan his response. His instinctive reaction was to counterattack.

After covering some routine matters with Haldeman, the President turned to the Watergate problem. Exactly what he said is unknown, because when the tape recording of the conversation was forced into the open by the Special Prosecutor, it had an eighteen-and-one-half-minute gap on it. The gap covered the period in which Watergate was discussed. Why that gap occurred cannot be said (it is unique; in no other tape is there such a gap).* People suspected Nixon, but he insisted he was innocent, and no proof has ever been produced.

Haldeman's notes of the meeting do exist. For the period of the gap, they read, in full: "be sure EOB office is *thoroughly* ckd re bugs at all times—etc.

"what is our counter-attack? PR offensive to top this—hit the opposition with their activities.

"Pt out libertarians have created public [illegible] do they justify this less than stealing Pentagon papers, Anderson files, etc [?]

"we shld be on the attack—for diversion

"what is sched on SFR [Senate Foreign Relations] SALT hearings?

"go to Calif. on Fri—w/PN—

"Julie come out later

"PN not to the shower." [33]

So Nixon's first response was to shore up his own defenses by making certain that *he* was not being bugged. The FBI regularly swept his offices to find hidden microphones; Alexander Butterfield, Haldeman's aide who directed the taping system, knew when the agents were coming, and somehow he managed to hide Nixon's own microphones.

---

* Al Haig said the tape had been erased by "some sinister force." Rose Mary Woods said she did it, accidentally; this generated considerable skepticism, because of her known unquestioning loyalty to Nixon and because of her known efficiency. Haldeman speculates that when the existence of the tapes was revealed, Nixon set out to destroy the evidence. He began by listening to the first recorded conversation he had on Watergate and erasing the eighteen and one-half minutes. But, still according to Haldeman, he botched the job, due to his ineptness with anything mechanical. And he quickly realized that it would take years of concentrated, full-time effort to erase everything about Watergate, so he gave it up.[32] This seems reasonable, but it is not conclusive. Still, the only people who had access to the tapes were Nixon, Haldeman, Butterfield, and Woods, and somebody erased the eighteen and one-half minutes.

Next, Nixon launched his counterattack. The objective was to show that bugging was an ordinary part of the political process; the method was to prove that the Democrats, and others, used the same techniques. To Colson, on the afternoon of June 20, Nixon sardonically suggested that he get someone to make a speech urging that the Watergate break-in crew be given a Pulitzer Prize.[34]

The previous day, McGovern had made a thrust: he called the break-in "shocking" and charged that it was the "legacy of years of snooping" by Mitchell and his subordinates. Nixon's counterthrust, scribbled on his News Summary, was: "Buchanan —Haven't there been some other break ins in political and govt'l offices [?]," and "C & B, Where were these cries of anguish when the *Times* & Anderson got prizes for Pentagon Papers and other gov't documents?"[35]

Complications ensued. Nixon could not trust his own troops, so he could not share with them his own plans or knowledge, either about his activities or what information the enemy had or might uncover. He had compartmentalized power and knowledge. As Ehrlichman put it, the top people in the Nixon White House were "unaware of what Nixon was ordering our colleagues to do."[36]

At 4:35 P.M. on June 20, Nixon met again with Haldeman.

He asked if Mitchell knew anything about this business.

To that improbable, indeed absurd, question, Haldeman answered, "No."

Then Nixon, playing the perfect innocent, asked Haldeman to tell him what had happened, and why. Haldeman gave a rambling answer that emphasized the Cuban connection. Nixon seized on the idea of passing off the break-in as something the burglars thought up themselves. Their motive, he suggested, was fear of a possible McGovern/Castro connection. That line, he suggested, would protect the White House from the political impact of disclosing CREEP's involvement, and it would help the counterattack, by drawing attention to the Cubans' fear of McGovern's naive policy toward Castro.[37]

That evening, Nixon called Mitchell. The dissembling continued, as Mitchell described himself as chagrined and embarrassed, and indicated that the whole thing came as a "complete surprise to him." This from the man who had approved Gemstone, had read the transcripts from the bug on Oliver's phone, and told Liddy to do better!

Next Nixon called Haldeman. He returned to his idea as to how to handle the PR. Nixon suggested that he would call Rebozo and have him get the Cubans in Miami to start a public bail fund for their arrested countrymen "and make a big media issue out of it." The President thought he could use the issue to revive the Democrats' inept handling of the Bay of Pigs. He said it might even be that he could "make Watergate work in our favor." Meanwhile, he said, "those people who got caught are going to need money. I've been thinking about how to do it." [38]

Nixon ended his day, at about 11:30 P.M. in his EOB office, with a diary entry. The last line read, "I felt better today than I have really for months—relaxed and yet able to do more work than even we usually do with far more enthusiasm." [39]

The following morning, June 21, Nixon met with Haldeman and Ehrlichman. They discussed, at length, how to maintain the cover-up. In so doing, they set a pattern for numerous future discussions, as they desperately sought some way to escape. They were like three men in a lifeboat, in the middle of the Atlantic, with a storm on the horizon, without paddles, a motor, or a sail, no food or water, discussing their options.

Ehrlichman had an idea. He would get Liddy to confess. Liddy would give as his motive a desire to be a big shot at CREEP. The three conspirators grew enthusiastic. Liddy's confession would cut off the Democrats' civil suit, it would divert the press and political attack, it would bring an end to the FBI investigation.

Haldeman made his contribution: once Liddy confessed, he said, the Republicans could make an appeal for compassion on the basis that he was a misguided zealot who had read too many spy stories.

Nixon was all for it, until he wondered, What if Liddy implicated Mitchell? That gave Haldeman pause; despite his negative answer the previous day, he now said he thought Mitchell might have been involved. So did Ehrlichman.

Still unwilling to give up the plan, Nixon said that taking a rap was common enough. Haldeman added that they could take financial care of Liddy. Nixon agreed; he said he was "willing to help with money for someone who had thought he was helping me win the election."

That still left the problem of Mitchell, plus another: What about Colson? Nixon expressed concern that because Colson had hired Hunt and Liddy, it could all come back to Colson. He asked Haldeman if he thought Colson was involved. Haldeman said that he was convinced that Colson was not, but he pointed to another danger, that Colson certainly was guilty of setting in motion other illegal activities carried out by Hunt and Liddy.

It was all very frustrating. Hunt and Liddy could not be thrown to the wolves because they knew too much. To attempt to pin it on either Colson or Mitchell brought the whole thing too close to the

Oval Office. In his frustration at being blocked at every turn, Nixon indulged himself in some righteous indignation; he complained that the Democrats had been doing this kind of thing for years and "*they* never got caught." The President suggested "that every time the Democrats accuse us of bugging we should charge that we were being bugged and maybe even plant a bug and find it ourselves!"

That afternoon, Nixon talked to Colson. "We didn't know a goddamn thing about it," Nixon said of Watergate. Colson said he certainly knew nothing about it, and volunteered that he could not believe that his friend Howard Hunt had had anything to do with it.[40]

By June 21, in short, the basic pattern of lies, deceit, and deception, even to one another, along with pointless discussions of nonexistent options, was established.

It continued at the Nixon-Haldeman meeting the next morning. Haldeman had good news: the FBI had no case on Howard Hunt. Nixon and Haldeman knew Hunt had been at the scene of the crime, but the FBI did not and had no warrant out on him. More good news: the FBI had been unable to trace the $100 bills. Further, the Cuban story was holding. The FBI thought the motive for the break-in was Castro. Haldeman observed that because of what Nixon and his top assistants knew about what had been done by Hunt and Liddy, they tended to read too much into what the press, FBI, and the Democrats had on them. They really had nothing to fear. He did suggest that Liddy join Hunt in hiding, even leave the country.[41]

That afternoon, June 22, Nixon held a news conference. There was but one question on Watergate. O'Brien had charged that the people caught in his office had a direct link to the White House. Was this true?

Nixon answered that both Ziegler and Mitchell had already responded in great detail to the charge. They had denied it. He went on: "This kind of activity, as Mr. Ziegler has indicated, has no place whatever in our electoral process or in our governmental process. And, as Mr. Ziegler has stated, the White House has had no involvement whatever in this particular incident." Nixon said the matter was under investigation by the proper authorities and thus he would not comment further. The news conference went on to questions about food prices and the defense budget.[42]

On June 23, at 10:04 A.M., Nixon and Haldeman met in the Oval Office. Haldeman's good news of the previous day had turned sour—it developed that the FBI had been able to trace the money right back to CREEP. Haldeman complained that "the FBI is not under control, because [Acting Director L. Patrick] Gray doesn't exactly know how to control them." But he had a new plan to propose. John Dean had cooked it up. Haldeman thought "we're set up beautifully to do it . . . to have [Vernon] Walters [deputy director of the CIA] call Pat Gray and just say, 'Stay the hell out of this . . . this is ah, business here we don't want you to go any further on it.' . . . That would take care of it."

Did Gray not want to do this? Nixon asked.

"Pat does want to," Haldeman answered. "He doesn't know how to, and he doesn't have any basis for doing. Given this [plan] he will then have the basis."

Nixon liked the idea of stopping the FBI operation in its tracks. "All right," he said. "Fine."

To carry out the plan, Haldeman passed on Dean's idea that he and Ehrlichman call in Walters and Richard Helms, the head of the CIA, and tell them to tell Gray to back off, because the FBI was getting into a CIA operation.

That suited Nixon, who thought it should work, because "we protected Helms from one hell of a lot of things." He felt Helms could be blackmailed into cooperating, because of Hunt's previous connections with the CIA. Exposing Hunt would "uncover a lot of things. You open that scab there's a hell of a lot of things . . . This involves these Cubans, Hunt, and a lot of hanky-panky."

Then Nixon asked, for the fourth time, in a tone of voice that conveyed innocence, curiosity, and befuddlement, "Well what the hell, did Mitchell know about this thing to any much of a degree?"

Haldeman thought he did not know the details.

"Well who was the asshole that did?" demanded the President. "Is it Liddy? Is that the fellow? He must be a little nuts."

"He is," said Haldeman.

"I mean he just isn't well screwed on, is he? Isn't that the problem?"

He was under pressure, Haldeman explained.

"Pressure from Mitchell?"

"Apparently."

Nixon asked a question. It is garbled on the tape and cannot be understood.

"Gemstone, yeah," Haldeman replied.

"All right, fine, I understand it all. We won't second-guess Mitchell and the rest. Thank God it wasn't Colson."

Haldeman said the FBI had interviewed Colson yesterday, and Colson convinced the agents that "it is a CIA thing, so the CIA turnoff will play."

"Good deal," said the President. "Play it tough. That's the way they play it and that's the way we are going to play it." To get started, Nixon told Haldeman what to say to Walters and Helms: "Don't lie to them to the extent to say there is no involvement, but just say this is sort of a comedy of errors, bizarre, without getting into it, [say] 'the President believes that it is going to open the whole Bay of Pigs thing up again. . . .' They should call the FBI in and say that we wish for the country, don't go any further into this case, period!" [43]

Haldeman and Ehrlichman met that afternoon with Walters and Helms. They discovered that Gray had already called Helms to say, "I think we've run right into the middle of a CIA covert operation," to which Helms had replied, "Nothing, nothing we've got at this point." Gray had answered, "Sure looks to me like that's what we got."

At the afternoon meeting, Haldeman told Helms that the problem was the FBI investigation would track back to the Bay of Pigs. He mentioned Hunt. Helms finally got the picture and said he would be happy to be helpful, but he wished to know the reason. Haldeman hemmed and hawed. Finally it was left at this: Walters would see Gray. When Haldeman so informed Nixon, the President sighed with relief. As he later wrote, he felt "this was the end of our worries about Watergate." [44]

Not quite.

Over the next few days, Nixon asked Haldeman repeatedly whether he thought Mitchell was involved. Meanwhile, John Dean had the Secret Service break into Hunt's safe in his White House office and remove the documents, which included faked cables linking the Kennedy Administration to Diem's assassination, papers related to various Gemstone activities, and items about the Plumbers. Dean gave the documents to Gray for destruction, telling him they were "political dynamite." On July 3, Gray—who when appointed had been told by Nixon to keep the FBI out of political matters—burned the files.

Magruder, meanwhile, acting under Mitchell's direct orders (Mitchell vehemently denied the accusation), had burned the entire Gemstone file. [45]

On June 30, Nixon learned about Hunt's safe, and that FBI agents were looking for Hunt, who was still in hiding. Annoyed, he asked Haldeman why the FBI was continuing the investigation. Haldeman said that Gray did not know how to follow through, that the U.S. Attorney's office at the Justice Department was pushing hard, making it difficult for the FBI to limit the investigation.

Nixon had an easy solution to that one: he told Haldeman to send Walters to see the Justice Department officials and tell them what he had told Gray, to back off.

Nixon asked again, for the sixth or seventh time, whether Mitchell knew in advance of Liddy's bugging plans. Not specifically, said Haldeman, but there was a further problem; it turned out Liddy had worked for Ehrlichman in the White House. Still, there was good news: Liddy was prepared to take the rap. He would write a "scenario" that would tie together all the loose ends and take full responsibility and say that no one higher up had authorized it. Nixon wished that the Cuban angle could be maintained, but told Haldeman to cut the losses and "get the damn thing done." As for Liddy, Haldeman said that the White House had access to funds—in Bebe Rebozo's safe, much of it contributed in cash by Howard Hughes—that could be used to take care of Liddy's family. If Liddy got a long sentence, the President could wait a discreet interval after the election and then pardon him. Nixon agreed.[46]

Meanwhile Mitchell's wife, Martha, was raising hell. Long since a celebrity in Washington, by far the most colorful of the wives of the leaders of the Administration, outspoken and highly quotable, she had had it with Nixon and his cohorts. She told her husband to either give up politics or her.

Nixon wrote later, "I considered John Mitchell to be one of my few close personal friends."[47] Listening to Nixon-Mitchell conversations on the tapes, this author gets the sense that Mitchell was the dominant personality in the relationship, that Nixon was even afraid of Mitchell, certainly afraid to argue with him or to cross him. On June 26 Nixon had told Haldeman, who had suggested that the only way to put an end to Watergate was to blame and then sacrifice Mitchell, "I won't do that to him. To hell with it. I'd rather lose the election."

On June 30, in the EOB, Nixon had lunch with Mitchell, who was obviously worn out, not only because of his wife's activities but because of all the time and effort he had put into defending the Justice Department in the ITT case. His hands were shaking. Mitchell said he was going to resign, because of Martha.

That afternoon, Nixon named Clark MacGregor, former Minnesota congressman, to replace Mitchell at CREEP, with Fred Malek from the White House staff as his assistant. "We'll clean that son of a bitch up," Nixon told Haldeman, "and we'll run this campaign."[48]

Nixon never did dare ask Mitchell if he was involved in the break-in. Nor did he ever put the blame directly on Mitchell. But he did find a convenient scapegoat. He wrote in his diary at the time something he repeated on a number of occasions after his retirement: "Without Martha, I am sure that the Watergate thing would never have happened."[49]

If not for Martha, or so Nixon's logic suggests, Mitchell would have been paying attention to business, and he would have . . . What? Resisted the pressure from Nixon via Haldeman and Colson to find out what O'Brien knew? Told Liddy to forget about Gemstone? Told Magruder to read the newspapers if he wanted to know what O'Brien was up to? Personally supervised the break-ins, to make certain nothing went wrong? Convinced Nixon that victory was a sure thing, so that it was unnecessary to spend CREEP's money on intelligence? To ask such questions is to answer them, and demonstrates how unjust and self-serving it was for Nixon to blame Martha (and thus Mitchell) for Watergate.

It was not the break-in that got Nixon into trouble. Had it been an isolated incident, it would have caused a scandal, but not a disaster. Besides, Nixon was well protected; no one has ever proved that he ordered it, or knew in advance about the tactics Liddy and Hunt would use to get information on O'Brien. Nixon's trouble came because the cover-up had to cover so much more than Watergate, and that was a consequence of a whole series of illegal activities over four years that all traced back to the White House. What made Watergate what it became was not the break-in, but the cover-up. And the one who instigated the cover-up, and tried desperately to maintain it for more than two years, was Richard Nixon. As his own words and actions show beyond doubt, he started the cover-up within minutes of reading about the arrest of the burglars. He planned it, supervised it, insisted upon it. Martha was uninvolved. The truth is that without Nixon, the Watergate thing would never have happened.

On July 1, Nixon flew to California for a two-and-a-half-week stay. He worked hard, concentrating on politics. As was his habit, he used his scribbled comments on the News Summaries to hand down orders and to set themes. When he read that McGovern had said he would end the war within ninety days of his inauguration, Nixon wrote, "C—He should be hammered—why *wait* 'till then? He delays end of war until *after* election." [50]

Nixon set out to undercut McGovern by presenting himself as the peace candidate, while simultaneously continuing and vigorously defending the ongoing bombing campaign against Hanoi. At a news conference just before leaving for California, he announced that peace talks would resume on July 13 and that negotiations would continue through the campaign season. Reporters later got Ziegler to confirm that the date had been selected by Nixon; it coincided with the climax of the Democratic Convention in Miami. Cynics noted that the negotiations "might disarm some of the doves who wished to engage him in political debate on the war," while his promise to continue the air offensive should the negotiations fail or flounder would please the hawks.[51]

Although Nixon wanted to concentrate on foreign-policy issues insofar as possible—almost daily he reminded his aides that the economy was the enemy's issue—he did all he could, which was considerable, to reduce inflation and unemployment. Along with such traditional methods as speeding up government spending projects, just before flying to California he signed a bill that increased Social Security benefits by 20 percent. It would become effective on September 1, so that checks mailed in early October to 27.8 million Americans would include the increase. The payroll taxes to finance the increase would not take effect until January 1, 1973.

Events were working for him. The economy was on an upswing; such major indices of productive activity as industrial output, retail sales, and nonfarm employment were pointing toward rapid and sustained economic expansion. The business reporters were using the word "boom." Nixon said that he expected, by the end of 1972, to reach a goal of 5 percent unemployment and 2.5 percent inflation.[52]

When he got to California, Nixon was upset to read that Citibank, which had just raised its prime rate to 5.25 percent a week earlier, had announced another raise, to 5.375 percent. He moved immediately: "Schulz [sic]—pass to Dr. Burns—I expect him to raise hell about this. If he doesn't I shall."[53]

There were areas in which Nixon refused to spend. One was public broadcasting. He vetoed a Democratic bill that provided two years of increased support for the Corporation for Public Broadcasting. Walter Cronkite, on CBS-TV, accused him of trying to place "a direct muzzle" on PBS. Nixon commented, "Z—Ridiculous. RN doesn't see or hear it. He only has time to follow networks."[54]

His conviction that the media were out to get him remained solid, indeed increased, as Colson, Buchanan, and others fed him tidbits designed to goad him. On July 7 Colson gave the President a long analysis of network coverage of the campaign. All three networks were judged guilty of bias in McGovern's favor and against Nixon's Vietnam policy, with ABC-TV being the worst. Nixon wrote on the memo, "H & E—a *very* important analysis. Required reading for those hold outs on our staff who think that bias against us is 'unintentional.' "[55]

Even more irritating to the President was the way the reporters were starting to ask leading and potentially embarrassing questions about the use of taxpayers' money to pay for improvements at his residences in San Clemente and Key Biscayne. Taken altogether, the sum was said to be $17 million, which at first glance looked like an outrageous amount. But by far the bulk of the money was spent to create Western and Southern White Houses; it included such items as helicopter pads, boat-docking facilities, road improvements, obviously necessary security measures, communication facilities, and the like. Not even the most anti-Nixon reporter could make much of a story out of those expenditures.

But the General Services Administration had spent money directly on Nixon's houses and grounds, $701,000 at San Clemente and $575,000 at Key Biscayne.[56] That did raise questions, but as Wallace Turner wrote in a *New York Times* piece, the GSA refused to answer them. Turner did some investigating and reported that Nixon's San Clemente neighbors were "suspicious about Mr. Nixon's property being benefited by permanent improvements financed from the Federal treasury." They pointed to the replacement of the tennis courts with a swimming pool and the building of gazebos and a gatehouse.[57]

That Nixon was fudging, that he was getting the government to pay for improvements that had nothing to do with security and that he should have paid for himself, is clear, but it is equally clear that no sharp distinction was possible and that the reporters were indulging in innuendo in their stories. For example, when Nixon complained that the fireplace at San Clemente did not draw well, Herb Kalmbach, Nixon's on-site representative at the Western White House, arranged to install a small exhaust fan in the chimney at a cost of $388.78. Kalmbach sent the bill to the GSA with instructions to pay it. GSA balked. Kalmbach's secretary then wrote GSA to say that the improvement certainly was linked to security; "How would [GSA] like it if you know who was asphyxiated?" GSA paid.[58]

FOR ALL OF Nixon's anger at the newspaper and television reporters in July of 1972, they were actually doing him the greatest possible service by concentrating on McGovern, Vietnam, and the financing of his home improvements while all but ignoring the Watergate story. It was not that there were no new developments, or even that they went unreported, but they were buried deep in the newspapers or received only passing mention on the television news programs. O'Brien sent Nixon two telegrams demanding the appointment of a special prosecutor for the case; the story appeared on July 4 at the end of an account of the search for Howard Hunt, and gave more space to Ziegler's reply (that had rejected the demand on the grounds that the FBI was conducting a thorough investigation) than to O'Brien's telegrams.[59]

Another story that got only passing mention on page 21 of *The*

New York Times and none in most other papers, even though it was one of the keys to the entire re-election effort, was a July 10 CREEP request to the U.S. District Court in Washington to postpone until after November 7 hearings in the Democrats' lawsuit for the Watergate break-in. CREEP argued that pre-election hearings could deter Nixon campaign workers, discourage campaign contributions, and force disclosure of confidential campaign information. CREEP also asserted that McCord's employment was but "coincidental." [60]

The court granted the delay. Watergate, in short, was being successfully contained. Colson's private polls showed that it was having no impact on the public perception of Nixon.

That did not mean Nixon had nothing to worry about. The cover-up had to hold through the Justice Department investigation, the FBI investigation, a grand jury proceeding, the trial of the burglars, and the Democrats' lawsuit, and because it was based on various fictions—the Cuban/Castro connection, McCord's "incidental" relationship to CREEP, the claim that Liddy was acting on his own, and so forth—that would not be easy.

On July 6, Nixon got a call from Pat Gray that crumbled his first line of defense. Gray said that he had just talked to Walters, who had told him that the CIA had no interest in the break-in and that pursuing the investigation would not be an embarrassment to the CIA.

Gray went on: "Walters and I feel that people on your staff are trying to mortally wound you by using the CIA and FBI and by confusing the questions of CIA interest in, or not in, people the FBI wishes to interview."

Nixon, the man who had ordered the CIA to tell the FBI to stay out of it, hardly skipped a beat. "Pat," he said to Gray, "you just continue to conduct your aggressive and thorough investigation," and hung up. [61]

That evening, Nixon made a diary entry. After blaming misguided but well-intentioned "subordinates" for the break-in, he continued, "In any event, as I emphasized to Ehrlichman and Haldeman, we must do nothing to indicate to Pat Gray or to the CIA that the White House is trying to suppress the investigation. On the other hand, we must cooperate with the investigation all the way along the line." [62]

Following the Gray phone call, Nixon's new line was full cooperation. The next morning, July 7, he met with Ehrlichman. "Gray and Walters must tell people that there is no effort to cover up either by the White House or the Committee to Re-elect," he said. "A cover-up is the worst thing; cover-up is how I nailed Truman [in the Hiss case]. It can hurt deeply." [63]

The next afternoon, walking along the beach, the two men returned to the subject. "We can't even *appear* to have a cover-up of anything," Nixon said. "Not a whiff of it." He began spinning out what his spokesmen should say: "The President said, 'Do it fully; let the chips fall where they may. There is to be no cover-up.' No one in the White House is involved. Our own investigation is completed, and that's the finding." Ehrlichman wondered what investigation he was talking about, as there was none going on, much less "completed."

Nixon brought up the subject of clemency for Hunt, explaining that Colson was concerned "about what Hunt might do . . . He's wondering about offering Hunt immunity in return for his silence."

Ehrlichman was aghast. "You simply can't let anyone talk to you about clemency," he said. "A conversation like that will bring it all into your lap."

But Nixon would not let it go. He argued that worse criminals had been pardoned (and that night, in his diary, Nixon wrote: "Everyone agrees that this incident was so clumsily handled that it probably doesn't deserve the criminal penalty that such incidents would ordinarily bring." In other words, because Hunt, Liddy, and their hired hands had screwed it up so badly, they did not deserve to be punished).

Ehrlichman advised the President, "Don't even think about it," at least not until after the election.[64]

Ehrlichman told Nixon that Magruder was in trouble, that he would have to testify and since he was the one who gave the direct orders to Liddy to break in and place the bug, he would probably have to take the Fifth Amendment to avoid incriminating himself. Nixon thought Magruder should voluntarily divulge what he had done and take the responsibility.[65]

Instead, Magruder went to work on concocting a story that would leave the responsibility with Liddy. His partner in putting it together was John Mitchell, who after resigning as head of CREEP had established his law office just across the hall from CREEP at 1701 Pennsylvania Avenue. What had to be explained away was the money; CREEP had given Liddy $199,000 in cash for Gemstone. The story Magruder made up was that $100,000 had gone for a surrogate protection program: ten young men had been paid $1,000 a month for ten months to infiltrate radical groups. The remainder had gone to provide security for the Republican Convention, and to investigate Jack Anderson, Democratic contributions, and so on. No one at CREEP had known that Liddy used some of the money to break in at the Watergate.[66]

Someone, perhaps Mitchell, perhaps Dean (who participated in making up the story), kept the President informed. One afternoon Dean came to Magruder's office. "Jeb," he said, "the President is very pleased with the way you've handled things. You can be sure that if you're indicted you'll be taken care of."[67]

Still, Nixon expressed the wish that Magruder resign from CREEP before he was indicted. Haldeman told the President there was a good chance Magruder's story would hold, and that there would be no indictment. The main thing, Nixon said, was that "Mitchell come out clean." He told Haldeman that whatever the actual case, "Magruder simply had to draw the line on anything that might involve Mitchell."[68]

In mid-July, one month after the break-in, the cover-up was in place and holding. Although the attempt to cut it off with McCord and the Cubans had failed, Nixon believed that Magruder's willingness to perjure himself before Justice Department proscecutors and a grand jury would cut it off with Liddy. Mitchell would not be touched. Magruder's story would explain away CREEP's money. Although Nixon had been unable to mount an effective counterattack, and although his outer lines of defense had crumbled with the demise of the Cuban angle and the refusal of the CIA to cooperate, his main line of defense was solid—no one in the White House was involved, CREEP's involvement was incidental, it was a bizarre business. Best and most important of all, no new information was likely to come out before November 7.

But because containment of the story rested on a pack of lies and a series of illegal actions by the President and his aides, because Nixon had constructed his defense on a scaffold so intricate that the slightest puff of wind could bring the entire edifice tumbling down, he had put himself in an exceedingly vulnerable position. He had refused to come forward with information at his disposal, for example, that Hunt was at the scene of the crime. His aides, acting under Mitchell's direct orders, had destroyed evidence; Pat Gray had burned the contents of Hunt's White House safe, Jeb Magruder had burned the Gemstone file, other documents had been shredded.

Nixon had actively attempted to obstruct justice by ordering the CIA to lie to the FBI and by buying the silence of the guilty through offers of clemency and financial support. In his public statements—that he had ordered a vigorous FBI investigation and that he had ordered an internal White House investigation that proved no one on his staff was involved—he had lied. He had also lied in private, to Haldeman, Ehrlichman, and Colson.

Eisenhower had once told Nixon that he had "learned a long time ago" that when you got caught, "don't try to be cute or cover up. If you do, you will get so entangled you won't know what you're doing." Nixon knew that was good advice; as he had reminded his aides on a number of occasions in the past month, Truman's at-tempt to cover up for Hiss had just made things worse.

But what choice did Nixon have? If McCord talked, he would reveal Liddy; if Liddy talked, he would reveal the Plumbers and Hunt's activities and Magruder; if Magruder talked, he might bring up Mitchell and Gemstone; if Mitchell talked, he might reveal Colson and the President. Nixon's only choice, short of telling the truth and then announcing that he would not seek re-election, was to cover up.

His great weakness was that he could not control Congress or the courts. His great piece of luck was timing. The arrest at the Watergate came too late for the Democrats to launch any full-scale congressional inquiries into the affair, using the power of subpoena and the threat of a perjury charge (techniques Nixon had used so well in 1948 in the Hiss case) to force Haldeman, Colson, Mitchell, Magruder, Ehrlichman, et al. to testify. The DNC civil suit had been contained until after the election. Grand jury proceedings were secret, and the burglars could avoid testifying by pleading guilty in return for private presidential promises of financial sup-port and ultimate clemency.

He could not control the press, and as he liked to say, there were so many reporters out there who wanted a Pulitzer Prize that it was almost impossible to cover up a scandal, and he believed, more or less correctly, that many of them would love nothing more than to bring Richard Nixon down.

Yet in this case, the press proved to be his invaluable ally. After the initial furor, the Watergate story not only failed to make the headlines, it did not even make the front pages. There were some obvious reasons for this development: hard news was difficult to come by; the business did seem bizarre; the President's reassur-ances were convincing because they made sense; not even the most crusted reporter could believe that Nixon would tell out-and-out lies; the media had been to some extent cowed by the Nixon Administration's assault on its objectivity and threats about license renewals; and there was so much else going on, such as bombing in Vietnam, peace negotiations, the aftermath of the China open-ing, SALT, détente, and most of all the disarray in the Democratic Party.*

---

* During the period Nixon was in California, the Washington *Post* carried three minor stories on the break-in, all concerning legal motions and pro-ceedings. It carried not one editorial or column on the event. In the first month following the break-in, *Time* and *Newsweek* each carried only a

In mid-July, that last was the big news, as the Democrats gathered in Miami to nominate George McGovern on a peace platform. To that event the President, like everyone else, turned his attention.

---

one-page report on the arrest of the burglars, *Time* in its section on "Politics," *Newsweek* under the heading "Capers."

CHAPTER TWENTY-FIVE

THE CONVENTIONS
July–August 1972

WATCHING THE 1972 Democratic National Convention on television from his living room at La Casa Pacifica gave Nixon great pleasure. By contrast, for many of the Democratic Party's professionals, also watching on television—because they had been excluded as a result of the McGovern reforms in the delegate selection process—viewing the proceedings gave them great pain. Amateurs had stolen their party. The delegates put on a show that almost seemed at times to have been scripted by Nixon. The speeches were too long and too strident and too negative. The Democrats gave an appearance of being anti-religion and pro-drugs, anti-profit and pro-welfare, anti-family and pro-abortion, anti-farmer and pro–migrant worker, anti-Saigon and pro-Hanoi, anti–armed forces and pro–draft dodgers. Delegates booed Hubert Humphrey; they booed the few times Johnson's name was mentioned; some were heard to cheer Ho Chi Minh.

The convention was the high-water mark of the New Left's participation in national politics. For the New Left, and for the Democratic Party, it was a disaster. The Democrats had not looked so bad, nor been in such disarray, since 1968. Which was a point worth noting; the professionals had run the 1968 convention in Chicago, and they had botched it almost as badly as did the amateurs in Miami in 1972.

The Democrats' catastrophe climaxed on July 12 and 13, with McGovern's nomination and his selection of Senator Thomas Eagleton of Missouri as his running mate. This was followed by an extraordinarily undisciplined scene, as thirty-nine additional vice-presidential candidates were nominated, including Mao Tse-tung and Martha Mitchell. McGovern did not get to give his acceptance speech until 2:30 A.M., July 14. Nixon was not impressed. He called Haldeman when McGovern finished and they agreed that the Democrats had nominated the wrong man. Teddy Kennedy would have been a much stronger candidate; so would Humphrey.

Nixon was moved by the sight of Humphrey, who looked dejected as the cameras panned his face. In a generous gesture, Nixon wrote Humphrey by hand to remind him of Churchill's response when his wife tried to console him after his election loss in 1945 by saying it might have been a blessing in disguise. Churchill had answered, "If this is a blessing it is certainly *very* well disguised." Nixon saluted Humphrey as a "gallant warrior," and concluded, "As friendly opponents in the political arena I hope we can both serve our parties in a way that will best serve the nation." [1]

The Democratic debacle, and McGovern's nomination, made Nixon exuberant. The best thing about it was that the Democrats themselves had turned back Humphrey and Kennedy and repudiated Johnson, which made it possible for Nixon to reach out to the millions of disgruntled Democrats and all but assured his re-election. It also set his strategy, which was to concentrate on attacking McGovern personally while shunning any mention of the Democratic Party.

"Avoid 'Republican' everywhere," Nixon instructed Haldeman four days after the convention. "Direct whole campaign to defecting Dems and Inds." In a meeting with Senator Hugh Scott, Haldeman, and Ehrlichman, the President ordered his people to never use the words "Republican" and "Democrat." "Don't blame the Democrats," he said. "Call them McGovernites." [2]

Nixon wanted not only to win, but to surpass Johnson's 1964 landslide and win by the biggest margin ever, thereby creating a "New Majority." He did not mean by that a Republican majority; he wanted a mandate that would make it possible for him to dictate to a Congress controlled by a coalition of Republicans and conservative, anti-McGovern Democrats. With that coalition, he intended to implement his "New American Revolution"—welfare reform, revenue sharing, reorganization of the government, and détente first of all. In 1972 America's most partisan politician since Harry Truman thus became the one least interested in party and most concerned about personality.

Immediately after the Democratic Convention, Nixon began to mount an all-out attack on McGovern, on the man himself as well as the issues on which McGovern was most vulnerable with mainstream Democrats, especially legalizing marijuana, busing, abortion, amnesty, and defense cuts. On July 17, he told Haldeman to concentrate on these issues, and to constantly use the word "dangerous." McGovern was dangerous to "our security, our economy, our way of life."[3]

In Nixon's view, his major obstacle in depicting McGovern as a radical was a fawning, liberal press. He told Haldeman that McGovern's "*great* advantage over Goldwater in '64" was that the press would not paint McGovern as an extremist.[4] When *Life* magazine expressed the hope that McGovern could make his campaign come alive, Nixon noted, "C—This is the fervent wish of the press."[5] The President anticipated the worst; when *Newsweek* cited columns by Reston, Braden, Joseph Kraft, and others attacking McGovern and noted, "If anything, the coverage of the McGovern campaign so far has demonstrated unmistakably that the press is beholden to no one," Nixon commented, "C & H—only an attempt to justify the vicious attacks they will make on us."[6]

ABC-TV reported that McGovern was "getting a hard look from the press." "H—This is crap," Nixon responded. "M's press is very good, ours is still lousy."[7]

Nixon expected McGovern to cultivate the press and the public by modifying his positions on issues. In the President's view, oft expressed, conservatives would rather be right than be victorious, but liberals would abandon principle for victory. As he put it in his diary a day or so after the convention, "The radicals of the left want power. They will compromise on issues in order to get power, recognizing that when they get power they can do what they want on the issues."[8] Nixon therefore instructed his aides to never let up on McGovern, to make him responsible for all his prenomination statements.

Nixon put his people to work on researching McGovern's positions. Shortly after McGovern's nomination, Kissinger gave Nixon a four-page, single-spaced memorandum on McGovern's defense proposals. Kissinger's analysis showed that the budgetary savings that would result from a full implementation of the McGovern cuts would not be $32 billion, as McGovern claimed, but only $15 billion. That was not what Nixon wanted to hear; he scribbled on Kissinger's memo, "(1) *Always* treat it as a $30 billion cut (2) *Then* point out what a cut of that magnitude would do."[9]

Along with defense, Nixon wanted to go hard after McGovern on amnesty. He had Ray Price prepare an analysis of Lincoln's amnesty policy; Price found that Lincoln had commuted the sentences of deserters who had been condemned to death and granted pardons to deserters who returned to their units. Price also noted that in 1947 Truman had pardoned 1,523 men who had evaded the draft in World War II, and commented that he thought Truman's approach "is much closer to what we'll actually end up doing." Nixon underlined that sentence and wrote, "E—*Never!*" He also complained, "This is a very weak memo from Price," and pointed out that Lincoln offered amnesty to deserters who went to Canada "*on condition* that they serve in prison for the time they were out of the country." [10]

Nixon told a news conference, "Those who chose to desert the United States or to break the law by dodging the draft have to pay the penalty . . . before they can obtain amnesty or pardon or whatever you want to call it. . . . The other side [McGovern] does not share that view. I say: Pay a penalty; others paid with their lives." [11]

Nixon saw in McGovern everything he despised. In his initial strategy session with Haldeman, Nixon said he wanted his supporters to always emphasize the differences between the candidates, concentrating on one point: the election offered "the clearest choice in a century," because it pitted the "strong vs. the weak." [12]

Nixon felt so intensely about the difference that he proposed using his own name in a negative way. In a hand-drawn design, he suggested a bumper sticker that would read, "NIXon McGovern." [13]

On July 25, Nixon got an incredible break. At a news conference, Senator Eagleton admitted that a story just revealed by Jack Anderson was true: he had undergone electroshock therapy for depression. McGovern's immediate reaction was that he would nevertheless keep Eagleton on the ticket. Nixon's immediate reaction was different; he told Connally that "McGovern would give him [Eagleton] four or five days and then have his major newspapers call for him to resign and then have him replaced by the national committee." [14]

To Nixon's surprise, the next day McGovern said he was behind Eagleton "1000 percent." To Nixon this was "a sign of a weak man or a very tricky one." [15] He wisely avoided any public comment as McGovern and the Democrats went through agony. When Senator Lowell Weicker (R., Conn.) praised Eagleton as a senator who was "sensitive to other people's problems and possessed of a keen ability to solve them," Nixon commented, "H—Can't our people just shut up for once?" [16]

The following week, as the controversy over Eagleton's mental health swelled, McGovern realized that unless he did something that issue would dominate the campaign. He therefore asked for Eagleton's resignation. [17] McGovern's hesitation to act made Nixon contemptuous of his opponent. "This tells us a hell of a lot about McGovern," Nixon wrote in his diary. "The main test of a man is whether he has the character to make tough decisions and then to lead his associates to follow him on those decisions." [18]

McGovern asked a number of prominent Democrats to take Eagleton's place, including Teddy Kennedy, Edmund Muskie, and Hubert Humphrey, only to be rebuffed. Finally Kennedy's brother-in-law and former Peace Corps director Sargent Shriver agreed to join the ticket. Nixon was contemptuous of Shriver too. "Destroy him," the President told Haldeman as they discussed the best way to deal with Shriver. "Kill him." McGovern-Shriver, said Nixon, was "a double-edged hoax." [19]

IN HIS PURSUIT of a New Majority, Nixon went after traditional Democratic voting blocs, including Jews, white southerners, organized labor, ethnic groups (especially those upset by busing), and small farmers. The ones he ignored were blacks, welfare recipients, left-wingers generally, social workers, teachers, and state and federal bureaucrats.

When Israel opened its first telecommunications ground station toward the end of July, Nixon made a highly publicized call to Prime Minister Golda Meir. In the course of a folksy conversation, the President pledged to protect "the integrity of Israel," and Mrs. Meir recalled the hours she had spent in the Oval Office. "I must say," she commented, "I always came out with the right answers." [20]

Nixon could threaten as well as promise. The president of the American Jewish Congress urged fellow Jewish leaders to remain neutral in the campaign, because both parties supported Israel and sympathized with Soviet Jews. Nixon commented, "C—our Israeli friends should be coldly told they can't have it both ways!" [21]

That same week, Nixon made a major production out of the signing of a bill extending federal crop insurance to farmers under twenty-one years of age. He invited television cameras, and 125 young farmers, to the East Room for the ceremony and delivered a stirring tribute to the capacity of youth "to build a better America." [22]

On July 8, Agriculture Secretary Earl Butz signed a three-year agreement with the Soviets. They agreed to purchase $750 million worth of grain in that period. It turned out that the Soviets had already been quietly making contracts with the American exporting companies, buying up grain at bargain prices and in wholly unexpected quantities. By early August they had already bought $1 billion in corn, wheat, and soybeans. This brought charges, never proved and probably untrue, of insider trading and other scandals. It also brought the largest farm export year in American history, raised grain prices substantially on the eve of the election, encouraged farmers to plan to put more land into production in 1973, and reduced government costs in the loan and storage programs. Taken altogether, the grain deal was a major plus for Nixon.[23]

Republicans in Congress had been pushing antistrike legislation, but in late July the President withdrew his support. Ziegler gave a convoluted explanation that was so absurd the White House reporters burst out in laughter. Nixon read about the incident and noted, "E & H—a phony issue—Washington libs care about it— Not the country."[24]

Ehrlichman prepared an "Economic Good News Kit" that went out to thousands of speakers and supporters. It claimed that the Nixon Administration had cut inflation from 6.1 percent to 2.7 percent, improved the GNP from a growth rate of 3.4 percent to 6.3 percent, increased real earnings from zero to 4 percent per year, and had done all this while reducing federal income taxes by 20 percent. "Fine job," Nixon told Ehrlichman.[25]

With all that good news, and with McGovern's unique ability to offend the power brokers in the Democratic Party, it was no surprise that organized labor decided to give its old enemy Dick Nixon a free ride in 1972, or even support him. On July 17 Nixon's favorite union, the Teamsters, endorsed him. He invited the Teamster president, Frank Fitzsimmons, and his board to San Clemente. Nixon told them that when the chips were down, at the time of the Cambodian invasion and during the mining of Haiphong harbor, businessmen, the media, members of the Cabinet, and most politicians were reluctant to stand with him, but he found that labor leaders "were really tough and strong in the crunch when the interests of the country were involved."[26]

Nixon frequently expressed such sentiments. In a diary entry later in the campaign, after a meeting with some hard hats in New York City, he wrote: "The American leader class has really had it in terms of their ability to lead. It's really sickening to have to receive them at the White House as I often do and to hear them whine and whimper and that's one of the reasons why I enjoy very much more receiving labor leaders . . . who still have character and guts and a bit of patriotism." He claimed to have more in common with labor leaders "than does McGovern or the intellectuals generally. They like labor as a mass. I like them individually."[27]

Perhaps that was true, but if it was, Nixon had managed to keep it hidden for decades. He had got his start in politics bashing organized labor; he had built his reputation before the Hiss case by managing the Taft-Hartley bill, anathema to labor, on the House floor; except for Jimmy Hoffa, Fitzsimmons, and a few other Teamsters, he had never spent any time with labor leaders or said a good word about them.

Especially not George Meany, the biggest labor leader of them all. Nixon and Meany had feuded for years; their antagonism had reached a climax in 1971, when Nixon imposed his wage freeze and Meany insulted him at the AFL-CIO convention. But in the summer of 1972, following McGovern's nomination, that changed. On July 19 the AFL-CIO executive council adjourned without endorsing McGovern. For Nixon, it was "a moment to ponder and savor." On July 28, he invited Meany to join him, Bill Rogers, and George Shultz for a game of golf at Burning Tree. After that improbable foursome finished, the men sat on the porch at the club, sipping drinks and smoking cigars. Meany told Nixon that McGovern was going to lose by a landslide and that the AFL-CIO was not going to waste any money on his campaign. He also said that he would not vote for Nixon, but he would not vote for McGovern either. His wife, he admitted, was going to vote for Nixon. But, he added, "Just so you don't get a swelled head . . . I want to tell you why—she don't like McGovern." [28]

Frank Rizzo, boss of the Democratic machine in Philadelphia and mayor of the city, was another defector from his party's ranks. He met secretly with Ehrlichman, Bud Krogh, and Nixon's friend Walter Annenberg, and predicted that Nixon would lose Philadelphia by not more than fifty thousand to seventy-five thousand votes. Ehrlichman assured Nixon, "We are continuing to devise ways of pumping money into Philadelphia." Nixon commented, "Good— go all out." [29]

Nixon was also putting money into Chicago, where the mayor was appropriately appreciative. When Pat made a visit to the city, Daley joined her on the platform. She told her friend Helene Drown, "Daley was friendly. He joked and told me to give his regards to my husband and that he has great admiration for him. When we were on the stands, some of Daley's henchmen came up and right in front of him said that Daley had given them permission to split their votes on election day . . . So if I can believe anything, at least they're not going to try to steal votes from us like they always have." [30]

One Democratic leader whose support for Nixon was no secret was John Connally. Nixon's admiration for Connally, already great in 1971, had grown to the point of adulation after Connally advised him to go ahead with the bombing of Hanoi and the mining of Haiphong and predicted that Brezhnev would not cancel the summit. By the summer of 1972, Nixon believed that Connally "was the only man in either party who clearly had the potential to be a great President." He talked to Haldeman about replacing Agnew with Connally on the 1972 ticket; he talked to Mitchell, telling him bluntly that he thought Connally should be his successor in 1976 and that he wanted to give him a head start by making him the running mate. He also discussed the proposition with Connally. All three men told him what was obvious, that Agnew had wide support in the Republican Party, so it would be a mistake to dump Agnew for the Democratic Connally.[31]

Connally instead went to work as chairman of Democrats for Nixon. He put his enthusiasm, his political skills, his money, and lots of other people's money into the task. Nixon sought and took his advice. When Colson sent in a long list of prominent Democrats he felt Nixon ought to personally call on the telephone, Nixon scribbled on the list, "If Connally wants calls made, I shall do so. Return to me with whatever calls Connally believes I should make."[32]

One call Connally urged Nixon to make was to Lyndon Johnson. Not to ask his support—that was unthinkable—but to seek his neutrality when Democrats inquired about the former President's attitude toward Connally's group. Nixon made the call. Johnson assured him that although he was going to support the Democratic ticket at all levels, he was telling his friends that "what an individual does in a presidential campaign is a matter of conscience, and I'm not going to interfere with that decision."

Later, Johnson gave Nixon some advice, via Billy Graham. "Ignore McGovern . . . but stay above the campaign, like I did with Goldwater. . . . And don't worry. The McGovern people are going to defeat themselves."

Graham asked Johnson what he thought of the Watergate business. Johnson laughed and said, "Hell, that's not going to hurt him a bit."[33]

So the two men generally acknowledged to be the greatest living political experts in the country agreed on how to run the campaign, and on the effect of Watergate.

With leading Democrats and labor leaders all but rushing into his arms, and the Eagleton affair further weakening the already badly damaged McGovern campaign, Nixon had to do some searching to find anything to worry about. There remained, however, one potentially grave problem, a Wallace third-party candidacy. Wallace was in a wheelchair, his recovery from the gunshot wound was slow, he had further operations to face, but he remained as feisty and thus as dangerous as ever. He had denounced the Democratic Party for nominating McGovern and was keeping his options open.

Nixon wanted Wallace's issue, busing, but not a Wallace candidacy. A week after the Democratic Convention, he moved on both fronts. On July 19 Nixon read an account of a Detroit case; a judge had ordered a stay on the purchase of 295 school buses. An attorney for the Detroit NAACP noted, "There's not enough time left to get the buses, and without the buses, there's no desegregation." Although this development meant no busing in Detroit that fall, Nixon was unhappy. He commented, "E—it looks like they are getting off the hook—We must have the issue *alive* in October —or it will not help us."[34]

The next day, Nixon read a memorandum that said it was possible the House Rules Committee would vote for Nixon's moratorium bill. The President wrote on the memo, "E—Maybe it is best *not* to get this. Then we will have the issue." The bill stayed buried in committee.[35]

That same day, Nixon met with Colson, Haldeman, and Billy Graham to discuss ways to keep Wallace out of the race. Colson said he had met with Wallace representatives to discuss issues and money. Wallace's people told him they were authorized to "cut a deal." They did not want to get into the money angle in any specific way, but they did want assurances on busing. Nixon, who wanted the issue more than he wanted to stop busing, was ready to give all the assurances they wanted.

Graham said he had talked to Wallace the previous day, after the governor came out of an operation. Wallace had assured him there was almost no chance that he would run. He did ask Graham whether he would take more votes from Nixon or McGovern if he did run; Graham replied that three out of four Wallace voters would otherwise go to Nixon. Wallace swore that he would never turn one hand to help McGovern.[36]

On July 25, Nixon sent Connally to make a deal. "Go down there and see him," Nixon instructed Connally, "and let me know what he wants." Connally reported by telephone: "All he really wants from you is to be sure that his message on the issues was heard." Wallace added that he would announce in a day or so that he definitely was not going to run. Connally told Colson, "We might well say that this was the day the election was won."

Nixon called Wallace to thank him. He had Haldeman send the movie *Sunrise at Campobello* to Wallace. He began looking into the possibility of getting a salt-water swimming pool for Wallace. He told Wallace that Connally was his closest political adviser and was available to Wallace at any time that he wanted to talk. He sent Al Haig down to Alabama to give Wallace foreign-policy briefings.[37] Anything he could do for Wallace, he was ready to do.

• •

ON AUGUST 3, he read that antiwar leader David Dellinger had urged a gathering of young men at Harvard to go to Miami in order to demonstrate at the Republican Convention. Nixon put out an order: "H & C—Be sure McG signs are plentiful with these people." [38] Senator McGovern was trying to encourage the press to make an issue of the Watergate break-in by stressing it continually in his speeches. In early August, McGovern charged that the incident was "the kind of thing you expect under a person like Hitler," and he demanded that Nixon's personal involvement in the affair be examined. Nixon wrote in his diary, "McGovern is striking out more wildly now, trying to say that I was indirectly responsible for the bugging of the Democratic headquarters." [39]

Nixon was also angry over Democratic attempts to make an issue about the anonymous campaign contributions CREEP had received before April 7. He wanted to counterattack, using the IRS as his weapon. There was an element of revenge involved; in 1952 IRS bureaucrats had leaked his tax returns to Drew Pearson, and Bobby Kennedy had launched an all-out audit on him in 1962. He believed most IRS agents were Democrats, which made him furious; he further believed that Republicans hesitated to use the IRS for political purposes, which left him frustrated. In his view, Republican efforts on those lines were "tentative and feeble and amateurish in comparison to the Democrats'." [40]

On August 3, Nixon told Haldeman and Ehrlichman he wanted IRS information on the Democrats. He found it "ironic that when we were out of office they really used to crucify us—now that we are in office they still do, due to the fact that the bureaucrats at the lower level are all with them."

As Nixon saw it, the problem was "that all of our people are gun-shy as a result of the Watergate incident and don't want to look into files that involve Democrats." Haldeman assured him that "after the election we really could then take the steps to get loyalists in various positions that were sensitive." [41]

Nixon did not want to wait. He "repeatedly urged" his aides to have IRS checks made on McGovern's staff and contributors. Most of all, he still wanted O'Brien. Even though going after O'Brien was clearly playing with fire, Nixon ordered Haldeman and Ehrlichman to get the IRS to conduct a full audit on O'Brien's tax returns. He hoped that the audit would establish that O'Brien had not reported or paid taxes on his retainer from Howard Hughes, although he was realistic enough to comment, "I would be very surprised if he [O'Brien] would have allowed himself to get in such a box." Evidently O'Brien did report the income; the IRS audit cleared him. [42]

Nixon's aides were getting better cooperation from the Justice Department and the FBI. Federal prosecutors in the Watergate investigation kept John Dean informed about witnesses to be called before the grand jury, and what they would be asked, information that was especially valuable with regard to Magruder, as it gave Mitchell and Dean time to prepare Magruder with his story about how Liddy spent $199,000. Dean asked Attorney General Kleindienst for copies of the confidential FBI reports on the investigation; when Kleindienst refused, Dean got eighty-two of the reports from Pat Gray.[43]

The break-in, meanwhile, remained a nonstory in the newspapers and on the evening television news. There was a flurry in late July when Walter Rugaber reported in *The New York Times* that "sources involved in the investigation" had revealed that Bernard Baker, one of the burglars and a former CIA agent, had made fifteen telephone calls to Liddy's office at CREEP between March and mid-June. But Liddy had been dismissed from CREEP and refused to answer FBI questions, and the sources told Rugaber that the investigation had been unable to establish a motive for the break-in. Thus it remained a "bizarre incident" and made no headlines.[44] At a July 27 news conference, Nixon was not asked a single question about Watergate.

What did make headlines was Nixon's announcement on July 22 that he had selected Agnew as his running mate. Conservative Republicans applauded, but Nixon immediately had cause to wish he had been able to pick Connally. At a Cabinet meeting on July 21, Nixon had given explicit orders to never use the words "Democrat" or "Republican" in the campaign, but in an evening speech in Oregon the next day, Agnew tore into the Democrats, by name. Nixon noted on the press report, "H—he seems to have taken our counsel about 50%!"[45]

IF AGNEW AND WATERGATE were minor problems for Nixon, Vietnam was a major one. The NVA ground offensive, though blunted and reduced, continued; the American air offensive continued; the ARVN counterattacks had failed to retake Quang Tri or relieve An Loc. Hanoi launched a propaganda campaign, charging that the U.S. Air Force was deliberately bombing the intricate dike system in North Vietnam in an effort to flood the countryside. A Swedish television film crew seemed to prove the charges with footage shown on the American networks. Former Attorney General Ramsey Clark joined the Swedes and said he saw with his own eyes where dikes had been bombed. He called for an end to the attacks. Senator Kennedy declared himself to be shocked by the revelations. When Clark returned to the States, Kennedy had him testify before a Senate committee on the good treatment American POWs were receiving in their camps.

As there was not a word of truth in the charges or the claim, Nixon was naturally incensed. He expressed his anger on his News Summary reports. "Haig—This sounds like a fix," he wrote on a description of civilian casualties. "Why not demand they [the North Vietnamese] let impartial foreign press in." On another, "K—See if we can discredit this,"[46] He made the most effective rebuttal himself, at his July 27 news conference. After calling attention to the civilian casualties inflicted by the NVA in its offensive, and to the hundreds of thousands made homeless by that offensive, he pointed out the obvious—that if the United States wanted to destroy the dike system of North Vietnam, it could do so in less than a day. A few dikes may have been hit accidentally, but the policy was to avoid them, even when the NVA put SAMs on them. As commander in chief, his orders to Air Force pilots were "to avoid civilian damage."

Nixon went on to give a ringing defense of the Air Force pilots. "We get the idea they are a bunch of savage flyboys, and they love to get down and machine-gun innocent little civilians and all the rest." But the truth was, from the top brass in the Pentagon to the pilots in Vietnam, the military did not want to bomb civilian targets. "They believe it would be counterproductive, and second, they believe it is not necessary. It might shorten the war, but it would leave a legacy of hatred throughout that part of the world from which we might never recover. So our military have not advocated bombing the dikes; they are doing their best to carry out the policy we want of hitting military targets only."[47]

The extreme charges from Clark, Kennedy, and others, which bordered on calling Nixon a war criminal, along with McGovern's comparisons of Nixon with Hitler, were unfair and unwise. They were also a reflection of the agony of the doves, who by the summer of 1972 had come to a point where they could not believe one word Dick Nixon said, and who feared that the war would go on for four more years. In their frustration, they were ready to do anything to take away Nixon's war-making power, even to the point of emasculating his role as commander in chief and subverting his power to conduct foreign policy.

In mid-July, Senator Cooper offered an amendment that called for total U.S. withdrawal if negotiations failed to end the war in four months. Unlike earlier versions, this one did not require North Vietnam to free the POWs as a condition. Nixon was aghast: "K— Good God! What does *this* do?"[48] The amendment passed the Senate by five votes, but only after a POW condition was added to it. Despite that small victory, it was clear that the Nixon Administration would soon face a crisis; Congress was on the verge of cutting off all funds to carry on the war.

Nixon was operating against a deadline. To forestall it, he appealed privately to the congressional leaders with a heartfelt letter. He pointed out that "End the War" amendments deprived him of any negotiating flexibility. "I recognize that there are differing views on how best to bring about the end to this war," he wrote, "but I am also conscious that the responsibility for doing so is above all mine, and I intend to carry out this obligation in a responsible way."[49]

In public, he was more impassioned. At his July 27 news conference, he warned that ending the war by simply walking away would result in a bloodbath in South Vietnam, "with perhaps at least a million marked for assassination. . . . That would be the height of immorality." He said the Senate had sent a message to Hanoi: "Don't negotiate with the present Administration; wait for us; we will give you what you want—South Vietnam." He charged that "those who say 'End the War' really should name their resolution 'Prolong the War,' " because "the chance for a negotiated settlement is better now than it has ever been." He expressed the hope that he could end the war before the election.[50]

Nixon slowed, but could not stop, the end-the-war movement in Congress. He did manage to persuade a majority of the public. Polls showed strong support for his basic position, that the United States would never agree to turn over the government in Saigon to the Communists, and that American forces would remain in action in Vietnam until the POWs came home.

But the polls showed something else too. Although they indicated that Nixon had a huge lead in his race with McGovern, and solid backing for his Vietnam policy, they also indicated that the voters were going to elect a Congress controlled in both branches by Democratic doves. It seemed almost certain that the first act of the new Congress coming to power in January 1973 would be to cut all funds for the war.

The mystery of how the American people could adopt such a split position highlights another mystery in the 1972 campaign: why did not Nixon do something about this situation? He was going to win, almost no matter what, but there was a big difference between winning and governing. To carry out his policies, he had to have the support of Congress; to get that, he had to have more Republicans than Democrats at the swearing-in ceremonies in January. Nixon told his aides, and Republican candidates, that a big win over McGovern would give him a mandate so powerful that Congress would be incapable of resisting him. That was a profound misjudgment, and a surprising one, coming from a man who had spent most of his adult life in Washington.

To Nixon, Congress—controlled by the Democrats for most of his lifetime—was an irritant, even an enemy, never a partner. Although he had begun his career in Congress, in his heart he was contemptuous of it as an institution, and he had little liking for most of its members. So he acted in 1972 as if the only election that counted was for the Presidency. The figures speak for themselves: of the $60 million Stans raised, only $1 million, about 1.5 percent of the total, went to Republican congressional candidates.

Of course, Nixon hoped to have the war over with before January, perhaps even before the election, and that accomplishment, combined with an overwhelming electoral mandate, could make it possible for him to rule free of restraint.

KISSINGER WAS RETURNING to Paris for more talks with Le Duc Tho. Although Hanoi was finally ready to compromise, because of the toll taken by the bombing, because of the failure of its go-for-broke spring offensive to overthrow the Thieu government, and because Nixon's triangular diplomacy threatened to lead to a Chinese and Russian withdrawal of support, the Communists were not ready to accede to all of Nixon's demands. Kissinger had already indicated that the United States would stop the bombing and withdraw its troops while allowing the NVA to stay in South Vietnam and the Vietcong to retain its gains, but the United States was not prepared to give the Provisional Revolutionary Government (PRG) a share in the government of South Vietnam, much less to overthrow Thieu. Le Duc Tho was prepared to yield on the last point, but he insisted on a role for the PRG.

Nixon was ambiguous about the negotiation process. "Henry," he had told Kissinger in the spring, "you tell those sons of bitches that the President is a madman and you don't know how to deal with him. Once re-elected I'll be a mad bomber."[51] By the summer, Kissinger believed, Nixon had become "convinced that he had narrowed McGovern's support to a far-out liberal fringe that would oppose him regardless of what he did on Vietnam. On the other hand, settling . . . might well put at risk his support among conservative groups whom he considered his base. Nixon saw no possibility of progress until *after* the election and probably did not even desire it."[52]

Still, there was pressure for peace, even beyond the doves in Congress. Budgetary realities, for example; Laird wanted to reduce the cost of Vietnam by withdrawing ninety-eight B-52s and three squadrons of F-4s. Without peace, Nixon would not be able to reduce taxes in his second term, or implement his welfare reform, or have any spare revenue to share with the states, or be able to concentrate on a major reorganization of the government. A continuation of the war would put his whole New American Revolution in jeopardy.

Other factors contributed to the confusion over negotiations. Although Kissinger assured Nixon that Thieu was being kept fully informed and was agreeable to compromise, Nixon had good reason to doubt that Thieu would accept a settlement that left large parts of his country in the hands of his enemies while giving them a share in governing the rest. Kissinger and Nixon also disagreed over timing; in Kissinger's view, Hanoi was up against a deadline, Election Day in the United States. He believed that the best chance for wringing concessions out of the Communists was to do it before November 7. Nixon was not so sure; he believed that his mandate would free him to carry out additional acts of war, at least in the period between the election and the start of the new Congress in January, which would force the enemy to accept his dictates.

Disagreements aside, the negotiations had to continue, for a variety of reasons. They provided Nixon with his best excuse for refusing to debate McGovern; they held out hope for peace and thus could be used to undercut the doves; they were necessary to finding out how far Hanoi and Saigon were willing to go to reach an accord. So, in late July, Kissinger set off for Paris. "I proceeded to the negotiations," he wrote, "with Nixon's acquiescence, if not his enthusiasm."[53]

The conflicting attitudes showed most clearly in Kissinger's report on his August 14 meeting with Le Duc Tho, and Nixon's marginal comments on it. Kissinger wrote, "We have gotten closer to a negotiated settlement than ever before; our negotiating record is becoming impeccable; and we still have a chance to make an honorable peace." Nixon commented: "Al—It is obvious that no progress was made and that none can be expected." Nixon said he was discouraged, and pointed out that "we have reached the stage where the mere *fact* of private talks helps us very little—if at all. We can soon expect the opposition to begin to make that point." Indeed, McGovern was already doing so, heaping scorn on the talks. Nixon feared that "disillusionment about K's talks *could* be harmful politically—particularly in view of the fact that [Kissinger's scheduled] Saigon trip, regardless of how we downplay it, may raise expectations."

Nixon concluded with a point that he regarded as basic: "What we need most now is a P.R. game plan . . ."[54]

To that end, the White House made a series of announcements in the two weeks before the Republican Convention. On August 12, Ziegler told the press that the last American ground combat troops had left Vietnam. A week later, Nixon said that in July 1973 the United States would be able to end the draft and go to an all-volunteer force. A few days later, he announced the withdrawal of twelve thousand men from Vietnam, leaving a residual force of twenty-seven thousand. And on August 22, en route to Miami for the convention, Nixon told Stewart Alsop, a *Newsweek* columnist, "I'm sure of one thing. The war will be over. The war won't be holding over us in a second term."[55]

But PR could not end the war. To achieve that, three things had to happen. The North Vietnamese had to abandon their most basic demand, that the Thieu government be removed; by August 1972 that appeared possible. The United States had to agree to allow the NVA to remain in South Vietnam, and to accept a cease-fire in Vietnam but not Cambodia and Laos; that too seemed possible. And Thieu had to accept the American concessions; that appeared unlikely, if not impossible.

On August 17, Kissinger went to Saigon to persuade Thieu to agree to compromise. The meetings did not go well. As Ambassador Bunker told Kissinger, Thieu was feeling strong, even cocky, as a result of the relative failure of the NVA spring offensive. Vietnamization had worked too well. The South Vietnamese President insisted on mutual withdrawal, and he would not accept Kissinger's proposed Committee of National Reconciliation that would oversee elections because it gave equal status to the PRG and the GVN.

In Yogi Berra's classic line, it was *déjà vu* all over again. Back in 1953, when Eisenhower was working for an armistice in Korea, it was South Korean President Syngman Rhee, not the Chinese, who refused to compromise. In 1972, once again it was the leader of a small Asian nation the United States had come to help who was blocking American efforts to make peace.

In 1953, Eisenhower had pressured Rhee to accept an armistice by threatening to withdraw support if he did not. Ike also promised Rhee that if he cooperated, the United States would guarantee South Korea's security. Nixon had been Ike's emissary. In 1972, Kissinger threatened Thieu: "I'm going to talk to Le Duc Tho again in Paris. This is the position you will agree to."[56] But Nixon was rather more inclined to side with Thieu than with Kissinger. Further, he was willing to consider an option that Ike had rejected, a drastic and dramatic escalation in the war. Kissinger wanted an agreement before the election; Nixon preferred to wait. He believed he could get better terms after he received his mandate and was thus free to become the mad bomber.

Meanwhile, Nixon gave Thieu reassurance. In an end-of-August letter, he assured Thieu "personally and emphatically, of the bedrock of the U.S. position." Nixon wrote, "The United States has not persevered all this way, at the sacrifice of so many American lives, to reverse course in the last few months of 1972. We will not do now what we have refused to do in the preceding three and a half years. The American people know that the United States cannot purchase peace or honor or redeem its sacrifices at the price of deserting a brave ally. This I cannot do and will never do."[57]

So Thieu received conflicting signals from the American President and his National Security Adviser. This reflected the ambiguity of the American position, and of Nixon himself. Kissinger knew what he wanted to do, but Nixon was not sure. On the eve of the Republican Convention, he did not know whether he wanted to rush into an agreement before the election, or be the mad bomber afterward, whether he wanted to join Kissinger in forcing on the GVN a less-than-satisfactory agreement, or to join Thieu in defiance.

IN OTHER AREAS of foreign policy, in the summer of 1972, Nixon was doing better. In July, he had a spectacular success, one that was a pure gift. President Anwar al-Sadat of Egypt expelled twenty thousand Soviet military advisers and technicians. This came as a complete surprise to the American government, which had done nothing to bring it about and never dreamed it was possible. It was nevertheless highly welcome and a major Cold War triumph.

In another part of the Middle East, the United States was more active. The day after the Moscow summit, Kissinger and Nixon had met with the Shah of Iran in Teheran. Although they had just signed the "Basic Principles of Relations" with the Soviets, which called for restraint and promised to eschew "efforts to obtain unilateral advantage," and although American policy in the postwar years had been to restrain the arms race in the Middle East, they promised the Shah virtually unlimited access to the products of the American arms industry. That meant, in effect, that the Shah could use his oil profits to build his armed forces. In the succeeding years, he did so at wholly unprecedented rates. In practice, this made Iran America's closest ally in the region.

In addition, Nixon agreed to give covert support to the Shah's allies in Iraq, the rebellious Kurds. Iraq had just signed a treaty of friendship and cooperation with the Soviet Union. The Shah persuaded Nixon to support the Kurdish rebellion with arms and other aid. In August, without consulting the CIA oversight committee, or the CIA director, or the Secretary of State, or the NSC, Nixon implemented the policy. Israel too supported the Kurds in order to tie down the Iraqis.[58]

Throughout 1972, Nixon also provided secret support to Allende's enemies in Chile in an effort to "destabilize" the government.

Simultaneously, Nixon continued triangular diplomacy. Kissinger made another secret trip to China. The grain deal with the Soviets went through. There was progress on granting the Soviet Union a Most Favored Nation trading status, and on holding a European security conference and opening negotiations on mutual and balanced force reductions (MBFR) in Central Europe. At the same time, the American and Soviet arms buildups, all but dictated by the SALT agreement, continued.

Taken altogether, Nixon had launched an activist foreign policy that went far beyond anything undertaken by his predecessors. It was often contradictory, and in some cases it violated Nixon's pledges in the Basic Principles of Relations, as well as the underlying principles of détente, but it certainly signaled that America was on the move, and it held out great promise for the "New Era" Nixon intended to establish in his second term.

PAT NIXON was an enthusiastic supporter of her husband's foreign policy, and he wanted the public to know it. Although she was willing enough to make trips and appearances at various women's and Republican gatherings, she disliked making speeches and disliked even more holding news conferences. But Nixon knew how valuable to him she was, and he insisted. On August 8, she agreed to hold a preconvention news conference. She was nervous before it began, but she did her usual excellent job.

For Nixon, the best moment came when a reporter asked his wife to comment on a charge Jane Fonda had recently made over Hanoi radio, that dikes had been "bombed on purpose" by the U.S. Air Force. Pat indignantly denied it and added, "I think she should have been in Hanoi asking them to stop their aggression. Then there wouldn't be any conflict. I'd have had her go over there and beg on bended knees."

Asked how she would define the campaign, she said she saw it as one that pitted "accomplishment against a promise." Then she made a promise; given four more years, her husband would top his trips to Peking and Moscow.

Would Chou En-lai come to Washington? "Well, that's it,'" she said, laughing. "We've got to be in the White House or he won't come." She refused to comment on Eagleton's health, but pointed out that her husband had been hospitalized only twice in the past quarter century, once with a knee injury during the 1960 campaign and earlier with a broken elbow when he was a congressman.[59]

The following morning, Rose Mary Woods sent a memo to Nixon. She said she had talked to veteran White House reporter Sarah McClendon, who told her "Mrs. Nixon was superb at her press conference yesterday. They asked her everything they could think of and she handled it all perfectly! Mrs. McClendon said . . . that Mrs. Nixon outdid anyone she has ever seen, men or women."

Nixon passed the memo to Pat and noted in his diary, "The only problem is that she goes through such agony in preparing it that I hate to have her take on the assignments."[60]

He did it anyway. He made up an extensive campaigning schedule for her, and for Julie, Tricia, and Ed Cox too. In his diary, he recorded, "I am going to hit Haldeman hard . . . [to] see to it that the Price shop does a better job in preparing [speech] material for Pat and the girls, and Ed, in the days ahead. It just seems that they won't really buckle down and get something done unless they think that they are doing it for me, which is a grievous error."[61]

Public speaking, even using material prepared by Price, continued to make Pat nervous. She explained to a friend, "I used to be a teacher, head of the pep squad, in lots of plays, and I was quite used to speaking and performing in public. But when Dick entered politics, we decided there would be only one public spokesman in the family. During the House, Senate, and vice-presidential days I didn't give speeches. Now here I am being asked to do more and more, and I'm just not comfortable with it."[62]

One subject she avoided was the Watergate break-in, but she did discuss it in a telephone conversation with Helene Drown, who noted, "Pat very disturbed about Watergate stories—says that Dick says that there is nothing to it. . . . Pat said that 'I suppose that every day they will come up with some new name and some new story—if it were the Democrats we were yelling about, the press would cry smear, etc.' "[63]

She resented being manipulated by Nixon's aides (they did not much like her, either; behind her back, Haldeman called her "Thelma").[64] She would take suggestions from her husband, but not from his aides. For his part, Nixon wanted her to concentrate on reading Price's speeches, not make suggestions. Just before the convention, after seeing a short film biography of her that was to be shown in Miami, she asked to preview the film prepared about her husband, as she had heard it was not very good and wanted to recommend changes. Nixon wrote in his diary, "Needless to say, I don't intend to look at mine and I'm going to see that some way we avoid her seeing it too."[65]

As for Julie, Tricia, and Ed Cox, Nixon had Haldeman put them before young audiences across the country at every opportunity. They were effective campaigners, clean-cut, photogenic, enthusiastic for Nixon, always positive and upbeat.

Not trusting Price, Nixon provided speaking material for his daughters. On July 24 he sent them a memo that began, "It occurs to me that from time to time you may be asked for anecdotes." Just in case they could not think of any, the President provided them with a couple: "You might mention some of our Christmas parties when I played the piano for group singing, etc., always by ear." Such events, he reminded his girls, "have been part of the Nixon story that is to you most heartwarming." They should also point out that at their birthday parties, "I from time to time played a Happy Birthday song for you."

Another heartwarming Nixon habit was to call people "who may be sick, who have had hard luck . . ." He wanted Julie and Tricia to emphasize that "these calls never are publicized because they are personal in nature." While they were publicizing the calls, they should also point out, "These personal calls never given to the press are the most rewarding ones I make from a personal standpoint."

There was a poignant side to this bit of Nixonian mawkishness. He claimed, with some truth, that he called fellow politicians who had just lost an election. He told his daughters that "everybody" calls a winner, but "I know from experience that you receive very few letters or calls when you suffer a defeat. It is in that period that you find out who your real friends are."

The girls did their best to tell the public what a wonderful, warm, human father Dick Nixon was, with great success.

On Election Day, James Reston commented, "It would be difficult to overestimate the political influence of the Nixon family in this campaign."[66]

David Eisenhower could not join his wife on the campaign trail, because of his active duty in the Navy. In a series of requests to Haldeman, Nixon tried to find some way around that legal restriction, without success. On July 20 the President sent a memo to Haldeman: "A suggestion has been made that David might say a word at the convention after the [film] tribute to his Grandfather. Some thought it would be political. However, I think it would be very appropriate for him to talk about his Grandfather. See what can be done to work this out."[67]

It proved to be impossible. David did, however, attend the convention, and was very much in evidence in the balcony, signing autographs. Nixon was able to arrange for Mamie Eisenhower to introduce the film about her husband.

THE 1972 REPUBLICAN CONVENTION in Miami presented a contrast to the Democratic Convention in the same city a month earlier that was so complete it was almost as if there were two Americas. Where the Democrats had been contentious, confused, and divided, the Republicans were cool, confident, and disciplined. Where the Democrats stressed what was wrong with America, the Republicans strutted about what was right. The Democratic nominee did not make it to the platform until the wee hours of the morning; the Republican nominee strode to the platform at precisely 10:30 P.M., Eastern time.

Two groups of young people in Miami provided a symbolic exclamation point to the contrast. At Flamingo Park, about three thousand war protesters set up a tent city, "the people's liberated zone of revolutionary living." The main street was named Ho Chi Minh Trail; on either side were, among others, the Women's Tent, the Free Berkeley Booth, the Neo-American Church tent, the Free Gays, the Jesus Freaks, the Society for the Advancement of Nonverbal Communication, and the Yippie Headquarters. At the end of the street, there stood the People's Pot Park. The long-haired youngsters needed a wash, as did their blue jeans, and the smell of marijuana hung heavy in the air. The exception was in the tent of the Vietnam Veterans Against the War, where leader Tim Butz tried to maintain some kind of decorum and to engage in meaningful political activity rather than mindless chanting.

Two miles away, some three thousand youthful Republicans, the Young Voters for the President, had their headquarters at Nautilus Junior High School. They slept in hotel rooms; they wore snappy Bermuda shorts; they were overwhelmingly white with neat haircuts; they were invariably polite and helpful; they were well organized to do volunteer work at the convention.[68]

The Young Voters for the President were concerned about the Vietnam War too, but their theme was that McGovern was sabotaging Nixon's efforts to negotiate an end to the war. They accused McGovern of having adopted Hanoi's terms for a settlement and thus inviting the North Vietnamese to hold out for a Democratic victory. They were also strong for the overall Republican theme, which was to come to Miami to celebrate the "saga of exhilarating progress" under the Nixon Administration.

As there was no business to do at the convention, no disputes, no divisive votes to take, it was more a coronation than a political gathering. "Adoration" was the best word to describe the delegates' feelings toward Nixon. "Four more years!" they chanted loudly, in unison, and all but continuously. Speakers vied with one another in expressions of fealty to the President. When Nixon arrived at Miami International Airport at 4 P.M. on the second day, the three giant screens behind the podium in the convention hall showed the event. As he smiled, and lifted his arms in his V-for-Victory sign, the delegates rose to their feet with a mighty roar, which lasted some minutes after he departed by helicopter for Key Biscayne.[69]

That evening, Governor Rockefeller placed Nixon's name in nomination. He had been preceded by Barry Goldwater and Ronald Reagan. It was an impressive reminder that Republican unity in 1972 stretched from coast to coast.

The Miami police easily handled the sole threat to the carefully scripted program. It came on August 23, as Nixon flew by helicopter to Miami to make his acceptance speech. A couple of thousand protesters from Flamingo Park tried to surround the convention hall to prevent the President from entering. Unlike the Chicago police at the Democratic Convention four years earlier, the Miami cops did not start beating on the kids; instead they used tear gas to scatter them. When a few of the protesters attempted to block traffic by slashing tires or ripping out the distributor caps of vehicles stopped at traffic lights, the police arrested them, but without using billy clubs. Television cameramen were kept at a distance. The protest turned out to be a nonevent.

This was Nixon's fifth acceptance at a Republican Convention. He reached back to 1960 and used his basic theme in the campaign against Kennedy: "A record is not something to stand on, it's something to build on."

He made the points he wanted to emphasize in the campaign: America was "a good and great country." Taxes were still too high, especially property taxes, which placed "such an unfair and heavy burden on the poor, the elderly, the wage earner, the farmer, and those on fixed income." He promised to reduce inflation even more than he already had done. He appealed to Democrats: "To those millions who have been driven out of their home in the Democratic party, we say, come home. We say come home not to another party, but we say come home to the great principles we Americans believe in together. . . . Join us as members of a new American majority bound together by our common ideals." He charged that McGovern would "destroy the system which has made America No. 1 in the world economically." He identified himself with FDR, Harry Truman, Eisenhower, JFK, and LBJ as a foe of isolationism.

He said he joined them in his determination to make certain that "the United States should have a defense second to none in the world." He showed that he was different from them: "In our relations with the Soviet Union, we have moved from confrontation to negotiation and then to cooperation in the interest of peace." But he pledged that he would not become complacent and would resist with all his might McGovern's "proposed massive cuts in our defense budget."

"Let us always be sure," he went on, "that when the President of the United States goes to the conference table he never has to negotiate from weakness." With regard to negotiations over Vietnam, he said he had gone the extra mile, and then some, in his search for peace, but there were three things he would never do: abandon the POWs, impose a Communist government on Saigon, or stain America's honor.

In his peroration, he strained to make the upcoming campaign into a crusade. He asked for support "not just in the cause of winning an election, but in achieving a hope that mankind has had since the beginning of civilization.

"Let us build a peace that our children and all the children of the world can enjoy for generations to come."[70]

There was nothing fresh and little that was quotable in the speech, and Nixon knew it. Going back on the helicopter he was depressed. Pat noticed it and tried to cheer him up, without much success.[71]

What did cheer him up was hitting the campaign trail. The next morning he flew west, stopping in Chicago, Michigan, and San Diego before reaching San Clemente. He brought the American Legion delegates in Chicago to their feet with a rousing, bellicose speech that emphasized peace with honor, crime, drugs, permissiveness, and "elitists who defied moral values." In an airport rally in San Diego, there were thousands of "Four More Years!" signs. The Nixon juggernaut was on its way.[72]

At the end of August, the Gallup poll reported 64 percent for Nixon, 30 percent for McGovern, 6 percent undecided. By contrast, at the same point in 1968 the polls had shown 43 percent for Nixon, 31 percent for Humphrey, and 19 percent for Wallace. And in 1968, Lyndon Johnson had controlled events; in 1972, Nixon did.

WITH SUCH a commanding lead, Nixon was even less sure that a pre-election peace in Vietnam was desirable. After the convention, Kissinger flew to Moscow to confer with the Soviet leaders. He wanted them to pressure Hanoi to compromise. Nixon did not. He had Al Haig send Kissinger a cable: "He [Nixon] stated that . . . the

American people are no longer interested in a solution based on compromise, favor continued bombing and want to see the United States prevail after all these years." Haig added that although he had managed to convince the President that the public's "attitude was fragile," Nixon wanted him to emphasize to Kissinger "that the record you establish tomorrow in your discussions be a tough one which in a public sense would appeal to the Hawk and not to the Dove." [73]

In an August 29 news conference, Nixon was equally tough. Asked about the prospects for negotiations, he pointed out that Vietnamization was working, that ARVN had stopped the NVA spring offensive, and that therefore the enemy ought to be willing to accept a negotiated settlement. But if "the enemy does not feel that way, then we are prepared to go on as we have indicated . . . [If] there is one POW in North Vietnam, or one missing in action, not accounted for, there will be an American volunteer force in South Vietnam." Would he slacken the bombing even without an agreement? "Absolutely not. . . . Unless there is progress on the negotiating front which is substantial, there will be no reduction of the bombing of North Vietnam and there will be no lifting of the mining."

He was reminded that he had said, in 1968, "Those who have had a chance for four years and could not produce peace should not be given another chance." Did he still feel that way?

Rather than answer the question, Nixon counterattacked: "I think there are those who have faulted this Administration on its efforts to seek peace, but those who fault it, I would respectfully suggest, are ones that would have the United States seek peace at the cost of surrender, dishonor, and the destruction of the ability of the United States to conduct foreign policy in a responsible way."

On another question, he did not counterattack, but simply lied. Asked if he thought a special prosecutor should be appointed for the investigation of the Watergate break-in, Nixon said it would serve no useful purpose. He claimed that the investigations by the GAO, the FBI, and the Justice Department "have, at my direction, had the total cooperation of the—not only the White House—but also of all agencies of the Government."

He went on: "In addition to that, within our own staff, under my direction, Counsel to the President, Mr. Dean, has conducted a complete investigation of all leads which might involve any present members of the White House Staff or anybody in the Government. I can say categorically that his investigation indicates that no one in the White House Staff, no one in the Administration, presently employed, was involved in this very bizarre incident." [74]

John Dean, watching the news conference on television in a hotel room, later wrote, "I damn near fell off the bed. . . . I had never heard of a 'Dean investigation,' much less conducted one." [75]

Nixon told another whopper when he claimed that CREEP itself was conducting an investigation in order "to clear the air." He said, "We are doing everything we can to take this incident and to investigate it and not to cover it up. What really hurts in matters of this sort is not the fact that they occur, because over zealous people in campaigns do things that are wrong. What really hurts is if you try to cover it up." [76]

It was often said of Nixon that while he was very good at handling the politics of his problems, he was not so good at handling the problems. This was a classic example. By using the words "cover up" himself, but pointing out how harmful an attempted cover-up would be to him personally, he was entirely convincing. In disarming the reporters, who could not believe he was engaged in a cover-up if he brought up the subject himself, he had dealt with the politics of his problem but done nothing about the problem.

He had achieved his immediate goal, which was to contain Watergate until after the election. With the mandate the polls indicated he was going to achieve, he could deal with it then.

CHAPTER TWENTY-SIX

THE LAST CAMPAIGN

PART ONE
September 1–October 8, 1972

THE 1972 CAMPAIGN, Nixon later wrote, "should have been the most gratifying and fulfilling of all my campaigns. Instead it was one of the most frustrating and, in many ways, the least satisfying of all." He felt the reason was that "against McGovern . . . it was clear that the less I did, the better I would do," which dictated a strategy of being presidential, staying in the White House, and having others do the speaking and attacking.[1]

Until the last couple of weeks before the election, Nixon planned to let Senator Bob Dole of Kansas, chairman of the RNC, and others do the campaigning for him. The team of surrogates included Cabinet members Butz, Kleindienst, Richardson, Shultz, and Ruckelshaus of EPA, Senators William Brock of Tennessee, Edward Brooke of Massachusetts, Goldwater, Jacob Javits of New York, William Saxbe of Ohio, Hugh Scott of Pennsylvania, and Robert Taft, Jr., of Ohio, Governors Reagan and Rockefeller, Congressmen Ford and Kemp, and many others. In what he called a "dramatic reversal" of his role as "party wheelhorse," Nixon would not appear in support of Republican congressional candidates. For the most part, he stuck with that strategy.

This did not mean, however, that he was uninvolved. As always, he set the agenda, picked the issues, gave the orders. And, as had been the case in his first campaign against Representative Voorhis in 1946, in his second campaign against Senator Douglas in 1950, and in every campaign since, his theme was attack.

McGovern was calling for an end to the price guidelines Nixon had established in his economic program. Nixon responded, "C—

crucify him on this—it means High Prices, High Taxes, High cost of living."[2]

Senator Scott, meanwhile, charged that "the McGovern campaign is the campaign of the three A's: acid, abortion, and amnesty."[3] Still Nixon's surrogate speakers were less vigorous than he wanted them to be. When Buchanan remarked in mid-September that "there is a political vacuum . . . no dominant attack stories coming from our side . . . McGovern has the offensive," Nixon commented, "C & H—This is my intuition also—the need for better *attack* is urgent—we are scattering the shots too much."[4]

Amnesty was a key target. When it appeared in mid-September that McGovern might modify his position, Nixon wrote, "C & H— we must not let him off the hook on this."[5]

Although Nixon wanted to keep the emphasis on McGovern, he was not averse to publicity about himself, with the emphasis on what he had accomplished rather than what he promised. In late September, *The Saturday Evening Post* gave him exactly what he wanted in a spread featuring the work of White House photographer Oliver Atkins. There was a Nixon portrait on the cover, and inside photos of Nixon dining with Chou En-lai, toasting with Brezhnev, in deep reflection, playing with his dog King (as it would never do to have an American President with a dog named King, the Irish setter was known to the public as Timahoe), and in a relaxed moment with Pat.

There were limits, however, even for Nixon. A magazine editor, Elizabeth Manning, started a drive to nominate Nixon for the 1972 Nobel peace prize. Nixon sent her a letter of support, saying that one of the compensations of public life was to have this kind of recognition for his prime goal, a lasting peace. Mrs. Manning admitted that "the Nobel people said nobody had ever tried anything like this before," but she nevertheless collected $20,000 to support the campaign and got twenty-eight heads of state and more than a thousand professors to agree to place Nixon's name in nomination. But when the press learned about the effort, Nixon feared ridicule and backed off. "This is silly," he wrote Haldeman. "Knock it off."[6]

For Colson, there were no limits. When in August he discovered to his dismay that about half his staff had taken the weekend off, he sent out instructions: "No one is to leave town without my permission. There are only seventy-one days left and every one counts. Ask yourself every morning what you are going to do to help re-elect the President today. . . . Many erroneous things about me have found their way into print lately—but last week's UPI story that I was once reported to have said that 'I would walk over my grandmother if necessary [to re-elect Nixon],' is absolutely accurate."

Nixon was delighted. When the memo kicked up a furor, the President defended his man. He told visitors, "Colson—he'll do anything. He'll walk right through doors."[7]

Among the people Nixon did not like were the bureaucrats and the reporters. When he learned that Shriver had used Peace Corps mailing lists, Nixon asked, "H & K—How in hell did he get them? It's time to clean all the holdovers out of the Peace Corps." When Cronkite reported that McGovern was drawing good crowds and that this would soon be reflected in the polls, Nixon commented, "C & H—a small idea of what they will say when there is any shift in polls!"[8]

Nixon was also unhappy with Republican candidates who were complaining that he had "scarcely lifted a finger against any Democrat except McGovern." Nixon's comment was not, We must do something about this. Instead, he wrote, "H—we can expect more of this," and chose to ignore it.[9]

Watergate continued to be a problem, but far more inside the Washington Beltway than in the country as a whole. The hometown newspaper, the Washington *Post*, was increasing the pressure, as young reporters Bob Woodward and Carl Bernstein, with help from Jim Mann, Lawrence Meyer, Sanford Unger, Ronald Kessler, and others, had the story on the front page almost every other day through September. But what they reported was more rumor than fact, with the emphasis on what was not happening. They did identify Liddy and Hunt as participants in the burglary, but those two no longer worked for CREEP and Hunt's previous employment in the White House was so relatively low level that nothing was sticking to the Administration. U.S. District Judge Charles Richey, a Nixon appointee hearing the Democrats' civil suit against CREEP, was taking depositions from Mitchell and others, but according to the leaks the *Post* was getting Mitchell had denied any knowledge of anything, and in order to protect the rights of the accused burglars, Judge Richey refused to make the depositions public.[10]

The *Post* was not even getting close to the real story. By concentrating on the money trail, in an attempt to prove that the $100 bills found on the burglars came from CREEP via a Mexican bank, Woodward, Bernstein, and the other reporters were doing Nixon a major favor. Mitchell's denials notwithstanding, a citizen would have to be blind and deaf not to know that CREEP was behind the break-in, which was not after all a burglary in the ordinary usage of the word, as nothing was taken out (except photographs of documents), nothing stolen, and something left behind (the telephone bugs). Who more than CREEP would want to know what Larry O'Brien was saying on his telephone?

The real story, that Nixon had ordered a cover-up, that he had involved the FBI and the CIA and his closest aides in that cover-up, that he had authorized the payment of hush money to the burglars, that Herb Kalmbach had raised $220,000 and disbursed $187,500 to the defendants, and that relevant documents had been destroyed by the President's counsel John Dean and by the director of the FBI, did not appear in the *Post*, much less in any other newspaper or on television.

The threat to Nixon came not from the media, but from the legal system and Congress. The Justice Department indictments stemming from the break-in were due in mid-September; there was a real danger that they might not cut off with Liddy and Hunt, but include Magruder. Judge Richey could seriously embarrass the Administration, at a minimum, by starting a public trial on O'Brien's civil suit before the election. The GAO was conducting an investigation into campaign financing that could be damaging. Texas Representative Wright Patman was threatening to hold hearings before his Banking and Currency Committee.

As against this, the good news was that the Gallup poll found that 48 percent of the American people had never heard of the Watergate break-in.[11] Further, the Justice Department leaks indicated that no one beyond Liddy and Hunt would be indicted, Judge Richey was cooperating with John Dean, and Nixon had ways of bringing pressure against the GAO and Congressman Patman.

So Nixon was feeling optimistic on September 11, when he met with Haldeman. They discussed the upcoming indictments. Nixon said he wanted to develop a "thorough game plan" for Watergate. The question was, "How to handle it PR-wise." Nixon told Haldeman to have Ziegler "take the offensive, call on the Democrats to apologize."[12] The following day, when the Democrats amended the civil suit to add Stans, his assistant Hugh Sloan, and Liddy to the list of defendants in the "political espionage conspiracy," and raised the damages asked to $3 million, Nixon took it in stride. "H & C," he noted, "obviously the 'establishment' has decided to go all out on this issue this week."[13]

Nixon's ho-hum attitude was justified. On September 15, the Justice Department announced the indictments. McCord and his team, plus Liddy and Hunt, were indicted. Magruder was not. Attorney General Kleindienst said the investigation was "one of the most intensive, objective, and thorough investigations in many years." The Justice Department said, "We have absolutely no evidence to indicate that any others should be charged." MacGregor demanded an apology from the Democrats for their reckless and unfounded charges. Senator Dole asserted that the indictments proved there was no evidence to support "any of the wild and slanderous statements McGovern has been making." Representative Ford, leader of the House Republicans, said the indictments reinforced his conviction that no one in the White House or in CREEP was involved.[14]

At 5:27 that afternoon, Nixon called John Dean into the Oval Office. Haldeman was already there. When Dean entered, Nixon was reclining in his swivel chair, feet propped up on his desk. The President looked at Dean through the V formed by his shoes.

"Well, you had quite a day today, didn't you?" the President said.

"Quite a three months," Dean answered.

They ran through the indictments. Haldeman observed that it was a good thing Liddy and Hunt were included, because "that takes the edge off whitewash really . . . to those in the country, Liddy and, and, uh, Hunt are big men."

Dean thought it was time to demand an apology from the Democrats.

"Fat chance," Haldeman remarked, laughing.

"Just remember all the trouble they gave us on this," Nixon said. "We'll have a chance to get back at them one day."

Dean pointed out that the FBI had put more agents on this case than on the inquiry after Kennedy's assassination.

"Isn't that ridiculous," Haldeman commented. "This silly ass damn thing."

"Yeah," the President added, "for Christ's sake. . . . Goldwater put it in context [when] he said, 'Well, for Christ's sake, everybody bugs everybody else.' We know that."

Nixon insisted, "It's true. It happens to be totally true." He said his airplane had been bugged in 1968, and that he had been bugged in 1962 running for governor of California. "God damnedest thing you ever saw."

Haldeman said he had proof of the '68 bugging.

"The difficulty with using it," Nixon noted unhappily, "is that it reflects on Johnson. He ordered it. If it weren't for that, I'd use it." He speculated on the possibility of pinning the '68 bugs on the DNC, but realized that would not work, as it was the FBI that did the bugging. To expose Johnson would be to jeopardize the whole Connally Democrats for Nixon operation, which was out of the question.

Dean wondered if it could be pinned on Humphrey.

"Oh, hell no," Nixon answered.

Haldeman pointed out that "he [Johnson] was bugging Humphrey, too."

Still Nixon would not let go of the thought. "I'll tell you who to call," he said. "I want you to ask Connally. Whatever he thinks, maybe we ought to just, just let that one fly." But finally he decided, "It isn't worth it. It isn't worth it. Damn it, it isn't worth— the hell with it." So, thanks to Nixon's need for Johnson's neutrality and Connally's support in 1972, LBJ's bugging operations in 1968 went unexposed.

Nixon and his aides discussed a second bug the Democrats had found in the DNC two days earlier, the one on Spencer Oliver's phone. The FBI had missed it in its original sweep of the office. Nixon hoped against hope that the Democrats had planted it themselves, and could be exposed.

The telephone rang. It was Clark MacGregor. Nixon picked it up and opened the conversation by asking, "Did you put that last bug in?" Whatever MacGregor's answer, Nixon responded, "Yeah."

MacGregor said something else. Nixon commented, "Well, I'll tell you, uh, just don't let this keep you or your colleagues from concentrating on the big game. . . . This thing is just, uh, you know, one of those side issues and a month later everybody looks back and wonders what the hell the shouting was about."

As he rang off, Nixon said, "Okay, well, anyway get a good night's sleep. And don't, don't bug anybody without asking me. Okay?" He spoke in a serious, matter-of-fact manner; there was not the slightest hint in his tone of voice that he was kidding.

The conversation in the Oval Office resumed. Dean said he thought they were safe, at least until Election Day. Nixon congratulated him. "The way you, you've handled it," the President said, "it seems to me, has been very skillful, because you—putting your fingers in the dikes every time that leaks having sprung here and sprung there."

Dean replied, "The only problems that, uh, that we have are, are the human problems and we'll keep a close eye on that." He explained that Stans and his associates were bitter. "They feel that they're taking all the heat, and, and, uh, all the people upstairs [at CREEP] are bad people."

"Ridiculous," Nixon interjected. "They're all in it together."

"That's right," Dean agreed.

"They should just, uh, just behave," Nixon went on, "and recognize this, this is, again, this is war. We're getting a few shots and it'll be over, and we'll give them a few shots and it'll be over. Don't worry. I wouldn't want to be on the other side right now. Would you?"

Dean shook his head.

"I wouldn't want to be in Edward Bennett Williams' position after this election," Nixon said. (Williams was representing the DNC in the civil suits.) "We're going after him," the President promised.

"That's the guy we've got to ruin," Haldeman agreed.

Nixon pointed out that Williams was an attorney for the Washington *Post*. "I think we are going to fix the son-of-a-bitch. Believe me. We are going to. We've got to, because he's a bad man."

Dean said he was keeping notes on the people "who are emerging as less than our friends."

"Great," said the President. "I want the most comprehensive notes on all of those that have tried to do us in. Because they didn't have to do it." He said that if it were shaping up as a close election, he could understand. "But now they are doing this quite deliberately and they are asking for it and they are going to get it."

The Oval Office had not heard such talk since Roosevelt and Churchill discussed Adolf Hitler, or Truman and Acheson expressed their feelings about Joseph Stalin, or since Jack and Bobby Kennedy talked about Dick Nixon.

Nixon lamented that his Administration had not used the FBI and the Justice Department and the IRS in the first term, "but things are going to change now. And they're going to change, and, and they're going to get it right—"

Dean interrupted. "That's an exciting prospect."

"It's got to be done," Nixon said. "It's the only thing to do."

"We've got to," Haldeman agreed.

Nixon said that "we've been just God damn fools," because they had done nothing with regard to Democratic senators who were up for re-election. "They're, they're crooks, they've been stealing, they've been taking [unintelligible]. That's ridiculous. Absolutely ridiculous. It's not going, going to be that way any more."

Pleased with themselves and the prospects of doing in their enemies, the three men turned to the GAO investigation. Haldeman thought they could cut that off by threatening House Speaker Carl Albert (D., Okla.) with exposing his drinking problem and some troubles he had had with the D.C. police as a result of drunk driving.

With regard to Patman and his Banking Committee, Nixon thought that Representative Ford could put some heat on, with threats to expose Democratic campaign violations.

Having settled those problems, the men returned to the "get them" theme. "The main thing is," Nixon said, "the *Post* is going to have damnable, damnable problems out of this one. They have a television station. And they're going to have to get it renewed. . . . The game has to be played awfully rough." They went on to relish the thought of Maurice Stans filing a countersuit against the DNC for libel.[15]

The conversation moved on to the IRS. Nixon complained about the failure to get anything on O'Brien and other Democrats. Dean explained that the IRS bureaucrats were all Democrats and would not cooperate. He could not get at the files.

"There are ways to do it," Nixon said. "Goddamnit, sneak in in the middle of the night. . . ."

Haldeman warned against taking such chances before the election.

Nixon referred to Secretary of the Treasury Shultz: "He's got to know that the resignations of everybody . . . The point is, I want there to be no holdovers left. The whole Goddamn bunch is to go out. And if he doesn't do it, he's out as Secretary of the Treasury. And that's the way it's going to be played. Now, that's the point. See."

And not just at Treasury, either. Nixon wanted to clean out the whole federal bureaucracy. Mitchell had not done it at Justice. Rogers "was totally captured by the American bureaucracy. Mel Laird, he didn't change anybody." He went on, "HEW, the whole damn bunch. . . . You've got to do it fast because . . . after the first of the year it's too late. You've got to do it right after the election. You've got one week, and that's the time to get all those resignations in and say, 'Look, you're out, you're out, you're finished, you're done, done, finished.' Knock them the hell out of there." He wanted to get at the Veterans Administration, the National Park Service ("they've been screwing us for four years"). It would be a complete housecleaning, because "it's time for a new team. Period. I'm going to say we didn't do it when we came in before, but now we have a mandate. And one of the mandates is to do the cleaning up that we didn't do in '68."[16]

Thus did Nixon plan to do in the men who were at that moment out on the campaign trail, knocking themselves out to give him the mandate that would be their dismissal warrant.

Nixon often indulged himself in rhetorical overkill when he was with Haldeman (or with Colson or Kissinger), hurling threats he did not mean. But in this case he was entirely serious. A few days later, Haldeman called Dean into his office. He said he wanted to talk about what Nixon had said the previous week about postelection plans.

"This is something that's being held very closely, John," Haldeman said, "and I think you'll understand why. I want you to make sure there's no legal problem in doing it. We are going to ask for the resignation of every single Presidential appointee as soon as the election is over. Every single one of them. And we're going to put our own people in there. Can you check it out for me?" Dean said he would.[17]

Nixon expressed his resolution in a diary entry. He wrote that Dean "had the kind of steel and really mean instinct that we needed to clean house after the election . . . There simply has to be a line drawn at times with those who are against us; and then we have to take the action to deal with them effectively. Otherwise, they will be around to deal with us when their opportunity comes to them."[18]

Nixon also brought Caspar Weinberger and John Ehrlichman in on his plans. On September 20, at Camp David, he subjected them to a two-hour monologue on how things were going to change after he got his mandate. He wanted Weinberger to prepare a radically austere budget for fiscal 1973. He wanted Ehrlichman to get cracking on the reorganization, not only of departments (Nixon wanted to reduce the Cabinet to eight departments; there would be four new ones, Economic Affairs, Human Resources, Natural Resources, and Community Development, plus four traditional ones, State, Defense, Justice, and Treasury) but by finding new people to replace the current officeholders.[19]

NIXON'S ANTICIPATED MANDATE not only strengthened his tough-guy and mean-streak attitude toward McGovern and the Democrats, and toward his own Cabinet and the federal bureaucracy, but toward the North and South Vietnamese as well. Events, and the polls, added to his determination. On September 15, ARVN recaptured Quang Tri. The Harris poll said that 55 percent of the American people supported continued heavy bombing of North Vietnam, 64 percent supported the mining of Haiphong, and 74 percent thought it was important that South Vietnam not fall into the hands of the Communists. In Paris, Kissinger rejected Le Duc Tho's demand for a coalition government; nevertheless, Tho proposed another meeting in eleven days, to discuss Kissinger's counteroffer, made formal for the first time, for a Committee of National Reconciliation. It would be one-third South Vietnamese, one-third Communist, one-third neutral, and operate under a principle of unanimity. Its function would be to "review" the constitution of South Vietnam and oversee elections.

Seymour Hersh sees this as "perhaps, the most fateful moment of the secret negotiations," because it gave the PRG legal status in the South.[20] It was equally fateful for South Vietnam, as it granted what Thieu had all along denied, that the Communists were a legitimate political force in his country. Kissinger and Tho made further progress at meetings on September 26 and 27. Most important, they agreed to get together again on October 8, for what promised to be the decisive meeting.

By this stage, Saigon was more an obstacle to peace than Hanoi. Kissinger had failed to keep Thieu adequately informed as to what he was agreeing to and it was obvious, although not admitted, that Thieu would oppose the deal with all his might. As Haig was on better terms with Thieu than Kissinger, because he was more sympathetic, and as Kissinger rightly feared that Haig was undercutting him with Nixon, Kissinger suggested sending Haig to Saigon to sell the proposal to Thieu. Nixon agreed.

In Saigon, Haig promised and threatened. The promise was that Nixon would not rush headlong into an unsatisfactory agreement. The threat was that if Tho made a "reasonable offer" and the Americans turned it down, the doves would raise such a storm in America that it would be impossible for the Nixon Administration to continue supporting South Vietnam. Thieu, visibly shaken, railed against Kissinger, who, he said, did not "deign" to take the South Vietnamese into his confidence. He broke into tears.

When Haig reported to Nixon, the President sent a personal message to Thieu: "I give you my firm assurance that there will be no settlement arrived at, the provisions of which have not been discussed personally with you well beforehand." He also threatened, reminding Thieu of the danger of stirring up the American doves through intransigence. Even more alarming, he urged Thieu to "avoid the development of an atmosphere which could lead to events similar to those which we abhorred in 1963"—a less-than-subtle reminder of what happened to Diem.[21]

Haig returned to the United States, over Nixon's objections. The President told Kissinger it was a mistake for Haig to leave Saigon; he should have stayed to work over Thieu. Nixon told Kissinger to have Ambassador Bunker talk "cold turkey" with Thieu. He also told Kissinger, "And we're just going to have to break it off with him [Thieu] after the election, I can see that. You know, if he's going to be this unreasonable, I mean the tail can't wag the dog here."

Kissinger liked the idea of hammering Thieu, but he feared Nixon's commitment to a pre-election armistice was less than firm. He did get the President to agree that if Tho accepted the offer he had made in September, he could go to Saigon to sell it to Thieu.

Nixon said that in that case Kissinger should "cram it down his [Thieu's] throat."[22]

Meanwhile, Gromyko arrived in the United States for the ceremony of signing the SALT agreements. Nixon took him to Camp David. The President warned the Soviet Foreign Minister that the offer Kissinger would make to Tho in Paris on October 8 was final. If Tho turned it down, Nixon said, "we would have to turn to some other methods after the elections."[23]

Kissinger's fears about Nixon's commitment were well founded. Colson originally sided with Kissinger: "I thought he'd [Nixon] be a hero with an agreement," Colson said in an interview. But then Nixon convinced him otherwise. "That son-of-a-bitch," Nixon said to Colson of Kissinger, "want[s] me to be in his debt for winning this election." Nixon said he had told Kissinger, "If we get it [an armistice], great. Right now, it won't help and it might hurt. We don't want to get it just to get it." Nixon added, "I can't convince Kissinger to slow down. Please tell him it will hurt—not help us—to get the settlement before the election."[24]

At a news conference on October 5, Nixon gave out mixed signals. Asked if there was any possibility of an agreement before the election, he said that "the settlement will come just as soon as we can possibly get a settlement which is right," but insisted that the timing would not be affected by the election date. The Democrats had tried a bombing halt on the eve of the 1968 election, he pointed out, and although "there are those who believe that they were motivated . . . by political considerations," he himself did "not claim that that was the case." He did charge that Johnson had "made a very, very great mistake in stopping the bombing without adequate agreements from the other side."[25]

Nixon hastened to add that he meant no personal criticism of Johnson, and immediately after the conference he had Ziegler call the former President to assure him of the current President's continued admiration and support.[26]

Kissinger set off for his October 8 climax meeting with Tho, accompanied by Haig. According to Kissinger, the reason Haig was along was that "he would be able to help sell any possible agreement to Nixon." Haig's presence in Paris had another advantage; he would not be in Washington, undercutting Kissinger.[27] As to what Nixon wanted, no one, including his emissaries, could say with certainty—not even the President himself.

GROMYKO'S VISIT, a month before the election, gave Nixon a welcome opportunity to act presidential and, as a bonus, in the cause of world peace. It was also an occasion, however, that should have reminded Nixon of the limits of his power, even in foreign affairs.

Nixon had been able to get the ABM Treaty, limiting each side to two ABMs defending national capitals and signed by the heads of government at Moscow in May, ratified by the Senate without undue difficulty. The interim agreement with the Soviet Union on limiting strategic offensive arms was another matter. As it was not a treaty, it did not require a two-thirds vote of the Senate for ratification, but Nixon did ask Congress for a joint resolution approving its terms. Senator Henry Jackson objected. He called it a "bum deal" on the grounds that it allowed the Soviets more throw weight in missiles, and he introduced an amendment that prescribed that any future agreements be based on what he called, rather equivocally, "equality."

Jackson had been one of John Kennedy's advisers in 1960; in that capacity, he had been prominent in support of Kennedy's charge that the Eisenhower Administration had allowed a "missile gap" to develop, a charge that hurt Nixon in the election. There was a danger that Jackson might repeat the performance in 1972. Nixon therefore opened secret negotiations with Jackson, using Kissinger as his emissary. Kissinger and Jackson talked over the telephone as often as three or four times daily, and had a weekend meeting at the White House. They worked out wording that both sides could live with, and in September the interim agreement, accompanied by the Jackson amendment, passed both Houses of Congress.[28]

Nixon signed the Joint Resolution on September 30.

On October 3, in the White House, Nixon and Gromyko signed documents that put into force the ABM Treaty and the interim agreement (which was subject to review in five years). In his remarks at the ceremonies, Nixon stressed that the agreements were but a "first step in reducing the danger of war." The next "vitally important" step was to consider the whole range of offensive nuclear weapons, and beyond that "we can look to the possibility of reducing the burden of nuclear arms and eventually to the possibility of limitations and restrictions on the use of such arms."[29]

The bright promise of the ceremony was duly trumpeted by the media; what reporters did not note was an intense conversation Nixon had with Senator Jackson in a forty-five-minute stroll through the Rose Garden after the signing. The subject was not nuclear weapons and the survival of the human race, but the rather more mundane topic of trade agreements with the Soviet Union. In Moscow in May, Nixon had put off signing such agreements with Brezhnev. One reason, openly stated, was congressional insistence that in return the Soviet Union agree to repay some part of the lend-lease debt from World War II. A second reason, more important if unstated directly, was Kissinger's insistence on linking trade with Soviet assistance in reaching a settlement in Vietnam. Gromyko was able to satisfy Nixon on both points, and the President was ready to grant the Soviets MFN status and implement a trade agreement. But two could play the linkage game, and on October 3, in the Rose Garden, Jackson told Nixon he wanted to link MFN to the issue of Jewish emigration from the Soviet Union.

Jackson had presidential ambitions of his own, for 1976. With McGovern as his party's candidate in 1972, he had milked defense for about as much as he could get with his amendment to the interim agreement. Nixon just was not vulnerable to charges of a missile gap. But the treatment of Soviet Jews was another matter. Nixon had never done very well with Jewish voters (he got 17 percent of the Jewish vote in 1968), nor been very popular with Jewish leaders, despite having Kissinger as his National Security Adviser and despite his record of support for Israel. In early September, he had slipped further following a massacre by terrorists of Israeli athletes at the Olympic Village in Munich. American Jews had urged the President to recall the American team and boycott the Olympics, but Nixon had refused to do so.

At about the same time, the Soviets had suddenly and unexpectedly imposed an "exit tax" on Jewish emigration. Nixon was "dumbfounded" by this development.[30] He had been urging Brezhnev to ease up on restrictions, with some success—Jewish emigration had increased from four hundred a year in 1968 to thirty-five thousand per year by 1972. What motivated the Soviets to impose the exit tax (designed, so they claimed, to get reimbursement for the expense of providing a higher education for the emigrants) when their friend Richard Nixon, the author of détente, was up for re-election remains unclear. The best guess is that it was a response to Sadat's action in throwing their troops out of Egypt; i.e., the exit tax was a pledge to the Arabs that the Soviets would limit the numbers of Jews emigrating to Israel.

For Jackson, it provided an opportunity he was quick to seize. In the Rose Garden on October 3, he told Nixon he intended to link the exit tax with the trade agreements. He had an amendment he would attach to the next available piece of legislation; the amendment would deny MFN status to the Soviet Union until it rescinded the exit tax. But Jackson had an offer for Nixon. He said he would not make his amendment into a campaign issue, nor force it to a vote in the 92d Congress, if Nixon would agree to release the fifteen to eighteen Republican loyalists in the Senate who resisted becoming cosponsors without Nixon's signal of assent. Nixon made the deal.[31]

The following day, Jackson introduced his amendment. He

had seventy-two Senate cosponsors, a stunning display of the power of the Jewish lobby in American politics. In the Soviet Union, however, the Jews had no political power, and Brezhnev took the position that he would not allow an American senator to dictate the internal policies of his country. But he was realistic enough to respond to Kissinger's private pleas to Dobrynin, and to help Nixon get re-elected; in October, the Soviets granted "exemptions" from the emigration tax for hundreds of Jews, and altogether allowed a record number of Jews, forty-five hundred, to leave in that month. All this was reported in the *The New York Times*, where it did Nixon the most good.[32] Nixon sent Haig a message: "Al—Tell Dobyrian [*sic*] a very shrewd move."[33]

In return, the Soviets got Nixon to sign a comprehensive trade agreement, in which the Administration promised to seek congressional approval for MFN status for the Soviet Union and the Soviets promised to pay $722 million of the lend-lease debt. Nixon also authorized the extension of Export-Import Bank credits to the Soviet Union; the loans were used to finance the Soviet grain purchases.

Taken altogether, Nixon had handled the problems raised by the SALT agreements, the MFN issue, and Jewish emigration about as adroitly as could be done under the circumstances. But he had not solved any of them. He could not, alone. He had to have the cooperation of Congress, especially the Senate, to do so. They were sure to be major sources of controversy with the 93d Congress, if for no other reason than because Jackson would see to it that they were. That only emphasized the importance to Nixon of getting more Republicans into the Senate. Nevertheless, he remained aloof from the congressional races.

To the extent that he did involve himself, it was via his News Summary comments, and moderate Republicans were his target as often as liberal Democrats. When he read that Senator Charles Percy had expressed his dismay over Nixon's refusal to support a consumer bill, Nixon noted that Illinois looked safe in the presidential race, then ordered, "H—Hack him [Percy] up a bit."[34]

BACK IN 1956, when Eisenhower had reluctantly agreed to run for re-election, he had insisted to the RNC that he would limit his campaign to four or five television speeches. In the event, however, Adlai Stevenson had goaded him into a much more active campaign. Nixon, in 1972, resisted any temptation to tour the country. His model was Roosevelt's 1944 re-election campaign—FDR had made a few radio addresses, and that was it.

Nixon's previous pattern had been three or four major

speeches on every weekend day, in different parts of the country. In 1972, Nixon spent his weekends at Camp David, relaxing. In previous campaigns, his mind worked nonstop on political problems; in 1972, it sometimes strayed into the most improbable areas. Floating on his back in the pool at Camp David one September weekend, Nixon got to thinking about the leaves overhead. He wrote in his diary, "I was reminded of the fact that in the spring the leaves turned over in the wind and the leaves in the spring and the fall were really so very much alike. One portrays the beginning of summer, the other the beginning of winter—one the beginning of life, the other the beginning of death."

Philosophical musings gave way to practical problems. Mc-Govern was stepping up his attacks, in Nixon's view "in a very vicious and irresponsible way." Nixon was unhappy with the response; he told Colson that his surrogate speakers were "reacting in their usual honest and stupid way, by defending rather than attacking."

Richard Nixon was a man so full of contradictions that he did not even recognize them when he made them. In his memoirs, after quoting his remark to Colson, he wrote, one paragraph later, and without any attempt at explanation or justification, "Ted Agnew, Clark MacGregor, Bob Dole, and their teams were doing a magnificent job. They were not only effective spokesmen for the administration but kept McGovern on the defensive with sharp thrusts against his far-left views." [35]

On September 22, Nixon made his first campaign appearance. He flew to Texas, not to speak to Texas Republicans in Houston or Dallas, but to go to Connally's ranch for a Democrats for Nixon barbecue. Guests included James and Elliott Roosevelt, Frank Fitzsimmons, Perle Mesta, some former and current southern governors, and Senator Lloyd Bentsen, who had in 1970 defeated George Bush for the Senate. While the guests ate and sipped their drinks around the swimming pool decorated with floating chrysanthemums, Nixon gave a tough law-and-order speech. But his main purpose in coming to Texas was to have a talk with Connally, not about 1972, but about 1976. Nixon said it was "vitally important" that Ted Kennedy "not pick up the pieces after this election." [36]

Nixon's wife and daughters, meanwhile, were crisscrossing the country. In the course of the campaign, they covered seventy-seven cities in thirty-seven states. Pat could not have been very happy about it. In mid-September, she set off on a tour of the western states. Julie wrote to David, who was on duty in the Mediterranean, "Poor Mom was so nervous this morning, according to Tricia . . . Six-day trip, with lots of speaking. *It is* difficult." [37]

Pat had misgivings about the tone of her husband's campaign. She told Helene Drown on the telephone, "If I were in charge of the campaign I wouldn't be running it the way it is being run." Years later Julie, writing a biography of her mother, asked Pat about that remark. Pat said that "it worried her that more and more power seemed vested in the handful of men around [Nixon] and that he had so little direct involvement in the campaign." She added, "I think I made a mistake protecting Daddy too much and in giving in too much, but I knew he was busy, the war was hanging over us . . ." [38]

Ken Ringle of the Washington *Post* covered Pat's western tour and produced a front-page feature piece on it. He wrote that "she shows no sense of urgency about the election and no hunger for the next four years. . . . She moves mechanically through the rituals of campaigning, hidden behind a shell of smiling reserve." On the 5,400-mile trip, she was filmed watching Old Faithful in Yellowstone, dedicating a school building in Idaho Falls, touring a research center in Sunnyvale, California, and visiting an old folks' home in Riverside. All this made the local news, and some of it the national news, but, according to Ringle, it also reinforced the "one-dimensional image of Pat Nixon that had stood before the public mind for more than 20 years: the slender, smiling embodiment of stoic wifely loyalty who endures and transcends the fire and rain of national politics." [39]

In the course of the tour, she endured freezing rain, gale-force winds, sleet, snow, and hail in Billings, Montana, and 102-degree heat in Riverside. She also went through a press conference that clearly made her uncomfortable, as reporters asked her about abortion, amnesty, the economy, and the war. Worst of all were questions about Watergate. Pat said she knew nothing about the break-in, but thought "it's been blown completely out of proportion." She was sure the people realized "Dick had no part in it." On Vietnam, she commented that she agreed with a recent remark Julie had made, that she was willing to die for South Vietnam. Pat said, "I would be willing to die to save freedom for 17 million people who are now having aggression against them with the idea of taking away their freedom and their country." [40]

In another conference, in Oklahoma City, she was asked whether the war would have an impact on the election. "There's not been any killing. We didn't have anyone die last week" was her response. Reminded that Vietnamese were still dying, that the United States Air Force was bombing Hanoi and elsewhere throughout Indochina, she said, "People do want a cessation to this war, but they don't want to lose their freedom." [41]

Throughout the campaign, wherever she went, protesters who were frustrated at being unable to heckle the President heckled her instead. In a New York City appearance, demonstrators chanted "Murderers!" and "Stop Nixon! Stop the bombing!" There were signs, too: "If Nixon Wins, Humanity Loses," "I'm Min-Li, Bomb Me" (on a picture of a Vietnamese child), and, simply, "Shame."[42]

Through it all, Pat kept smiling and being her usual gracious self.

LIKE THE HECKLERS, McGovern was frustrated by Nixon's absence from the podium. He called Nixon's team of speakers "lackeys" and "second-rate bureaucrats" and tried, unsuccessfully, to taunt the President into campaigning. When the Watergate indictments were announced, McGovern charged "whitewash." He contended that "this blatant miscarriage of justice was ordered by the White House." He said the unanswered questions were "staggering in scope," and demanded to know who ordered the break-in, who paid for it, and who was reading the transcripts of the taped conversations.[43]

On October 3, McGovern got massive coverage around the country when he said that Nixon was the most deceitful President and the head of the "most corrupt administration in history." He also charged that Nixon's Vietnam policy was the worst crime since the Nazi extermination of the Jews, and that Nixon was the number-one war maker in the world.

Nixon announced a news conference for October 5, then went into his EOB office to meet with Haldeman to plan his response. They considered two approaches: to ridicule the charges as those of a "desperate drowning politician" or to hit McGovern for character assassination. But Nixon decided instead to ignore McGovern. He recalled Eisenhower's remark about Joe McCarthy— "I'm not going to get in the gutter with that guy"—and said, according to Haldeman's notes, "N not off high road of statesmanship to get in gutter with McGovern." But he did want his team of speakers to defend him by hitting McGovern "on his low-road, gutter approach." More important, he wanted the speakers to turn the debate around by concentrating on other issues, especially amnesty, marijuana, taxes, surrender in Vietnam, and so forth. He told Haldeman to have the team "go with the issues that get to people," amnesty above all.[44]

The first question at the news conference was on McGovern's charges. "Needless to say," Nixon answered, "some of my more partisan advisers feel that I should respond in kind. I shall not do so—not now, not throughout this campaign. I am not going to dignify such comments." He added, "I think the responsible members of the Democratic Party will be turned off by this kind of campaigning, and I would suggest that responsible members of the press, following the single standard to which they are deeply devoted, will also be turned off by it." [45]

Nixon's comment about the press was unusual for him; not since his "last press conference" ten years earlier had he been so sarcastic in public. In private, he was bitter as always, convinced that the reporters had a double standard and were out to get him. In the first week in October, for example, the media pushed hard on the supposed scandal in the grain deal. Cronkite was especially critical. Nixon struck back: "Z—Turn Walter down coldly whenever you feel it is best time to do so. H & C & Z, We are underestimating the damage he did in '68—we must have a strategy for discrediting the T.V. Media immediately." [46]

The New York Times endorsed McGovern. Nixon told Haldeman "there should be a letter to the *Times* or a statement that the *Times* basically *should* endorse McGovern because he stood for everything they stood for—permissiveness, a bug-out from Vietnam, new isolationism, etc." [47]

In fact, the press was helping far more than it was hurting Nixon, because of its failure to pursue the Watergate break-in story. The Washington *Post* was an exception. Woodward and Bernstein stayed on the money trail. On September 18 they reported that Magruder had control of a secret CREEP fund, and Liddy had access to it. On the twentieth, they charged that financial records at CREEP had been destroyed after the arrest of the burglars. On the twenty-eighth, they quoted unnamed but "reliable" sources who said that Mitchell "personally approved withdrawals from the fund." (When Bernstein called Mitchell for a comment, the former Attorney General said, "All that crap, you're putting it in the paper? It's all been denied. Katie Graham's gonna get her tit caught in a big fat wringer if that's published.") [48]

On October 4, the Los Angeles *Times* made a contribution when Jack Nelson and Ronald Ostrow revealed that logs of conversations monitored by the bugs in the DNC had gone to "an official of CREEP who is not among the seven defendants indicted in the case."

Hints, rumors, unnamed sources, unnamed recipients of the fruits of the bugging—there just was not enough that was solid in what the investigative reporters were finding to make a national story with any impact. Buchanan and Allin were able to note, happily, on Nixon's October 3 News Summary, "Watergate is out of the news."

The relative silence on what should have been one of the big issues in the campaign was not entirely the fault of the press. Republican congressmen, led by Ford, plus Administration threats, had managed to turn off the GAO investigation and Chairman Patman's proposed hearings before the House Banking Committee. Equally valuable to Nixon, two Republican judges made important contributions. On September 20, Judge Richey announced that it would be impossible to bring the Democrats' civil suit against CREEP to trial before November 7. He added that none of the depositions taken in the case would be made public until the trial.[49]

On October 4, Chief U.S. District Court Judge John J. Sirica (an Eisenhower appointee), in charge of the trial of the burglars, issued an order prohibiting anyone connected with the case from making public statements about it. Sirica prohibited all law-enforcement agencies, defendants, witnesses, alleged victims, their attorneys, and all persons acting for or with them in connection with the case from making statements to anyone. The order was so broad it apparently applied to McGovern and other Democratic candidates. When the Democrats howled in protest, Sirica backed down a bit; on October 6 he advised McGovern and other Democrats that they should not feel bound by the order. Still, the overall effect was to close off leaks from FBI agents and Justice Department lawyers who were unhappy with the way their bosses were handling the case.[50]

Senator Sam Ervin (D., N.C.) was furious. On October 7, he said that if the trial of the burglars did not begin immediately, he would press for a congressional investigation of the whole Watergate affair. Ervin characterized as "inexcusable" the idea that the burglars could not be tried before November 7 and added, "Anybody who can't prepare the case in 15 minutes ought to have his law license taken away." He ridiculed the claim that the delay was necessary in order to protect the rights of the defendants.[51]

At his October 5 news conference, Nixon took a different view. He thought the whole thing should be left to the courts, and that they should proceed in an orderly manner, giving due consideration to the rights of the defendants.

A reporter asked if he did not think the defendants would be better served "if you people would come through and make a clean breast about what you were trying to get done at the Watergate?"

"One thing that has always puzzled me about it," Nixon replied, "is why anybody would have tried to get anything out of the Watergate." He said that the decision to break in was made at "lower levels, with which I had no knowledge." He pointed out that the FBI had assigned 133 agents to the investigation; they followed eighteen hundred leads and conducted fifteen hundred interviews. He said he had conducted the Hiss investigation (a claim that stretched the truth considerably), and it "was basically a Sunday school exercise compared to the amount of effort that was put into this [Watergate affair]."

Nixon expressed his approval of the massive effort made by the FBI. He said, "I wanted every lead carried out to the end because I wanted to be sure that no member of the White House Staff and no man or woman in a position of major responsibility in the Committee for the Re-election had anything to do with this kind of reprehensible activity."

He was satisfied that no one working for him was involved. The grand jury had handed down its indictments. "It is now time to have the judicial process go forward." He added, "I am going to follow the good advice, which I appreciate, of the members of the press corps," advice given him when he commented on accused murderer Charles Manson, and was widely criticized for doing so. This time he would keep silent in order not to prejudice the rights of the defendants.[52]

To Nixon's disappointment, he got no questions on busing. So, when the traditional "Thank you, Mr. President" signaled the end of the news conference, he put up his hand to stop the outrushing reporters. "One more thing," he said. If Congress did not pass the moratorium he had requested (as it obviously was not going to do, because on his instructions the bill had been held up in committee), he was going to support a constitutional amendment prohibiting busing. It was, he pointed out, a clear-cut issue in the campaign, like amnesty, spending, and defense cuts.[53]

The following week, Nixon spent a day campaigning in Ohio. It included a long motorcade. There were protesters carrying signs along the route. When he spotted them, he raised and extended his arms, spreading the first two fingers in the "V-for-Victory" sign. "This really knocks them for a loop," he remarked, "because they think this is their sign." In a diary entry, he went on to analyze the antiwar protesters.

"I think as the war recedes as an issue," he wrote, "some of these people are going to be lost souls. They basically are haters, they are frustrated, they are alienated—they don't know what to do with their lives." He thought the "saddest group" would be the professors, particularly the younger ones. "They wanted to blame somebody else for their own failures to inspire the students," and they wanted the government to take responsibility for the youngsters. They were going to have a hard time in Nixon's second term, because "the black power thing is gone—the environment has fizzled out—the war will be gone—the question is, what next? I suppose it will be big business or corruption or what have you, but it will be difficult to find one that emotionally will turn the kids on like the war issue."

Nixon thought it would be a good thing to force the professors to "look within themselves—look in the mirror—and realize that it is they who have the responsibility—that they are at fault if the young people are not inspired. They can't blame it on government or anybody else." [54]

THERE WAS SOME TRUTH in Nixon's musings, and some falsehood, and much that was questionable. By no means were all the professors of the early seventies, even the younger ones, monolithic in their views. And certainly thousands of students were inspired by their teachers, inspired to a greater patriotism, a greater love of their country, a desire to serve. If Nixon doubted that, all he had to do was ask his daughters and sons-in-law.

But his thoughts, as he recorded them, were an accurate reflection of his lifelong penchant for indulging himself in generalizations, especially about his opponents. He had always practiced the politics of divisiveness. He wanted to isolate his foes from the body politic. In 1972, goaded by McGovern's aggressive attacks, especially the comparison with Hitler and the accusation that he was using KKK tactics, Nixon brought this practice to its pinnacle. This reflected and reinforced the inner contempt and hatred he felt for those who disagreed with him.

"They are asking for it," he had told Dean and Haldeman three weeks earlier, "and they are going to get it."

And who were "they"? They were the college professors, and their students. The editors and reporters, especially those on the staffs of The New York Times and the Washington Post. The television newscasters, led by Walter Cronkite and Dan Rather. All Democrats from outside the South. All Republicans from east of the Ohio and north of the Potomac. Most members of his Cabinet. The "American leader class" with its whining and whimpering. Big-business men. All bureaucrats, especially those in the State Department, the IRS, the Justice Department, the Park Service, HEW, and the CIA. Welfare recipients. Blacks. Social workers. It was an astonishingly long list. Nixon hated them all.

And whom did he like? Labor leaders, especially the Teamster bosses and, at least in 1972, George Meany. Texas Democrats particularly, southern Democrats generally. A handful of reporters and conservative columnists. Republicans from west of the Mississippi River, especially those from Southern California. Small-business men, at least as a group. The men and women serving in the armed forces. The courtiers on his White House staff.

And, again as a group, those white, middle-class Americans who were enthusiastic recruits for his New American Revolution.

And whom did he love? His family, most of all. Bebe Rebozo. Robert Abplanalp. Perhaps John Connally and John Mitchell. It was an astonishingly short list. His closest advisers—Haldeman, Kissinger, even Colson—were not on it.

And what did he love? His country, certainly, most of all its armed forces and the institution of the Presidency. But as his own words to Haldeman and Dean on September 15 demonstrated, his feelings about the rest of the government, including its executive branch, were decidedly negative. His actions in the 1972 campaign showed how little he cared for the Republican Party. He was contemptuous of Congress, angry at the courts.

And whom did he trust? Haldeman a bit, and Connally a lot, and Rebozo and Abplanalp, but—except for his family and himself —that was about it.

Yet this man, who could trust almost no one and love only a few, inspired among his countrymen an outpouring of trust, admiration, and even affection. It was all the more remarkable considering that he had been unable to deliver on many of the promises he had made in 1968, including an end to busing, getting tougher with criminals, prayer in the schools, welfare reform, an end to the war in Vietnam, and a halt in the growth of government. It was ironic that his great achievements, the ones he was proudest of, including the opening to China, détente, and the beginning of arms control, had more appeal to his opponents than to his friends, as Senator Jackson's amendments in the fall of 1972 demonstrated.

On the great domestic issues of the day, however, Richard Nixon was obviously in much closer touch with his fellow countrymen than was George McGovern. On busing, amnesty, drugs, defense spending, taxes, even Vietnam, he was speaking for a large majority of the people, while McGovern was talking to a shrinking minority. The polls told the story; by the end of the first week in October, after the voters had had a chance to hear both sides for six weeks, they favored Nixon more than 2–1.

In a memo that he titled "General Philosophy and Themes" Haldeman described the difference between Nixon's supporters and McGovern's backers: "Our New Majority are people who are Americans to the core. Southerners, for instance, are more so than the rest of the United States because they are not poisoned by the elitist universities and media. Also, we are strong with Polish, Italian, Mountain State, and farm-type people. We're weak in suburbia and big cities because the people there are soft." [55]

In the last month of the campaign, Nixon prepared to further isolate those who were "soft" from real Americans. Insofar as he was already all but assured of victory, and thus would be President of all the people for four more years, that was as questionable a judgment as his decision that the congressional races did not matter.

CHAPTER TWENTY-SEVEN

THE LAST CAMPAIGN

PART TWO
October 8–November 7, 1972

ON OCTOBER 8, Kissinger and Haig arrived in Paris for what they hoped would be the last round of talks with Le Duc Tho. They worked out an agreement that involved concessions on both sides and included the following major points: the United States would withdraw all its armed forces, but it could continue to supply ARVN; there would be a National Council of Reconciliation, with PRG representation; Hanoi would release the American POWs; the Thieu regime would remain in place in Saigon; the NVA would remain in place in South Vietnam; the United States would contribute to the economic reconstruction of North Vietnam (but not as an admission of guilt or for reparations, but as a gesture of humanity).

For Kissinger, it was a great moment. "I have participated in many spectacular events," he wrote in his memoirs; "I have lived with power; I have seen pomp and ceremony. But the moment that moved me most deeply has to be that cool autumn Sunday afternoon" when the agreement was reached. He called it "my most thrilling moment in public service."[1]

Nixon was equally euphoric. When he saw the provisions of the accord, he described them as "a complete capitulation by the enemy; they were accepting a settlement on our terms." Even the agreement to provide reconstruction aid to Hanoi seemed to Nixon to be a victory, because "however they tried to justify it, taking money from the United States represented a collapse of communist principle."[2]

Kissinger set up a tight schedule for tying up loose ends and arranging for a signing ceremony. He would return to the United

States, get Nixon's approval, then fly to Saigon to get Thieu's approval. On October 21, the United States would stop bombing North Vietnam; Kissinger would fly to Hanoi the next day to initial the peace accord. Formal signing of a peace treaty would come on October 31 when Secretary of State Rogers and the North Vietnamese and South Vietnamese Foreign Ministers met in Paris.

If the timetable held, the war would be over in three weeks. It seemed too good to be true.

On October 10, with Kissinger still working on details with Tho in Paris, McGovern made the major speech of his campaign on Vietnam. He said that on the day he was inaugurated he would stop all bombing and begin the immediate withdrawal of all American troops from Indochina. He would expect Hanoi to return all POWs within ninety days. He would not impose a political settlement, because "I say General Thieu is not worth one more American prisoner, one more drop of American blood. . . . Our problem is that we have asked our armed forces to do the impossible—to save a political regime that doesn't even have the respect of its own people."

McGovern, himself a bomber pilot in World War II, spoke with great depth of feeling about the bombing. "The reality of this war," he said, "is seen in the news photo of the little South Vietnamese girl . . . fleeing in terror from her bombed-out school. She has torn off her flaming clothes and she is running naked into the lens of that camera. That picture ought to break the heart of every American. How can we rest with the grim knowledge that the burning napalm that splashed over [her] and countless thousands of other children was dropped in the name of America?" [3]

The following day, Kissinger cabled that he was staying in Paris for an extra day because he was on the verge of a major breakthrough on the details and wanted to seal the deal. Nixon thereupon announced that he was stopping the bombing of Hanoi and its immediate vicinity.

On October 12, Kissinger and Haig returned. They went immediately to Nixon's EOB office to report. Kissinger was wearing the broadest smile Nixon had ever seen. "Well, Mr. President," he began, "it looks like we've got three out of three!" First China, then the Soviet Union, now Vietnam. He outlined the agreement, and the schedule for the cease-fire and the signing ceremony in Paris. Nixon ordered steaks and a bottle of Château Lafite-Rothschild to toast the success.

But Haig seemed less enthusiastic. Nixon asked him how he felt about the terms from Thieu's point of view. Haig said he honestly felt they were a good deal for Thieu, but confessed that he doubted Thieu would see it that way. [4]

Haig's response dampened Nixon's mood. Ambiguity set in again. The following day he sent a message to the North Vietnamese delegation in Paris. He said that while he accepted the basic draft of the agreement, there were "technical issues" that needed to be clarified, and "substantive changes" that he had to insist upon. These concerned the PRG's status and the nature of the duties of the National Council of Reconciliation, points that were certain to be crucial to Thieu. The North Vietnamese replied that Nixon was demanding changes in points already agreed upon, which they could not accept.[5]

That cooled Nixon considerably. He told Kissinger that a settlement before the election "would not particularly help us . . ." Kissinger suggested that a complete bombing halt would be a great help, as it would demonstrate America's good faith to Hanoi. Nixon had already decreased the level of bombing from 200 to 150 sorties per day, but he was "absolutely opposed" to a complete halt. He said that if everything worked out and Kissinger did go to Hanoi to initial the agreement, he would "consider a bombing *pause* for the few days he was there. But there would be no bombing *halt* until the agreement was signed. I was not going to be taken in by the mere prospect of an agreement as Johnson had been in 1968."[6]

On October 15, Nixon met with Kissinger, who was off the next day for Paris. Haldeman took notes. Nixon expressed his concern: "Will it look like we've given in to Jane Fonda?" They discussed the PR aspects of the accords. Nixon, Haldeman's notes recorded, was worried "re: q[uestion] of appearance of P[resident] crawling."[7]

According to Colson, while Kissinger pushed for a quick, pre-election settlement, the President wanted to delay. "Our great fear," Colson said in an interview, was that a settlement "would let people say, 'Well, thank goodness the war is over. Now we can go on and worry about peace and we will elect a Democrat because Democrats always do more in peacetime.' The other thing was that we didn't want to appear to be exploiting, as Johnson had done in '68 with the bombing pause, which was so blatantly and transparently political. After the fifteenth of October it was definitely contrary to our interest to get an agreement."[8]

On October 16, Kissinger met with the President from 10:15 to 11 A.M. Nixon gave him a handwritten note of instructions. "Do what is right without regard to the election," it said. "At all costs we must avoid the fact or the impression that we have imposed or agreed to a coalition government." Then Kissinger flew off to Paris.[9]

As Kissinger left, Nixon drove over to the Statler-Hilton, where he substituted for Kissinger as the principal speaker to a thousand members of the National League of Families of American Prisoners and Missing in Southeast Asia. He used the occasion to reply to McGovern's campaign speech on Vietnam.

He made a blistering attack on "the so-called opinion leaders of this country" for not supporting him on May 8 when he ordered the bombing of Hanoi and the mining of Haiphong. He denounced the "leaders of the media, the great editors and publishers and television commentators and the rest . . . the presidents of our universities and the professors and the rest . . . our top businessmen" for giving him "precious little support" when he made the most difficult decision of his Presidency.

But the POW families had supported him, and he thanked them for that, saying it was "heartwarming." He pledged that the fate of the POWs would not be left "to the goodwill of the enemy" and that draft evaders and deserters "will pay a price for their choice." These barbs directed at McGovern brought the audience to its feet for a standing ovation.

As to negotiations to end the war, Nixon said, "I shall not and cannot comment," because "I would not want to raise false hopes." He did promise, "We shall not stain the honor of the United States." [10]

In Paris, hitches developed. The North Vietnamese wanted a promise to release all Vietcong civilian prisoners held by the Thieu government; Kissinger would not give it. There was disagreement over the provisions for resupply of ARVN and NVA forces in South Vietnam, and over the language regarding American POWs held in Laos and Cambodia. Nixon sent a note to the Communists, telling them he thought another meeting would be necessary before Kissinger could go to Hanoi and the United States stopped the bombing. As a sign of goodwill, he added, he would maintain the current restrictions on bombing sorties.

The North Vietnamese replied that they accepted Nixon's position on arms replacements and they agreed to an unconditional release of POWs in North Vietnam. Nixon sent a cable to Hanoi saying that the agreement could now be considered complete.

It was not, however. The problem of the American POWs in Laos and Cambodia remained, along with the much greater stumbling block of obtaining Thieu's acceptance of the overall accord.

On October 18, Kissinger flew to Saigon. He carried with him a letter from Nixon to Thieu. Nixon wrote, "I believe we have no reasonable alternative but to accept this agreement." [11]

Thieu did not agree. He proved to be exceedingly difficult. Kissinger was beside himself. Having achieved so much, in his own view, he was being undercut by the very people he had saved.

He compared the Vietnamese, North and South, to tigers balanced on stools in a cage, with himself as the animal trainer, cracking the whip to force them to go through their paces. "When one is in place, the other jumps off. If it was only the U.S. and the North Vietnamese, it would be easier to reach agreement," he complained.[12]

To Nixon, Kissinger said he was caught in a paradoxical situation "in which North Vietnam, which had in effect lost the war, was acting as if it had won; while South Vietnam, which had effectively won the war, was acting as if it had lost."[13]

Had Thieu seen that message, he would have exploded in laughter or broken down in tears. How could Kissinger say such a thing? The accord gave the NVA the right to keep 150,000 troops in South Vietnam and the PRG the right to play a role in the political life of Thieu's country, because no matter how brilliantly Kissinger defended his National Council proposal, he could not cover the truth: it meant a coalition government, with Communist participation. Meanwhile, the Americans would be leaving.

Nixon began to realize that he had been premature in calling the agreement complete, and the doubts that he had had all along about the wisdom of settling before the election began to strengthen. Three developments reinforced those doubts.

First, Haig had stayed behind when Kissinger went to Paris and then Saigon, and Haig was using his access to Nixon to undercut his boss. Haig told the President that the Communists were on the move militarily, seizing as much territory around Saigon as they could before the agreement was signed. Haig warned that the Communists intended to kill all their opponents in the areas that they controlled when the cease-fire was announced. "This would be a murderous bloodbath," Nixon wrote in his diary; if it happened, the bloodbath would make it difficult if not impossible to justify the settlement.[14]

(The United States, meanwhile, was moving to strengthen ARVN before the accord was signed on October 31 and the provisions for limited material replacement went into effect. On October 20, Operation Enhance Plus began; it was a massive airlift of military equipment and supplies to South Vietnam. The emphasis was on air power; Enhance Plus, when completed, gave the South Vietnamese the fourth-largest air force in the world.)

Second, Nixon was under pressure from the right wing in the United States. *National Review*, William F. Buckley's magazine, warned that any settlement must not be a cover for a coalition government, and must include a public pledge to continue all-out military aid to South Vietnam. It added, "Be steadfast, Doc [Kissinger]. Don't give it away. Don't be seduced by dreams of an even greater victory for RN [in the election]. We want to be gentlemanly about it, but we promise you the biggest backlash you ever saw, if you falter now." [15]

Third, General Westmoreland told Nixon he was opposed to the agreement. Although Westmoreland had recently completed his four-year tour as Army Chief of Staff and retired, on October 20 Nixon called him to the White House for consultation. When the President finished briefing the general on the proposed settlement, Westmoreland urged him "to delay action on the new agreement and to hold out for better terms." He believed that more bombing of Hanoi and continued mining of Haiphong would force the Communists to make "meaningful concessions." He emphasized that it was "vital" that North Vietnamese troops be compelled to withdraw from South Vietnam. As to the National Council of Reconciliation, Westmoreland thought it was "impractical, almost absurd, nothing more than a facade." [16]

Westmoreland was not the only high-ranking officer to oppose the agreement. The American military had fought long and hard in South Vietnam, under severe restrictions and at the cost of many a reputation. To a number of senior officers, the idea that the politicians were ready to make deals—that they, like Thieu, believed would all but certainly lead to the eventual collapse of the Saigon government—was galling. Admiral Zumwalt made a bitter comment: "There are at least two words no one can use to characterize the outcome of that two-faced policy. One is 'peace.' The other is 'honor.' " [17]

After his meeting with Westmoreland, Nixon sent a cable to Kissinger: "As you continue discussions with Thieu, I wish to re-emphasize again that nothing that is done should be influenced by the U.S. election deadline . . . a settlement which takes place before the election which is, at best, a washout, has a high risk of severely damaging the U.S. domestic scene, if the settlement were to open us up to the charge that we made a poorer settlement now than what we might have achieved had we waited until after the election." [18]

The great danger, at this point, was that if the Americans went back on the agreement because of Thieu's refusal to accept it, Hanoi would go public with the details of the settlement. Such an action would show that the Communists had accepted the terms Nixon had proposed on May 8, down to the details, only to have the Americans reject the deal. Nixon faced that danger in the last sentence of his cable to Kissinger: "I am aware of the risk that Hanoi might go public but am confident that we can handle this eventuality much easier than we could handle a pre-election blow-up with Thieu or an agreement which would be criticized as a pretext for U.S. withdrawal." [19]

On October 21, Kissinger met with South Vietnamese leaders, but not Thieu; they demanded twenty-three changes in the draft agreement, most importantly, a requirement that the NVA withdraw from their country and the elimination of the National Council. Kissinger argued, to no avail. He advised Nixon, by cable, that he wanted to go to Hanoi anyway, as scheduled, even without Thieu's agreement. Nixon refused. The President feared that the Communists would exploit Kissinger's presence in Hanoi and use it to turn American public opinion against Thieu. He told Kissinger there would be no trip to Hanoi unless and until Thieu agreed to the settlement.[20]

To pressure Thieu, Nixon sent him a warning, via Kissinger: "Were you to find the agreement to be unacceptable at this point and the other side were to reveal the extraordinary limits to which it has gone in meeting demands put upon them, it is my judgment that your decision would have the most serious effects upon my ability to continue to provide support for you and for the government of South Vietnam." [21]

But even as he put pressure on Thieu to accept, even as he encouraged Kissinger to push the settlement, Nixon was drawn increasingly to the option Westmoreland had recommended, especially when Haig joined in. Haig said that after the election Nixon would be armed with a mandate that he could use to force concessions from Hanoi, because he would "be less constrained." Nixon noted in his diary, "Immediately after the election we will have an enormous mandate . . . and the enemy then either has to settle or face the consequences of what we could do to them." [22]

But the enemy already *had* settled, on the terms Nixon had offered on May 8, terms that he had characterized as "a complete capitulation by the enemy." It was Thieu who refused to settle, not Hanoi.

Kissinger's manipulations, and Nixon's policies, had put Nixon in the damnedest position. If Hanoi went public at this point, the negotiating record would show that the Communists had agreed to everything Nixon had required, and would prove that Saigon, not Hanoi, was blocking peace. The tail was wagging the dog. Thieu had a veto power that he was determined to use. But if he used it, Nixon knew that the doves would stir up American public opinion against Saigon. The 93d Congress would refuse to give the President any funds to continue the war. Hanoi would then win everything. All the sacrifices would have been in vain. Instead of peace with honor, there would be defeat with humiliation. On October 22, the worst happened. Thieu absolutely refused to accept the settlement. Kissinger informed the President by cable, and commented, "I need not tell you the crisis with which this confronts us." In a second cable, he added, "It is hard to exaggerate the toughness of Thieu's position. His demands verge on insanity."[23]

Thieu demanded total withdrawal of the NVA forces from his country and the elimination of the National Council from the settlement. Nixon knew there was no possibility of the Communists accepting such terms. But he could not bring himself to confess, two weeks before the election, that the negotiations had failed. He therefore sent a cable to Hanoi, requesting one more meeting. He said that the text of the meeting would be considered final, and as a token of goodwill he offered a bombing halt north of the twentieth parallel.

Nixon's message crossed wires with a cable from Hanoi. The North Vietnamese insisted that the agreement was complete and no further meetings were necessary. They were ready to receive Kissinger in Hanoi as scheduled.

Nixon replied on October 25. He said he regretted that a "brief delay" in the signing was necessary, but pointed out that he could not accept an agreement that Thieu had rejected. He repeated his request for one more meeting. Then the man who had sworn on a number of occasions that under no circumstances would he follow the Johnson precedent and institute a pre-election bombing halt said that if Hanoi would agree to another meeting, as soon as the text had been completed and even without Thieu's acceptance of it, he would completely stop the bombing of North Vietnam.[24]

Instead of flying from Saigon to Hanoi, as planned, to sign the agreement, Kissinger flew home from Saigon. He and Nixon now had to await Hanoi's response. They had to know that it would be negative, not necessarily to the proposal for another meeting, but certainly to any acquiescence to Thieu's demands. In any case, they could only wait for events they could not control.

Rumors about an imminent peace, meanwhile, were filling the American newspapers and television news programs. There were all sorts of guesses as to what was contained in the deal. *Newsweek* said that the POWs would be freed and a coalition formed until national elections could be held. Nixon circled "coalition" and scribbled beside it, "K—the code word we must knock down." Dan Rather reported that the North Vietnamese were skeptical that any pre-election accord would be long-lived and were saying that if Nixon was negotiating for any other purpose than the election, it would be "incredible." Nixon commented, "K—good—if they believe this—we can tell them we should wait."[25]

Bernard Kalb said on CBS radio that Thieu was reported to have said that if the NVA remained in South Vietnam "the war will have proved to be only a U.S. war of aggression and the GI and ARVN sacrifices will have proven unnecessary and a betrayal." Nixon winced at the force of that one. He wrote, "K—a dangerous charge."[26]

So what did the President want? A settlement or a chance to bomb Hanoi into further concessions? Did he want Thieu to accept the Kissinger deal or reject it? It is impossible to say, because he himself did not know. In any case, he had put himself in a position in which it was no longer his decision to make. After all those lives sacrificed, all those bombs, all that money spent, all that effort, the United States had lost control of events. It was up to the Vietnamese, North and South, to settle their war.

BACK IN 1962, during the race for governor of California, Pat Brown had charged that Nixon had no heart, and claimed that he was a better American than Nixon. In all Nixon's campaigns prior to 1972, no one had gotten to him as Brown did with those statements. In his own way, Nixon had liked and respected some of his opponents (Kennedy, Johnson, Humphrey); he was contemptuous of others (Voorhis, Douglas, Stevenson); he attacked them all; but Brown was the one who got him so angry that he lost control. Brown's remarks were what had set him off at his "last press conference." He had been talking about Brown—"I believe Governor Brown has a heart, even though he believes I do not. I believe he is a good American, even though he feels I am not"—when he lost his temper completely and started in on the press, charging that while he defended Brown's patriotism, "you gentlemen [the press] didn't report it."

In 1972, McGovern got to Nixon even more than Brown had done. But this time around, Nixon kept control. He never once mentioned McGovern in public. But in private he was furious. What upset him were McGovern's remarks about Nixon as a person. It was not so much the "most corrupt Administration in history" charge, or even the accusation that Nixon's tactics were those of the KKK; the charge that cut was the comparison of Nixon with Hitler. Insofar as no one in human history, not even Attila the Hun, not even Stalin, can be compared to Hitler, who was pure evil and who did more harm to more people than any other human being, the comparison was blatantly unfair, unjustified, below the belt, inexcusable. Nixon had every reason to be furious.

Further, Nixon could not abide McGovern's moralism. It was not just that he disagreed with McGovern so strongly on such issues as amnesty, abortion, and marijuana; McGovern had a "holier-than-thou" attitude that Nixon despised.

Nixon's feelings were so strong that he did things he had not done in previous campaigns. For example, he kept after Colson to get the IRS to run checks on McGovern's contributors.[27] When the New York *Post* began a story, "According to McGovern, the President of the United States is a liar, barbarian, immoral, cruel and murderous," Nixon underlined the sentence and commented, "H & C—I believe he must be *taken apart*."[28]

McGovern felt he had to use harsh and strident language; as O'Brien explained, "We must create a public demand that Nixon come out of the White House and campaign. The only way we can do that is through the media."[29] But Nixon would not come out; instead he issued daily instructions to his surrogate speakers to "hit McGovern harder."

It bothered Nixon that not only the elite newspapers but also the elite college students favored McGovern. He tried to dismiss this fact with sarcastic remarks, but clearly he was disturbed, enough so that he launched a major counterattack.

A campus poll found that McGovern was ahead of Nixon by an 8–1 ratio among student-body heads and campus editors. Nixon commented, "H—note—the *activists* and those most influenced by professors."[30] Harvard law students favored McGovern 698–131, while Harvard law faculty were 34–4 for McGovern. Nixon wrote, "H—E—note—not a good area for future recruitment!"[31] Talking to Haldeman about his postelection reorganization plans, Nixon thundered, "None of them in the Cabinet, do you understand? None of those Harvard bastards!"[32]

In 1962, Nixon's anger had hurt him. In 1972, he used it effectively. He saw clearly that while McGovern's approach appealed to the Harvard types, it hurt him with a majority of Americans. On his News Summary on October 20, he circled a comment about McGovern's "pretentious moralism" and wrote, "C—H—His real weakness." He set out to exploit it.

In the last weeks of the campaign, Nixon delivered a series of nationally broadcast radio addresses. On October 21, his subject was his philosophy of government. He could as well have entitled it his answer to McGovern's preaching. In preparing the talk with Safire, Nixon remarked, "Leadership requires character, and too much education today destroys character." At another point he told Safire, "Try this: 'People who have had the advantage of a superior education think that gives them the right to lead.' Well, the hell with that, education's more of a liability these days." [33] McGovern had a Ph.D. in American history from Northwestern University. His mentor had been Ray Allen Billington, one of the greatest historians of the American West and a student of the legendary Frederick Jackson Turner.

In the radio address, Nixon went after McGovern and his elitism and moralism—without ever mentioning his opponent by name—to a fare-thee-well. He said there were "a great many people in politics . . . who believe that the people just do not know what's good for them. Putting it bluntly, they have more faith in government than they have in people. . . . To them, the will of the people is the 'prejudice of the masses.' "

When a citizen complained about high taxes, Nixon said, "I don't think it is right to charge him with selfishness, with not caring about the poor and the dependent.

"When a mother sees her child taken away from a neighborhood school and transported miles away, and she objects to that, I don't think it is right to charge her with bigotry.

"When young people apply for jobs . . . and find the door closed because they don't fit into some numerical quota, despite their ability, and they object, I do not think it is right to condemn those young people as insensitive or racist.

"There is no reason to feel guilty about wanting to enjoy what you get and get what you earn, about wanting your children in good schools close to home or about wanting to be judged fairly on your ability. Those are not values to be ashamed of; those are values to be proud of. Those are values that I shall always stand up for when they come under attack."

Nixon said that when a father tried to tell his children what to do, it was paternalism. When an employer tried to tell his workers that he knew what was best for them, that was paternalism. And when government tried to tell people how to conduct their lives, that too was paternalism. But, he went on, "most Americans don't like to be under anybody's control, no matter how benevolent that control may be." [34]

Ten days later, in an exclusive interview for the Washington Star, Nixon returned to the theme, although not so adroitly. "The average American is just like the child in the family," he said. "You give him some responsibility and he is going to amount to something. He is going to do something. If, on the other hand, you make him completely dependent and pamper him and cater to him too much, you are going to make him soft, spoiled and eventually a very weak individual." [35]

"Soft" and "weak" were words Nixon used frequently in characterizing McGovern in private, and might have used in public to good effect, but that "child in the family" business could have hurt Nixon. Fortunately for the President, the interview—which when it appeared did cause commentators to charge that Nixon had callously shown his contempt for the American people—was not published until after the election.

By OCTOBER OF 1972 Nixon was totally addicted to his daily News Summary. Although it had grown in scope, size, and depth of coverage, he read the fifty or more pages (single spaced) carefully. Toward the end of the campaign, he noted on one issue, "Buchanan—Tell Mort [Allin] et al that I am constantly amazed at the brilliant work done in preparing the News Summary. It is invaluable . . . RN." [36] He underlined passages and made innumerable marginal comments; he continued to issue orders through those comments, and to pass on his instinctive reaction to events or the statements of others. More than ever, that marginalia revealed the real Nixon.

On October 9, Nixon read that Hugh Sidey had said that the Administration controlled the media better than any of its predecessors. Nixon could hardly believe his eyes. "C & H & B," he wrote, "*We* control the media?! The biggest joke of the year." [37]

Insofar as the Washington *Post* and *The New York Times* were concerned, Nixon for once was not exaggerating. In the last month of the campaign, those two newspapers hammered away at Nixon, most of all on Watergate and other excesses. On October 10, Woodward and Bernstein got one of their first banner headlines above the fold: "FBI FINDS NIXON AIDES SABOTAGED DEMOCRATS." The story began, "FBI agents have established that the Watergate bugging incident stemmed from a massive campaign of political spying and sabotage conducted on behalf of President Nixon's re-election and directed by officials of the White House and the Committee for the Re-election of the President."

According to the unnamed agents, what Nixon's people had done was not new, but it was "unprecedented in scope and intensity." It included following members of the families of Democratic candidates and assembling dossiers on their personal lives, forging letters and distributing them under the candidates' letterheads, leaking false and manufactured items to the press, throwing campaign schedules into disarray, seizing confidential campaign files, and planting provocateurs in the ranks of potential demonstrators. The White House refused to comment on the story; an unnamed official at CREEP said, "The *Post* story is not only fiction but a collection of absurdities."

Five days later, Woodward and Bernstein named Donald Segretti as the head of the dirty-tricks operation, and wrote that Segretti reported to Nixon's appointments secretary, Dwight Chapin. *The New York Times* did a feature article on Segretti, charging that he had told contradictory stories about whom he was working for and who was paying for his activities.[38]

Unlike the *Post*'s stories about the money trail of the Watergate burglars, the Segretti items got a big play in the national media. In the October 16 News Summary, Buchanan wrote, "The Left elite is humping for all it is worth this weekend, and this morning, to tie the Watergate to the White House, via the 'Chapin Connection.' This morning's Today Show led with the Time Magazine story, this morning's CBS AM news gave us all that came out of the weekend." He worried that an effort was being made to tie the White House not simply to Segretti's "hanky-panky—but directly to an operation of which the Watergate was an integral part." He thought another danger was that the story was designed "to tear RN down, rather than try the impossible of building McGovern up." Buchanan concluded, "The question of how to handle this seems the present major political decision, on our part, of the campaign."

Despite Buchanan's fears, Nixon took it in stride. He underlined Buchanan's last sentence, then commented, "H—*no*—That occurred when Wallace got out." [39]

The reason Nixon was so calm was that he realized something Buchanan had missed, which was that the American people were likely to regard Segretti's and Chapin's activities as the pranks of a couple of USC fraternity boys. In a sense, the spying and sabotage stories were helping Nixon. Few doubted that they were true, but few doubted that the Democrats did the same kinds of things, or that the Federalists and nineteenth-century Jeffersonian Republicans had engaged in similar actions, come to that. That was why the Segretti story got picked up while the Watergate money trail story sank of its own weight—there was nothing inexplicable here, no mystery, no doubt about motive or who ordered it or why.

There was danger to Nixon in the story; the Chapin connection brought it out of CREEP and into the White House, and Segretti had got his funds from the same account that supported the burglars, before and after the break-in. Because of those vulnerabilities, Segretti could not be produced to deny the stories, or to defend himself with a "so's your old man" argument. So he was told to disappear until after the election.[40]

Nixon instructed Haldeman on how to carry on. First, he wanted his surrogate speakers to ignore the spy and sabotage stories and continue to attack McGovern, "more in sorrow than in anger. Hit hard on the issues." As to the "most corrupt Administration" charge, Nixon wanted the surrogates to emphasize that "in not one instance in four years has there been any personal corruption." As no one had been caught stealing any money, or gotten rich through his association with the Administration, no one was guilty.[41]

Still the reporters pressed on. Woodward and Bernstein charged on October 16 that Nixon's personal attorney, Herb Kalmbach, authorized payments from CREEP's secret intelligence-gathering and espionage fund. Two days later *The New York Times* revealed that Segretti had made frequent telephone calls not only to Chapin but also to Howard Hunt. Segretti was not available for comment; Ziegler and MacGregor accused reporters of printing "hearsay," "innuendo," and "unsubstantiated rumors."

Nixon made no public comment, but he recorded his reaction in his diary. He characterized the charges against Segretti, Chapin, and Kalmbach as "McCarthyism at its very worst."[42] As always, in his view, the media were indulging themselves in a "double standard that permitted massive and frequently distorted coverage of Watergate while virtually ignoring the many serious violations of law and ethics committed against us."[43] For example, he noted, the reporters "excused [Democratic prankster] Dick Tuck and other operations as being just good clean fun, but where we are doing it, it is grim and vicious espionage and sabotage of the worst type." He consoled himself with a thought that he passed on to Haldeman in a midnight telephone call: "The latest attack on Chapin et al. was the 'last burp' of the Eastern establishment."[44]

On the morning of October 25, Woodward and Bernstein broke the biggest story yet. The *Post* headline read, "TESTIMONY TIES TOP NIXON AIDE TO SECRET FUND." The story said that Haldeman was one of five men authorized to approve payments from the CREEP espionage and dirty-tricks fund. It therefore tied Watergate not just to the White House but to the President's personal chief of staff. The *Post* charged that Hugh Sloan, Stans's assistant, had testified that Haldeman had approved the expenditure of hundreds of thousands of dollars for spying and sabotage activities.

Ziegler issued an immediate denial. He said the story was "untrue" and accused the *Post* of "shabby journalism" and "a blatant effort at character assassination." McGovern tried to put the spotlight on Nixon. He declared that the United States faced a "moral and a constitutional crisis of unprecedented dimensions" because of "widespread abuse of power" by the Nixon Administration.[45]

Haldeman, Nixon wrote in his diary, "is a strong man and took it very, very well. He says that the story was inaccurate insofar as the Hugh Sloan testimony was concerned."

The President noted something else: "Haldeman spoke rather darkly of the fact that there was a clique in the White House that were out to get him. I trust he is not getting a persecution complex."[46]

What Haldeman's suspicions portended was simple enough: as the investigative reporters got closer and closer to the Oval Office, Nixon's aides were beginning to scramble to protect themselves. There was still almost two weeks to go in the campaign; they had to hold it together until November 7.

There was another aspect to the infighting, backbiting, and intrigue going on among the courtiers in the Nixon White House, and it had nothing to do with Watergate. Kissinger had just returned from Saigon, empty-handed. His fellow courtiers, led by Haldeman, Ehrlichman, Colson, and Haig, were increasingly jealous of and angry with him. They were also suspicious that he was trying to set up a situation in which he could claim what he did not have, a settlement, and thus seize the credit for the coming election victory. They also feared that he had given away too much, which raised the possibility of right-wing opposition.

What Kissinger did have, which his White House critics did not, was access to the media, and his own power base, one that rested on the adulation the reporters felt for him. And Kissinger was a man who always used all his assets in promoting himself.

IN THE TWO WEEKS between Kissinger's return and the election, Nixon's obvious best course of action was to attempt to do with Vietnam what he was doing with Watergate, keep it out of the news. Accordingly, he instructed Kissinger to "keep things quiet."[47]

Instead, Kissinger undertook a round of background briefings to the press. One theme was how much he had accomplished in spite of his unnamed opponents in the White House. "You can't believe how hard it is, especially for a Jew," he told a Jewish journalist. "You can't begin to imagine how much anti-Semitism there is at the top of this government—and I mean at the top."[48]

James Reston, one of Kissinger's favorite recipients of his leaks, took up Kissinger's theme: "And it is also true that there are influential men around the President who are arguing that he doesn't need a cease-fire before the election and will get a better settlement later on. . . . Well, nobody knows in this capital these days because—and this is the heart of the Washington problem—

there is mistrust in the President because he trusts no man, even many of the men in his official family." [49]

On October 25, Kissinger had lunch with Max Frankel, Washington bureau chief of *The New York Times*. When Kissinger told Nixon that afternoon, "I've just briefed Max Frankel on the general agreement," Nixon "was so mad his teeth clenched," Colson recalled. "He was furious." Nixon later complained to Colson, "I suppose now everybody's going to say that Kissinger won the election." [50] And Frankel's article, the following day, carried on the front page, was headlined: "AIDES SEE A TRUCE IN FEW WEEKS; MAYBE BY ELECTION DAY." Kissinger's defense of his leaks was the need to preempt Hanoi, to get out the American version before Hanoi made the negotiating record public.

Around midnight, October 25–26, Hanoi radio began broadcasting the terms of the settlement. The Communists said they had reached an agreement, but "the United States has not respected [it]. The Democratic Republic of Vietnam denounces the frivolous attitude of the Nixon Administration."

The news quickly spread around the world and started intense speculation. The most important discussion took place in the Oval Office, where Kissinger and Nixon assessed the situation. In Nixon's words, they agreed that Kissinger would use a previously scheduled press conference that morning "to undercut the North Vietnamese propaganda maneuver and to make sure that our version of the agreement was the one that had greater public impact." [51]

Kissinger had given hundreds of backgrounders by this time and had held dozens of on-the-record press conferences, but he had never before appeared live on television, because the White House press people were convinced that his heavy German accent would not play well in Middle America. But this occasion was so important that the decision was to go live. [52]

The Briefing Room was jammed with reporters, confused and skeptical. Kissinger, calm and professorial, appeared confident.

In his opening remarks, he declared, "We believe that peace is at hand. We believe that an agreement is within sight, based on the May 8th proposal of the President . . . which is just to all parties." Only minor details remained before the settlement was signed.

The clause "peace is at hand" made banner headlines around the world. An enormous wave of relief swept over the country, tempered by skepticism from those who had got their hopes so high before, exactly four years earlier, when Johnson announced the bombing halt, only to have those hopes dashed. Still, overall, Kissinger's announcement created euphoria similar to that following Prime Minister Neville Chamberlain's post-Munich conference claim to have achieved "peace in our time."

Inside the White House, however, there was more anger than euphoria. Haldeman and Ehrlichman, among others, felt that Kissinger was forcing his way into the center in an election that was already won. He had violated a cardinal rule, calling attention to himself and distracting it from Nixon. They suspected, rightly, that Kissinger had been saying in his private briefings that Nixon could not have achieved the breakthrough, that Kissinger had indicated that Nixon was so belligerent that he had failed to pick up the nuances of Le Duc Tho's position, that he had even accused Nixon of slowness of thought. Only Kissinger had the subtlety of mind to discern the changes in Hanoi's attitude. And if Kissinger had actually concluded an agreement, Haldeman and Ehrlichman wondered, where was it? [53]

When they wrote their memoirs, neither Nixon nor Kissinger gave any details as to Nixon's reaction to "peace is at hand." Evidently Nixon used some strong language; he wrote that "Kissinger himself soon realized that it was a mistake to have gone so far . . ." Nixon pointed out that Kissinger's pronouncement had created a serious diplomatic problem: "I knew immediately that our bargaining position with the North Vietnamese would be seriously eroded and our problem of bringing Thieu . . . along would be made even more difficult." [54]

But Nixon, typically, was more worried about the PR problem the promise created. His first concern was, Who will get the credit? On his News Summary the next day, he instructed on a page quoting reactions from around the country, "C—must have positive comments across board—This is RN's settlement." MIA and POW families, according to the AP wire, "reacted with prayers and crossed fingers." Nixon noted, "C—be sure they praise it." [55]

Republican senators were lavish in their praise, some Democrats only slightly less so. Frank Church said, "If it [peace] is now to be reached at a highly opportune time for Nixon, I can only say I hold peace more dear than politics." Senator William Proximire was more cautious: "I hope we will not delay or kill this opportunity by demanding further negotiations." McGovern thought it was all over for him, but indicated he wanted peace more than the Presidency. Senator Eugene McCarthy was one of the few to raise a critical note; he demanded an explanation as to why "this was not done four years ago." [56]

That, indeed, had been the first question asked of Kissinger at his televised press conference. Kissinger had replied that there was "no possibility of achieving this agreement four years ago" because of Hanoi's demand that Thieu be overthrown. The South Vietnamese disagreed violently with Kissinger on this point; in their view, there was no significant difference between Kissinger's 1972 agreement and what the Communists had demanded of the Nixon Administration in May of 1969. Thieu and his advisers felt that Kissinger's National Council of Reconciliation was exactly the coalition government Hanoi had always wanted, while on the military side the Communists were getting more than they would have settled for in 1969, because the NVA was now in force in South Vietnam.[57]

Kissinger anticipated this criticism from Saigon. He spent the afternoon of October 26 dealing with it in advance, beginning with another background briefing for television reporters, followed by an hour of telephone calls to columnists, an hour-long conference with Joseph Kraft, and a final hour taking calls from reporters. The next day he talked to senior representatives from the newsmagazines, the wire services, and *The New York Times*.[58]

All that effort paid off. Polls showed Kissinger was almost as popular as the President. And Reston, in his October 27 column, wrote, "It has been a long time since Washington has heard such a candid and even brilliant explanation of an intricate political problem as Henry Kissinger gave to the press on the peace negotiations."

But all the brilliance in the world, all the good PR notwithstanding, could not disguise Kissinger's duplicity. He had described as a dramatic diplomatic breakthrough what was in fact a diplomatic failure. In the process, he had put his boss in a highly vulnerable position, not necessarily for the election, but afterward.

President Thieu made this clear on October 27, when he declared that South Vietnam would not be bound by any peace agreement that he did not sign. He repeated his demands, that North Vietnam withdraw its troops from the South and that Hanoi recognize South Vietnam as a sovereign nation without PRG participation in the government. He rejected the National Council out of hand.

Hanoi also undercut Kissinger's claims; the North Vietnamese government announced that its negotiators would not meet with Kissinger to discuss the "minor details" that needed ironing out, but only to sign the already agreed upon settlement. Le Duc Tho said "peace is at the end of a pen."[59]

Nixon was in a bind. He could not fire the popular Kissinger, or repudiate the agreement that he himself had called "complete." The President struggled to extricate himself from a bad situation.

In an October 29 briefing for his surrogate speakers, he stressed that he had achieved "peace with honor—not surrender—not begging." He spoke of the "historic year of 1972," in which he had given the world "a chance for peace for a generation." [60]

That same day, he put pressure on Thieu. In a letter to the South Vietnamese President, Nixon defended the National Council idea, calling it "a face-saving device for the communists to cover their collapse on their demands for a coalition government and your resignation." He added a warning, "If the evident drift towards disagreement between the two of us continues . . . the essential base for U.S. support for you and your Government will be destroyed. In this respect the comments of your Foreign Minister that the U.S. is negotiating a surrender are as damaging as they are unfair and improper." [61]

There was irony here: exactly four years earlier, Nixon had urged Thieu not to go to Paris for negotiations with the North Vietnamese; now he was trying to force Thieu to go to Paris to accept a settlement.

But Thieu would not cooperate. As a result, a backlash, similar to the one that had hit Humphrey in 1968, began to appear possible. As the details of the agreement began to sink in, McGovern and others joined Senator McCarthy in demanding to know what had been gained that could not have been achieved four years earlier. McGovern's aides were cheering up at news that polls were indicating people had doubts as to how close peace really was. Mary McGrory wrote in the Washington *Star* that there was a "bewildering adverse reaction [to 'peace is at hand']. Canvassers reported even among the Silent Majority, there was indignation about the timing." An unhappy Nixon commented, "H—K—C—Note. This time she is reporting what we are finding." [62]

Nixon did what he did best. He counterattacked. On November 2, in his first televised political broadcast of the campaign, he said he was determined that "the central points be clearly settled, so that there will be no misunderstanding which could lead to a breakdown of the settlement and a resumption of the war.

"We are going to sign the agreement when the agreement is right, not one day before—and when the agreement is right, we are going to sign without one day's delay." That dealt with those who wanted to know why more negotiations were necessary if peace was really at hand. To appease the hawks, Nixon had the White House leak information about Enhance Plus, with the stress on the hundreds of fighter-bombers going to Saigon. [63]

The next day, in Rhode Island, Nixon again defended the settlement. He said, "We have made a breakthrough in the negotiations which will lead to peace." The agreement met "the three major principles that I laid down in my speech of May 8." First, he said, there would be a cease-fire throughout Indochina, not just in Vietnam but in Cambodia and Laos. "We have agreed on that." (In fact, Hanoi insisted that the agreement did *not* cover Laos or Cambodia.) Second, all POWs would be returned and all MIAs accounted for. Third, "we have reached agreement on the principle that the people of South Vietnam shall determine their future without having a Communist government or a coalition government imposed upon them against their will." (He did not mention what Kissinger was now calling that "miserable little council.") There were details to be worked out, Nixon admitted, and they were important, "but the most important thing is we are going to end this war and end it in a way that will lay the foundation for real peace in the years to come. This is what all Americans want." [64]

Nixon's speech was a *tour de force*. His explanation was satisfactory to a majority of the American people and rescued him from the potential trap Kissinger had created. He had solved his political problem.

The problem itself remained. In facing it, Nixon was hardening in his attitude toward Thieu. He noted in his diary that "we are now in a position where if he [Thieu] doesn't come along after the election we are going to have to put him through the wringer. . . . We simply have to cut the umbilical cord and have this baby walk by itself. If they can't do it now, with all we have fed it in the way of arms and ammunition and training, etc., they will never be able to do it."

But his method of putting pressure on Thieu was to increase the bombing pressure on North Vietnam. On November 2, even as he was preparing his Rhode Island speech that defended an agreement Hanoi had all but begged him to sign, he ordered an intensification of the bombing of North Vietnam. [65]

It had been a difficult week for the President. One good thing, however, had happened. All the furor over "peace is at hand" had effectively ended comment and speculation about the Woodward and Bernstein charge that Haldeman had authorized payments from the secret CREEP fund for spying and sabotage efforts. Watergate could not compete with the Vietnam War for the nation's attention.

ON OCTOBER 30, McGovern charged that "for the first time in the history of this country, we have had a Presidential campaign with only one candidate." He castigated Nixon for letting Agnew do the speaking for him, and warned that the Republicans were preparing for eight years of a Spiro Agnew Presidency. "If that isn't enough to make you tremble," he said, "I don't know what is."[66]

Someone else was disturbed by this new, noncampaigning Nixon. She had been with him for almost a quarter century, longer than any other person except Pat Nixon. She had seldom offered advice, but in the closing days of the 1972 campaign Rose Mary Woods was so upset that she sent Nixon a memorandum full of suggestions.

"I strongly urge you in the last two to three weeks of this all-important campaign to make brief appearances in the large states," she began. She feared that he was giving "our own people across the country the feeling that you are so sure of the election that you do not have the time—or do not feel so inclined—to even make a brief appearance in their state/city, etc.

"Above all, please do not let the PR types talk you into using film on the television the night before Election Day. Please speak to the people of this country—in your own calm, reassuring manner and ask for their votes—their help."

She concluded, "Please forgive me—but after campaigning with you every two years from 1952 on—I couldn't resist sending this memo."[67]

Nixon did not respond, either in writing or by changing his campaign plans.

What he did do was more of the same, which was to urge his surrogate speakers to greater efforts. On October 25, Buchanan wrote that while the "Eastern media" were still trying to make something out of Watergate, the issue was not catching on in the country as a whole. Therefore "it would seem that the best defense on this is a good offense." Nixon commented, "C—H—Correct. Step up attacks."[68]

Watergate was almost turning into a plus for Nixon. Walter Rugaber noted in *The New York Times* on November 1 that none of McGovern's charges had been proved: "There has been no public indication that either the President or any of his close advisers played roles in or had advance knowledge of an illegal assault upon the opposition party. . . . With the election only a week away, there are still no definitive, conclusive answers to either of the key questions posed by the Watergate affair from the beginning: What are the limits in assessing blame? What were the intentions and actions of those involved?"[69]

The cover-up Nixon had started the day the burglars were arrested had worked. As the campaign approached its climax, there were no ongoing investigations of the break-in. Not by Justice, not by the FBI, not by the GAO, not by the House Banking Committee, not by the Senate. In the courts, Judge Sirica had set January 8 as the trial date for the burglars. Judge Richey had decided he would not proceed with the Democrats' civil suit against CREEP until the criminal case was finished.

On the November 3 News Summary, Buchanan did a "Political Media Analysis." He was euphoric. "The McGovern campaign cannot be a very pleasant place this morning," he began. "Reports of disaster are coming in from everywhere in the media. . . . Political analysts, state polls, and press reports all are pointing to an unprecedented Nixon landslide. . . . McGovern himself seems on the verge of a breakdown. . . . In this observer's judgment we have an excellent opportunity in McGovern's current state of bitchiness and exhaustion and in his increasing bitterness toward the President personally."

Nixon underlined the last sentence and wrote, "C & H— I agree."

Buchanan thought that the "special hatred which McGovern and his staff have felt for us, which has been revealed from time to time, is an ugly and unattractive aspect of their campaign which might just be exposed by a little discreet needling—and calling on them to join us in a call for national unity after we clean up the floor with them on Tuesday." [70]

WITH WATERGATE DEAD in the water as an issue, McGovern concentrated in the last week of the campaign on Vietnam. His theme was that the President had deliberately misled the nation into believing peace was near. The truth was, he said, that on Saturday, November 4, the Air Force had dropped four million pounds of bombs on Vietnam, that the United States was rushing additional American aircraft to South Vietnam, and that the Pentagon's claim that some North Vietnamese units were withdrawing from the South was "completely false." He asserted, "The fact is that the war is now intensifying." [71]

The President responded the next day in a five-minute nation-wide television address. He claimed he had achieved a "break-through" in the negotiations, that both Hanoi and the United States had a settlement under which "the people of South Vietnam will determine their own future." Nixon admitted that there were "some details that we are insisting still be worked out," but only because he wished to be certain "this will not be a temporary peace but a peace that will last." He expressed himself as "completely confident" that he would soon reach an agreement "which will end the war in Vietnam." [72]

Nixon's emphasis was entirely personal. It was *his* agreement.

He had negotiated it. *He* was proud of it, and would stand by it, once those minor details had been worked out.

Kissinger took a different view of where the credit belonged. On November 4, he gave an exclusive interview to Italian journalist Oriana Fallaci. She asked him to explain his remarkable popularity.

"I'll tell you," Kissinger responded. "What do I care after all? The main point stems from the fact that I've always acted alone. Americans admire that enormously. Americans admire the cowboy leading the caravan alone astride his horse, the cowboy entering the village or city alone on his horse. Without even a pistol, maybe, because he doesn't go in for shooting. He acts, that's all: aiming at the right spot at the right time. A Wild West tale, if you like.

"This romantic, surprising character suits me," he told Fallaci, "because being alone has always been part of my style. . . . Independence, too. Yes, that's very important to me and in me."

As to the future, Kissinger said, "I've by no means decided to give up this job yet. You know, I enjoy it very much. . . . You see, when one wields power, and when one has it for a long time, one ends up thinking one has a right to it." [73]

As Nixon had been with his "the average American is just like the child in the family" interview, Kissinger was lucky that the Fallaci interview was not published until after the election.

ON NOVEMBER 4, Nixon flew to San Clemente. At the Ontario, California, airport, he spoke to an overflow crowd. He was less than twenty miles from Pomona, where he had made his first campaign speech, twenty-six years earlier. In almost every speech in the quarter century of chronic campaigning since then, he had attempted to divide the electorate. Now, in his last appearance as a candidate, he made an effort to bring the nation together.

"I want to tell you something about this country," he said. "There was a time, and it was not too long ago, when if you traveled through the country, you would see it deeply divided—the West against the East, the North against the South, the cities against the farms, and so forth. But let me tell you, wherever you go across America, this nation is getting together." [74] In a statement released at the airport, he claimed, "When it comes down to the important things, Americans still stand together—we are one America in conscience, in purpose, and in inspiration." [75]

On election eve, November 6, Nixon spent the afternoon making a film recording of a short address to be shown on nationwide television that night (so much for Rose Woods's plea that he speak live in his "own calm, reassuring manner"). He concentrated on Vietnam. "As you know," he said, "we have made a breakthrough.

... We have agreed on the major principles that I laid down in my speech to the nation of May 8. ... There are still some details that I am insisting be worked out and nailed down because I do not want this to be a temporary peace. ... I can say to you with complete confidence tonight that we will soon reach agreement on all the issues and bring this long and difficult war to an end."

His concluding words, the last he would ever speak as a candidate, were "Let's make the next four years the best four years in America's history." [76]

After the filming, Nixon went for a walk on the beach. There was an ebb tide, "out further than I have ever seen it," he wrote in his diary. He wondered whether this was a good or a bad omen. He went on to the spot where a peace sign had been carved in a red sandstone cliff. The sign was worn down by weather. "It looked like a man with a frown on his face. This may be an indication that those who have held up this sign finally have had their comeuppance and they are really in for some heavy depression." [77]

Election Day, after voting, he spent the morning working. He sent a memorandum to Haldeman and Colson: "The opposition line will be: 1, Mc'G's mistakes lost it, not his views & not RN's strength. 2, The low vote proved no one liked either candidate. 3, RN let down his party." [78]

Point three was beginning, finally, to worry him. He had been informed on October 20 that his newfound friends among the labor union leaders were beginning to work for the Democrats, and had commented, "C—We may see more of this in final two weeks because of need to save local candidates." [79] On November 7, he read in his News Summary that Republicans were complaining about his indifference to the congressional races. The Cleveland *Plain Dealer* quoted a disgruntled conservative who was "mad as hell" at Nixon's "pallid efforts" to assist the Republican Party and who warned that "Nixon is going to have to sleep in the bed he made— the Hill." Nixon commented, "H—we need a PR program—by Bush—et al—to knock this down." [80]

Kissinger noted that "as his hour of triumph approached, Nixon withdrew ever more, even from some of his close advisers [read Kissinger]. His resentments, usually so well controlled, came increasingly to the surface. It was as if victory was not an occasion for reconciliation but an opportunity to settle the scores of a lifetime." [81]

Kissinger had it right. Nixon had instructed Ehrlichman, in a reference to the Antitrust Division of the Justice Department, to "clean out this gang on November 8." [82] And on Election Day, Haldeman sent an identical order to every presidential appointee in the executive branch. He said the President requested a memo "regarding your possible service in the next Administration . . . no later than Friday, November 10. This should accompany your pro forma letter of resignation to become effective at the pleasure of the President." [83]

THE AFTERNOON of Election Day, Nixon flew to Washington. When he went to his bedroom, he found a handwritten note propped on his pillow. It was from Kissinger. The National Security Adviser wanted to let the President know, "before the votes are counted," what a privilege it had been to serve him. Kissinger said he was confident of the outcome, but no matter how the vote turned out, "it cannot affect the historic achievement—to take a divided nation, mired in war, losing its confidence, wracked by intellectuals without conviction, and give it a new purpose and overcome its hesitations." Nixon's accomplishments, Kissinger predicted, "will loom ever larger in history books."

Kissinger concluded, "It has been an inspiration to see your fortitude in adversity and your willingness to walk alone. For this —as well as for the unfailing human kindness and consideration— I shall always be grateful." [84]

Nixon spent the evening in the Lincoln Sitting Room. His sons-in-law came in from time to time with the early returns. Haldeman gave him more detailed reports, via telephone.

For Nixon, it was a triumph. He got 47 million votes, or 60.7 percent of the total, to McGovern's 29 million, or 37.5 percent. He carried every state but Massachusetts. He was the first Republican ever to win a majority of the Catholic vote and of the blue-collar vote. The labor-union vote split evenly. McGovern won easily among black and Jewish voters, but his majorities were much lower than Humphrey's in 1968. McGovern also carried the youth vote, but Nixon far exceeded even his own expectations, winning 46 percent of the first-time voters.

Only 54 percent of the eligible voters had gone to the polls, however, as compared to more than 60 percent in the previous five elections. In 1960, more than 64 percent had voted. Nor did Nixon win a historic landslide. Johnson held the record (data on popular votes dates back to 1824) with his 61.1 percent in 1964; Franklin Roosevelt had won 60.8 percent in 1936. Nixon fretted that he had not set a record, but what disturbed him even more was the failure of his coattails to bring in Republicans. Although the party gained twelve seats in the House, the Republicans were still more than fifty votes short of a majority. In the Senate, the Republicans actually lost two seats, giving the Democrats a 58–42 majority. [85]

Nixon, who had so badly wanted a historic first in the 1972 election, had achieved the one he did not want. He was the first President ever to win two elections without once having his party achieve a majority in either the House or the Senate.

The stark meaning of the figures was that the Democrats would control the 93d Congress, and thus they had the subpoena power to back their right to instigate congressional investigations. And although Nixon had carefully avoided the word "Democrat" throughout the campaign, the Democrats were nevertheless furious with him. They suspected that he had not achieved peace in Vietnam. They wanted to know more about CREEP's dirty tricks and fund-raising activities. They were eager to force Administration officials to explain the ITT and Russian grain deals. They were convinced that Nixon had not told the truth about the Watergate break-in.

Just as Nixon could hardly wait to get started firing people, the Democrats could hardly wait for the gavel to bang down on January 3, 1973, so that they could start their investigations.

CHAPTER TWENTY-EIGHT

NIXON'S FIRST TERM:
AN ASSESSMENT
1969–1972

NIXON'S STUNNING TRIUMPH in the 1972 election marked the climax of his political career. It was a compound of many factors, not least the inept performance of the disaster-prone McGovern campaign. But although some part of Nixon's total came from citizens who were against McGovern rather than for Nixon, the stark fact remains that six out of ten Americans who cast a vote in 1972 did so for Richard Nixon.

This came after four years of the Nixon Presidency, and after twenty-five years of Nixon at or near the center stage of national politics. Undoubtedly the American electorate had seen more of Nixon, heard more from him and about him, and read more about him, than any other person in the world. People knew Nixon's good and bad sides, his strengths and weaknesses, his complexities and contradictions. They were not manipulated into voting for him, or fooled into it by some made-for-TV image, or sold on Nixon by CREEP's media, billboard, telephone banks, volunteer, and organizational overkill. Nixon's 1972 victory must be recognized as a tremendous vote of confidence that reflected a deep and widespread approval of his leadership in his first term.

Thus the assessment that mattered most to Nixon, that of the American people, was overwhelmingly favorable.

Nixon did not earn that judgment by being a bland, middle-of-the-road, take-no-chances kind of politician. To the contrary, he was a bold, innovative, high-risk President who had succeeded in bringing a majority of his countrymen with him on adventures into wholly new areas—most obviously, the opening to China, détente with the Soviets, and the beginning of arms limitations.

654 | NIXON'S FIRST TERM: AN ASSESSMENT

These were his special triumphs, and uniquely his. No one else could have done what he did. To be sure, this was in large part because only President Nixon did not have to deal with Nixon as a critic; without Nixon to lead it, the right wing of the Republican Party, which opposed all three initiatives, could not mount an effective opposition. Although Nixon had hinted at his intentions in his 1968 campaign, by no means had the initiatives toward the Chinese and the Russians been a major feature of that effort. Critics of America's Cold War policy had been advocating a normalization of relations with China and peaceful coexistence with the Soviet Union for two decades, but by no means was there a consensus for such changes. In these fundamental areas of foreign policy, Nixon provided real leadership that went beyond anything any of his predecessors had dared to try. Rather than wait for a constituency to develop behind such policies, Nixon acted, and by acting, created a constituency for them.

For this reason, he had earned and deserved his triumph in the 1972 election.

There were problems. Nixon's penchant for secrecy and surprise, his overreliance on Kissinger, his refusal to involve the State Department, the Pentagon, Congress, and the people in his initiatives, precluded the development within the government and among the public of a base to guarantee that his changes would become permanent. He used tactics that were more appropriate to Metternich in early-nineteenth-century Austria than to the President of a democratic republic in the second half of the twentieth century. By presenting the Republican Party with a *fait accompli* in China and Russia, instead of persuading it to adopt new policies, he endangered the survival of those policies.

Of course, he expected to complete his revolution in foreign policy in his second term. He anticipated in SALT II the achievement of real arms control, far beyond the purely symbolic agreement that there could be some limits placed on the arms race that he had reached in SALT I. He believed that in his second term he could broaden and deepen détente, building on an ever-increasing flow of trade and scientific and cultural exchanges between the U.S. and the U.S.S.R., and China as well, to create a genuine new era in international politics.

The danger was that it all depended on him; if he lost his political base, not only Nixon, but his policies, would go under.

Just before the Moscow summit, in early May 1972, when Nixon was in a depression because of the NVA offensive and thought he could not be re-elected, he had said that if Kissinger would remain in the government, he could provide continuity in foreign policy. This was not true, as the events of 1975 and 1976 proved (President Ford went so far as to ban the use of the word "détente" in the White House; SALT II, negotiated by Nixon, could not be ratified). This was because Kissinger had neither an institutional nor a political base. He had risen to his key position in opposition to rather than in cooperation with the State Department. He had no claim on the Republican Party, and few supporters in it.

Nevertheless, Kissinger's unflagging energy, his willingness to spend nearly half his time in airplanes, his skills as a diplomat and negotiator, his knowledge of the world, and his unique relationship with Nixon, plus his personal flair, all combined to make him crucial to Nixon's foreign-policy triumphs. His role, however, was as agent, tool, and sometimes adviser, not as a generator of ideas. The basic thrust of Nixon's innovations came from the President, not the National Security Adviser. Further, Kissinger's love of intrigue, surprise, and conspiracy, his egomania (a strong word; no other will suffice), his refusal to take advice from the State Department and other experts, his backbiting, and his habit of saying one thing to one man, another to the next, made a dangerous combination that played on Nixon's worst instincts, as was seen most clearly in the policy toward Allende in Chile, India in the Indo-Pakistani War, and Thieu and Le Duc Tho in October 1972.

Vietnam showed Nixon and his associate at their best and worst. By November 1972, Nixon had managed to reduce the American ground forces commitment from 550,000 to 20,000. More than any other single factor, this achievement had insured his re-election. He had done what LBJ had not been able to do. Johnson, who like Nixon had recognized in February 1968 that the war could not be won, had cut and run on Vietnam. Nixon, who inherited the quagmire, was the one who extracted the troops, and he had done so without abandoning the South Vietnamese to the Communists.

He had not, however, ended the war, as he had promised to do in the 1968 campaign. The fighting continued, with American armed forces heavily involved in the air and at sea, and as the sole supplier of ARVN. But the American casualties were down to almost nothing, for which the American people were exceedingly grateful, while the ARVN, as a result of Vietnamization, was larger and more powerful that it had ever been.

Nixon's original goal in Vietnam had been to achieve an armistice, with the NVA withdrawn to North Vietnam, the Viet Cong destroyed or disbanded, and the pro-American government in Saigon intact. That goal was so important to him that he was ready to sacrifice his China initiative and détente with the Soviets to achieve it. But it was an impossible goal, as Nixon came to realize, although only after four years of fighting. Had he seen that truth earlier, and made the necessary concessions to Hanoi, much of the bitterness and divisiveness that characterized his first term could have been avoided.

But he did eventually modify his negotiating position, and agreed to make concessions to the enemy. The most important was to indicate to Hanoi that he was willing to allow the NVA to stay in South Vietnam, and the VC to hold to its gains, in return for a cease-fire, the release of the POWs, and the retention of the Thieu government in power, albeit with the National Council to dispute that power. Whether Hanoi would have agreed to such a deal earlier or not is problematical; we cannot know because it was not tried. We do know that not until the Chinese and Russians began to pressure the North Vietnamese to compromise and not until Nixon launched the bombing and mining campaigns against Hanoi and Haiphong did the North Vietnamese drop their insistence on the removal of Thieu as a precondition to a cease-fire. Whatever the might-have-beens, by November of 1972 the main outline of a commonsense deal had been worked out.

Still, much remained to be done. Thieu had not agreed to the deal, indeed had made his opposition clear. The Communists were seeking more ironclad guarantees about their participation in a new government via the National Council.

Into this delicate situation, Kissinger had jumped with both feet and the full force of his ego. Nixon did not claim on the eve of the election that peace was at hand, but Kissinger did. It gave him headlines, and it got him wholly undeserved credit in many quarters for Nixon's election victory. But it also created a potential problem for Nixon of the first magnitude. If Kissinger could not come through, if Thieu and Le Duc Tho refused to cooperate, if Nixon had to escalate once again in the war, there was a real chance that the American people would feel betrayed, fooled, misled. If that happened, they would be taking out their anger on Nixon, not Kissinger.

Two other points need to be made about Nixon and Vietnam. First, he was by no means a free agent. His policies did not reflect his best judgment about what should be done. His options were increasingly limited by the ever-growing strength of the doves, especially in Congress. Ironically, his success in driving the anti-war demonstrators off the streets contributed to this growth, by making the dove cause respectable. The result was that the 93d Congress was not going to let him have one penny to carry on the war. He had to make peace before January 1973 or face the impossible situation of trying to carry on the war without funds.

Second, nearly all the names on the left-hand side of the Vietnam Wall in Washington commemorate men who died in action while Richard Nixon was their commander in chief, and they died after he had decided that the war could not be won.

ON THE DOMESTIC SIDE, Nixon had tried to be as bold and innovative as on foreign policy, but without success. His major bids had been FAP and reversing the flow of power to Washington. On the first, he had failed utterly; on the second, his revenue-sharing program had marked a beginning. As with détente and SALT, he expected in his second term to make real progress on welfare reform, and to bring about a fundamental change in the relationship between state and local governments on the one hand, and the federal government on the other. Still, in assessing his first term, it must be said that he had no achievement worthy of note.

His best-known actions, positions, and policies tended to be negative. The wage-and-price freeze, for example, which Nixon had to be forced into accepting and of which he said later he wished he had not done it, was a temporary measure that treated the symptom of inflation while leaving the causes untouched. Nixon's adamant stand against busing amounted to not much more than simply saying "NO!" While it certainly was popular, it offered nothing in the way of a solution to the immediate problem, how to desegregate America's schools, and far from dealing with the broader problem of how to improve race relations in the United States, it added to it.

Nixon expected to make his domestic contribution in his second term. He planned to return to state and local governments the powers they had lost over the past four decades. This was certainly bold and imaginative; whether it was wise was not so clear. He also intended to reorganize the federal government, starting at the top. The need for such a reorganization was obvious, but how to go about it had not produced a consensus. It was in these areas that Nixon anticipated providing the kind of leadership that would mark him as a great President. He called his program the New American Revolution.

He had not campaigned on these issues, and thus had not created a constituency for them. Although he could count on the support of state and local politicians, he could also count on the entrenched opposition of the federal bureaucracy and Congress. It was therefore uncertain whether or not he could reverse not only a forty-year trend in American history, but a two-centuries-old trend throughout the world—that of centralization of power within nations. His goal was so ambitious, the changes he sought so fundamental, that he would need all his political skills and an unassailable political base to succeed.

How difficult it would be for him to put over what was essentially his personal program can be seen with a glance at his relations with the other two branches of government in his first term. Democratic control of Congress meant, in general, that he had governed in spite of, or even in opposition to, rather than in cooperation with Congress. Congress would not give him a free hand in Vietnam, it would not give him FAP, it cut back sharply on his revenue-sharing proposal, it forced him to adopt the wage-and-price freeze, it resisted his demand for a moratorium on busing and, at the end of 1972, it was threatening to devote its energies in the next term to cutting off all funds for Vietnam while launching a potentially embarrassing, even devastating, investigation into Watergate and Nixon's campaign.

With regard to the Supreme Court, things were only slightly better. In 1968, Nixon had made the liberal trend of the Warren Court one of his most profitable issues. He had promised to nominate strict-construction conservatives to the bench. With Carswell and Haynsworth he had done so, only to suffer embarrassing reverses, but he did manage to put four men who met his standards on the Court, including the Chief Justice.

That did not, however, lead to a reversal of the landmark decisions of the Warren Court. The Burger Court did not overturn *Miranda* v. *Arizona*, it did not restore prayer in the schools, it did not outlaw pornography, it struck down state laws that banned the distribution of contraceptives, in a series of decisions it upheld the rights of welfare recipients, it struck down all Nixon's attempts to soften the impact of *Brown* v. *Topeka*, it ruled in favor of busing, it refused to allow prior censorship of the Pentagon Papers, and it told the Nixon Justice Department that it had no right to wiretap domestic radicals.

Taken altogether, this was a most discouraging record for Nixon and his supporters. Whatever a majority of Nixon's voters wanted, the Court followed instead the main lines of thought that had developed over the past twenty years in jurisprudence.

As Nixon knew painfully well, the President could not dictate Supreme Court decisions, but as George Wallace knew, and exploited, many voters thought of the government as a single entity, so that when things went wrong, they blamed the man at the top. And the Court was currently hearing a case that was as emotionally charged as school prayer or busing. Called *Roe* v. *Wade*, it concerned abortion. If the ruling followed current judicial trends, it would affirm the right of the woman to decide whether or not to terminate a pregnancy. There would be no profit for Nixon in such a decision. As things stood at the end of 1972, the Court promised to be as much of a problem to Nixon in his second term as did Congress.

With regard to the fourth estate, Nixon had no cause for complaint. In the 1972 campaign, American newspapers had overwhelmingly endorsed him (753 daily newspapers endorsed Nixon, to 56 for McGovern). Both the press and the television news had given him magnificent coverage of his trips to Peking and Moscow. In addition, they had supported him on the opening to China, on détente, and on SALT. And they had cooperated in downplaying Watergate.

Yet complain Nixon did. He accused the press of being liberal, softheaded, idealistic, and out to get him. Hardly a News Summary went by on which he did not instruct his aides to knock this reporter, or cut that one, or freeze him, or smash him. Nixon saw all criticisms of his policies as a criticism of his person, brought on by the reporters' hatred of him. This *idée fixe* of Nixon's, that the press hated him, was a consequence of his own hatred of the press.

He also badly exaggerated the importance of the press. In Nixon's view, it could make or break a President. He went to extraordinary lengths to manipulate the press. After announcing a major decision, such as the incursion into Cambodia, he had Colson and his people send in sacks and sacks of favorable mail, so that he could claim to the press that he had widespread approval for his action. He despised leakers, but he leaked himself, or had Kissinger and others do it for him, on a regular basis. He used exclusive interviews with conservative columnists to put forward his point of view, while ordering no more backgrounders for liberal writers. His war with the press was never-ending.

Every President is at war with the press to some extent, and all of them try to manipulate it. Nixon went farther than any other President, because of the immense importance he ascribed to the media. In this he was as one with the right wing of the Republican Party (and, come to that, with the press itself), which vastly overrated the power of the press.

The truth of the matter, however, was best expressed by Dwight Eisenhower. At his last press conference, in January 1961, Robert Spivack asked Eisenhower if he felt the reporters had been fair to him over the past eight years. "Well," Ike replied, "when you come down to it, I don't see what a reporter could do much to a President, do you?"[1]

But whereas Eisenhower downplayed the importance of the press, Nixon exaggerated it; whereas Ike wooed the press, Nixon went to war with it.

NIXON'S HATREDS extended far beyond the reporters. He was constantly railing at "they," threatening to "get them."

One day late in the first term, Nixon was sitting around with Kissinger, Haldeman, Ehrlichman, and Colson. They were discussing some of Nixon's enemies (in this case, antiwar Democratic senators). Nixon said, "One day we will get them—we'll get them on the ground where we want them. And we'll stick our heels in, step on them hard and twist—right. Chuck, right?"

Colson nodded his assent.

"Henry knows what I mean," Nixon went on. "Get them on the floor and step on them, crush them, show no mercy."

Kissinger smiled and nodded.[2]

That such attitudes were inappropriate for the leader of a democracy hardly needs saying. What is worthy of remark is the effect those attitudes had on Nixon. Because of his hatred of so many people, because of his war with the press, because of his intense desire to take revenge for all the slights and hurts he had suffered for so many years, he seethed with anger. Because he so often acted on his impulses, he was incapable of uniting people and groups behind his policies. Combined with his inability to control the Supreme Court and his failure in the 1972 election to bring Republicans along to Washington on his coattails, these characteristics led to a paradox. Nixon could get the people to vote for him overwhelmingly, but on many crucial issues he could not lead the nation in the directions he thought it ought to go. Congress blocked him on revenue sharing, on Vietnam, on détente; the Court blocked him on busing, pornography, getting tough with criminals, raising welfare requirements; the State Department and the Pentagon blocked him on his bold initiatives; the press blocked him on getting his story out to the people.

As President, Nixon had struck back at his perceived enemies by going outside the law. He had used illegal wiretaps and other forms of electronic surveillance to spy on government employees and newspaper reporters. The Justice Department, at his urging, had undertaken a widespread program of bugging and infiltrating radical groups (which was declared illegal in June 1972). Nixon created, set the tone for, and gave the objectives to the Plumbers, an unauthorized, unknown intelligence-gathering and covert-operation unit operating from within the White House. It was in an atmosphere established and encouraged by Nixon that agents of the President of the United States made forcible illegal entries into Dr. Fielding's office in Los Angeles, and Larry O'Brien's office at the Watergate in Washington, in the first instance to try to steal material that would incriminate or embarrass Daniel Ellsberg, in the second instance to leave a bug that would allow Nixon's people to listen to O'Brien's phone conversations.

Nixon compounded his criminal liability in these cases by withholding information in his possession from federal prosecutors, and in the Watergate case by launching an active cover-up the day of the arrest of the burglars. In the course of carrying out his obstructions of justice, he used the FBI, the Justice Department, his closest White House aides, the high officials at CREEP, and he attempted to use the CIA. He had offered, and his agents had paid, money to the burglars to purchase their silence. He had acquiesced in, if he had not actually initiated, perjured testimony from Jeb Magruder.

He had broken the law, and was still breaking the law at the time of the election, and intended to go on breaking the law, as the cover-up continued. For those reasons, he deserved to be repudiated by the American people.

IT IS MEALYMOUTHED, even cowardly, to end an assessment by saying that Nixon deserved to be re-elected and deserved to be repudiated. But a contradictory judgment seems inescapable with this contradictory man, the author of détente and the author of the Watergate cover-up.

A vote for Nixon in 1972 was a vote for détente, for expanded relations with China, for arms control, for a whole new era of world peace. It was also a vote for government reorganization at home, and revenue sharing, and another attempt at welfare reform, and an end to busing, and a balanced budget, and lower taxes.

A vote for Nixon in 1972 was also a vote for a continued cover-up, not only of the Watergate break-in but all the illegal activities of the past four years. It was a vote for wiretapping by the White House of Nixon's perceived enemies, for more break-ins, for an attempt to use the IRS and the Justice Department to harass and punish the people on John Dean's list, for wholesale firings in the federal bureaucracy, up to and including the Cabinet. A vote for Nixon was a vote for aggressive use of the licensing power of the FCC to force the television networks, as well as newspapers like the Washington *Post* that owned television and radio stations, to modify, or even eliminate, their criticisms of and negative reporting about Nixon.

A vote for Nixon in 1972 was a vote for the principle Nixon

stated so succinctly in a 1977 interview with David Frost: "Well, when the President does it, that means that it is not illegal." [3]

So he deserved to win, and he deserved to lose.

ON ELECTION NIGHT 1972, Nixon made two public appearances. The first was a televised statement from the Oval Office, the second a brief appearance at a victory celebration at the Shoreham Hotel. In both, he was subdued. He confessed in his diary, "I was not as upbeat as I should have been," but he hoped that "the very fact that the victory was so overwhelming made up for any failure on my part to react more enthusiastically than I did." [4]

In fact, on this night on which one would have thought he would be supremely happy, he was furious. In his memoirs, he described his feeling as "melancholy," and wrote that he was "at a loss" to explain it. But the melancholy masked an anger that knew no bounds. He expressed that anger the next morning, when he abruptly demanded the resignations of all the men who had just worked so hard and so successfully in his behalf.

His anger resulted from the frustrations that he knew lay ahead. He had done a magnificent job on the politics of his problems in 1972, but all the problems remained. He did not have peace in Vietnam, and the 93d Congress was not going to give him any funds to continue the war. He could use busing as a vote-getting issue, but he could not get the courts to stop busing. Senator Jackson was blocking him on arms control and détente. The CIA had refused to cooperate in the Watergate cover-up, and FBI agents were pressing their investigation and leaking to the press.

Nixon, on election night, 1972, could anticipate that despite his overwhelming victory, the Democrats, the bureaucracy, the media, and the courts were all going to go after Watergate as hard as they could. And Nixon knew, better than any other individual in the country, how much there was in the Watergate break-in affair and related activities for them to find.

So on election night, Nixon could not enjoy his triumph. He was not planning how to bring people together, to create a consensus behind his New American Revolution, but rather how to destroy his enemies before they destroyed him. In his own immortal phrase, "They are asking for it, and they are going to get it."

That was going to be the real theme of his second term, if Nixon could get his way.

NOTES

*The following abbreviations are used throughout
the Notes:*
EL—Eisenhower Library, Abilene, Kansas
JL—Johnson Library, Austin, Texas
*NPMP—Nixon Presidential Materials Project, Alexandria,
Virginia*
*NS—News Summaries, found in Nixon Presidential
Materials Project*
*PP—Public Papers of the President, Government Printing
Office, Washington, D.C.*
*VPP—Richard M. Nixon Vice-Presidential Papers, Laguna
Niguel, California*

CHAPTER ONE

1. Safire, *Before the Fall*, 21.
2. *New York Times*, 1/22/63.
3. Eisenhower to Brownell, 11/17/63, EL.
4. *New York Times*, 3/13/65.
5. Witcover, the closest student of this period of Nixon's life, insists that Nixon ran for governor precisely to avoid the 1964 nomination, with his eye on 1968. Witcover, *Resurrection of Richard Nixon*, 25.
6. *Ibid.*, 36–38.
7. *Ibid.*, 38.
8. Klein, *Making It Perfectly Clear*, 133.
9. Woods note on call from Harlow, 1/2/63, VPP.
10. Witcover, *Resurrection of Richard Nixon*, 41.
11. Nixon, *Memoirs*, 248.
12. Eisenhower, *Pat Nixon*, 216.
13. Witcover, *Resurrection of Richard Nixon*, 42.
14. Nixon to Harlow, and Nixon to Hess, both 2/19/63, VPP.
15. *New York Times*, 3/15/63.
16. Nixon to E. C. Gerhart, and Nixon to C. E. Daniel, both 3/11/63, VPP.
17. Nixon, *Memoirs*, 247.
18. Nixon to Eisenhower, 3/18/63, and Eisenhower to Nixon, 3/25/63, both in EL.
19. Witcover, *Resurrection of Richard Nixon*, 43.
20. *New York Times*, 4/21/63.
21. Nixon to William Pawley, 5/8/63, VPP.
22. See the Nixon–Virginius Dabney correspondence for May 1963, VPP.

23. Hess interview.
24. Nixon to Hess, 2/19/63, VPP, and Hess interview.
25. Eisenhower, *Pat Nixon*, 216.
26. *New York Times*, 5/7 and 5/14/63.
27. *Ibid.*, 5/2 and 5/3/63.
28. Chicago *Tribune*, 5/16/63.
29. Nixon, *Memoirs*, 248.
30. Eisenhower, *Pat Nixon*, 217.
31. See Nixon to Phil Watts, 4/9/63, VPP.
32. *New York Times*, 6/13, 6/16, 6/17, 7/18/63.
33. *Ibid.*, 7/21/63.
34. *Ibid.*, 7/26/63.
35. *Ibid.*, 7/29/63.
36. Nixon, *Memoirs*, 248.
37. *New York Times*, 8/2/63.
38. Nixon, *Leaders*, 62.
39. *New York Times*, 7/26/63.
40. Kissinger, *White House Years*, 20. Stephen Jones, who worked for Nixon as a political aide in 1964, and who has given me basic information on Nixon during this period, recalls many prominent New Yorkers who called on Nixon.
41. *New York Times*, 10/23/67.
42. *Ibid.*, 12/29/63; Nixon, *Memoirs*, 250.
43. Witcover, *Resurrection of Richard Nixon*, 52–53.
44. *Ibid.*, 49–50.
45. Eisenhower to Nixon, 9/25/63, EL; Witcover, *Resurrection of Richard Nixon*, 56.
46. *New York Times*, 9/30/63; private information.
47. Witcover, *Resurrection of Richard Nixon*, 56.
48. *New York Times*, 10/25/63.
49. *Ibid.*, 10/27/63.
50. Nixon, "Khrushchev's Hidden Weakness," 59–64.
51. Nixon, *Memoirs*, 251.
52. Baldwin, "Managed News," 54.
53. Lasky, *It Didn't Start with Watergate*, 55–56.
54. See Gill, *Ordeal of Otto Otepka*.
55. Nixon to Karl Mundt, 11/13/63, Karl Mundt Papers, University of South Dakota.
56. Eisenhower to Nixon, 11/5/63, EL.
57. Nixon to Robert Humphreys, 11/7/63, VPP.
58. Eisenhower to Nixon, 11/11/63, EL.
59. Witcover, *Resurrection of Richard Nixon*, 58.
60. Or so Mrs. Oswald told the Warren Commission; she has since denied this.
61. *New York Times*, 6/5/63.
62. Dallas *Morning News*, 11/22/63.
63. Witcover, *Resurrection of Richard Nixon*, 60; Nixon, *Memoirs*, 252–253.
64. Hess interview.
65. *New York Times*, 11/24/63.
66. Witcover, *Resurrection of Richard Nixon*, 61–62.
67. Nixon, *Memoirs*, 253.
68. Hess interview; Witcover, *Resurrection of Richard Nixon*, 63–64.

69. Ambrose, *Eisenhower,* Vol. II, 227.
70. Witcover, *Resurrection of Richard Nixon,* 60.

CHAPTER TWO

1. *New York Times,* 12/7/63.
2. Witcover, *Resurrection of Richard Nixon,* 69; Jones interview.
3. *New York Times,* 2/11/64.
4. *Ibid.,* 3/6/64.
5. *Ibid.,* 3/12/64.
6. *Ibid.*
7. Nixon memo, 3/12/64, Fred Seaton Papers, EL.
8. Nixon to Eisenhower, 3/13/64, EL.
9. *New York Times,* 3/23/64.
10. *Ibid.,* 3/24/64.
11. *Ibid.,* 4/2/64.
12. Nixon, *Memoirs,* 257–258.
13. *New York Times,* 4/5 and 4/6/64.
14. *Ibid.,* 4/10/64.
15. Witcover, *Resurrection of Richard Nixon,* 77.
16. *New York Times,* 4/20/64.
17. Fred Seaton memos, 4/20, 4/21, and 4/22/64, EL.
18. *Ibid.*
19. *New York Times,* 4/28/64.
20. *Ibid.,* 5/16/64.
21. Eisenhower/Nixon phone call, 5/19/64, EL.
22. Nixon, "Needed in Vietnam: The Will to Win," 37–43.
23. Nixon, "Cuba, Castro and John F. Kennedy," 283–300.
24. Reinhard, *Republican Right since 1945,* 185; Goldwater, *Goldwater,* 169–170.
25. Goldwater, *Goldwater,* 162–163.
26. Witcover, *Resurrection of Richard Nixon,* 85.
27. *Ibid.,* 85–86.
28. *New York Times,* 6/14/64.
29. Witcover, *Resurrection of Richard Nixon,* 93.
30. *New York Times,* 6/13/64.
31. Los Angeles *Times,* 7/14/64.
32. Witcover, *Resurrection of Richard Nixon,* 97.
33. Nixon, *Memoirs,* 259.
34. Witcover, *Resurrection of Richard Nixon,* 99.
35. Nixon, *Memoirs,* 261; *New York Times,* 8/10/64.
36. Witcover, *Resurrection of Richard Nixon,* 100–101.
37. *Ibid.,* 110.
38. *New York Times,* 10/4/64.
39. Nixon, *Memoirs,* 263.
40. *New York Times,* 11/6/64.
41. *Ibid.,* 11/11/64.
42. *Ibid.,* 11/16/64.

Chapter Three

1. Nixon, *Memoirs*, 266; Jones interview.
2. Nixon to Jack Olson, 1/19/65, Wisconsin State Historical Society.
3. Nixon, *Memoirs*, 272.
4. *New York Times*, 1/23/65.
5. *Ibid.*, 1/27/65.
6. Reinhard, *Republican Right since 1945*, 219.
7. *Ibid.*
8. *New York Times*, 2/8/65.
9. *Ibid.*, 2/11/65.
10. *Ibid.*, 2/14/65.
11. Donovan, "Over-Nominated, Under-Elected, Still a Promising Candidate," 14–15.
12. Eisenhower, *Pat Nixon*, 222.
13. *Ibid.*, 225.
14. *Ibid.*, 227.
15. *Ibid.*, 227–228.
16. Nixon, *Memoirs*, 265.
17. *New York Times*, 4/2/65.
18. Safire, *Before the Fall*, 6.
19. *New York Times*, 4/11/65.
20. *Ibid.*, 4/17/65.
21. Merriam interview.
22. Stans, *Terrors of Justice*, 128–129.
23. Safire interview.
24. *Ibid.*
25. Hess interview.
26. Safire, *Before the Fall*, 26.
27. *New York Times*, 8/29/65.
28. *Ibid.*, 8/28/65.
29. *Ibid.*, 9/6/65.
30. *Ibid.*, 9/8/65.
31. *Ibid.*, 9/13 and 9/15/65.
32. Witcover, *Resurrection of Richard Nixon*, 115–116.
33. *New York Times*, 7/6/65.
34. *Ibid.*, 10/25/65.
35. *Ibid.*, 10/27/65.
36. Safire, *Before the Fall*, 22.
37. *New York Times*, 10/29/65.
38. Nixon to Eisenhower, 11/8/65, EL.
39. *New York Times*, 11/7/65.
40. Benson to Nixon, 11/10/65, and Nixon to Benson, 12/22/65, EL.
41. *New York Times*, 11/22/65.
42. *Ibid.*, 11/25/65.
43. *Ibid.*, 11/29/65.
44. Nixon, "Why Not Negotiate in Vietnam?"

Chapter Four

1. *New York Times*, 1/31/66.
2. *Ibid.*, 5/1/66.

3. *Ibid.*, 3/9/66.
4. Witcover, *Resurrection of Richard Nixon*, 149–150.
5. Brodie, *Richard Nixon*, 464–465; Safire, *Before the Fall*, 23, 26.
6. *New York Times*, 6/6/66; Safire, *Before the Fall*, 24.
7. Eisenhower to Nixon, 6/13/66, EL.
8. Los Angeles *Times*, 6/24/66, and *New York Times*, 9/17/66.
9. Nixon, *Memoirs*, 272; Safire, *Before the Fall*, 27; Witcover, *Resurrection of Richard Nixon*, 123–124; Stans, *Terrors of Justice*, 130–131.
10. Witcover, *Resurrection of Richard Nixon*, 127.
11. Ehrlichman, *Witness to Power*, 37–38.
12. Haldeman, *Ends of Power*, 45.
13. Witcover, *Resurrection of Richard Nixon*, 139.
14. *New York Times*, 2/10/66.
15. Nixon to Eisenhower, 7/23/66, EL.
16. *New York Times*, 8/6/66.
17. *Ibid.*, 8/8/66.
18. *Ibid.*, 8/14/66.
19. *Ibid.*, 2/10/66.
20. *Ibid.*, 9/4/66 and 9/16/66.
21. Witcover, *Resurrection of Richard Nixon*, 142, 146.
22. *New York Times*, 9/16/66.
23. *Ibid.*, 9/24/66.
24. *Ibid.*, 2/10/66.
25. *Ibid.*, 10/28/66.
26. *Ibid.*, 9/25/66.
27. *Ibid.*, 10/14/66.
28. Witcover, *Resurrection of Richard Nixon*, 137.
29. *New York Times*, 10/30/66.
30. *Ibid.*, 9/1/66.
31. Witcover, *Resurrection of Richard Nixon*, 147.
32. *New York Times*, 10/28/66.
33. *Ibid.*, 5/7/66.
34. *Ibid.*, 5/8/66.
35. *Ibid.*, 5/7/66.
36. *Ibid.*
37. Witcover, *Resurrection of Richard Nixon*, 130.
38. *New York Times*, 8/26/66.
39. Nixon to Eisenhower, 10/4/66, EL.
40. *New York Times*, 8/25/66.
41. *Ibid.*, 8/27/66.
42. *Ibid.*, 9/4/66.
43. *Ibid.*, 9/12/66.
44. *Ibid.*, 9/29/66.
45. *Ibid.*, 9/30/66.
46. *Ibid.*, 10/2/66.
47. Nixon to Eisenhower, 10/4/66, and Eisenhower to Nixon, 10/7/66, EL.
48. *New York Times*, 10/2/66.
49. Nixon to Eisenhower, 10/13/66, EL. Nixon enclosed a copy of his remarks.
50. Chicago *Tribune*, 10/7/66.
51. *New York Times*, 10/8/66.
52. *Ibid.*, 10/15/66.
53. *Ibid.*, 11/1/66.

54. Safire, *Before the Fall*, 36–38.
55. *Ibid.*, 38–39; *New York Times*, 11/4/66.
56. *New York Times*, 11/5/66; Safire, *Before the Fall*, 39.
57. Safire, *Before the Fall*, 40; *New York Times*, 11/5/66.
58. Safire, *Before the Fall*, 38–39.
59. *New York Times*, 11/5/66.
60. Nixon, *Memoirs*, 276; Eisenhower to Nixon, 11/5/66, EL.
61. *New York Times*, 11/7/66.
62. *Ibid.*, 11/6/66.
63. Safire, *Before the Fall*, 33.
64. *Ibid.*, 41.
65. Witcover, *Resurrection of Richard Nixon*, 170; Klein, *Making It Perfectly Clear*, 148.
66. Nixon, *Memoirs*, 277.
67. *New York Times*, 11/8/66.
68. *Ibid.*, 11/9/66.
69. Weaver, "Four Hearties of the Good Ship G.O.P."
70. *New York Times*, 11/13/66.
71. Witcover, *Resurrection of Richard Nixon*, 152.
72. Eisenhower, *Pat Nixon*, 230.
73. *New York Times*, 12/30/66.

Chapter Five

1. Safire, *Before the Fall*, 42–43.
2. *Ibid.*, 45; Nixon, *Memoirs*, 279.
3. Eisenhower to Seaton, 1/31/67, and to John D. Lodge, 3/7/67, EL.
4. Stans, *Terrors of Justice*, 132–133.
5. *New York Times*, 3/6/67.
6. Nixon, *Memoirs*, 281.
7. *New York Times*, 3/17/67.
8. *Ibid.*, 3/19/67.
9. *Ibid.*, 3/21/67.
10. *Ibid.*, 3/22/67.
11. *Ibid.*, 3/26/67.
12. Price, *With Nixon*, 21–25.
13. *New York Times*, 4/18/67.
14. Nixon, *Memoirs*, 282.
15. *New York Times*, 2/22 and 5/9/67.
16. Eisenhower, *Pat Nixon*, 230–232.
17. *Ibid.*, 231–232.
18. *New York Times*, 5/14/67.
19. *Ibid.*, 5/8/67.
20. *Ibid.*, 5/16/67.
21. Nixon to Eisenhower, 9/26/67, EL.
22. Ambrose, *Eisenhower*, Vol. II, 378.
23. *New York Times*, 6/1/67.
24. *Ibid.*, 6/22/67.
25. *Ibid.*, 5/7/67.
26. Nixon, *Memoirs*, 284.
27. Ambrose, *Eisenhower*, Vol. I, 493–494.
28. Nixon, *Memoirs*, 284–285.

29. Nixon, "Asia After Viet Nam," 111–125.

30. In a draft of the article that Nixon sent to Eisenhower for comment, he had used the phrase "non-nuclear armed forces." Ike had pointed out that the logic of Nixon's position that Japan should assume responsibility for its defense led to the conclusion that it had to have its own nuclear capacity. In the printed article, Nixon removed the "non-nuclear" that Ike objected to. Nixon to Eisenhower, 8/15/67, EL.

31. See Ambrose, *Nixon: Education of a Politician*, 324.

32. Nixon, "Asia After Viet Nam," 111–125.

Chapter Six

1. *New York Times*, 7/24/67; Nixon, *Memoirs*, 286.
2. *New York Times*, 8/22/67.
3. Cannon, *Reagan*, 148.
4. *Ibid.*, 151.
5. *New York Times*, 10/28/67.
6. *Ibid.*, 5/28/67.
7. Witcover, *Resurrection of Richard Nixon*, 211–212.
8. *New York Times*, 7/20/67.
9. *Ibid.*, 7/23/67.
10. *Ibid.*, 10/19/67.
11. Nixon to Glenn Davis, 10/24/67, Davis Papers, Wisconsin State Historical Society.
12. Stans, *Terrors of Justice*, 134.
13. Witcover, *Resurrection of Richard Nixon*, 209–210.
14. *New York Times*, 10/23/67.
15. *Ibid.*, 12/20/67; Ewald, *Eisenhower the President*, 305.
16. *New York Times*, 12/20/67.
17. Nixon, "What Has Happened to America?"
18. Milwaukee *Journal*, 10/29/67.
19. *New York Times*, 12/9/67.
20. Chicago *Tribune*, 10/28/67.
21. *New York Times*, 10/29/67.
22. *Ibid.*, 9/5/67.
23. Cannon, *Reagan*, 136.
24. *New York Times*, 11/28/67.
25. Nixon, *Memoirs*, 287–288; Chicago *Tribune*, 10/1/67.
26. Nixon, *Memoirs*, 289.
27. *New York Times*, 11/29/67.
28. Eisenhower, *Pat Nixon*, 232–233.
29. *New York Times*, 12/1/67.
30. *Ibid.*, 12/25/67.
31. *Ibid.*, 12/10/67.
32. Nixon, *Memoirs*, 291.
33. Eisenhower, *Pat Nixon*, 233–234.
34. Nixon, *Memoirs*, 292–293.
35. Eisenhower, *Pat Nixon*, 234.
36. Nixon, *Memoirs*, 294.
37. Eisenhower, *Pat Nixon*, 234.

CHAPTER SEVEN

1. Nixon to Glenn Davis, 1/16/68, Davis Papers, Wisconsin State Historical Society.
2. Stans, *Terrors of Justice*, 135.
3. *New York Times*, 2/2/68.
4. *Ibid.*
5. Witcover, *Resurrection of Richard Nixon*, 234–235; Eisenhower, *Pat Nixon*, 236.
6. *New York Times*, 2/4/68.
7. Witcover, *Resurrection of Richard Nixon*, 239–240.
8. *New York Times*, 2/4/68.
9. White, *Making of the President, 1968*, 131.
10. Eisenhower to Nixon, 2/8/68, EL.
11. *New York Times*, 2/18/68.
12. White, *Making of the President, 1968*, 131–134; Witcover, *Resurrection of Richard Nixon*, 237–238.
13. Stans, *Terrors of Justice*, 136, 141.
14. Nixon, *Memoirs*, 298.
15. *New York Times*, 3/3/68.
16. Witcover, *Resurrection of Richard Nixon*, 257.
17. *New York Times*, 3/6/68.
18. *Ibid.*
19. *Ibid.*, 3/8/68.
20. *Ibid.*, 3/11/68.
21. Nixon to Eisenhower, 3/17/68, EL.
22. *New York Times*, 3/7/68.
23. *Ibid.*, 3/8/68.
24. Nixon to Eisenhower, 3/6/68, EL.
25. *New York Times*, 3/13/68.
26. Ehrlichman, *Witness to Power*, 40.
27. Eisenhower, *Pat Nixon*, 238.
28. *New York Times*, 3/22/68.
29. Nixon, *Memoirs*, 300.
30. *New York Times*, 3/15/68.
31. Safire, *Before the Fall*, 47–48.
32. Hammond, "The American Withdrawal from Vietnam." This is a brilliant piece of work, and I have drawn on it heavily.
33. *New York Times*, 4/2/68.
34. White, *Making of the President, 1968*, 147–148.
35. Safire, *Before the Fall*, 48–49.
36. *Ibid.*, 48.
37. Nixon, *Memoirs*, 304.
38. Witcover, *Resurrection of Richard Nixon*, 289.
39. Eisenhower to Nixon, 4/23/68, EL.
40. Eisenhower, *Pat Nixon*, 237.
41. *Ibid.*, 238.
42. *New York Times*, 7/3/68.
43. *Ibid.*, 5/5/68.
44. Witcover, *Resurrection of Richard Nixon*, 298.
45. *New York Times*, 5/9/68.
46. *Ibid.*, 5/15/68.

47. Safire, *Before the Fall*, 49–50.
48. *New York Times*, 5/29/68.
49. Nixon, *Memoirs*, 305.
50. *New York Times*, 6/2/68.

CHAPTER EIGHT

1. Nixon, *Memoirs*, 305.
2. *New York Times*, 6/15/68.
3. Witcover, *Resurrection of Richard Nixon*, 322.
4. Eisenhower, *Pat Nixon*, 241.
5. *New York Times*, 6/15/68.
6. Stans, *Terrors of Justice*, 143.
7. *New York Times*, 6/28/68.
8. Klein, *Making It Perfectly Clear*, 27.
9. *New York Times*, 6/22/68.
10. *Ibid.*, 6/27/68.
11. *Ibid.*, 6/15/68.
12. Nixon, *Memoirs*, 307; Goldwater, *Goldwater*, 257.
13. Nixon to Eisenhower, 7/15/68, EL.
14. *New York Times*, 7/19/68.
15. Nixon, *Memoirs*, 312.
16. Witcover, *Resurrection of Richard Nixon*, 350.
17. *Ibid.*, 321.
18. Nixon, *Memoirs*, 311–312.
19. Haldeman interview.
20. Witcover, *Resurrection of Richard Nixon*, 351.
21. Klein, *Making It Perfectly Clear*, 26.
22. *New York Times*, 7/21/68.
23. *Ibid.*, 7/25/68.
24. Rostow interview.
25. Nixon, *Memoirs*, 308.
26. *New York Times*, 8/3/68.
27. *Ibid.*, 8/4/68.
28. *Ibid.*, 8/7/68.
29. Nixon, *Memoirs*, 309.
30. Witcover, *Resurrection of Richard Nixon*, 343.
31. *New York Times*, 8/8/68.
32. Witcover, *Resurrection of Richard Nixon*, 349.
33. *New York Times*, 8/7/68.
34. For the record, Nixon had not yet met Henry Kissinger, except once, for a moment or two, at a Clare Luce party in 1967. Nixon told Kissinger at that time that he had read *Nuclear Weapons and Foreign Policy*, Kissinger's first book, and had sent Kissinger a congratulatory note on it. Kissinger, embarrassed, said he had forgotten the note. Kissinger, *White House Years*, 9.
35. Witcover, *Resurrection of Richard Nixon*, 354.
36. Finch interview; Nixon, *Memoirs*, 312–313.
37. Witcover, *Resurrection of Richard Nixon*, 355–356.
38. Nixon, *Memoirs*, 313–314.
39. *New York Times*, 8/9/68.

Chapter Nine

1. *New York Times,* 8/21/68.
2. *Ibid.,* 8/10/68.
3. *Ibid.*
4. Bob Fleming to LBJ, memo, 8/19/68, JL.
5. Stans interview; Witcover, *Resurrection of Richard Nixon,* 367.
6. *New York Times,* 8/25/68.
7. Witcover, *Resurrection of Richard Nixon,* 364.
8. Safire, *Before the Fall,* 63–65.
9. Witcover, *Resurrection of Richard Nixon,* 370.
10. *New York Times,* 9/5/68.
11. *Ibid.,* 9/7/68.
12. Billy Graham notes, 9/17/68, JL.
13. *New York Times,* 9/7/68.
14. *Ibid.,* 9/14/68.
15. *Ibid.,* 10/8/68.
16. Ehrlichman, *Witness to Power,* 50.
17. *New York Times,* 9/16/68.
18. *Ibid.,* 9/13/68.
19. *Ibid.,* 9/22/68.
20. *Ibid.,* 9/24/68.
21. *Ibid.,* 9/29/68.
22. *Ibid.,* 9/9/68.
23. *Ibid.,* 9/11/68.
24. *Ibid.,* 10/5/68.
25. Ehrlichman, *Witness to Power,* 55.
26. *New York Times,* 9/10/68.
27. *Ibid.,* 9/23/68.
28. *Ibid.,* 9/27/68.
29. Los Angeles *Times,* 9/17/68.
30. *New York Times,* 9/23/68.
31. *Ibid.,* 9/16/68.
32. Witcover, *Resurrection of Richard Nixon,* 386–388.
33. Safire, *Before the Fall,* 75.
34. Nixon, *Memoirs,* 319.
35. *New York Times,* 9/18/68.
36. *Ibid.,* 9/28/68.
37. Los Angeles *Times,* 10/4/68.
38. *New York Times,* 10/6/68.
39. *Ibid.,* 10/13/68.
40. *Ibid.,* 9/30/68.
41. *Ibid.,* 10/10/68.
42. Safire, *Before the Fall,* 78.
43. Nixon, *Memoirs,* 323–324.
44. *New York Times,* 9/25/68.
45. *Ibid.,* 9/26/68.
46. *Ibid.*
47. *Ibid.,* 10/1/68.
48. *Ibid.,* 10/5/68.
49. *Ibid.,* 10/8/68.
50. *Ibid.*

51. *Ibid.*, 10/13/68.
52. *Ibid.*, 10/14/68.
53. Nixon, *Memoirs*, 324.
54. Johnson, *Vantage Point*, 547.
55. *New York Times*, 10/9/68.
56. Los Angeles *Times*, 10/15/68.

CHAPTER TEN

1. Witcover, *Resurrection of Richard Nixon*, 424–425; Los Angeles *Times* and *New York Times*, 10/15 to 11/2/68.
2. Witcover, *Resurrection of Richard Nixon*, 424.
3. *Ibid.*, 426.
4. *New York Times*, 10/18/68.
5. Author's recollection.
6. *Ibid.*
7. *New York Times*, 10/25/68.
8. *Ibid.*, 10/26/68.
9. *Ibid.*, 10/27/68.
10. *Ibid.*, 11/2/68.
11. Eisenhower to Nixon, 10/24/68, EL.
12. Nixon to Eisenhower, 10/27/68, EL.
13. *New York Times*, 10/17/68.
14. *Ibid.*, 10/28/68.
15. *Ibid.*, 10/22/68.
16. *Ibid.*, 10/21/68.
17. *Ibid.*, 10/31/68.
18. *Ibid.*, 11/4/68.
19. Unsigned memorandum, "Notes of the President's Meeting with RN," 11/11/68, JL.
20. Nixon, *Memoirs*, 325.
21. *New York Times*, 10/18/68; Nixon, *Memoirs*, 325.
22. Hung and Schecter, *The Palace File*, 23.
23. *Ibid.*, 24; Hersh, *Price of Power*, 21–22.
24. Nixon, *Memoirs*, 326.
25. *Ibid.*
26. Memo, "Notes of the President's Meeting with RN," 11/11/68, JL.
27. *New York Times*, 10/24/68.
28. Nixon, *Memoirs*, 327.
29. Safire, *Before the Fall*, 85–86, reproduces the Harlow draft with Nixon's changes; see also Nixon, *Memoirs*, 327–328.
30. *New York Times*, 10/28/68.
31. *Ibid.*
32. Memo, 11/11/68, JL.
33. Johnson, *The Vantage Point*, 520–521.
34. Hung and Schecter, *The Palace File*, 25.
35. Witcover, *Resurrection of Richard Nixon*, 431–432.
36. Johnson, *The Vantage Point*, 528.
37. Washington *Post*, 11/1/68.
38. Witcover, *Resurrection of Richard Nixon*, 437.
39. Hung and Schecter, *The Palace File*, 28; White, *Making of the President, 1968*, 381.

40. *New York Times*, 11/3/68.
41. *Ibid.*, 11/4/68; Witcover, *Resurrection of Richard Nixon*, 438–439.
42. Nixon, *Memoirs*, 329.
43. Witcover, *Resurrection of Richard Nixon*, 442.
44. White, *Making of the President, 1968*, 381.
45. Witcover, *Resurrection of Richard Nixon*, 441.
46. Hersh, *Price of Power*, 22.
47. Papers of Clark Clifford, Box 6, Presentation on Paris Peace Talks, Nov. 11, [1], JL.
48. *New York Times*, 11/5/68.
49. David Eisenhower interview.
50. Washington *Post*, 11/6/68.
51. *Ibid.*
52. White, *Making of the President, 1968*, 385.
53. Witcover, *Resurrection of Richard Nixon*, 446.
54. *Ibid.*, 447.
55. White, *Making of the President, 1968*, 388–389
56. *Ibid.*, 390–394.
57. Eisenhower, *Pat Nixon*, 246.
58. Nixon, *Memoirs*, 334.
59. Eisenhower, *Pat Nixon*, 247.
60. Nixon, *Memoirs*, 335.

CHAPTER ELEVEN

1. Haldeman, *Ends of Power*, 83.
2. Miami *Herald*, 8/7/68.
3. *New York Times*, 11/7/68.
4. *Ibid.*
5. Eisenhower, *Pat Nixon*, 226.
6. *New York Times*, 11/24/68.
7. Ehrlichman, *Witness to Power*, 69; *New York Times*, 12/22/68.
8. Eisenhower, *Pat Nixon*, 226.
9. Safire, *Before the Fall*, 112.
10. *Ibid.*, 113.
11. Nixon, *Memoirs*, 337.
12. Haldeman, *Ends of Power*, 72.
13. Klein, *Making It Perfectly Clear*, 32.
14. Nixon, *Memoirs*, 354–355.
15. Ambrose, *Eisenhower*, Vol. II, 614.
16. Nixon, *Memoirs*, 355; Klein, *Making It Perfectly Clear*, Ch. 3.
17. Clifford handwritten memo, "Notes of Pres's Meeting with President-Elect Richard Nixon," 11/11/68, JL.
18. *New York Times*, 11/12/68.
19. Hung and Schecter, *The Palace File*, 29.
20. *Ibid.*, 30; William Hammond, U.S. Army Center of Military History, letter to the author, 2/11/88.
21. Hersh, *Price of Power*, 23.
22. Kissinger, *White House Years*, 11, 15.
23. Nixon, *Memoirs*, 341.
24. Garthoff, *Détente and Confrontation*, 27.
25. *Ibid.*, 69–70.

26. Kissinger, *White House Years*, 26; Garthoff, *Détente and Confrontation*, 70.

27. *New York Times*, 12/3/68.

28. *Ibid.*

29. Powers, *Secrecy and Power*, 440.

30. Nixon, *Memoirs*, 358.

31. Ehrlichman, *Witness to Power*, 156.

32. Haldeman, *Ends of Power*, 80; Lasky, *It Didn't Start with Watergate*, 215.

33. Haldeman, *Ends of Power*, 81.

34. Nixon, *Memoirs*, 338–339.

35. *Ibid.*, 342.

36. Moynihan interview.

37. Nixon, *Memoirs*, 342.

38. Hess interview.

39. Safire, *Before the Fall*, 108.

40. Ehrlichman, *Witness to Power*, 77.

41. Nixon, *Memoirs*, 339.

42. Safire, *Before the Fall*, 108.

43. Nixon, *Memoirs*, 339.

44. *New York Times*, 12/12/68.

45. Nixon, *Memoirs*, 338.

46. *Ibid.*, 352.

47. *New York Times*, 11/27/68.

48. *Ibid.*, 12/21/68.

49. *Ibid.*, 12/23/68.

50. Nixon, *Memoirs*, 361.

51. Hersh, *Price of Power*, 55.

52. Kissinger, *White House Years*, 241.

53. Nixon, *Memoirs*, 357–358.

54. *Ibid.*, 357.

55. Los Angeles *Times*, 1/2/69.

56. *New York Times*, 1/10/69.

57. Price, *With Nixon*, 42–44.

58. Nixon, *Memoirs*, 365–366.

59. Price, *With Nixon*, 49.

60. *New York Times*, 1/21/69.

61. *Ibid.*

62. Eisenhower, *Pat Nixon*, 253–254.

Chapter Twelve

1. Washington *Post*, 2/25/69.

2. Eisenhower, *Pat Nixon*, 267; Washington *Post*, 6/30/69; Haldeman to Klein, 6/30/69, NPMP.

3. Washington *Post*, 5/1/69.

4. NS, 5/19/69.

5. *Ibid.*

6. Washington *Post*, 2/19/69.

7. Nixon, *Memoirs*, 368.

8. Klein, *Making It Perfectly Clear*, 197, 322, 418.

9. NS, 2/22/69.

10. *Ibid.*, 2/23 to 3/11/69.
11. Butterfield to Klein, 6/2/69, NPMP.
12. Safire, *Before the Fall*, 152.
13. Garment to Haldeman, with RN notation, 6/21/69, NPMP.
14. Ehrlichman to RN, with RN notation, 2/1/69, NPMP.
15. Haldeman to Klein, 2/5/69, NPMP.
16. Harlow to Haldeman and Klein, with RN notation, 3/10/69, NPMP.
17. NS, 1/30/69.
18. *Ibid.*
19. Nixon to Ehrlichman, 6/16/69, NPMP.
20. Safire, *Before the Fall*, 343.
21. NS, 3/26/73.
22. *Ibid.*, 4/10/69.
23. PP (1969), 15–17.
24. See Chang, "JFK, China, and the Bomb," 1287–1310.
25. NS, 5/19/69.
26. PP (1969), 19.
27. Garthoff, *Détente and Confrontation*, 57.
28. Hersh, *Price of Power*, 104–105.
29. Nixon, *Memoirs*, 370.
30. Dean Acheson, "The First Hundred Days," remarks to the American Society of Newspaper Editors, 4/16/69. In Acheson collection, Princeton University. My thanks to Douglas Brinkley for bringing this and other Acheson material to my attention.
31. Kissinger, *White House Years*, 93.
32. Nixon, *Memoirs*, 371; Kissinger, *White House Years*, 95.
33. Klein, *Making It Perfectly Clear*, 133.
34. Haldeman, *Ends of Power*, 71.
35. Washington *Post*, 3/19/69.
36. PP (1969), 183–184.
37. *Ibid.*, 185.
38. *Ibid.*, 189.
39. *Ibid.*, 210–211.
40. Hersh, *Price of Power*, 61–64; Nixon, *Memoirs*, 380–381; Kissinger, *White House Years*, 245–247.
41. PP (1969), 208–212.
42. Acheson notes of meeting, in Acheson collection, Princeton University.
43. NS, 1/22/69.
44. *New York Times*, 1/22/69.
45. *Ibid.*, 1/28/69.
46. Washington *Post*, 3/6/69.
47. NS, 1/24/69.
48. PP (1969), 235–237.
49. *New York Times*, 4/30/69.
50. *Ibid.*, 6/4/69.
51. Ehrlichman to RN, with RN notation, 6/5/69, NPMP.
52. PP (1969), 258.
53. *Ibid.*, 365–366.
54. Huston to RN, with RN notation, 6/18/69, NPMP.
55. Burns to RN, with RN notation, 6/9/69, NPMP.
56. Nixon's chattel deed, dated December 30, 1968, and an amend-

ment, in a letter to Joel Solomon, Administrator of the General Services Administration, dated March 22, 1978, are in VPP.

57. Nixon, *Memoirs,* 375.
58. Price, *With Nixon,* 61.
59. *New York Times,* 3/31/69
60. Burke and Burke, *Nixon's Good Deed,* 9.
61. *Ibid.,* 42.
62. *Ibid.,* 45.
63. *Ibid.,* 67.
64. Nixon, *Memoirs,* 382–383; Hersh, *Price of Power,* 72–73.
65. Garthoff, *Détente and Confrontation,* 75.
66. Nixon, *Memoirs,* 384.
67. Haldeman, *Ends of Power,* 85.
68. Kissinger, *White House Years,* 316, 319.
69. Nixon, *Memoirs,* 385.
70. Hung and Schecter, *The Palace File,* 31.
71. NS, 3/23/69.
72. PP (1969), 300.
73. Nixon, *Memoirs,* 391.
74. *Ibid.*
75. Hersh, *Price of Power,* 75.
76. Safire, *Before the Fall,* 166.
77. Nixon, *Memoirs,* 389.
78. Hersh, *Price of Power,* 84; Powers, *Secrecy and Power,* 446.
79. Hersh, *Price of Power,* 94.
80. Safire, *Before the Fall,* 167–168.
81. Ehrlichman, *Witness to Power,* 174–175.
82. Powers, *Secrecy and Power,* 447; Nixon, *Memoirs,* 389.
83. Hersh, *Price of Power,* 96.
84. Eisenhower to RN, 12/13/68, EL.
85. Nixon, *Memoirs,* 419.
86. Warren to RN, 4/25/69, NPMP.
87. Ehrlichman, *Witness to Power,* 114.
88. Burger to RN, 5/8/69, NPMP.
89. Nixon, *Memoirs,* 420.
90. *New York Times,* 5/23/69.
91. PP (1969), 369–374.
92. *New York Times,* 5/16/69.
93. NS, 6/11/69.
94. *Ibid.,* 5/19/69.
95. *New York Times,* 6/5/69.
96. *Ibid.,* 6/6/69.
97. Kissinger, *White House Years,* 272.
98. PP (1969), 443.
99. Nixon, *Memoirs,* 392.
100. Kissinger, *White House Years,* 274.
101. PP (1969), 472.

Chapter Thirteen

1. NS, 7/15/69.
2. Kissinger, *White House Years,* 276.

3. *Ibid.*, 247–249.
4. Nixon, *Memoirs*, 393.
5. PP (1969), 910.
6. Hersh, *Price of Power*, 120.
7. Kissinger, *White House Years*, 261–263.
8. Nixon, *Memoirs*, 396.
9. See RN to LBJ, 7/16/69, JL.
10. Safire, *Before the Fall*, 149.
11. Ehrlichman, *Witness to Power*, 292.
12. Ehrlichman to Kissinger, 12/10/69, NPMP.
13. Safire, *Before the Fall*, 155.
14. *New York Times*, 7/19/69.
15. PP (1969), 530.
16. *Ibid.*, 541–543.
17. NS, 7/30/69.
18. *New York Times*, 8/1/69.
19. *Ibid.*, 7/27/69.
20. Washington *Post*, 8/2/69.
21. *Ibid.*, 7/31/69.
22. *New York Times*, 7/31/69.
23. RN to Haldeman and Ehrlichman, 8/7/69, NPMP.
24. PP (1969), 549.
25. Kissinger, *White House Years*, 223–224; Garthoff, *Détente and Confrontation*, 74.
26. Haldeman, *Ends of Power*, 91.
27. NS, 6/6/69.
28. Kissinger, *White House Years*, 156.
29. *Ibid.*, 180–181.
30. Nixon, *Memoirs*, 395.
31. *New York Times*, 6/20/69.
32. Ambrose, *Rise to Globalism*, 315.
33. Nixon, *Memoirs*, 418.
34. Harlow to RN, with RN notation, 7/1/69, NPMP.
35. RN to Harlow, 8/5/69, NPMP.
36. Butterfield to Kissinger, with RN notation, 4/25/69, NPMP.
37. Nixon, *Memoirs*, 418.
38. Butterfield to Klein, with RN notation, 7/2/69, NPMP.
39. Moynihan to RN, with RN notation, 4/11/69, NPMP.
40. Burke and Burke, *Nixon's Good Deed*, 87.
41. *Ibid.*, 90.
42. Washington *Post*, 12/3/69.
43. Burke and Burke, *Nixon's Good Deed*, 93.
44. *Ibid.*, 90, 91.
45. Harlow to Ehrlichman, 7/28/69, NPMP.
46. Burke and Burke, *Nixon's Good Deed*, 104–107.
47. NS, 10/10/69.
48. PP (1969), 637–645.
49. Burke and Burke, *Nixon's Good Deed*, 125–128.
50. Press release, 5/12/69, NPMP.
51. Eisenhower, *Pat Nixon*, 271.
52. Washington *Post*, 6/29/69.
53. Eisenhower, *Pat Nixon*, 272.
54. Washington *Post*, 8/20/69.

55. Ehrlichman, *Witness to Power*, 118.
56. *Ibid.*, 118–119.
57. Safire to RN, with RN notation, 7/3/69, NPMP.
58. Safire, *Before the Fall*, 227.
59. Magruder, *An American Life*, 78–79.
60. *Ibid.*, 79–81.
61. *Ibid.*, 68.
62. Nixon, *Memoirs*, 397.
63. NS, 9/8/69.
64. *Ibid.*, 9/15/69.
65. Kissinger, *White House Years*, 284–285.
66. Laird to RN, 9/4/69, NPMP.
67. PP (1969), 718.
68. NS, 9/30/69.
69. PP (1969), 748, 752–753.
70. *Ibid.*, 749.
71. Nixon, *Memoirs*, 400.
72. Harlow to RN, with RN notation, 10/6/69, NPMP.
73. RN to Kissinger, 10/1/69, NPMP.
74. *New York Times*, 10/5/69.
75. Nixon, *Memoirs*, 401.
76. *New York Times*, 10/12/69.
77. Magruder, *An American Life*, 85.
78. Washington *Post*, 10/7/69.
79. *New York Times*, 10/10/69.
80. Caulfield to Ehrlichman, with RN notation, 10/10/69, NPMP.
81. PP (1969), 798–800.
82. Safire, *Before the Fall*, 172.
83. *Ibid.*
84. Nixon, *Memoirs*, 403.

CHAPTER FOURTEEN

1. Magruder, *An American Life*, 87–90.
2. Kissinger, *White House Years*, 285.
3. Nixon, *Memoirs*, 405.
4. Schell, *Time of Illusion*, 56.
5. Nixon, *Memoirs*, 406–407.
6. Garthoff, *Détente and Confrontation*, 253–254.
7. Nixon, *Memoirs*, 407–408.
8. Acheson notes, in Acheson collection, Princeton University.
9. PP (1969), 901–909.
10. Nixon, *Memoirs*, 409.
11. *New York Times*, 11/4/69.
12. Nixon, *Memoirs*, 410.
13. Klein, *Making It Perfectly Clear*, 279.
14. *New York Times*, 11/9/69.
15. Nixon, *Memoirs*, 410–411.
16. Rostow to Nixon, 11/12/69, JL.
17. Nixon to Rogers, 11/17/69, NPMP.
18. Author's recollection.
19. Nixon, *Memoirs*, 499.

20. *New York Times*, 11/18/69.
21. Garthoff, *Détente and Confrontation*, 135.
22. Nixon to Haldeman, 12/1/69, NPMP.
23. PP (1969), 815.
24. Ehrlichman, *Witness to Power*, 119–120.
25. *Ibid.*, 122.
26. Nixon to Buchanan, 10/21/69, NPMP.
27. *New York Times*, 11/22/69.
28. PP (1969), 957.
29. *Ibid.*, 750.
30. *Ibid.*, 1010.
31. Nixon, *Memoirs*, 440.
32. Washington *Post*, 7/22/69.
33. *Ibid.*, 7/3/69.
34. *Ibid.*, 12/1/69.
35. *Ibid.*, 9/5/69; *New York Times*, 7/16/69.
36. PP (1969), 1027.
37. *Ibid.*, 1007.
38. *Ibid.*, 1013.
39. *Ibid.*, 1011.
40. Nixon, *Memoirs*, 433.
41. PP (1969), 1032.

CHAPTER FIFTEEN

1. Kissinger, *White House Years*, 780.
2. NS, 3/12/70.
3. Kissinger, *White House Years*, 436.
4. NS, 1/12/70.
5. *Ibid.*, 1/16/70.
6. Hersh, *Price of Power*, 168; *New York Times*, 1/30/70.
7. NS, 2/2/70.
8. *New York Times*, 2/1/70.
9. NS, 2/5/70.
10. *Ibid.*
11. Magruder to RN, 2/23/70, NPMP.
12. NS, 10/27/70.
13. *Ibid.*, 4/1/70.
14. Brown to Magruder, 4/2/70, NPMP.
15. Haldeman memo, 2/27/70, NPMP.
16. Krogh to Ehrlichman, with RN notation, 1/24/70, NPMP.
17. PP (1970), 8, 15.
18. *New York Times*, 2/9/70.
19. PP (1970), 10–11.
20. Ehrlichman to RN, with RN notation, 2/25/70, and Butterfield to Ehrlichman, 2/27/70, NPMP.
21. Garthoff, *Détente and Confrontation*, 223–224.
22. Byrd to Nixon, 1/12/70, NPMP.
23. Ehrlichman, *Witness to Power*, 126.
24. *Ibid.*, 126–127; NS, 3/1/70.
25. NS, 1/9/70.
26. *New York Times*, 3/4/70.

27. NS, 1/16/70.
28. Buchanan to RN, with RN notation, 1/30/70, NPMP.
29. Nixon, *Memoirs*, 441.
30. NS, 3/25/70.
31. Moynihan to RN, with RN notation, 1/16/70, NPMP.
32. *New York Times*, 2/23/70.
33. *Ibid.*, 1/26/70.
34. Washington *Post*, 3/6/70.
35. *Ibid.*, 3/4/70.
36. Nixon, *Memoirs*, 456.
37. Eisenhower, *Pat Nixon*, 282, 290; Ehrlichman, *Witness to Power*, 62.
38. Buchanan to RN, with RN notation, 3/16/70, NPMP.
39. Nixon, *Memoirs*, 481–482.
40. Kissinger, *White House Years*, 563.
41. *New York Times*, 2/19 to 2/26/70.
42. *Ibid.*, 3/7/70.
43. Hersh, *Price of Power*, 171; Kissinger, *White House Years*, 455–456.
44. Nixon, *Memoirs*, 447; Kissinger, *White House Years*, 463.
45. Kissinger, *White House Years*, 465.
46. Nixon, *Memoirs*, 447.
47. *New York Times*, 4/2/70.
48. *Ibid.*, 4/3/70.
49. PP (1970), 345–346.
50. *New York Times*, 4/11/70.
51. Nixon, *Memoirs*, 447–448.
52. Ehrlichman, *Witness to Power*, 62.
53. Nixon, *Memoirs*, 448.
54. Kissinger, *White House Years*, 473.
55. *Ibid.*, 474.
56. Nixon, *Memoirs*, 448.
57. Kissinger, *White House Years*, 481.
58. PP (1970), 373–377.
59. Kissinger, *White House Years*, 481.
60. *Ibid.*, 484; Nixon, *Memoirs*, 448–449.
61. Nixon, *Memoirs*, 449; Kissinger, *White House Years*, 490–491.
62. Kissinger, *White House Years*, 491.
63. Nixon, *Memoirs*, 450.
64. Kissinger, *White House Years*, 495.
65. Hersh, *Price of Power*, 187–188.
66. Kissinger, *White House Years*, 495.
67. Hersh, *Price of Power*, 109.
68. *Ibid.*, 190; Morris, *Uncertain Greatness*, 147; Brodie, *Richard Nixon*, 477.
69. Kissinger, *White House Years*, 498.
70. *Ibid.*
71. Nixon, *Memoirs*, 450.
72. Kissinger, *White House Years*, 501–502.
73. *Ibid.*, 1485.
74. Nixon, *Memoirs*, 451.
75. *Ibid.*
76. *New York Times*, 4/30/70.

77. PP (1970), 405–410.
78. Nixon, *Memoirs,* 452–453.

CHAPTER SIXTEEN

1. Nixon, *Memoirs,* 453.
2. *New York Times,* 5/2/70.
3. Nixon, *Memoirs,* 454.
4. *New York Times,* 5/2/70.
5. PP (1970), 417.
6. HRH notes, 5/1/70, NPMP.
7. *New York Times,* 5/3/70.
8. Hersh, *Price of Power,* 193–194.
9. *New York Times,* 5/5/70.
10. *Ibid.*
11. PP (1970), 411.
12. *New York Times,* 5/8/70.
13. Mrs. D. P. Moynihan interview.
14. *New York Times,* 5/6/70.
15. *Ibid.,* 5/7/70.
16. *Ibid.,* 5/6, 5/7, 5/8/70.
17. *Ibid.,* 5/8/70.
18. PP (1970), 413–419.
19. Price, *With Nixon,* 170–174; Safire, *Before the Fall,* 204–208; Nixon, *Memoirs,* 459–466.
20. Safire, *Before the Fall,* 209–210; Nixon, *Memoirs,* 460.
21. Nixon, *Memoirs,* 460.
22. Price, *With Nixon,* 169.
23. Hersh, *Price of Power,* 196.
24. HRH notes, 5/11/70, NPMP.
25. *New York Times,* 5/13/70.
26. HRH notes, 5/20/70, NPMP.
27. *New York Times,* 5/17/70.
28. *Ibid.,* 5/21 and 5/24/70.
29. *Ibid.,* 5/24/70.
30. Nixon, *Memoirs,* 467.
31. Ambrose, *Eisenhower,* II, 361.
32. Nixon to LBJ, 5/22/70, JL.
33. PP (1970), 476–480.
34. Hersh, *Price of Power,* 202.
35. *New York Times,* 6/4/70.
36. *Ibid.,* 5/20/70.
37. Haldeman, *Ends of Power,* 107.
38. Nixon, *Memoirs,* 471.
39. Powers, *Secrecy and Power,* 450.
40. *Ibid.,* 451.
41. Eisenhower, *Pat Nixon,* 290–291.
42. Klein to Gorkin (editor of *Parade*), 5/28/70, NPMP.
43. *New York Times,* 7/18/70.
44. Haldeman to Klein, 8/4/70, NPMP.
45. *New York Times,* 5/21/70.
46. Nixon, *Memoirs,* 443.

47. Finch interview.
48. Ehrlichman, *Witness to Power*, 230–231.
49. *Ibid.*, 233.
50. *New York Times*, 6/7/70.
51. Dent to Nixon, 6/16/70, NPMP; Nixon, *Memoirs*, 442.
52. Ehrlichman, *Witness to Power*, 227.
53. HRH memo, 8/4/70, NPMP.
54. Garment to RN, with RN notation, 8/5/70, NPMP.
55. *New York Times*, 8/15/70.
56. *Ibid.*, 8/20/70.
57. Moynihan to RN, with RN notation, 8/24/70, NPMP.
58. Moynihan to RN, 7/1/70, NPMP.
59. *New York Times*, 8/29/70.
60. Powers, *Secrecy and Power*, 453–454.
61. *Ibid.*, 456.
62. Nixon, *Memoirs*, 475.
63. *New York Times*, 7/31/70.
64. *Ibid.*, 8/4/70.
65. Butterfield to RN, with RN notation, 8/12/70, NPMP.
66. *New York Times*, 6/23/70.
67. Haldeman to Klein, 7/20/70, NPMP.
68. *New York Times*, 7/26/70.
69. *Ibid.*
70. Klein, *Making It Perfectly Clear*, 125–128.

CHAPTER SEVENTEEN

1. *New York Times*, 8/28/70.
2. NS, 9/1/70.
3. *Ibid.*, 9/10/70.
4. *Ibid.*, 8/1/70.
5. Dean to RN, with RN notation, 8/4/70, NPMP.
6. Nixon, *Memoirs*, 491.
7. NS, 9/22/70.
8. *Ibid.*, 10/17/70.
9. Magruder memo, 9/23/70, NPMP.
10. PP (1970), 757–763.
11. RN to McCain, 9/18/70, NPMP.
12. *New York Times*, 9/21/70; RN to Jack Olson, 9/20/70, Wisconsin State Historical Society.
13. RN to Olson, 9/26/70, Wisconsin State Historical Society.
14. This paragraph is based on the author's personal experience at Kansas State and the University of New Orleans.
15. PP (1970), 758.
16. Kissinger, *White House Years*, 653.
17. *Ibid.*, 654.
18. *Ibid.*, 673; Hersh, *Price of Power*, 273.
19. Hersh, *Price of Power*, 273–274; Kissinger, *White House Years*, 673.
20. Garthoff, *Détente and Confrontation*, 76, note 27.
21. Kissinger, *White House Years*, 632–633.
22. Garthoff, *Détente and Confrontation*, 79–81.

23. *Ibid.*, 82.
24. Haldeman, *Ends of Power*, 85–86.
25. Kissinger, *White House Years*, 638.
26. *Ibid.*, 639.
27. Nixon, *Memoirs*, 486.
28. *Ibid.*, 487; Kissinger, *White House Years*, 642–643.
29. *New York Times*, 9/25/70; Smith, *Doubletalk*, 215.
30. Kissinger, *White House Years*, 646–647; Nixon, *Memoirs*, 487–488.
31. Nixon, *Memoirs*, 488–489.
32. Hersh, *Price of Power*, 256.
33. NS, 12/1/70.
34. Nixon, *Memoirs*, 483–484.
35. Haldeman to Klein, 9/22/70, NPMP.
36. *New York Times*, 9/30/70.
37. *Ibid.*, 10/4/70.
38. Acheson memo, 12/7/70, in Acheson collection, Princeton University.
39. Garthoff, *Détente and Confrontation*, 122.
40. NS, 3/20/70.
41. *New York Times*, 9/2/70.
42. Nixon, *Memoirs*, 468.
43. Safire, *Before the Fall*, 385.
44. *Ibid.*, 384–385.
45. PP (1970), 821–822.
46. *New York Times*, 10/8/70.
47. Karnow, *Vietnam*, 627.
48. PP (1970), 830–832.
49. *New York Times*, 10/9 and 10/11/70.
50. Nixon, *Memoirs*, 469.
51. NS, 10/17/70.
52. *New York Times*, 10/2, 10/13, and 11/24/70.
53. Magruder, *An American Life*, 137.
54. *New York Times*, 10/18/70.
55. *Ibid.*, 10/20/70.
56. PP (1970), 940–941.
57. *New York Times*, 10/25/70.
58. NS, 10/21/70.
59. Safire, *Before the Fall*, 328.
60. PP (1970), 1023.
61. Nixon, *Memoirs*, 492.
62. Safire, *Before the Fall*, 330.
63. PP (1970), 1027.
64. Magruder, *An American Life*, 140.
65. *New York Times*, 10/31/70.
66. *Ibid.*, 11/1/70.
67. PP (1970), 1069.
68. Haldeman to Klein and Ziegler, 11/27/70, NPMP.
69. NS, 12/27/70.
70. Nixon, *Memoirs*, 495–496.
71. Price to RN, 11/13/70, NPMP.
72. *New York Times*, 11/21/70.
73. PP (1970), 1095–1096.

74. Schoenebaum, *Profiles of an Era,* 140. This is an invaluable reference work.
75. Moynihan to RN, with RN notation, 11/30/70, NPMP.
76. *New York Times,* 12/2/70.
77. PP (1970), 1101–1110.
78. Nixon, *Memoirs,* 546.
79. *Ibid.*
80. *Ibid.,* 546–547.
81. PP (1970), 1110.

Chapter Eighteen

1. *New York Times,* 1/3/71.
2. *Ibid.*
3. Moynihan interview. Bill Safire, who was present, heartily agreed with Senator Moynihan's remarks.
4. NS, 1/4/71.
5. PP (1971), 7–22.
6. Buchanan to RN, with RN notation, 1/6/71, NPMP.
7. Klein, *Making It Perfectly Clear,* 371.
8. Dean to staff, 8/15/71, NPMP.
9. RN to Haldeman, 6/16/69, NPMP.
10. RN to Haldeman, 5/9/71, NPMP.

Chapter Nineteen

1. *New York Times,* 4/1/71; Lukas, *Nightmare,* 8; Nixon, *Memoirs,* 497.
2. Moynihan to RN, with RN notation, 3/8/71, NPMP.
3. NS, 2/1/71.
4. *Ibid.,* 5/7/71.
5. *Ibid.,* 3/12/71.
6. *Ibid.,* 6/5/71.
7. *Ibid.,* 2/28/71.
8. *Ibid.,* 2/11/71.
9. RN to Haldeman, 6/1/71, NPMP.
10. Haldeman to RN, with RN notation, 6/11/71, NPMP.
11. Price to RN, with RN notation, 4/11/71, NPMP.
12. Finch to RN, with RN notation, 4/15/71, NPMP.
13. Nixon, *Memoirs,* 502–503; Eisenhower, *Pat Nixon,* 309–310.
14. Flanigan to Nixon, 2/22/71, NPMP.
15. NS, 3/18/71.
16. LBJ to Nixon, 3/31, 4/12, and 6/1/71, JL; *New York Times,* 5/23/71.
17. NS, 5/28/71.
18. *Ibid.,* 11/25/71.
19. *Ibid.,* 5/28/71.
20. Karnow, *Vietnam,* 631.
21. PP (1971), 605–610.
22. *New York Times,* 5/30/71.
23. Kissinger, *White House Years,* 999.
24. *Ibid.,* 994.

25. Nixon, *Memoirs*, 498.
26. Kissinger, *White House Years*, 999.
27. NS, 3/8/71.
28. *Ibid.*, 2/22/71.
29. PP (1971), 160.
30. Timmons to RN, 4/1/71, NPMP.
31. Bush to RN, 4/5/71, NPMP.
32. MacGregor to RN, 4/5/71, NPMP.
33. Nixon, *Memoirs*, 499.
34. Kissinger, *White House Years*, 986.
35. NS, 4/12/71.
36. Colson to Chapin, 12/12/70, NPMP.
37. Drosnin, *Citizen Hughes*, 412.
38. Dean, *Blind Ambition*, 66.
39. Drosnin, *Citizen Hughes*, 412.
40. Dean, *Blind Ambition*, 67–70.
41. Nixon, *Memoirs*, 501–502.
42. Ambrose, *Eisenhower*, II, 203.
43. Haldeman, *Ends of Power*, 195.
44. Eisenhower, *Pat Nixon*, 307.
45. *Ibid.*
46. Nixon, *Memoirs*, 501.
47. Eisenhower, *Pat Nixon*, 307.
48. Moynihan to RN, with RN notation, 3/8/71, NPMP.
49. Lukas, *Nightmare*, 60.
50. PP (1971), 545–550.
51. *New York Times*, 3/1/71.
52. *Ibid.*
53. Dean to Ziegler, 3/3/71, NPMP.
54. PP (1971), 391.
55. Nixon, *Memoirs*, 547.
56. PP (1971), 160.
57. *New York Times*, 2/26/71.
58. *Ibid.*, 4/11/71.
59. NS, 1/22/71.
60. Hughes to RN, with RN notation, 2/26/71, NPMP.
61. PP (1971), 162.
62. *New York Times*, 2/27/71.
63. PP (1971), 524–526.
64. *New York Times*, 4/15/71.
65. PP (1971), 530–531.
66. *Ibid.*, 541–542.
67. Nixon, *Memoirs*, 549.
68. PP (1971), 394.
69. NPMP.
70. *New York Times*, 1/30/71.
71. PP (1971), 53.
72. *New York Times*, 6/19/71.
73. PP (1971), 597.
74. Lukas, *Nightmare*, 18–19.
75. *New York Times*, 3/25/71.
76. NS, 5/26/71.
77. McCracken to RN, with RN notation, 4/26/71, NPMP.

78. Ehrlichman to RN, with RN notation, 6/29/71, NPMP.
79. Transcript, 3/23/71, NPMP.
80. Lukas, *Nightmare*, 124.
81. *Ibid.*, 131–132.
82. NS, 6/7/71.
83. PP (1971), 188.
84. *Ibid.*, 593–595.
85. *New York Times*, 6/1/71.

CHAPTER TWENTY

1. Garthoff, *Détente and Confrontation*, 127–147; Hersh, *Price of Power*, 336–337; Kissinger, *White House Years*, 812–818; Nixon, *Memoirs*, 523; Smith, *Doubletalk*, 147–148.
2. PP (1971), 648.
3. Garthoff, *Détente and Confrontation*, 150.
4. Kissinger, *White House Years*, 819.
5. Haldeman notes, 5/20/71, NPMP.
6. Scali to RN, with RN notation, 5/26/71, NPMP.
7. NS, 6/1/71.
8. *Ibid.*, 6/5/71.
9. *Ibid.*, 3/11/71.
10. RN to Acheson, 5/23/71, Acheson Papers, Yale University.
11. Eisenhower, *Pat Nixon*, 312.
12. *New York Times*, 6/13/71.
13. Eisenhower, *Pat Nixon*, 313–314; Nixon, *Memoirs*, 507.
14. Hersh, *Price of Power*, 385.
15. Haldeman interview.
16. Hersh, *Price of Power*, 384–385.
17. Karnow, *Vietnam*, 63.
18. Haldeman, *Ends of Power*, 110.
19. NS, 7/5/71.
20. Haldeman, *Ends of Power*, 111.
21. Nixon, *Memoirs*, 512; Hersh, *Price of Power*, 387.
22. Ehrlichman, *Witness to Power*, 165.
23. Nixon, *Memoirs*, 596.
24. Hersh, *Price of Power*, 392.
25. *New York Times*, 6/24/71.
26. Haldeman, *Ends of Power*, 112.
27. Colson to Ehrlichman, 7/22/71, NPMP.
28. Haldeman, *Ends of Power*, 115–116.
29. *Ibid.*, 117.
30. PP (1971), 695.
31. Nixon, *Memoirs*, 551–552.
32. Hersh, *Price of Power*, 345.
33. Kissinger, *White House Years*, 716.
34. Nixon, *Memoirs*, 553.
35. Hersh, *Price of Power*, 367.
36. *Ibid.*, 370–376; Garthoff, *Détente and Confrontation*, 232–233.
37. PP (1971), 819–820.
38. *New York Times*, 7/17/71.
39. *Ibid.*, 9/6/71; Goldwater, *Goldwater*, 259.

40. RN to Kissinger, 7/19/71, NPMP.
41. NS, 8/2/71; PP (1971), 850.
42. Ehrlichman to RN, with RN notation, 9/11/71, NPMP.
43. NS, 9/23/71.
44. *Ibid.;* Haldeman notes, 7/25 and 9/13/71, NPMP.
45. Haldeman, *Ends of Power*, 59.
46. Schoenebaum, *Profiles of an Era*, 95.
47. *Ibid.*, 96.
48. Safire, *Before the Fall*, 519.
49. Klein, *Making It Perfectly Clear*, 286–287; Safire, *Before the Fall*, 492–493.
50. Schoenebaum, *Profiles of an Era*, 96; Safire, *Before the Fall*, 493–495.
51. Safire, *Before the Fall*, 497.
52. Ehrlichman, *Witness to Power*, 261.
53. Kissinger, *White House Years*, 951.
54. Gulley, *Breaking Cover*, 201.
55. Schoenebaum, *Profiles of an Era*, 140; Safire, *Before the Fall*, 509.
56. PP (1971), 886–890.
57. *New York Times*, 8/17/71.
58. *Ibid.*, 8/16/71.
59. *Ibid.*, 8/17/71.
60. Ehrlichman to RN, with RN notation, 8/5/71, NPMP.
61. Safire to Ehrlichman, and Ehrlichman to RN, with RN notation, 7/2/71, NPMP.
62. NS, 9/23/71.
63. Klein to RN, with RN notation, 7/3/71, and Morgan to Nixon, 7/6/71, NPMP.
64. *New York Times*, 8/8/71.
65. *Ibid.*, 8/15/71.
66. *Ibid.*, 9/17/71.
67. *Ibid.*, 4/25/71.
68. Milwaukee *Journal*, 3/4/71.
69. Hersh, *Price of Power*, 442; Garthoff, *Détente and Confrontation*, 255.
70. Kissinger, *White House Years*, 1025.
71. *Ibid.*, 1026.
72. Hersh, *Price of Power*, 424.
73. PP (1971), 953–954.
74. Kissinger, *White House Years*, 799–833; Garthoff, *Détente and Confrontation*, 117–120; Hersh, *Price of Power*, 415–422.
75. Lukas, *Nightmare*, 94.
76. *Ibid.*
77. Nixon, *Memoirs*, 514.
78. Haldeman, *Ends of Power*, 114–115; Ehrlichman, *Witness to Power*, 401.
79. Lukas, *Nightmare*, 94.

CHAPTER TWENTY-ONE

1. *New York Times*, 9/17/71.
2. PP (1971), 949–950.

3. Buchanan to RN, 9/29/71, NPMP.
4. Garment to RN, 9/30/71, NPMP.
5. Ehrlichman, *Witness to Power*, 134–135.
6. *Ibid.*, 137–138.
7. *Ibid.*, 136.
8. NS, 10/13/71.
9. Eisenhower, *Pat Nixon*, 321.
10. *Ibid.*; Ehrlichman, *Witness to Power*, 137.
11. NS, 12/3/71; *New York Times*, 12/12/71.
12. NS, 11/5/71.
13. *New York Times*, 10/22/71; NS, 10/15/71.
14. Jaworski to RN, 10/25/71, NPMP.
15. RN to Jaworski, 11/30/71, NPMP.
16. Ehrlichman to RN, 9/24/71, NPMP.
17. Ehrlichman to RN, 10/23/71, with Liddy enclosure, NPMP.
18. Ehrlichman, *Witness to Power*, 166.
19. Ehrlichman to RN, 11/6/71, NPMP; Nixon, *Memoirs*, 597–599.
20. Ehrlichman, *Witness to Power*, 166–167.
21. Safire, *Before the Fall*, 587.
22. *Ibid.*, 588–589.
23. NS, 8/1/71.
24. Safire, *Before the Fall*, 585.
25. PP (1971), 955.
26. NS, 11/15/71.
27. Safire, *Before the Fall*, 590.
28. *New York Times*, 11/20/71.
29. NS, 11/20/71.
30. Klein to RN, with RN notation, 12/8/71, NPMP.
31. Price to RN, with RN notation, 12/16/71, NPMP.
32. *New York Times*, 11/10/71.
33. NS, 12/3/71.
34. Lukas, *Nightmare*, 154.
35. *New York Times*, 12/5/71.
36. Lukas, *Nightmare*, 136–139.
37. PP (1971), 1030–1031.
38. Hersh, *Price of Power*, 346–348.
39. *New York Times*, 5/1 and 11/6/71.
40. NS, 11/1/71.
41. Nixon, *Memoirs*, 556.
42. *New York Times*, 10/28 and 10/30/71.
43. Nixon, *Memoirs*, 525.
44. Wayne to RN, 12/1/71, NPMP.
45. PP (1971), 1104–1107.
46. Kissinger, *White House Years*, 856.
47. Hersh, *Price of Power*, 450.
48. Garthoff, *Détente and Confrontation*, 265.
49. Kissinger, *White House Years*, 866.
50. Garthoff, *Détente and Confrontation*, 267.
51. Nixon, *Memoirs*, 526.
52. Kissinger, *White House Years*, 877; Hersh, *Price of Power*, 456.
53. Nixon, *Memoirs*, 525–526.
54. Hersh, *Price of Power*, 456.
55. Nixon, *Memoirs*, 531.

56. Kissinger, *White House Years*, 897.
57. Nixon, *Memoirs*, 527.
58. Hersh, *Price of Power*, 456.
59. Nixon, *Memoirs*, 527.
60. Kissinger, *White House Years*, 904.
61. Garthoff, *Détente and Confrontation*, 270–271; Hersh, *Price of Power*, 457.
62. Kissinger, *White House Years*, 905.
63. *Ibid.*, 910–911.
64. Garthoff, *Détente and Confrontation*, 277.
65. Kissinger, *White House Years*, 916.
66. Nixon, *Memoirs*, 529.
67. *Ibid.*, 532.
68. Ehrlichman, *Witness to Power*, 305.
69. *Ibid.*, 306.
70. Hersh, *Price of Power*, 476.
71. Kissinger, *White House Years*, 912.
72. NS, 11/5/71.
73. *Ibid.*, 10/15/71.
74. *Ibid.*
75. Hersh, *Price of Power*, 474.
76. Ehrlichman, *Witness to Power*, 306.
77. *Ibid.*, 307.
78. Hersh, *Price of Power*, 475.
79. Ehrlichman, *Witness to Power*, 308.
80. Joan Hoff-Wilson paper at June 9, 1971, meeting of the Society of Historians of American Foreign Relations, American University, Washington, D.C.
81. *New York Times*, 12/20 and 12/25/71.
82. *Ibid.*, 6/22/71; Schoenebaum, *Profiles of an Era*, 303.

CHAPTER TWENTY-TWO

1. PP (1972), 1–9.
2. Hallett to Colson, with RN notations, 1/3/72, NPMP.
3. Colson to RN, with RN notation, 1/6/72, NPMP.
4. NS, 3/11/72.
5. *Ibid.*, 2/2/72.
6. Richardson to RN, with RN notations, 1/8/72, NPMP.
7. See Nixon's comments on Dean to Richardson, 1/5/72, NPMP.
8. Mark, *The Space Station*, 45; *New York Times*, 1/6/72.
9. Safire, *Before the Fall*, 533–537.
10. Lukas, *Nightmare*, 147; Nixon-Dean transcript, 3/21/72, NPMP.
11. Schoenebaum, *Profiles of an Era*, 653.
12. Lukas, *Nightmare*, 148–149.
13. Schoenebaum, *Profiles of an Era*, 653.
14. NS, 3/11/72.
15. Colson to RN, 1/12/72, NPMP.
16. *New York Times*, 1/16 and 1/17/72.
17. Drosnin, *Citizen Hughes*, 419–420; Klein, *Making It Perfectly Clear*, 328–329.
18. Dean, *Blind Ambition*, 390; Drosnin, *Citizen Hughes*, 421–422.

19. Drosnin, *Citizen Hughes*, 422.
20. Haldeman interview.
21. Ambrose, *Nixon: Education of a Politician*, 599–600.
22. Drosnin, *Citizen Hughes*, 425.
23. Lukas, *Nightmare*, 178–179; Magruder, *An American Life*, 196.
24. Haldeman, *Ends of Power*, 11.
25. NS, 3/11/72.
26. Nixon, *Memoirs*, 582.
27. Dean, *Blind Ambition*, 58.
28. Nixon, *Memoirs*, 583; *New York Times*, 3/10/72.
29. Haldeman, *Ends of Power*, 155.
30. Drosnin, *Citizen Hughes*, 427.
31. Magruder, *An American Life*, 197.
32. Lukas, *Nightmare*, 185.
33. PP (1972), 488–489, 491.
34. Drosnin, *Citizen Hughes*, 429.
35. Nixon, *Memoirs*, 584.
36. See Hersh, *Price of Power*, Chapter 34.
37. Safire, *Before the Fall*, 400–401.
38. Hersh, *Price of Power*, 481.
39. *New York Times*, 1/9/72.
40. NS, 1/7/72.
41. *Ibid.*, 1/13/72.
42. Safire, *Before the Fall*, 402.
43. *Ibid.*, 406.
44. PP (1972), 100–105.
45. *New York Times*, 1/26/72.
46. *Ibid.*
47. *Ibid.*
48. Hersh, *Price of Power*, 485–486.
49. *New York Times*, 2/8/72.
50. PP (1972), 351, 358.
51. Hersh, *Price of Power*, 485.
52. *New York Times*, 2/17/72.
53. NS, 3/18/72.
54. *New York Times*, 2/18 and 2/20/72.
55. Kissinger, *White House Years*, 1054.
56. Nixon, *Memoirs*, 559.
57. *Ibid.*, 561; Kissinger, *White House Years*, 1058.
58. Safire, *Before the Fall*, 413.
59. Nixon, *Memoirs*, 561–564.
60. Kissinger, *White House Years*, 1067, 1082.
61. PP (1972), 376–379; Nixon, *Memoirs*, 571–579; Kissinger, *White House Years*, 1075–1079; Hersh, *Price of Power*, 497.
62. Hersh, *Price of Power*, 497–499; Kissinger, *White House Years*, 1082–1083.
63. PP (1972), 379.
64. Safire, *Before the Fall*, 411.
65. *Ibid.*
66. Kissinger, *White House Years*, 1093–1094.
67. Washington *Post*, 2/28/72.
68. NS, 3/2 and 3/11/72.
69. Kissinger, *White House Years*, 1094–1095.

70. Eisenhower, *Pat Nixon*, 335–336.
71. Washington *Post*, 3/1/72.
72. *New York Times*, 3/16/72.
73. Washington *Post*, 1/11/72.
74. *New York Times*, 3/16/72.
75. Moynihan to RN, 1/3/72, NPMP.
76. NS, 1/13/72.
77. *Ibid.*, 1/15/72.
78. RN to Ehrlichman, 1/28/72, NPMP.
79. Ehrlichman to RN, 2/16/72, NPMP.
80. *New York Times*, 3/5 and 3/15/72.
81. *Ibid.*, 3/7/72.
82. *Ibid.*, 3/17 and 3/18/72.
83. *Ibid.*, 3/17/72.
84. Ehrlichman, *Witness to Power*, 221.

CHAPTER TWENTY-THREE

1. RN to Haldeman, 3/11/72, NPMP.
2. NS, 4/3/72.
3. Nixon, *Memoirs*, 587.
4. Kissinger, *White House Years*, 1113.
5. Hersh, *Price of Power*, 506.
6. Nixon, *Memoirs*, 588–589.
7. *New York Times*, 4/11/72.
8. *Ibid.*, 4/15/72.
9. *Ibid.*, 4/16/72; Nixon, *Memoirs*, 590.
10. Nixon, *Memoirs*, 590.
11. *Ibid.*, 591.
12. Kissinger, *White House Years*, 1128.
13. Garthoff, *Détente and Confrontation*, 96–99.
14. Nixon, *Memoirs*, 592.
15. Kissinger, *White House Years*, 1136–1137.
16. *Ibid.*, 1155.
17. *Ibid.*, 1160.
18. *Ibid.*, 1162.
19. Nixon, *Memoirs*, 592.
20. PP (1972), 550–555.
21. Nixon, *Memoirs*, 593–594.
22. *New York Times*, 5/1 and 5/2/72.
23. *Ibid.*, 5/2/72.
24. Nixon, *Memoirs*, 595.
25. *Ibid.*, 599–600; Colson, *Born Again*, 67.
26. Zumwalt, *On Watch*, 399.
27. Nixon, *Memoirs*, 601; Kissinger, *White House Years*, 1176.
28. *New York Times*, 5/6/72.
29. *Ibid.*, 5/5/72.
30. *Ibid.*, 5/7/72.
31. Kissinger, *White House Years*, 1177.
32. *Ibid.*; Nixon, *Memoirs*, 601–602.
33. Nixon, *Memoirs*, 602.
34. Kissinger, *White House Years*, 1179.

35. Nixon, *Memoirs*, 602–603.
36. Kissinger, *White House Years*, 1184–1186; Haldeman interview.
37. Nixon, *Memoirs*, 604; PP (1972), 583–587.
38. Nixon, *Memoirs*, 606–607.
39. *New York Times*, 5/9/72.
40. Nixon, *Memoirs*, 607.
41. *Ibid.*, 544.
42. *New York Times*, 5/18/72.
43. Colson to RN, with RN notation, 5/14/72, NPMP.
44. *New York Times*, 5/17/72; RN to Haldeman, 5/18/72, NPMP.
45. Nixon, *Memoirs*, 599.
46. *New York Times*, 5/5/72.
47. *Ibid.*
48. Lukas, *Nightmare*, 175–177, 199–201.
49. Nixon, *Memoirs*, 609.
50. *Ibid.*, 619.
51. *Ibid.*, 610.
52. PP (1972), 633.
53. Hersh, *Price of Power*, 535.
54. Smith, *Doubletalk*, 376.
55. *Ibid.*, 377.
56. RN to Kissinger, 6/12/72, and Kehrli to Haldeman, 8/17/72, NPMP.
57. Hersh, *Price of Power*, 530.
58. Garthoff, *Détente and Confrontation*, 162, 191.
59. Nixon, *Memoirs*, 615.
60. Kissinger, *White House Years*, 1233.
61. Safire, *Before the Fall*, 451.
62. Nixon, *Memoirs*, 617–618.
63. Garthoff, *Détente and Confrontation*, 190.
64. *New York Times*, 6/2/72.
65. Kissinger, *White House Years*, 1246; Ambrose, *Rise to Globalism*, 243; Smith, *Doubletalk*, 459–460.
66. Zumwalt, *On Watch*, 407.
67. NS, 6/20/72.
68. PP (1972), 711–712.
69. *New York Times*, 6/2/72.
70. Garthoff, *Détente and Confrontation*, 259.
71. NS, 6/23/72.
72. *New York Times*, 6/29/72.

CHAPTER TWENTY-FOUR

1. NS, 6/10/72.
2. *Ibid.*, 6/27/72.
3. *Ibid.*, 6/10/72.
4. *Ibid.*, 6/29/72.
5. *Ibid.*
6. Ehrlichman, *Witness to Power*, 326–327.
7. NS, 6/29/72.
8. *Ibid.*, 6/10/72.
9. *Ibid.*, 6/20/72.
10. Nixon, *Memoirs*, 624.

11. *New York Times*, 6/11/72.
12. Price to RN, with RN notation, 6/14/72, NPMP.
13. Haldeman notes, 6/19/72, NPMP.
14. NS, 6/29/72.
15. PP (1972), 703.
16. NS, 6/27/72; Washington *Post*, 6/22/72.
17. NS, 6/23/72.
18. *Ibid.*, 6/26/72.
19. *Ibid.*, 6/27/72.
20. *Ibid.*, 6/28/72.
21. *Ibid.*, 6/29/72.
22. Ehrlichman, *Witness to Power*, 327–328.
23. Stans, *Terrors of Justice*, 142, 169, 173.
24. *Ibid.*, 177–178.
25. Safire, *Before the Fall*, 549.
26. Magruder, *An American Life*, 229–230.
27. See Carter, "Nixon Cover-up Goes On."
28. Nixon, *Memoirs*, 626.
29. Haldeman, *Ends of Power*, 13; Haldeman's summary notes, 5/7/73, NPMP.
30. RN to Haldeman, 8/9/72, and Haldeman notes, 3/28/73, both NPMP.
31. Haldeman, *Ends of Power*, 13.
32. *Ibid.*, 207.
33. Haldeman notes, 6/20/72, NPMP.
34. Nixon, *Memoirs*, 630–631.
35. NS, 6/20/72.
36. Ehrlichman, *Witness to Power*, 342.
37. Nixon, *Memoirs*, 631–634.
38. *Ibid.*, 634–635; Haldeman, *Ends of Power*, 23–24.
39. Nixon, *Memoirs*, 635.
40. *Ibid.*, 635–637.
41. *Ibid.*, 638.
42. PP (1972), 690–691.
43. Transcript of 6/23/72 meeting, NPMP.
44. *Ibid.*; Nixon, *Memoirs*, 642.
45. Magruder, *An American Life*, 247–248.
46. Nixon, *Memoirs*, 644–645.
47. *Ibid.*, 648.
48. *Ibid.*, 648–649.
49. *Ibid.*, 649.
50. NS, 7/1/72.
51. *New York Times*, 7/2/72.
52. *Ibid.*
53. NS, 7/1/72.
54. *Ibid.*
55. Colson to RN, with RN notation, 7/7/72, NPMP.
56. Lukas, *Nightmare*, 350.
57. *New York Times*, 7/11/72.
58. Lukas, *Nightmare*, 351.
59. *New York Times*, 7/4/72.
60. *Ibid.*, 7/11/72.
61. Lukas, *Nightmare*, 235; Nixon, *Memoirs*, 650.

62. Nixon, *Memoirs*, 651.
63. Ehrlichman, *Witness to Power*, 354.
64. *Ibid.*, 354–355; Nixon, *Memoirs*, 653.
65. Nixon, *Memoirs*, 652.
66. Magruder, *An American Life*, 251, 266–267.
67. *Ibid.*, 268.
68. Nixon, *Memoirs*, 662.

CHAPTER TWENTY-FIVE

1. Nixon, *Memoirs*, 653–656.
2. Haldeman notes, 7/17 and 7/21/72, NPMP.
3. *Ibid.*, 7/17/72.
4. *Ibid.*, 7/19/72.
5. NS, 8/8/72.
6. *Ibid.*, 8/11/72.
7. *Ibid.*
8. Nixon, *Memoirs*, 657.
9. Kissinger to RN, with RN notation, 7/14/72, NPMP.
10. Price to RN, with RN notation, 7/14/72, and Ehrlichman to RN, 7/26/72, NPMP.
11. PP (1972), 836.
12. Haldeman notes, 7/17/72, NPMP.
13. The Nixon document is filed under 8/3/72, NPMP.
14. Nixon, *Memoirs*, 663.
15. NS, 7/26/72.
16. *Ibid.*, 7/29/72.
17. McGovern interview.
18. Nixon, *Memoirs*, 664.
19. Haldeman notes, 8/15/72, NPMP.
20. *New York Times*, 7/30/72.
21. NS, 8/8/72.
22. *New York Times*, 7/30/72.
23. Butz to RN, 8/9/72, NPMP.
24. NS, 8/4/72.
25. Ehrlichman to RN, with RN notation, 7/29/72, NPMP.
26. Nixon, *Memoirs*, 658.
27. *Ibid.*, 670.
28. *Ibid.*, 672–673.
29. Ehrlichman to RN, with RN notation, 7/20/72.
30. Eisenhower, *Pat Nixon*, 349.
31. Nixon, *Memoirs*, 674–675.
32. Colson to RN, with RN notation, 8/18/72, NPMP.
33. Nixon, *Memoirs*, 673–674.
34. NS, 7/19/72.
35. Timmons to RN, with RN notation, 7/20/72, NPMP.
36. Haldeman notes, 7/20/72, NPMP.
37. Nixon, *Memoirs*, 657–658.
38. NS, 8/3/72.
39. Nixon, *Memoirs*, 675.
40. *Ibid.*, 676.
41. *Ibid.*

42. *Ibid.*, 677.
43. Lukas, *Nightmare*, 241, 243.
44. *New York Times*, 7/25/72.
45. NS, 7/24/72.
46. *Ibid.*, 7/19 and 7/20/72.
47. PP (1972), 752.
48. NS, 7/20/72.
49. RN to Hugh Scott and others, 7/27/72, NPMP.
50. PP (1972), 747–749.
51. Hersh, *Price of Power*, 568.
52. Kissinger, *White House Years*, 1308.
53. *Ibid.*, 1309.
54. *Ibid.*, 1319.
55. *Newsweek*, 9/4/72.
56. Hung and Schecter, *Palace File*, 66–67.
57. *Ibid.*, 68.
58. Garthoff, *Détente and Confrontation*, 316.
59. Washington *Post*, 8/9/72.
60. Eisenhower, *Pat Nixon*, 347.
61. *Ibid.*, 346–347.
62. *Ibid.*, 347.
63. *Ibid.*, 349.
64. Ehrlichman, *Witness to Power*, 81.
65. Eisenhower, *Pat Nixon*, 346.
66. *New York Times*, 11/7/72; RN to Julie and Tricia, 7/24/72, NPMP.
67. RN to Haldeman, 7/20/72.
68. *New York Times*, 8/22/72.
69. *Ibid.*, 8/23/72.
70. *Ibid.*, 8/24/72.
71. Eisenhower, *Pat Nixon*, 345.
72. *New York Times*, 8/26/72.
73. Kissinger, *White House Years*, 1331.
74. PP (1972), 827–831.
75. Dean, *Blind Ambition*, 129.
76. PP (1972), 828.

Chapter Twenty-six

1. Nixon, *Memoirs*, 665.
2. NS, 9/16/72.
3. O'Brien, *No Final Victories*, 333.
4. NS, 9/18/72,.
5. *Ibid.*
6. *Ibid.*, 9/29/72.
7. Colson, *Born Again*, 71–72.
8. NS, 9/15/72.
9. *Ibid.*, 9/19/72.
10. Washington *Post*, 9/1 to 9/15/72.
11. Lukas, *Nightmare*, 276.
12. Haldeman notes, 9/11/72, NPMP.
13. NS, 9/12/72.
14. Washington *Post*, 9/16/72; Dean, *Blind Ambition*, 133.

15. Transcript, 9/15/72, NPMP.
16. Haldeman, *Ends of Power*, 169–172.
17. Dean, *Blind Ambition*, 141.
18. Nixon, *Memoirs*, 682.
19. Ehrlichman, *Witness to Power*, 361.
20. Hersh, *Price of Power*, 577.
21. Hung and Schecter, *Palace File*, 73–74.
22. Kissinger, *White House Years*, 1339–1340.
23. Nixon, *Memoirs*, 689.
24. Hersh, *Price of Power*, 581–582.
25. PP (1972), 953–954.
26. Memo, 10/5/72, Walt Rostow Papers, JL.
27. Hersh, *Price of Power*, 583.
28. Stern, *Water's Edge*, 41.
29. PP (1972), 947.
30. Kissinger, *White House Years*, 1271.
31. Stern, *Water's Edge*, 42.
32. *Ibid.*, 45.
33. NS, 10/19/72.
34. *Ibid.*, 10/7/72.
35. Nixon, *Memoirs*, 683.
36. Washington *Post*, 9/22/72; Nixon, *Memoirs*, 683.
37. Eisenhower, *Pat Nixon*, 347.
38. *Ibid.*, 348–349.
39. Washington *Post*, 9/27/72.
40. *New York Times*, 9/19/72.
41. *Ibid.*, 9/24/72.
42. *Ibid.*, 9/17/72.
43. *Ibid.*
44. Haldeman notes, 10/5/72, NPMP.
45. PP (1972), 952.
46. NS, 10/7/72.
47. Nixon, *Memoirs*, 684.
48. Lukas, *Nightmare*, 270.
49. Washington *Post*, 9/21/72.
50. *Ibid.*, 10/5 and 10/7/72.
51. *Ibid.*, 10/8/72.
52. PP (1972), 957.
53. *Ibid.*, 958–960.
54. Nixon, *Memoirs*, 685.
55. Haldeman memo, 10/15/72, NPMP.

Chapter Twenty-seven

1. Kissinger, *White House Years*, 1345–1346.
2. Nixon, *Memoirs*, 692.
3. *New York Times*, 10/11/72.
4. Nixon, *Memoirs*, 691, 693.
5. *Ibid.*, 693.
6. *Ibid.*, 694.
7. Haldeman notes, 10/15/72, NPMP.
8. Hersh, *Price of Power*, 591.

9. Kissinger, *White House Years*, 1364.
10. PP (1972), 986–988.
11. Nixon, *Memoirs*, 695–696.
12. Hung and Schecter, *Palace File*, 109.
13. Nixon, *Memoirs*, 696.
14. *Ibid.*, 697.
15. NS, 10/19/72.
16. Westmoreland, *A Soldier Reports*, 393–394.
17. Zumwalt, *On Watch*, 413.
18. Nixon, *Memoirs*, 697.
19. Kissinger, *White House Years*, 1377.
20. Nixon, *Memoirs*, 698–699.
21. *Ibid.*, 700.
22. *Ibid.*, 701.
23. *Ibid.*, 702.
24. *Ibid.*, 703–704.
25. NS, 10/23/72.
26. *Ibid.*, 10/25/72.
27. *Ibid.*, 10/9/72.
28. *Ibid.*
29. *Ibid.*
30. *Ibid.*
31. *Ibid.*, 10/23/72.
32. Haldeman, *Ends of Power*, 69.
33. Safire, *Before the Fall*, 647.
34. PP (1972), 997–998.
35. Washington *Star*, 11/12/72.
36. NS, 10/25/72.
37. *Ibid.*, 10/9/72.
38. Washington *Post*, 10/15/72; *New York Times*, 10/16/72.
39. NS, 10/16/72.
40. Dean, *Blind Ambition*, 144.
41. Haldeman notes, 10/16/72, NPMP.
42. Nixon, *Memoirs*, 710.
43. *Ibid.*, 713.
44. *Ibid.*, 710.
45. *New York Times*, 10/26/72.
46. Nixon, *Memoirs*, 711.
47. Kissinger, *White House Years*, 1395.
48. Hersh, *Price of Power*, 603.
49. *New York Times*, 10/22 and 10/25/72.
50. Hersh, *Price of Power*, 604.
51. Nixon, *Memoirs*, 705.
52. Kissinger, *White House Years*, 1399.
53. Schulzinger, *Doctor of Diplomacy*.
54. Nixon, *Memoirs*, 705.
55. NS, 10/27/72.
56. *Ibid.*
57. Hung and Schecter, *Palace File*, 112–113.
58. Hersh, *Price of Power*, 606.
59. Washington *Post*, 10/28/72.
60. Haldeman notes, 10/29/72, NPMP.
61. Hung and Schecter, *Palace File*, 114.

62. NS, 11/1/72.
63. *New York Times*, 11/3/72.
64. PP (1972), 1108.
65. Nixon, *Memoirs*, 706–707.
66. *New York Times*, 10/31/72.
67. Woods to RN, 10/10/72, NPMP.
68. NS, 10/25/72.
69. *New York Times*, 11/1/72.
70. NS, 11/3/72.
71. *New York Times*, 11/6/72.
72. *Ibid.*, 11/7/72.
73. Quoted in Hersh, *Price of Power*, 608–609.
74. Nixon, *Memoirs*, 713.
75. PP (1972), 1128.
76. PP (1972), 1138–1139.
77. Nixon, *Memoirs*, 714.
78. NS, 11/7/72.
79. *Ibid.*, 10/20/72.
80. *Ibid.*, 11/7/72.
81. Kissinger, *White House Years*, 1406.
82. NS, 10/25/72.
83. Haldeman memo, 11/7/72, NPMP.
84. Nixon, *Memoirs*, 715.
85. All figures from *New York Times*, 11/8 and 11/9/72.

CHAPTER TWENTY-EIGHT

1. Ambrose, *Eisenhower*, II, 614.
2. Colson, *Born Again*, 45.
3. Frost, *"I Gave Them a Sword,"* 183.
4. Nixon, *Memoirs*, 717.

BIBLIOGRAPHY

Ambrose, Stephen E. *Eisenhower: Soldier, General of the Army, President-Elect*, Vol. I. New York: Simon and Schuster, 1983.
———. *Eisenhower: The President*, Vol. II. New York: Simon and Schuster, 1984.
———. *Nixon: The Education of a Politician, 1913–1962*, Vol. I. New York: Simon and Schuster, 1987.
———. *Rise to Globalism: American Foreign Policy since 1938*. New York: Penguin Books, 1985.
Baldwin, Hanson. "Managed News." *Atlantic*, April 1963.
Brodie, Fawn M. *Richard Nixon: The Shaping of His Character*. Cambridge, Mass.: Harvard University Press, 1983.
Burke, Vincent J., and Vee Burke. *Nixon's Good Deed: Welfare Reform*. New York: Columbia University Press, 1974.
Cannon, Lou. *Reagan*. New York: G. P. Putnam's Sons, 1982.
Carter, Dan. "The Nixon Cover-up Goes On." *New York Times*, July 25, 1988.
Chang, Gordon. "JFK, China, and the Bomb." *Journal of American History*, March 1988.
Colson, Charles W. *Born Again*. Old Tappan, N.J.: Chosen Books, 1976.
Dean, John W., III. *Blind Ambition*. New York: Simon and Schuster, 1976.
Donovan, Robert. "Over-Nominated, Under-Elected, Still a Promising Candidate." *New York Times Magazine*, April 25, 1965.
Drosnin, Michael. *Citizen Hughes*. New York: Holt, Rinehart and Winston, 1985.
Ehrlichman, John. *Witness to Power: The Nixon Years*. New York: Simon and Schuster, 1982.
Eisenhower, Julie Nixon. *Pat Nixon: The Untold Story*. New York: Simon and Schuster, 1986.
Ewald, William Bragg, Jr. *Eisenhower the President*. Englewood Cliffs, N.J.: Prentice-Hall, 1981.

Frost, David. *"I Gave Them a Sword": Behind the Scenes of the Nixon Interviews*. New York: William Morrow, 1978.

Garthoff, Raymond L. *Détente and Confrontation: American-Soviet Relations from Nixon to Reagan*. Washington, D.C.: The Brookings Institution, 1985.

Gill, William J. *The Ordeal of Otto Otepka*. New Rochelle, N.Y.: Arlington House, 1969.

Goldwater, Barry M., with Jack Casserly. *Goldwater*. New York: Doubleday, 1988.

Gulley, Bill, with Mary Ellen Reese. *Breaking Cover*. New York: Simon and Schuster, 1980.

Haldeman, H. R., with Joseph DiMona. *The Ends of Power*. New York: New York Times Books, 1978.

Hammond, William. "The American Withdrawal from Vietnam: Some Military and Political Considerations." Southeast Asia Branch, U.S. Army Center of Military History. A paper read at the Hofstra University Conference on Nixon in November 1987.

Hersh, Seymour M. *The Price of Power: Kissinger in the Nixon White House*. New York: Summit Books, 1983.

Hung, Nguyen Tien, and Jerrold L. Schecter. *The Palace File*. New York: Harper & Row, 1986.

Johnson, Lyndon Baines. *The Vantage Point*. New York: Holt, Rinehart and Winston, 1971.

Karnow, Stanley. *Vietnam: A History*. New York: Penguin Books, 1984.

Kissinger, Henry. *White House Years*. Boston: Little, Brown, 1979.

Klein, Herbert G. *Making It Perfectly Clear*. Garden City, N.Y.: Doubleday, 1980.

Lasky, Victor. *It Didn't Start with Watergate*. New York: The Dial Press, 1977.

Lukas, J. Anthony. *Nightmare: The Underside of the Nixon Years*. New York: The Viking Press, 1976.

Magruder, Jeb Stuart. *An American Life: One Man's Road to Watergate*. New York: Atheneum, 1974.

Mark, Hans. *The Space Station: A Personal Journey*. Durham, N.C.: Duke University Press, 1987.

Morris, Roger. *Uncertain Greatness: Henry Kissinger and American Foreign Policy*. New York: Harper & Row, 1977.

Nixon, Richard. "Asia After Viet Nam." *Foreign Affairs*, October 1967.

———. "Cuba, Castro and John F. Kennedy." *Reader's Digest*, November 1964.

———. "Khrushchev's Hidden Weakness." *Saturday Evening Post*, October 12, 1963 (reprinted in *Reader's Digest*, January 1964).

———. *Leaders*. New York: Warner Books, 1982.

———. *The Memoirs of Richard Nixon*. New York: Grosset & Dunlap, 1978.

———. "Needed in Vietnam: The Will to Win." *Reader's Digest*, August 1964.

———. "What Has Happened to America?" *Reader's Digest*, October 1967.

———. "Why Not Negotiate in Vietnam?" *Reader's Digest*, December 1965.

O'Brien, Lawrence F. *No Final Victories: A Life in Politics—From John F. Kennedy to Watergate*. Garden City, N.Y.: Doubleday, 1974.

Powers, Richard Gid. *Secrecy and Power: The Life of J. Edgar Hoover.* London: Hutchinson, 1987.

Price, Raymond. *With Nixon.* New York: The Viking Press, 1977.

Public Papers of the President (1969–1972). Washington, D.C.: Government Printing Office.

Reinhard, David W. *The Republican Right since 1945.* Lexington, Ky.: University Press of Kentucky, 1983.

Safire, William. *Before the Fall.* Garden City, N.Y.: Doubleday, 1975.

Schell, Jonathan. *The Time of Illusion.* New York: Vintage Books, 1976.

Schoenebaum, Eleanora W. *Profiles of an Era: The Nixon-Ford Years.* New York: Harcourt Brace Jovanovich, 1979.

Schulzinger, Robert. *The Doctor of Diplomacy.* New York: Columbia University Press, 1989.

Smith, Gerard. *Doubletalk: The Untold Story of SALT.* Garden City, N.Y.: Doubleday, 1981.

Stans, Maurice H. *The Terrors of Justice.* New York: Everest House, 1978.

Stern, Paula. *Water's Edge: Domestic Politics and the Making of American Foreign Policy.* Westport, Conn.: Greenwood Press, 1979.

Weaver, Warren, Jr. "Four Hearties of the Good Ship G.O.P." *New York Times Magazine,* November 27, 1966.

Westmoreland, William C. *A Soldier Reports.* Garden City, N.Y.: Doubleday, 1976.

White, Theodore H. *The Making of the President, 1968.* New York: Atheneum, 1969.

Witcover, Jules. *The Resurrection of Richard Nixon.* New York: G. P. Putnam's Sons, 1970.

Zumwalt, Elmo R., Jr. *On Watch.* New York: Quadrangle, 1976.

MANUSCRIPTS

The Nixon Presidential Materials Project (NPMP), in Alexandria, Virginia, is the basic documentary collection of the Nixon Administration. It includes the News Summaries, Haldeman's handwritten notes on his daily meetings with Nixon, memorandums from and to Nixon, Haldeman, Ehrlichman, Safire, Price, Colson, Magruder, and others, and much else. As noted on page 558, the National Archives and Richard Nixon are locked in a legal struggle over the release to the scholarly community of the record of his Administration. Although Nixon has managed to block access to tens of thousands of documents, the Archives has managed to open significant sections of the basic record.

NPMP also holds the tape recordings made in the Oval Office, Nixon's EOB office, the Cabinet Room, and over the telephone. A few of these tapes, covering Watergate-related conversations, are available to scholars, along with transcripts.

Other manuscript collections used include the Walt Rostow, Clark Clifford, and presidential collections at the Lyndon Baines Johnson Library in Austin, Texas; the Nixon collection at the John Fitzgerald Kennedy Library in Boston; the Fred Seaton Papers and the Nixon-Eisenhower correspondence at the Dwight David Eisenhower Library in Abilene, Kansas; the Dean Acheson collections at Princeton University and at Yale University; the Glenn Davis Papers at the Wisconsin State Historical Society, Madison; the Nixon Vice-Presidential Papers in Laguna Niguel, California; and the Karl Mundt Papers at the University of South Dakota.

NEWSPAPERS

Chicago *Tribune*
Dallas *Morning News*
Los Angeles *Times*
Miami *Herald*

Milwaukee *Journal*
New York Times
Washington *Post*
Washington *Star*

INTERVIEWS

Mort Allin
John Ehrlichman
David Eisenhower
Robert Finch
H. R. Haldeman
Steve Hess
Joan Hoff-Wilson
Stephen Jones
George McGovern

Robert Merriam
Daniel Patrick Moynihan
Mrs. Daniel Patrick Moynihan
Ray Price
Elliot Richardson
Walt W. Rostow
William Safire
Maurice Stans
Ron Ziegler

ACKNOWLEDGMENTS

IT IS MY GREAT FORTUNE to have Alice Mayhew of Simon and Schuster as my editor. She is outstanding, as a source of ideas, an inspiration, a guide, a teacher of writing, a judge of what works and what does not, a critic, and a friend. She is also demanding and can be difficult, but as time goes by she becomes easier to work with (this is our fifth book together), because I have learned that she is always right (well, almost) and that by doing what she says/suggests rather than fighting her, the book is vastly improved.

David Shipley oversaw the transformation of this work from manuscript to book, a daunting task carried out with the professionalism and good humor I have come to expect from Simon and Schuster. Patricia Miller, who has now done the copy-editing on five of my manuscripts, has put me ever more deeply in her debt.

Ever since I began writing American history, three decades ago, I have known that the best friend any historian has is the archivist. In the case of Nixon, it is the people at the Nixon Presidential Materials Project in Alexandria, Virginia, who make a study of his career possible. Their quarters are less than grand, not to be compared to the magnificent presidential libraries in Abilene, Hyde Park, Independence, Austin, and elsewhere. The cooperation they receive from the man himself is nonexistent; indeed, the National Archives' relationship with Nixon is antagonistic. Despite these handicaps, the archivists at the Nixon Project have managed to make the basic documentation of the Nixon Administration available to scholars, in an atmosphere conducive to research. Without their efforts, it would not be possible to undertake a serious study of the Nixon Presidency.

Jim Hastings, the director, Joan Howard, his assistant, Maarja Krusten, Frederick J. Graboske, Nick Lemann, Ray Geselbracht, and the others on the staff at the Nixon Project are all archivists of the highest professional quality. They meet the standard I have come to expect and to rely upon from those who work for the National Archives.

So do Harry Middleton and his staff at the Johnson Library, and John Wickman and the staff at the Eisenhower Library. In addition, I have drawn on the resources and benefited from the cooperation of the staffs at the Wisconsin State Historical Society, the Milwaukee Public Library, the Public Library in Bay St. Louis, Mississippi, and most of all my home library at the University of New Orleans.

Mrs. Carolyn P. Smith transferred the manuscript from yellow legal pads covered with innumerable cross-outs and handwritten additions to computer-printed clean copy in an exemplary manner.

My agent, John Ware, did his usual superb job of handling the myriad details that inevitably accompany the creation of a manuscript of this size. He was also a sounding board and a provider of ideas and encouragement. He is a good friend who never lets me down, no matter how heavily I lean on him.

In the fall of 1987, Hofstra University sponsored a conference on Richard Nixon's Administration. It brought together more than two dozen members of that Administration, including Henry Kissinger, H. R. Haldeman, John Ehrlichman, Maurice Stans, Charles Colson, Ron Ziegler, Robert Finch, Elliot Richardson, Egil Krogh, Ray Price, and Jeb Magruder. The conference gave me an opportunity to hear these men speak in a formal, academic setting about their experiences, and a chance to meet with them informally and ask questions. It was an invaluable experience and I want to thank Hofstra for providing it.

In January 1988, I held the Nixon Chair at Whittier College. I taught a seminar on the Nixon Administration, and was fortunate enough to have Haldeman, Finch, and Stans visit the seminar to answer questions from the students and from me. This was also an invaluable experience.

I owe a special debt to Steve Hess. In the fall of 1987, he invited me to a small dinner party at his Washington home. The other guests were Pat Moynihan, Bill Safire, and Mort Allin. We talked about Nixon, virtually nonstop, for nearly six hours. Of course I learned a great deal, but it was the overall impression I took away that had the biggest impact on me.

Steve Hess, by this time, was at the Brookings Institution. Moynihan was a Democratic senator from New York. Safire was a senior columnist for *The New York Times*. Allin, younger than the others, was still rising in the federal government; he was just back from an extended tour in Russia with the USIA.

All four men, in short, were at (or almost at) the absolute top in their professions. None of them owed anything to Richard Nixon, and there was nothing Nixon could do for or to any of them. Each had some reason to feel that Nixon had let him down.

Further, the four men represented four very different political perspectives, ranging from pretty far on the Right to pretty far on the Left. Their prejudices are strongly held and strongly stated. There is little that they agree upon.

But they agreed that Richard Nixon was a kind man, a considerate man, a rewarding man to work for, and a good if not great President. That Nixon could so impress these men, who had worked with him so closely, naturally impressed me. Although in the course of doing my research, I seldom found the man they talked about so positively, I kept their feelings in mind when writing about President Nixon. Since I had never met

Nixon, and held negative feelings about him, the dinner at Steve Hess's provided me with a necessary corrective.

H. R. Haldeman gave generously of his time and knowledge. He read the entire manuscript and made hundreds of comments. He too provided a needed corrective in perspective. He remains as completely loyal to the former President today as he was twenty years ago. I adopted many of the changes he suggested, and rejected as many more. He strongly, vigorously, and bluntly disagrees with many of my interpretations, most especially on the role and importance of the media, on the Watergate break-in and subsequent attempts to cover up or contain the scandal, and on the character of Richard Nixon.

Michael Beschloss also read the manuscript and gave me valuable suggestions. Equally helpful was his willingness to talk over the telephone about Nixon. Michael is not only a brilliant young historian but also an inside-the-Beltway addict, who, like me, is ready, nay eager, to talk politics from noon until MacNeil-Lehrer comes on.

Finally, I want to thank those readers who have taken the time and trouble to write me about the first volume of this biography. They have given me a much-needed boost. For the past two years, I have spent at least five and often ten hours a day, six days a week, with two or three short breaks, at the typewriter. This is a lonely way to live. Inevitably, as I got to page 500, or 700, or 800, I would wonder, Who on earth is going to read all this stuff? Can there be any living person who wants to know this much about Richard Nixon?

Time and again, just when those feelings of loneliness and "nobody will ever read this anyway" got almost unbearable, a letter would arrive from a reader who said he or she could not wait for Volume Two. There is nothing like that to keep a writer going.

I have had research help from three talented women, each of whom I love very much. My daughter Grace Veronica Ambrose was a history major at the University of New Orleans and is now a schoolteacher. She went through the Washington *Post* for me, making copies of articles on the Nixons from the "Style" section. Grace has a good eye for the usable article; she found for me, among much else, that wonderful headline that begins Chapter Twelve.

My daughter Mrs. Stephenie Ambrose Tubbs, who worked for me on the first volume after earning her M.A. in history from the University of Montana, went through *The New York Times,* the Los Angeles *Times,* and other newspapers, hunting Nixon items. She also collected government documents and examined various manuscript collections. As a researcher, she is first-rate; as the mother of my first grandson, she is outstanding; as a daughter she is, like Grace, perfect.

My wife, Moira Buckley Ambrose, did all the things she has done on every one of my books. She participates actively in the research in the Nixon archives, she does the collating, and she is my first and most valuable critic.

Without Moira, I could never get through any book; for Moira, this one has been especially difficult, because of her passionate opposition to the war in Vietnam. Although she supported Nixon in 1960, his Vietnam policy set her teeth on edge. Often when I finished reading to her a section dealing with Nixon and Vietnam, she would spit out the words, "Oh, how he's disappointed me!"

Sometimes I would respond, "Honey, it was as much Lyndon's fault as it was Dick's."

Other times I would say, "How can you, a writer's wife, say such a thing when he is giving me all this great material to work with?"

For myself, I don't claim to have attained a position of indifference or neutrality. What I do claim is to have made my best possible effort to be an objective, careful, honest, and fascinated observer of the life of Richard Nixon.

STEPHEN E. AMBROSE
The Cabin, Dunbar, Wisconsin
(God's Country, North)
May–August 1987, 1988

Merry Weather, Bay St. Louis, Mississippi
(God's Country, South)
September 1987–April 1988
September–December 1988

INDEX

ABC-TV, 249, 262, 271, 572, 581
Abernathy, Ralph, 247–48, 331
ABM system, 258–59, 260, 276, 277
    cost of, 290
    SALT and, 288–90, 313, 441–42, 444,
        545, 548, 615
ABM Treaty, 548, 615
Abplanalp, Robert, 226, 625
Abrams, Creighton, 210, 278, 280–81,
    309, 535, 551
academic freedom, 72–74, 76, 82–83
Acheson, Dean, 77, 254, 259–60, 302,
    307–8, 386, 387, 444
Adams, Duque, and Hazeltine, 16
Adams, Sherman, 228
Adenauer, Konrad, 107, 386
Ad Hoc Inter-Agency Group
    Concerning Prisoners of War, 429
AFL-CIO, 473–77, 479, 585
Africa, 253–54
    Nixon in, 112–13
    Pat Nixon in, 519
Agnew, Spiro, 99, 241, 454
    background of, 163, 170
    as embarrassment to Nixon, 191–92,
        457, 589
    finances of, 174
    Finch compared with, 173–74
    in 1968 campaign, 146, 158, 161, 162–
        163, 172–75, 177–78, 179, 181, 191–
        194, 200, 202, 217, 218, 220, 222, 243
    in 1970 campaign, 390
    in 1972 campaign, 493, 500, 554–55,
        586, 589, 646–47
    Nixon's praise of, 493, 497
    racial issues and, 162–63, 174
    as possible Supreme Court
        appointee, 469
    as Vice-President, 270, 293, 297, 307,
        311, 338, 341, 353, 374, 397, 457,
        493
Agronsky, Martin, 211
Aid to Families with Dependent
    Children (AFDC), 268
    see also welfare system
Air Force, U.S., 77, 215, 242, 258, 272,
    481, 488, 493–94, 505, 507, 589,
    590, 648

Air Force Academy, Nixon's speech at,
    277
Alabama, politics in, 499–500
Albert, Carl, 610
Aldrin, Edwin, 284–85
Alexander v. Holmes County, 316
Allen, Richard, 158, 230
Allende, Salvador, 378–79, 396, 404
Allin, Mort, 248–51, 280, 325, 409, 455,
    621, 638
Alsop, Stewart, 594
American Bar Association (ABA), 469,
    470
American Conservative Union, 90
American Independent Party, 141, 163–
    165, 181–86, 191–94, 555
American Jewish Congress, 583
American Law Institute, Burger's
    address to, 361
American Legion Convention, Nixon's
    speech to, 88
Americans for Conservative Action, 90
American Society of Newspaper Editors
    (ASNE), Nixon's appearances at,
    19–21, 151, 430
amnesty, 581–82, 620
Anderson, Jack, 422, 487, 488, 500, 501,
    508
    Hughes and, 501, 502
    ITT case and, 502–3
Anderson, John, 444
Anderson, Martin, 124
Anne, Princess of England, 362–63
Annenberg, Walter, 585
anti-Communism, 35, 471, 479
    Diem and, 30–31
    of Nixon, see Nixon, Richard Milhous,
        anti-Communism of
antisatellite (ASAT) weapons, 548
anti-Semitism, 470, 641
antitrust laws, 436, 455
    ITT and, 502–5
antiwar movement, 68, 70–75, 85, 103,
    109, 223, 225
    Cambodian incursion and, 350–53,
        355–57
    Moratorium and, 299–300, 302–6
    My Lai massacre and, 312–13

antiwar movement (*cont.*)
  in 1968 campaign, 165, 166, 185, 201
  in 1972 campaign, 599, 620
  in Nixon Administration, 245, 256,
    261–65, 281, 299–306, 312–13, 333,
    343–44, 350–53, 355–57, 369, 374,
    392–95, 414–15, 437–38
Apollo program, 283–86, 314, 339
Arab-Israeli conflict, 112–13, 188, 251,
    334–35, 383–84
Arends, Leslie C., 122
arms control, 203, 313–14, 653–54
  nuclear test ban treaty, 23, 50
  see also SALT; SALT I; SALT II
Armstrong, Neil, 284–85, 363
Army, U.S., 75, 144, 147, 426
  all-volunteer, 190, 265, 467
  morale problems of, 417–19
  politics in, 322–23
  racial tension in, 418
Army of the Republic of Vietnam
    (ARVN), 91, 94, 147, 148, 215, 216,
    280, 358, 387, 541, 551, 589, 635
  in Cambodia, 339–41, 343–45, 347–
    348, 360
  in Laos, 419–21, 428, 505
  NVA spring offensive and (1972), 527,
    529, 530, 533, 535, 536, 602
  in peace agreement, 627, 630, 631
  strengthening and improvement of,
    168, 224, 257, 278, 309, 324, 388,
    505–7, 655
Ash, Roy, 398
Ashbrook, John, 61, 497
"Asia After Viet Nam" (Nixon), 115–16,
    453
Asia policy:
  Nixon's reversal of, 319–20
  see also Korean War; Vietnam War;
    specific countries
Associated Press (AP), 45, 128, 476
Astor, Mrs. W. Vincent, 332
Atkins, Oliver, 605
Atlantic, 29
atomic bomb tests, 501–2
Australia, 78, 115
automobile industry, 458

Baby Boomers:
  as bums vs. heroes, 348, 349, 354
  diversity of, 189
  Nixon's courting of, 190–91
  see also antiwar movement; student
    radicalism
Bahamas, Nixon in, 13–14, 16–17
Baker, Bernard, 589
Baker, Bobby, 47
Baker, Howard, 301, 421
Baker, Russell, 40, 245

Baldwin, Hanson, 29
Ball, George, 208
Bangladesh (East Pakistan), 482–86
Barnett, Ross, 74
"Basic Principles of Relations," 545,
    595, 596
Bassett, Jim, 52, 65
Bayh, Birch, 296, 315, 337
Bay of Pigs invasion, 20, 27, 33–34, 49,
    379, 563, 566
Beecher, William, 272
Bennett, Donald, 362
Bennett, Robert, 421, 423, 450, 501
Benson, Ezra Taft, 75
Bentsen, Lloyd, 534, 618
Beria, Lavrenti, 65
Berkeley, University of California at,
    119–20, 333
Berlin:
  détente and, 464–65
  Kennedy in, 24
  Nixon in, 23, 24
Berlin Wall, 24, 33–34, 464
Bernstein, Carl, 606, 621, 638–40,
    646
Bernstein, Mrs. Leonard, 332
B-52s, 241–42, 258, 335, 336, 339, 420,
    529, 530, 535–36, 593
Biafra, 253–54
Billington, Ray Allen, 637
Birdwatchers of '66, 67, 83–84, 99
Black, Hugo, 468
Blackmun, Harry, 338, 563
Black Panthers, 332, 333, 367
blacks, 236, 243, 474
  Agnew and, 162–63, 174
  first use of term, 103
  Moynihan's views on, 331–32, 366
  Nixon's relationship with, 247–48
  Nixon's views on, 124–26, 186–88,
    244, 249
  riots and, 55, 68, 103, 125, 144–45,
    163
  in Vietnam War, 349
  see also busing; civil rights
    movement; desegregation; racism;
    segregation
Bliss, Ray, 84, 98
Blough, Roger, 25, 33
Blount, Winton, 237
B'nai B'rith, Nixon's speech to, 188
Bobst, Elmer, 17, 25, 84, 241
Bobst, Mrs. Elmer, 239
Boeing, 433
Bohemian Grove, 114, 118
bombing policy, bombing:
  Johnson's halt in, 196, 256, 494, 614,
    629
  in Laos, 242, 325, 344

of North Vietnam, *see* North Vietnam,
 U.S. bombing of
 secret, of Cambodia, 256–57, 270,
 272, 281, 325
 in South Vietnam, 241–42
Borman, Frank, 287
Boston *Globe*, 218
Boyarsky, Bill, 212
Boys Clubs of America, 82
Bradley, Omar, 323
Brandeis, Louis, 82, 316
Brandt, Willy, 385–87, 464–65
Brazil, Nixon in, 111–12
Bremer, Arthur Herman, 541
Brewer, Albert, 499–500
Brewster, Kingman, Jr., 351
Brezhnev, Leonid I., 526, 531, 532,
 615–17
 Moscow summit and, 544–45, 547,
 550
 Nixon's correspondence with, 484,
 485
Brinkley, David, 290–91, 326, 414
Brock, William, 604
Broder, David, 85, 88–89, 302, 495–96
Brooke, Edward, 179, 183, 186, 236, 604
Brookings Institution, 448
Brown, George, 534
Brown, Pat, 15, 104, 119, 635
Brownell, Herbert, 25, 142, 274, 311
Brown v. *Topeka*, 187, 274, 316, 520,
 523, 658
Buchanan, Pat, 84, 96, 98, 112, 149, 248,
 298, 331, 362, 409, 455, 460, 510,
 621, 638
 in 1968 campaign, 145, 153, 163, 170,
 179–80, 193
 in 1972 campaign, 554, 556, 572, 605,
 639, 647, 648
 Nixon criticized by, 405, 407
 Nixon's relationship with, 67, 410
 as Nixon's speech writer, 67, 193, 297
 Supreme Court appointments and,
 468
Buckley, William F., Jr., 61, 231, 251,
 277, 289, 378, 410
Buffalo *Evening News*, 325
Bundy, McGeorge, 448
Bunker, Ellsworth, 210, 211, 613
bureaucracy:
 Nixon's criticism of, 328–29
 Nixon's postelection plan for, 611–12
Bureau of Labor Statistics, 457
Burger, Warren E., 274–75, 295, 315,
 346, 361, 445, 469, 470, 563
Burns, Arthur, 237, 249, 265–66, 269,
 292, 455–58
 Colson and, 455–56
Bush, George, 158, 398, 421

business, 238, 435–36
 antitrust laws and, 436
 investment and, 125
busing, 125, 169–70, 393, 433, 460–61,
 500, 657
 in 1972 campaign, 520–24, 542, 553,
 555–56, 586–87, 623
 Nixon's call for moratorium on, 523–
 524, 555–56, 587, 623
Butterfield, Alexander, 329, 423, 564
Butz, Earl, 583, 604
Butz, Tim, 599
Byrd, Robert, 330, 469
Byrnes, James F. (Jimmy), 30

Cabinet, Nixon:
 Family Security System and, 292–93
 place and function of, 238–39
 selection of, 236–38
 shifts in, 365, 398, 542, 636
 see also specific Cabinet members
Calhoun, Jesse, 479
Califano, Joseph, 97, 208
California, 16, 118, 119, 242
 gubernatorial races in, 11–13, 15, 80,
 83
 Nixon's house in, 294–95, 371
 primaries in, 46, 50, 104, 157, 554
 split of Republican Party in, 16
California, University of, 119–20, 333,
 434
Callaway, Howard, 164
Calley, William, Jr., 428
Cambodia, 76, 78, 103, 104, 129, 147,
 339, 407, 462, 507, 594, 646
 Cooper-Church amendment and, 358,
 367
 Lon Nol coup in, 336–37
 material captured in, 360–61
 Nixon's views on, 242, 256, 344–46,
 352, 354, 360–61
 POWs in, 630
 U.S. aid to, 399–400
 U.S. secret bombing of, 256–57, 270,
 272, 281, 325
Canteen Corporation, 436
Carmichael, Stokely, 103
Carswell, G. Harrold, 330–31, 337–38,
 495, 658
Case, Clifford, 72
Casey, William, 45, 46
Castro, Fidel, 19, 42, 44, 49, 379–81,
 480
 Watergate motive and, 565, 567
Caulfield, Jack, 273, 303
CBS-TV, 248–49, 299, 429, 449, 572
Ceauşescu, Nicolae, 107–8, 288, 400
Central Intelligence Agency (CIA), 106,
 232, 273, 336, 361–62, 422, 450

Central Intelligence Agency (*cont.*)
  in Cambodia, 339–41
  in Chile, 378–79, 396
  Cuban operations of, 379–82
  FBI relations with, 471, 473
  formation of, 35
  Haldeman's shake-up of, 543
  operations methods of, 35–36
  Watergate and, 568, 569, 574, 576,
    661, 662
  youth rebellion and, 262, 264
Central Office for South Vietnam
    (COSVN), 103, 256–58, 272
  Cambodian incursion and, 341, 345,
    347, 352, 354, 360
Chafee, John, 72
Chamberlain, Neville, 48, 355, 643
Chamber of Commerce, U.S., 263–64
Champion, George, 25
Chancellor, John, 403, 414
Chapin, Dwight, 123, 124, 158, 170,
    219, 311, 356–57, 461
  in dirty-tricks operation, 477, 639, 640
  Peace Movement memo of, 305–6
Chappaquiddick Island, 283–84
Charles, Prince of Wales, 362–63
Chennault, Anna Chan, 207–8, 210,
    213–16, 231, 235
Chennault, Claire, 207
Chiang Kai-shek, 44, 68, 108, 207, 480,
    514
Chicago, Democratic Convention in
    (1968), 181–82, 265
Chicago *Daily News*, 325
Chicago Executives Club, Nixon's
    speech to, 126
"Chicago Seven," 265
Chicago *Sun-Times*, 436
Chicago *Tribune*, 294, 518
child rearing, Nixon's views on, 470
Chile, 404
  CIA in, 378–79, 396
China, People's Republic of, 24, 262,
    324
  Cuba's relations with, 379, 380, 439
  Kissinger's visits to, 450–53, 479–80,
    512, 513, 517
  Nixon-Chou communiqué and, 515–
    17
  Nixon's views on, 44, 68, 81, 116, 150,
    168, 191, 252–53
  Nixon's visit to, 168, 287, 450, 453,
    480, 512–19, 525–26
  nuclear weapons of, 81
  Pakistan and, 482–83
  Romania and, 288, 427
  Soviet relations with, 23, 44, 75, 428
  United Nations and, 44, 400, 428,
    452, 486
  U.S. relations with, 44, 116, 150, 191,
    224, 233, 252–53, 288, 307, 320,
    329, 400, 427–28, 430, 450–54, 483,
    485–86, 494, 514–18
  Vietnam War and, 76, 78, 166, 224–
    225, 452, 507, 515, 516, 551, 592,
    656
Chisum, 369
Chotiner, Murray, 69, 90, 158, 219, 392
Chou En-lai, 323, 400, 427, 428, 430,
    450–54, 479, 506, 519, 526, 545,
    597
  Kissinger's gift to, 452–53
  Nixon's meeting with, 512–16, 518
Chrysler Corporation, 16
Church, Frank, 335–36, 358, 509, 643
Churchill, Winston, 11, 13, 23, 24, 34,
    218, 320, 355, 580
  Nixon compared with, 180, 191
CIA, *see* Central Intelligence Agency
Citibank, 572
Civil Rights Act (1964), 41–42, 50, 89
civil rights movement, 36, 41, 373
  in Johnson Administration, 41–42, 50,
    55–56
  in 1968 campaign, 66, 162–65, 169–
    170
  Nixon's lost opportunity in, 406–07
  Nixon's views on, 42, 43, 61, 89, 331,
    363–66, 407
  white backlash and, 42, 55–56, 89
  see also busing; desegregation
Clark, Ramsey, 589, 590
Clay, Lucius, 386, 444
Clean Elections Legislation, 266
clean-water bill, 553
Cleveland *Plain Dealer*, 650
Clifford, Clark, 203, 237–38, 501
  Vietnam policy and, 147, 196–97,
    208, 210, 215, 230, 231, 278–79,
    324, 340, 448
Cold War, 34, 367
  Berlin Wall and, 24
  New Left view of, 71
  Nixon's views on, 20, 23, 49–50, 168
  see also specific events
Colorado, University of, 333
Colson, Charles (Chuck), 298, 311, 392,
    397, 410, 414, 501, 614, 629, 642,
    660
  advancement of, 421
  Gleason and, 479
  ITT case and, 503–4
  leaks prevention and, 449–50
  in 1972 campaign, 495, 496, 499, 556,
    572, 574, 586, 587, 605–6, 618, 636,
    641, 650
  Nixon's correspondence with, 474–
    475, 510, 542

Nixon's relationship with, 410, 411, 455–56, 625
Watergate and, 560, 562, 563, 565–68, 571, 574, 576, 577
"Come-Back Theme," 180
Committee of National Reconciliation, proposed, 594, 612
Committee to Re-elect the President (CREEP), 497–99, 502, 552, 557, 588–89, 603, 606–9
DNC suit against, 563, 574, 577, 607, 610, 622
espionage activities of, 502, 505, 543–544, 558
see also Watergate affair
Common Cause, 414
Communism:
academic freedom and, 83
Du Bois Clubs and, 81–82
Nixon's revised views on, 168
youth rebellion and, 262
see also specific countries
Communist Party, U.S., 36, 109, 303
Congress, U.S., 55, 122–23, 188, 192, 242, 261, 265, 364, 545
ABM system and, 258, 288–90
arms control and, 549, 550
busing moratorium and, 523–24
Nixon's inability to work with, 406–7, 413, 433, 444, 658
political contributions limits and, 266
public election funds and, 477–78
tax issues and, 290–91
Vietnam War and, 76, 257, 276, 281, 299, 301, 311, 358–59, 367, 420–21, 461, 467–68, 506, 539, 590–91, 656–57
see also House of Representatives, U.S.; Senate, U.S.
Congress of Racial Equality (CORE), 235
Connally, John, 31, 398, 456–59, 534, 537, 625
milk price supports and, 434–35
in 1972 campaign, 542, 554, 561, 582, 585–87, 589, 608, 609, 618
Nixon's respect for, 535, 537, 542, 585–86
resignation of, 542
Constitution, U.S., 358, 370
executive privilege and, 426–27
containment, 20
Cooke, Terence Cardinal, 247
Cooper, John Sherman, 358, 590
Cooper amendment, 590–91
Cooper-Church amendment, 358, 367, 391
Corporation for Public Broadcasting, 572

Cost of Living Council, 458
COSVN, see Central Office for South Vietnam
Cotton, Hamilton, 294
Council of Economic Advisers, 238
Court of Appeals, U.S., 554
Cox, Edward F., 58, 170, 445, 491, 538
in 1972 campaign, 597, 598
Cox, Tricia Nixon, 13, 17, 63, 111, 131, 242, 294–95, 491, 538
dating of, 317, 445
at Debutante Ball, 58
education of, 16, 26, 62–63
father's views on, 317–18
marriage of, 445–46
in 1968 campaign, 152, 155, 161, 170, 220
in 1970 campaign, 391
in 1972 campaign, 597, 598
in White House, 247, 416
Cranston, Alan, 277
CREEP, see Committee to Re-elect the President
crime:
as 1970 campaign issue, 391, 393
Nixon's denunciation of, 87, 90
poverty and, 154, 202, 373
students and, 262–63
see also law and order
Crime Control Act (1968), 273
Cronkite, Walter, 22, 248, 283, 325, 429, 449, 455, 508, 572, 606, 621, 624
Crosby, James, 133
Cuba, 18–21, 44, 379–83, 480
Bay of Pigs invasion and, 20, 27, 33–34, 49, 379, 563, 566
as campaign issue, 13, 379
"Cuba, Castro and John F. Kennedy" (Nixon), 49–50
Cuban missile crisis, 12, 18–21, 49, 379
Curtis, Charlotte, 189
Cushman, Robert, 280–81, 341
Czechoslovakia, Soviet invasion of, 225

Daley, Richard, 181, 182, 183, 219, 220, 585
Daniel, Aubrey, 428–29
Davies, John S., 13–14
Davis, Rennie, 334
day-care, 470, 495, 497
DDT, banning of, 553
Dean, John, 374, 409, 422–23, 426–27, 465, 502
Irving investigation and, 501
ITT case and, 503
Supreme Court appointments and, 469, 470
Watergate and, 558, 562, 568, 569, 575–76, 589, 602–3, 607–12

Defense Department, U.S., 15, 103, 237–38, 271, 289, 336, 350, 380–81, 397, 529, 648
Moscow summit and, 547, 548, 549
defense spending, 553, 601
in Kennedy Administration, 34
in Nixon Administration, 259, 290, 327, 433
de Gaulle, Charles, 23–24, 34, 88, 254
Dellinger, David, 588
Democratic National Committee (DNC), 246, 422
countersuit proposal and, 611
CREEP break in at, see Watergate affair
CREEP sued by, 563, 574, 577, 607, 610, 622
Democratic National Convention:
of 1968, 181–83, 265
of 1972, 554, 555, 578, 579–80, 599
Democrats, Democratic Party, 15, 326–327, 328, 349, 425, 432, 455, 456, 459
Chappaquiddick incident and, 283–284
news media as supporter of, 12
in 1960 campaign, 15, 19, 20, 44, 84, 104, 127, 138, 202, 204, 205, 221
in 1962 campaign, 440
in 1964 campaign, 33, 39, 41–43, 47–51, 54, 57, 60, 202
in 1965 campaign, 72, 74
in 1966 campaign, 80, 81, 86
in 1968 campaign, 90, 97, 102, 127–128, 130, 141, 145, 146, 149, 151, 155–56, 157, 160, 164, 165–66, 181–86, 188, 191–99, 207–214, 216–17, 243, 375
in 1970 campaign, 391–92, 396
in 1972 campaign, 496, 499, 500, 503, 522, 541–42, 544, 552–65, 571, 572, 578–88, 591–93, 599, 600, 601, 604–6, 608, 618, 620–21, 622, 624, 625, 628, 630, 635–38, 640, 646–48, 651–52
in Nixon Cabinet, 236–37, 398
Nixon compared with, 88
Nixon's attacks on, 12, 13, 19–21, 23, 27, 28, 34, 41, 43, 44, 47–50, 56, 62, 64, 68, 69, 75–76, 81, 89, 136; see also specific Democrats
Nixon's intelligence-gathering on, 242; see also Watergate affair
public election funds and, 477–78
Republicans compared with, 30, 88, 164, 243, 246, 599
secret peace talks and, 509–10
Southern, 89, 165
split in, 185
weakness of, 12

Democrats for Nixon, 542, 586, 608, 618
Dent, Harry, 365
desegregation, 297, 301, 331, 364–66, 406–7, 433, 460–61
in Alabama, 500
Brown v. Topeka and, 187, 274, 316, 520, 523, 658
see also busing
détente, 439–44, 526
Brandt's development of, 385–86, 464–65
defined, 439
economic, 143
Ford's views on, 655
Nixon's strengths in promoting of, 440–41
U.S.-Chinese, 171, 233, 254, 439, 440, 450–54, 512–19, 525–26, 653–54, 656
U.S.-Soviet, 171, 233, 254, 307, 320–321, 439–44, 462, 478–79, 526–27, 653–54, 656, see also Moscow summit; SALT; SALT I; SALT II
Détente and Confrontation (Garthoff), 233
deterrence concept, 548
Detroit, race riot in, 103
Dewey, Thomas E., 17, 28, 33, 80, 90, 241, 274
death of, 416–17
Dickerson, Nancy, 320, 403, 404
Dicks, Randy, 303
Diem, Ngo Dinh, 28, 36
overthrow and assassination of, 30–31, 33–34, 36–37, 48, 464
Dirksen, Everett, 30, 208–9
Dobrynin, Anatoly, 275, 307, 528–31
Kissinger and, 271–72, 382, 427, 441–442, 446–47, 528, 531, 535, 541, 617
Dole, Robert, 445, 476
in 1972 campaign, 503, 604, 608
dollar, U.S., fixed vs. floating, 459
Domestic Council, 328
domino theory, 48, 78
Donovan, Robert, 62
Doolittle Committee, 35
Doubleday, 21, 32, 33
Doubletalk (Smith), 546
Douglas, Helen, 104, 121, 604
Douglas, William O., 315
Doyle, James, 218
draft, 264–6, 300, 414, 444, 467–68
abolishing of, 190, 265
Draft Rockefeller Committee, 146
Drown, Helene, 22, 111, 220, 241, 520, 597, 619
Drown, Jack, 22, 241
Drown, Maureen, 22

drugs, 71, 418
Drummond, Roscoe, 280, 281
Du Bois, W. E. B., 81
Du Bois Clubs, 81–82
Duchin, Mrs. Peter, 332
Duck Hook, 282, 299–301, 306–7, 310,
  319, 320, 407, 463
Dulles, John Foster, 92, 230, 233, 512
Dumont, Wayne, 72–74

Eagleton, Thomas, 579–80, 582–83, 597
EC-121 reconnaissance aircraft, North
  Korean downing of, 269–71
"Economic Good News Kit," 584
economy, U.S.:
  blacks and, 187–88, 249
  1972 campaign and, 498, 554, 572,
    581, 584, 604–5
  Nixon's views on, 19–20, 87–88, 124,
    154, 187–88, 397, 403, 431–36,
    457–70, 475
  Safire's memorandums on, 296–97
  Vietnam War and, 142, 225
  see also inflation; taxes
Eden, Anthony, 359
education, 326, 373
  desegregation of, see desegregation
  Nixon's views on, 124–25, 169–70,
    187, 555–56
  see also academic freedom
Edwards, Agustín, 378
Egypt, 112–13, 334
  Nixon in, 23
  Soviet relations with, 383, 595, 616
Ehrlichman, John, 84, 272–73, 297, 303,
    328–31, 357, 362, 410, 446–49, 455,
    457, 488, 491, 501, 612, 643, 660
  appointed White House counsel, 237
  black issues and, 247–48, 521–22
  busing issue and, 421–22, 553
  Family Security System and, 291
  Harlow's memo to, 292
  Hoover and, 471–73, 503
  Kissinger and, 284, 489–90
  milk price supports and, 434–35
  in 1968 campaign, 145, 172, 186, 190
  in 1972 campaign, 556, 580, 584, 588,
    641
  Nixon's correspondence with, 248–
    251, 264, 284, 287, 329, 364, 459–
    460, 521–22
  on Nixon's drinking, 84, 342
  Nixon's relationship with, 410, 411
  personality of, 172
  Plumbers operation and, 449, 465
  Supreme Court appointments and,
    296, 315, 330, 469
  Watergate and, 558, 565, 566, 568,
    569, 574–76

Eisenhower, Barbara, 362
Eisenhower, David, 101, 242, 245, 295,
    338, 362–63, 391, 538, 598
  engagement of, 129–30, 136, 204
  Julie's correspondence with, 618
  in Navy, 334, 446, 491, 498, 598
  in 1968 campaign, 131–32, 135–36,
    152, 157, 161, 170, 182–83, 189–90,
    204, 218
  in 1972 campaign, 498, 598–99
  Nixon's correspondence with, 131–
    132
  wedding of, 240–41
  in White House, 247, 317
Eisenhower, Dwight D., 12–13, 15, 17,
    23, 31, 44, 72, 80, 90, 96, 98, 114,
    147, 224, 274, 290, 659–60
  Army politics and, 322–23
  death of, 266–68
  executive privilege and, 426–27
  foreign policy views of, 18–19, 35,
    128–29, 152, 319, 427–28
  on getting caught, 576–77
  health problems of, 160–61, 162, 175,
    203–4, 240
  inauguration of, 243, 244
  Johnson's relationship with, 283
  in 1956 campaign, 493, 617
  in 1964 campaign, 27, 31, 47, 54
  in 1968 campaign, 105–6, 130, 135–
    136, 151–52, 160–62, 183, 203–4,
    218
  Nixon compared with, 213, 238–39,
    243, 244, 267, 328–29, 408–9, 412,
    442, 472, 544, 594–95
  Nixon endorsed by, 160–62
  Nixon's correspondence with, 27, 30,
    74, 83, 92, 112, 137, 143, 151–52,
    161, 203–4
  Nixon's criticism of, 27, 28
  Nixon's disagreement with, 129
  Stalin's views on, 383
  tape recording of, 423
Eisenhower, John, 203–4, 362
Eisenhower, Julie Nixon (daughter), 13,
    17, 22, 63, 131, 227, 294–95, 362–
    363, 445, 491, 538
  biography of mother by, 619
  as celebrity sweetheart, 189
  cooking abilities of, 242
  at Debutante Ball, 101
  diary of, 63, 131, 132
  education of, 16, 26, 62–63, 101, 242,
    334, 338
  engagement of, 129–30, 136, 204
  on father, 403
  father's correspondence with, 130
  father's views on, 317–18, 343–44
  marriage of, 239–41

Eisenhower, Julie Nixon (*cont.*)
in 1968 campaign, 135–36, 152, 155, 170, 182–83, 189–90, 220
in 1972 campaign, 498, 597, 598, 618
Rebozo and, 111, 241, 362
on tapes, 424
in White House, 247, 317, 416
Eisenhower, Mamie, 129, 152, 175, 203, 208, 240, 244, 267, 599
Eisenhower, Milton, 362
Eisenhower, Susan, 362
Eisenhower Administration, 15, 25, 35, 69, 198, 215, 615
election of 1946, 473
election of 1952, 17, 156, 159, 204, 213
election of 1956, 493, 617
election of 1960, 15, 19, 20, 44, 84, 104, 127, 204, 379
    Haldeman's criticism of, 137–38
    King and, 150–51
    1968 campaign compared with, 171– 172, 179–80, 191, 202–3, 221
election of 1962, 11–13, 15, 104, 440
election of 1964, 13, 21, 39–58, 202, 235
    California primary in, 46, 50
    Goldwater in, 20, 22, 23, 27, 28, 39– 47, 50–54, 56–58, 89, 95, 96, 105, 179, 379, 554
    Kennedy's death and, 33
    Nixon in, 13, 20, 23, 27, 28, 31, 33, 39–58, 84, 379
    polls in, 27, 39, 45
    primaries in, 40–41, 45–47
    Rockefeller in, 20, 22, 27, 28, 31, 39– 41, 44–47, 50, 53, 54, 57, 95
    Vietnam War and, 42–45, 48–49
election of 1965, 72–74
election of 1966, 80–101, 119
    Nixon's role in, 60, 80–101
    Republican preparation for, 59–79
election of 1968, 13, 102–222, 243, 375
    Agnew controversy and, 174–75, 177–78, 179
    August 9 to October 14 in, 177–200
    civil rights and black issues in, 66, 162–65, 169–70, 186–88
    conventions in, 169–70, 172–77, 181– 183
    Eisenhower endorsement and, 160– 162
    Election Day in, 218–19
    equal-time rule and, 192, 199
    fundraising in, 123, 133, 140, 178–79
    Haldeman memoranda in, 137–38, 180
    Hillsboro approach in, 139–41, 151
    law-and-order issue in, 125–26, 144– 145, 154, 174, 182, 184, 187, 201
    new coalition in, 178

    1960 campaign compared with, 171– 172, 179–80, 191, 202–3, 221
    1972 campaign compared with, 217, 600, 601
    Nixon/Chennault/Thieu intrigue in, 207–8, 210, 213–16
    Nixon's acceptance speech in, 166– 167, 175–76
    Nixon's doubts in, 131–32
    Nixon's refusal to debate in, 184, 192–93
    Nixon's strategy and tactics in, 133– 141, 151, 155, 179–81, 186, 190–91, 221–22
    Nixon's turnaround in, 11–12, 61, 65
    October 15 to November 6 in, 201–22
    Operation Candor in, 121–22
    polls in, 120, 141, 160, 164, 172, 177, 183, 193, 194, 199, 205, 212, 216
    primaries for, 104–5, 121, 133–56
    results of, 219–21
    rough-them-up tactics in, 186
    telethons in, 216, 218
    television's role in, 138–40, 165, 170, 202, 216–17
    Vietnam War and, 66, 75–76, 78, 104, 115, 126–29, 134–35, 137, 141–44, 146–50, 166–69, 180, 190–91, 193– 198, 206–18, 655
    Waldorf group and, 102, 104–5
election of 1970, 281, 373–97
    campaign funds in, 391
    Social Issue in, 392–96
election of 1972, 242, 375, 431, 493– 512, 552–654
    campaign funds in, 391, 476–77, 498
    civil rights and, 364, 520–24, 542, 553, 555–56, 586–87
    conventions in, 436, 502, 503, 554, 555, 578, 579–80, 588, 599–601
    détente and, 440–41
    dirty tricks in, 500, 505, 543–44; *see also* Watergate Affair
    economics and, 498, 554, 572, 581, 584, 604–5
    Election Day in, 650–51, 662
    Hallett's approach to, 495–96, 497, 499
    New American Revolution in, 580, 593, 662
    New Majority in, 580, 583, 625
    1968 campaign compared with, 217, 600, 601
    Nixon's acceptance speech in, 600– 601
    Nixon's fears about, 413, 522
    Nixon's independence in, 557, 580, 600

Nixon's strategy and tactics in, 604, 617–18
October 8 to November 7 in, 627–52
polls in, 496, 507, 511–12, 591, 601, 636
primaries in, 497, 498, 500, 508, 522, 541–42, 554
results in, 651–52
Richardson's approach to, 497, 499
September 1 to October 8 in, 604–26
vote of confidence in, 653
voters' split position in, 591–92
voting blocs in, 496–97, 499
election of 1976, 618
Elementary and Secondary Education Act (1965), 523
Elizabeth II, Queen of England, 385
Ellington, Duke, 247
Ellsberg, Daniel, 447–49, 465–66, 490, 508
Ellsworth, Robert, 106, 107, 153
entente, 439
environmental movement, economic impact of, 459–60
Environmental Protection Agency (EPA), 553
Equal Educational Opportunities Act (1972), 523
equal-time doctrine, 192, 199, 327, 328
Ervin, Sam, 523, 622
Evans, Daniel, 158, 179
Evans, Rowland, 301
Evans, Tom, 102
Evers, Medgar, 36
excise tax, 458
Executive Office, reorganization of, 328
executive privilege, doctrine of, 426–27

"Face the Nation," 31, 75–76, 91, 211
Fallaci, Oriana, 649
Family Assistance Plan (FAP), 293–94, 298, 314–15, 328, 366–67, 391, 402, 404, 405–6, 657, 658
Family Security System (FSS), 269, 291–93
farmers, 583–84
Far Right:
China policy and, 454
in 1962 campaign, 440
in 1964 campaign, 53–54
in 1968 campaign, 141, 163–65, 181–186, 191–94
in 1972 campaign, 440–41
Nixon's criticism of, 23, 75
SALT opposed by, 442
"Fascism is Here" letter (Moynihan), 413, 425

Federal Bureau of Investigation (FBI), 29, 32, 36, 47, 234–36, 425, 448–49, 564
Chennault wiretap of, 208, 210
Ellsberg and, 448
Gray appointed director of, 543
Huston Plan opposed by, 368
Nixon Administration wiretaps of, 272–74, 350, 361
Nixon's criticism of, 361–62
Nixon's problems with, 471–73
Watergate and, 567–69, 573, 574, 576, 588, 602, 608, 609, 622–23, 638, 661, 662
youth rebellion and, 264, 265
Federal Communications Commission (FCC), 661
Federal Corrupt Practices Act, (1925), 478
Federal Reserve Board, 225
Field, George, 77
Fielding, Lewis J., 466, 661
Finch, Robert, 39, 66, 84, 99, 543 as
Counsel to the President, 365, 416
in 1968 campaign, 102, 104, 173–74, 212, 213–14, 219
Nixon's relationship with, 173, 174
resignation of, 365
as Secretary of Health, Education and Welfare, 237, 268–69, 297, 301, 331, 362, 364–65
Finkelstein, Louis, 247
Finney, John, 350
Fisher Island, 110, 227, 294
Fishhook, 341, 342, 344, 345, 347–48
Fitzsimmons, Frank, 491–92, 584, 618
Flamingo Park, 599, 600
Flanigan, Horace, 25
Flanigan, Peggy, 416
Flanigan, Peter, 66, 83, 416
in 1968 campaign, 102, 104, 105, 106, 123
Flemming, Arthur, 124
Florida, primary in, 523–24
Fonda, Jane, 414–15, 596
Ford, Gerald R., 76–77, 315, 421, 445, 540, 622, 655
in 1972 campaign, 604, 608, 610
Ford Foundation, 265
Foreign Affairs, 115–16, 232, 278, 453, 494
Formosa, see Taiwan, 95
Fortas, Abe, 159–60, 183, 199, 200, 274, 275
resignation of, 295, 296, 316
fragging, 418
France, 88
Nixon in, 23–24, 27–28, 254

Franco, Francisco, 23
Frankel, Max, 344, 360, 443, 512, 536–
    537, 642
freedom, 112, 114
    academic, 72–74, 76, 82–83
    new, Nixon on, 136, 137
Freedom Foundation, 16
Freedom House, 77
freedom of speech, 72–74, 82–83, 391
Freeman, John, 255
Free Society Association, 90
Free Speech movement, 119
Freeze List, 409
Frelinghuysen, Peter, 421
Frick, Mrs. Henry Clay, 240
Friday, Herschel, 469
Friedman, Milton, 124
Fritchey, Clayton, 470
Frost, David, 662
FSS (Family Security System), 269,
    291–93
Fulbright, J. William, 44, 249, 258, 277,
    510
    executive privilege and, 426, 427
    Vietnam policy and, 77, 78, 79, 81,
        301, 302, 350, 359, 518
Fund for the Republic, 16

Galbraith, John Kenneth, 284
Gallup polls, 90, 287, 294, 311, 359,
    413, 414, 436, 511, 601
    in 1964 campaign, 27, 39
    in 1968 campaign, 177
    Pat Nixon in, 318
Gandhi, Indira, 482–85
Gardner, John, 325, 414
Garment, Leonard, 82, 124, 138, 150,
    170
    Supreme Court appointments and,
        468–69
Garthoff, Raymond, 233, 253, 329, 381,
    443, 451–52, 486
    Moscow summit and, 546–48, 550
Gates, Thomas, 25
Gaunt, Loie, 26
Gayler, Noel, 362
Gemstone, 502, 505, 543–44, 562, 565,
    569, 575, 576
General Accounting Office (GAO), 602,
    607, 610, 622
General Beadle State College, 264
"General Philosophy and Themes"
    (Haldeman), 625
General Services Administration (GSA),
    362, 573
generation gap, 70–71, 189, 225, 352
Genovese, Eugene D., 72–74, 76, 82
German Democratic Republic (East
    Germany), 386, 464–65

German unification, Nixon's views on,
    23, 24
Germany, Federal Republic of (West
    Germany), 517
    Nixon in, 23, 107
    Ostpolitik of, 385–86, 464–
        465
Gestapo, 35
Gifford, Frank, 25
Gleason, Thomas (Teddy), 479
Goldberg, Arthur, 91–92
Goldwater, Barry, Jr., 317
Goldwater, Barry, Sr., 15, 54, 60, 80,
    454, 600
    acceptance speech of, 53–54
    in 1964 campaign, 20, 22, 23, 27, 28,
        39–47, 50–54, 56–68, 89, 95, 96,
        105, 179, 379, 554
    Nixon compared with, 51
    Nixon supported by, 60–61
gold window, closing of, 459
Goodell, Charles, 300, 302
Goodpaster, Andrew, 423, 424
Gore, Albert, 249, 258, 277
government reorganization, Nixon's
    views on, 158–59, 189, 328
Graham, Billy, 128, 131, 183–84, 240,
    247, 283, 285, 445, 555
    in 1972 campaign, 586, 587
Graham, Katherine, 621
grain sales, 478–79, 526, 545, 583–
    584
Gray, Beatrice, 543
Gray, L. Patrick, 543, 567–68, 569, 574,
    576
Great Britain, 428
    India and, 482, 483
    Nixon in, 255, 385
Great Society, 41–42, 61, 142, 326, 327,
    432, 433
Greece, Nixon in, 113
Greenspan, Alan, 158
Greenspan, Hank, 501, 502, 504
Gregory, Dick, 312
Griffin, Robert, 159, 315
Grinnell Corporation, 436
Gromyko, Andrei, 544, 614–16
Groves, B. Allen, 415
Grubb, Dale, 56
Gruening, Ernest, 55
Guam, Nixon in, 287
Guam Doctrine, 287
Guantanamo, 42
Gulf of Tonkin Resolution, 55, 58, 61,
    338–39, 367
Gulley, Bill, 457
GVN (government of Vietnam), 206,
    207, 209, 210, 211, 212, 215–17,
    241, 324–25, 594, 595

Hagerty, James, 229
Haig, Alexander, 273, 281–82, 324, 350,
    419–20, 451, 463, 529, 537, 564n,
    587, 617
  Kissinger and, 490, 532, 601–2, 613,
    614, 631, 641
  Nixon's relationship with, 532, 535,
    613, 531
  peace agreement and, 627–29, 631,
    633
Haiphong harbor, 69, 76, 103, 282, 301,
    342
  U.S. mining of, 537–42, 612, 632
Haldeman, H. R. (Bob), 39, 236, 266–
    267, 302, 326, 348, 356–57, 361–63,
    370, 410, 420, 457, 465, 504, 529,
    660
  appointed chief of staff, 228
  black issues and, 247–48
  China policy and, 454, 512
  on Colson, 455
  CREEP and, 502
  Cuba policy and, 381
  Hughes-Nixon dealings and, 501–2
  Kissinger and, 357–58, 489–90
  Middle East policy and, 384
  in 1968 campaign, 137–40, 153, 158,
    162, 163, 166, 170, 172, 179–80,
    189–90, 204, 219, 224
  in 1970 campaign, 391, 396
  in 1972 campaign, 496, 500, 561, 580–
    583, 587, 588, 597, 598, 605, 620,
    636, 641, 650–51
  Nixon's correspondence with, 137–
    138, 248, 249, 250, 287, 297–98,
    314, 411, 414, 415, 417, 510, 526,
    542–543, 605
  on Nixon's drinking, 84–85
  Nixon's "firings" handled by, 409–
    410
  Nixon's relationship with, 410, 411,
    560, 625
  on Nixon's turning point, 361
  O'Brien-Hughes matter and, 422–23
  Pentagon Papers and, 446–48
  taping system and, 423–25
  Vietnam policy and, 510, 511, 537,
    538–39, 629, 643
  Watergate and, 558, 560–71, 574, 576,
    607–12, 639–41
Hallett, Doug, 495–96, 497, 499
Halperin, Morton, 272–73, 289
Hanoi:
  bombing of, 103, 282
  Spring of 1972 bombing, 530
Hardin, Clifford M., 434–35
Harlan, John, 468, 471
Harlow, Bryce, 16, 160, 208, 209, 292,
    296, 297, 301, 330, 406, 457

ABM and, 289, 290
  on Colson, 298
Harriman, Averell, 149, 206–7, 209
Harris polls, 199, 212, 413, 507, 511–12,
    612
Harsch, Joseph, 410
Hartford Fire Insurance, 436
Harvard University, 351
Hatfield, Mark, 158, 358
Hauge, Gabriel, 25
Hayes, Woody, 242
Haynsworth, Clement F., 296, 301,
    315–17, 330, 337–38, 658
Health, Education and Welfare
    Department, U.S. (HEW), 331,
    460–61
Heard, Alexander, 369
Heath, Edward, 486
Helms, Richard, 178, 230, 253, 379,
    419–20, 568–69
  Cambodia policy and, 337, 340, 341
Herbers, John, 87
heroin, 418
Hersh, Seymour, 214, 451–52, 485, 547,
    550, 612–13
Hershey, Lewis B., 303
Herter, Christian, 22
Hess, Steve, 14, 21, 26, 32, 39, 237
  on Nixon's relationship with speech
    writers, 67–68
Hickel, Walter, 237, 398
Higby, Larry, 158, 372
Higher Education Act (1968), 262–63
Hill, James, 82
Hill, Robert, 56
Hillings, Pat, 66
Hillsboro approach, 139–41, 151
Hiss, Alger, 426
Hiss case, 234, 251, 427, 574, 577, 623
Hitler, Adolf, 34, 35, 48, 77–78, 191,
    590, 635
Ho Chi Minh, 34, 78, 224, 226, 304, 579
  Nixon's correspondence with, 281–
    282, 299, 309
Ho Chi Minh Trail, 44, 104, 207, 217,
    256, 257, 272, 280, 325, 335, 339,
    404, 419, 481, 507
Hoffa, James (Jimmy), 491–92
Hoff-Wilson, Joan, 490
homosexuality, 47, 127
Honecker, Erich, 464–65
Hong Kong, 44, 115
Hook, Sidney, 377
Hoover, Herbert, 114
Hoover, J. Edgar, 32, 75, 109, 122, 234–
    236, 361–62, 377, 425, 445, 503
  blackmail threatened by, 448–49
  death of, 543
  Huston Plan opposed by, 368

Hoover, J. Edgar (*cont.*)
  Nixon's problem with, 471–73
  wiretaps and, 235, 272–73, 361
Hope, Bob, 414–15, 476
House of Representatives, U.S., 55, 57, 205–6, 221, 311, 405, 455, 461
  Banking and Currency Committee of, 607, 610, 622
  Judiciary Committee of, 558
  1966 campaign and, 80, 99, 100
  1970 campaign and, 391, 396
  revenue sharing and, 433
  Rules Committee of, 587
  Ways and Means Committee of, 433
housing, integration of, 521–22
Housing and Urban Development Department, U.S. (HUD), 329
Hruska, Roman, 330
Hughes, Charles Evans, 470
Hughes, Howard, 18, 47, 123, 391, 421–423, 504, 561, 570
  "autobiographical" revelations of, 501–2
Hughes, James (Don), 429
Hughes, Richard J., 72, 74
Hughes Tool Company, 561
Hultman, Evan, 56
Hume, Brit, 503
Humphrey, Hubert H., 56, 90, 236, 242, 244, 253, 523, 609
  Agnew's criticism of, 191
  humor of, 204, 206
  in 1968 campaign, 149, 156, 157, 160, 164, 165, 172, 177, 181–86, 188, 191–214, 216–21, 235, 391
  in 1972 campaign, 522, 554, 579–80, 583, 586, 597
  Nixon compared with, 193
  Nixon criticized by, 184, 192, 193–94, 206
  Vietnam policy and, 194–99, 207–14, 216–17, 301–2, 426, 509
Humphreys, Robert, 30–31
Hungary:
  Nixon in, 23
  revolution in, 28, 65
Hunt, E. Howard, 449–50, 466
  CREEP and, 502, 543–44, 558, 561
  Watergate and, 543, 561–63, 566–69, 571, 573, 575, 576, 577, 606–8, 640
Hunt, H. L., 123
Hussein, King of Jordan, 384
Huston, Tom Charles, 90, 264, 265, 362
Huston Plan, 367–69

ICBMs, *see* intercontinental ballistic missiles

income tax, 18, 50, 290, 584
  negative, 124, 269, 294
  surcharge on, 134
India, 482–86
  Soviet relations with, 483–85
  U.S. relations with, 483–85
Indonesia, 78, 286
Indo-Pakistani War, 484–86
inflation, 134, 142, 225–26, 326–27, 392, 572, 584
  Nixon's views on, 87, 90, 458–59
intercontinental ballistic missiles (ICBMs), 134, 259, 276
  SALT and, 289, 441–42, 546
interest rates, 225, 572
Internal Revenue Service (IRS), 18, 172, 265, 455, 500, 561, 588, 611
International Debutante Ball, 58, 101
International Telephone and Telegraph (ITT), 435–36, 502–5
investment, 125, 458
Iran, U.S. relations with, 595–96
Iraq:
  Kurdish rebellion in, 595–96
  Soviet relations with, 596
Ireland, 334, 385
Irving, Clifford, 501, 504
Israel, 112–13, 596, 616
  Nixon's views on, 188, 251, 334–35
  Soviet Jews and, 479
  U.S. relations with, 188, 251, 384, 583
"Issues and Answers," 81, 98, 100
Issues Research Council, 66
Italy, 107, 378
ITT (International Telephone and Telegraph), 435–36, 502–5

Jackson, Henry, 236, 522, 523–24, 615–617, 662
Jackson amendment, 615–17
Japan, 428
  Nixon in, 44, 58, 68
  rearmament of, 115–16
  U.S. relations with, 314, 517
Javits, Jacob, 179, 604
Jaworski, Leon, 470
Jenkins, Walter, 47
Jews, 316, 334–35, 470
  Nixon's criticism of, 272–73, 296, 457
  Soviet, 479, 616, 617
  U.S., as voters, 583, 616
J.F.K.: The Man and the Myth (Lasky), 29
Job Development Credit, 458, 459
jobs, 125, 225, 432
John Birch Society, 53, 64, 75, 83
Johnson, Jim, 89
Johnson, Lady Bird, 67, 243, 245, 248, 283, 318

Johnson, Luci Bird, *see* Nugent, Luci
Johnson
Johnson, Lynda Bird, 67, 446
Johnson, Lyndon B., 16, 36, 90–99,
102–4, 108, 130, 157, 178, 243, 246,
378, 393, 478
Apollo program and, 283, 284
bombing halt ordered by, 196, 256,
494, 614, 629
in decision not to run, 149, 151
Great Society program of, 41–42, 61,
142
humor of, 204, 205
Manila meeting of, 92–93
memoirs of, 200, 423
in 1964 campaign, 39, 41–43, 47–51,
54, 57
in 1968 campaign, 90, 97, 102, 127–
28, 130, 141, 145, 149, 151, 157, 200
in 1972 campaign, 579, 580, 586, 608–
609
Nixon compared with, 78–79, 147,
248, 264, 266, 269, 534, 544, 655
Nixon criticized by, 92–93, 96–98,
200, 209–10
Nixon's correspondence with, 359–
360, 417
Nixon's criticism of, 41, 43, 47–50,
56, 62, 64, 68, 69, 75–76, 81, 85, 88,
91–93, 97–98, 136, 167–68, 614
Nixon's goading of, 90–92, 97
Nixon's honoring of, 283
Nixon's relationship with, 417
Nixon's respect for, 183–84, 205, 614
Nixon's visit to ranch of, 178
overselling techniques of, 78
Sentinel program of, 258–59
speeches of, 147, 149
Johnson, Samuel, 558
Johnson Administration, 172, 225
civil rights in, 41–42, 50, 55–56
foreign policy in, 41–44, 47–50, 54–
55, 61–62, 64, 188, 252, 253; *see
also* Vietnam War, in Johnson
Administration
Israel policy in, 188
school desegregation and, 187
wiretapping in, 208, 210, 214, 235–
236, 248, 423, 424, 608–9
Lyndon B. Johnson Library, 209, 215,
417
Joint Chiefs of Staff, U.S., 207, 257,
486–88
Cambodia policy and, 340–42, 347–
348
SALT and, 547
Jones, Stephen, 39
Jordan, 112–13
U.S. relations with, 384

Justice Department, U.S., 18, 29,
30, 275, 316–17, 364, 436, 611,
660
antiwar movement and, 265, 425
busing and, 460–61
Irving and, 501
ITT case and, 502–5
Pentagon Papers and, 447
Watergate and, 563, 569, 574, 576,
589, 602, 607, 622, 661

Kalb, Bernard, 490, 635
Kalb, Marvin, 299, 420, 490
Kalmbach, Herb, 573, 607, 640
Kansas State University, Nixon's lecture
at, 375–77
Kaplow, Herbert, 212–13, 259, 353
Karnow, Stanley, 447
Keating, Kenneth, 72
Kendall, Donald, 17–18, 25, 326, 378
Kennedy, Caroline, 416
Kennedy, David, 237, 292, 397
Kennedy, Edward (Ted), 218, 250, 258,
297–98, 300, 334, 541, 618
Chappaquiddick incident and, 283–
284
China policy and, 453, 480
in 1972 campaign, 541, 580, 583
Vietnam policy and, 297, 589–90
Kennedy, Jacqueline, *see* Onassis,
Jacqueline Kennedy
Kennedy, John, Jr., 416
Kennedy, John F., 13, 15, 18–21, 31–
38, 235, 243, 246, 378, 414, 498
Apollo program and, 283, 284
assassination of, 32–33, 36, 37, 38, 65
Connally and, 398
hostility toward, 31–32
in 1960 campaign, 15, 19, 20, 44, 84,
104, 127, 138, 204, 221
Nixon compared with, 24, 34, 36,
136, 171, 221, 327–28, 383, 408–9,
544
Nixon's criticism of, 12, 19–21, 23,
27, 28, 34, 49
Nixon's resentment of, 33–34
speeches of, 23
Kennedy, Robert F., 90–91, 414, 491
on academic freedom, 73
assassination of, 157
as Attorney General, 18, 29, 30, 502
in 1964 campaign, 33
in 1968 campaign, 145, 146, 149, 151,
155, 156, 157, 182, 185, 375
Nixon investigated by, 18, 29, 502,
588
Vietnam policy and, 106–7, 109, 141
Kennedy Administration, 36, 172
defense spending in, 34

Kennedy Administration (*cont.*)
  foreign policy in, 12, 18–21, 27, 30–
    31, 33–34, 36–37, 40, 49, 142, 252,
    253; *see also* Vietnam War, in
    Kennedy Administration
  political power abused in, 18, 28–29
  wiretapping in, 28–30, 33–34, 172,
    235
John F. Kennedy Center, 417
Kennedy-Krushchev agreement, 379–
  383
Kent State University, student deaths
  at, 350–51
Kessler, Ronald, 606
Key Biscayne, Nixon in, 226, 241, 242,
  269
Khrushchev, Nikita, 23, 24, 107, 464
  Cuba policy of, 12, 42, 379, 380
  memoirs of, 383
  Nixon and, 64, 544
Kihss, Peter, 26
Kilpatrick, James J., 121
Kim Il-Sung, 269
King, Coretta, 151
King, Martin Luther, Jr., 36, 77, 79, 109,
  172, 235, 331, 414
  assassination of, 150–51, 162–63
Kirk, Claude, 118
Kissinger, Henry A., 25, 231–34, 243,
  252
  back-channel messages of, 231, 427,
    441–42, 446–47, 464, 545
  Chile policy of, 378, 379
  China policy and, 253, 287, 446, 450–
    454, 479–80, 485–86, 512, 513, 517
  on Connally, 457
  Cuba policy and, 380–82
  Dobrynin and, 271–72, 382, 427,
    441–42, 446–47, 528, 531, 535, 541,
    617
  EC-121 incident and, 270–71
  Fallaci's interview with, 649
  foreign-policy ambitions of, 196
  Indo-Pakistani policy and, 482–86,
    488–89
  memoirs of, 232, 381, 451, 462, 513–
    514, 519, 627, 643
  mood swings of, 489–90
  Moscow summit and, 530–36, 541,
    544–48
  as National Security Adviser, 232–33,
    270–73, 280–82, 284, 297, 299, 306,
    324, 336, 339–43, 348, 350, 357–58,
    380–82, 387–89, 408, 410, 419–21,
    425–27, 441–44, 446–47, 450–54,
    462–65, 479–80, 482–91, 507–9,
    512, 513, 517, 519, 528–41, 592–96,
    601–2, 612–16, 627–35, 641–44,
    646, 650, 651, 654–56, 659, 660

1972 campaign and, 581, 650, 651
  Nixon compared with, 232–33, 447,
    490–91, 655
  Nixon criticized by, 270–71
  Nixon's correspondence with, 242,
    262, 334–35, 380, 400, 454, 519,
    532–33, 546–47, 632–33, 651
  Nixon's relationship with, 231–34,
    254–55, 357, 410, 411, 480, 488–91,
    533, 546–47, 625, 641, 644, 650,
    654
  paranoia of, 447
  Rogers's relationship with, 321, 357–
    358, 489, 508–9
  SALT and, 441–44, 446, 545–48
  secrecy of, 231, 233, 271, 387–88,
    408, 441–42, 446–47, 451
  Vietnam policy and, 196, 208, 256,
    258, 278, 280–82, 299, 306, 324,
    336, 339–43, 387–89, 408, 419–21,
    426–27, 462–63, 507–9, 528–29,
    531–32, 534–41, 550, 592–95, 612–
    614, 627–35, 641–44, 646, 656
  wiretapping ordered by, 425
Klein, Herb, 15, 99, 124, 159, 227–30,
  249–51, 255, 291, 297, 325, 362,
  363, 384, 460, 476, 501
  appointed director of
    communications, 230
  background of, 228–29
  memoirs of, 409
  in 1968 campaign, 138, 164
  Nixon's image and, 370–72
Klein, Marge, 255
Kleindienst, Richard, 169, 261, 330,
  436, 522, 604
  ITT case and, 503–4
  Watergate investigation and, 589,
    607–8
Kopechne, Mary Jo, 283
Korean War, 35, 69, 76, 94–95
  Vietnam War compared with, 198,
    224, 226, 238–39, 260, 324, 594–95
Korry, Edward, 378
Kosygin, Aleksei, 350, 385–86, 544, 545
Kraft, Joseph, 273, 644
Krause, Allison, 351
Krogh, Egil (Bud), 449, 465, 585
Ku Klux Klan, 53, 64
Kurdish rebellion, 595–96

labor, 584–85
  anti-Communism of, 479, 480
  Nixon's views on, 473–74, 624
La Casa Pacifica, 295, 371
Laird, Melvin, 196, 197
  Nixon's relationship with, 410
  as Secretary of Defense, 238, 257,
    258, 259, 269–70, 276, 277, 280–81,

299, 301, 307, 337, 340–41, 343, 349–51, 357–58, 410, 419–20, 487–488, 530, 538, 549, 592–93, 611
Lake, W. Anthony, 273
Lakeside Speech, 114
Lam Son Operation, 419–21, 428, 429
Lansdale, Edward, 447
Laos, 44, 76, 78, 104, 129, 147, 462, 594, 646
   Lam Son Operation in, 419–21, 428, 429
   North Vietnamese offensive in, 335–336, 507
   POWs in, 630
   U.S. bombing in, 242, 325, 344
LaRue, Fred, 102
Lasky, Victor, 29, 172, 251, 410
Latin America, Nixon in, 110–12
"Laugh-In," 202
law and order:
   in 1968 campaign, 125–26, 144–45, 154, 174, 182, 184, 187, 201
   in 1970 campaign, 373–77, 392, 394, 396
   in Nixon Administration, 260–65, 369–70
Lawrence, Bill, 100
Lawrence, David, 158
Leaders (Nixon), 24
leadership, 320
   new, Nixon's call for, 134, 135, 136, 153–54
League of Women Voters, 470
leaks, 301, 332, 399, 659
   Cambodian incursion and, 350, 351
   investigation of, see Plumbers operation
   Johnson's warning about, 242
   Nixon's obsession with, 249, 271, 272, 291, 350, 446, 449–50, 513
   of secret talks, 508–10
Lear, William, 84
Lebanon, Nixon in, 43
Le Duc Tho, 463, 507, 509, 528, 535, 592–93, 612–13, 614, 627–28, 643, 644, 656
LeMay, Curtis, 193–94
Lewis, Hobart, 66, 445, 476
Lewis, Ted, 489
Liddy, G. Gordon, 449, 466, 471, 504
   CREEP and, 502, 505, 543–44, 558, 561–62, 621
   Watergate and, 543, 561–63, 566–68, 570–71, 574–77, 588, 606–8, 621
Life, 82, 325, 501, 581
Lilley, Mildred, 469
Lincoln, Abraham, 36, 310, 581, 582
Lincoln Memorial, 355–57
Lindsay, John, 158, 169, 174, 179, 352

Linkletter, Art, 445
Lippmann, Walter, 77, 251
Lisagor, Peter, 443
Loan, Nguyen Ngoc, 134–35
Lodge, Henry Cabot, Jr., 43, 172
   in election of 1964, 40, 41, 46–47
Lon Nol, 336–37, 339–41, 344–45, 360, 399, 463
Los Angeles Times, 336, 421, 621
Love, John, 179
Luce, Clare Boothe, 241
Lukas, J. Anthony, 466

MacArthur, Douglas, 43, 44, 69
McCain, James, 377
McCarthy, Eugene, 335–36, 643, 645
   in 1968 campaign, 141, 145, 155–56, 157, 160, 164, 165, 181, 182, 185, 197
McCarthy, Joseph, 414, 426
McClendon, Sarah, 597
McCloskey, Paul, 415, 497
McCloy, John, 386, 444
McCord, James, 558, 574, 576, 577, 607
McCracken, Paul, 238, 434, 460
McGee, Gale, 391
McGinniss, Joe, 14
McGovern, George, 315, 358, 414, 426, 459, 469, 477, 509, 523, 565
   in 1968 campaign, 165–66, 181, 182
   in 1972 campaign, 496, 522, 541–44, 552–57, 561, 571, 572, 578–88, 591, 592, 593, 599, 600–601, 604–6, 608, 618, 620–21, 622, 624, 625, 628, 630, 635–38, 640, 646–48, 651
   Vietnam policy and, 506–7, 509, 540, 542, 553, 571, 578, 628, 645
McGovern-Hatfield amendment, 358, 387, 391, 509
McGraw-Hill Book Company, 501
MacGregor, Clark, 421, 467, 478, 557, 609
   CREEP and, 570, 608, 621, 640
McGregory, Mary, 261, 645
McLaren, Richard, 436
McNamara, Robert, 68, 88, 134, 203, 224, 508
MacNeil, Robert, 455
MacPherson, Myra, 246, 247
McWhorter, Charles, 25, 56, 66, 84
Maddox, Lester, 89, 164
Madman Theory, 224, 256, 258
Magruder, Jeb Stuart, 298, 311, 326, 346, 395, 504
   CREEP and, 502, 505, 558
   Watergate and, 558, 561, 562, 569, 571, 575, 576, 588, 607, 621, 661
Maheu, Robert, 421–22, 501
Mahoney, George, 89

Mai Van Bo, 282
Making of the President, 1960, The (White), 21
Malaysia, 115
Malek, Frederick, 457, 570
Manila Communiqué, 93–94, 96, 100, 275
Mann, Jim, 606
Manning, Elizabeth, 605
Mansfield, Mike, 109, 299, 307, 336, 350, 444, 454, 509
Mansfield amendment, 444
Manson, Charles, 369–70
Mao Tse-tung, 400, 454, 580
  Nixon's meeting with, 512–15
Marble Collegiate Church, 240
Marcos, Bong Bong, 286
Marcos, Ferdinand, 286
Mardian, Robert, 448
marijuana, 71, 87, 418
Marshall, John, 470
Marshall, Thurgood, 103
Martin, Laurence, 549
Marx, Louis, 448
Maryland, primary in, 541–42
Mathias, Charles, 302
Mayo, Robert, 292
Mazo, Earl, 251, 298, 410
Mazurov, Kirill, 225
Meany, George, 316, 459, 500, 585, 624
  Nixon's problems with, 473–76, 480
Meany, Mrs. George, 585
"Meet the Press," 69, 212–13, 306–7
Meir, Golda, 384, 583
mergers and takeovers, 436
Merriam, Robert, 66, 83, 84
Mesta, Perle, 618
Meyer, Lawrence, 606
Miami:
  Democratic Convention in (1972), 554, 555, 578, 579–80, 599
  Republican Convention in (1968), 169–70, 172–77
  Republican Convention in (1972), 436, 502, 503, 588, 599–601
Miami *Herald*, 169
Michigan, primary in, 541
Middle East:
  Arab-Israeli conflict in, 112–13, 188, 251, 334–35, 383–84
  see also specific countries
Middleton, Drew, 172
Midway Island, 277–78
Milbank, Jerry, 102
milk price supports, 434–35
Miller, William E., 52
Mills, Wilbur, 433, 478
Milwaukee *Journal*, 461

MIRVs, *see* multiple independently targeted reentry vehicles
missile gap, 202, 203, 615
missiles:
  Cuban missile crisis, 12, 18–21, 49, 379
  ICBMs, *see* intercontinental ballistic missiles
  see also ABM system
Mississippi, race relations in, 89
Mississippi, University of, 74
Mississippi Freedom Democratic Party, 36, 235
Mitchell, John, 457, 517, 529, 538, 625
  as Attorney General, 238, 246, 270, 272–75, 280–81, 297, 330, 342, 343, 365, 374, 379, 410, 425, 455, 468, 469, 432, 611
  background of, 123
  Chennault and, 208
  Gemstone and, 502, 505
  Kissinger's approach to, 196
  news conference of, 261
  in 1968 campaign, 123–24, 133, 150, 158, 162–63, 167, 169, 172–75, 179, 196, 219
  in 1970 campaign, 374–75
  in 1972 campaign, 497, 502, 503, 505, 554, 558, 570, 586
  Nixon's loyalty to, 228
  Nixon's trust in, 238, 410, 570
  resignations of, 497, 570, 575
  Supreme Court appointments and, 330, 468–70
  Watergate and, 558, 562, 565, 571, 575, 576, 577, 606, 621
  wiretaps and, 272, 273
Mitchell, Martha, 570–71, 580
Moley, Raymond, 39
Monde, Le (Paris), 454
Moonglow, 285–87
Moore, Richard, 470
Moorer, Thomas, 419–20, 485, 487–88, 490
Moratorium, 299–300, 302–6
Morse, Wayne, 55
Morton, Rogers, 174
Moscow summit (1972), 478–79, 484, 485, 489, 525–26, 530–37, 541, 544–50
  arms control and, 478–79, 526, 532, 545–50
  Kissinger and, 530–36, 541, 544–48
  Nixon's instructions for, 531–32
  Nixon's visit and, 544–48
Moscow University, 64–65
Moyers, Bill, 94, 97
Moynihan, Daniel Patrick, 124, 243, 244, 351, 457

Family Security System and, 269, 291
farewell address of, 402–3
in Nixon cabinet, 236–37, 249, 268–
269, 291, 294, 331–32, 366, 402–3
Nixon's correspondence with,
413, 425, 521
resignation offer of, 331–32
on revenue sharing, 398
Moynihan, Mrs. Daniel Patrick, 351
Mudge, Stern, Baldwin, and Todd, 17–
18, 21, 24–27
multiple independently targeted
reentry vehicles (MIRVs), 276–77
SALT and, 288–90, 313, 441, 443, 546
Mundt, Karl, 29, 30, 264
Munich Olympics, 616
Murchison, John, 534
Murphy, George, 394
Muskie, Edmund S., 243, 290, 396, 413,
425, 453, 461, 477
in 1968 campaign, 201, 202, 218
in 1972 campaign, 496, 499, 500, 507,
522, 541, 562, 583
Vietnam policy and, 510–11
Muskie, Mrs. Edmund S., 500, 522
mutual and balanced force reductions
(MBFR), 596
My Lai massacre, 312–13, 428–29

NAACP (National Association for the
Advancement of Colored People),
32, 523, 587
Nader, Ralph, 414, 445
Nasser, Gamal Abdel, 23, 334, 383, 384
National Alliance of Postal and Federal
Employees, 374
National Archives, 558–59
National Association of Manufacturers,
Nixon's speech to, 126
National Command Authorities (NCAs),
441
National Commission on Obscenity and
Pornography, 393
National Conference of Christians and
Jews, Nixon's speech to, 46
National Council of Reconciliation, 627,
629, 631, 632, 633, 634, 644, 645,
646, 656
National Education Association (NEA),
556
National Guard, 350, 352
Nationalist China, see Taiwan
National League of Families of
American Prisoners and Missing in
Southeast Asia, Nixon's speech to,
630
National Liberation Front (NLF), 169,
195, 216, 241
National Review, 61, 444, 631–32

National Security Council (NSC), 232,
253, 281, 340–41, 382, 488, 489
student rebellion and, 262, 264
National Student Association, 352–53
National Welfare Rights Organization,
315
NATO (North Atlantic Treaty
Organization), 28, 35, 88, 107, 191,
254
Navy, U.S., 269–71, 485, 488
Nazi Germany, 34, 35, 77
NBC-TV, 240, 249, 290–91, 320, 453,
511
Nebraska, primaries in, 41, 45–47, 121,
541
"Needed in Vietnam" (Nixon), 48–49
"negotiations, new era of," 225, 313
Nelson, Jack, 621
"New Alignment for American Unity,
A" (Nixon), 154–55
New American Revolution, 580, 593,
657, 662
New Hampshire:
Nixon's letter to, 133–34
primaries in, 40–41, 105, 121, 133,
135–37, 139–41, 145, 497, 498,
508
New Left, 71–75, 165, 181
in 1972 campaign, 579–80
Newlin, Melvin, 256
Newlin, Mr. and Mrs. Joseph, 256
Newman, Ralph, 266
"New Nixon, The" (Reston), 86–87
New Republic, 249, 470
news media, 283, 297
China trip and, 512, 514
Cuban Missile Crisis and, 19
Eisenhower's views on, 229
guilt of, 13
Nixon's criticism of, 12–13, 229, 310–
311, 325–26, 538
Nixon's image problem and, 138–40,
248–51, 370–72
Nixon's need for, 17
Nixon's obsession with, 248–51, 411,
412, 572, 659
Nixon's positive coverage by, 21, 22
Watergate story ignored by, 573, 577,
589, 621–22
News Summary, 248–53, 261, 262, 276–
277, 280, 285, 293, 325, 331, 373–
375, 391, 394, 433, 455, 460, 474,
475, 489, 549, 571, 638, 648, 650
censorship of, 411
Nixon's personality revealed in, 409–
412
Vietnam War in, 271, 291, 300, 403,
421, 429, 590, 643
Watergate in, 565, 621

Newsweek, 39, 248, 250, 293, 301, 325, 421, 577n–78n, 581, 594, 634
Newton, Isaac, 363
New York City:
  Nixon household in, 21–22
  Nixon's decision to live in, 16–18, 22
  Nixon supporters in, 25, 352, 359
  Nixon's views on, 16, 17, 26, 62
New York *Daily News,* 489
New Yorker, 518
New York *Post,* 636
New York Stock Exchange, 459
New York Times, 21, 25, 26, 62, 69, 74, 85–86, 88, 93–94, 96, 99, 100, 122, 130, 134, 193, 250, 260, 272, 284, 288, 294, 302, 310, 316, 320, 325, 332, 335, 341, 344, 350, 351, 360, 382, 446, 461, 479, 502, 508, 512, 535, 536–37, 542, 573–74, 617, 621, 624, 638, 639, 640, 647
New Zealand, 115
Ngo Dinh Diem, *see* Diem, Ngo Dinh
Nguyen Van Thieu, *see* Thieu, Nguyen Van
Nixon, Donald (brother), 18, 47, 172, 273, 422, 501–2
Nixon, Frank (father), 128
Nixon, Hannah (mother), 356, 502
  death of, 128
Nixon, Harold (brother), 128
Nixon, Julie, *see* Eisenhower, Julie Nixon
Nixon, Mudge, Rose, Guthrie, and Alexander, 38, 56, 63, 82
Nixon, Pat (Thelma Catherine) Ryan (wife), 13, 16, 17, 101, 242, 519–20
  Asian travels of, 285, 286, 519
  background of, 291
  in China, 519
  daughters' weddings and, 240, 241, 445–46
  European travel of, 22, 385
  house decorating of, 294–95
  humor of, 519, 597
  husband advised by, 416, 469
  at inauguration, 243–45
  as "Miss Ryan," 63
  mistake of, 619
  in New York City, 21, 26, 62–63, 491
  in 1968 campaign, 132, 152–53, 170, 182, 218–20
  in 1972 campaign, 556, 585, 596–98, 618–20
  politics disliked by, 17, 26, 63, 111
  press criticism of, 248, 318–19, 333
  Supreme Court appointments and, 416, 469
  volunteerism of, 318–19, 333

  in White House, 247, 248, 317–19, 332, 416, 445
Nixon, Richard Milhous:
  acting ability of, 560
  African travels of, 112–13
  aides' loyalty to, 227–28
  anger of, 409–10, 411, 516–17, 527–528, 543, 572–73, 588, 635–36, 642, 660, 662
  anti-Communism of, 12, 18, 20, 23, 28, 30, 41, 43–44, 48–50, 55, 61, 73–74, 81–82, 94–95, 171
  antiwar movement opposed by, 70–75, 85, 109, 261–65, 299–300, 302–306
  anxiety of, 239, 413
  appearance of, 14, 59, 86–87
  Asian travels of, 43–44, 68–69, 85, 107–10, 285–87
  assessment of first term of, 653–62
  awkwardness of, 255, 285
  bid for greatness of, 405–6
  book contract of, 21, 32, 33
  business-world friends of, 14, 15, 17–18, 25, 110–11
  campaign strategy and tactics of, 133–141, 151, 155, 179–81, 186, 190–91, 221–22, 392–96, 604
  campaign style of, 15, 32, 56–57, 136–37
  canvassing technique of, 258
  career opportunities of, 16
  as centrist Republican, 15, 45, 61
  contemplative style of, 14, 82
  contradictions of, 618
  cynicism of, 13, 89, 124, 215, 264, 411, 416, 491
  dancing of, 241, 445–46
  debating of, 107, 127–28, 138, 184, 192–93, 206
  depressions of, 131, 529, 531, 601, 654
  diary of, 487, 503, 504, 529, 530, 535, 538, 544, 566, 570, 574, 575, 581–584, 597–98, 612, 618, 623, 631, 633, 641, 646
  distrustfulness of, 232, 233, 513, 516–517, 625, 642
  doubts of, 131–32
  drinking of, 84–85, 342, 533
  driving of, 226
  emotional changes of, 481–82
  enemies of, 25, 172, 624, 660
  European travels of, 22–24, 27–28, 51–52, 64–65, 85, 106–8, 254–55, 384–85
  on "fast track," 16–17, 24–28, 59, 62, 121
  firings by, 409–10, 472, 517, 652

first term of, 246–662
foreign policy briefings of, 230, 241–242
foreign press conferences of, 23, 24, 27–28, 43, 52, 69, 85, 109, 112, 113
frankness and candor of, 121–22, 135
gossip enjoyed by, 447–48
grace of, 255–56
as hard worker, 13, 24–25, 100, 122, 243, 307
health of, 14, 138, 597
heckling, demonstrations, and pickets opposed by, 32, 90, 185–86, 303, 334, 376, 395, 437–38
heroes of, 26, 322–23
as his own Secretary of State, 230, 232
image problem of, 138
imagination of, 412, 518
impeachment call and, 415
inauguration of, 243–45
intelligence of, 96, 163, 232, 412, 518
investments of, 110, 227, 561
jokes of, 87, 130, 190, 204–5, 255, 285, 320
lack of administrative experience of, 15
lack of privacy of, 317
last press conference of, 11–13, 15, 19, 28, 135, 138
Latin American travels of, 110–12
as lawyer, 16, 17–18, 21, 24–27, 38–39, 82, 457
liberalism attributed to, 405, 407
as loner, 410–11
loser image of, 15, 28, 104, 135, 138
lying of, 213–14, 336, 344, 367, 576, 602–3
madman image of, 224, 256, 258, 592
mail's importance to, 415
as man of substance, 113–17
as master politician, 122
memoirs of, 28, 32, 110, 166, 207, 209, 229, 232, 254, 278, 368–69, 383, 421, 424, 451, 465, 480, 508, 513–514, 560, 618, 643
midterm assessment of (1969–1970), 402–12
mood changes of, 108
in 1960 campaign, 15, 19, 44, 84, 104, 127, 137–38, 150–51, 171–72, 179–180, 221, 379
in 1962 campaign, 11–13, 15, 104, 379
in 1964 campaign, 13, 20, 23, 27, 28, 31, 33, 39–58, 84, 379
in 1966 campaign, 80–101
in 1968 campaign, 11–12, 61, 65, 69, 78, 89, 90, 97, 100, 102–222

in 1970 campaign, 390–97
in 1972 campaign, 391, 431, 440–41, 482, 493–512, 552–88, 654
obsessions of, 248–51
outstanding speaking qualities of, 138–39
overexposure feared by, 137
patriotism of, 73, 90, 342, 348–49, 486, 499
personal papers of, 266, 558–59
political assets of, 13, 14–15, 59–60, 120, 122
political favors owed to, 15, 60
political liabilities of, 15, 59, 104
in political polls, 27, 39, 45, 120, 141, 160, 162, 172, 177, 183, 193, 294, 311, 359, 413, 453, 496, 507, 511–512, 532, 591, 601
post-crisis behavior of, 14
power motive of, 13, 17, 513
pragmatism of, 171, 498–99
as President-elect, 223–42
Presidential news conferences of, 252, 253, 254, 257–58, 270–71, 300, 353–54, 369, 389–90, 399–401, 426–27, 429, 430, 437–38, 450, 454, 463–64, 467–68, 480–81, 504–5, 511, 549–50, 567, 571, 590, 591, 602–3, 614, 620–23
public's distrust of, 130, 367, 495–96
as Quaker, 355, 472
reading of, 26, 227
relaxation of, 227, 295, 410–11, 618
revenge seeking of, 19–20, 588, 611
as "Richard the Chicken-hearted," 184, 192–93, 206
risk taking of, 13, 90, 105, 126–27, 182, 254, 653
salary and finances of, 11, 16, 17, 59, 174, 227, 240, 294
secrecy of, 231, 233, 242, 258, 271, 281, 291, 300, 320–21, 350, 387–88, 408, 446–47, 451
"secret fund" of, 174
self-confidence of, 136, 166, 219, 232, 253
self-delusion of, 411–12
sensitivity of, 109, 403
shyness of, 232, 472
sincerity of, 95–96, 136–37, 213
Southern Strategy of, 330–31
speeches of, 19–21, 27, 39, 40, 46, 56–57, 65, 81, 82–83, 87–88, 98–99, 113–14, 126, 133, 136–37, 138, 142–43, 146–47, 154–55, 166–67, 171, 175–76, 187–88, 242–44, 262–264, 267–68, 276–77, 282, 293–94, 304–11, 327–28, 343–46, 375–77, 388–89, 394–96, 417, 418–19, 432,

Nixon, Richard Milhouse (*cont.*)
  458–59, 507–10, 523, 533, 539–40,
  600–1, 617–18, 629–30, 645–46,
  648, 649–50
 sports interest of, 25, 227, 242
 State of the Union addresses of, 327–
  328, 432
 stoning of, 394–95
 tax audit of, 18
 as toastmaster, 109, 255, 363, 517
 tough talking of, 342, 384, 407, 518,
  611
 travel style of, 371
 as Tricky Dick, 121, 365, 455, 477
 as Vice-President, 15, 17, 22, 87, 98,
  159, 162, 171, 232, 239, 266, 326,
  473, 501
 vice-presidential choices considered
  by, 157–58
 vindictiveness of, 172, 271
 vulnerability of, 387
 Watergate and, 271, 558–71, 573–77,
  588–89, 606–10, 621–23, 638–41,
  646, 661–62
 writing of articles by, 21, 28, 48–50,
  68, 77–78, 113, 115–16, 125, 232,
  453, 494
Nixon Administration:
 antiwar movement in, 245, 256, 261–
  265, 281, 299–306, 312–13, 333,
  343–44, 350–53, 355–57, 369, 374,
  392–95, 414–15, 437–38
 budgets in, 327, 431–34
 defense spending in, 259, 290, 327,
  433
 law and order in, 260–65, 369–70
 police-state charges against, 425–26
 wiretapping in, 235, 272–74, 350,
  361, 423–26, 434, 448–49, 559–60,
  564, 658, 660
"Nixon Big Charge," 342
Nixon Doctrine, 287, 309, 319, 400, 497
Nixon for President Committee, 123–24
Nixonomics, 392
"Nixon's the One," 141, 164, 181
Nofziger, Franklin (Lyn), 298
North American Newspaper Alliance,
  68
North Korea:
 U.S. reconnaissance aircraft shot
  down by, 269–71
North Vietnam, 54–55, 452
 in Cambodia, 339–41, 360–61, 399
 Laotian offensive of, 335–36
 Nixon's views on, 44, 45, 49, 61, 68–
  69, 76, 88, 198
 Paris peace talks and, 154, 166, 168–
  169, 195, 206–7, 241, 271, 288, 463,
  627–30

 proposal for declaration of war
  against, 76–77
 spring offensive of (1972), 526–30,
  532, 533, 536
 two-party peace talks and, 271–72,
  275, 282, 309, 387–89, 507–10, 528,
  535, 592–93, 612–13, 614, 627–28
 U.S. bombing of, 43–44, 49, 61, 62,
  68, 77, 88, 91–92, 103, 104, 106–7,
  149, 166, 178, 182, 194, 206–7, 241,
  257, 282, 299, 349–50, 404, 426,
  481, 493–94, 505, 550, 612, 628,
  629, 632, 634
North Vietnamese Army (NVA), 141,
  147, 256, 257, 275, 282, 324, 387–
  389, 399, 505–7, 539, 550, 589–90,
  592, 594, 635, 655–56
 Cambodia incursion and, 339, 341,
  347, 354, 507
 in Laos, 419–20, 507
 in peace agreement, 627, 630, 631,
  633, 634, 644
 in spring offensive (1972), 527–30,
  532, 533, 602, 654
Novak, Robert, 301
Nuclear Nonproliferation Treaty, 313–
  314
nuclear test ban treaty, 23, 50
nuclear weapons, 202, 252
 of China, 81
 control of, *see* arms control; SALT;
  SALT I; SALT II
 first-strike capability and, 253
 Kissinger's views on, 270
 Nixon's views on, 48, 95, 203, 253,
  430
 of Soviet Union, 134, 224, 289, 439
 U.S. superiority in, 203, 288–89,
  439
 Vietnam War and, 193, 223, 282
Nugent, Luci Johnson, 67, 240
NVA, *see* North Vietnamese Army

O'Brien, Larry, 198, 218, 402, 421–23,
  446, 450
 Gemstone and, 502, 505
 Maheu and, 421–22, 501, 504
 in 1972 campaign, 500, 544, 558, 561–
  562, 611, 636
 Nixon criticized by, 391–92, 395, 396,
  429
 Nixon's fear of and anger at, 502–5,
  561
 public election funds and, 477
 tax audit of, 588
 Watergate and, 544, 558, 561–62, 567,
  571, 573, 607, 661
O'Donnell, Peter, 102
Office of Economic Opportunity, 249

Office of Management and Budget (OMB), 328
oil companies, Vietnam War and, 444
Oishi, Gene, 191–92
Okinawa, 314
Oliver, R. Spencer, 544, 609
Onassis, Jacqueline Kennedy, 33, 248, 318, 416
Onganía, Juan Carlos, 112
Operation Candor, 121–22
Operation Enhance Plus, 631, 645
Opponents List, 409
Oregon, primaries in, 41, 45, 46, 47, 105, 121, 146, 153–56
Osborne, John, 249
Ostpolitik, 385–86, 464–65
Ostrow, Ronald, 621
Oswald, Lee Harvey, 31n, 37
Otepka, Otto F., 29–30, 172, 446
Overseas Press Club, Nixon's speech to, 91

Paar, Jack, 18
Pacific Charter, proposed, 92
Packard, David, 249
Pakistan, 286, 427, 450, 482–85, 488
Palestinians, 383
Panama, 42
Parade, 362, 480
Paris Air Show, 433
Paris peace talks, 154, 166–69, 194–98, 206–17, 241, 288, 388, 463, 627–30
controversy and, 241
Nixon's undercutting of, 271–72
parity concept, 203, 253, 430, 526, 545
Parrot's Beak, 341–45, 347–48
Patman, Wright, 607, 610, 622
patriotism, 70, 71
of Nixon, 73, 90, 342, 348–49, 486, 499
Patton, 337, 343
Patton, George S., Jr., 322–23, 337, 346
Peace Corps, 606
peace movement, see antiwar movement
" 'Peace' Movement and November 15, The" (Chapin), 305–6
Peale, Norman Vincent, 25, 240, 247, 445, 491
Pearson, Drew, 127, 588
Pentagon Papers, 446–48, 455, 465, 535, 658
Pepsi-Cola, 17–18, 43, 68
Percy, Charles, 99, 302, 617
in 1968 campaign, 104, 105, 121, 158, 161, 167, 179
Peru, Nixon in, 112
Philadelphia Inquirer, 280
Philadelphia Plan, 474

Philippines, 34, 78, 115, 286
Phillips, McCandlish, 56, 57–58
Phouma, Souvanna, 335, 463
Plumbers operation, 449, 465–66, 471, 487, 489, 502, 577, 660–61
Supreme Court appointments and, 468, 469
Podgorny, Nikolai, 544, 545, 550
Poff, Richard, 468–69
Poland, 106, 386
police, 125, 181, 182, 183, 186, 261, 366, 600
police states, Nixon's views on, 425–26
"Politicians and the People, The" (Broder), 495–96
politics, politicians:
lying of, 214
1968 as low in, 217–18
soldiers compared with, 322–23
see also specific politicians
pornography, 393, 394
Porter, William, 270
Portland Oregonian, 324
Potter, Phil, 354
poverty, 187, 291, 326–27, 332, 373
crime and, 154, 202, 373
War on, 41, 55–56, 86, 268
see also welfare system
Powell, Lewis, 470–71, 563
Pravda, 65
Presidential Records and Materials Preservation Act (1974), 558–59
President's Advisory Council on Executive Organization, 398
President's National Advisory Commission on Civil Disorders, 144
"preventive detention," 261
Price, Raymond, 115, 236, 243, 244, 267, 297, 357, 410, 415–16, 476
Asian travels of, 108–9
background of, 106
in 1968 campaign, 106, 108–9, 146–147, 151, 153, 167, 170
in 1972 campaign, 555, 581–82, 597, 598
Nixon criticized by, 397
Nixon's mail and, 415
price freezes, 458–59, 657
price supports, 434–35
Priscilla of Boston, 240
prisoners of war (POWs), 429, 462, 463, 480, 481, 494, 495, 505–7, 511, 539, 602, 656
Cooper amendment and, 590–91
McGovern's charges about, 506–7, 509
peace agreement and, 627, 628, 630, 634, 643, 646

"Profile of Pat" (Smith), 318–19
property taxes, 432–33, 600
Prouty, Winston, 392
Provisional Revolutionary Government
  (PRG), 592, 594, 613, 629, 631,
  644
Proxmire, William, 397, 643
public opinion, U.S.:
  Eastern Europe and, 28
  Vietnam War and, 257–58, 359, 421,
    511–12
  see also antiwar movement; Gallup
    polls; Harris polls

Quemoy-Matsu question, 427–28

racism:
  in Army, 418
  Carswell accused of, 337
  in 1972 campaign, 500, 522
  Nixon campaign charged with, 164,
    165
  see also segregation
Radford, Charles, 486–90
Rapoport, Dan, 212
Rather, Dan, 248, 493–95, 507, 624,
  634–35
Reader's Digest, 28, 48–50, 77–78, 125,
  476
Reagan, Ronald, 57, 351, 460
  campus radicals criticized by, 119–20
  in 1966 campaign, 80, 83, 99, 100, 119
  in 1968 campaign, 104, 118–21, 127,
    153, 155, 157, 162, 167, 169, 170,
    173, 179
  in 1970 campaign, 394, 396
  in 1972 campaign, 405, 600, 604
  popularity of, 119
Real Majority, The (Scammon and
  Wattenberg), 374
Rebozo, Bebe, 14, 110–12, 226–27, 241,
  341–42, 445, 455, 561, 625
  Cuba policy and, 379–80
  fundraising of, 391, 501
  Hughes and, 422–23, 501, 502
  make-believe graduation and, 362
  Nixon's friendship with, 226, 232,
    410–11, 532, 533
  Watergate and, 565–66, 570
Rehnquist, William, 261, 470–71, 563
Reid, Mrs. Ogden, 25
Reinhard, David, 61
religion, Nixon's views on, 476
"Report from Saigon," 324
Republican National Committee (RNC),
  45, 56, 60–61
  1966 campaign and, 83–84, 90, 98
Republican National Convention:
  of 1964, 52–54
  of 1968, 169–70, 172–77
  of 1972, 436, 502, 503, 588, 599–601
Republicans, Republican Party, 349,
  459
  conservative, Nixon supported by,
    60–62
  Democrats compared with, 30, 88,
    164, 243, 246, 599
  Johnson's criticism of, 92–93
  liberal, ABM opposed by, 289–90
  liberal, Agnew opposed by, 174–75
  news media's relations with, 12–13
  in 1964 campaign, 13, 20, 22, 23, 27,
    28, 31, 33, 39–58, 84, 202, 379
  in 1965 campaign, 72–74
  in 1966 campaign, 80–101
  in 1968 campaign, 11–12, 61, 65–69,
    78, 89, 90, 97, 100, 102–222
  in 1970 campaign, 390–97
  in 1972 campaign, 242, 391, 431, 440–
    441, 476–77, 482, 493–512, 552–
    654
  Nixon as 1968 choice of, 11–12
  Nixon as spokesman of, 15, 18, 62, 86
  Nixon as unifier of, 52, 53, 86, 90, 179
  nuclear test ban treaty and, 23
  preparation for revival of (1965), 59–
    79
  on Senate Internal Security Sub-
    committee, 29, 30
  southern, 89–90, 118, 121, 155
Republican Volunteer Women, 415
Republican Women for Nixon, 207–8
resentment, politics of, 165, 178
Reston, James, 41, 86–89, 229, 310, 443,
  510, 598, 641–42, 644
  on 1968 campaign, 113, 130–31, 178
  on 1970 campaign, 373
revenue sharing, 297, 398–99, 404, 413,
  432–33, 458, 657
Rhee, Syngman, 594
Rhodes, James, 158, 161, 179
Richardson, Elliot:
  in 1972 campaign, 497, 499, 604
  as Secretary of Health, Education and
    Welfare, 365, 553
Richey, Charles, 606, 607, 622, 648
right-wing extremists, see Far Right
Ringle, Ken, 619
riots, race, 55, 68, 103, 125, 144–45, 163
Rizzo, Frank, 585
Robb, Chuck, 446
Roberts, Chalmers, 443
Roche, John, 410
Rochester, University of, 82–83
Rockefeller, Happy, 50
Rockefeller, Mary Clark, 22
Rockefeller, Nelson, 15, 22, 72, 87, 238,
  396

Kissinger and, 232, 233
New York as base of, 16, 17, 25
in 1964 campaign, 20, 22, 27, 28, 31,
  39, 41, 44–47, 50, 53, 54, 57, 95
in 1966 campaign, 80
in 1968 campaign, 89, 104, 105, 118,
  120, 135, 141, 145–46, 153, 155,
  157, 160, 162, 164, 165, 169, 170,
  179, 220
in 1972 campaign, 498, 600, 604
Nixon's correspondence with, 99
Rockefeller, Winthrop, 99
Roe v. *Wade*, 658–59
Rogers, William, 11, 25, 585
China trip and, 512, 513, 516–17
Kissinger's relationship with, 321,
  357–58, 489, 508–9
Moscow summit and, 531
Nixon's correspondence with, 312
Nixon's relationship with, 410
as Secretary of State, 233–34, 257,
  258, 269–70, 276, 301, 307, 336–37,
  340–41, 343, 349–51, 357–58, 382,
  410, 419–20, 426, 454, 490, 512,
  513, 516, 531, 538, 611, 628
"Role of Women in the Administration,
  The" (Finch), 416
Romania:
China and, 288, 427
Nixon in, 107–8, 287–88
Romney, George, 22, 27, 51, 72, 89, 237,
  329
in 1966 campaign, 80, 99, 100
in 1968 campaign, 89, 104, 105, 118,
  120, 127, 135, 137, 141, 157, 158,
  167, 174–75, 179
in 1970 campaign, 393–94
Roosevelt, Elliott, 618
Roosevelt, Franklin D., 408, 544, 651
Roosevelt, James, 618
Roosevelt, Theodore, 26, 151, 406
"Rose Mary's Baby," 478
Rostov, Walt W., 29, 49, 78, 166, 230,
  311–12, 446
Royster, Vermont, 410
Rubin, Jerry, 334
Ruby, Jack, 37
Ruckelshaus, William, 261, 553, 604
Rugaber, Walter, 589, 647
Rusher, William, 61
Rusk, Dean, 157, 166
Vietnam policy and, 78, 79, 88, 230
Rutgers University, 72–74
Ruwe, Nick, 56

Sadat, Anwar al-, 595, 616
Safeguard, 259, 260, 441
Safire, William, 66, 68, 74, 94, 97, 250,
  251, 456, 460

on Connally, 457
economics memorandums of, 296–97
at Moscow summit, 547, 548
in 1968 campaign, 102, 105, 138, 142,
  146–47, 150, 153, 179–80, 193, 220,
  221
in 1970 campaign, 394, 395
in 1972 campaign, 497, 499, 636
Nixon's relationship with, 67, 410
as Nixon speechwriter, 11, 67, 193,
  220, 297, 304, 388–89, 507–8, 636
Vietnam policy and, 388–90, 507–8,
  510
wiretap of, 273
Sainteny, Jean, 282
St. Louis *Post-Dispatch*, 250
Salisbury, Harrison, 94, 186–87, 191,
  443
SALT (Strategic Arms Limitation
  Talks), 225, 252, 288–90, 350, 404,
  413, 430, 446, 596
détente and, 441–44
Moscow summit and, 478–79, 526,
  532, 545–50
opening of, 313, 320
SALT I, 546–50, 615–17, 654
interim agreement and, 550, 615, 616
SALT II, 548, 654, 655
Sanchez, Fina, 22, 132, 241
Sanchez, Manolo, 22, 132, 241, 355, 356
San Francisco, Republican Convention
  in (1964), 52–54
Satellite reconnaissance, 452–53
Sato, Eisaku, 314
Saturday Evening Post, 21, 28, 68,
  605
Saxbe, William, 289–90, 337, 604
Scali, John, 443
Scammon, Richard, 293, 364, 542
Scanlan's Monthly, 374
Schmitz, John, 454
Scott, George C., 323
Scott, Hugh, 53, 445, 580, 604, 605
Scranton, William, 72, 179
in 1964 campaign, 41, 51, 52
Sears, John, 100, 153, 273
Seaton, Fred, 39, 41, 45–46, 83, 105,
  106
Secret Service, 186, 226, 245, 273, 317,
  334, 338, 355, 362, 423, 569
security gap, Nixon's charges of, 203
Seelye, Gloria, 520
segregation, 89, 274, 316, 330, 331, 349,
  364
Segretti, Donald, 461, 477, 500, 639,
  640
Selling of the President 1968, The
  (McGinniss), 140
Semple, Robert, 126–27, 320, 393

Senate, U.S., 55, 57, 221, 311, 388, 461, 477, 617
  ABM and, 276, 288–90
  Armed Services Committee of, 358, 549
  Cooper amendment and, 590–91
  Finance Committee of, 366, 391
  Foreign Relations Committee of, 254, 299, 338–39, 358–59, 367, 426–27
  Haynsworth rejected by, 315, 316, 337–38
  Internal Security Subcommittee of, 29–30
  Judiciary Committee of, 503–4
  1966 campaign and, 99, 100
  1970 campaign and, 391, 396
  Nixon testimony to, 40
  Select Committee of, 558
  SST opposed by, 397–98, 413, 433
  Supreme Court appointments and, 199, 296, 315, 330, 337–38, 468, 469
  treaty ratification and, 18–19, 314, 380, 615
"Send Them a Message," 164
Sentinnel ABM program, 258–59
Sequoia, 342–43, 348–49, 456
Sevareid, Eric, 403–4
Shafer, Raymond, 158, 179
Shaheen, John, 64
Shakespeare, Frank, 138, 139, 231
Sherman, John, 436
Shivers, Allan, 534
Shriver, Sargent, 284, 583, 606
Shultz, George, 328, 434, 457–58, 585
  appointed Secretary of Labor, 237
  in 1972 campaign, 604, 611
  as Secretary of Treasury, 542, 611
Sidey, Hugh, 229, 326, 638
Sihanouk, Norodom, 272, 336
Silent Majority, 311–13, 325, 412, 432, 645
Simpson, O. J., 242
Singapore, 115
Sino-Soviet split, 44, 440
Sirica, John J., 622, 648
Six Crises (Nixon), 11–12, 49, 67, 514, 519
Sixth Fleet, U.S., 384–85
Skelton, Red, 445
Slater, Ellis, 241
SLBMs, *see* submarine launched ballistic missiles
Sloan, Hugh, 607, 640
Smathers, George, 14
Smith, Gerard C., 313, 382, 441, 442, 526, 546, 549
Smith, Howard K., 404, 518–19
Smith, Margaret Chase, 290

Smith, Marie, 318
Smith, Merriman, 258
Smith, Terence, 351
Smith, William French, 470
Snow, Edgar, 400
Social Issue, in 1970 campaign, 392–96
Socialist Party, U.S., 303
Social Security, 50, 88, 188, 327, 432, 572
Societa Generale Immobiliare (SGI), 246
Sokolniki Park, 107
Son Tay prison, U.S. raid on, 399
South, 365–66
  Carswell rejection and, 337–38
  as Nixon political base, 89–90, 118, 155, 170, 316, 317
Southeast Asia Treaty, 55
South Korea, 115, 515
South Vietnam, 28, 30–31, 42, 91, 104, 115, 197, 198
  Army of, *see* Army of the Republic of Vietnam
  bombing in, 241–42
  corruption in, 147–48, 215, 417–18
  Diem overthrown and assassinated in, 30–31, 33–34, 36–37, 48, 464
  elections in, 275, 282, 389, 463, 505
  Nixon in, 43–44, 69, 85, 109–10, 286–287
  U.S. advisers to, 54
  see also GVN; Vietnam War
Soviet-American relations, 233, 258–60, 313, 379–85, 400–401, 462, 525–33, 544–50
  arms control and, 23, 225, 252, 288, 313, 320, 350, 441–44, 525–26, 532, 545–50, 596, 615–17, 654, 655
  China and, 307, 451, 453, 515, 525–26
  coexistence, 545, 654
  détente and, 171, 233, 254, 307, 320–321, 439–44, 462, 478–79, 526–27, 653–54, 656; *see also* Moscow summit; SALT; SALT I; SALT II
  grain sales and, 27, 478–79, 526, 545, 583–84
  Kennedy-Khrushchev agreement and, 379–83
  Most Favored Nation (MFN) status and, 545, 596, 616, 617
  nuclear test ban treaty and, 23
  see also Cold War
Soviet-Indian Friendship Treaty, 483
Soviet Union, 34, 114, 262, 433
  as arms supplier, 334, 528
  China's relations with, 23, 44, 75, 429
  Cuba and, 18, 19, 20
  Egypt's relations with, 383, 595, 616
  "freeing" of, 20

India's relations with, 483–85
Iraq's relations with, 596
Jewish emigration from, 479, 616
MIRVs and, 276, 277
1972 campaign and, 552–53
Nixon in, 64–65, 106, 107, 544–48
nuclear weapons of, 134, 224, 289, 439
Syria's relations with, 383
Vietnam War and, 143, 146, 168, 191, 224–25, 307, 309, 387, 462, 505, 506, 507, 526–32, 535–37, 539–40, 550–51, 592, 601–2, 614, 656
World War II debt of, 545, 615, 617
space program, 283–86, 314, 339, 498
Spain, Nixon in, 23
Spanish-American War, 319
Spivack, Robert, 229, 659
Srinivas, M. N., 333–34
SST (supersonic transport airplane), 397–98, 413, 433
Stalin, Joseph, 34, 35, 383
Stanford University, 333–34, 496
Stans, Maurice, 25, 66, 83, 84, 237, 246, 557
in 1968 campaign, 106, 123, 133, 140, 153, 158, 178–79
Watergate and, 607, 609, 611
Stassen, Harold, 162
State Department, U.S., 19, 22–23, 254, 271, 321, 329, 350, 380, 427, 448, 485, 553, 654, 655
China trip and, 512, 513, 516–17
Nixon's distrust of, 232, 233, 513, 516–17
Nixon's insulting of, 531, 548
SALT and, 443
wiretapping of, 29–30
Stevenson, Adlai, 31, 33, 156, 198, 204, 259, 617
Stewart, Potter, 274
Stoessel, Walter, 329
Stokes, Carl, 265
stop-Goldwater movement, 51
Strachan, Gordon, 461, 562
Strategic Arms Limitation Talks see SALT; SALT I; SALT II
Strauss, Lewis, 160
student radicalism, 119–20, 165, 261–265, 333–34, 376, 377, 623–24
Mitchell's criticism of, 375
see also antiwar movement
Students for a Democratic Society, 351
Studies on the Left, 71
submarine launched ballistic missiles (SLBMs), 289, 441, 442
SALT and, 546, 547
Sullivan, Rev. Leon, 188
Sullivan, William, 272, 471

Sulzberger, C. L., 382, 410
supersonic transport airplane (SST), 397–98, 413, 433
Supreme Court, U.S., 82, 103, 170, 273, 373, 447, 658–59
appointments to, 159–60, 183, 199, 200, 201, 274–75, 295–96, 315–17, 330, 337–38, 416, 468–71, 563, 658
school desegregation and, 187, 433, 460, 520
surface-to-air missiles (SAMs), 505
survival gap, 203, 204
Symington, Stuart, 426
Syria, 112–13, 334
Soviet relations with, 383

Taft, Robert, Jr., 604
Taft, William Howard, 470
Taiwan, 68, 95, 115, 400, 427–28, 450, 452
Nixon in, 44, 68
Nixon's visit to China and, 453, 515–517
United Nations and, 480, 506
Task Force, 74, 485, 487
Tate, Sharon, 370
taxes, 88, 290–91, 553
cuts in, 290
excise, 458
income, see income tax
Nixon residence improvements and, 572–73
property, 432–33, 600
Vietnam War and, 94, 142, 225
teach-ins, 72
Teamsters, 491–92, 584–85
television, 248–50
in 1968 campaign, 138–40, 165, 179, 202, 216–17
Nixon image and, 138–40, 314
race riots and, 103
see also ABC-TV; CBS-TV; NBC-TV
Tennessee Valley Authority, 50
terrorism, Huston Plan vs., 367–69
Thailand, 78, 115
Thieu, Nguyen Van, 92, 134, 194, 195, 206–16, 222, 241, 257, 299, 387, 388, 462, 551, 593–95
bombing halt and, 206–11
Chennault and, 207–8, 210, 213–16, 231
corruption and, 147–48
in elections, 463–64, 481
Haig and, 613, 628
Kissinger and, 613–14
Nixon's meeting with, 277–78
peace agreement and, 627, 628, 630–635, 644–46

Thieu, Nguyen Van (*cont.*)
  peace talk participation refused by, 212–16, 230–31
  step-down offer of, 509
Tho, Le Duc, *see* Le Duc Tho
Thomas, Helen, 399, 403, 504
Thompson, Llewellyn, 208
Thompson, Sir Robert, 306, 310
Thurmond, J. Strom, 61, 141, 155, 164, 170, 330, 444
Time, 301, 325, 494, 577*n*–78*n*
Time v. *Hill,* 82
Timmons, Bill, 420–21
Tito (Josip Broz), 385
Tkach, Walter, 266–67
"Today" Show, 91, 511
Tonkin, Gulf of, 55
  see also Gulf of Tonkin Resolution
Tower, John, 61, 118, 155, 159, 164, 180
Treleaven, Harry, 138, 139
triangular diplomacy, 483–85, 525–26, 551, 592, 596
Trotsky, Leon, 65
True Grit, 323
Truman, Bess, 417
Truman, Harry S., 15, 19, 35, 46, 141, 198, 204, 243, 260, 378, 408
  executive privilege and, 426, 427
  Hiss case and, 574, 571
  Nixon compared with, 408–9, 557
  Nixon's criticism of, 94–95
  Nixon's relationship with, 416–17
  pardons granted by, 581–82
Tuck, Dick, 640
Turner, Frederick Jackson, 637
Turner, Wallace, 573
TWA, 501

unemployment, 392, 397, 403, 432, 459, 572
Unger, Sanford, 606
United Nations:
  China and, 44, 400, 428, 452, 480
  Indo-Pakistani War and, 484
United Press International (UPI), 251, 552–53
United States:
  arms sales of, 188, 251, 335, 384
  foreign policy of, *see specific countries*
  foreign prestige of, 19, 28
  moral superiority of, 34–35
  sense of power of, 35–36
  weakness and vulnerability of, 49–50, 134–35, 203, 288–89
Universal Military Training and Service Act (1951), 467
Urban Affairs Council, 237

Urban League, 366
U.S. Table Tennis Association, 430

Vanocur, Sander, 455
Vietcong, 49, 62, 64, 77, 94, 103, 104, 313, 339, 550, 592, 630, 655–56
  New Left view of, 71, 72, 74
  in peace talks, 210, 211, 212, 216
  political arm of, *see* National Liberation Front
  Tet offensive of, 134–35, 137, 141–142, 147–48, 150
Vietminh, 34
Vietnam Veterans Against the War, 265, 461, 599
Vietnam War, 42–45, 126–29, 141–50, 222–26
  appeasement line on, 77–78, 81
  bipartisan support and, 93, 97
  cease-fire in place offer and, 389–90
  China and, 76, 78, 166, 224–25, 452, 507, 515, 592, 656
  de-Americanization of, 168, 180, 196–197, 277–78
  death tolls in, 75, 241, 256
  de-escalation of, 148–49, 199, 299, 300, 319–20, 551
  Diem assassination and, 30–31, 34, 36–37
  domino theory and, 48, 78
  Duck Hook and, 282, 299–301, 306–307, 310, 319, 320, 407
  escalation of, 44, 49, 54–55, 61, 62, 64, 77, 94, 100, 103, 104, 129, 142, 144, 299, 319, 536, 648
  Fishhook and, 341, 342, 344, 345, 347–48
  in Johnson Administration, 42–44, 48, 54–55, 61, 62, 64, 68–69, 73–79, 86–87, 88, 91–98, 103, 104, 106–7, 126, 129, 134–35, 137, 141–44, 146–50, 166, 167, 178, 182, 194–98, 200, 206–17, 230–31, 232, 241–42, 260, 275, 278, 311–12, 319, 338, 446, 494, 506, 614, 629, 655
  in Kennedy Administration, 28, 30–31, 34, 36–37, 142, 215, 319, 446
  Korean War compared with, 198, 224, 226, 238–39, 260, 324, 594–95
  Manila Communiqué and, 93–94, 96, 100
  morale problem and, 417–19
  in 1964 campaign, 42–45, 48–49
  in 1968 campaign, 66, 75–76, 78, 104, 115, 126–29, 134–35, 137, 141–44, 146–50, 166–69, 180, 190–91, 193–198, 206–18, 655
  in 1972 campaign, 494, 499, 505, 505–512, 571–72, 578, 589–95, 601–2,

619–20, 623–24, 627–35, 641–46, 648–50
in Nixon Administration, 252, 254, 256–58, 260, 275–82, 295, 297, 299–313, 319–20, 324–25, 333–55, 373, 387–89, 403, 404, 407, 413–15, 417–21, 428–29, 436–38, 461–64, 467–68, 480–81, 487–88, 493–95, 505–12, 527–42, 550–51, 589–95, 612–14, 627–35, 641–46, 648–50, 655–57
Nixon/Chennault/Thieu intrigue in, 207–8, 210, 213–16
Nixon's China trip and, 515, 516
Nixon's inheritance of, 223–26, 338–339, 358
Nixon's Nov. 3, 1969 speech and, 304–11, 319
Nixon's promise of honorable end to, 190–91, 195, 223–24
Nixon's views on, 43–45, 48–49, 61–62, 64, 68–69, 73–79, 88, 90, 91–92, 95–96, 100, 103, 04, 106–7, 109–10, 115, 126–27, 129, 142–50, 154, 166–69, 180, 182, 193, 195–98, 209, 210, 233, 236
Operation Enhance Plus in, 631, 645
Parrot's Beak and, 341–45, 347–48
peace negotiations and, 54, 77–78, 91–92, 144, 148–49, 506, 528–29, 627–35, 642–46; see also Paris peace talks
Pentagon Papers and, 446–48
Reagan's views on, 120
SALT linked to, 441, 444
secret talks in, 271–72, 275, 282, 309, 387–89, 507–10, 528, 535, 592–93, 612–13, 614, 627–28
Tet offensive in, 134–35, 137, 141–142, 147–48, 150
U.S. bombing halt in, 196–99, 206–213, 216–17, 230, 241–42, 256, 494, 614, 629
victory in, 69, 76, 77, 90, 93, 96, 115, 144, 148, 282, 302
Vietnamization of, 277–78, 306, 309, 324, 339, 388, 419–20, 426, 429, 461, 480, 505, 506, 627, 602, 655
see also antiwar movement; specific countries
Volpe, John, 237, 246
Voorhis, Jerry, 104, 228, 604
voting age, 370
Voting Rights Act (1965), 89, 370

wage-and-price controls, 458
wage freezes, 458–59, 474–75, 657
Wallace, DeWitt, 84
Wallace, George, 331, 365, 461, 658

in 1968 campaign, 141, 163–65, 177, 181–86, 191–94, 204, 205, 206, 220–21
in 1972 campaign, 497, 499–500, 507, 522, 541–42, 555, 562, 586–87, 639
shooting of, 541–42
Wallace, Gerald, 500
Wallace, Henry, 141
Wallace, Lurleen, 89, 499
Wall Street Journal, 389, 456, 557
Walters, Barbara, 511
Walters, Vernon, 252–53, 568–69, 574
Warner, Denis, 324
Warner-Lambert Pharmaceutical Company, 17
War on Poverty, 41, 55–56, 86, 268
Warren, Earl, 159, 199, 243, 274, 521
Washington, D.C., crime in, 260–61
Washington, George, 342
Washington Daily News, 454
Washington Post, 211, 246, 247, 250, 251, 261, 296, 302, 317, 318–19, 446, 495, 518, 606, 607, 611, 619, 621, 624, 638–40
Washington Special Action Group (WSAG), 483, 485, 486
Washington Star, 637–38, 645
Watergate affair, 271, 278, 558–71, 621–623, 638–41, 646
break in and bugging in, 544, 558, 560–63, 565, 567, 570–71, 573–76, 577n, 588–89, 597, 602, 606–7, 619, 621–22, 661
cover-up in, 558–60, 563, 566–69, 571, 574–77, 607–10, 647–48, 661
Justice Department investigation of, 574, 576, 589, 602, 607–8, 622, 661
Watergate apartments, 246, 261
Wattenberg, Ben, 374
Wayne, John, 323, 480
Weathermen, 367, 369
Weaver, Warren, 121
Weicker, Lowell, 582
Weinberger, Caspar, 431, 456, 612
Welander, Robert O., 486–89
Welch, Robert, 75
welfare system, 124–25, 237, 268–69, 291–94, 327, 460, 495, 657
West Berlin, Ostpolitik and, 464–65
Westmoreland, William, 103, 134, 137, 141–42, 144, 147, 278, 419, 420, 632, 633
West Pakistan, 482–85, 488
West Point, Nixon's speech at, 418–19
Whalen, Richard, 146–47
"What do you believe the principles underlying the form of government of the United States to be?" (Nixon), 38–39

Wheeler, Earle, 157
Whitaker, John C., 19, 39, 51
White, Theodore, 21, 136, 139, 150, 168, 214
white backlash, 58
    civil rights and, 42, 55–56, 89
White House:
    bugging and wiretapping in, 235–36, 248, 272–73, 423–26, 448–49
    liveliness of (1970), 332
    Republican changes at, 246–48
    wedding at, 445–46
White House Correspondents' Dinner, 411
White House staff, 602
    changes in, 297–98
    competition of, 228, 230
    Nixon's dissatisfaction with, 297–98
    Nixon's selection of, 228–30
Whitman, Ann, 326
Wicker, Tom, 88–89, 100
Wilkins, Roy, 370
Wilkinson, Bud, 155
Williams, Edward Bennett, 610
Williams, William A., 71
Wilson, Harold, 255
Wilson, Woodrow, 26, 136, 437
Woodrow Wilson International Center for Scholars, 437
wiretapping, 154, 208
    of CIA, 36
    in Johnson Administration, 208, 210, 214, 235–36, 248, 423, 424, 608–9
    in Kennedy Administration, 28–30, 33–34, 172, 235
    in Nixon Administration, 235, 272–274, 350, 361, 423–26, 434, 448–49, 559–60, 564, 658, 660
Wisconsin, primaries in, 105, 121, 146, 541

Witcover, Jules, 26–27, 82, 88–89, 101
Wold, John, 391
Wolfson, Louis E., 275
women:
    in Nixon Administration, 416, 469–470
    Nixon's views on, 470
Women's Wear Daily, 374–75
Woods, Rose Mary, 16, 26, 33, 46, 63, 132, 170, 228, 246, 343, 362, 647
    burglary in apartment of, 261
    Julie Nixon's wedding and, 240, 241
    1972 campaign and, 478, 597
    tapes and, 564n
Woodward, Bob, 606, 621, 638–40, 646
World War II:
    Soviet debt from, 545, 615, 617
    U.S. legacy from, 34–35
    Vietnam War compared with, 77–78, 81, 147, 148

Xuan Thuy, 282, 509

Yahya Khan, 400, 450, 482–84
Yeats, William Butler, 263
Young, David, 449, 465, 469
Young, Whitney, 236, 366
Young Americans for Freedom, 454
Youth for Nixon, 190
youth rebellion, 119–20, 165, 261–65, 369–70, 373
Yugoslavia, Nixon in, 385

Ziegler, Ron, 158, 204, 250, 251, 348, 350, 356–57, 461, 490, 492, 523, 571, 584, 594
    appointed press secretary, 229–30
    Watergate and, 560, 567, 573, 607, 640
Zumwalt, Elmo, 485, 535, 549, 632